INSIDE THE ARMY
OF THE POTOMAC

Inside the Army of the Potomac

The Civil War Experience of
Captain Francis Adams Donaldson

Edited by J. Gregory Acken

STACKPOLE
BOOKS

Published by
STACKPOLE BOOKS
5067 Ritter Road
Mechanicsburg, PA 17055

Grateful acknowledgment is made to the University of California Press for permission to
quote from *The Road to Richmond: The Civil War Memoirs of Major Abner R. Small of the
Sixteenth Maine Volunteers. Together with the Diary Which He Kept When He Was a Prisoner of
War,* edited by Harold Adams Small (Berkeley, CA: The University of California Press,
1939).

Printed in the United States of America

10 9 8 7 6 5 4 3 2 1

FIRST EDITION

Library of Congress Cataloging-in-Publication Data

Donaldson, Francis Adams, 1840–1928.
    Inside the Army of the Potomac : the Civil War experience of Captain Francis Adams
Donaldson / edited by J. Gregory Acken. — 1st ed.
        p.   cm.
    Includes bibliographical references and index.
    ISBN 0-8117-0901-9
    1. Donaldson, Francis Adams, 1840–1928—Correspondence.   2. United States.
Army. Pennsylvania Volunteer Infantry Regiment, 118th (1862–1865).   3. Soldiers—
Pennsylvania—Philadelphia—Correspondence.   4. Pennsylvania—History—Civil War,
1861–1865—Personal narratives.   5. United States—History—Civil War, 1861–1865
—Personal narratives.   6. United States. Army. Pennsylvania Infantry Regiment, 71st
(1861–1864).   I. Acken, J. Gregory.   II. Title.
E527.5 118th.D66   1998
973.7'448—dc21   98-17111
                                                                                   CIP

All editor's proceeds from the sale of this book are being donated to The Civil War Library and Museum. Located at 1805 Pine Street in Philadelphia, Pennsylvania, The Civil War Library and Museum is a nonprofit institution that houses the papers and personal effects of Capt. Francis Adams Donaldson as well as thousands of books and artifacts related to the United States Civil War.

CONTENTS

List of Maps

List of Illustrations

FOREWORD

In late November 1996 I received a letter from J. Gregory Acken inviting me to read and comment on a manuscript that he had recently completed. The core of the manuscript, he said, was the Civil War correspondence of Capt. Francis Adams Donaldson of the 118th Pennsylvania Infantry—better known as the Corn Exchange Regiment—which, in transcribing and editing, he had lived with for more than seven years. The Donaldson Papers, Acken noted, were in the collections of The Civil War Library and Museum in Philadelphia, of which he was on the Board of Governors. Long familiar with the museum and its outstanding collections of Civil War manuscripts, artifacts, and iconography, I told Greg Acken I welcomed the opportunity to examine his manuscript.

Over the Christmas holiday, I had the privilege of spending many hours with "Old Soldier Donaldson." I use the word *privilege* after considerable thought. Since reporting for duty at Vicksburg National Military Park on September 28, 1955, through a forty-year career in the National Park Service and beyond, I have immersed myself in the Civil War as a researcher, author, lecturer, and battlefield guide. During these years, I have read thousands of soldiers' letters, journals, and reminiscences, both published and in manuscript form. The Donaldson manuscript, unlike so many soldiers' collections which add little to our knowledge of the war or the soldiers' personalities, excites interest. Here is a soldier who writes well, is a talented observer, and served with two of the Army of the Potomac's better-known regiments. He was an enlisted man in the 71st Pennsylvania (the 1st California) until wounded at the battle of Fair Oaks on May 31, 1862, and then served as a captain and company commander in the Corn Exchange Regiment until his discharge from the army in January 1864.

Donaldson, for most of his two and a half years in the military, was an enthusiastic and exemplary Union soldier. An antislavery Democrat and an admirer of Maj. Gen. George B. McClellan long after his departure as commander of the Army of the Potomac, the twenty-one-year-old soldier first saw combat at Ball's Bluff on October 21, 1861. He was one of the large number of Federals captured in that disaster and spent the next four months as a prisoner of war in Richmond.

His fortunes and hopes for advancement in the military, a career in which he represented the best and the brightest, changed in the months after he joined the Corn Exchange Regiment. Initially, there is an erosion of the respect he has for longtime regimental commander Lt. Col. James Gwyn, which results in his earning the colonel's enmity. The denouement comes when good soldier Donaldson challenges Gwyn's authority, which ultimately leads to his departure from the service.

Spiced by his bitter interpersonal relations and conflicts with Colonel Gwyn and his sycophants, the story of Donaldson's decision to self-destruct is reminiscent of a Greek tragedy. Donaldson's letters and journals lend excellent insights into camp life, marches, and battles. There are human interest stories, some poignant, others laced with humor. These provide the grist for a better understanding of what it was like to be a line officer in an unhappy regiment, as Donaldson and his friends gather in the evenings to sit around and talk, gripe, and share another "Joe Hooker."

As one who has spent more than two score years immersed in the Civil War, my thanks to The Civil War Library and Museum for its good work in preservation and education and for sharing the Donaldson journal and correspondence. A special plaudit to Greg Acken for the long hours spent with Captain Donaldson and his correspondence, readying them for publication. As an editor, he is in that special class, providing excellent background and explanatory information without overwhelming the reader with trivia. Scholars, buffs, and casual readers will find *Inside the Army of the Potomac: The Civil War Experience of Captain Francis Adams Donaldson* enjoyable and informative.

Edwin C. Bearss
Historian Emeritus
National Park Service

ACKNOWLEDGMENTS

I am indebted to the following individuals for their assistance with this work: Russ Pritchard, former Executive Director of The Civil War Library and Museum, who gave his enthusiastic endorsement of the project when I first approached him with it, and John J. Craft, the museum's current Executive Director, who has been highly supportive throughout its continuance. Steve Wright, Curator of Collections at the museum and Dale Biever, Registrar of the Museum, provided much helpful advice and pointed me to some little-known source material that proved valuable. The Presidents of the Board of Governors of The Civil War Library and Museum who have served during my preparation of the Donaldson Papers, George J. Lincoln, III, H. Sinclair Mills, Jr., Alan E. Hoeweler, and Richard W. Czop, all took a sincere interest in the project, as did the various board members whose term of service covered the period.

For reading rough drafts of the manuscript and offering their expertise and criticism, I am indebted to John J. Hennessy, Fredericksburg, Virginia; James M. McPherson, Princeton, New Jersey; Brian Pohanka, Alexandria, Virginia; Wiley Sword, Bloomfield Hills, Michigan; and Jeff Wert, Centre Hall, Pennsylvania. Special thanks go to Edwin C. Bearss, Historian Emeritus of the National Park Service, for a particularly thorough review of an early draft and for his preparation of the foreword.

Many others assisted with their time, effort, and guidance: Mike Cavanaugh, Philadelphia, Pennsylvania; Blake Magner, Cinnaminson, New Jersey, who photographed images from The Civil War Library and Museum; Don Enders, Harrisburg, Pennsylvania, who allowed me to use images from his collection housed at the U.S. Army Military History Institute, Carlisle, Pennsylvania, and Jim Enos, of Carlisle, who ably photographed them for me;

Mike Musick of the National Archives was constantly helpful. Gary Lash of Fredonia, New York, provided me with a treasure trove of information from his ongoing research of the 71st Pennsylvania; Laura Katz Smith of Virginia Polytechnic Institute and State Library, Blacksburg, Virginia, facilitated the reproduction of John Donaldson's photograph from the University's collections; Ed Hagerty, Philadelphia, Pennsylvania, shared research from his study of the 114th Pennsylvania. George Skoch, Cleveland Heights, Ohio, skillfully prepared the maps from my rough sketches and outlines; Mike Benson of Glen Riddle, Pennsylvania, was helpful in accessing the letters of Lt. Henry Peck in the collections of the 1st Regt. NGP Library in Philadelphia; Lil Miller, Lansdale, Pennsylvania, was patience personified as she typed, from my longhand, the initial draft of the manuscript, as well as my innumerable revisions. Michelle Simmons of Stackpole Books patiently answered an unending string of questions I posed to her. My editor at Stackpole, William C. Davis, an unparalleled scholar of the Civil War, did much to bring this project to fruition. After kindly reviewing an early draft of the work, he saw the merit of Donaldson's writings, and offered to publish them.

Finally, to my wife, Regina, go my love and thanks for her understanding of the many hours that were devoted to Captain Donaldson and of the importance of the project to me. Without her selflessness, it would not have been possible.

INTRODUCTION

For thousands of men in the North and South, the outbreak of the American Civil War signaled the beginning of the most important experience of their lives. For Francis Adams Donaldson, his enlistment in the Union Army was a change that could not have come at a more propitious moment. Bored with the workaday routine of life as a clerk in the Philadelphia shipping concern of Alexander Heron, Jr. & Co., he found the escape he had been looking for in the prospect of a military career. "I like the life of a soldier more and more," he wrote soon after he joined the army, "and would not give it up for anything in the world. It is just what I have been longing for and dreaming about all my life. It suits me and I it."[1] While Donaldson's enthusiasm for life as a soldier would wane perceptibly over the course of the thirty-two months he served, there was no hint of its lessening in the momentous days that followed the firing on Fort Sumter.

When word of the onset of hostilities reached Philadelphia in April 1861, Donaldson immediately determined to enlist. He was not an abolitionist, though, and like many of the volunteers who signed on early in the war, he was prompted to fight more by what he perceived as the effrontery of the newly formed Confederacy and the desire to uphold the Constitution than he was by any desire to put down slavery. "I burn with indignation when I think of the outrageous conduct of the South," he would later write, "and I for one will never be able to give up the fight until they are chastised into submission to the laws."

Assisted by his friend William Harris, who was a member of a local militia unit called the Blue Reserves, the pair canvassed the streets of Philadelphia, accompanied by a fife and drum corps, gathering recruits and adding generally to the patriotic atmosphere then prevailing. In due time, they had enough men to fill out a company, the services of which they had previously pledged to an unidentified regiment that was forming for service in western Virginia. But after a short time, Donaldson and Harris grew disenchanted with the leadership of the organization and transferred their company en masse to the headquarters of Capt. Garrick Mallery, who was mustering men for service in what was to become Company H of the California Regiment, later to be known as the 71st Pennsylvania Volunteers. "The price of this defection," Donaldson wrote, "was a 2nd Lieutenancy for Harris, and—nothing—for myself, having told Capt. Mallery I was not after any position." Donaldson did not go completely unrewarded, though, as he was soon appointed 5th sergeant of the company.

So began the Civil War experience of Francis Adams Donaldson. He was born in Philadelphia on June 7, 1840, the third and youngest son of John Plankenhorn Donaldson and Matilda Nice, both of whom died during his adolescence. Donaldson traced his paternal lineage back to Capt. Andrew Donaldson, who had served as an officer during the French and Indian War, and to William Townsend Donaldson, who was high sheriff of Philadelphia in the early 1800s. His maternal ancestors were instrumental in establishing the Nicetown section of Philadelphia in 1704, and his great-grandfather, George Nice, had served as a captain in the Pennsylvania state forces during the Revolutionary War.

After the death of his parents, Donaldson and his two brothers, Jacob, who was five years his senior, and John, who was two years older, were raised by their mother's sister, Eliza Ann Nice. In the wartime letters he wrote to Eliza, Frank Donaldson addresses her as "Auntie," but there is no doubt that the brothers considered her as their mother, and in their letters they refer to her as such to anyone other than family members. Little is known about Eliza, though Donaldson does mention that he entered the service against her wishes and that she was constantly worried about the safety of her boys. The basis for this worry was not without foundation, because Eliza would see two of her nephews in armed conflict during the war, one serving the Union and one the Confederacy.

In 1858, at the age of twenty, John Donaldson had moved from Phila- delphia to Charleston in the Kanawha Valley of what is today West Virginia. He had gone there seeking employment and began working as a salesman in the general merchandise firm of John Goshorn. Outgoing and handsome, John soon found himself accepted among the social circles of Charleston, and in the course of time he joined the local militia company, the Kanawha Riflemen. The Riflemen were led by a Virginia Military Institute graduate and transplanted Richmond attorney, Capt. George S. Patton, who had set up his law practice in the city, and whose grandson and namesake would gain fame during World War II.[2] When Virginia seceded and the war began, recalled one of John Donaldson's fellow Riflemen, "this company volunteered to a man in the cause of Virginia and the Southland, and none more eagerly than did Donaldson, whose association and identification with its Southern-born members had been so intimate and of such duration that no one of his associates ever thought of his Northern birth. . . ."[3] The Kanawha Riflemen were mustered into the Confederate service as Company H of the 22nd Virginia Infantry, and John Donaldson was elected second sergeant. Captain Patton was eventually promoted to the colonelcy of the regiment, and in May 1862, John was elected captain of the company, which he led through numerous battles and skirmishes until he was captured at Cold Harbor, Virginia, on June 3, 1864.[4]

Frank Donaldson, although in complete disagreement with John's decision to side with the South, understood his brother's motives. "When you write to John," he told their brother, Jacob, in June 1861, "tell him that now that he is a soldier, even though it be in a bad cause, to try and distinguish himself, and

Capt. John P. Donaldson, 22nd Virginia Infantry.
THE CIVIL WAR LIBRARY & MUSEUM.

also say that I do not blame him, because he believes he is right." In his letters, Frank expresses anxiety about the possibility of opposing John on the battlefield, and when the opportunity arose, he would question prisoners taken in battle as to the whereabouts of his brother's regiment. Frank and John never did meet in combat, though, as the 22nd Virginia campaigned for the most part in the western regions of Virginia through early 1864, while Frank's actions were directly tied to the Army of the Potomac, fighting predominantly in eastern Virginia and Maryland. No lasting animosity resulting from their divided loyalties appears to have existed between Frank and John, and even as the war progressed and Frank adopted a more hardened attitude toward the South, he continued to express his love and concern for his "misguided" brother.

The oldest of the Donaldson brothers, Jacob, was born in 1835. Jacob was a Philadelphia merchant and was Frank's principal correspondent during his war service. Although none of Jacob's letters to Frank have survived (when

Jacob Donaldson, Frank's oldest brother and principal correspondent. The Civil War Library & Museum.

necessity dictated it, Frank would erase Jacob's letters and use the paper to respond), it is clear from Frank's replies to his brother that he looked up to Jacob and valued his guidance, especially on nonmilitary matters. From time to time, Jacob would offer an opinion on the Army of the Potomac or one of its commanders, but these opinions seemed to invariably contrast with Frank's views, and the young soldier would usually suggest that Jacob confine his letters to news from home. Despite their occasional differences, however, Jacob was by far Frank's closest confidant throughout his term of service. Jacob was the sole supporter of Eliza Nice and, as a result, saw little war service, spending time briefly in the state militia during the Antietam Campaign.

Frank Donaldson served during the Civil War in two of the more well-known regiments of the Army of the Potomac, initially as a sergeant and second lieutenant in the California Regiment of the 2nd Corps, which was to become officially known as the 71st Pennsylvania Volunteers, and later as captain in the Corn Exchange Regiment, which was the nickname of the 118th Pennsylvania Volunteers of the 5th Corps. While some of the notoriety attached to these two organizations resulted from their distinctive names, they were also famed, and rightfully so, for the severity of battles they passed through and the number of casualties they suffered as a result. Donaldson served with the California Regiment until May 1862, fighting at Ball's Bluff and participating in the Peninsula Campaign until the Battle of Fair Oaks. With the Corn Exchange Regiment, he was present for many of the landmark battles and campaigns in the east, including Antietam, Fredericksburg, Chancellorsville, Gettysburg, Bristoe Station, and Mine Run.

Donaldson's Civil War experiences were diverse, and his letters, as they convey the details of what he passed through, chart the course of his transition from a naive, enthusiastic recruit into a war-wearied, somewhat cynical veteran and, at the same time, mark the passage of a youth maturing into manhood. He labored during his first few months in the California Regiment to hold himself to the high standard that he felt characterized what he above all desired to become: "a complete and finished soldier."

When his brother asked him in July 1861 if he would accept a furlough were it offered, Donaldson wrote that he "would decline it, no matter how dearly I would love to see you all. I would feel a greater pride in stifling and subduing these feelings, which should not be allowed a place in a soldier's breast . . . than in gratifying my longing to be again with my loved ones at home. This is what I interpret as discipline, this is what [I] would do to crush out the tenderheartedness . . . which must be put aside for sterner and more soldierly thoughts."

When Jacob and Eliza contemplated visiting him at the encampment of the California Regiment outside of Washington in August 1861, Donaldson was against it. "I have fought down my homesickness," he told Jacob, "and am wholly and truly a soldier—without ties of any kind, so far as I can master my feelings, and should Auntie come to see me, I fear I would lose control of myself and give way to feelings I would rather keep in subjugation. . . . I am determined to be a soldier in all things—cost what it may to my hearts longing."

On another occasion, while the regiment was posted outside of Hampton, Virginia, in July 1861, Donaldson was returning to camp from a remote picket outpost one evening. As he walked along a dark, backwoods road, he was startled by a stone thrown at him. "Instantly I sprang into the bushes," he admitted to Jacob, "and stood for a moment with hair on end and knees knocking together with fright." He soon recovered his senses, though, and "felt a glow pervading my body . . . and once more brought under control my other faculties. The glow . . . was from shame that I should have been tried and found wanting."

Donaldson would wait several more months before he was able to prove to himself that he possessed the requisite inner strength to stand up to the enemy in combat. His first taste of action came at the disastrous Union defeat at the Battle of Ball's Bluff on October 21, 1861. He was captured there and spent the ensuing four months as a prisoner in Richmond, albeit under less than normal circumstances. His first two months were spent in one of the jails that had been established in the tobacco warehouses of the city, but in early January 1862, his Confederate brother, John, was able to secure his release on the condition that he be confined to the limits of Richmond. Donaldson moved freely throughout the Southern capital over the next month and a half, clad in a gray uniform coat that one of John's comrades had given him, and boarding with a former Confederate soldier from his brother's 22nd Virginia. Interestingly, during this time, Donaldson was offered a position in the Confederate Postal Service, which he declined. When he had occasion to attend church, he could look down from the balcony where he sat and see Confederate president Jefferson Davis worshiping below. Though his experience as a prisoner was not nearly as harrowing an ordeal as it was for Union soldiers captured later in the war, it was a trial he did not ever want to relive. As he passed near the Ball's Bluff battlefield while on the march northward during the Gettysburg Campaign in mid-1863, the familiar setting conjured up unpleasant memories for him. "I determined then and there," he wrote, "never to be taken prisoner again." Donaldson was exchanged and sent north in February 1862, and by March he was back again with his regiment, now known as the 71st Pennsylvania Volunteers.

Upon his return, Donaldson was delighted to be advanced personally by the commander of the 71st to the rank of sergeant major, with the promise of another promotion at the first available vacancy. He would freely state at times throughout the war that he was eager for promotion, as he felt that by virtue of his knowledge of tactics and experience he could handle larger responsibilities. "I admit that I am ambitious and want to rise higher," he wrote in December 1862 while serving with the 118th Pennsylvania, "feeling confident of my ability as an officer of higher grade than captain." Early in his service with the 118th, he felt that his competence was underappreciated and talked of a desire to be transferred to the Regular Army. "There I could be what my dearest ambition longs to realize—[to be] an efficient, capable soldier, deserving recognition by these qualities." Notwithstanding these complaints, Donaldson did, in fact, rise fairly rapidly for a man of his age, in spite of a self-described "youthful appearance," which he thought "mitigated against him" and prevented more rapid advancement.

Soon after his promotion to sergeant major, Donaldson was advanced again, this time to the second lieutenancy of Company M, and it was with no little pride that he conveyed the news to his brother, Jacob. When Jacob mistakenly addressed a subsequent letter to him using his previous rank, Donaldson was mortified. "I . . . will caution you against putting any further indignity upon me by addressing your letters to Sergt. F. A. Donaldson, as you are now doing, as I will return all such unopened."

As the Army of the Potomac advanced up the Virginia Peninsula during the spring of 1862, Donaldson was shocked at times by the severity and seeming wantonness of what he saw, and he struggled to come to terms with it. While occupying the entrenchments fronting Yorktown one day in April, he watched aghast as Federal sharpshooters first shot down a Confederate work detail, and then proceeded to pick off the stretcher bearers sent to the stricken men's aid. "These are some of the horrible incidents having official sanction that I have as yet been unable to reconcile in my mind with what I consider honorable warfare," he wrote, "but I am constantly told by those better posted than I that war is a terrible arbitrament, and must be made as dreadful as possible while it lasts. . . . "

As the prospect of battle again loomed closer, Donaldson turned introspective and confided to his brother how he felt before a fight: "I freely admit that during an engagement or when one seems imminent, I have the most annoying feelings. Not exactly fear, but a longing desire that either the battle will terminate, the sun go down, or that I be detailed for some duty to the rear, but I act the other and more soldierly one of obeying orders and doing my duty no matter how unpleasant or what the consequences. These feelings are my true ones, which I do not disguise from you, but to my comrades and the men under me, I present a calm, unmoved demeanor during times of trouble, and when in actual battle, all thought of self is lost in my desire and anxiety to have those under me do their work and behave well. Could they but know my inward thought at such times, could they see beneath the apparently brave exterior, the fluttering heart, the quickened pulse, I fear the regard they have for my courage would be but short lived. . . ."

Donaldson was also anxious to prove to his men that he was worthy of the leadership role he had been placed in, and he felt the quickest way he could do that was to set an example by rashly exposing himself to enemy fire at the earliest opportunity. He soon had his chance, but he paid a price for his recklessness. On the first day of the Battle of Fair Oaks on May 31, 1862, Donaldson was shot through the arm. He would never again serve in the 71st Pennsylvania.

Donaldson spent the early summer of 1862 recovering from his wound in Philadelphia. While he healed, the 71st Pennsylvania reduced its number of companies from fifteen to ten, leaving Donaldson, as one of the most recently commissioned officers in the regiment, without a command. A second generation of regiments was forming throughout the North at this time, though, and Donaldson was able to secure a captaincy in one of these new units, the 118th Pennsylvania Volunteers. From the very beginning, his transfer to the Corn Exchange Regiment would prove to be an unhappy change for the young soldier. Throughout the next year and a half, Donaldson would make known a great deal of personal dissatisfaction with his new command, reserving especial invective for the officers of the 118th, who he felt were generally inexperienced and too presumptuous. "A great drunkard and decidedly on the borrow," was how he described one officer. Another he thought "rough and grossly ignorant, fond of whiskey, but a good soldier." Of one of the field officers, he noted that "arrogance is his substitute for force of character," and he found a fellow captain to be "an old grandmother."

At twenty-two, Donaldson was the youngest captain in the regiment (only two other officers, both lieutenants, were younger), but he possessed more battle experience than any other line officer. This fact did not, to Donaldson's annoyance, seem at first to make any impression on the other officers. "They rather look on me as a boy," he wrote soon after joining the regiment, "to be treated as such." His youthful appearance may have contributed to this impression of him, as he later wrote disdainfully that his company referred to him as the "Little Captain."

Not surprisingly, Donaldson found it difficult to make friends among the officer corps of the 118th. In mid-November 1862, he confessed to Jacob, "I do not like service in this regiment. Everything is so entirely different from the California Regiment that I can not endure it." His disillusionment would only deepen over time. "I am very unhappy here," he wrote in October 1863. "With exception of a very few officers I have no friends in this regiment. I do not and cannot mingle and associate with all the officers, and my inter-course with some of them is so very limited that it amounts to positive unfriendliness. . . ."

While some of Donaldson's unhappiness as a member of the 118th resulted from his own predispositions and the high standards of honor and refinement he felt his fellow officers should aspire to, much of his dissatis-faction could be traced directly to the man who would ultimately lead the regiment for most of the time he served in it, Lt. Col. James Gwyn. The first colonel of the 118th, Charles M. Prevost ("a polished gentleman," Donaldson noted approvingly), was severely wounded during the regiment's first engage-ment at Shepherdstown, Virginia, on September 20, 1862, and except for several weeks in May 1863 and a stretch that fall, Gwyn commanded the 118th for the balance of Donaldson's term of service.

On meeting him for the first time in August 1862, Donaldson was almost instantly put off by what he considered Gwyn's coarseness and rough, uncouth manners. As time passed, his unfavorable opinion of Gwyn grew, and the feeling was returned in kind by the lieutenant colonel. "I despise him," Donaldson would eventually write, "he is a drunken, dictatorial, worthless fellow, not a gentleman, [and] not fit to command gentlemen." Gwyn was fully aware of the contempt in which Donaldson held him, and he went to great lengths at times to make life miserable for the headstrong young captain and several other officers of the regiment who felt the same way. As a result of this internal feuding, the 118th Pennsylvania became divided into two separate cliques: the officers who supported Gwyn and were willing to overlook his faults (Donaldson would refer to them as the "rum drinkers") and those who, like Donaldson, maintained a strictly professional relationship with the lieutenant colonel and had little interaction with him otherwise. In a passage from the Regimental History of the 118th Pennsylvania, Gwyn's attitude toward Donaldson and those of his ilk is described in the following way:

> Colonel Gwyn was intelligent, of fair tactical acquirement, and anxious to secure for his regiment the reputation it earned. But he was unhappily liable to be influenced by violent and unjust prejudices. While he was courteous and obliging to his friends, he too often acted oppressively and with wholly unwarranted severity towards others whom he conceived to be unfriendly to him. Some of the most manly spirits in the regiment were crushed by this oppressive conduct. They submitted uncomplainingly to injustice and oppression, rather than bring disgraceful criticism upon the command by an exposure of its internal disorders.[5]

Donaldson attempted several times, through both official and unofficial channels, to be transferred away or resign from the 118th, but Gwyn would refuse to sanction any of his efforts. Eventually, Donaldson became frustrated by his inability to break free from Gwyn's overbearing grasp, and finally, in December 1863, he took what he felt to be the only remaining course of action to remove himself from the control of his superior. Exactly what he did is fully spelled out in a letter written to Jacob soon after the incident.

By virtue of the 118th Pennsylvania's posting to the 5th Corps of the Army of the Potomac, Donaldson experienced a good deal of combat during his service in the regiment, and he left a remarkable written record of what he observed. Despite his lack of advanced education (his formal schooling had ended at the equivalent of the high school level), he wrote full, descriptive accounts of his adventures, occasionally sprinkling his letters with references to Shakespeare or the Napoleonic Wars. As a rule, within several weeks of the close of a particular battle or campaign, Donaldson would have a lengthy (in several instances more than fifty pages) narrative of what he passed through dispatched home to either Jacob or Eliza, in addition to his regular correspondence.

He was a prolific writer, but it was not an undertaking he relished. "Letter writing to me is a task," he wrote while with the 71st Pennsylvania.

"I go about it pretty much as I suppose clergymen do when writing their sermons. I first think over what I am about to write, then note it down and afterwards write my letter." "I could no more sit down and write off hand as you could fly," he told Jacob in May 1862. "All my letters, without exception, are first written in the rough, and then copied." Although he writes that he strove to portray only what came under his observation ("I merely state facts as they occur and I see them, giving my own impression only of my sur-roundings"), Donaldson appears to have been guilty, on several isolated occasions, of embellishing details in his letters, and in these instances he seems to have chosen to do so in order to impress his older brother. Donaldson was also sensitive about the content of his missives, as is evidenced by his reaction when Jacob told him he wanted to give his letters to the editor of a Philadel-phia newspaper for publication. "For heaven sake, do not give him my letters, can't you see they are written in the fullest confidence? Were they published, people would think me the veriest egotist alive. There is nothing in them but self. While you and I know exactly the reason for this, others would say 'this fellow carries on the whole campaign himself—alone.' While my letters are merely discriptive [*sic*] of my personal experience, and are literally true, anyone reading them would feel that I said too much about myself."

He also admitted that while his letters and diary entries accounted for the doings of his brigade, division, corps, and army as a whole, there was little in them on the men he commanded. The reason for this, he told Jacob, was because "It is the same with them, one day with another. They are like all others, a shiffless [*sic*] set, so unthinkingly improvident. They would try the patience of Job himself, for they are a childish set of babies, so dependant [*sic*] . . . I am in a measure to blame for this—I have spoiled them." Despite these seemingly disparaging comments, when the time came for Donaldson to part with them, he would speak of his men with pride: "They are my creation, they are soldiers of my own making . . . a braver, better, or more honorable set of men no captain ever commanded. I have great respect for my company."

Although dismayed that at five feet, eight inches tall and weighing 160 pounds, he was known to his company as their "Little Captain," Donaldson handled the physical rigors of active campaigning remarkably well, never spending a single day, except the time he was wounded, in the hospital. When his messmates and he were able to arrange it, they dined sumptuously, espe-cially while in a permanent encampment, but Donaldson found no difficulty subsisting on the plainer fare of army food. "It makes very little difference what I have to eat," he wrote to Jacob. "When nature informs me that my stomach is empty, I can make as enjoyable a meal on crackers as others can on roast chicken and trimmings." Although he was not overly fond of alcohol, he was no teetotaler, and he expressed surprise and disgust at the amount of alcohol his brother officers imbibed and the frequency with which they drank. "It is astonishing the extent to which drinking is carried on in camp," he told his brother in December 1862. "It appears to be a qualification in certain quarters to be able to carry an enormous amount of beverage with the least possible exhibition of its side effects. It is a bad business, I think."

Throughout his service, Donaldson was unabashedly proud to be a member of the Army of the Potomac, and he was not hesitant to share with his brother his thoughts on the men who commanded it. Like many of the veterans of the Peninsula Campaign, he was utterly devoted to the army's first commander, George B. McClellan. "Give us him back," he wrote while en route to Gettysburg a full seven months after McClellan was relieved, "and the Johnnies will soon show a clean set of heels." He found Ambrose Burnside "comically incompetent," had no love for Joe Hooker, and after some initial skepticism, grew to respect George Meade. Of his 5th Corps commanders, he held Charles Griffin in high esteem but felt that although George Sykes was capable, he was too cold and distant to be liked.

While Donaldson would infrequently allude to his dislike for the Southern civilians he came in contact with, he had nothing but praise for the combat abilities of the Confederate soldiers he faced. "They are splendid fighting men," he wrote in September 1862, and several months later he said he found them "energetic, brave, [and] wonderful."

Politically, he identified himself as a Democrat, "first, last, and all the time," but as the conflict wore on, Donaldson's convictions gradually shifted. Shortly before election day 1863, he wrote that he "would dearly love to be at home" to cast a vote for the staunchly pro-Republican governor of Pennsylvania, Andrew G. Curtin, adding that ". . . as long as the Rebels are in arms, I will sustain the government's efforts to put down rebellion with my life if necessary."

The sum total of the rigors of the campaigns he participated in combined with the human cost of the battles in which he fought came to harden Donaldson and at the same time changed the way he viewed the war. In September 1863, he reflected on what he had been through: "I do not think I am now as reconciled to Army life, after an experience of nearly three years, as I was at first. It is, of course, a free and easy way of living, but the surroundings tend to develope [sic] all that is bad in human nature, and the little good there is in man has a sorry chance among soldiers." In a diary entry written around the same time, Donaldson noted that his brother chided him in a letter for what he called Frank's "degeneration" since his enlistment. "Well," he admitted, "there is a good deal of truth in what he says. I believe I have changed; the poetry has been rudely taken out of me, all sentiment gone, and I see things differently." He attributed this in part to the way the war was being waged. "I believe the battle of Fredericksburg first gave me an insight into the way with which the war was prosecuted. The Army of the Potomac is merely a political machine. We are moved forward and backward to suit the political situation. Earnest men like Genls. Meade, Hancock, and Sedgwick, all true soldiers, are given to understand that strategy will be supplied from Washington. . . . As it is, backing and filling, racing to the Rappahannock and back again to the Potomac will never end the war. I, an humble line officer with no military training, but as earnest in the cause as when I first entered the army, can see these things and I am discouraged, or as my dear brother says, 'luke warm.' . . . I have degenerated, and so has the army. . . .'"

His combat experiences also served to desensitize him. He related to Eliza after the Battle of Gettysburg that he viewed with indifference the sight of two of his fellow officers shot down on either side of him, "an occurrence that at any other time would have horrified me."

His changing attitudes and outlook on the war, combined with Gwyn's undisguised animosity and the continuing alienation Donaldson felt within the 118th Pennsylvania, ultimately took their toll and led to the termination of his Civil War service. He gave vent to the bitterness he felt soon after. "I want to get away, I am unhappy here. It is without exception the most dreadfully demoralized command in the service. Bickerings and quarrelings, hatred, jealously and malice are abroad among us everywhere. All the officers are at loggerheads . . . they cordially hate and despise one another. I doubt whether throughout the Army of the Potomac or indeed the whole Army of the United States there exists a regiment so torn to pieces by internal discentions [*sic*] as this famous Corn Exchange Regiment—and all brought about by its disreputable commanding officer."

⊱┤◆⟩─◦─⟨◆├⊰

With several exceptions, the Donaldson letters have never appeared in print, at least not in their current format. The Regimental History of the 118th Pennsylvania Infantry was published in three separate editions, first in

1888 as the *History of the Corn Exchange Regiment 118th Pennsylvania Volunteers,*
then in 1892 as *Antietam to Appomattox with the 118th Penna. Vols. Corn Exchange Regiment,* and finally in 1905 as the *History of the 118th Pennsylvania
Volunteers Corn Exchange Regiment.* The book itself, comprising an average of
six hundred pages of text, plus a roster in each edition, is one of the better
written and more thorough unit histories on the Union side, and many
modern students and historians have consulted it for details of the battles,
campaigns, and attitudes of the soldiers of the Army of the Potomac. Bruce
Catton, in his highly influential trilogy on the Army of the Potomac, consulted
it extensively. John J. Pullen, in his masterful history of the 20th Maine, cited
it frequently in his early chapters as the basis for some of what he wrote.
John Bigelow and Harry Pfanz, in their superlative studies of the Battles of
Chancellorsville and Gettysburg, respectively, also used the work. What
these writers, along with a host of others who have referenced it did not
know, however, was that when quoting from the Regimental History of
the 118th, they were in fact quoting indirectly from Donaldson's letters.

Donaldson served with the 118th from its formation in August 1862
through early January 1864, and in the Regimental History, the seventeen
months covering his term of enlistment account for the initial two-thirds
of each edition. These 375 pages are based to a large extent on the letters
Donaldson wrote home to his family. But where the Regimental History
glosses over or leaves entirely unmentioned the darker side of life in the
Army of the Potomac, Donaldson speaks of it with unvarnished candor in
his correspondence, and it is herein that the value of his observations lies.
Incompetence and drunkenness abound. Rivalries fueled by resentment
and jealously are commonplace. Officers resort to fisticuffs and brawling to
settle their differences. Subalterns who turn and run in the face of enemy
fire are discharged; naive recruits who desert are put to death. Though
Donaldson wrote plainly of these occurrences and many others, most of
these unsavory incidents never made it to the printed pages of the history
of the 118th.

The introduction to each edition of the Regimental History states that
it was compiled and authored by the "Survivors' Association" of the regiment and goes on to list seven veterans who "aided materially" in the
preparation of the work. Conspicuously absent from this list is Donaldson,
and it is uncertain why this is so. Possibly it was in deference to Colonel
Gwyn, who was alive when the first two editions were published. Gwyn
does not appear in the most benevolent light in the pages of the book, and

had he known that Donaldson was one of the principal contributors, he might have strongly objected to its content. Or maybe Donaldson simply did not want any of the notoriety that might have come from identifying himself as a contributor. There were many cabals and divided loyalties among the officers of the 118th throughout their war service. Rivalries ran deep and feelings ran high, and Donaldson may have wanted to avoid becoming once again embroiled in any sort of controversy. Whatever the reason, although his name is occasionally mentioned in the body of the work, it is not listed among the contributors, even though I strongly suspect that he actually wrote much of what was contained in the book.

Several pieces of Donaldson's correspondence have previously appeared in print. An unincluded letter from early in his enlistment was published, in an edited form, in the *Philadelphia Daily Evening Bulletin* of September 12, 1861. There is little doubt that Jacob passed this letter on to the paper, with or without his brother's permission. A postwar letter to a young friend (not a part of the collection) in which Donaldson described a reconnaissance by the 118th Pennsylvania in late December 1862, appeared in the January 1961 issue of *Civil War Times Illustrated*. His letter of December 6, 1862, which was missing from the collection since the mid-1970s but has since been restored, was reprinted in *North-South Trader* in the January–February 1982 issue. Overall, remarkably little of what Donaldson recorded has previously been seen in print.

Donaldson wrote 169 letters, dozens of pages of diary entries, and several separate narratives during the course of his service. Included in this work are 117 letters, two postbattle narratives, and his diary entries. Donaldson's letters were carefully saved by his brother Jacob, who presented them to him several years after the war, and Donaldson painstakingly placed them in three large, black, leather-bound volumes. Each of the volumes measures 15½ by 11½ inches and contains on average 250 pages. The spines bear the gold-stamped title *Army Letters of Francis Adams Donaldson, 1861–1864*. Interspersed throughout his writings are photographs, personal papers, official documents, newspaper clippings, and in several places, correspondence with fellow soldiers that sheds light on details contained in the letters. In only three instances did Donaldson alter the content of his letters, blacking out or erasing passages. Almost every letter is accompanied by the post-marked and dated envelope in which it was mailed, although most of the stamps have disappeared. Roughly half of his correspondence was written in pencil and half in dark ink.

That Donaldson realized the importance and historical value of the collection is apparent by the care with which he arranged and preserved it. Although it was suggested to him on at least one occasion that he publish his letters, there is no record of any attempt to do so. Shortly before he died, Donaldson made it known to his oldest son, Francis Jr., that he wanted the volumes to be donated to The Civil War Library and Museum in Philadelphia (then known as the War Library and Museum), the welfare of which he was keenly interested in. Upon his passing in 1928, his wish was fulfilled, and his letters, photographs, and correspondence, along with other war-related personal effects, became a part of the holdings of the museum, where they can be studied by qualified scholars. The collection remained in the vaults of the museum, for the most part untouched, until I found it there in 1989. Donaldson surely would be pleased to know that the publication of the letters he treasured was being undertaken to benefit the institution he revered.

In editing the Donaldson letters, I have taken scrupulous care not to materially alter any of what he has recorded. Twenty letters from his first three months in service have not been included. Little of note happened to Donaldson during that time, and it is not until just before the Battle of Ball's Bluff that the present work begins. Portions of letters dealing with personal matters, entire letters that deal solely with personal matters, and material of a repetitive nature has been deleted. Additionally, due to space constraints, it was necessary to omit paragraphs and passages that might otherwise have added to the reader's insight into Donaldson. All told, roughly 35 percent of his writings were left out.

Like any writer, Donaldson occasionally misspelled words. In many places his errors can be attributed to several factors—fatigue, time constraints, or simple carelessness. This is evident from the fact that words that are misspelled in certain instances are, at other times, spelled correctly. I have corrected the majority of these misspellings, but, for the purpose of retaining some of the nineteenth-century flavor of his writing, I have kept his original spelling for some words, such as *bivouaced* for bivouacked and *centre* for center. In cases where proper or place names were misspelled, I have let the name or place stand initially as Donaldson wrote it, endnoted the error, and in subsequent mentions have silently corrected it. An occasional comma or apostrophe has been added or deleted, paragraphs formed, and proper punctuation has been added to the conversations he records. Words have been added in brackets where their presence is necessary to convey the meaning of a sentence. Ampersands replace the plus signs that Donaldson used as a substitute for the word *and*. Complimentary closes at the end of letters have been excised. I have added endnotes and explanatory paragraphs as necessary and have provided chapter introductions to help the reader more clearly follow Donaldson in his battles and campaigns. In no instance have I rewritten, modified, or changed anything that Donaldson wrote.

In conclusion, I would like to add a personal note, a justification, and a comment. It has been an unmitigated pleasure for me to have spent a portion of the last seven years in the company of Captain Donaldson, and it is with regret that I part with him. Given the multitude of firsthand accounts by participants in the American Civil War, one might ask why we need another one. Harold Adams Small, in the preface to his father's engagingly written memoir of service in the Army of the Potomac, answered the question best when he wrote:

> Because if we read only the latest Civil War novel or the latest Civil War history, we may lose as much as we gain. It is true that as time creates a perspective through which we look upon the past, we are better able to discern the relations of things and to judge men and motives more justly; but the gain in coolness of judgment is likely to be accompanied by a fatal loss in warmth of fellow feeling. The historian unhappily may be the first to suffer, and on his pages heroes will stiffen into statues, tides of anger and pride and fierce animosity will congeal as 'trends,' and pretty soon it will all be reduced to a 'complex of forces' and the war—the shouts and yells, the blood, the pain, the exultation and despair—will have become a 'study.' . . . As the years carry us farther and farther away from the Civil War, the more we lose in actual nearness to what was once as near as a trigger to the finger. The only way for us to reach back to it, now, is through a book; and the surest way is through a record set down by one who was there.

Small had prefaced these comments with an observation on the relative skill of the Civil War memoirist: "If he writes well, so much the more enjoyment for us. Even if he writes badly, something will shine through, and we will see for a moment what he saw and in the sunlight of his day."[6]

Fortunately for us, Donaldson wrote well, and the tides of anger and pride, the shouts and yells, and the exultation and despair all shine through in his letters.

CHAPTER 1

Ball's Bluff,
Captivity, and Return

September 28, 1861–March 20, 1862

*T*he 1st California Regiment was raised under the authority of President Abraham Lincoln by his close friend and former Illinois Whig party confidant, Edward D. Baker. Baker, fifty, was an English-born lawyer-politician known for his brilliant oratorical skills. He also possessed military experience, having commanded an Illinois regiment, and later a brigade, in the Mexican War. After serving several terms as a congressman representing Illinois in the 1840s, Baker relocated to San Francisco in 1852 to resume his law practice.

Over the course of the decade that preceded the Civil War, Baker had become a leader in the California Republican party, and in the months leading up to the Rebellion he had worked tirelessly to ensure that the western U.S. territories would remain loyal to the Union. When the conflict began in April 1861, Baker was in Washington, D.C., serving as the first senator from the newly admitted state of Oregon.

Initially dissatisfied with the speed with which troops were arriving to defend the capital, Baker hastened to New York City in mid-April, hoping to attract enough men from California then present in that metropolis to complete his regiment, but he met with only limited success.[1] Not willing to concede defeat, he contacted his former San Francisco law partner, Philadelphia native Isaac J. Wistar, and promised him a lieutenant colonelcy if he would help him to fill out the regiment by recruiting in Philadelphia. "Within six months I shall be a major general," Baker promised Wistar, "and you shall have a brigadier general's commission and a satisfactory command under me."[2]

Wistar took on the task in earnest, and by late May he had forwarded over one thousand Philadelphians to Fort Schuyler, New York. Included among them was 5th Sergeant Francis Adams Donaldson of Company H.

Donaldson was immediately taken with his new vocation. "The life of a soldier as thus far experienced," he wrote Jacob early in his service, "has every charm for me, and

19

I tell you frankly that I like it and strive with all my energy to be a soldier in everything." The young recruit apparently excelled at his duties, as by mid-June he had been promoted to third sergeant of his company.

The California Regiment remained at Fort Schuyler, drilling and training under the direction of Lieutenant Colonel Wistar (Baker had retained his senate seat and split his time between the regiment and his obligations at Washington) until June 28, when they were ordered to Fort Monroe, Virginia.

Outfitted in what Donaldson described as a "gray light jacket, gray pants with red stripe down the leg, gray felt overcoat, [and a] very heavy and entirely impervious fatigue cap," which had originally been earmarked for a Confederate artillery regiment,[3] the regiment paraded through the streets of New York and headed south. On passing through Philadelphia, five additional companies were added to the ten already in place, and the men arrived at Fort Monroe on July 6.

The regiment continued its instruction and training near Fort Monroe, which was located on the tip of the peninsula formed by the York and James Rivers, and conducted occasional picket and scouting forays inland, although they fought nothing more substantial than the insects of Virginia. "My dear brother," wrote Donaldson, "the bite of the bold Virginia Secesh mosquito is as unlike the gentle puncture of the educated abolition mosquito of the good old Quaker City as is the kick of a mule to a gentle tap from the paw of a kitten. . . . My head looks like a big plum pudding."

The California Regiment's stay in Virginia was short-lived. In late July, following the Confederate victory at First Bull Run, they were rushed to Washington to help bolster the defenses of the capital against an expected Rebel attack. The Southerners failed to take advantage of the disorder their triumph had wrought, however, and they settled into a defensive position near Manassas.

Donaldson and his fellows were soon set to work building fortifications and manning the defenses surrounding the city. Like many of his comrades who were seeing their nation's capital for the first time, Donaldson was unimpressed. "I don't think much of Washington City," he wrote in August. "It may be pleasant in winter, but in summer it is both scorchingly hot and very dusty. Apart from the public buildings, there is really nothing to see here."

Maj. Gen. George Brinton McClellan, a thirty-four-year-old West Pointer who had recently met with success in several minor battles in western Virginia, was placed in command at this time by Lincoln. McClellan was a skillful administrator and organizer, and he immediately set about molding the disheartened troops encamped around the capital into a cohesive fighting force. Within a few short months, he was able to take a defeated, dispirited mass of men and instill in them pride, discipline, order—and an *identity: They would ever after be known as the Army of the Potomac. In the process, McClellan earned from many of the men who served under him, including Donaldson, an unswerving devotion. "He is . . . ," Donaldson would write in early November 1862, "the greatest military chieftain of the age."*

In October, the 1st California Regiment was brigaded with the Philadelphia-raised 2nd and 3rd California Regiments, and all were placed under the command of Colonel Baker. Following a reconnaissance and foraging expedition to Lewinsville, Virginia,[4] on September 11, Baker's brigade was posted in reserve outside of Washington on the Virginia side of the Potomac River. On September 28, the brigade was ordered on a nighttime advance to Munson's Hill, a commanding eminence several miles southwest of Ball's Cross Roads that was occupied by the Confederates. In what proved to be a deadly mix-up, the gray-clad California Regiment and its supports were fired on by advanced Union pickets who mistook them for the enemy in the moonlight. "Was there ever such a mixed up affair?" lamented Donaldson. "Who is responsible for sending upon such an expedition men dressed in the garb of the enemy?"

Camp near Monocacy, Md.
Oct. 15, 1861

Dear Jacob:

Yes! it has been a long time, indeed, since I last wrote you, and, as you say, a perfect age has passed by, with its stirring incidents, while pages have been added to the military biography of your younger soldier brother. It will be utterly impossible to chronicle all the many stirring scenes encountered during this time, and the brief mention of them in my letter to Auntie, is, I fear, all that I will be able to do. I have been unable to keep a correct journal owing to our rapid movements, and the want of paper to note my daily experiences upon. But I will try and give you a hasty review of our doings to date, and only regret Capt. Tomlin's[5] inability to see and give you a personal account of the "Midnight horror at Munson's Hill."[6] . . .

Nothing of moment ocurred until Sept. 28th, when after retreat had sounded, orders came for the regiment to prepare for immediate marching orders, and at 10 p.m. with the balance of the brigade we started, with the California Regiment and a battery of artillery in the van. There were a good many surmises as to our probable destination, but from the fact that knapsacks had been left behind, the one day's cooked rations alone told it to be a midnight attack upon the enemy. It was soon learned that many other troops, beside those of our brigade, were marching also, and the mystery attending the expedition, together with the celerity of our movement, caused us to be keenly on the alert.

At first the night was extremely dark but towards midnight the moon came up and illuminated the woods and fields through which we passed, making distant objects distinctly clear to our vision. . . . Just at the place where the outposts were met, and where we halted for a little rest, ran a road at right angles with the one on which we were traveling, and out which the picket posts at short intervals extended along the worm fence bordering the side of it nearest the enemy's country. The fences on the opposite side had been taken to form rude shelters. The now thoroughly amused sentinels, near us, stood in front of their posts with every look and appearance of astonishment at our sudden advent. In conversation with them I learned the enemy were abt. a mile further on, and that Munson's Hill was abt. a mile and half out the road on which we then were. Again we moved forward, but no skirmishers were thrown out, which suprised me a good deal. I could not

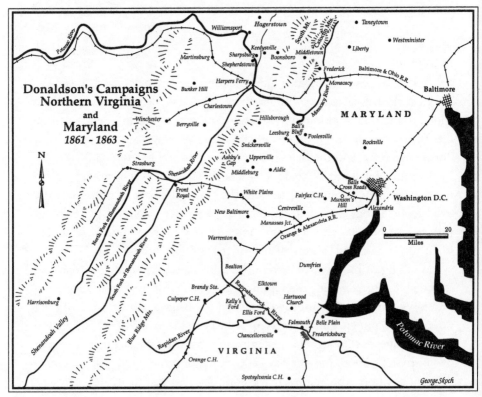

understand how it was we could move in the enemys country without the protection of a skirmish line. I will confess that I felt nervous and excited, but the comforting assurance that we were commanded by an able and experienced officer, Genl. W. F. Smith,[7] went a great deal towards quieting my apprehensions.

Orders were now received for the men to cease talking and to make as little noise as possible. In our company were a number of unruly men who either could not or would not understand the importance of religiously observing this order, and among them, Private Joseph Pascoe[8] seemed, in this occasion, to be possessed by an uncontrollable demon. He was spoken to a number of times by Capt. Mallery,[9] but nothing could stop his low jests and blasphemy. At length, after lighting his pipe, contrary to the most positive orders not to strike matches, he finished a long speech in a merry burst of low humor and a string of oaths that appalled me. We were then at a halt so I went up to [him], and in as forcible a manner said to him, "Pascoe—be careful that the Almighty God, whom you have just asked to damn your soul, don't take you at your word." Said I, "We are apparently upon some desperate undertaking, and you, among others of us, may be called suddenly to meet this God above you so grossly defy, so cease your cursing and act as a man."

With all his indifference, bluster, and noise, Pascoe was a man well liked by every man, and his great fault of profane swearing was more a habit than otherwise, but it was exceedingly uncalled for and out of place at this time. This conversation had taken place within the hearing of the whole company and had a very salutary effect upon the men. I heard no more loud talking from any of them save Pascoe, who kept it up despite all efforts to still him.

The road now led through dense forests and after a further march of about ½ hour we came to a halt near a place called Falls Church, when the order was given to load our muskets. The moon was now shining brightly, and our regiment, with its gray uniforms, looked, for all the world, like the rebels. As we stood in the roadway, the silence of death prevailing and not a sound disturbing the tranquil midnight air, the sudden & incessant barking of a dog in the distance jarred uncomfortably upon our sensitive ear, as strained to its utmost tension, we listened for the slightest sound that would apprise us of the nearness of the enemy. I will never forget the tones of that terrible beast, and though it must have been at least a ¼ mile away, its dreadfully plaintive whine and sharp bark made me feel that the creature had scented us and was giving the alarm to our foes.

We were now wrought up to a great state of excitement by the conflicting orders passed along the line, while the death like stillness, the uncertainty as to our position, and what was expected of us all tended to increase the uneasiness of the men. How it came about will probably never be known, but suddenly a panic and a stampede took place on the right of the line, and the rushing sound made by the frightened men as they pushed and crowded each other in one wild endeavor to escape some impending and unforseen danger was the most harrowing and blood curdling I ever heard. The alarm extended along the whole line, and like sheep they broke for the woods back of the regiment, and instantly all organization and discipline was lost. Each man struggled to be the first to climb the worm fence between him and safety.

At this instant a rapid discharge of musketry came from the woods opposite, which added to the horror and confusion. My heart was paralyzed with a dreadful fear and my hair stood on end. Whether it was that I was unable to move, I cannot say, but I stood still in the middle of the road for a moment and looked right into the flaming tongues of fire as they came from the muskets of the unseen hands that fired them. I was very speedily knocked down, however, and lay in the roadway with the body of a man across me. The men, as they gained the shelter of the trees, commenced returning the fire, and a fierce fusillade ensued, which lasted a few minutes and then ceased altogether. Speaking to the man that lay so heavily across me, I told him to get up as all danger was past. Yes! all danger had passed for him—poor fellow, for he was dead—shot in the throat—his warm blood flowing over my pants. Would you believe it, Jacob, when I tell you it was Pascoe, who was even now standing in the presence of that God he so lately defied, and shot in the throat too, how dreadful—how awfully swift the avenging hand of the almighty.

Disengaging myself I sprang to my feet, and owing to the absence of Sloanaker[10] who was home sick, I was acting orderly sergeant, & commenced calling the roll from memory. As the men responded to their names they came over the fence and took place in line. When I called the name of Ed. Ford,[11] there was no response, which surprised me somewhat, so I called again "Ed. Ford," when someone in the ranks called out, "hasn't got the order to halt yet." I afterward learned that at the first alarm he had taken to his heels and ran away, never stopping until the old camp was reached. This was most mortifying to me, as Ford had been considered one of the brave and reliable men of the Co. I will state here, that his conduct, on this occasion, alienated his friends and caused the dissolution of the "House of Lords."[12]

Ford rapidly lost cast and there after was of no account except to be company clerk for Captain Mallery. He still tents with me, however—but as he is a non-combatant and not subject to drills or duty of any kind—he makes himself generally useful about home—as it were.

When Joseph Payran's[13] name was called, the same answer was given, "No order to halt yet," but daylight found the poor fellow, with one leg thrown over the top rail of the fence from whence came the firing, and so nicely was he balanced that, although he was stone dead, one would have supposed him to be merely resting preparatory to leaping over. The ball that had slain him had [pierced] his eye, passing through the glass of a pair of spectacles, but leaving them still adjusted with one glass yet perfect. Joseph White[14] lay dead in the middle of the road, amid a pool of blood, with his brains all scattered around. Many of the men did not put in an appearance until daylight, but at morning roll call all were accounted for except Ford.

Scarcely had order been somewhat restored when a second panic seized the men, and again a stampede took place. There were a few, however, who merely crouched down in the road as the firing again commenced, among whom were myself and Lieut. Harris,[15] and we discovered that it was our own men who were firing on each other. It appears the Berdan Sharpshooters,[16] a part of the same expedition, had been marching out another road, and their skirmishers, discovering us as we stood in the moonlight and mistaking our uniforms for that of the rebels, had fired into us. They now, at this second stampede, moved over the fence in order to attack, and as they gained the road we discovered their true character and called out they were firing in their own people. Maj. Parish[17] and Adjutant Newlin[18] now came riding along the road, calling loudly for the California Regiment to fall in and cease firing.

To add still further to the commotion, the battery was heard to get into position to rake the road, and only for the forethought and promptness of Lt. Wm. C. Harris, a terrible slaughter would have ensued. Hastily calling upon those near him, he ordered a charge upon the guns and with a yell of despair we cleared the intervening space and actually took them, the gunners running in all directions and leaving their half loaded cannons in our hands. I ran still further to the rear in order to give notice of the mistake that was happening, when I found the road choked with abandoned ammunition wagons and artillery. Had the enemy been near, and understood the situation, a large capture could have been made by them. The alarm extended far to the rear and troops were hurried out of Washington and the adjacent Forts to repel the attack of the enemy. I never beheld such confusion.

The finale to this disgraceful affair was in my meeting with a squadron of the Cameroon Dragoon's picking their way along the road to charge our poor regiment.[19] These I stopped and fortunately recognized in their orderly Sergeant my old friend Billy Bird,[20] who speedily recognized me, and an explanation took place. His orders were to support the battery and by charging clear the road. Was there ever such a mixed up affair? Was there ever in the annals of War, such a disgraceful disorder? And pray who is responsible for the great loss of life—Who is responsible for sending upon such an expedition men dressed in the garb of the enemy? There had been 20 men killed and 50 wounded among our men and the Berdan men.[21]

The regiment was now reassembled and after a little rest again moved forward a short distance and encamped on the road and in the wood where the Berdan men had been. The presence of other troops were discovered which at day break proved to be those of the 9th Massachusetts Regiment, the van of another column of the same expedition.

The dawn showed a most curious sight. Very many of the men in their fright had lost their caps, and in seeking others had taken any that had come handy, and the gray felt, green plumed, stiff brimmed hat of the sharpshooter was freely found among the gray forage cap of the regiment. There were also found very many of the curious globe-sighted weapons of the Berdan men, and during the course of the morning quite a time was had exchanging these articles. Munson's Hill was found abandoned by another column, and it is supposed the enemy, hearing the firing and suspecting its cause, prudently retreated. So Ended the Night of Horrors.

Immediately after their mishap, Baker's Brigade was ordered to join Brig. Gen. Charles P. Stone's division guarding the upper fords of the Potomac near Poolesville, Maryland. Stone had been charged with monitoring Confederate infantry posted in the vicinity of Leesburg, Virginia, and on October 20 was ordered to make a "slight demonstration" across the Potomac in hopes of forcing the Rebels to withdraw.[22] Stone, in turn, gave Colonel Baker discretionary orders on October 21 to either withdraw a small reconnaissance force that was already across the river near Leesburg or, if he encountered an inferior enemy force and felt that he might gain an advantage, reinforce the detachment. Unknowingly faced by a numerically superior Confederate force, Baker ill-advisedly chose to ferry his command piecemeal across the Potomac and fight. The resulting Battle of Ball's Bluff cost Baker his life and the Union 49 killed, 198 wounded, and 714 missing and captured. Among the captives was Donaldson, who would spend the next four months as a prisoner in Richmond.

On Sunday Sept. 30th our Brigade recrossed the Potomac and marched to Great Falls, Md.—a distance of about 10 miles. Again we had no idea of the object of our movement, but as we packed up and took everything along, a permanent change of camp was thought to be most likely.

Oct. 1st. At noon, we again took up line of march and at dark halted at Rockville. This was a glorious march through a glorious civilized country, at least the cultivated fields and well kept towns along the route told us that war's rude blast had not yet swept over this portion of the country. We saw very few people on the way and these betook themselves in doors as we passed their farm lands.

Oct. 2nd. We marched to Seneca Mills, through a drenching rain storm. This was a pretty place with its Great Flouring Mill in full operation, the workmen coming to the open door ways of each floor in front of the building, down which the hoisting rope hung idly, and gazed in silence as our wet, muddy and forlorn brigade passed by. Certainly there was no enthusiasm manifested, and one would have supposed, from the stoical indifference that we were looked upon as intruders. It will be well for them if the ravages of war does not reach this place and lay it waste.

Oct. 3rd. We reached here and encamped. It is near Pollsville,[23] Montgomery Co. Md., but I do not know whether we are to locate permanently or not. Col. Baker gave orders that private property should be respected and that each company would be allowed 10 fence rails for fuel. Since then, from the appearance of the country I should judge that after the first 10 had been used, the Co.'s began a new count, as there are none left.

We have pitched camp according to regulations, and have had work since at drills and other camp duties. Col. Baker and Lt. Col. Wistar have had the officers in hand, and the principles of battalion drill and other duties incumbent upon commissioned officers have been gone through with daily. It is a fine sight to us men of the ranks to see the company officers ordered around and hectored as the drill masters instruct them in the practical workings of tactical movements. The sergeants, also, have been in constant course of instruction by Maj. Parrish as to their particular duties, especially in that of guide, and I must confess I have learned much from him. Maj. Parrish is a stern, strict disciplinarian who requires the closest attention to his orders, and as he imparts the knowledge of his much studied tactics, he hammers home each lesson with the final injunction that he will make us thorough soldiers—"by the Eternal," he will. Upon several occasions I have been out on officers drill, and now feel quite at ease in giving commands, as it frequently happened, in order that officers should properly understand the practical meaning of "facings" and "wheelings," I have been put in command of a platoon of them. I made no bones in keeping them up to the work, I can tell you.

An incident lately occurred upon one of the Sunday morning drills, when the regiment was out for "Divine Worship" which made me somewhat conspicuous against my will, and, I fear, hurt the feelings of a really worth[y] man. It appears that we were performing a movement by inversion, and I, in the absence of Lt. Harris, had charge of the 2nd platoon of the Co. Immediately on my right was Capt. Keffer,[24] who, by the way, is a most excellent man, but a poor tactician, and is constantly getting mixed up when on drill. We were in column of platoons when by inversion were marching rear rank in front, and the order was given to form Company while on the march and then to halt. Capt. Keffer got his company so thoroughly tangled up that Col. Wistar, who was in command, halted the column, and after a volley of oaths, called the Captain to the front, and told him to hold up his right arm. When he had done so he said, "Captain that is your right arm, now hold up your left. That, Sir, is your left arm, now don't again forget your left from your right, or else I will take your company from you and give it to Sergeant Donaldson, who is more fitted to command it than you are." Can you imagine the utter humiliation of the poor man, to be thus disgraced before the whole command? And can you imagine my feelings at being so complimented? Why Jacob, I felt my face burn with shame at the indignity put upon the Captain, and the prominence given to my knowledge of the tactics.

However, things are now looking nicely, and the regiment is looking in tip-top condition in its new uniforms, which I am glad to state have at last been issued. It consists of a dark blue jacket, light blue pants and dark blue fatigue cap. They are of a very superior and substantial quality and add greatly to our appearance. Indeed we look like a new regiment just come out. I feel sure, also, that the boys appreciate these good things, and work better and behave better, too. The fine crisp weather we are having may have something to do with their behavior, and I often look at their glowing, healthy countenances, and feel that an army composed of such material as Baker has under him could over-run the whole country without hindrance.

Maj. Chas. Smith[25] continues his kindness to me and upon every available occasion stops his horse and has something kindly to say. I wish he would not do so as I have no desire to be considered as attempting familiarity with my superiors. I avoid him always, and when it cannot be helped and I have to respond to his kind words, I invariably stand in the position of a soldier and salute him in the most respectful & soldierly manner. If he can forget that army discipline changes the relations of former acquaintance & friendship I can not.

Our tent is a marvel of neatness and comfort and was made so by dint of hard work and the practical experience gained in former campaigns. Sergeant Stiles[26] was the architect and straw the material used. By a complete system of organized raids upon a neighboring farm, we borrowed (some would call it stealing) a dozen "battons" of straw, which, after being matted together, were spread along the sides and floor. We also made a door of straw, well bound together and fastened by straps, in an ingenious manner, to the front pole. This was the happy work of old "limp-and-go-fetch-it" Chapman,[27] and all his idle moments are now spent in swinging it backward and forward to see whether the "hinges" creak—so he says. Over the top we fastened our oil cloth blankets, and are now able to bid defiance to the rude blasts of "old Boreas." Stiles has given birth to an underground plan for a house, which should the supply of straw fail or the present arrangement not prove a success, we will put into execution, when assured our stay will be a permanent one, or at least for the winter.

We have also built an <u>oven</u>, and the manner in which old Stiles divided up the work among us was most creditable to his Yankee ingenuity. Stiles himself was the master builder and stone mason, Ed. Ford mortar maker, Jimmy Chapman hod carrier, and myself, water carrier and wood chopper. We commenced in good earnest after reveille on the morning of the 13th, Ford & I . . . getting up a lot of the most superior mortar ever seen on Mason & Dixon's line. It consisted of well mixed soft mud, and after we were through, samples of it in great profusion covered our shoes and clothing. Stiles broke and fitted the stones that Chapman brought him, and before breakfast we had the foundation formed and lain, and by 12M the whole structure finished and ready for the fire. We inaugurated its completion by heating it hot and baking a prodigious mess of pork and beans, which required all night to thoroughly cook. The next morning, upon removing the door, we found the savory dish done to a turn. In fact, my dear brother, in order to form anything like a proper appreciation of our luxury and grandeur, you must visit our encampment and see for yourself. Our tent is celebrated for its good cheer and hospitality, the latch string always hanging out, and a dish of "Sheet Iron" bread awaits the visitor who chances to call.

At night a knot of friends gather around the oven drawn thither by the glowing fire and genial warmth, while levity and mirth claim the happy hours until "tattoo." . . .

The other day I witnessed, for the first time, a regular nigro dance, or break-down. Some darkeys from a neighboring plantation, having come into camp to see what could be picked up in the old cloths line, and to take a look at Massa Lincum's soldiers, chanced into our streets, and the boys got around and set them to dancing. I never saw such dancing in my life—how they did jump and throw themselves about, and with it all, seemed so happy that it was with difficulty we could get them to stop. They appeared to be quite amused at our ignorance of such matters, and one of them said contemptuously, "sho' you nebber seed a smot nigger affo'." They promised to come again on Sunday, and as their dancing and singing is of the nature of a religious worship, no harm can be done in starting them up.

Speaking of Sunday, we have on that day a very interesting discourse by our chaplain, and as the regiment is paraded for that purpose, the speaker is gratified by the presence of a large congregation. However, as he generally manages to make his sermons interesting, he is complimented still further by the close attention of the men, who remain silent and respectful listeners.

The country round about us is very beautiful, and the farmers continue plowing as though there was no such thing as an army near them. I am very thankful for this, as we feel we are among civilized people, while in Virginia everything looks so desolate and forsaken. I will now have to say good bye, because of an invitation to spend a little time with Lieutenants Harris and Urie[28] at their quarters. The latter gentleman is rapidly gaining in the flesh, which he attributes to the amount of dirt eaten, the limit of the traditional pick having long since been exceeded. . . . My health and spirits are good, and I begin to believe what every one says is so, that I am at last gaining weight. Upon looking at my watch I find it is so late, everyone having long since retired, that I will have to abandon my contemplated visit to Lieut. Harris' quarters—and say good night—I am so sleepy although it is a splendid night and one to enjoy around the oven fire.

> The very pen within my hand
> Its sabbath seems to keep,
> And sinks in the accustomed stand
> To gauge the sable deep,
> Men, company, camp, mess and
> Your scribes are Fast asleep.

Oct. 16th. . . . I am sorry I cannot answer your query as to the object of our movement to this point, but presume it is to meet the enemy should they attempt a raid into Maryland. We have also reinforced Genl. Stone,[29] under whose command we now are, and with the other forces he has, make up a respectable division. I am sorry to learn of the bad opinion the people have formed of Col. Baker, and fail to understand it at all. His men love him devotedly, and I feel sure he will never again leave us.

In regard to a furlough, it is simply impossible to get one, and it is therefore useless to try—Again, I do not care to leave, when there is a prospect of a forward movement. You must recollect we have never had orders to go into Winter Quarters, and are still, a moveable column, as it were. . . .

. . . Captain Collis[30] has been over on a visit, and I find him the same gay fellow as ever. That is, I stood off and looked on his reception by the officers. I am an enlisted man, you know, and keep my place accordingly.

Tell Harry Donaldson[31] not to take anything along with him but what is absolutely necessary, as every little thing in his knapsack will weigh a pound on a long march. I could make use of a good army blanket and think it would reach me by Adams Express—would also like to have a good pair of buckskin gloves. The Express reaches and if you think you can secure these things for me, will be very glad to get them.

Enclosed find a lock of my hair; I had it cut in the "plug" fashion today, and send you this lest an occasion might arise when it would be a comfort to you all to have it. I send it as a remembrance. . . .

Donaldson's description of his experiences at the Battle of Ball's Bluff is made up from notes he took following his exchange in March 1862. His narrative was supplemented by a volume of recollections, which a friend and fellow prisoner, 2nd Lt. William C. Harris of Company H, published soon after his return from Richmond. Donaldson wrote the account while at home in Philadelphia during the summer of 1862.

On October 3rd, 1861 the California Regiment, afterwards the 71st Pennsylvania Volunteers marched to and encamped at Poolesville, Montgomery County, Maryland, having left Camp Advance, Virginia, the extreme outpost of the Union Army, beyond the defenses of Washington, Sunday morning September 30th. Here it remained in the usual course of active and incessant instruction and training until the morning of October 21st when at one o'clock it was suddenly aroused by hasty marching orders.

One half of the regiment was on picket along the Monocacy River, and Companies A, C, D, G, H, L, N, P alone made up the command. While the regiment was preparing to move, Colonel E. D. Baker, commanding, visited each company street and talked with the men. We had lately received new uniforms, regulation, including overalls, instead of gray in which we had been clothed, and I asked the Colonel if we should wear the overalls with the new clothes. "Yes," said he, "put on all the uniform that you have as it will be none too good to die in." This remark rather surprised me at the time but I soon forgot it and did not recall it until some days afterward.

Just before the regiment marched I was directed by Lieutenant William C. Harris to go to a farm house beyond Poolesville where a friend of his resided and notify the family of our hasty movement. I did so but was prevented from approaching the house by two vicious dogs, and so, stopping at the fence gate, I called lustily and tried to awaken someone in the house. Finally hearing a window raised, I said the regiment had moved away towards the Potomac and then made haste back to camp, but on the way I learned the regiment had moved at 2 o'clock and was a long way ahead of me, but I succeeded in overtaking it. It was a cold gray morning. At daylight we found many inhabitants of the various houses passed awake and at doors and windows. When asked how far it was to the Potomac, "about two miles" was the invariable answer, and it was always "two miles" until we reached the river. At 7 A.M. Conrad's Ferry was reached where we rested on the banks of the Chesapeake and Ohio Canal skirting the Maryland shore, and awaited.

Immediately across the river rises abruptly Ball's Bluff, covered with trees, undergrowth and rocks, making it impassable for artillery and almost so for infantry. It commands Harrison's Island, a narrow track of land a mile or two in length, midway the stream. The river was high from recent storms, flowing with great rapidity and very deep. The means of crossing was altogether inadequate, being two scows for crossing to the Island, one scow, one boat, and two small skiffs for crossing to the Virginia side. We commenced crossing to the Island at about nine o'clock and then over to the Virginia side. There were two cannon on the Island, a few wounded and a number of men from other regiments when I crossed. As fast as each boat reached the shore, the men scrambled and climbed the Bluff nearly to the top where we awaited further orders. We had about, or, a little more than 1,500 men in the line, composed of parts of the California, 15th and 20th Massachusetts, and 42nd New York regiments.

About noon skirmish firing commenced and the battle was on at about 2:30 P.M. I was greatly excited throughout the entire action, especially at first, and much annoyed because our muskets fouled so.

The first one killed in my company (H) was Private Morris Stradling,[32] a man of magnificent physique and a fine soldier. I was near him at the time. Lieutenant Urie, late a sergeant of Co. H, but now in command of Co. L, was on the right of the regiment and I ran along in rear of the battle line and told him of the death of Stradling. "Get down," said he, and pulled me beside him on the ground close to his company, now loading and firing with great coolness and deliberation.

Urie was a man who always saw the humorous, as I had often observed, and he now pointed to one of his men, an old fellow with spectacles, who would wipe his glasses before firing to make sure of his aim, but while talking to me [he] was shot in the shoulder and rolled down the hill a short distance to near where one of the assistant surgeons had established himself to be near at hand in assisting the wounded, and [who], with my help, took charge of Urie, bound up his shoulder as best he could, gave him a big drink of whiskey, and started us both down the Bluff. I had the satisfaction of assisting him into a barge that, with many wounded, was leaving for Harrison's Island.

I now made my way to the front where the battle was fiercely waging and when nearing the top I met Private Marsden coming down, very seriously wounded, his lower jaw having been shot away.[33] As I passed the two cannon, (small Howitzers) which had been dragged up the hill along a rough path the artillerymen had made, I found but one in service, the other disabled, the gun crew killed or wounded, and it was being served by a few infantrymen as best they could, and I assisted in filling it with stones and dirt, as, with the exception of a few flannel powder bags, all ammunition had been expended. Then I returned to my company and continued with it until the end, frequently near Colonel Baker and Lieutenant Colonel Wistar, who were constantly in advance of the line of battle.

About this time I noticed many wounded of Co. H either lying on the ground or crawling to gain cover below the hilltop, and that Privates Harvey, Johnson, and Survey were dead.[34] Private Jaggard[35] I saw shot and carried off the field by two soldiers, his legs over one of the muskets which both held and [his] arms around their necks. He recognized me as they passed. He died, I believe, when they got to the river bank. His loss was a very sad one to me as he was a kind friend and jovial comrade.

The battle ground was an open space on top of the Bluff, surrounded on three sides by dense woods which concealed and covered the movements of the enemy occupying them, while we held the other side at the edge of the Bluff. At intervals there would be a lull in the fighting, and as strange as it may appear, at times there would come from across the river strains of music from a band on the canal bank. Notwithstanding the turmoil, noise and confusion, I was conscious of the music and repeatedly recognized the airs played.

About 4 o'clock Colonel Baker was killed immediately in front of Company H. There had been fierce fighting and part of our line had been driven to and below the hill top. I did not see Colonel Baker killed, although but a short distance from him, because of the smoke that hung along our line, but saw him immediately after he fell, stretched full length on his side, with his head resting on his hand and elbow. Captain Beirel,[36] Co. G came running toward the group of Company H and others that were still on the hill top and implored those below to join with those at the top in recovering the body of Baker. "Do you wish to leave the body of our beloved Colonel in the hands of the enemy?," said he. This brought a number of men forward, a rush was made which drove off the rebels, but not before they had despoiled the body of its overcoat and hat. Shortly after, the Massachusetts men formed and made a charge, forcing the enemy from the clearing back into the woods again, but it was only momentarily, for the 8th Virginia, 17th & 18th Mississippi again assumed the offensive and charged, finally driving us off the hill. Colonel Cogswell,[37] 42nd New York, now ranking officer present, gave the order to retire and the line gave way and rushed down the Bluff in a wild, disorderly retreat, amidst the relentless firing of the enemy from the top. The only boats between the Virginia side and the Island had been sunk while returning with wounded; communication being thus cut off many tried to save themselves by swimming, but the current was too swift and cold, and but few succeeded. So those who escaped this terrible affair, shivering with cold, many with but scanty clothes, having discarded their uniforms in endeavor to swim, had to surrender. The battle of Ball's Bluff was over and I became a prisoner of war.

It was late when I was captured. Private Whitehouse[38] and I after the retreat hurried along the river bank in an endeavor to reach our lines at Edwards Ferry, seven miles below, and after proceeding rapidly for at least an hour, sat down on a fallen tree trunk to rest. We were both wet, having waded out in the river, but did not part with any of our equipments. The moon was brightly shining making objects for a considerable distance quite distinct. We had been seated probably five minutes when a voice called out from the hill above, "Don't move, Yanks, stay right where you are, how many are you?" I replied, "There are but two of us." "Come up here one at a time." I told Whitehouse I would go up first and did so. When I reached the top I found about 100 men in line drawn up to receive us. Without waiting for Whitehouse I was told to pass to the left of the line, and when I reached there I was stopped by a mounted officer who proved to be Col. Fetherson,[39] 17th Mississippi, who asked if I had any side arms. The moon was shining brightly on me as I turned to answer and hand him a bayonet I still held, when he asked my name, home regiment and age. Just then Whitehouse came along and we were ordered to fall in to the front of the detail, which we did, and the line of march was taken up to near the late battlefield where many other prisoners, officers and men, were assembled, and the whole moved on to Leesburg, some two or three miles beyond.

One of the sergeants of the 17th Mississippi marched alongside of me and in conversation with him I learned that the Colonel of the 18th Mississippi had been killed[40] and casualties were so severe in his regiment that it had been consolidated with the 17th under command of Colonel Featherston towards the close of battle. As we proceeded towards Leesburg he told me to give him my canteen, and upon hesitating to do so, demanded it. Shortly after he left me. This incident caused me to scatter along the road the musket caps I had, fearing trouble should they be found on me. Presently the sergeant rejoined the column and returned my canteen with directions to use its contents sparingly. I found it half filled with whiskey the kind fellow had secured somehow. Upon my thanking him for his generosity and goodness, he said that during the battle he had noticed me at the cannon and could not make sure how it was that I had not been shot, as he knew I had been fired at repeatedly. Of course he was mistaken as I was but a very short time at the guns and doubtless he mistook me for an artilleryman because of the overalls I had on, similar to those worn by the artillery. He also claimed me as his personal prisoner, I do not know why, but he seemed to feel that in some way he owned me. However, I was very grateful for his kindness.

Upon reaching Leesburg we were at once surrounded by a howling, frantic mob, the townspeople appearing perfectly maddened at the sight of us, and with yells of ecstasy and derision, crowding and shouldering each other in herds to get a glimpse of us, shouting "We got 'em this time," "Oh you infernal Yankees," "Make way there, I want to see a Yankee," and it was not until we were taken off the street that the wild uproar of the furious multitude quieted. To their credit it must be said the rebel soldiers, our late antagonists, protected us from physical violence.

My dear friend, my late enemy the sergeant, took me away with him, and after bidding me goodbye, passed me into a brilliantly lighted building hard bye, which proved to be the headquarters of General Evans,[41] commanding the rebel forces, and now occupied by the captured Union officers. As soon as I perceived this I sought Lieutenant Harris and had him pass me out to the guard, where I explained that I was not an officer but an enlisted man, and was at once taken to the Court House which, by the way, was filled with prisoners, so I was put into the gallery, which was not so crowded.

About 10 o'clock bread was distributed, hot, newly baked, a half a loaf to each man, those in the gallery, where I was, received theirs from the point of a bayonetted musket reached up to them. By some chance I was handed a full loaf, and without being sure of it have always credited my rebel friend, the sergeant, with this further evidence of his kindness. Water was also served. Here we remained until 12 o'clock when we were ordered out on the street, assembled in column of fours and marched about two miles, halting in an open field to await arrival of our officers. Shortly after they joined us, the march was resumed to Manassas, 25 miles away, the prisoners still in column, the officers in front and as many as possible of them crowded into the only wagon provided as a convoy.

The roads from recent rains had become ankle deep with mud, and although the moon had been brightly shining, it clouded up and commenced raining before daybreak, and continued throughout the day, rendering the march slow [and] tiresome, with much suffering from the sharp October air. We were guarded on the front, rear, and flanks, under command of Captain Singleton,[42] 18th Mississippi, and Captain Jones,[43] 17th Mississippi. Captain Singleton was a very humane man and won our regard by his efforts to cheer and help us keep up, frequently dismounting and putting a weary, worn out soldier on his horse, and many times taking a man up behind him. Upon one occasion, he rode beside and invited me to ride, saying "Here youngster, put your foot on mine and get up behind me, you seem very tired." I thanked him and replied that there were many others more weary than I, and many times during the day he would talk with me evincing interest not only in me but in other youthful prisoners. Upon one occasion towards noon he spoke rather energetically to the stragglers, saying in his broad southern dialect, "Look here you men, I have been doing all that I can to help you to get along, and I must insist that you keep up, for we are obliged to lose as little time as possible. I call you men as we call our troops, all gentlemen, not boys, as you call all your soldiers, we call our niggers boys.

Now see here, I have done nothing for my men and they are just as tired and worn out as you are, besides, very few have overcoats as you have." (He pointed to the splendid waterproof French Chausseur overcoats worn by our regiment.) I replied that while it was true his men did not lag nor complain, they were buoyed up by pride and the consciousness of having won a great battle, while we, the losers, were dispirited, discouraged and altogether uncertain as to our future. It is really a fact, I did not see one of his men with an overcoat. Gradually the officers' wagon became filled with sick and weary privates, the officers trudging through the mud to relieve them. . . .

At one or two halts we made, lasting a few minutes each, Captain Singleton told us to gather persimmons from trees that seemed to abound in this section, but would not allow his men to take any. I know that I had a goodly quantity. At near four o'clock in the afternoon we halted at a large mill near Bull Run; the privates were placed in the mill and the officers in the miller's house. Here we expected rest and food, having marched without halting, except for a few moments to enable the line to close up, for sixteen hours, during which time we had not received any food. An incident occurred on the march that greatly excited and angered the men. One of the prisoners belonging, I am sorry to say, to the California Regiment, and to my company, had in his posession the field glasses of Colonel Baker which he picked up as his body was borne from the field, having fallen unnoticed by those carrying him. On the march this man showed the glasses to me, hidden in his overcoat, and we talked over what had better be done with them. Towards noon I saw him, as did others, part with the glasses to a rebel soldier for a small portion of the ration the man possessed. This Esau like conduct estranged his fellow comrades from all intercourse with him. It illustrates the effect the longing desire for food and keenness of appetite had at times upon some men under trying conditions such as ours.

We were sadly disappointed as in a few minutes orders came to resume the march and we were again formed and marched three miles nearer Manassas, to an old stone house on the battlefield of Bull Run. It was here that our wounded at that battle were brought and on the field directly in front of the house the main struggle of the day was made. Many marks of cannon and rifle balls were to be seen, one, a rifled cannon shot, had gone directly through the building. At the stone house we halted, the privates bivouacing in the open air, the officers in the open house. At eleven o'clock at night rations of fat pork and corn bread were served, and I never tasted anything so palatable as this luscious diet. We had been for forty-eight hours without sleep, twenty four hours without food, and had marched seventeen hours without halting to rest, besides having been in action at Ball's Bluff moreover from early morning until dark.

At daybreak on the 23rd October, our march was continued to Manassas, a distance of seven miles, where we arrived at 10 o'clock A.M. We were halted at the headquarters of the provost marshal where the names, rank, and regiments were registered, during which process we were surrounded by a dense mass of soldiers, civilians, and a few ladies. Although no abusive language was used, there was a peculiar smile of delight and contempt upon every lip. We were arranged in single file in a long line, and passed before an officer sitting at a wooden table at the entrance of "The Pen" as the rebels termed the long fenced enclosure, which covered a space large enough to accommodate at least several hundred men without too much crowding, and as each man's description was recorded, he was passed in. It had a large shed across one end for shelter from the weather, and had been constructed for disciplining their own unruly people. There were at this time about thirty rebel prisoners confined there who had built themselves a fire, around which they loitered, and from which, with threats and curses, they drove away any having the temerity to approach its genial warmth.

As I stood in line awaiting my turn to register, I noticed a distinguished clerical gentleman who, with hands behind his back, was continually passing up and down inspecting the long line of prisoners. Once or twice as he approached he would slow up in his walk and look at me with [the] evident intention of speaking. Finally he did so, and asked if I thought my mother knew where I was. "Surely not," said I. "Would you like her to know?" "Most dearly," I replied. He then asked my name and home address and said "She shall know where you are." He was the Rev. Mr. Smith, an Episcopal clergyman I believe. He did send the message to my mother but it had been anticipated by a small slip of paper similarly addressed, given [to] Solomon McDonald,[44] Company H, enclosed in a note to his father and given a rebel soldier to mail. . . .

At seven P.M. we were placed under guard and taken to the cars for Richmond—they were freight cars, at the doors of each two guards were stationed. The guard from Manassas was commanded by Lieutenant Colonel Johnson,[45] 19th Georgia, and Captain Andrews,[46] 4th North Carolina. We arrived without incident at 9 A.M. on the 24th of October. Buckets of water were handed into the cars before we alighted, which was most acceptable.

We found the depot and adjacent streets thronged with a dense mass of people. The crowd surrounding the cars and crowding the depot and platforms was very abusive.

After a short delay, we were assembled and marched in detachments and formed on Broad Street, eight abreast. The new guard commanded by Captain O'Neill, of what regiment I could not learn, surrounded us front, rear, and both flanks, we occupying the centre of the street. As far as the eye could reach the populace were thronging. In the street, pressing on the guard, on the side walk, in the trees, on the balconies, and on the housetops, were crowding the eager people. Frequently, triumphant yells would be heard, "I say Yanks, how do you feel?" From the depot through the main thoroughfare we were paraded guarded by soldiers, escorted by the mob, until we arrived at our future prison, a tobacco warehouse, southwest corner of 25th and Main Streets. As we halted on the pavement of the warehouse, every window was crowded by Federal prisoners, mostly Bull Run captives. We were counted and ordered into the building. For some unknown reason about one hundred, myself among the number, were put into a building on Cary Street, afterwards known as "Castle Thunder," but in the course of a week we were transferred to Liggon & Co.'s warehouse where the others of our regiment were and without further incident I commenced my Prison Life.[47]

>─┤─◆>──O──<◆─┤─<

Richmond, Va.
November 13th, 1861

Dear Brother:

Having permission from the authorities to write home, I avail myself of the opportunity to acquaint you of my continued good health. I have nothing to complain of except the confinement, which you know to a person of my active habits was, at first, a source of much worriment. Please tell Aunty to give herself no uneasiness about me, and, as far as circumstances permit, am treated as a gentleman. A letter, I think, will reach me, if addressed to

Sgt. F. A. Donaldson (Prisoner of War)
California Regiment Co. H
Richmond, Va.

I have written to Charleston, Va. but have no tidings of John.

A few citizens of Charleston, West Virginia, including John Goshorn, a retail and dry goods merchant who was the prewar employer of Donaldson's Confederate brother, John, learned of Frank Donaldson's captivity and visited him while in Richmond. A member of the group, J. E. Caldwell, wrote to John soon after their interview with his brother.

Richmond, Va.
Dec. 13, 1861

Jno. P. Donaldson Esq.
Floyds Brigade –
Friend Jno,

I intend leaving here in the morning with Wm. Goshorn but will drop you a few lines this eve—Goshorn, Joel Shrewsbury & myself went this morning to call on your Bro. Frank who we had learnt was a prisoner taken at Leesburg. Col. Tompkins[48] got us the permit to see him & intended going with us but did not find us when he called so we went without him. He was very much surprised to see & very glad to see us. He is a nice looking fellow & we were very sorry to see him a prisoner. He has been sick but is very well now, though looking thin. He says he is treated very well and has nothing to complain of. We told him that you expected to come and see him & he was very much pleased to hear it. When you come on Joel Shrewsbury who is in the P.O. Department will go with you to see him. Col. Tompkins who lives on 7th St. between Carey & Marshall I believe will get you a permit & render you any assistance he can. He expressed a desire to do anything he could to alleviate his condition. I think you might through Col. Tompkins get him released on parole although I do not know.

Donaldson wrote as frequently as permissible to his family while in captivity, but not all of his letters may have reached Philadelphia. The correspondence below appears to be the first to reach his family since the letter he wrote five weeks earlier.

Richmond, Va.
Dec. 20th, 1861

Dear Brother,

Tomorrow will be exactly two months that I have been a prisoner, and is that all? Why it seems to me that I have been here six months at least. How many more weary months am I to remain a captive?

The monotony of my everyday life was somewhat agreeably interrupted last Friday by a visit from Mr. John Goshorn and two of brother John's friends, who together with himself are exiles from Charleston Va. I had quite a lengthy talk with them all and received most flattering accounts of John, who they say will shortly be promoted to the rank of Major. They offered to assist me in any way that was in their power, but I politely declined any assistance, accepting only a package of reading matter which they kindly offered to send. They told me that John would come on here immediately on receipt of a letter from them which they intended to write that same evening, and as a matter of course he would call at once to see me. They all wish to be remembered to you and Mother. You can imagine with what joy I looked forward to a meeting with a brother I love so well, and one who has gone so far astray as he has done, even to lifting his hand against a government that has protected him from his youth up. Unfortunately after anticipating with much pleasure his arrival I saw, two days after, a notice of the removal of his regiment far, far away from my direct communication with this city.[49] Oh, how hard it was for me thus to have my hopes and wishes dashed at once to the earth, and now he has gone, and I may never see our dear brother in life again. It is strange he did not write me. . . . I am still in good health and along with my fellow prisoners put great faith in our government knowing full well that if not released by an exchange it will be done by its strong and mighty arm; such a release would be more agreeable to my tastes than any other. Love to mother and all inquiring friends and when next you write don't forget the 10¢ postage.

John Donaldson soon learned of his brother's imprisonment, and in late December, accompanied by his friend Adj. Noyes Rand of the 22nd Virginia, he journeyed to Richmond from his camp at Lewisburg, Virginia, to try to secure Frank's parole. In 1904, Rand wrote the following recollections of their efforts:

Hon. John Letcher was the war governor of Virginia at that time, and a resident of Lexington, Va., where the writer had attended Washington College immediately prior to the war and was well acquainted with the Governor and his family; a fact well known to John Donaldson, through the intimate friendship existing between us. Finding a rocky road to travel in his efforts in behalf of his brother through his own individual exertions, he appealed to the writer (then Adjutant of the 22nd Virginia Infantry, C.S.A.) to come to his aid in Richmond; which was done. I interviewed Governor Letcher and personally requested as a favor the parole of Francis A. Donaldson, and, after meeting many difficulties, finally succeeded in obtaining a letter to the War Department, which upon attempting to deliver I was most fortunate in finding in the person of one of the assistants in the War Department an old college-mate, through whose aid I finally, on January 1st,

1862, secured an order for the parole of the prisoner. John Donaldson and I had rooms at the Spotswood Hotel, one of the nicest in the city. We secured a carriage and drove down to Libby Prison,[50] presented our order to the official in charge and soon had the pleasure of meeting Francis A. Donaldson, who was brought out and turned over to us and taken to our quarters at the hotel, or as Francis said at the time, "taken from Hell into Heaven." We then spent some days walking about the streets of Richmond, and the prisoner, being the only one in Federal uniform outside of Libby, was often guyed by the crowds on the streets, until I suggested the idea of his changing coats with me,—we being about the same size and our caps and pants very near the same,—as the terms of his parole would not permit the idea of retaliation in any measure to any guying or insults he might be subjected to, whilst I could resent same with impunity. We had quite a pleasant association of a week or so in Richmond, when John Donaldson and I were obliged to rejoin our commands, and leave the paroled prisoner to await exchange. During our stay in Richmond, John Donaldson and I had our daguerreotypes taken to give to Frank as a souvenir of the incident.[51] . . .

Richmond, Va.
January 22nd, 1862

My dear Brother:

Do not think me neglectful in not writing you, as it is one thing to write and another to get you the letter. As it is merely my desire to acquaint mother and yourself of my continued good health and spirits, I try every known means of so doing, trusting that should the communication fall into the hands of the Confederate Government, they will be generous enough to let the same go through. Indeed, Jacob, I would be an ingrate should I try to communicate to the authorities at Washington, or even to you, what I incidentally see and hear daily in this Capital of the Confederacy, because I am deeply grateful for the uniform kindness received at the hands of John's friends here (now mine, also). I am grateful, also, to the Confederate Government officials with whom I have come in contact, and will say that I am treated with great consideration by them all. There are many things I would like to say to you, but I fear I might be betrayed into saying something which I know to be a sacred trust—even to the mentioning of names, and I wish to act as honorably as possible, for I feel that it may not be considered just the thing to try to get a letter home "sub-rosa" when I am denied the privilege by those who have the power to grant it. Still for your sake and mother's I will venture this stretch of my obligations.

Need I say my thoughts are constantly with you all, and how I long to be once again at home. Oh! how utterly desperate and lonely I am. Could I but once again get a glimpse of our dear Flag, I would feel that all is not utterly lost. How ardently I love my country's flag and my heart yearns for its dear presence more and more as I am denied the blessed privilege of seeing it—can this be treason thus for me to write? I know should I openly express

Lt. John P. Donaldson (left) and Adj. Noyes Rand (right) of the 22nd Virginia presented a copy of this image to Frank as a memento of their successful attempt to obtain his parole from prison at Richmond in January 1862. Rand noted that they gave a daguerreotype of themselves to Donaldson, but no copy exists in what remains of Donaldson's papers and personal effects. This ambrotype, which is hand colored, was located at Virginia Polytechnic Institute. LOUISE TESTERMAN PAPERS, SPECIAL COLLECTIONS DEPARTMENT, UNIVERSITY LIBRARIES, VIRGINIA TECH, BLACKSBURG, VIRGINIA.

such sentiments here, it would be so considered, and yet I am putting myself in jeopardy by writing just what I feel. I must not do so, as I desire to have this letter get to you, and I will not hazard its chances for doing so by any further untimely allusions.

Our dear brother John left for his regiment this morning, and it was a very sore trial to part with him. Indeed, I fear I made myself quite contemptible in the eyes of the bystanders at the Depot, as I clung to him and implored him not to leave me. I could not help it—my feelings got the better of my manhood, and I wept like a child. My good dear brother. My splendid hero brother. Oh! God! I may have parted from him forever. He goes to battle against his people, his kinsfolk and the flag that has watched over him since his infancy. Is it not strange, is it not passing all understanding the inscrutable ways of Providence? To think of it, brother against brother. Still for all that I love him so tenderly, and had he been less honorable than he is, this very heart's tenderness could have been worked upon to have had me remain here and await the termination of the bloody arbitrament of war. Need I say that he has ever urged my return to duty as soon as I am exchanged, and has rudely refused the tempting offers of the officials for an appointment for me in the Post Office Department of the Confederate States, should I desire to remain. Even now, I am utterly powerless to control my feelings and as I write my eyes are blinded with the tears that refuse to be stayed and I write I scarcely know what.

John has left me quite comfortably located in a private boarding house, and I have for a room mate a most excellent gentleman and a dear friend of his— Levi Welch[52] by name, a former member of his company, whose brother was lately killed in battle. He is now preparing for admission into the military school here with a view of entering the regular Confederate Army. Welch is a kind hearted gentleman and quite literal in his interpretation of the duties of the soldier, that is, he respects my feelings, but as did John, urges me to again to return to my post of duty as soon as I am able to do so and not abandon the colors I have sworn to protect. He is also able to engage me in quiet argument as to the merits of the Confederate Cause, and combats, without heat, the various opinions I advance in sustaining my view of the situation.

The package of clothing you so kindly sent me I have received in perfect condition, thus showing that it had not been opened by the Confederates for examination. I also acknowledge receipt of your letter of January 11th together with one from Julian Wright. They came through by flag of truce and were received promptly. It was like hearing from the otherworld, and

I have read and re-read and kissed the pages again and again. The knowledge of mother's good health comforts me so much, and the loving anxiety of all my friends is very precious and dear to me. The greater part of the underwear together with the boots I gave to John, knowing that he stood in great need of them. The little gold coins is a priceless gift, the display of which is the "open sesame" to the hearts of this worthless paper currency ridden community. One dollar of my gold is nearly equal to a basket-full of the curious circulation they call money. My friend Levi Welch desires to enclose in this a letter to his friends in Kanawha, and I have assured him of its prompt mailing should this letter be fortunate enough to get through the lines. <u>Please see to this</u>!

My health is excellent and I have nothing in the world to complain of except the separation from you all. Some idea of my personal appearance can be had when I tell you that I look not unlike an "undertaker" with my black cloths, black hat, and were it not for the Confederate overcoat which John gave me, in exchange for my splendid one, I fear I would be so mistaken. . . .

Any additional letters Donaldson may have written during his captivity in Richmond have not survived, and along with many of the other Ball's Bluff prisoners, he was exchanged on February 19, 1862. After a brief reunion with his family in Philadelphia, he reported back to his command, where many changes had taken place.

Following the Ball's Bluff disaster, the California Regiment, along with the other Philadelphia-raised regiments that made up Baker's Brigade, was claimed by Pennsylvania as part of its quota of men for three years' service and was, to Donaldson's displeasure, officially designated as the 71st Pennsylvania Volunteers. "What a pity the old name could not have been kept," he complained to his brother, "and how shabby of California not to recognize us."

Together with the renumbered 69th, 72nd, and 106th Pennsylvania Volunteers, the brigade, which was destined to become known as the Philadelphia Brigade, was placed under the command of Brig. Gen. William W. Burns and assigned to duty in Brig. Gen. John Sedgwick's division.

In late February, the division had been sent to support a Federal move against Confederate forces posted near Winchester, Virginia, but the Southerners retreated. As Donaldson relates, he reported back to the 71st Pennsylvania as they were returning to Harpers Ferry from Winchester, the first of the Ball's Bluff captives to do so. His celerity in returning was rewarded soon after, as in late March Colonel Wistar appointed him to act as sergeant major, with the promise of a commission should a vacancy occur.

Harpers Ferry, Va.
March 12th, 1862

Dear Jacob:

Just arrived safe and sound after a <u>short</u> ride of nearly <u>six</u> hours. It is dreadfully warm and I have discarded several articles of my clothing. This is a wretched town and I cannot see where the beauty is I have heard so much of. I find that my regiment is but a short distance from Winchester, and about 17 miles from this place. I will start tomorrow early and try to reach the encampment by nightfall. I am stopping at the sutler's and will sleep there tonight. I will have to "hoof" it all they way. Have left all my baggage at the sutler's, it being too heavy to carry, and I do not care whether I lose it or not. Will write as soon as I reach a resting place.

P.S. . . . This is written in great haste as I stand at the sutler's counter where I am jostled and pushed about by the men who frequent the place.

><▷•◦•◁>◁

Bolivar Heights, Va.
March 15, 1862

Dear Brother:

Here I am once again on Old Virginia's sacred soil. In the few lines written from Harpers Ferry, I said I did not think much of the place. That was literally true as regards the town itself, but as to the beauty of the country, the magnificence of the surrounding landscape, there can be no question. Harpers Ferry is situated at the junction of the Shenandoah and Potomac Rivers, and is probably one of the most picturesquely located places in America. I can conceive of no more beautiful scene than just here. Then too it is full of memories of the stirring past, although desolation and ruin reign everywhere. There is scarcely anything beside a few standing walls to remind one of the busy arsenal where so many muskets, now in the hands of its enemies, as well as its own troops, were made by the government. The Engine House where John Brown battled for abolition's cause is still standing, but the citizens of the town itself have deserted it. The only places of business opened are by our own people, and the only customers, too, are our own army. Everything wears an aspect of utter decay and destruction. I was glad to get away.

I left on Thursday morning and rode as far as Charleston,[53] a distance of 9 miles, in the Sutlers Wagon, when finding he was not going further,

I took up my journey on foot for Berryville, a distance of a trifle less than 13 miles. Charlestown is a pretty place, with numberless frame cottages painted white with green venetian shutters. I did not have time to go all over the place, but a number of historical places were pointed out to me, notably the Court House where old John Brown was tried and the Jail where he was kept a prisoner. . . .

All along the good solid turnpike to Berryville there were evidences of the passing of large bodies of troops, there being scarcely a fence-rail left in the whole distance, and the sod house made with the woods where our encampment had taken place was most marked. I saw no soldiers during this tramp. The farmers appeared to have been at work, and the country as far back as I could see was well cultivated and full of fine looking wheat, at least to my unpracticed eye it looked remarkably good and heavy.

I arrived at Berryville about 2 P.M., and after stopping long enough to get something to eat, pushed on again for Winchester, which I understood to be at least 10 miles further on. After proceeding about half that distance, I met the brigade returning, and learned that, owing to the crowded condition of Winchester and its vicinity, they had to return for a place to bivouac. Everyone was glad to see me and I had quite an ovation, being the first of the Ball's Bluff prisoners to return to the old California, now the 71st Penna. Regt. What a pity the old name could not have been kept, and how shabby of California not to recognize us. Had we hailed from Pennsylvania in the first place, we would now be 1st Penna. Regt., as we were the 1st 3 years men mustered into the service. Captain Urie's welcome I shall never forget. By the way, he has been promoted to captaincy of Company L—think of that! He caught me in his arms and after a close embrace said I should never leave him again. I fell in with the old Company H and found it commanded by Lt. Marine C. Moore,[54] a son of the old stationer on Chestnut Street. He was very kind to me.

As soon as tents were pitched Captain Urie made me occupy his with him, and since then I have continued to do so. This is a great privilege, I assure you, as a Captain appears to be a sacred being so far as an intimacy with him is concerned. No one is allowed that privilege except officers of his grade, and his Lieutenants are never permitted to associate, mess, or quarter with him.

I have not yet reported for duty and Col. Wistar, upon my reporting my arrival to him, said not to report to Lt. Moore, as he intended giving me a commission for my excellent conduct on the Balls' Bluff Battlefield, where he had noticed my behavior particularly. I felt most gratified to be thus spoken to by my colonel, although I felt that I deserved it, as I did my whole duty on that occasion, and have ever since wondered whether the Colonel remembered having praised me during the heat of the engagement, saying, "Well done Sergeant, you are a Lieutenant today." But he did remember it, and I have felt brim full of joy and happiness ever since he recalled it to me.

Since then I have been with Capt. Urie, talking, sleeping and marching with him. He is a great favorite with the Colonel and appears to be the leading Captain in the command. Captain Mallery is at home, and will not rejoin the regiment for a week or two as he is quite sick. Had he been here I verily believe I would have gone into the ranks again, as there appears no other place is open, the sergeants vacancy being filled during my absence. The next day we marched back again as far as Charlestown and encamped for the night, and this A.M. again took up line of march reaching here amid a drenching rain storm. I don't think I ever saw it rain so hard, why the very windows of heaven appear to be opened and the water just pours down in sheets. Oh! how miserable it makes everything.

Harpers Ferry is just below us and crowded with marching troops, our whole division being among them. It is a wonderfully grand sight to see, the 20,000 men in motion, with accompanying artillery and baggage wagons filing along the road and across the pontoons. Our destination I believe to be Alexandria, or Annapolis, where a fleet is fitting out to transport us to some other field of operations in support of the movement from Manassas for the reduction of Richmond. I find the brigade commanded by Brig. Genl. W.H. Burns of the Regular Army and is in the 2nd Division, 2nd Army Corps. This Corps is commanded by Maj. Genl. Edwin V. Sumner, and is composed of 3 Divisions, 1st Genl. Richardson, 2nd Genl. Jno. Sedgwick, a regular and an old Mexican vet, the 3rd by Genl. Blenker.[55] Our brigade consists of the 69th, 71st, 72nd, & 106th Penna. Reg.

As we moved away from the vicinity of Charlestown, we saw a number of nigroes leaning on the fence surrounding a neat little house on what appeared to be a large plantation. Capt. Urie spoke to one of them and asked whether he would like to join the army. Replying that he would, the Captain told him to come along and he and two or three others did so. In conversation with him I learned his name to be George Slow,[56] and that he had been a slave, but on joining the Confederate Army, his master, knowing he could not keep his slaves, had given them their freedom, and he (George) would like me to go back and corroborate what he said. He had been a house servant and nicely brought up. Indeed, for that matter, his conduct and manners soon bespoke him a "quality dark." We like him very much, as he is a first rate cook and very handy generally.

>─┼◆>─O─<◆┼─<

Bolivar Heights
March 18, 1862

Dear Jacob:

We move today, I believe, for Washington and from that point I scarcely know where, but, of course, it will be upon some expedition toward Richmond. As to the displacement of Genl. McClellan, I gave no credence to the report, as it would be a hazardous undertaking to remove so renowned & competent a General upon the eve of a campaign. Certainly the men, who love him dearly, would resent such an outrage. I do not believe any other living man could handle this army successfully were he removed.

I have been appointed 2nd Lieutenant of Co. M with prospects of higher grade. Capt. Hills,[57] its commander, is the same who was 1st Lt. Co. H so that I will be pleasantly situated. So sensitive, however, am I, that I greatly prefer you would address me as Sergeant until I get my commission in hand, and would rather you would not mention this yet, awhile, to Sloanaker, as I fear he would feel badly about it. I will write from Washington—am still living with Capt. Urie, who continues his kindness unabated, and I feel so grateful. My health continues good and I have not taken the least cold these wet days. . . .

>─┼◆>─O─<◆┼─<

Bolivar Heights, Va.
March 20th, 1862

Dear Jacob:

Your most interesting letter of the 18th inst. was received, and I can scarcely express my happiness at again getting one of your dear, <u>old time</u>, letters, so full of news and so long too, although I thought it short enough. . . . If the people at home only knew how little it takes to encourage the soldier, or how little to depress him, they would be very careful of what they write.

So my friends were astonished at my sudden departure? Well the sequel proved that I left not a day too soon, as I have shown in former letters. Again this morning in conversation with Col. Wistar he reiterated what he had before said, and urged the importance of hard work at my tactics, so that I will be prepared for the examination which I now believe is required of all those receiving promotion or appointment. He further said he desired me to pass this examination not only with credit to myself but to the regiment also, and that I could now consider myself permanently detached from Co. H, and pending the arrival of my commission he would have me act as Sergeant Major, of which duty I would shortly receive notice. Meantime I will continue to devote myself to Capt. Urie, with whom I still mess, and do all his writing.

Donaldson's first cousin, Sgt. Henry Clay Donaldson, Company R, 72nd Pennsylvania Volunteers (Baxter's Fire Zouaves). He was killed at Savage's Station, June 29, 1862.

THE CIVIL WAR LIBRARY & MUSUEM.

I frequently see Harry Donaldson, and only yesterday paid him a long visit. He is rejoiced at my prospects and urges me to deport myself with becoming dignity. He looks in splendid health and feels so I am sure. . . .

Our camp is filled with "contrabands" and everyone now has his "George" to pull off his boots and to wait upon him. My George has proved a treasure and by his conduct commands respect, not only from the soldiers, but from the nigroes, also, the latter, however, he is too swell a "dark" to notice. Harry Donaldson is much amused at my "body" servant as he calls him and thinks I am commencing rather soon to assume the privilege of an officer. . . . P.S. In regard to our movements all that I know about it is as stated in previous letters. We are attached to Gen'l. Sumner's Corps. and are under marching orders.

CHAPTER 2

Yorktown and Fair Oaks

March 24–June 8, 1862

*A*s the winter of 1861 melted into the spring of 1862, the North watched anxiously
for McClellan and his superbly equipped Army of the Potomac to finally take the
offensive. None waited more impatiently than President Lincoln, and in late January,
distressed with his commanding general's secrecy and inactivity, he issued a series of orders
directing McClellan to begin his advance on Richmond via Manassas no later than
Washington's birthday, February 22. Finally spurred to action, McClellan revealed his
strategic plan to the administration for the first time since being named general in chief.

Rather than attack overland toward Manassas, as Lincoln had wished, "Little
Mac" instead favored sailing his force down the Chesapeake Bay to Urbanna, on the
south bank of the Rappahannock River, in the process outflanking Confederates
under Gen. Joe Johnston posted near Manassas. Once at Urbanna, McClellan would
take advantage of Union control of the waterways to keep his supply lines short and
communications intact, and strike directly west at Richmond. On March 9, however,
Johnston vacated Manassas and fell back below the Rappahannock, forcing McClellan
to move his stepping-off point to Fort Monroe on the Peninsula.

In late March the laborious process of moving the 105,000 soldiers of the Army
of the Potomac to Virginia commenced, and by April 4 the vanguard of the Union
forces, comprising some 53,000 men, began the advance on Richmond. The Rebels,
though outmanned, were waiting, and only one day after starting their forward movement,
the lead elements of the army bumped up against Confederate works stretching from
Yorktown on the York River all the way across the Peninsula to the James River.
Through the skillful manipulation of his 11,000-man force holding the Yorktown-
Warwick line, Maj. Gen. John Magruder was able to fool the overcautious McClellan
into believing that he was opposed by superior numbers and forced him to enter into a
tedious month-long siege operation. "No one but McClellan could have hesitated to
attack," commented Johnston when informed that his adversary was digging in.[1]

The 71st Pennsylvania, placed as it was in the Philadelphia Brigade of Brig. Gen. John Sedgwick's division, formed a part of Brig. Gen. Edwin Vose Sumner's 2nd Corps and saw little combat outside of skirmish duty in the operations around Yorktown. Though the siege dragged on throughout April, accompanied by mud, sniper fire, and exhaustion brought on by physical labor, Donaldson's morale never faltered. "I am happy and well," he wrote on April 21, "although one of the dirtiest men in the whole army." His physical appearance notwithstanding, his qualities as a soldier never suffered, and on April 15, having spent the previous month assuring his brother that he was to be promoted, Donaldson was advanced to the second lieutenancy of Company M. "You can . . . state to my admiring friends," he intoned sarcastically soon after, "that the war will now be ended right away."

Washington D.C.
March 24th, 1862

Dear Jacob:

We arrived here this A.M. after a most uncomfortable experience of 12 hours in a freight car. We struck tents at 7 o'clock A.M. on the morning of the 23rd and marched to Harpers Ferry where we loitered around loose until 6 P.M. During the day I had an opportunity of seeing, for the first time, our Division General. He was sitting on his horse watching the brigade file past him, and at first I thought him to be a Quarter Master or other non-combatant officer, as he was without staff, had on a blouse and appeared merely to be passing away time. When I learned it was our distinguished General Sedgwick, I took a searching look at him, and the impression his face and appearance made upon me was altogether favorable. He is quite a stout man, with beard all over his face, but cropped close. . . .

At 6 P.M. we were packed like herrings in freight cars and after poking all night long finished a most tedious and annoying journey at this 7 A.M. As it was impossible to sit down with any degree of comfort, I stood all the way, and as a consequence was quite used up when we arrived, being scarcely able to move one foot before the other. I soon recovered vitality enough to skip around and hunt up my friends in the city. We are encamped at the lower, or upper, I do not know which, end of Massachusetts Avenue, in rear of the depot. . . .

On board U.S. Transport
"Louisiana"
March 29, 1862

My dear Brother:

. . . On Wednesday last I left camp and proceeded to Washington, where I paid several visits to friends and acquaintances, among them Mrs. Kendall, who urged me so warmly to return and spend the evening and night with them that I did so. In the evening, with the whole family, I visited cousin Lambert Free's and received a cordial welcome, a great fuss being made over me—the returned prisoner of war—the lion of the evening. Mr. Free has two lovely daughters, of the ages of 18 and 20 years, who are both pretty and attractive. I immediately made myself agreeable to them, and met with a somewhat flattering success, as the enclosed photograph of one of them will bear testimony. As this trophy was attained after a <u>protracted argument</u> you will at once understand the debate to have been a <u>close</u> one. I mark this evening as one of the brightest and happiest I have ever passed.

After a refreshing nights sleep I made an early start for camp, with pockets full of sardines and arms full of brandy peaches, periodicals, illustrated papers and other reading matter enough to gladden the eye and cause the cockles of the heart to rise up in the needy and greedy soldier at the bare sight of them all. When I arrived at the place where the camp ought to have been, lo! and behold!, there was no camp there. The regiment had packed up and gone—whither—not one of the darkies picking up camp trash could tell. I at once became demoralized and gave away the sardines and peaches, and, after firing the periodicals and reading material down a contiguous sewer, started off at a quick pace to find the command.

As luck would have it I found the brigade on the march up Pennsylvania Avenue and succeeded in joining the regiment during a temporary halt, just in time to witness Capt. Urie discipline one of his men, who, having succeeded in obtaining a canteen of whiskey, had the temerity to offer him a drink of it. Snatching the canteen from his hand he poured its contents on the ground, much to the horror of the man, the dismay of the company, and a most wonderful display of nerve power in the Captain. He has since confessed to me, which I repeat parenthetically, that it caused him many a sigh of regret as he contemplated with what horrid greed the thirsty earth absorbed the fragrant and exhilarating fluid. . . .

Our march was continued to Alexandria, a distance of six miles from the [Long] Bridge, when we encamped just outside the town. I believe I told you I have been acting in the capacity of Sergeant Major, but the Colonel has since said that he wanted me to assume permanently the duties of that office, for a short time, until my appointment as 2nd Lt. was confirmed, as he desired all promotions to come regularly through that office. . . .

In the afternoon we again took up the march and after passing through the town, embarked on this boat. We slept aboard but did not leave the wharf until next day at about 4 P.M. All our regiment is on this one boat, which is considerably crowded, but I fortunately succeeded in getting a bunk and slept quite comfortably. We have two large schooners in tow, filled with cavalry horses and men, and our captain says we will not be able to reach our destination before tomorrow some time. There appears to be a total ignorance as to our destination, but I presume it must be Fort Monroe or Newport News—but no matter where—it is evident there is warm work before us sooner or later. As we passed Mount Vernon the men became silent and stood uncovered, while the band played the Star Spangled Banner, Hail Columbia and other stirring and patriotic airs. . . . We also passed the terrible batteries erected by the energetic secesh along the river, but which are now silent and deserted, much to the disgust of a number of the impatient ones who are ever anxious for a brush with the enemy.

There are at least 5000 men in our brigade, which as I have before stated, consists of Morehead's, Owen's, Baxter's,[2] and our own regiment, a battery of artillery and several companies of cavalry, all commanded by Genl. Wm. W. Burns, and attached to Genl. Sedgwick's Division, Genl. Sumner's Corps, which consists of Sedgwick's, Heintzleman's, Blenker's and Richardson's Divisions, in all about 20 to 25,000 men.[3] I do not know the exact amount of artillery attached to the corps, but I feel it is all sufficient to "knock the chivalry." . . .

I hardly think it necessary to send me the papers as I receive them sooner than by mail. As to keeping my dignity—which you so kindly suggest should be done, I have but to quote my friend Capt. Urie, who exclaims at my want of liveliness and rails at my "official manner." . . .

Camp near Hampton, Va.
April 2, 1862

My dear Brother,

Your letter of the 27th inst. duly received, contains so many questions, the answers to which you so persistently insist upon, that I must confess, without exception [you are] the most exacting elder brother I ever heard of. However, I will do my best to satisfy you as fully as can be, with some of the questions, but there are others that will have to remain unanswered until I see you, as I do not care to put in writing some of my private affairs. . . .

In regard to my acting as Sgt. Major, although I believe I have already stated the reason, I will again say that the Colonel desires all promotions to come through that office, and I merely act [as such] until Sloanaker arrives, when I will join Co. M, and Sloanaker will act as Sgt. Major. Please let him know this and urge his return to the regiment, when after serving a week or so he will receive a commission. . . .

I trust you received the letter I wrote from on board the transport "Louisiana." I still continue in good health, but with the new office comes additional cares and duties, which require constant labor and toil to the exclusion of all but mere business letters to you in the future, so please make allowance for brevity, at least for a time. Write often and keep me posted in all that pertains to home and friends.

>─◆>─○─<◆─◁

Camp near Yorktown, Va.
April 11th, 1862

Dear Jacob:

By the above heading you will perceive that we have moved nearer the enemy. I do not remember whether I mentioned in my last letter that the beautiful little town of Hampton, whose neat white houses, lovely abundant foliage and magnificent shade trees, which so impressed me when here before, is now one vast charcoal heap, having been destroyed by Genl. McGruder shortly after we withdrew from its vicinity last summer. I cannot understand the strategy developed by such wantonness, neither can I see the importance of this particular region, anyway.[4] It has been a puzzle to me, ever since we landed at Fortress Monroe on the 31st of March, and found the country filled with soldiers and artillery which had preceded us, to know why such a God forsaken country should be selected for the manoeuvering of vast armies and the possible fighting of bloody battles. Still I am mindful of the fact that Lord Cornwallis selected this very country also, and I can only account for it under the supposition that it is accessible to the fleets which must supply this great army, and in that respect its importance becomes of moment. It is true the same conditions apply to the enemy, and unfortunately for Cornwallis were used by the French fleets to destroy him, but with us the enemy have no navy and therefore cannot annoy us.

April 4th. We commenced the forward movement, and with Genl. McClellan in our midst, reached and bivouaced at Big Bethel. I shall never forget my feeling as I stood upon the formidable works the enemy had constructed at this place and pictured to myself the battle fought here, the death of the noble and brave Greble,[5] and the discomfiture of our people. I also stood in wonderment at the strategy which caused such a defensive place to be abandoned, and I feel that the science of war was indeed to be acquired only after a close study of its principles and a thorough knowledge of engineering, such as only those who pass through the 4 years tuition at the Military School at West Point can hope to attain. These reflections have raised the standard of the Regular officers (which was always high) very considerably in my estimation.

I wish I could convey to you a description of the abounding enthusiasm the presence of Genl. McClellan has upon the troops. After we had started upon our forward movement he was seen approaching along the road, when the soldiers lined each side of it and as he passed cheered and crowded around him in the wildest frenzy of joy such as I have pictured to myself the French soldiers displayed in the presence of the Great Napoleon. Although not very demonstrating, I too felt the influence and cheered as lustily as any of them.

On the 5th we moved to this camp in the vicinity of Yorktown. The country through which we passed was heavily wooded, low, flat, marshy and intersected by streams, and to add still further to the disagreeableness of our surroundings, it rained for a week until today, when hearing loud cheering I came out of my quarters to learn the cause, and found to my amusement that the men were cheering the appearance of the sun, and, indeed, I felt like joining in with them, as I at last saw a prospect of getting my wet cloths dryed. We are entirely without shelter, or at least might as well be, as we have no tents and nothing to protect us from the weather, except blankets. Capt. Urie and I succeeded in securing a small piece of canvas which we use as a roof to the 4x6 mud house we have constructed. We have a large chimney in its rear, and as wood is very abundant, we contrive to keep one side dry while the other is getting wet from the leaky roof, so that we really fare much better than the average officer. The mud is something stupendous and in places is nearly knee deep, thus ending all camp duties save those of "guard mount" which must be performed without considering the elements.

Yesterday the 15th Mass., 106th Penna. and our regiment made a reconnaissance towards the enemy. Such marching I never witnessed. It was every man for himself in the struggle against mud, swamps, rivers, hills and dense woods, while ever and anon the enemy's pickets, which retired before us, would stop to exchange a shot with our advance. We were brought unceremoniously to a halt by the shot from a hidden battery which caused us to about face and scamper home again, amidst the blinding drenching rain. Apart from the <u>valuable</u> information obtained our captures consisted of one prisoner. During all this experience in which I have been constantly soaked to the skin my health has remained marvelously good, and I appear to thrive on it. I have but one change of clothes with me, as before moving, Genl. McClellan issued an order reducing officers baggage, and Capt. Urie kindly took my surplus things, packed them with his own and shipped his trunk per Adams Express to his home, where I trust it is now all safe and snug. . . .

I do not know whether letters will reach you from here, hence the meager description of movements and camp life, but I trust the means and the way will be found to forward promptly soldiers letters. I visited Harry Donaldson today and found him in good health and spirits, and looking remarkably well. . . .

><del>+</del>+‹›+O+‹›+<del>+</del>‹

Camp "Winfield Scott" Va.
Near Yorktown, Va.
April 14th, 1862

My dear Brother,

. . . You ask what is my opinion of the expected battle at Yorktown. Well, as you are aware, my opinion does not go for much, still I am happy to give it, for all that, as it will convince you that I do some little thinking of my own and am not biased by newspaper editorials which, by the way, are very ridiculous sometimes, as <u>they</u> explain the <u>Situation</u>. From the elaborate preparation, the vast number of troops constantly arriving & which now fill the country from Fortress Monroe to this place, a distance of 24 miles, I think Yorktown will be the "Waterloo" of the war. There is no denying that a monster task is before us, but our sagacious little General has the confidence and there are no impossibilities to him. From what you say, I should judge that General McClellan is being severely criticized by the Stay at home Masters of the Art of War, but for all that we, who are at the front, feel every confidence in him. However I agree with you that this campaign will either be the making or the breaking of Genl. McClellan, and I doubt not the result. I will also add, since I have made such pointed allusions to the "Stay at Home Warriors" that there are a few officers with us who doubt the ability of this army to drive out of such formidable works the devils who are behind them, but these doubters, fighting men all, are willing to try, and will do all they can to make it a success.

We still remain at the same camp, altho' the name "Camp Winfield Scott" has been applied to the whole army, by General Orders, as you doubtless know. The levies are being drawn closer upon the soldiers, no permits being granted to leave camp, no beating of drums, no sounding bugles, no cheering—no demonstration of any kind allowed whereby the enemy can gain a knowledge of our numbers or what we are doing. We expect daily orders to move up close to the enemy and if a regular siege is undertaken some experience will be had in the manner of running parallels and digging trenches, which must be a terrible duty if my recollection of the Crimean War serves me. Thus far we are out of reach of their shells, and witness only their effects, as the wounded and mangled are daily carried by in ambulances.

We are now blessed with delightful weather, which improves our health and spirits, making life once again worth living for, and causing us to almost forget the missing of the past week or two. Soldiering, with the exception of a short allowance of hard bread and "salt horse," is again quite endurable, and savors of the picknick order of things just now. Further on as the siege progresses I may write differently, but I will wait and see. . . .

In future you can address me as Lieutenant F. A. Donaldson Co. M as I enter upon my duties as such tomorrow the 15th inst. I trust all doubting will now be ended, and you can imagine to yourself, and in fact describe an imaginary hulking officer, with a drawn scimitar in his right hand, and state to my admiring friends that the war will now be ended right away. Poor Sloanaker by his delay in reporting has lost his chance for promotion, as I have been relieved of the duties of Sergt. Major by Winfield Scott Batchelder,[6] a Sergt. of F Co. who will be promoted in due time. Batchelder's duties will not be as arduous as mine were, as the signal box will be discarded.

This was an immense leather box—on the cartridge box pattern—containing 24 different colored explosives, which some fool invented for the avowed purpose of using when two columns approach from opposite directions, and it being uncertain as to their character, an explosive was to be dashed upon the ground, which was to be properly answered by the other column, or else a fight would ensue. The Sergt. Major was the custodian of this useless article and upon him devolved this duty. He was to furnish transportation for this box to the exclusion of all personal effects. To my mind this was all bosh, just as though two belligerent forces would stop long enough to fire off a few blue or red lights before engaging. Why, even the instincts of brutes are keener than this, they know an enemy in each other at sight—why then should the reason of man be duller. I don't credit myself with too much penetration but I really think I can tell a secesh as far as I can see him. . . .

For some time I have been laboring under a great depression of mind owing to the fact that I was obliged to shave off my mostache, as its great length strains the already thin soup issued us, and I thus lose much nutricious food that would otherwise help to keep up my strength and courage. However, as a compromise, I have started a bold pair of side whiskers, which, although extensively laid out, are very poorly settled, but strong hopes for the future are entertained. Capt. Urie advises me to shave them also, as he fears the mental anxiety consequent on their development may cause brainfever, and thus would be lost to the service a bold and sagacious blade. Satire, aint it? All this is levity, but reflects the exuberance of spirits occasioned by the genial sunshine and the successful issue of battle to our arms hoped for. . . .

>-+→•O•-<+-+-<

Camp California Regt.
Near Yorktown, Va.
April 17th, 1862

My dear Brother:

. . . We have not been paid yet, and God only knows when the "spons"[7] will be forthcoming. You are mistaken in supposing that we are permanently with Heintzleman's Corps. We have only been temporarily detatched from Sumner. Genl. McClellan is quartered in our midst and the honor of guarding his person and Head Quarters have been ours for some time. We have also been placed with the Regulars, which is not only an honor, but tends in a great measure to improve the discipline of the command. . . .

Among the many rumors stirring is that . . . the disposition our Brigade in the coming battle is prominent. It is said that Baxter's Regt. has been selected to do the storming of the position in our front, while the California Regiment will be kept in close reserve and support. How true this may all be—time alone will tell. That our regiment will do its duty well is the unanimous opinion of its officers and not the least among them—the junior 2nd Lt. I will be glad when the issue is made, as I would just as soon settle the war here as anywhere else.

You speak of the grandeur of the warlike scene—how can I depict it? My pencil fails to convey one iota of the wonderful panorama, surrounded as we are by thousands (some say 150,000) infantry, cavalry, and artillery. One can scarcely realize that there should be a doubt as to our final success, but nothing is certain in war, as everything depends on the ability of our commander and the morale of the troops at his disposal. Of these I feel assured and so should you and all our friends at home. . . .

We have just received orders to camp at this point until the arrival of the siege guns from Fortress Monroe.

>─◄◊►─O─◄◊►─I─◄

Camp before Yorktown, Va.
April 21st, 1862

Dear Brother:

Your letter of the 15th received while I was on Picket, and its contents rather discouraging. To think that my statements are questioned seems to me to cancel any obligation of duty resting upon me to write home at all. I hardly know how to proceed, but will caution you against putting any further indignity upon me by addressing your letters to Sergt. F. A. Donaldson, as you are now doing, as I will return all such unopened. It is very humiliating to have to verify any facts stated by me in previous letters, beside it entails additional trouble and labor, which I do not care to take, but of one state- ment which <u>you insist</u> upon as doubting—my appointment as 2nd Lieut. Co. M, I desire you to have confirmed by addressing Col. Isaac J. Wistar or else Harry Donaldson. I know you well enough to feel assured that you will disdain all intention to wound my feelings, but I tell you Jac, I do feel it when you make light of anything written by me, as I have no desire or intention to deceive you. I merely state facts as they occur, and as I see them, giving my own impressions only of my surroundings. This I believe you have often asked me to do, but I now feel sorry that I have been led into making them. The result of all this will be to make me more guarded in entering into details, which I would otherwise do, of matters that I think would be of interest to you, my family and friends.

Note what you say relative to Genl. Patterson,[8] and thank you for the suggestion, although the experience thus far gained of the character of such exclusive and exalted beings as general officers, will go far towards intimidating one of so humble a rank as myself from approaching him. But as you say he is very well acquainted with you, it may be of service to me, if he permits me the honor of a personal interview. I will make the attempt, I assure you, as soon as he arrives at this camp.

Lieut. Kenney,[9] Co. P—late of Libby Prison, Richmond, again reported for duty, and has been promoted. This I am glad of as he is a good little fellow, not much of a tactician, but brave and unassuming. . . .

A week ago we broke camp and moved up closer to the works, being now just one mile from the enemy's batteries. The dense woods between them and us partially shelters us from their fire, although a shell now and then finds its way into our camp, very greatly to the annoyance of the soldiers and to the utter demoralization of the colored camp followers and servants. Every third day our brigade is on picket, which will illustrate the urgency, severity and danger of the service which occasions the presence of such large bodies of men. There being but three brigades in our division, the duty becomes very laborious.

I will cite as an illustration of this duty the fact that for the past two days I have been without sleep. This was occasioned by the enemy making a sortie and attack upon Gorman's Brigade,[10] night before last, which was upon picket at the time, and a fight ensued, which for the space of a half hour threatened to involve the greater portion of the army. We were ordered under arms and moved up in support, and although it was raining hard, so urgent was the necessity that we were hustled to the front at the double quick, time not even being given the men to get their overcoats. Although not called into action we were compelled to take the drenching all the same, and at early dawn were withdrawn to camp, where after breakfasting we again returned and relieved Gorman. We in turn have just been relieved by Genl. Dana[11]—thus making, as I have said, two nights without sleep for this command. Of course we are not alone in this, as other portions of the line are subjected to similar duty and annoyances, and I am told, as the parallels of siege approach closer [to] the enemies works, the duty continues both night and day without intermission or relief.

Our picket line is in the woods, about 100 yards from the rebel batteries, but our sharp shooters have driven their people completely behind their works, from which they dare not stir, until after dark, when the placing of their pickets occasions the various fights which constantly take place after nightfall.

Our guns keep up a constant shelling both day and night, which is seldom responded to by the rebels, because of the terrible Berdan sharp shooters who cover their guns to such an extent that they can not work them. I never before saw such a set of men as these same Berdan sharp shooters. They are armed with the telescope sighted rifles peculiar to their calling, some of which weigh the extraordinary heft of 57 to 60 pounds. These men speak confidently of killing, without the slightest difficulty, at a mile distant. The impression left upon the minds of the soldiers by these people is not at all a pleasant one, and as they come out each morning after breakfast strutting leisurely along, the men look askance and rather shrink from them. As far as I am able to judge, although receiving a general order to occupy certain portions of the line, it is left discretionary with them to select their own position. So that good service is done, the method is with the individual. It has frequently occurred that one or more of them have occupied my post, and I have watched their proceedings very closely. They remind one of the spider who, hour after hour, so patiently waits for the unhappy fly. These men will, after cutting crotches and resting their rifle on them, coolly take a camp stool, and adjusting the telescopic sight, wait for some poor devil to show himself, when, quick as a flash, bang goes the rifle, and the soldier has solved the Trinity. I have often looked through their sight pieces, and been amazed at their power and the distinctness with which objects of at least a mile distant are brought under the eye of the observer.

Yesterday four of these demons occupied the post with me, and after busying themselves with suitably and satisfactorally adjusting their rifles, sat down to await a victim. They had not long to wait however, as soon were seen four men leaving the enemies works, who proceeded towards the works on our left, apparently with no thought of danger at least so early in this day. At their distance they would have been perfectly secure from our muskets, but were in easy range of the murderous Berdan rifle. The sharp shooters consulted for a moment, and three of them, removing the rear most support from their rifles, brought them to bear upon the men, and at the word from the fourth, fired. Three of them dropped instantly, while the fourth, after standing in apparent bewilderment suddenly [fell] beside his dead comrades, adjusted their bodies as a protection, and stayed there <u>all</u>

day long. The enemy immediately opened upon our post, which made it pretty hot, but which in no wise disconcerted the sharp shooters, who, taking advantage of their position, picked off the gunners quite lively. As for my men, they were completely demoralized and driven off by the fire, and took shelter further in the woods. Shortly after firing having ceased, four other men bearing stretchers were seen to suddenly leave the works and approach the dead men. I can scarcely bring my pencil to write it, but these inhuman fiends, these vaunted brave Berdan sharp shooters, murdered these poor fellows also. I will add that there was a good deal of feeling displayed by my men, and Mr. Rifleman was requested to go somewhere else, as their presence was distasteful.

These are some of the horrible incidents having official sanction that I have as yet been unable to reconcile in my mind with what I consider honorable warfare, but I am constantly told by those better posted than I that war is a terrible arbitrament and must be made as dreadful as possible while it lasts, hence the necessity of seeming wantonness in the taking of life.

There are, in a Wisconsin Regiment of our division, two regularly enlisted Indians,[12] who make it a practice of sleeping by day and of prowling at night beyond our pickets, their object can well be imagined, as it of course means assassination. Still this is also <u>sanctioned</u>—as war must be made terrible.

Day before yesterday the enemy hoisted a white flag and sent a woman over to ask permission to bury their dead, and also to return prisoners held by them. That afternoon, the truce being granted, both parties availed themselves of the opportunity to take a good look at each other. They sent us over 40 dead of our brave soldiers who, while prisoners, had died of their wounds. This will illustrate the closeness of our positions and the deadly character of the encounter, which occasion the abandonment of the wounded and dead.

McClellan is evidently faced by a soldier who is his equal in ability both as an engineer and tactician, and to answer your question frankly, I cannot see how it will be possible to capture the enemy, we can only drive him out of Yorktown, and then catch him on the retreat. But then, don't you know, their brave general will no doubt take up a new line of defense, and the work will have to be done all over again. However, I am not capable of reasoning these things, and you should not expect from me a correct diagnosis of the case, as the doctors say, for my humble position in this army gives me few opportunities of learning the art of war, other than the manual labor part. Had I the chance of being brought in contact with the <u>brains</u> of the army or of the colonels of regiments, or men in high rank, I firmly believe a good organizer, a good planner, and a good officer and soldier could be made of me, or in other words, I take to the trade and like it.

As an illustration of the manual labor part of the war I as one of the atoms of this vast host am called upon to perform, I will say that my place being constantly with the enlisted men in all their exposure, privations and dirt, that I, like them, have not washed my face, or had my clothes off since Wednesday, and for the last two weeks have lived on crackers and coffee, eaten out of vessels which it was impossible to find time to clean other than by a wipe now and then with dried leaves, and fed myself with hands black with dirt and smoke. Still, I am happy and well, although one of the dirtiest men in the whole army. Even my hair has been uncombed for a long time, as I had the misfortune to lose the comb Mary Landell[13] so kindly gave me, and which I trust you will speedily replace with one from home. The seat of my trousers and both knees are out and I am doing my level best to walk upon the uppers of my boots. I am not alone in this deplorable condition however, as Frank Urie is as bad, and in fact, owing to the severity of the service, both officers and men of our brigade are in rags and tatters, so that no one can possibly call the other names. Harry Donaldson is in pretty much the same condition as myself and, like me, is well and healthy. . . .

>—·—‹›—O—‹•—·—‹

On picket before Yorktown, Va.
April 29th, 1862

My dear Brother:

This morning I was posted at this spot with 12 men under my immediate command, and now avail myself of a little quiet to acknowledge your letter of the 21st duly received. This picket post is within 50 yards of the Rebel pickets, or to put it more intelligently, within murdering distance, for that is about what picket duty, as now conducted, amounts to. As yet, this is as near as I have been to the enemy, and about as near as I care to get on duty such as this. During the day it is bad enough, but at night the situation is anything but agreeable. . . . I frankly confess to a morbid hatred of night work, and sincerely trust I may come safely out of it, as I do not care to be killed or wounded in such duty.

This post has become famous because of the number of men killed here at various times. It is the first time I have been called upon to occupy it, and the force of 12 men I have under me will illustrate its importance as well as the danger attending its occupancy. Its peculiar situation makes it an unenviable place. Occupying the point of a heavily wooded angle, along the side of which a road leads on the other and to the front clear up to the rebel earth works, an open country gives full scope to the vision, while to the left the heavy timber at a right angle closes in the open for a considerable distance, from whose fastness and from the rifle pits and two lonely chimneys immediately in front of the earth works, many a fatal shot of the sharp shooter has been fired.

There is now, immediately in the open field in front of us, a rifle pit, wherein sits an old gray haired Berdan sharp shooter, who has been detailed to locate the spot in the chimneys from whence, at long intervals, comes the unnerving shot that has done so much damage to our people. Although the old man has been two days on this duty he has as of yet failed to find the man who so safely conceals himself. This post is always the first to be engaged in the heavy firing that occasionally bursts forth, but I feel confident of holding it with the material I have, as they constitute the best of the 60 men comprising Co. M. I think I can count on a score of the enemy should they attack me today.

We have been fired at several times by the rebel sharp shooters, and, although the smoke of their rifles could be plainly seen, have not fired a shot in return, as my orders are not to do so, for fear of provoking an artillery fight, which I believe is just not now desired. The Confederates seem to be in a musical mood today, and I have quite enjoyed the playing of their brass band. The Marseilles Hymn, and afterwards the "Dead March" from Saul, which succeeded it, leads me to believe that probably the funeral of an officer has just taken place. I have heard their soldiers singing and could distinctly make out the words of the chorus in The Happy Land of Canaan—

Oh! Oh! Oh! Ha! Ha! Ha!
The Louisiana boys air a coming,
Never mind the South
They are bound to fight it out,
As they roll around the Happy Land of Canaan

. . . Speaking of dangerous consequent on picket duty—yesterday, a shell fired from the rebel battery struck and killed three men of the regiment then on picket, wounded another, then burst and wounded six others.

This, however, is fortunately an exceptionable accident. The rebels had their balloon up yesterday and from the length of time it stayed up, I presume they were having a pretty good view of our encampments and field works.[14] I am delighted with your letter and trust you will always write in the same strain and at the same length, please, also enclose a stamp or two, as I cannot get them here. . . .

I saw Harry Donaldson yesterday and can report him to be in good health and excellent spirits. He had a good laugh at my deplorable condition. . . .

I am in splendid health and as happy as the day is long. . . .

2 Hours Later

Shortly after closing my letter, and while I was still thinking of you and of home, a shot was fired by the enemy and a 32 pound shell came tearing and crashing through the trees where I then was, and exploded to the rear directly among Co. A., Baxter's Fire Zouaves, wounding a corporal and a private, the latter seriously. This appeared to be the signal to let loose the "dogs of war," as our artillery immediately opened and in a short time both sides were heavily engaged in the artillery duel which ensued. The Berdan men came running to the front and were soon busy at the work of death, trying to drive off the enemy's gunners. Whether they succeeded in this or whether the enemy tired of the fight, certain it is that they first ceased firing and soon again <u>all nature smiled</u>.

Very near to my position but further in the woods to the rear, out of sight, is the great observatory, built of logs, from the top of which our general officers obtain good and correct views of the enemy.[15] It would be a bad thing for these same generals should the enemy, by their promiscuous manner of throwing shell about, chance to hit this tower, but as yet no harm has come to it. I noticed today how easily information could be given the enemy without our people knowing about it. An officer of the battery near us dug up a rebel shell which had not exploded, and after emptying, put into it a copy of the New York Herald, when after plugging he fired it back again to the enemy, where I presume it has been received and <u>contents noted</u>.

There is a good deal of activity to the rear of us, men in great numbers making "gabions," or hollow wicker-work cylinders, to be filled with earth as a protection for the gunners at the batteries. Indeed, everything indicates activity and warm work for the near future. I have just been handed yours of the 25th, which was mailed the 26th inst., also the Philada. Inquirer of yesterday, and again thank you for the lengthy letter, and am filled with enthusiasm over the newspaper account of the capture of New Orleans by our glorious Navy.[16]. . .

Well, I presume I will have to stop again, as nature admonishes me it is time for my "square meal," as we call eating our hard crackers. Still, we have abundant delicious spring water, which you know is very filling only a fellow don't appear to fatten much on such diet. Were Capt. Urie here he would remark that in case I felt myself starving I might fall back upon my cheek, where there would be enough and to spare, for a good hearty meal. However the poor fellow is not here, and I may be doing him a great injustice. I am mindful of what you say about John, and should fate cast him a prisoner among us, he will receive an ovation from the California Regiment for his treatment of me when a prisoner in Richmond. Love to all the multitude. . . .

>—◦—⟨⟩—◦—⟨⟩—◦—⟨⟩—<

April 30th, 1862

After writing the forgoing, we were suddenly and mysteriously relieved by Paddy Owens' 69th P.V., reassembled and marched further towards the right, where we awaited the approach of darkness. I can scarcely give you a correct idea of my peculiar sensation at this time—That we were about to undertake some desperate service all felt, but what was the nature of it none knew. My mind was filled with thoughts of night attacks, and of storming earth works, and I noticed one particular fact—that I was continually reasoning out the possibility of leading a headlong charge of M Co. and the success attending the same. That there was a probability of the men not following me was never for a moment thought of, but that the Junior 2nd Lieut. would do something with the command I was determined.

I hadn't long to speculate however, for as soon as it was dark, picks, shovels and spades were distributed to all. The men were then ordered to leave behind everything that would make a noise, such as tin cups & scouse pots, and to sling their muskets over their backs, ready for instant use, and to be careful not for a moment to lay them aside. After all was ready we were moved out in line of battle from among the sheltering woods, and into the open field, over which we stealthily proceeded to within 600 yards of the enemy, when after spreading out we commenced to throw up an entrenchment clean across the open. Just where my Co. rested the ground was very marshy, and it was with the greatest difficulty our part of the line was anything like completed. Still, before we were through a big pile of dirt was raised. Along towards the centre and right of the command daylight showed good heavy entrenchments or "parallels" as the army term goes. . . .

At dawn there arose a perfect howl as the enemy discovered the handy work of the "damned Yanks" during the night past, and their attempts at shelling out the troops who then occupied them was of short duration, as the ever dreaded sharp shooters soon cleared the guns of their workers, and the enemy could do nothing. In a few days this same parallel will be transformed into a "breaching battery" with guns of heavy calibre mounted and mortars and other devices for driving out the devils who so boldly confront us.

Before daylight we were withdrawn to our camp where I now am toasting my shins before a blazing wood fire in front of my tent, preparatory to a visit to the paymaster where, with becoming modesty I will draw my dirty little $34 and then have a full stomach for once, if fortune favors my weak endeavors to find a toothsome meal. If not, with accustomed obedience to discipline and sublime submission to fate, I will again approach with humility the despised sheet iron cracker, the scouse pot of coffee and the plentious spring water.

McClellan had hoped to begin shelling the Confederate works around Yorktown on May 5, but Joe Johnston, who had assumed overall command of the defenses in mid-April, knew he was outnumbered by almost two to one and evacuated his lines on the evening of May 3–4, retreating toward Richmond. McClellan initiated an ineffectual pursuit, sending a portion of his force overland to attempt to catch Johnston, and another part, which included the 71st Pennsylvania, by transport up the York River to West Point to try to cut off the Rebels. Battles were fought at Williamsburg on May 5 and West Point on May 7, but Johnston escaped, and by mid-May he had fallen back into a defensive position south of the Chickahominy River covering Richmond.

The Pennsylvanians saw no action in the pursuit of Johnston, and by late May, along with the balance of the Army of the Potomac, they had advanced to within five miles of the Confederate capital. "You cannot possibly conceive how very anxious I am for this battle," Donaldson wrote his brother on May 25, as he was eager to prove himself in his new position and "show my company that I can handle them." He had not long to wait.

McClellan's position at this time was astride the Chickahominy, with three of his five army corps, including Sumner's 2nd Corps, north of the swampy river, and the remaining two on the south side. A heavy rainstorm on the night of May 30 rendered the normally tepid river nearly impassable, turning it into a seething torrent and leaving the Federal 3rd and 4th Corps south of the river unsupported. Joe Johnston seized the opportunity thus given him and attacked the two isolated corps on May 31 near Fair Oaks Station on the York River Railroad. Late in the day, with the Union lines threatening to break under Rebel assaults, Sumner and his 2nd Corps were ordered south of the river as reinforcements.

For Donaldson, the opportunity he had sought to establish himself in the confidence of his men was at hand. Sedgwick's division led the way across the river, and the 71st Pennsylvania was soon on the battlefield at Fair Oaks supporting elements of the hard-pressed 4th Corps.

Camp Winfield Scott
May 4th, 1862

My dear Brother:

Herewith I send you a sprig of lilac taken from within the enemy's entrenchments, which they evacuated before dawn this A.M. Last evening and pretty much all night they kept up a fearful artillery firing which, of course, is now understood to have been intended to conceal their preparations for leaving. There was also large fires to be seen from within their works during the night. Before daylight, however, this morning, our people discovered their retreat and our dear glorious old flag now waves where the rebel banner fluttered defiantly for so long a time. Of course a column in pursuit was immediately started after them and as they have not so much of a start after all, they will very likely be brought to bay and engaged forthwith. From what I can see and hear, the rebels got away with all their movable equipment, but, of course, had to leave their heavy guns, many of which are spiked and therefore useless to us. . . .

While I cannot help admiring the enemy for their energy, pluck and bravery, there are many things done by them which I do not consider honorable and which, I am sure, the humblest among us would scorn to do. I refer to the planting of percussion shells about their works, which have caused the mangling and death of quite a number of our men.[17] This only displays the hatred these people have for us, which feeling does not exist with our army, on the contrary, we are actuated by love for our government and pity for our foes—a pity akin to the feelings for a misguided brother. Of course, this conduct on their part will only reflect upon their cause, which must indeed be a bad one when such mean measures of revenge are resorted to. I do not think their retreat will be stayed short of Richmond, which means for us a long and fatiguing march in pursuit, and my next letter will, in all probability, be from "on the march to Richmond." Still I am glad our trench digging and vile picket duty is at an end, at least for a time.

Our regiment is now packing up preparatory to moving and before night I presume we will be well on our way towards the rebel capital. As I write, regiment after regiment is now passing to the front, together with a perfect rush of artillery and ammunition wagons. All firing has ceased and you cannot imagine how different things appear. Just to think I can now cross and recross those dreaded open fields with perfect impunity, where but a few hours ago, to show oneself even at the edge of the woods was to be the object of several shots from the enemy's sharp shooters. Why when I first attempted to cross the open, it being so natural for me to dodge and skulk, that I actually did so without thinking, as did others with me, much to each other's amusement.

The enemy before leaving set fire to their quarters and there remains nothing now but smoldering ruins of what was a vast city of wooden houses. I have been over their encampment and found a number of tents still standing, all marked "Florida Troops," with curious devices in charcoal upon them, representing the "Yankees" in anything but flattering positions, intending to represent the triumph of the South over the North. They were very amusing however, and notwithstanding their coarseness and vulgarity, displayed not a little artistic skill. I saw also quite a number of their unburied dead, which spoke plainly of the haste of their departure.

If you remember in my last I spoke plainly of an old Berdan sharp shooter, who was watching the chimneys. Well, he actually succeeded in killing the rifleman hidden there—his body, which proved to be that of a nigro, was found in the fireplace just as it had fallen. The old Berdan man, however, lost his life also, for as was often his custom, upon staying out all night in the pit for the avowed purpose of "catching the early bird," he was found the next morning, still in his pit, but with his throat cut and his rifle gone. Someone as bold as he had stolen in upon him during the night and murdered the poor old fellow.[18] . . .

Just received orders to move with 3 days cooked rations. This indeed looks like a march. The men are filled with enthusiasm and can scarcely be restrained. . . .

>-+-♦>-O-<♦-+-<

Camp at West Point, Va.
May 8th, 1862

Dear Jacob:

We reached this place last evening, just about dark, and found it occupied by Franklin's Division[19] and Dana's Brigade of our division. There had been a big fight with the enemy for its possession in the morning in which although successful, our troops had been roughly handled, losing several hundred men, many of whom, I am told, were killed after being severely wounded and while prisoners in the hands of the enemy. I am also told that some of our men and all colored servants captured were hanged by the rebels, and their suspended bodies afterwards found by our people. I do not know how true this is, but it appears to be current report and has caused a feeling of resentment for which I am sorry.[20] I am free to confess that the contemptible and unsoldierly conduct of the Confederates is fast taking the poetry off the honorable conduct which I always believed actuated belligerents, and I certainly feel apprehensive lest our foes develop into fiends, cruel and unmerciful.

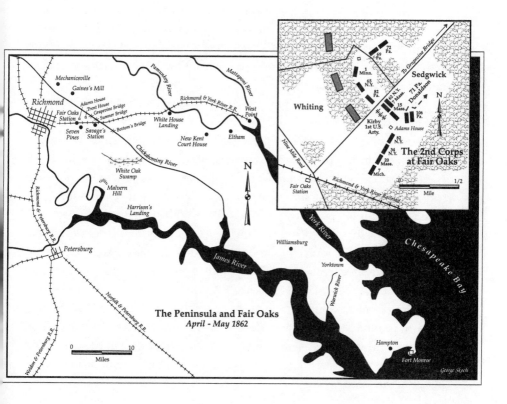

The 2nd Corps at Fair Oaks

The Peninsula and Fair Oaks
April - May 1862

George Skoch

White House is situated at the terminus of the York River, where two smaller rivers, Mattapony and Pamunkey, flow into one wide channel forming the York. The Pamunkey appears to be a very crooked stream. The White House, property of General Lee, stands about a mile from the Pamunkey River and is quite picturesque and beautiful.[21] All night there was signaling by lights with other portions of our army, and away off in the distance we gazed for a long time at the flashing lights in response, and I will add that a feeling of security permeated the division as thus noticing this, to us, unintelligible conversation with the advance of our friends. . . .

. . . I [have] again visited the rebel works and, like the others of which I wrote an account, found them to be of the most substantial kind. Our men appropriated the tents also found standing here, and all commissary stores and other useful things they could find. Enclosed I send you some cotton taken from a bale which, with many others, formed a part of their principal fortification. I also send one or two scraps of letters found within the entrenchments. Again I have to record the savage and cowardly action of the enemy. Around the principal objects of interest, such as the large guns and tents, were planted percussion shells and torpedoes, which continually exploded injuring many poor fellows whose inquisitiveness led them to be incautious. One man of Owen's 69 Regt. P.V.[22] had both legs blown off, and in less than an hour died and was buried. Quick work that—within an hour from robust life and health to death and the grave.

The next day we started for the town and arrived there after about [a] half hour's march. I found Yorktown to be a wretchedly miserable place, and now that it was deserted it presented a deplorable appearance. Availing myself of the halt here, I rambled about sight seeing. At length feeling tired, I seated myself upon what I thought to be a small hillock, but soon discovered it to be the grave of a Confederate officer, named Lieut. Greenhill,[23] 12th Mississippi troop. As I lingered I was filled with feelings of sadness, and could not but sorrow over the untimely death of this man, and of his lone grave so far away from friends and his native place. I sorrowed because of the useless sacrifice he had made in upholding an unholy cause. The ground near and around where I stood struck me as being a burial place, for there were hundreds of just such hillocks on every side, although arranged in something like order, while this one was apart by itself. It seemed to me that these graves in a measure represented the loss of the enemy during the siege. The rebel entrenchments, as I have said, were most formidable and of a character never before known on this continent. Their capture by storm, in my judgment, would have entailed a slaughter amounting to a fourth part of our army. . . .

From Yorktown, that day, we took transports for this place and are now encamped on the field so hotly contested for yesterday. The ride up the river was grand, and the scenery beautiful beyond conjecture. The grassy slopes and lovely scenes which from time to time unfolded themselves made many a heart long to tarry amid so much picturesque loveliness. Here and there along the river were cottages of snowy whiteness in the midst of clusters of trees, and in many places the banks were low and bushy trees grew in wild luxuriance to the waters edge. Each house as we passed displayed the white flag, a token of submission which will be speedily forgotten as soon as we leave here. Troops are constantly arriving and artillery in untold numbers also. The transports as they unload the troops take on board the wounded who crowd the hospitals. I presume this will continue until an immense force is concentrated, when the advance will be again taken up. I forgot to mention that rumour also has it that General Lee was severely wounded in the engagement of yesterday by the limb of a tree striking him.

Our gun boats took an active part in this fight, and I have examined with wonderment and fear the immense cavities their shells have, in many places, made in the ground. One in particular, I assure you, a six mule team could have been driven through so great was the effect of the explosion of their ponderous shells. My man George continues to give me close attention and I fear that his usefulness has made it impossible to endure this life without him. He is faithful, honest, thoughtful and brave, and I am deeply attached to him. . . .

>-+-+>-+-O-+-+>-+-<

Bivouac (for the night) of the California
Regiment <u>somewhere in Virginia</u> and
not many miles from West Point—
May 10th, 1862

My dear Brother:

Yesterday the 9th inst., in the afternoon, our whole division moved to this place and are now encamped in regular order as though for a stay of some days. As usual our regiment is on picket and I am writing this at the extreme outpost of the army. I do not fear interruption as it would be impossible for the enemy to penetrate the dense jungle by which we are surrounded. I can give you no description of the place as I have no view beyond a few yards distant, so heavy is the timber and underbrush. A short distance to the rear there is a house or two and some cleared ground. I have not yet learned the name of "the City" as large towns down here with big sounding names experience has taught me consists of no more buildings than this one. When I learn the name I will make it known to you. . . . I am seated on an old Corn Crib, and have for my desk a shingle torn from its roof, while mosquitoes and gnats are swarming upon me, causing my disengaged hand to be in incessant motion protecting face and eyes. This paper is held in place by my knife blade and my position and attitude denotes anything but comfort and ease.

I am sorry to learn that the evacuation of Yorktown causes dissatisfaction and that the press and people indulge in such ungrateful attacks on Genl. McClellan and that rumor speaks of his removal. Why, my dear brother, if Yorktown was not a victory, it certainly was not a defeat. The rebels retreated, not we. Why did they leave? Because their works were no longer tenable. The people may be dissatisfied and grumble, but I tell you, in all candor, that the soldiers of this army will not stand a stab in the back by those from whom they expect encouragement and support. Remove McClellan and you disorganize the army, changing it from a unit into demoralized factions. From the tenor of your letter, I judge you have also imbibed these cruel feelings. Now to my mind the solution of this clamor is as plain as the nose on your face. McClellan is a Democrat, and as such, must be removed. Republicanism is the fashion, and all who are not of the persuasion must go, no matter how much the service suffers, no matter that the interests of the country demand support and confidence in the commander of its great army. I can speak with certainty of our regiment, where the situation, as you picture it, has been discussed, and the officers, one and all, are determined to resign should such rank injustice be done "Little Mac."

A "reliable contraband," just arrived from the enemy's lines, confirms the report of the wounding of Genl. Lee at West Point. A shot struck a tree, shivering it to pieces, a large limb striking the general, bruising him and tearing his cloths badly. His horse was dreadfully mangled and killed. He also reports that Genl. Lee is very much discouraged and says that the general states the game to be up should he fail at Richmond where a stand will be made. It is surprising how communicative General Officers of the Confederate States are with the "reliable contrabands.[24]". . .

May 11th. I have just learned this place to be Eltham. Direct as before, adding California Regiment (71st P.V.)

>─┼─◆>─○─<◆┼─<

Camp near White House, Va.
May 18th, 1862

My dear Brother:

I say "Camp near White House" because I do not know what else to call it. We are at least 3 miles from that place however, and bivouaced in the centre of a large wheat field, the owner of which is highly indignant, and has vehemently protested to Genl. Burns against its occupancy, and the destruction of his grain. Poor man, we have indeed outraged him, laid waste to his fields, used his fences for fuel and even as I write, the crash of falling trees is plainly heard as our pioneers, with untiring swing of the axe, are destroying a grove of fine timber upon which the owner prides himself. Need I add, his protests were of no avail and that he had to content himself with the fact that <u>as yet</u> his house remains intact.

We arrived this A.M. from our late "Camp near New Kent Court House"[25] (Official) and thanks to delightful weather had quite a pleasant march. All along the route, white flags were displayed at the houses passed in token of submission, which means submission while we are here to enforce it, and rank rebellion, aid, and comfort to the enemy as soon as we are gone. I do not think much of this "trimming" policy on the part of the natives, but it has the effect of protecting their property, which is all they care about. This portion of Virginia is perfectly beautiful, everything so green and lovely. How soon all would be changed should it please our general to have us remain a week or two with the <u>friendly disposed citizens "who always were loyal and against secession.</u>" They would then find that it would be better for that people that an army of locusts had come upon them for even a short space.

Where are the Sesesh! is the question now most frequently asked. We neither see nor hear anything of them. In fact, were it not for the newspapers, we would be loath to believe there was any war, any sesesh, or anything else to make us realize that it was not a gigantic picnic we are on. . . .

<u>May 19th</u>. Genl. Frank Patterson with his staff and brigade passed our camp yesterday. He is certainly a fine looking soldier, especially on horseback.

If I can sum up courage enough to do so, I will call upon him at his camp which is but a short distance from us.

About 5 P.M. yesterday the weather being so balmy and delightful I took a stroll along the country road up the side of which we are camped, and came to a house where the usual emblem of submission—white flag—was flying from a window on the second floor. It was quite a pretty place and the nigro quarters the best that I had seen in sesesh-land. Seeing the lady of the house at the door I stopped and asked how long the Confederates had encamped here. She replied, "About a week." I asked if there were many of them. She said, "I did think there was right smart of them until you all came." To my question whether she observed any difference between the two armies she said, "No, there are good and bad on both sides, since you all have been here we have lost quite a large drove of swine, and a calf." Her property, however, is now protected by a strong guard, and she has no complaint to make, but it seemed strange to her that we waited until everything worth carrying off had been stolen by the soldiers before a guard was put on her property. Her husband is in the rebel army.

This will illustrate the tenor of feeling held by all the people, here abouts, that I have spoken with. They are anxious to have their property preserved and take it as a great hardship if a few fence rails are taken and destroyed, but make no moment of the fact that they themselves are trying to destroy the country that has always protected and given them the best of government. They do not feel that their soldiers are armed rebels, but think only that they are defending homes from invasion by a horde of plunderers, and when they find out that we are not as they had been taught to believe, they ask in wonderment "What then did you all come down here for?," plainly showing that they do not know for what they are fighting. Well they will soon understand what it is all about, as troops were pouring in by thousands all night long, and as I write are still passing to the front. Notwithstanding, the people feel confident that we will get dreadfully whipped this side of Richmond as the rebels have a trap for us there, and that our forces will meet with disaster at Corinth.[26]

I presume our turn will soon come to move on. It is dreadfully hot during the daytime and I am burned as brown as a nut. Capt. Urie still continues dangerously ill and for several days past requires the constant muscular attention of myself and the doctor to confine him to bed. I do wish we could get him home, as the attempt to keep him with the command only protracts his sickness. This is a dreadful country to get sick in anyway, and the captain, being such a big strong fellow, requires the most powerful medicines to make an impression, and these the hospital department have not got. . . .

>—+—<>—+—O—+>—+—<

Camp in the Field before Richmond, Va.
May 23rd, 1862

Dear Brother:

We retired from Bottom's Bridge where we had been encamped since the 21st inst. and reached this place an hour or two ago.[27] As we are bivouaced in an open country no official name has yet been given to the camp, hence I say "before Richmond" as we are but a few miles from that city. . . . We are abundantly supplied with artillery on flank and centre, much dependence apparently being placed in that terrible arm of the service. I am told that the whole division could be put into battle array and ready for the fight inside of five minutes.

Genl. Burns has been and is now as I write with the men speaking to them. He said in my hearing when passing a group who, with hands at the visor of their caps, stood in respectful military attitude as he passed, "Men,— I hope to have the opportunity within the next few days of heading my brigade in a bayonet charge. I feel confident there is nothing that can stand before you, and should it be necessary, I will lead the California Regiment in person." The men are very fond of him, and feel great confidence in his skill and judgment.

The scene is wonderfully exciting as the whole camp is astir, men busily engaged in drying cartridges and cleaning their muskets. I also have been similarly engaged, having reloaded and freshly capped my pistol and otherwise girded up my loins for the fray. I forgot to mention that the sword I carry was loaned me by Co. F and was captured when the company was skirmishing on the advance from Bethel. It was just after daybreak on that occasion when the company moved forward and took the enemy so completely by surprise that a rebel officer had to abandon his sword, belt and coat to make good his escape. My pistol was presented by Co. H so that as far as armament is concerned I will bear inspection.

Speaking of inspection, to show you the condition I am in and the figure I cut, I will mention an incident that will probably have the effect of hastening the finish and delivery of my uniform. While at Camp near [New] Kent Court

House, Genl. Sumner inspected the division, and as is the custom on such occasions, with his staff the general, from the right first, rode down the front as the men, in line of battle, stood at shoulder arms. Ever attentive to all matters of discipline and soldierly bearing, I was, along with the other officers, in front of the regiment, standing rigidly with eyes to the front, neither did I notice the approach of the old warrior, but was mindful only of his proximity by the screeching fifes and roll of drums as our Drum Corps gave "Hail to the Chief" with resounding vigor. Suddenly the dear old General was before me and with all the energy of my nature I tried to look the soldier when, reining in his horse, to my intense mortification he demanded "Who in the devil" I was. "2nd Lt. Co. M," cried I with vehemence, as saluting I looked straight at him. "You are, are you?" said he, "I thought you were a bundle of rags." With that he rode on. Since then I have had a good deal of fun poked at me which has now become somewhat tiresome, so hurry along my clothes.

We moved from Camp near White House on the 21st and reached Bottom's Bridge on the Chickahominy same day. This was a dreadful march, the worst we have as yet experienced. The weather was extremely hot and there had been so much rain of late that the earth was saturated, heavy and soggy. The hot sun evaporated this moisture so rapidly that it was like marching through steam, which made the atmosphere oppressive and hard to bear. As far as I have been able to judge the Chickahominy is an exceedingly sluggish stream, more like a big swamp than anything else I can liken it to, and, I presume, from the heavy rains lately fallen in this latitude, has overflowed its banks, thus accounting for the marsh like appearance the country presents. All along the 15 miles marched to Bottom's Bridge, which by the way is 13 miles from Richmond, there was every evidence of the passage of large bodies of troops, as on every side overcoats, blankets and all manner of clothing were strewn. During the march many men were overcome by heat and two of the brigade have since died from its effects.

Yesterday I took a lovely bath in the Chickahominy at Bottom's Bridge and enjoyed it hugely. Genl. McClellan passed us yesterday and but few recognized him in the slouched hat and old blue blouse he wore—no one could have told him from an ordinary cavalryman. The country is more cultivated and presents a better appearance as we approach Richmond. Indeed in some places it is perfectly lovely and as beautiful and romantic as can be found anywhere in Pennsylvania.

As I write heavy firing is heard on our left and I should judge by its long continuance and rapidity that our advance is engaged.[28] I feel a little exercised about the impending battle, and as it will be the first regular engagement in which I appear as an officer, I am exceedingly anxious to make a name for myself and to be worthy [of] the good opinion I feel the officers generally have of me. My only regret is that Col. Wistar is not here, as I am sure he would take occasion to observe me closely.[29] As for my reputation as a soldier, that is established, at least with Co. H, and my character for coolness and courage is generally understood by the whole command who know why I was promoted. Still I have never fought Co. M, and apart from severe picket duty have never had opportunity to show them just what I can do as an officer. It is true that Capt. Hills has left matters pretty much in my hands and I have improved the occasion by making myself familiar with the character of each individual member of the Co., and I am convinced I can fight the Co. to its best advantage if I have the opportunity, feeling assured the men will follow me anywhere. Of one thing they are sure, that never shirking myself, I will certainly see that none of them do so. However, time will tell and all that I can promise is to do my best.

Now I do not want you to suppose I am making too much of myself and of what I have done and what I will do. There is nothing further from my thoughts than seemingly to brag. On the contrary, I freely admit that during an engagement or when one seems imminent I have the most annoying feelings. Not exactly fear, but a longing desire that either the battle will terminate, the sun go down, or else that I be detailed for some duty to the rear, but I act the other and more soldierly one of obeying orders and doing my duty no matter how unpleasant or what the consequences. These feelings are my true ones, which I do not disguise from you, but to my comrades and the men under me, I present a calm unmoved demeanor during times of trouble, and when in actual battle, all thought of self is lost in my desire and anxiety to have those under me do their work and behave well. Could they but know my inward thought at such times, could they but see beneath the apparently brave exterior, the fluttering heart, the quickened pulse, I fear the regard they have for my courage would be but short lived. Oh! how I envy the brave fellow officers by whom I am surrounded, what would I not give to be like them—indifferent, insensible to all fear, but I will never attain to that happiness. I will never overcome the certain positive feeling of desire to be anywhere but in the battle's front. Still it being my duty to go there, go I will, and fight down all other feelings. . . .

I hope you will soon hear something from John. I always make inquiries of the prisoners as to the whereabouts of the 22nd Virginia Regt. but never have yet learned anything of them, so I feel certain they are not in our front. Capt. Urie left for home a day or two ago. He is a very sick man needing the care and attention of his family. . . . I am in splendid health and feel equal to any emergency. Love to Auntie and tell her to write soon. . . .

>-+-•>-•O-•<•+-<

Camp in the Field near Richmond, Va.
May 25, 1862

Dear Brother:

There being nothing special to do this morning, I asked and obtained permission from Maj. Smith to absent myself from Camp for a few hours in order to carry out a plan I had formed of visiting one or two of the fine old country mansions I had seen in the distance as we marched to this place. Hunting up my chums, Lt. A. P. Schurtz,[30] Co. P. and Lt. G. W. Kenney, Co. N, whom I found, after diligent search, stowed away busily engaged in a quick game of 10 cent ante, I made known my plans and readily got their consent to accompany me. After they too getting permission from the Major, we started off in gay spirits determined to enjoy to the full the delightful day and this bewitching anticipation of again seeing and talking to the gentler sex I was sure these lovely old houses would contain.

It is true my companions were not noted among the command for their beauty, and that they were not handsome was the only serious regret I had in view of the anticipated pleasure of meeting with some of the lovely maidens believed to inhabit this beautiful country. But I also knew that they were quick, smart, agreeable fellows who would make an impression where others more favored by good looks would be scarcely noticed. Especially is this true of Schurtz, a more engaging and brilliant talker I never met with, but he is extremely homely, and beside close curly sandy hair, although but a few years older than myself he has had the misfortune of losing all his teeth, and now sports a beautiful set of china ones which are quite stunning. Kenney is not quite so brilliant a fellow, but has a face that would not at first strike you as anything but ordinary, but by the peculiar sad expression habitually resting on it, would attract your attention if you were at all an observer of countenances. Then too when he talks and laughs, which latter he seldom does, he displays a set of teeth beautifully white and even which goes a long way to make him noticeable. He, unlike my Bucks Co. friend Schurtz, is small in stature and is always well dressed, neat and natty, although how in the world he manages to keep himself so I cannot conceive.

The road we took ran through a rich level country, divided into such extensive plantations that only two or three dwellings were anywhere visible. After a little consultation we concluded to proceed to one which could just be seen afar off, and for the purpose of avoiding the heat of the sun, made a cut through an intervening woods. After proceeding a mile or two in the direction of the house, enjoying the woods and here and there gathering wild flowers, we came upon a lovely sheet of water which was fragrant with the spicy pine and beautiful with aquatic plants, the names of which I did not know, but which the more gifted Schurtz easily recognized and explained. In the center of a cleared space which ran a little way back into the woods stood the old house, a fine old mansion with a veranda extending around the first story, and trees embowering the broad roof. Glimpses could be had of the outbuildings and nigro quarters farther back. Bent upon knowing who occupied the building, we entered a half opened gate and made a short cut through an apple orchard, in the center of which was

Lt. George W. Kenney, Company N, 71st Pennsylvania Volunteers. He was killed at White Oak Swamp, June 30, 1862. THE CIVIL WAR LIBRARY & MUSUEM.

a bower of young beautiful trees, and as we drew nigh, the lovely form of a woman burst upon our view. . . .

In what was surely a postwar alteration, the next two and a half pages of this letter have been blotted out. Historical accuracy appears to have suffered at the expense of discretion in this instance.

. . . for instead of the beautiful lady my Fancy pictured, there came forth a light mulatto girl, a slave, who said, "Is you hungry marster soldier man?" She was a beautiful light colored nigro girl, of the color of a new saddle, and I looked at her in wonderment. Suddenly getting my thoughts together I asked her name and learned it to be "Jennie Dixey," Virginia Dixey, waiting maid to a young lady residing in the house. Believing it to be no harm, I gave Virginia a rousing Yankee hug and two or three sound Union kisses, and then proceeded to call up my companions, but the effect of the entrance was so electrical that before doing so I thought to indulge myself with one or two more tender moments spent with the graceful girl, when lo! those delectable gentlemen, having from afar observed the peculiar turn affairs had taken, came rushing to the spot, and forcing me violently aside, fairly divided between them the poor girl. Virginia appearing to enjoy the society of the Yankee soldiers so much, that fearing to lose any further time, I asked her to conduct us to the house and inform her master that we were there. The old man appeared and invited us into the parlor and tried to make us comfortable.

He appeared to be about 55 years of age and had quite a venerable look. He informed us that he was a good Union man, and in fact had voted the Bell & Everett ticket,[31] but was sorry to state that his youngest boy had been drafted into the Confederate States service. He had, also, six sons in New York State. His name was Master, and upon informing him that we would take a letter and mail it North for him if he would write it at once, he was overjoyed, and proceeded alone to do so, leaving us with his daughter, who though not very pretty was a perfect lady and entertained us delightfully. The house was very plainly furnished but had an appearance of neatness corresponding with the outside looks of the place. The entry or hall, rather, during the whole of our stay, was crowded with dusky forms all eager to gaze upon the Yanks, we being the first Union soldiers to visit this place, and our friend Jennie had quite a crowd around her in the yard telling them of how we had acted. We were invited to dinner which we gladly accepted, and although there was nothing very grand, everything was good and substantial. We informed the old gentleman that if he would come down to our camp we would supply him with coffee and sugar. This made the old patriarch fairly jump and commence looking around for his hat to go immediately, but not being in any hurry ourselves we just faced it out for an hour longer, talking and having a good time. Altogether we had an enjoyable visit and were sorry to come away, and when we did so I hung back and fooled along considerably in hopes of again seeing Miss Virginia Dixey, but I was disappointed as she was not about and I saw no more of her. Indeed I fear I have quite lost my heart with this pretty yellow girl. My gracious! Jack, were she at home with us, what a heap of trouble Auntie would have with us all.

Well, we loaded the old gentleman and his darky with crackers, coffee, sugar and pork and sent him off to think, I hope, that the Yankee troops are not the villains and scoundrels the people are taught to believe, or else to chuckle and smile over the adroit manner with which he profited by the presence of the invaders; either way he put it, I will always personally feel his debtor for a pleasant hour or two spent in the agreeable society of his entertaining daughter, and for the quiet enjoyment of his hospitality away from the scenes of rude war with which for a long time I had been familiar.

I must bring this lengthy letter to a close as we have just had orders to prepare to march; beside too I am out of paper. We are to take nothing but our muskets, cartridge boxes, haversacks and canteens, all other baggage to be left behind in camp. I presume Genl. McClellan is about to storm the rebel Capital, and I think we will just go right over the works, for I do not think it possible to stay this enthusiastic army. There is now, as I write, a slight firing ahead. You cannot possibly conceive how very anxious I am for this battle, not only because I think the war can be settled by it, but also because I want to show my company that I can handle them and I am determined to make a big name on this field. One would think that I am in command of Co. M. but such is not the case. Capt. Hills is with us, but somehow I scarcely ever see him as he is seldom with the Co.

Later—Just returned from forming Regiment. We have stacked arms and the men are to have a ration of whiskey issued to them so that we will be off before long. There are immense bodies of troops passing and much artillery, while the heavens have become overcast threatening a stormy night. Everything looks weird and strange. I wonder whether we will fight tomorrow, certainly it is now too late to do so today, although the long roll is sounding. Give my love to Auntie—God bless her and you too Jacob.

Donaldson wrote the following narrative of his experiences in the Battle of Fair Oaks while at home in Philadelphia in the summer of 1862.

. . . <u>May 28th</u>. Lt. Kenney and I went across Bottom's Bridge and took a delightful bath in a mill dam, 12 miles from Richmond. It was perfectly lovely at this place. Indeed, for that matter, ever since leaving West Point we had been marching through a beautiful country, with everything in nature in a state of most luxuriant bloom. The fields were green with the new spring grass, and the trees were covered with rich leaves and blossoms, making glad the eye of the observant soldier if at all influenced by surroundings so lovely.

Since the 22nd our corps was busily engaged in building bridges across the Chickahominy, which was anything but an easy task. After great exertions, two bridges were completed, one the Sumner and the other the Grapevine Bridge, so called because vines had been largely used in binding the logs together. We also did some pretty severe picket duty. I was mostly detailed with a detachment in building corduroy approaches to the bridges. The banks of the Chickahominy, on our side, were swampy lowlands. Indeed for that matter there were no banks at all. But just beyond, across the river were bluffs of considerable height. At this work we continued until May 29th.

In the afternoon, our brigade was suddenly returned to camp, and were soon again busy in making ourselves comfortable. That is, our regiment. I was not on this expedition but remained in camp, except to visit Bottom's Bridge, as stated. Baxter's, however, were not so fortunate. Whether it was because the men were slow in executing the orders, or whether Col. Baxter was too particular as to the alignments, considerable delay was occasioned in getting the "Fire Zouaves" into bivouac, so much so as to attract attention from the other regiments of the brigade. Indeed we had long been dismissed and were making coffee before the poor Zoo Zoo's received the order to rest.

<u>May 30th</u>. It had been stormy all day, with occasional sun shine, long enough to make the steam arise, and then rain again. In the afternoon there had been a general clearing of the weather—so we thought—and men were drying their clothes, when it suddenly clouded up again and a most terrific thunder storm burst upon us. We seemed to be in the very midst of it. The lightning ripped and tore along the ground and rent the heavens with its dazzling flashes, while the thunder crashed in deafening peals that seemed to make the earth tremble beneath our feet. Great blinding sheets of rain fell and rushed through our camp, turning the country around us into a perfect river. I never before experienced such a storm. We were speedily soaked to

the skin, but made every exertion to keep dry our muskets and ammunition. This state of affairs continued with but slight intermission, all night long.

Early the next day, Saturday, May 31, the rain ceased and the sun once more appeared. The whole country was flooded, the ground being so saturated & soaked as to make it impassable for troops. About noon, firing was heard from across the river. First the booming of cannon, then the prolonged roar of musketry. This continued uninterruptedly, thus making it appear that a heavy engagement was being fought.

About 1 P.M. we were ordered to fall in, and remained some time in readiness for the order to march. I took occasion to look closely after the men, and to see that they were in good fighting condition, both as to muskets and ammunition, and to say to them that I trusted, should we become engaged, they would make me feel proud of the honor of being their lieutenant. I then called my man George Slow, and taking him aside, told him I thought it likely we would soon be engaged, and as it was the first time, as an officer, I would appear in action with the company, I, of course, would make an effort to establish myself in the confidence of the men. This would lead me to expose myself more than I otherwise would do, but that I was determined to show the company I was worthy to be their officer. I also said I thought it not unlikely I would be hurt, and taking from off my finger a heavy gold ring, I gave it to him to keep for me, adding that should I be killed, I wanted him to send it home to my family, as I greatly prized it. I also gave him my pocket book, reserving a small sum of money, which I also instructed him to send home. Finally I said I desired him, should I meet with misfortune, to go over the battlefield and find my body and give it decent burial, and to be sure and mark the spot plainly, so that my people could at some future time, recover my remains. I also said I wanted him to remember this conversation. Poor fellow, he cried bitterly at what I said and urged me to be careful and not expose myself. I felt confident I would be shot in this battle, not that I had a presentiment, but that my position as an untried officer would necessarily expose me to more than ordinary danger.

Shortly before two o'clock the march was begun, our division, Sedgwick's, in advance, Gorman's brigade leading. Then came ours, Burns, with Dana's brigade following. Richardson's division came after. Kirby's 1st U.S. Artillery, a battery of Napoleon guns, were between Gorman's and our brigade. We headed for the Grapevine Bridge, which we found almost submerged by the rushing water, and it was only by the weight of our troops that it remained long enough in place to permit the crossing. The mud was something appalling. When we reached the opposite side of the Chickahominy, the cannon were found mired to the hub, the horses being utterly unable to get them along. Long ropes were attached to the pieces, and the men swarming upon them, assisted the horses in getting four of them out of the mire and up the bluffs. Baxter's 72nd P. V. Philada. Fire Zouaves led our brigade, and as we debouched from the bridge they and the cannon were found floundering in the mud just in advance.

I noticed far to our left Major DeWitt[32] of the 72nd wading through the mud, trying to catch his horse which had broken away from him, and I thought it rather a strange coincidence that he should follow it, instead of detailing a man to effect its capture. It certainly looked as though the Major preferred to follow his horse rather than continue with his regiment to the front. To my mind, his conduct was anything but dignified, or that of a brave soldier. He escaped the battle, at all events.

The roar of musketry and the booming of cannon was deafening. Proceeding slowly until the whole of our brigade had crossed the bridge, we then commenced a rapid march to the front. Very soon we passed a large fine country dwelling, owned and occupied, I believe by Mr. Trent,[33] then through his wheatfield and fording a small stream beyond to a straggling strip of timber, we came in sight of the raging battle. What a sight it was. Our army was retiring, though slowly, round shot and bullets were tearing through the trees above us, and the whole plain was spread over by stragglers and wounded men.

Genl. Burns formed the brigade in line of masses, while Genl. Gorman, in line of battle, moved forward into the whirl of battle. At this time, Kirby arrived on the ground with four pieces of artillery and went into battery near a fence behind which the 23rd Penna. & Cochran's U.S. Chasseurs[34] were hotly engaged. Genl. Burns now detached the 72nd & 69th regts. and led them to our right while Genl. Sedgwick appeared on the ground and took immediate command of our 71st & the 106th P.V. and led us into battle. Just as we commenced to move forward a round shot came tearing along the ground in direction of my company and a panic seized the men which well nigh stampeded them. At least one half the company had broken to the rear before I discovered what they were doing. Instantly drawing my pistol I rushed after them, and seizing by the throat a red haired fellow by name of Jones,[35] held on to him, and flourishing my pistol called to the men in a most excited manner to be steady. I succeeded in bringing them back to their places thus arresting a wavering movement among the companies near me.

I was dreadfully excited and tore up and down the rear of the company threatening instant death to any who made the slightest movement towards the rear. Meanwhile, the advance was being continued under Genl. Sedgwick, who, with hat in hand, rode his fine horse upon the flank of our battalion on a line with the leading division.

We now passed over a field from which the timber had but lately been cut and piled into cordwood. It was on what is known as Allen's Farms.[36] There was an empty building near, probably a saw mill, as quite a pile of sawdust and other matter lay immediately to our right—at least, this is my remembrance of this place, although my attention was so fully occupied with watching the behavior of the men and taking orders from Capt. Hills that I paid very little attention to the surroundings.

We halted at this place directly to the rear of the U.S. Chasseurs, with Kirby's guns slightly in advance on our left flank. The battle was surging and raging just ahead. The Chasseurs, occupying the line of a fence, were loading and firing like demons. The battery was being served with great rapidity, the smoke in thick clouds hung over the field, while above, all the ringing cheers of the enemy could be heard as they came rapidly onward in a grand rush for the guns. Just beyond the fence, at about 50 yards distant, was a piece of timber amid which the enemy were, and from which they were pouring a heavy fire upon us. We were halted but a short distance in rear of the Chasseurs and the guns and ordered to lie down. A perfect storm of bullets tore over our heads and solid shot rent the air above us. In the formation of column my company occupied the left of the 2nd division,[37] with Co. A immediately in front and Co. P in back of us. When the order came to lie down, with exception of Capt. Jno. Markoe[38] & myself, all did so. Maj. Chas. W. Smith, who was in command, got off and squatted behind his horse for shelter. The poor beast was shot through the stomach and died shortly after the battle.

Now when the order came to lie down I ordered my end of the company flat upon the ground, but remained standing myself. It was the opportunity I had sought to fix myself in the men's confidence. Of course I at once became the observer of all to the rear of me, and was called upon to get down by a number of the officers. Immediately in front of me, as I have stated, lay Co. A, with 1st Lt. Thos. Ashton[39] in command; his captain, Jno. Markoe, having command of the division, was at this time standing at the right of it. There being no orders, I now turned my attention to the battle, and saw the enemy's column coming up to the guns in splendid order, notwithstanding the fire of canister poured into them. The U.S. Chasseurs were upon their feet behind the fence loading and firing as fast as they could, while the enemy were pouring a deadly fire upon us from the woods in front. At each discharge of the guns I called out to Lt. Ashton, "By George Ashton! you ought to have seen that shot, here they come again."

Shortly after noticing my friend Ashton as close to the ground as he could get, his undignified and comical position suddenly dawned upon me, causing a fit of laughter I could not suppress. I upbraided him for lying down at all, and had just said, "Great Scott Ashton!, why don't you stand up?," when I received a musket ball through my left arm, about three or four inches below the shoulder joint. It went clean through, smashing the bone and carrying portions of my undershirt & woolen blouse into the wound. The force of the blow turned me completely around. The sensation was that of having struck my elbow, or crazy bone. I was instantly aware of my mishap, but did not for a moment lose my self possession. I am not aware of whether I was the subject of any special shot from a sharpshooter, or whether I was wounded by a chance shot. . . . So close was the man who shot me that the bullet, after passing through my arm, continued on to the rear with a whizzing noise. Ashton said he never before beheld so complete and rapid a change of the human countenance as took place in my face. I was at a broad grin when hit and the instant change to the serious left an expression on my features most curious to behold.

Looking down at my hand which hung helpless at my side I strove to see whether it also had been hurt as the tingling sensation in my fingers gave the impression that I had been struck there too. In an endeavor to raise my arm I now noticed where the wound was. Reaching around with my right I caught hold of my left hand and drawing it up in front of me let it fall, when the arm swung about utterly useless. The blood ran down my fingers in streams, when again turning to Lt. Ashton, I said, "See how the soil of Old Virginia drinks up the Yankee blood." During this time no one moved to give me the least help. Everyone was kept down by the storm of bullets that still swept over the regiment. Becoming somewhat uneasy at the rapid loss of blood, I asked whether someone would kindly help me bind up my arm. Still not a man from my company or any other moved to assist me. I now drew out from my breast pocket a red bandana handkerchief, and still standing, tried to pass it around my arm. At this, 1st Sergeant Burt Schurz,[40] Company P, sprang to his feet and said, "I'll help you Lieutenant." Dropping his musket, he tightly bound my handkerchief above the wound and suggested my going to the rear. I then moved out to the flank and leisurely walked to the rear, still amid a storm of bullets which whistled around and ploughed up the ground in all directions.

After proceeding a short distance I came to a pile of cordwood behind which a young surgeon was busy in spreading out a case of instruments, who, upon my approach, ordered me to lie down while he examined my hurt. This brave fellow had certainly selected an exposed position for his hospital, as the bullets were striking the wood and sending the bark and splinters in all directions. Whether it was the danger he was in, or whether the nervousness, it certainly happened that the doctor ripped up the sleeve of my right arm in his haste to get at my wound. His hasty manner and nervous actions caused me to laugh and I said, "Confound it man, it is the other arm that is hurt," whereupon he cut up the other sleeve and made an examination, when finding the bone completely broken, he said, "You will have to go to the house in the distance where they will amputate the arm." This was the first intimation I had I was to lose my arm and I may add it depressed me a good deal. During all this time I had kept my overcoat with me, and at the time I was shot, it was rolled and thrown over my shoulder. The surgeon now undid it and throwing it over my shoulders buttoned it around my neck.

I now noticed for the first time several of Baxter's men lying behind the wood pile, and asked the doctor whether these men were dead. He said no!, there was nothing the matter with them, they were merely seeking shelter. As I soon after observed a good many of this same regiment tearing across the country to the rear, it struck me that all the good places for shelter had already been occupied by others of the same command to have caused these fellows to go so far to seek cover.

I now started for the house indicated by the surgeon as the field hospital and had proceeded but a short distance when I saw Major Robb Parrish of our regiment coming up at a brisk trot, leading his pack horse. He halted at meeting me, dismounted, and taking his holster pistols, turned his horses over to a <u>shelter seeking</u> Zouave and ordered him to lead them out of danger. From the prompt manner with which the man obeyed, I could not but admire the thorough discipline of Col. Baxter's men. The Major now asked about my hurt and examined my arm, which I was holding across my body with my right hand. He expressed much sympathy and trusted I would not lose my arm. He said he had been denied the privilege of fighting with his own command, being under arrest, and was about to join the brave fellows who were so hotly engaged at the fence. Bidding me good bye, I saw him walk boldly forward, with pistols in both hands, until lost to view in the smoke from the cannon.

At this moment, I saw four men coming from the front bearing a stretcher, upon which lay Capt. Markoe, wounded in two places, the most serious of which was an ugly hurt in the groin. Brave fellow, he had been standing at the right of his division, and by his conspicuous bravery giving confidence and steadiness to his men. . . .

Again moving off towards the hospital, I noticed at but a short distance a mounted officer attempting to stop a group of stragglers. After a free display of his pistol he succeeded in turning the men back towards the battle. He now rode up to me, and with a volly of blasphemy wanted to know what I, an officer, meant by going to the rear. Greatly surprised at his profanity and manner of authority, I stood still for a moment and tried to reconcile his words to his rank, believing it impossible that a staff officer, and a captain at that, could assume so much, as this blackguard did. I replied, and I fear I was led into language somewhat stronger than was my want, for intense indignation bristled all over me, "Damn you, you cowardly skulker, had you been where your brave general now is, you would not have dared to offer so gross and uncalled for insult to one so utterly unable to resent it as I am." With that I threw back my overcoat and displayed my bloody arm. The fellow had some sense of decency left, for he said quickly upon perceiving that I was wounded, "Oh!, excuse me," and before I had time to ask his name, put spurs to his horse and made off, but not towards the front, however. This officer I think was on Genl. Sumner's staff, and no doubt was incensed at the vast number of unhurt armed men running to the rear. I can make allowance now for his vehemence, but at the time I was very much angered at his ungentlemanly language. . . .

It was a sickening scene that presented itself upon arriving at the little two story and attic frame house now being used for surgical operations on the desperately wounded that needed immediate attention. The ground around was strewn with mangled fellows while away off, towards the front, streams more were either walking or else being carried to this spot. The house had a one story extension back, used as a kitchen, a window on either side, and a door in the rear with steps leading down to the yard. The principal operations were being carried on in this small room, as I could judge from the pile of arms and legs that, on the ground outside the window, reached nearly up to it as they had been thrown out after amputation. As I came towards the front of the house I noticed we were still within reach of artillery, as a round shot came howling along and struck a gray horse standing tied to a tree near the front door, completely carrying away his muzzle. The poor creature presented a most horrible appearance as he stood trembling while the blood streamed from his torn and bleeding head.

Seeing that I was an officer, an attendant took me inside, and as the lower rooms were loaded with wounded, I went back to the rear and found four tables being used as operating tables, each of which was occupied, while the surgeons with sleeves rolled up were literally working up to their elbows in blood, so busy were they with knife and saw. One of the subjects then undergoing amputation seemed to be put partially under the influence of chloroform, he struggled so. One of the surgeons, upon examining my arm, said it would have to come off. I had made up my mind to the fact, but could not get over the horrible thought of it being taken off at the socket, there not being room to cut it below. I was wondering what the sensation would be, as waiting my turn I stood in the doorway watching the busy doctors, when Doctor Rizer[41] of the 72nd P.V. came into the house, and recognizing me, made an examination of my hurt. He said that if I could get home, I would have a chance for my arm, as I was in a state of such perfect health. He took me to the attic and put me on a blanket that lay on the floor, then, bringing a feather pillow from the room below, he put it under my arm and detailed a man to pour cool water on it, while he went after splints. Returning soon after with a few pieces of shingle he had found, he bound up my arm as well as he could, then administered a pill opei[42] and ordered the man to keep my arm wet. He said that I must try and get some sleep, while he hunted up Mr. Clem. Barclay,[43] a Philadelphia Philanthropist who was then with the army and who would at once return home with as many wounded Philadelphians as he could take care of. I had known Mr. Barclay personally before enlisting, and I felt assured if he but knew of my mishap he would surely take me with him. With the happy thought of soon again being at home, and with a sense of great relief at the bare chance of saving my arm, I thanked the good doctor for his kindness and soon fell asleep. I awakened but once during the night and found another soldier by my side pouring water on my arm, which now pained me a good deal. I went to sleep again, however, and did not awaken till the booming of cannon announced daylight and the renewal of the battle. I laid in this house all day Sunday, June 1st.

Mr. Clement Barclay left early in the morning taking Capt. Markoe with him. He failed to learn of my being in the building. I was a good deal depressed when I heard of his departure, although Dr. Reizer did all he could to cheer me and said he would personally see that I should be sent to the transports that were taking on board the wounded for removal North. During the night several wounded men had been brought into the room where I was. They were very chatty fellows, and tried hard to get me into conversation, but I never replied to any of their numerous questions, but lay quite still enveloped in my own gloomy thoughts.

During the morning the sounds of battle were very distinct, and some fool of an ambulance attendant started the report that our army was being cut to pieces, that the enemy were taking no prisoners, but were bayonetting all, including the wounded, that they would soon be at this house when all our throats would be cut. He urged all that could possibly do so to leave. As we all were too badly hurt to avail ourselves of this timely information, a general howl and cry of despair ensued. Men in the shattered, wounded, nervous condition these poor fellows were in are quite ready to believe anything told them. I will confess that I, too, felt a little anxious, but after reflecting awhile, soon realized how utterly ridiculous was such a report. Beside, if my ears did not deceive me, the battle was receding, clearly proving that our army was anything but cut to pieces, but was at this very time driving the enemy. Addressing my bewailing comrades, I made known to them my deductions, and was gratified shortly after to hear one of them laugh. The sounds of battle ceased altogether during the afternoon, and nothing was heard excepting the continuous rattle of ambulances past the house. The soldier who first did duty with me was again in attendance and was very assiduous in gratifying as well as he could my wants. He kept my arm wet and cool and fanned and bathed my face continually. I am very grateful to him and regret that I do not know his name or regiment.

Nothing of note occurred during the night and I awakened June 2nd to find the sun shining brightly and a warm though refreshing breeze blowing on me through the window. This morning I had a good breakfast of fresh beef, coffee, and bread, furnished by the U.S. Christian Commission[44] who were busily engaged in establishing field depots for the relief of the wounded. About 9 A.M. Dr. Reizer came in, examined my pulse, looked at my arm and then helped me to my feet, saying, "I have an ambulance at the door to take you away." When I reached the door, I saw the grounds surrounding the house were literally one vast hospital. The ambulances, as fast as they could, were removing the wounded, while details were taking away for burial those who had died through the night. The ambulance to which I was taken was a "double decker," two beds below and two above. The two lower and one upper were occupied, and the remaining bed was pulled out, upon which I was put, when it was again slid into place. As my wounded arm was next [to] the side of the wagon, I was tied to the wagon bows to keep me from jolting. Next [to] me was a very agreeable gentleman who, after witnessing in silence the operation of tying, said "Now then youngster, as long as you are so secure just be kind enough to help keep me steady with your free arm." I learned his name to be Cross,[45] Colonel, 5th New Hampshire, and that he was wounded in the thigh, a very painful hurt. The subsequent jolting of the ambulance caused him to use some strong adjectives by way of easing his pain, as he put it.

It was a rough road over which we went, corduroy nearly the whole way to Savage Station on the Richmond and York River R.R., and I had to abandon the poor Colonel and look out for myself. I could do very little however, with only one arm towards keeping myself steady. At intervals of a quarter of a mile along the road were A tents with barrels of lemonade, claret punch, and liquors, together with oranges, lemons, and other refreshments. This was the work of the Christian Commission. At each of the tents the ambulance would halt and refreshment administered. I was invariably given claret punch, while to Col. Cross was given lemonade, much to his disgust. He always asked for a stimulant but was always refused, as his appearance and indeed his pulse indicated a high state of fever. As for me, I needed stimulating, being quite reduced from loss of blood.

On reaching the station, we were put aboard a train of box cars, which after being filled to their utmost, without further delay were taken to White House, where we found quite a number of transports loading the wounded. The boat to which I was directed looked like one of our Delaware River pleasure steamers, with its great paddle boxes and long sharp bow built for speed on smooth water. It was a shocking sight to see the mass of wounded and mangled soldiers congregated at the landing. Those able to walk were slowly moving along in line aboard the boat, while those who had to be carried were patiently waiting their turn. Many were sitting around on stumps and boxes, and all wore a look of dejection sad to behold. There was one man in particular who had been shot full in the face, the ball going through the bridge of his nose and lodging in the back of his head. Since then the wound had blackened while the rest of the face was chalky white. He presented the most repulsive, hideous countenance I ever beheld, anything but human. I saw hundreds with arms and legs off, many with loss of eye, and one man whose lower jaw had been shot away, a horrifying object to look at. There were some, too, slightly wounded, too slight to be sent away. One in particular, a captain, [was] wounded in the thumb of [his] left hand. His hurt was not serious, and had he been of true grit he would have stayed with his command.

When I got aboard the sight that met me was most sickening. The deck was filled to its utmost capacity with the desperately wounded, and for the first time, I heard the groans of men hurt in battle. I had often read about the groaning wounded on the battlefield, and although I had been on several, had never yet heard any myself. But here, on this hospital ship, I did hear the agonizing cry of anguish. Poor fellows, no wonder. Such a multitude of them, and so many who had not yet received attention. I noticed one man, a huge fellow with leg amputated above the knee, sitting up screaming for help, saying the maggots were eating him alive, and it was so. I saw them creeping in and out of the bandages covering his bloody stump. Sick and weak I was led to a state-room on the port side and was helped into a lower berth, where for a long time I lay, overcome by fatigue and the horrifying sights surrounding me.

There were two state rooms on either side [of] the boat, and the one I occupied had two comfortable berths, the upper one was not occupied while I remained aboard. I was so fatigued that I fell asleep directly. I don't know exactly how long I slept, but I was finally awakened by severe pains in my arm, which upon investigation I found had fallen out and was hanging over the side of the berth. The temporary dressing made by Dr. Reizer being unable to withstand an accident of this kind, the broken portions of the bone were, therefore, forced through the wound, occasioning the pain that awakened me. Upon trying to arise, the pain was so severely increased that I was glad to recline again. I now resorted to all manner of expedients to get my arm up again. The last and most feasible one was to pass a string I had in my pocket through the slat of the bed above me, then, letting the noose end down, try to swing my hand so as to catch it. Whether it was that I had lost feeling or that the pain was so great, I could not tell when I touched the string. Anyway, this bright expedient failed also. I now became very much alarmed, and as the sun had gone down and darkness would soon be upon us, I cryed lustily for help! help! I kept this up without cessation for a long time, when finally the door opened, and a young doctor, putting his head in, asked what was the matter. Not waiting a reply, he sprang to my side and lifted my arm into the berth. Noticing the contrivance I had arranged to do a like service for myself, he laughed a good deal and said he would put a permanent dressing on my arm that would prevent all accidents in the future. A little while after he returned with a soldier bearing a basin of water and proceeded to take off the old bandages & splints. He made an examination of my hurt, inserting his finger into the wound, and after a thorough sponging and cleaning with soap and water, proceeded to mould my arm into proper shape and then to put on patent Kid lined splints, which he cut into suitable lengths, and then made openings for the wounds to slough. After all was done he bandaged my arm and fastened it to my side. In fact I was in skillful hands, and when he left me, I felt so comfortable and easy that I again fell asleep. And here, at this time, I lost the reckoning by days.

From one ship to another I went and knew nothing positively certain until informed by an attendant that we were off Norfolk, Va., our place of destination, but that the hospital at Portsmouth being too full to receive us, it was uncertain where we would be ordered.

After about two hours delay our boat steamed over to the R. S. Spaulding, a large ocean steamer belonging to the Christian Commission. This vessel was fitted up in the most complete manner as a floating Hospital. Every available space was occupied by comfortable berths, with every appliance for the comfort of the wounded. A large corps of lady nurses were also in attendance, together with skillful doctors and helpers in sufficient number so that all the 1,500 patients this splendid ship was said to accommodate could receive constant and unremitting attention.

I was much amused at the business like way with which the crew of the "Spaulding" handled the living freight taken aboard. As the patient, after hoisting from our boat, would swing over the rail of the "Spaulding," the man at the hatch would call out "Right Stump" or "Left stump," or "Right Fracture" or "Left fracture" as the case might be. Then the attendants, or more properly the starboard or port gang, would be on hand to take the man to the proper side of the boat. As they brought me over the side, the man called out "Left fracture," and as I landed 'tween decks, I was at once taken to the port, or left side of the vessel, and put into an upper berth with my left arm out. All around me were rows of berths either filled or being filled by the wounded, while the helpers lost no time in attending to the needs of the poor fellows as fast as they were received aboard.

Shortly after I was placed in my bunk, a middle aged lady came along with sleeves rolled up and commenced to "clean me up" as she said. Without ceremony or asking whether I liked it or not, she deliberately took a pair of scissors and, commencing at my neck, cut my clothes, both outer and under, completely off me. She then, with assistance of an able bodied Christian Commission nurse, washed me from head to foot. I was then put into clean new clothes. The shirts were a marvel of ingenuity, and were made to give the sufferer as little trouble and pain as possible. They were in halves. First the back of the flannel undershirt was put under me, then the other half over my breast and arms, after which, by tapestrings, they were tied together. So also with the outer shirt. I shall never forget this dear lady's kindness. She seemed to feel so much interest in me, and as she toiled and labored over me, I could hear her say repeatedly, "How could his mother let him go in the army?," "What a pity, What a shame." I did not tell her that I went against my mothers wishes. After I was washed and dressed the surgeon came along and examined me. He said I had received skillful treatment and needed nothing except a little wine, which was given me. I then fell asleep.

When I awakened, by the rolling of the vessel, I knew we were at sea. I had no idea of our destination, and the nurses, if they knew, did not tell it. Immediately across the aisle from me was a wounded man, who, by the constant attention of the doctors and several nurses, I knew to be in desperate condition. I became much interested in witnessing the care given him by all. From a lady nurse, I learned this man was so desperately hurt that death was momentarily expected. Yet strange to say, he had rallied so often and had remained so intently conscious that the doctors were using every effort to prolong his life. He was a thoroughly religious man and spoke so beautifully to those around him that every one was moved to tears. Upon inquiring his name I learned that it was Capt. Glenny,[46] Company E, 64th N.Y., of Elmira, N.Y., wounded on the morning of June 1st. I will add that he recovered sufficiently before I left the ship to make my acquaintance, and for hours we would talk together. He was a cultured gentleman, and I shall ever look back with thankfulness to the hours and days spent in listening to his agreeable and instructive conversation, which made me forget my pain and which went so far to give me hope and encouragement. . . .

After tossing about for some days, a report reached me that we had passed the Delaware breakwater. I then learned our destination had been New York, but owing to the storm blowing us out to sea our coal was well nigh exhausted. It had then been determined to proceed to Philadelphia for orders. This news nearly overcame me. I could scarcely credit it. I waylayed everyone for information and finally was compelled to believe it true. Oh! how glad I was, and, I will add parenthetically, I shed a few tears, joyful ones though, tears of emotion.

Capt. William Glenny, 64th New York Volunteers.
THE CIVIL WAR LIBRARY & MUSUEM.

<u>Sunday morning, June 8th</u>. We arrived at Race St. wharf. News of our coming had been telegraphed, and the wharves, buildings and shipping were crowded with people eager to catch a glimpse of men wounded in battle. Prior to this but few had been seen in Philadelphia, hence the arrival of a large ship filled with wounded created an intense excitement. As soon as we made fast to the wharf I was assisted to the deck where I stood for some time gazing upon the sea of upturned faces and tried to recognize any familiar one among them. My bandaged arm and shoulder attracted attention from all and I had so many questions called to me that I did not attempt to answer any of them. While standing here, I heard my name loudly called from among the crowd and very soon saw a man making his way towards me, the crowd kindly giving way for him to approach the ship. It was George Miles, an old friend who just stood and shouted for joy

at seeing me. He said my family was in great distress, as apart from a newspaper statement that I was severely wounded, nothing else had been learned of me since the battle. When he had finished, someone asked my name, and then bawled, "Three cheers for Lieutenant Donaldson," which were given with a perfect roar. Miles now said he would hurry off and notify my family I was here. Overcome by emotion and trembling with excitement, I asked to be taken below and was led back to my bunk again, where I told Capt. Glenny of my good fortune, and then lay still awaiting developments.

About two hours after I had the unspeakable joy to see my brother Jacob coming along the aisle. I was so happy that speech failed me, and I turned away my head to hide the tears that in spite of all I could do welled up in my eyes. How changed my dear brother seemed, he had grown so stout and looked so handsome in his summer clothes and straight brimmed straw hat. He was accompanied by his friend David Wolff and I was delighted to once again see his handsome, cheery face. My brother at once got permission from the surgeon in charge to take me home, as I was the only Philadelphian aboard, and after bidding good bye to Capt. Glenny and the good kind ladies and nurses of my ward, I ascended the gang plank to the wharf to again meet the crowd that had greeted me before. But their behavior was now entirely different. They fell back in respectful silence and opened a path for me to the carriage in waiting at the foot of the wharf. But as soon as I was comfortably propped up with the pillows sent I was again the subject of vociferous cheering which made known to me my welcome home and the sympathy of the people for my hurts. I pause here—because language fails to describe the meeting with my mother. I will just quote her words as she fell upon her knees as I entered the room, "Thank God, thank God! I have him once more!"

Dr. Jno. Neil, Surgeon U.S.A.[47] was sent for and I was placed under his care. He had charge of the Cherry Street Hospital and I was entered on the books there. My recovery was slow but sure. Dr. Neill pronounced the dressing of the arm at White House to be most excellent and never changed it.

CHAPTER 3

Antietam and Shepherdstown

August 27–October 28, 1862

*W*hile Donaldson spent the months of June and July recuperating from his wound, his comrades in the Army of the Potomac struggled to capture Richmond, but it was not to be. Robert E. Lee had assumed command of the Army of Northern Virginia when Joe Johnston was wounded at the Battle of Fair Oaks, and in late June Lee initiated a series of hard-fought battles known as the Seven Days' Campaign, forcing McClellan back from the environs of Richmond to Harrison's Landing on the James River. At Harrison's Landing, the battle-worn 71st Pennsylvania disbanded five of its original fifteen companies, including Donaldson's Company M. The enlisted men and several of the senior officers were absorbed by the remaining ten companies, and the excess officers were discharged. As one of the most junior officers of the regiment, Donaldson was left without a command.

Donaldson's wounded arm healed slowly but steadily, and while he convalesced he acted as adjutant of the Broad Street Military Hospital, conducting guard mount and occasionally drilling companies of recovering soldiers.[1]

Due in large part to the reverses suffered by the Army of the Potomac near Richmond, President Lincoln issued a call on July 1 for an additional 300,000 volunteers to prosecute the war. New regiments began forming throughout the North, and seasoned, combat-tested officers were in demand. By the middle of August, although his wounded arm remained in a sling, Donaldson had recovered sufficiently to again serve in the army. An influential family friend and Philadelphia businessman, Thomas Sparks, recommended him for a captaincy in a new organization, the Corn Exchange Regiment, which was being raised under the auspices of the Philadelphia Corn Exchange. Members of the Exchange assumed much of the expense associated with recruiting and equipping the regiment, and in addition offered bounties of $160 to each enlisted man.

While he would later lament that he grieved "over the misfortune of having been ordered" to his new command, Donaldson must have realized that this was his *best opportunity for again serving in the army, as it was clear there was no longer room for him in the 71st Pennsylvania. In early August his transfer to the Corn Exchange Regiment, which would be officially designated as the 118th Pennsylvania Volunteers, was approved. By August 20 the youngest captain in the command and the ninety-eight noncommissioned officers and privates that made up his Company H were working through the intricacies of drill and guard duty at Camp Union, located just west of Philadelphia overlooking the falls of the Schuylkill River.*

Donaldson was not overly impressed with many of his new brother officers, only six of whom had seen any previous service, but he reserved special comment for his three superiors in rank, Col. Charles M. Prevost, Lt. Col. James Gwyn, and Maj. Charles P. Herring. Prevost, forty-four, had been active in the state militia before the war and served on the Peninsula on the staff of Brig. Gen. Frank Patterson before being chosen by the members of the Corn Exchange to lead the 118th. Although favorably relating that he was a "polished gentleman," Donaldson found him "too easy, by half. . . . He appears to think that officers and men alike are filled with the love for duty that he is and that this ought to so stimulate them that, without orders to do so, they ought to comprehend everything and live up to the true ideal soldiers life."

Major Herring, thirty-two, a Philadelphia businessman, had joined the Pennsylvania militia at the outbreak of the war but had not seen active service. Although noting his lack of experience, Donaldson thought him "a thorough soldier, and a man who will do the regiment and service great credit." A close friendship soon began between Donaldson and Herring and continued until Herring's death in 1889.

His military opinion of Colonel Prevost notwithstanding, Donaldson viewed both him and Major Herring in a generally positive light. But the same could not be said of the lieutenant colonel of the 118th, James Gwyn. Gwyn, a thirty-four-year-old Protestant native of Ireland, had, like Prevost and Herring, been engaged in business in Philadelphia before the war, and was serving on the Peninsula as a captain in the 23rd Pennsylvania when he was commissioned in the 118th. The Regimental History of the 118th Pennsylvania notes that Gwyn was "by nature impulsive and sometimes revengeful, with likes and dislikes characteristic of his race, strong and exacting. These traits won him many warm friends, and at the same time made him many bitter enemies."² Included among his enemies would be Donaldson. Indeed, from almost the first moment the two men met, a mutual hostility began to develop. After an acquaintance of only two weeks, Donaldson would write to his brother that Gwyn was "a very low person. . . . He is not a gentleman and the close companionship with such a man which of a necessity is forced upon the other field officers must be exceedingly annoying to men like Col. Prevost and Maj. Herring." The animosity between Donaldson and Gwyn only worsened over time, and the emotions it produced would eventually nearly consume the young captain, drive a wedge through the officer corps of the 118th, and ultimately lead to Donaldson's departure from the service.

The military situation in the East had changed considerably by the time Donaldson was commissioned in the Corn Exchange Regiment. McClellan had failed to respond to the administration's gentle prods to resume operations against Richmond from his base at Harrison's Landing, and on August 3 he was ordered to forward his troops north so that they might cooperate with Maj. Gen. John Pope's troops against an advancing Rebel column under Stonewall Jackson. With the threat to the Confederate capital thus gone, Lee marched north, united with Jackson on the old Bull Run battlefield and inflicted a lopsided defeat on the Federals at the Second Battle of Bull Run on August 29–30. For the North, it was yet another calamitous loss; for the South, prospects for independence had never looked brighter.

Following the setback at Second Bull Run, many of the new Union regiments that had been forming under Lincoln's July call were rushed to Washington. On August 31, just eleven days after completing its organization, the 118th Pennsylvania was sent to join the Army of the Potomac.

Camp at Arlington Heights, Va.
September 4th, 1862

My dear Brother:

I scarcely know how to write a resumé of the past few days, there having been so much excitement attending the hurried move to this place, together with such great fatigue and brain worry, that time has been wanting to note all the events as they occurred. I will therefore merely mention them without entering into any extended account.

You, of course, know of my muster into the service by Col. Ruff,[3] U.S.A. August 27th and that we struck tents and left Camp at Indian Queen Lane at 10 P.M. August 31st, reaching Baltimore Depot, Broad and Prune Sts. at midnight, of my hurried notice to you and Auntie, and of you witnessing the departure of our regiment at 5 A.M. Sept. 1st. Well! we arrived without accident at Baltimore at 2 P.M. that day, and halted at the Washington Depot. During [the] balance of the day [we] were busily engaged cooking and keeping the men together, a most difficult task as the men were green at soldiering and had not yet come under discipline. . . .

Sept. 2. Lt. Col. Gwyn arrived with the balance of the command and at 10 o'clock A.M. we left Baltimore for Washington. Before leaving I met with a slight accident which rather disfigured me somewhat, and which might have been a very serious one indeed. I had had great difficulty in teaching the men to stack arms and to break the stack again. Just before leaving, in giving my personal attention to one stack in particular, one of the men let his musket fall over, the bayonet striking me in the face just under the right eye, cutting it pretty badly. I had considerable difficulty in staunching the blood, which, however, I finally did by scooping lint from off my felt hat and applying it to the hurt. It, of course, made a very ugly appearance but I didn't mind it as I was grateful for not losing my eye.

We arrived at Washington at 4 P.M. and quartered at the Soldiers Retreat until dark, when we moved and bivouaced near the government corral, amid wagons, mules and dirt, but I slept soundly the night through.

Sept. 3rd. We moved this A.M., crossing Long Bridge and bivouaced at Fort Albany,[4] Arlington Heights, where we are now. Now, with all due respect to Col. Prevost, this camp is the most dreadfully situated one I ever saw. Whether the colonel of his own volition ordered it here, or whether he was instructed by higher authority to do so, certainly he ought to protest against the outrage of encamping men in a swamp when other dry and healthy localities are near at hand. There is no necessity or urgency for its present position. It is an actual fact that we are at the foot of the hill upon the top of which Fort Albany is built, and that some of the tents are pitched in the swamp where it is impossible to keep the men dry. Fortunately for my company, we are a little higher than some of the others and are not inconvenienced. All the leisure time we have is spent in drilling in order to prepare the men for active service, which all the war like surroundings leads me to believe will be soon. My company has been reduced to 89 men by reason of sickness, fatigue, and heat. I think, however, that some of the absent will turn up again.

The regiment being without National Colors, I this day presented it with the beautiful silk flag Aunt Sophia gave my company at Philadelphia.[5]

We are constant witnesses of the sad plight of the Army of the Potomac, as thousands of Genl. Pope's troops in great demoralization are ever passing the Fort in retreat to Washington. The poor old Army of the Potomac, how I pity it. What a dreadful mistake to give Genl. Pope the command of it. Just see the humiliating position it today holds before the country since Genl. McClellan was relieved from command. What a ridiculous order that was of Pope's "Head Quarters in the Saddle."[6] Well, he has been kept in the saddle ever since he issued it, making good his retreat to Washington. We want no more of him. . . .

Camp near Fort Cochran, Va.[7]
Sept. 10th, 1862

Dear Brother:

At last I have a little leisure which I will devote to you, but recollect, it is indeed a very little time, so do not complain if this letter is a short one. We are hard at it, and constant drilling is the order of the day, and it takes plenty of solid work to instruct the men in the duties of the soldier, so that morning, noon, and I may add, night too, it is drill and instruction all the time. I will let you into a secret. It would be vastly more to the purpose if some of the officers of the regiment were put through the manual of arms and company movements before they are intrusted with the instruction of others. Happily there are very few old soldiers among the enlisted men, and the great bulk of the command are imbued with the idea that their officers are little McClellan's in disguise.[8]

I have done my best to make soldiers out of the material I have, and with one or two exceptions, will have a pretty fair company. I daily instruct them in what I consider to be essentially the first duty of the soldier— never to lose anything, and by a rigid daily inspection find out whether they have all the accoutrements belonging to them. When I find a breast plate or any other article gone, I charge it against their pay until I see they have found others. Not that I desire to have my men thieves, but I want them to be self reliant and not come running to me with an account of every little article lost or stolen. Let them find others, or in other words, never lose anything. However, they have found out pretty well by this time that I never forgive a man for losing his musket or any part of his equipments.

I have made one or two changes in the non-commissioned officers. I have made Private John Montieth[9] corporal and put him in charge of the foraging detail. He is a bright good fellow and when on duty is extremely dignified and I think will make a capital good officer. Corporal Wheeler, the delicate fellow Auntie was so concerned about and took such an interest in will have to give place to some other and a more capable man. He is no good, always sick and was so when he enlisted and is a "shister," at least I think so.[10] I am unable to account for Lieut. Smith's[11] urgent and persistent pressure for his appointment. I also fear my orderly sergeant, Keener, is a fraud and a whiskey drinker. I am not sure, but just as soon as my suspicions are confirmed as I think they will be, I will reduce him to the ranks and put him at all the dirty work I can find. I do not like the man anyway, he is too cringing.[12] I am gradually studying the character of the men, and have gotten their measure pretty well. There is one thing I do not exactly like, however; they appear to fear me. I attribute this to my arm being in a sling and they thus put me down for a regular "fire eater," because I have been through the Peninsula Campaign and wounded in battle.

I have not made much headway in my acquaintance with the officers. They are all strangers to me, and all the captains and lieutenants, with two exceptions only, are older men. They rather look upon me as a boy, to be treated as such. That is they did act so, at first, but not so much now. Capt. Passmore[13] I know rather better than the others, that is, I know him, but not he me. He treats me pretty much as he did when I first met him at the camp on Indian Queen Lane—patronizingly. I say I know him, which is capable of two meanings. I know him because Aunt Sophia is well acquainted with his family, and Mr. Sparks, when speaking of him to me gave him such a handsome endorsement and vice-versa. Afterwards I met him officially. The occasion was my first arrival in camp. Col. Prevost took me to his quarters and introduced me, stating I was also the friend of Mr. Sparks. He was, as senior captain, in command of the camp, and wore the sash of officer of the day. Drawing himself up, and with his bulky figure towering away above me, he said, "How do, Captain, Mr. Sparks has spoken of you to me, and I will look you up when I have time," or words to that effect. I was then dismissed. Since then he has looked me up occasionally to talk of himself and the girl he left behind him, some neighbor's daughter of whom he is enamored and about whom he delights to speak whenever he finds as good a listener as myself, which is seldom. Again, I know him to be a blatant no account fellow, although a good tactician. He thinks he is the very personification of dignity, while I think him insufferably impertinent and overbearing.

His officer, 1st Lieut. Hunterson,[14] is a rough and grossly ignorant fellow, fond of whiskey, but a good soldier. Saml. Lewis,[15] 2nd Lieut., is the son of our friend Geo. T. Lewis and a mere "fledgling." He is one of the two officers alluded to as being younger than I.

Captain Henry O'Neill,[16] the "wild Irishman of the Gangees" as he ought to be called, is the most overrated man in the command, and was simply an "immense thing" in Philada. upon the reputation of having served 20 years in the British Army in "Injie" as he calls India. Why he knows nothing, absolutely nothing at all about military movements and company drills. Upon one occasion I actually saw him standing in front of his company instructing his men in the principles of the "direct step." He said, with a twinge of Irish brogue, "Yees will throw the weight of your body upon the right hip at the command forward, and extend the left foot well to the front, the point of the toe downward thus," and with that he did the very reverse, throwing the weight of his body upon the left hip and advancing the right foot. "Again," he continued, "at the command march, yees will bring the flat of the foot smartly to the ground and advance the right foot and so on. Now then, all together, forward!" The men at this command did as they were told and advanced the left foot, toe downward. He then ran to the left of the company and commanded "Left dress, toes on a line, out there!" or "down there!," as some poor fellow, getting tired, lowered or lifted his foot. Failing to get them in proper alignment, he said, "As you were, mark time! Ye are nothing but a parcel of lame ducks, ye are, disperse, and to the divil with ye!," meaning to break ranks and go to their quarters. When spoken to about the use of the tactics he replied, "I don't care a divil for the tactics. Sure this is the way we used to do it in Injie and they ought to know."

To think that it is not unlikely a contingency may arise whereby this man would be in command of the regiment makes one feel a little bit discouraged. Still I like O'Neill very much, apart from his military knowledge he is an uncomplaining, good natured fellow, always making light of trouble, and satisfied with everything and everybody, except his own company, which he persists in designating "lame ducks" and firmly believing their only aim in life is to shirk duty. When accounting their various failings, he laughs immoderately, wipes his huge nose on the back of his hand, and takes a heavy pinch of snuff, adding that the only duty they are capable of performing promptly is falling in for their "grub."

Among the privates of his company is my old friend Tom Scout,[17] who used to be 2nd mate of the steamer "Keystone State" when I was with Alex. Heron Jr. & Co., and his name appears to strike O'Neill as a particularly funny one, and he yells and bawls at Scout, whether he is performing his duty or not, and is frequently heard during drills calling "Out Scout" or "Back Scout" until the men of the regiment have noticed it, and poor Scout's life is made miserable by them whenever he appears in public. I do not know his officers, Wilson[18] and Schaefer,[19] but the latter is another one of those alluded to as being younger then myself.

Capt. Sharswood[20] I seldom, if ever, see, and do not remember to have addressed him a single word since I have been in the regiment. Indeed I scarcely know whether he is in the regiment or not, as he is generally at Head Quarters, where I never go, except when sent for.

Capt. Donegan[21] is an old grandmother, and like O'Neill knows absolutely nothing about soldiering or the Tactics, and in my opinion never will be better posted. I am exceedingly sorry that I waived rank with him. He and I were mustered in the same day, but I ranked him because of previous service, but gave way on account of his age, and, as I thought, it would please Mr. Sparks. I have since learned my mistake, but should trouble arise because of it, will do my own thinking in regard to obeying an order from him. His officers, Richard W. Davids[22] and Horace Binney[23] are true gentlemen whose society I seek and whose company I greatly enjoy. Neither of them know much about soldiering, but being educated gentlemen they will soon learn and make capital officers.

In regard to Sharwood's officers, Crocker[24] and McCutchen[25], I should have added that I like the appearance of the former very much, and think he will be a good officer, although just now he knows nothing about the tactics. I will add too that I do not know him, having never yet been in his company. The other gentleman has not yet joined us but, I am told, will do so as soon as he gets his discharge from Knap's Battery, where I understand he is serving as a private soldier.

Capt. Saunders[26] I meet with quite often and like him. He is a finished gentleman, but frightfully enthusiastic, always volunteering for special duty. He will get over that before the campaign is through with.

Ricketts[27] I meet very seldom, but like him, if not for his own, for his brother Charley's sake. Charley Ricketts, you know, is my friend, and he and I have had many a good time together. By the way, I wonder if he ever enlisted? I will ask Capt. Ricketts some day when I have a opportunity. His officers, McKean[28] and J. Mora Moss Jr.[29] are both nice fellows and will make good officers as soon as they get better posted.

Capt. Saunders' officers Wm. West[30] and Ruddy White[31] are both first class men. West has a great deal of dignity and is pretty well up on tactics, while Ruddy White is beloved by both officers and men, and is a good officer. I know West, of course. He is the only companion I have and our interests being the same and our families related we are therefore much together.

Capt. O'Callaghan[32] is a sterling good fellow, and I think will be very companionable. He is disposed to be quite sociable and is a really good soldier, well up [on] the battalion and company movements. His lieutenant, A. N. Wetherill[33] I do not think much of, as he is a great growler and grumbler, never satisfied, only when telling about his "sparring" and the number of able bodied men he has whipped in his time. I may be deceived, but to look at him, I think I could clean him out in short order, but I may be mistaken, you know. I think he will give O'Callaghan a good deal of trouble.

Capt. Fernald[34] I have found a pleasant and agreeable person. He is not what you would call a gentleman, but he is a man of considerable force, a good tactician, apparently a good soldier, very full of dignity and, whenever he can get it, very full of "oscafoodle," as he calls whiskey. He has a fine voice for command and handles his company very well. Walters,[35] his 1st Lt. has not yet put in appearance. He is to be transferred from the 23rd P.V., I believe. McIntyre,[36] his 2nd officer is a little bit of a whiffet, and like all little men, full of pomposity and blow. He is no good.

Capt. Bankson[37] of Co. F strikes me as a very austere man, a hard worker, indefatigable in looking after the wants and comforts of his company, and as at Camp Indian Queen Lane, dignified and unapproachable. He makes considerable bluster when upon drill, about which he knows nothing. I have not addressed any conversation to him, trusting to the future to give me a better insight into his character, as I am, at present, greatly prejudiced against him. The reason of this is that upon the occasion of my first appearance at camp in Philada., Col. Prevost, in introducing me to the officers who were present at the time, presented me also to Capt. Bankson, who very promptly, with undisguised disappointment of manner and without acknowledging the introduction said, "Colonel, I am sorry to see so many boys in the regiment as officers, we want better material and older heads as captains." This was such a grievous affront that I walked away, leaving the Colonel remonstrating with Bankson, and I was only restrained from openly resenting the indignity by a desire to please Mr. Sparks, who would have been greatly distressed had any difficulty then arisen.

Bankson's officers are Henry K. Kelly[38] and Charly Hand,[39] the latter joined us at Arlington and the former is at home sick.

Perney Smith of my company will never in the world do for a soldier. I think I will urge him to resign as I do not think he will be able to stand the hardships, and I feel confident he will be of no earthly good to me. He is a nice little fellow but was not cut out for a soldier, and I do not want such people around me. I expect to do my duty and I am determined that others in my command will do theirs. It being out of his power to ever succeed as a soldier, he must go.

Batchelder, my 1st Lieut. is in hospital, sick, for which I am very sorry, as having been comrades in the California Regiment, we know each other thoroughly and will work well together. Beside were he here now, a great deal of hard work would be taken off my shoulders and I would feel so satisfied knowing his ability and capacity. As a military man, he is the superior of any company officer here, and in handling a skirmish line, has no equal. As it is I cannot and do not allow Perney Smith to drill the company at all, but personally take sole charge of everything pertaining to their instruction which entails a tremendous amount of labor, [for] which even their perceptible improvement does not compensate.

On the 8th inst. Private Chas. F. Dare,[40] a most excellent soldier of my company, was detailed as Hospital Steward, and I fear Head Quarters have their mind settled upon one other good man from me as clerk in the adjutant's office. While I dislike to stand in the way of deserving men getting good appointments, I dislike very much to lose them.

From the foregoing you can perceive how isolated I am and, I will confess, homesick too. I am like a cat, a strange garrett, and not being one to easily make friends, I keep to myself and grieve over the misfortune of having been ordered to this regiment. I am yet unable to see why the governor so willed it, and why he heeded not the importunities of myself and Col. Wistar to let me remain with my old regiment and take me from home, as it were. I do not yet know what will be the upshot of this whole business, but as a general rule, I do not like the companionship of the officers of this regiment. It may be because I know them to be so woefully ignorant as to military matters, and I catechize myself repeatedly because of this very idea. It is true I learned the duties of a soldier in a good school under the tuition of a thoroughly practical officer, Lt. Mears[41] of the Regular Army, who was detailed as instructing officer of the California Regiment, hence, it is, that seeing everything now going at 6's and 7's, with no authority to appeal to, I feel sick at heart. Things are so different.

Now as to the Field Officers, I have to say that while Col. Prevost is a polished gentleman, he is too easy, by half. He does not grab the situation exactly. He appears to think that officers and men alike are filled with the love for duty that he is and that this ought to so stimulate them that, without orders to do so, they ought to comprehend everything and live up to the true ideal soldiers life. Now the Colonel will find that this will not be done, and he should get right up and jump on the one, whoever he may be, that is at all remiss in his duty. Were it Col. Wistar, he would make the fur fly and darken the atmosphere with blasphemy.

Col. Charles Mallett Prevost, 118th Pennsylvania Volunteers. The Civil War Library & Musuem.

I can tell you Lt. Col. Gwyn, I will frankly say, I do not like. He appears to know the tactics, although I am not so sure of it either, as I have known him to make many serious mistakes while on drill, notably the very first one I attended at Camp Union, where he was in command. He gave the order to "Double column at half distance." I, being in command of the centre division, which at that command becomes the 1st division of the column, slipped out and gave the cautionary command for my division to "stand fast." [He then] called out in a loud one of voice so that the whole assembled audience could hear, "Captain, move your division forward, sir," which he repeated several times as I hesitated to obey a wrong order, and only did so to avoid a controversy and to be strictly on the safe side. I afterwards showed him his error when he admitted his mistake, but the people thought I was wrong all the same.

Again, he did a very undignified thing when visiting my quarters at the same camp. It was my misfortune on that occassion to break the gallon

demijohn holding the beverage which I invariably extended to those who
then visited me, and as quick as thought Gwyn grasped my tin wash basin,
and holding it under the broken demijohn caught the liquor in it. After
that, without ceremony, he raised the basin to his mouth and took a long
draft from it, much to my disgust, which stamped him in my estimation a
very low person. I am of the opinion that he dislikes me simply because he
feels that I avoid him, which I certainly do, although to do him justice he
is a most agreeable and entertaining person with a cheerful smile to greet
you, and a pleasant tone of voice to put you at ease. Still, for all that I don't
like him. I don't like his name—Gwyn! Gwyn!, let me see, that is a Welsh
name, I believe, although he certainly is of Irish extraction. It is a peculiar
name and I have never heard it before, except in reading one of Lever's
novels, entitled "The Knight of Gwyn." To sum up, he is not a gentleman
and the close companionship with such a man which of a necessity is
forced upon the other Field Officers must be exceedingly annoying to men

Maj. Charles P. Herring, 118th Pennsylvania Volunteers. Don Enders
Collection, U.S. Army Military History Institute.

like Col. Prevost and Major Herring. Like the other Field Officers he is of a remarkable presence and a very handsome man. Indeed I verily believe we have three of the finest looking men in the service as Field Officers and I challenge any regiment in the Army of the Potomac to produce their equals for looks.

Maj. Herring you know as well as I, and being an old "Phoenix Hose boy,"[42] it is equivalent to being what he really is, an A1 good fellow, a thorough soldier and a man who will do the regiment and service great credit. Like the other Field Officers he is not yet perfect in battalion movements and I have known him to make errors. But what I like about him is that he does not set himself up for a tactician and is open to correction when ever he makes a mistake, but rigidly insists upon the obedience of orders first and appeal afterwards, a qualification that marks the instincts of a true soldier. I like him also because he is extremely sociable and polite to me, and does not attempt to make me feel my subordinate position as Gwyn does. He is always glad to see me, and from his manner I feel he is sincere in proferring friendship. I will observe him closely and take great interest in noting his character, which, as near as I am able to judge, is a manly one. I believe this judgment of personal worth and character to be an instinct with me. I have never yet failed in my estimate of men. You can put this down as conceit, if you will, but I feel my ability to read men in a very short time; to me the countenance is an open book.

The surgeons I know very little about, not yet having occasion to seek their society professionally, socially, or otherwise. Dr. Thomas,[43] I learn, was a Bucks County school teacher, whether before or since he practiced medicine I do not know. He is a fine looking and grave man who appears perfectly assured in his knowledge of the healing art. Time will show and that soon too, whether he is a competent "saw bones" or not, as there is an atmosphere surrounding us indolent of bloody battles yet to be found. Dr. Kollock,[44] assistant surgeon, strikes me as being one well up in his profession. However I am unable to judge positively as I do not see much of him and cannot say whether he has been with us all the time or is now with us. Dr. Rowland[45] the other assistant surgeon is a <u>fool</u>, and is entirely out of place as an army surgeon, and is only worth mentioning because he appears to be the "<u>bust</u>" of the regiment.

Adjutant Jas. P. Perot[46] is more of a sailor than a soldier and is entirely out of place in his present position. He is a jovial good natured man, with a voice like a hurricane, but no soldier, and worse still, no adjutant. It is a great mistake to suppose anyone can be an adjutant. A man to fill that position must be adapted for it by nature. You can't make an adjutant of any officer that comes along, and Perot is about as fit for the position as I would be to navigate a ship. Now Batchelder would make a rattling good adjutant, but I would not mention this above my breath for fear that after they find out that Perot won't do, as they surely will, he might be detailed for the position. Were there such an office as "Regimental Mentor," Perot would be just the man for it, as he has most excellent judgment, his advice is always sound, and his head is wrapt up in the success of the command.

Quarter Master Addicks[47] is a drunken loafer and of no earthly good to the service. He is never on hand when wanted and is the cause of much of the discomfort we all suffer from. Col. Prevost will surely bring him to task for his delinquencies, and the sooner the better.

I believe I have answered categorically your questions, but as my comments upon my superiors are treasonable ones, I rely upon your judgment whether it would be prudent to show this letter to others than Auntie, Mr. Sparks and one or two discreet friends, certainly not to any member of the Corn Exchange. . . .

. . . My health is excellent, and as I still have everything I brought from the old camp I am quite comfortable, but the experience gained in the Peninsular Campaign makes me feel certain that our present comforts will have to be disposed with, and that soon too. Give my best love to Auntie and say that my daily prayer is that she becomes reconciled to this separation, and that it adds to my comfort to know she keeps well and is not so distressed as when I last saw her. . . .

Soon after their arrival in the capital, the green Pennsylvanians were assigned to the veteran 1st Brigade, 1st Division of Maj. Gen. Fitz John Porter's 5th Army Corps. The 1st Brigade had seen hard service on the Peninsula and in the recent Bull Run battle, losing more than 1,400 men in the combined actions. As veterans are inclined to do, they cast a skeptical eye at their untried comrades, greeting them with insults and open ridicule. "My blood fairly boiled," Donaldson wrote of the reception the 118th endured, "and I could not help replying that probably there were some among us who had seen quite as much service as they." There was little time, however, to nurse wounded pride.

After his victory on the plains of Manassas, Lee set his sights on an invasion of the North. On September 4, after allowing for several days of rest, Lee sent the vanguard of his hard-marched Army of Northern Virginia across the Potomac and into Maryland. For Lincoln, a crisis was at hand. Dispirited remnants of Pope's defeated army, dislocated troops from the Army of the Potomac, and numerous newly raised regiments were thronging the capital. The president reluctantly turned to the one general who, at that moment, could bring order out of the chaos, placing McClellan in command of all of the forces around Washington. The "young Napoleon" took charge quickly, breathing new life into his troops and restructuring the Army of the Potomac as he began to chase Lee.

McClellan's pursuit of the advancing Confederates was cautious, and as Lee penetrated deeper into the western Maryland countryside, McClellan followed in his wake, all the while keeping between the Southern army and Washington, D.C. Five days into his march, McClellan was fortunate enough to secure a copy of an order that gave the location of Lee's widely scattered units. Moving with uncharacteristic alacrity, the Union leader attempted to permanently divide and defeat in detail the separate Confederate commands, and as a result, the Battle of South Mountain was fought on September 14. The Southerners held the passes at South Mountain long enough to allow Lee to unite his forces, and by September 15 the Confederate army was drawn up along Antietam Creek, defiantly offering battle.

McClellan, again moving deliberately, brought his army up to the east side of Antietam Creek late on September 15, and two days later fought the Battle of Antietam. By the time the sun set on September 17, there were more than 23,000 casualties, making it the costliest one-day battle in American history.

The bulk of the 5th Corps played a supporting role during the bloody encounter, and as such, Donaldson and the 118th Pennsylvania could only watch in awe as the combat unfolded before them.

Camp 118th P.V. near Sharpsburg, Md.

September 23rd, 1862[48]

Dear Brother:

My last was from Fort Corcoran, in which I gave my opinion of the officers of this regiment. How little I knew of the sad fate awaiting so many of them but a few days hence. I have had no opportunity of writing, and indeed of making very full notes of our movements, so hurried have they been. The newspapers, however, no doubt have kept you posted as to our daily doings in this wonderful campaign, and of the hardships and fatigue we have undergone, culminating in the slaughter of our brave regiment at Shepherdstown. I say it is impossible to give anything like a detailed account of all that has transpired since we left Fort Corcoran, but I will add that I have seen nearly as much service in the last two or three weeks as I did during the whole time I was with the 71st. We have made such long dusty marches that men have dropped dead from the heat and fatigue and exhaustion. We have done dreadful picket duty and have lost several men by sharp shooters of the enemy. We have fought a second Ball's Bluff and been defeated with fearful slaughter. But to take up in regular order the narrative which I copy from notes made each day:

September 8th. We left "camp in the swamp" at Fort Albany and moved to Fort Corcoran where we encamped on the side of a hill overlooking the valley approaches to Washington. Everything had a sunburned, dirty, dusty and forlorn appearance consequent upon the destruction of woods, the opening of innumerable roads hither and thither, and the debris of a large army scattered far and near. Our camp lay upon the side of a hill amid tree stumps and camp trash, which latter had to be cleaned away before we could be at all comfortable. Here we remained four days living on the plainest of army fare.

On the 11th, together with Quarter Master Sergeant John J. Thomas,[49] upon the broad back of his fine horse, we scoured the adjacent country in search of something to eat and drink. We found some canned goods, and upon the way back, through the kindness of George Agnew,[50] with whom we fortunately met, got some "spirits" also. George looked very rough but was smilingly good natured as ever. He belongs to Butler Price's cavalry stationed near here.

September 12th. This day we were brigaded with Brig. Genl. Martindale's 1st Brigade, Maj. Genl. Morrell's 1st Division, Maj. Genl. Fitz John Porter's 5th Army Corps,[51] and at 7 A.M. proceeded to take position with them. The Brigade consisted of the 22nd Massachusetts, Lt. Col. Tilden commanding. (This regiment was raised for Senator Wilson, and although he is still its colonel, with exception of passing through Philadelphia at its head, he has never been with it.) The 18th Mass., Col. Barnes, an old West Pointer, now in command of the brigade; 13th New York, Col. Marshall, also a West Pointer; 25th New York, Col. Johnson; 1st Michigan, [Capt. Belton]; 2nd Maine, Lt. Col. Varney.[52]

As soon as we put in an appearance and proceeded to take the position assigned us, we were greeted by these "heroes," these "veterans" with laughter and cries of "here comes the $200 boys," referring to the bounty paid recruits. My blood fairly boiled and I could not help replying to some of the officers of the N.Y. regiments who were particularly conspicuous and insulting, that probably there were some among us who had seen quite as much service as they. My impressions were certainly unfavorable to these new associates. However, I was given very little time to nurse my indignation as we at once took up the line of march, passing over the Aqueduct Bridge crossing the Potomac, and marched through Washington where everything wore the appearance of fright, haste, and disorder, few if any of the inhabitants witnessing our passage. For a time it seemed we were the victims of some practical joke, as we were marched backwards and forwards, up one street and down another until the men were heart sick and weary with the conflicting orders and the backing and filling policy which seemed to possess our commanders. Finally after all possible hope of ever getting out of the city had take possession of us, we finally headed for and proceeded out the road leading from 7th Street. . . .

We halted and bivouaced at Silver Spring, Md. This day was particularly hard on the boys and the whole regiment was completely used up, they with but few exceptions falling out along the road-side, Col. Prevost himself finally bringing the colors into camp, the color sergeant and color guard having been compelled to give them up owing to extreme exhaustion. The heat was something fearful and overpowering. I was one of the few who kept up and actually came into bivouac with but three of my company with me. Our regiment certainly presented a marked contrast to the others of the brigade when we joined them, each man having a knapsack, whereas the older troops had merely the green blanket roll. Of course, we too will come to this as the march progresses, as there is nothing [that] so soon brings about a literal compliance with the order given on the march of "route step-arms at will," as an intimate acquaintance with old mother necessity, and our boys will soon learn to discard all surplus and needless wearing apparel, and get down to light marching order. Silver Spring is about 7 miles north of Washington, but don't amount to more than a hamlet. During the night very many of the men came into camp, but when we started the next day at least one half were absent, necessitating the return of Maj. Herring to collect the stragglers and bring them up with the regiment.[53]

September 13th. We were up at daybreak and after cooking coffee took up line of march about 7 A.M. and marched through and bivouaced about half mile beyond Rockville. This was a hot dusty march and as I had anticipated the men commenced getting rid of their surplus clothing, throwing them away as they hourly felt the increasing power of old sol's rays. I heard many of the older troops say they hoped the $200 boys would be placed on the lead tomorrow so that the balance of the brigade might procure new outfits from them. Rockville is quite a smart little village and is the capital of Montgomery Co. It is about 16 miles from Washington and I am told about 30 miles from Baltimore. It has a court house, jail, and I believe several churches, but I cannot speak positively as to these, as I was not able to see much of the place. I usually derive information about the little towns through which we pass from the women who habitually stand in their doors and scowl at us as we pass by. There is not much Union sentiment in this county, I fear. The population of Rockville, when it is at home, I am told is between 4 and 5 hundred, may be more.

September 14th. We again took up the march at about 7 A.M. and at 6 P.M. bivouaced at Monocacy. This was a most oppressive and sultry day. I never saw anything like the dust that in hot suffocating clouds enveloped us all day long. Being saturated with perspiration, the dust clung to the cloths until the men looked as though they were clad in gray. Overcome by heat and dust, many fell out and lay scattered along the road. But a few officers, among them only one captain, and that one myself, reached the bivouac with the regiment. During the night however, the men came up and the command presented its usual appearance the next day. I should mention that all day long we heard the dull heavy sound of distant cannonading, which in the afternoon became prolonged and heavy, indicating a battle.

Among the men of my company who always kept up was Corporal John Montieth, and a more thoroughgoing fellow I never saw. He was jolly and lively all the time, making light of fatigue, and when the men were nearly used up, would inspire the whole command by singing a rattling good soldier song, called "I Come From the Old Granite State," with a chorus of boom! boom! boom! in an imitation of the bass drum, which had a most curious effect and was at once taken up by the regiment and rendered with a will. Indeed, the brigade took up the air and long after we were through, they could be heard shouting the boom! boom! chorus. Montieth had a rich, melodius voice and sang with great feeling. I mention him particularly as I desire to call your attention to his subsequent fate. In my judgment, had he been spared, he would have soon worn the shoulder straps, as he was a thorough solider, one sure to attract attention.

Monocacy is a little village in Frederick Co. Md., about 4 miles from Frederick City. I did not see much of the place as I was too hot and tired to notice its few houses as we passed through.

This evening, as is always my custom whenever I have the opportunity, I strolled off to a little stream of water, and took a good wash, feeling greatly refreshed thereby. The men, meanwhile, scattered far and near in search of something to eat, and shortly after, hearing several musket shots and inquiring the cause, I noticed several of my company dragging two wild hogs they had killed in the woods, and that night they had a rousing barbecue, thus ended this Lord's day—what a Sunday to be sure.

September 15th. We took to the road again about 8 A.M. and after a repetition of the previous days trials and fatigue, at 6 P.M. halted at the foot of the Catoctin Mountains, near Middletown, which is just beyond on the other side of the mountains. This was another scorching hot day, with clouds of fine dust permeating the air and enveloping us the whole time. All along the road travelled, ever since our first start, the near presence of the enemy was manifested on every side by broken telegraph poles and wires, broken fences and trampled fields where their infantry had marched in parallel columns. Broken wagons and quantities of debris of one kind and another strewed the road, showing haste in their movements.

We learned that the firing heard yesterday was from a heavy battle fought at South Mountain, between our advance and the enemy's rear guard, in which we completely defeated them with severe loss.[54] On our side too the loss was heavy, Genl. Reno[55] being killed and many other valuable lives lost. This action, to my mind, makes it clear that the enemy is being pressed so closely that I presume he will be obliged to deliver a battle. It is quite evident that our persistent and relentless pursuit is with evident intention of compelling him to halt and fight. But of course this is conjecture as I have no means of knowing what our general proposes doing. At all events if such be the case Genl. Lee is too good a soldier to do so other than on his own terms. Again this day cannonading was heard to the front showing our people were up with the Confederates and making it lively for them.

About 10 A.M. we passed through Frederick City, which is the largest place yet reached since leaving Washington. It is the capital of Frederick Co. and is about 45 miles from Washington. It is a beautiful place, with stone and brick houses, paved side walks, and straight streets, a court house, of course, 8 or 10 churches, "And," said the lady who gave me this information as I stood upon the cellar door talking to her through the quaker like curtains of her kitchen window, "a college of considerable reputation." A clean, beautiful city, nestled in as fertile and lovely a country as one cares to look at. I was sorry we were so soon compelled to leave, as the little halt made in its clean streets only gave the desire to see more of the place. The straggling this day, although considerable, was not near so bad as the day before, but our regiment is very much reduced in numbers, which will take a halt of some days to recruit.

September 16th. We were at it again at the early hour of 6 A.M. and soon reached and crossed the Catoctin Mountains. These mountains, or series of hills, run parallel with the Blue Ridge, between which two ranges lay the fertile Catoctin Valley. How beautiful the distant Blue Ridge appeared from the summit of the Catoctin Mountains, and how lovely the landscape. Down in the valley lay Middletown, as pretty a little village as there is in Frederick Co. I presume the pretty little Catoctin Stream, close to the rich grassy banks of which the village lay, derives its name from these picturesque mountains. We soon reached Middletown, and a near approach did not, in the slightest degree, lessen the beauty of the place. In the piping times of peace, I should judge this to be a sweet little country loafing place worthy a lengthy visit. It has a population of several hundred, I am told, but we did not see as many as a dozen single individuals.

While passing through this place the passions of the men were greatly inflamed against it by an act of hostility on the part of its citizens most uncalled for and rarely equalled. Indeed I wondered at the forebearance of the men and can only account for it because of the hurried march and the influence of the officers. It seems the citizens of this contemptible place had removed every handle from off the pumps along the street through which the army passed, and not a drop of water was to be had by the parched and thirsty troops. Our brigade was loud in its declarations of vengeance, and tarried long enough to fill each pump with stones and dirt so that the natives would feel some of the discomforts of the thirsty soldiers. This was the first time I ever heard threats of vengeance against a town, and I feel satisfied should the army have occasion to again pass this way they will destroy it.

Continuing on we soon reached South Mountain, which is a part of, or continuation of, the Blue Ridge. It is cultivated nearly if not quite to the top on both sides of the rigid roadway leading over it. We passed near the battlefield of the 14th and saw many newly made graves, silent witnesses of the fierceness and bloody character of the engagement. On reaching the summit, or Boonsborough Gap as it is called,[56] a sight unfolded itself that probably was never before witnessed on this continent—80 to 100,000 armed men assembled together. Down in the valley lay the Army of the Potomac, massed, the whole face of the country being covered with troops. I never before saw such a sight. From where I stood the men below looked like ants, and indeed the writhing mass resembled that of an ant battle, seemingly to work around and over one another like them, so closely were they packed. To the right was seen a dark line of men moving off in evident intention of taking position in line of battle, as it was clear the enemy had halted to deliver a battle. The stacks of muskets gave back flashes of fire as a passing cloud, unveiling the sun, would let its rays strike them. Curls of thin blue smoke from the camp fires ascended and permeated the atmosphere, only to make the panorama more wonderful without obscuring it in the slightest degree. How very inadequate this poor attempt of mine at a description of this marvelous scene, and how utterly impossible to convey the impression so grand a spectacle made upon me. Think of it! At my feet lay the whole Army of the Potomac, cavalry, artillery and infantry, in mass. What a picture, what an awfully grand spectacle.

Just at the base of the mountain, which was not cultivated like the other side, but more wooded, lay Boonsboro, a thriving village of Washington Co. of about 6 or 8 hundred inhabitants. On reaching this place we learned that our advance had overtaken the enemy's cavalry rear-guard the day before, hurling them through town, killing and wounding many and taking a number of prisoners, also capturing a battery of artillery. This and yesterdays news tended greatly to inspire the troops, whose voices giving forth the boom! boom! chorus was once again heard along the line.

We pushed on to Keedysville, another smart little village of Washington Co. lying close to Antietam Creek, and at about 5 P.M. halted for the night in a field beyond but near to the creek. A short distance to the front a battery occupied the high ground and was firing slowly, as we came into bivouac, keeping it up 'til the enemy replied, and their shells bursting in the air near us, while they did no harm, certainly made the men feel a little anxious. It was the first experience for many of them of actual hostile firing. We here learned that the enemy were well posted on the other side of Antietam Creek, about 3 miles from Keedysville, at a place called Sharpsburg. We also learned that the heavy firing heard all the afternoon arose from an attack made by Genl. Hooker upon the enemy, resulting in a heavy engagement.[57] I spent the interval between our halt and darkness in hunting up information, and, I will add, I got a prodigious amount of it, I can tell you. Every one had so much to repeat of what this or that corps or division and general was doing or saying, so that when I came back to camp I was fairly bewildered, but with the exception of the engagement that was kept up into darkness, I concluded to consider all other news as "Cook house."[58]

September 17th. A clear sky greeted us as we early moved up to the front in support of the 1st New York Artillery, occupying ground overlooking and commanding a great expanse of country on the other side [of] the Antietam Creek. Our army had been deployed during the night and early this morning and was now in line of battle, although the constant stream of troops continued pouring to the right. The incessant roar of musketry in the woods in this direction told plainly that the battle was on, the awful peculiar roar producing an effect on the men always noticeable with new troops on the eve of an engagement. I hardly know what to call this emotion, but "blood curdling" I think will nearest describe the feelings of those, both old and new soldiers, who stood this morning and listened to the harrowing sounds that smote upon the ear. Very little artillery was at this time being used, so that the dreadful musketry firing alone was heard. A cheer or a shout would have been welcome sounds, but there was neither, the continuous rattle alone attesting the closeness and bloody nature of the engagement.

It was soon noticeable that our whole Corps was here assembled, at least the enormous number of troops appeared to indicate it. The sight was certainly a martial one, as massed on the slopes of the hill sides Fitz John Porter's magnificent Corps of 30,000 men lay all day long ready to be called into battle. Back of this mass, Rush's Lancers,[59] with their long spears and red pennants, added picturesqueness to the scene. Away off, back of us, upon the very summit of the wood covered Blue Ridge, could be seen, alike by friend and foe, the ever bobbing flag of our energetic Signal Corps, as it telegraphed the movements of the Confederates which could be plainly seen by them. What a source of annoyance this little signal station must have been to Genl. Lee.

After listening a long time to the prolonged sound of the battle, I with some others went up to the artillery to see what was going on, and was at once ordered back by the battery officer who, after stating that a Major of a New York regiment had just been killed while standing among the guns,[60] also added that he did not want to draw the enemys' fire. As he spoke a shot came whistling along and passed to the rear over the regiment, and as I turned to see its effects, I saw the whole line "duck" in a very ridiculous manner. This however is but natural. I have always noticed a tendency to do just this thing, even though it is known positively the missile is beyond the possibility of harm. The sound of a solid shot tearing through the air in one's direction certainly contracts the sciatic nerve in about the shortest possible time on record. . . .

So the battle roar continued until night put [an] end to the fighting. We remained all day in position of support, not having been called upon for any active part in the battle. During the night we learned that General Lee had suffered a defeat and had been driven all along his line. This made us feel good and our slumbers were peaceful and undisturbed. We bivouaced where we had been all day—in rear of the 1st New York Battery.

September 18th. We were moved to the left towards the bridge crossing Antietam Creek, for the possession of which Genl. Burnside[61] had made so desperate a fight the day before. It was a horrifying sight that met us all along the route, especially in a cornfield through which we passed. Here our people had been subjected to a dreadful fire and the ground was thickly strewn with mangled bodies. The sight being new to our men, there was extreme silence in consequence among them as they contemplated this evidence and realized what war really was. So on down the slope to the bridge the dead lay everywhere, and vast quantities of muskets, cartridge boxes and debris encumbered the ground. Dismembered arms and legs lay about in surprising numbers, and at a little level space just before crossing the bridge, I halted at a spot where some poor fellow had had his leg torn off above the knee. It was lying there with shoe and stocking on the foot, the bloody and ragged end of the thigh showing the terrible force of the missile. Vast quantities of fore arms and hands lay near, a little old frame shanty near by having evidently served as a hastily improvised field hospital for the desperately wounded. The ground was much torn up and furrowed by the shells, and the old stone bridge was literally covered with bullet marks. There were a good many dead Confederates lying around both on this and the other side of the bridge.

It must have been a desperate charge that could have carried this bridge, as immediately upon the other side of Antietam Creek the ground rises abruptly, even almost perpendicularly. During the battle the enemy occupied this commanding ground and I cannot understand how they could have been driven off it. As you debouch from the bridge, a roadway leads back up and down the stream, along which our brigade at once deployed and then clambered up nearly to the top of the bluff, where a line was established. It was a very uncomfortable position, I can assure you, as it seemed almost like hanging on to the side of the hill. Some idea can be had of the situation when I add that in order to make myself secure and prevent sliding down hill, I was obliged to drive my sword into the ground as a foot hold. The men used their bayonets for a like purpose.

After seeing the men placed as comfortably as possible, I climbed up to the top and peeped over the edge. I found a worm fence extended along the edge, and beyond an open field intervened as far as the town of Sharpsburg, which was in plain view. The straggling houses on its edge were filled with sharpshooters who, knowing the Yanks occupied the brow of the hill, kept up a constant firing. I stayed at this place a long time, being protected from the enemy's sight by an angle of the fence and took in the situation. At length I discovered that the rebels had knocked off several shingles from the roof of a house nearer than any other to our line and from the interior were firing upon us, unseen, even the smoke from their rifles being hidden from us.[62] To all intents and purposes the house, upon casually looking at it, would strike one as being entirely unoccupied, but after a closer scrutiny to understand why it was that this particular house contained no sharpshooters, I discovered smoke issuing from a side window which had evidently been opened for the comfort of those within. The whole thing dawned upon me like a flash, so calling up several of my men, I directed a fire to be opened upon the house, taking the roof for a target, for I was sure the enemy were just under the shingles. Soon after, the regiment very generally moved cautiously up to the top of the hill, and a lively fire was inaugurated. After a time I returned to my first position— my sword hilt, and took a view of the surroundings.

I here enclose a sketch of the bridge which lay at our feet. This bridge is a strong stone arched country bridge, with stone parapets, and how in the world our troops could have passed over it in sufficient numbers to drive the enemy's artillery and infantry off the top of the bluff I cannot conceive. Possibly and most likely, the stream is fordable, but of this I cannot say positively, yet it must have been so, else our people could never have succeeded. This bridge is situated in a ravine, down the sides of which our troops had to move without shelter of any kind, as there were no trees or anything else to shelter them from the awful fire of the enemy's guns opposite.

About noon Genl. Burnside, with his jovial happy face passed along the foot of the hill. He was unattended by either staff or orderly. When passing the regiment some of the men called to him and wanted to know whether the rebels were still about. "Still about," said he; halting his horse and turning towards us he raised his right arm to give emphasis to his words, "Still about, why, there are thousands of them, just over the hill, and they will be coming for you pretty soon. In the meantime," continued he, "I am going to get out of this, as it is no place for me, I don't want to see any more of them." So saying he gave a hearty laugh and a good bye wave of his hand, and putting spurs to his horse was soon lost to view. We all felt animated by his presence and assured by his joking manner.

About 4 P.M. the first casualty occurred in the regiment. Private Sanford, Co. E, having doubted the existence of sharp shooters in the house of which I have mentioned, mounted the worm fence to prove his convictions and was immediately shot through the thigh from this very building. He was taken to the rear where his limb was soon added to those so thickly strewn about.[63] After that the firing became so severe that our men were gradually driven below the bluff and so continued until nightfall.

After it had become fully dark, orders were received to be extremely watchful, as it was feared the enemy would attempt to retake our position. I divided my company into reliefs and posted them along the fence, relieving the pickets every hour. It was a night of anxiety and horror. The firing was incessant all along our line, and, indeed, to the right of us amounted almost to a battle. With us too, a lively fusilade was kept up, and I candidly confess I passed a wretched and miserable night. I felt there was a good deal of responsibility resting upon me, as I was the only old soldier among the officers experienced in such work. Before morning, however, I found the majority of Captains, having every confidence in their own abilities, were doing well with their companies. While I felt relieved at this, I must add, in all candor, that I thought it a little strange that no thought as to my opinion of the situation seemed to trouble them, I and my previous service evidently being of very little account with these gentlemen. Of course my youth had much to do with this as they (the Captains) were all older men.

This nights work taught me one lesson at least, and that was to rely entirely upon myself, consult no one, and to keep my opinions to myself. It also confirmed me in my conduct of keeping to myself, seeking the companionship of no one, but rather to let the future develop the ones most likely to be my friends and associates. These reflections and determinations, together with constant attention to my men, caused the long night to pass with a better feeling as to my surroundings, and on the morrow's dawn to feel free from the isolation that hither to annoyed me so much.

McClellan had eked out a strategic victory at Antietam, and Lee, bloodied but unbowed, recrossed the Potomac on the night of September 18–19. McClellan ordered a half-hearted pursuit of the retreating Confederates on September 20, directing Maj. Gen. Fitz John Porter to send two divisions of his 5th Corps to cross the river and feel for the enemy.

Brig. Gen. George Sykes's division of Regulars crossed the Potomac first, using the same ford—Blackford's—that Lee had utilized for his retreat. As the Regulars advanced to the west out the Charlestown Road, they encountered the Rebels in much heavier strength than was anticipated and began to fall back toward the river. Maj. Gen. George Morell's division had been ordered to follow Sykes across the Potomac, but once they reached the Virginia shore, they were to scout north in the direction of the nearby village of Shepherdstown. The troops of the 1st Brigade, containing the rookies of the 118th Pennsylvania, led the division across the river and began to advance toward the town. They had not gone far, though, when they were quickly ordered to scale the steep bluffs that line the Potomac south of Shepherdstown to support the withdrawal of the Regulars. Sykes's division had stirred up a hornet's nest when it collided with the Confederate rear guard, and unknown to the Pennsylvanians as they worked their way to the plateau above the cliffs, Lee had ordered six brigades under Maj. Gen. A. P. Hill to push the menacing Federals back across the river.

Although they would go on to fight for two and a half more years in numerous battles and skirmishes, the defining moment of the 118th Pennsylvania was at hand. With a scant two weeks of field service under their belts, facing a foe who outnumbered them tenfold, and armed with defective rifle-muskets, the odds were against them. To add to their problems, at a critical point in the fight, Col. Prevost chose not to obey an order to withdraw because it was not delivered through what he considered the proper channels. In the rout that ensued, more than 35 percent of the regiment became casualties.

September 19th. Shortly before dawn the firing of the enemy ceased altogether and after daylight had fully come, it was discovered they had retreated and withdrawn across the Potomac. The heavy picket firing throughout the night was to mask the movement. However, before leaving they made it pretty hot for our pickets, having occupied a portion of the line to the right of us, capturing over one hundred prisoners.

After cooking coffee, about 9 o'clock the regiment was moved out upon the open, and for a long time drilled by Col. Prevost in the movements of battalion, especially in that of "Right by file into line." Before finishing however, we were moved off with the rest of the brigade and passed through Sharpsburg, where we were received by the inhabitants with every demonstration of joy, men, women and children vying with each other in their desire to make us welcome. It was quite evident in my mind that the rebels had not made a very good impression during their occupancy. How ridiculous seemed the bombastic order of General Lee, published upon his arrival on Maryland's soil. He had come to stay, he had come to give them freedom, and right here, in this town, close to the border of Virginia, were the people he had come to liberate, hailing with joy the expulsion of these "liberators"—very curious and funny to us narrow minded Yanks.[64]

Sharpsburg, Washington Co. Md. is a very pretty place and is situated on the Antietam Creek about 3 miles from Keedysville and 9 or 10 from Harpers Ferry. It has a number of churches and stores and a population of about 1000. It is beautifully situated. We found the houses crowded with wounded Confederates, and, indeed, every available place turned into a hospital. Even in some of the yards of the houses the poor fellows were lying on litters of straw, attended only by a few of their surgeons who had remained behind. Continuing on through the town, we bivouaced near Blackford's Ford on the Potomac, where we rested the balance of the day. . . .

September 20th. Opened bright, warm, and clear, not a cloud to be seen anywhere. After cooking coffee, orders were received to pack up, and shortly after we were at the Ford on the banks of the Potomac, having crossed the intervening canal. A short distance above us was a dam, over which very little water was flowing, and this only in places where the boards were off. At the far end, or Virginia side, it had either been broken, or else left open purposely, as there was a space of at least 20 feet where the water rushed rapidly through. I mention these facts now, although I did not notice them particularly at the time, but later on.

It was soon known that we were to cross the river by wading and the men at once commenced taking off shoes and stockings, it being understood the water was quite shallow. I kept boots on as I feared I would be unable to replace them should I take them off. A little before this, and when the order came to cross the river, my acting 1st sergeant, Thomas M. Coane, became perfectly demoralized, and in the face of the company, was taken <u>suddenly sick</u> and went to the rear, and throughout this eventful day, was not with the regiment. Such abject cowardice on the eve of an important reconnaisance by a man of his ability, respectability and understanding was most discouraging to me. His family, should I pursue the course his conduct deserves, would be humiliated in the dust, and his brother Charlie, whom both you and I know well, would be overwhelmed with mortification.

Thomas M. Coane, Donaldson's second lieutenant throughout most of his service in the 118th. The Civil War Library & Musuem.

It was particularly bad for Coane to act in this manner just at this time, when it was known to me that he would have received a lieutenancy upon the first vacancy, the Corn Exchange being desirous of it, and his soldierly ability entitling him to it.[65] I can account for his conduct only in one way, and that was his youth.

I was singularly unfortunate in being without help at this time. Lieut. Batchelder was taken sick at Fort Corcoran and was left behind, since which I have been without his valuable services. 1st Sergt. Keener, the fraud, I don't know what has become of him, I will make him feel the rigor of the service without fail. Lt. Perney Smith, although a good, willing little fellow, is of no earthly good to me, and requires as much attention and looking after as the whole company. Altogether I have been unhappily situated, and the amount of labor devolving upon me has been enormous.

Everything being in readiness, at 9 A.M. we headed the brigade across the river. There was much merriment, laughter and fun among the men as they waded this river, especially when some more unfortunate one, losing balance, would fall in the water. We reached the other side without accident and very little inconvenience, and after a little time spent in allowing the men to get on shoes and stockings, proceeded along the river road towards Shepherdstown, which was said to be but a short distance above. Just before fording the river, a battery of Genl. Sykes' Regulars under command of Capt. Gibson,[66] E 3rd Arty., came down the opposite bank, and without halting commenced fording to our side. We met midway in the river, and learned from them that they had been on a reconnaisance, and there were no enemy anywhere around.

During all this time I had felt very uneasy at the apparent want of caution displayed by our commander, and remarked to Lieut. Crocker, who happened near, that the place called vividly to mind Ball's Bluff. The face of the hill, where we landed, and indeed all along the road as far as could be seen, was like that place—too steep for ascent, and we had to move along the river bank towards the dam to find a road leading to the top. We passed a large empty brick mill built in the side of the hill, and further on at the dam, three large stone arches, or lime kilns. Then came a ravine and a rough winding road leading between the hills up till near the top when it turned abruptly to the left until the top was reached.

Just before entering this ravine, a staff officer came dashing up to Col. Barnes, the brigade commander, and told him the enemy were approaching in heavy force on the other side [of] the hill. Turning to Col. Prevost,

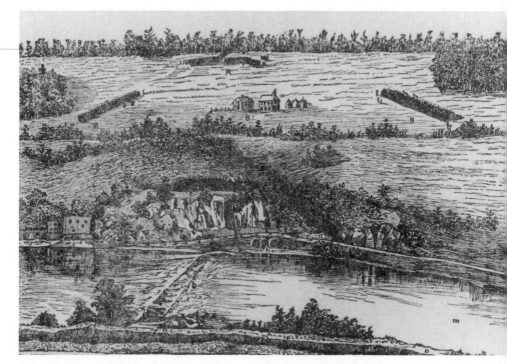

The Battlefield at Shepherdstown. The view in this pen-and-ink sketch, which was published in
History of the 118th Pennsylvania Volunteers Corn Exchange Regiment, *is looking from the*
Maryland shore across the Potomac into present-day West Virginia. The Pennsylvanians crossed
the river at lower left via Blackford's Ford (marked a), then turned north and advanced up River
Road, past Boteler's cement mill (seen at left) toward Shepherdstown, the outskirts of which are
visible at right. As they reached the point marked d on River Road, they were ordered to scale the
bluffs on their left to cover the retreat of other 5th Corps units. The dark mass at the top of the cliff,
with two battle flags barely visible, is the 118th. A. P. Hill's division, which is shown advancing on
the 118th from three sides, soon enveloped the regiment, forcing it back down, and in some cases,
over the rock facings. Some men huddled in the lime kilns at the river's edge (marked h) to escape
misdirected Federal artillery fire, while others either swam the Potomac or, like Donaldson, dashed
across the exposed wooden planking of the dam (marked b, directly opposite the cliffs). As they
made for the Maryland shore, the survivors were exposed to the fire of Confederates who crowded
the hilltop or protected themselves in the cement mill, but they were covered in part by Federal
sharpshooters posted in the dry bed of the Chesapeake and Ohio Canal, visible at the bottom of
the illustration. At present, the battlefield proper is heavily treed and covered with undergrowth;
however, many of the prominent features of the fight, including Blackford's Ford, the ruins of the
cement mill, the lime kilns, and the dam are easily identified.

Col. Barnes said, "Can you get your regiment on the top of the bluff?" "I will try," said Col. Prevost, and dismounting, he led the command up the road. On the way up I noticed in the ravine below a battery wagon with 4 horses attached that had evidently fallen in their endeavor to ascend the path. They of course must have belonged to the rebels. The horses appeared to be suffering intensely from their awkward situation, and Captain Ricketts clambered down the hillside and cut the traces. How little I then thought as I watched him do this act of humanity that it would be the last time I would ever look upon him, dead or alive, in this world again. Moving on I again

Capt. Levis Passmore, Company E, 118th Pennsylvania Volunteers. The Civil War Library & Musuem.

met with Lt. Crocker, and again repeated that this rough, winding roadway and the surroundings generally recalled Ball's Bluff. They were very similar.

As our regiment debouched on top of the hill, the enemy were in plain view, large bodies of them, seemingly a division being massed in front of a range of woods at least a mile away, while to the right, at about half a mile, a brigade of troops were moving towards us, their skirmishers well in advance, many of them firing as they came on. Immediately in front of our position, and at about a half a mile distant, was a farm house, barn, and several stacks of hay. The ground was well cleared of timber, and we had a good commanding view of the country. Col. Prevost gave the order to "right by file into line," the same movement learned in the morning battalion drill the day before in the fields before Sharpsburg, and ordered Capt. Passmore to throw out his Company as skirmishers. This fellow, this pompous, ranking captain, who would "some day look me up"—not only did not obey the order, but actually turned [his] back upon the enemy, abandoned his company and regiment, ran down the bluff to the road below, thence to below the dam, where wading and swimming he reached the other side and awaited in safety the issue of the battle. Meantime Lt. Hunterson, assisted by Lt. Saml. Lewis (Passmore's Company officers), moved the Company out and a savage skirmish at once commenced, the enemy, however, continuing to advance.

As I came upon the ground with my company, continuing the movement of right by file into line, the Companies already in line were firing by file, and the battle was on. Taking a hasty look over the field, I took in at a glance the situation, and ordered my men to kneel and commence firing. I was the only Captain in line that took advantage of this position to steady the men, and to shelter them from the terrible fire of the enemy. The slaughter immediately commenced to the right and left of me, and men were stricken down by the dozens, where a smaller loss would have been sustained had the other officers known how to fight their companies. The fire of the enemy was appalling; they seemed to fire by Companies as the rush of bullets sounded like a hurricane.

For a time things went on well with me, my men behaved gloriously and seemed to rely so upon my judgment; while others had suffered considerably, I had not lost a man. Lt. Col. James Gwyn coming along at this time, shouting and yelling in the rear of the line, noticing the position of my Company said to me, "Make your men stand up Captain, make them stand up like men," and without waiting for any action on my part, he drove into them with his sword shouting, "Damn you, stand up and act like men." In the midst of much confusion, noise and slaughter, I rushed at him in an agony of despair saying, "Let my company alone Colonel, I know how to fight them, don't you see I am doing more execution than anyone else and haven't lost a man?" But he was too excited to hear, and I do not remember to have seen him again while the battle lasted.

Of course my company was now in great confusion, as upon obeying the order of the Lt. Colonel they came to their feet, and like the rest were at once cut down. At this time, too, something got wrong with the muskets, they became defective and I was soon surrounded by the poor fellows asking what they should do. Taking a nipple pick from one of them, I found, in many cases, in their haste and confusion they had put the bullet in first, and of course, the gun became useless. One man said that something was the matter with his musket because he couldn't get the ram rod down. On examination I found he had, in the first instance, put the bullet in first, and the cap exploding, thought he had fired it off, so rammed another and another cartridge until the gun was full. It was the same thing throughout the regiment, a vast majority of the Belgian muskets became useless, and men were seen running hither and thither without pieces and loudly calling for them. God! just think of it!—sending such troops to fight the veterans of A.P. Hill and Stonewall Jackson.

The enemy now commenced ascending the hill upon which we were, and soon shots coming from our rear, it was noticed they had actually flanked us and were upon the road up which we came. Col. Prevost, noticing this, withdrew several of the right companies, faced them to the right, and soon cleared the road. This movement, however, being misunderstood at the centre, they commenced giving ground which, Col. Prevost seeing, [he] seized the colors and advanced boldly to the front, ordering the men to follow. Before he had gone many feet, he received a severe musket shot through the shoulder, and was taken to the rear. At this time, and while I was busily engaged supplying, as best I could, my men with other muskets, I met Lieut. Crocker, who, intent on the same object, was reaching about for any disused piece he could find. Looking up, and seeing me standing with a musket in my hand, he said "God! Captain, was Ball's Bluff like this?" I said, "Crocker, we are beaten and you had better look to the rear for a safe retreat for the men."

Just as he left me, the enemy came upon the ground in perfect line, with their Red Cross battle flags waving, and peculiar cheer rending the air. At that moment I received an order from some one, I cannot tell who, to retreat by companies from the right, and seeing the company next me leave, I called to Co. H to be steady and follow me. I have said that all along the disaster at Ball's Bluff was ever before me, and as I ascended to the top of the hill, I noticed well a line of retreat should it be necessary to make one. Therefore, heading my men and passing Co. C, who seemed to be undecided what to do or which way to go, I cut through the woods, struck a path leading into the one up which we had come, and in dashing furiously down it, I was almost killed by coming unexpectedly upon a fallen tree which lay across the roadway, but managed, without stopping my momentum, to slide under it, closely followed by Corporal Danl. B. Cobb[67] and the rest of the company.

The enemy were now pretty well on top [of] the hill, and commenced a plunging fire after our retreating boys. The slaughter became dreadful, men being shot as they ran, and their bodies, left supported by the trees, were afterwards seen by us from across the river when the fight was over. Others again were driven headlong over the bluff, and dreadfully mangled or else killed outright. Among these were Capt. O'Callaghan, who I fear is dreadfully if not fatally injured.

As soon as the last of the regiment were drawn off the hill, the enemy crowded along the top and into the old brick mill, of which I spoke, from the windows of which they picked off our poor fellows as they ran along the river bank and over the dam. Many, fearing to recross, huddled into the three arches near the dam, while others took to the water where with heads only exposed they essayed to escape the murderous bullets. For a time I stood near the sluice way which intervened between the dam proper and the river bank, seeing to the passage of the same by such of my company willing to venture across, and with aching heart witnessed the utter demoralization and rout of this fine body of men, who, beaten, dismayed, wild with fright, all order and discipline gone, were rushing headlong towards the dam, across which alone lay safety and escape. I did not stop long to contemplate the scene, however, as noticing bullets striking the ground thickly around me, I for the first time became aware that the enemy were in the brick mill. Hastening to where Lt. Purnell Smith and a few of my company stood not knowing what to do, I pointed out the fact of their being a conspicuous mark from the mill, and directed the men to cross the dam.

At this moment a battery of artillery from <u>our</u> side [of] the river opened a heavy fire on the enemy, but owing to the shortness of the fuses, the shells fell among our people, intensifying the dreadful scene. A cry of horror went up from our men, heard across the river. I was just preparing to recross the river, over the dam, and was standing in the water up to my knees, when noticing the men crowding the arch-ways were waving white handkerchiefs on the ends of ram rods in token of submission, I was about to order them out when a shell entered one of the arches, tearing to pieces 12 or 15 of the poor devils crowded therein. Quite a number immediately thereafter, headed by one man with a white handkerchief on his musket, ran out from the arches along the bank into the winding path up which we had ascended but so short a time before, and actually surrendered to the enemy on top of the hill. By heavens! think of it! these poor fellows had to run for safety to the enemy, lest their own people would kill them. God! the stupidity and gross ignorance of an artillery officer who could not judge of the distance across this river, no wider, I should say, than our Schuylkill. They kept pounding away for a long time, thinking they were having magnificent practice, until some compassionate officer rode up to them and explained the situation, when the length of the fuse being changed, better firing was made, and the enemy raked off the hill.[68]

I said I was standing partly in the water as these things occurred, while the dam was filled with fugitives, towards the centre of which I noticed Col. Prevost being supported across, with Maj. Herring closely following him. The dead and wounded lay all along, and the splinters were flying as the bullets ripped and tore the planks, while the men were dropping in quick succession. Lt. Smith, declining to cross because of his uniform and sword, I told him I would be obliged to leave him, as I was determined to make an effort for my escape, and the poor fellow actually abandoned his sword and put on a private's overcoat to hide his uniform, although, for that matter, I did the same thing, or nearly as bad shortly after, as I will state.

At this time I noticed our flags floating in the water near the shore above the dam, and seeing a man near the place, I called to him to stop and get them, which after a little wading he did and carried them safely to the other side. As I turned to start myself, Private John Fisher[69] of my Co., who had all along followed me closely wherever I went, now ran to a dead man lying at the waters edge, and pulling off his overcoat, brought it to me, and throwing it over my shoulders, buttoned it around my neck, saying that I would surely be killed by reason of my bright shoulder straps and sword and officers uniform. Without making any effort to prevent this act of kindness, or indeed, thinking much about it, I started off through the swift water-way, where I found the current to be very strong, reached the dam in safety, and ran as fast as the slippery and broken boards would admit. At this time, the Berdan Sharpshooters had lined the bank of the

canal and were keeping up a pretty lively fire in order to protect our crossing, there being no less than 10 or twelve men in front, rear and immediately around me, the others having gotten over or else been shot.

I shall never forget the scene as I worked my way across the dreadful
causeway. The bullets struck all around me, men were shot in various
places of the body, some falling, others again staggering and struggling to
make the other side, and all hurrying wildly on with the consciousness of
the desperate chances they were taking. When nearly midway across, one
poor fellow just ahead was shot, and in falling rolled over and over. As I
came up to where he was lying, he clutched the tail of my overcoat, and in
piteous accents called out, "Help me Captain, for God's sake don't leave
me here." Without stopping, I unfastened the overcoat from around my
neck and left it in his death grip, saying I couldn't help him then, but
would send after him as soon as I got across. I pushed on, but the poor fellow's soul had reached the presence of the Great Commander before I got
to the other side. On reaching the shore I rushed hurriedly up to and
crouched down behind the canal bank where I lay for a little while, utterly
exhausted.[70]

After resting somewhat I hastened to near where we had encamped in
the morning and found the survivors assembled in the woods near a barn,
from where a view could be had of the other side of the river and what
was still going on there. Meantime, the whole 5th Army Corps, and
indeed, troops from other corps, had been ordered up, and the face of the
country was covered with them. Just as I reached a group of officers, a
number of men appeared bearing in a blanket a wounded officer, who I
learned to be Lt. Ruddy White, Co. G, shot after having escaped across the
river and while in fancied security. It appears he was standing talking to
some of the men, when a sharpshooter, at nearly a mile distant, killed him,
the bullet tearing through his groin, causing hemorrhage of which he died
while being borne along in the blanket. They carried him to the barn and
laid him on a table there. . . .

. . . I proceeded to a clump of trees where I saw Lt. Col. Gwyn and
many of the officers assembled. I could not but notice how warmly I was
received by them, and by Col. Gwyn last of all, who turning to the officers
as he took my hand, said, "Gentlemen, I believe I am the only one who
made any very serious mistake today, and I now believe that Capt. Donaldson, in fighting his men kneeling, was doubtless right, and I am man
enough to say that I regret having interfered with him." I thanked him and
said I was glad to know that my conduct was approved. I have met with a

Lt. Col. James Gwyn, 118th Pennsylvania Volunteers. THE CIVIL WAR
LIBRARY & MUSUEM.

number of friends from other commands whose regiments had been ordered
up in support, and for quite a time was handed around among them as
though I was something wonderful. Afterwards I hunted up my company
and was again made aware of a most singularly cordial greeting, the men
crowding around me as though I was some object to be worshipped. I also
noticed that whenever I approached the other men of the regiment I was
saluted and spoken to in the most deferential manner. The officers too
treated me so very differently that I was forced to notice their changed
manner. I was greatly surprised at all this, as I was not conscious of having
done anything particularly brilliant in the late fight, yet still, the change of
sentiment was so marked towards me that I would have been a dull fellow,
indeed, had I not noticed it. It was clear to my mind that by some process
unknown to me I stepped conspicuously to the front from a most <u>obscure</u>
rear position in the regiment, and my own company was most fulsome in
its desire to show appreciation of its "little captain," as they called me.

After making what arrangements I could towards the comforts of my company, I proceeded to hunt up Col. Prevost and learn the nature of his wound. I was directed to a haystack where they had lain him, but I found he had been taken to a house near by and that he was too severely hurt to be seen. Capt. Passmore was at the haystack very sick but I did not see him, neither did I want to. With this days work ended this terrible and eventful campaign. Our loss had been nearly 300 in killed, wounded and missing. My loss was 12 killed and severely wounded, 8 or 10 slightly wounded, and several missing.[71] Among the mortally wounded was John Montieth, who was shot through the lungs and had been taken to Sharpsburg.

The 118th Pennsylvania lost 269 of the 737 men they had crossed the river with, including, as Donaldson has told, Col. Charles Prevost, who was seriously wounded by a bullet that shattered his shoulder blade. His injury would keep him away from the regiment for the next seven months, and to Donaldson's chagrin, Lt. Col. Gwyn ascended to the command of the 118th.

Meanwhile, McClellan, seemingly content to let the Army of Northern Virginia slip away, settled down to a month-and-a-half-long period of inaction on the banks of the Potomac.

September 21st. I was detailed on picket, and, with a portion of the poor disheartened fellows, posted along the canal opposite the battle ground. We were a sorry lot, I can tell you. With exception of an occasional shot from the enemy's sharpshooters, which kept us pretty close, we were not otherwise molested all day. Our dead were plainly in view, and the sorrowing sight of their quiet forms added still further to our discomfiture. . . .

An incident occurred today which I deem of too much importance to be overlooked. Lt. Crocker crossed the river alone and recovered the bodies of Capt. Saunders, Capt. Ricketts and Lt. Moss, which he brought over in a boat. This was a most daring act and was performed, I believe, without authority, orders, or instruction, and only at the dictates of a brave and generous heart. While on the enemy's side of the river, Crocker was approached by a general officer who demanded his authority for coming within their lines. Upon being told he came without authority and only upon an errand of mercy, the general, who was most likely A .P. Hill or Stonewall Jackson, told him to go ahead and do what he could, meanwhile he would be protected by their cavalry. Afterwards, an orderly sent by General Fitz John Porter told Crocker to come back to our lines or else he

(Porter) would shell him out if he did not instantly obey. Crocker failed to obey, however, until he had looked over the whole field, and upon returning to our side was at once arrested and taken before Genl. Porter, who rated him severely, adding that we were not down here upon any such business as mercy, and then allowed him to depart. The daring of this man Crocker is beyond all precedent. Think of it. Crossing the dam alone, exposed the while to the sharp shooters deadly aim, and why they did not fire upon him is beyond my comprehension.

The next day, <u>Sept. 22nd</u>, I went to Sharpsburg to hunt up my wounded. I found them in the little Episcopal Church there, and with the exception of Corporal John Montieth, appeared to be doing well. Corporal Wm. Pheeney[72] and Private James McLenaghan[73] are dangerously hurt. Jas. Nelson,[74] Chas. O'Neill,[75] George Steinmayer,[76] and H. T. Gale[77] [wounded] slightly in the arms.

Monteith had an ugly wound through the lungs, the ball passing entirely through him. He was shockingly emaciated and was rapidly sinking, being unable to speak or move, but just lay upon his bed of straw breathing in little rapid fitful gasps, rolling his eyes, which now looked unusually large and brilliant, about in a nervous and restless manner. As soon as he saw me approaching his whole countenance changed and lit up with unmistakable delight, which settled into impatience at my delay in reaching him. This was occasioned by the crowded condition of the floor upon which the wounded lay, the pews having been removed to make room. My progress was otherwise slower than I intended because so many poor fellows reached out their hands for me to shake, which could not be refused, besides the innumerable questions asked by others that had to be answered, so no wonder the poor corporal thought I was a long time in getting to him. Finally I reached him, and falling upon my knees beside him, clasped both his hands in mine and pressed them firmly, not saying one word, for I was in the presence of death, and that speedily too was stamped upon his countenance. "My brave fellow," said I after a while, "what do you want me to do for you, what shall I say to your family, for you have but a little while to live?" I then found he could neither speak nor move, and that although his mouth moved and his brows knitted together in endeavors to speak, yet not a sound came from his lips, although I put my ear close down to him. "Never mind," said I. "I will tell your wife how nobly you behaved, and how had you lived, a sergeants stripes awaited you" etc, and then I tried to comfort him, but I will never forget his look when I could not understand something he desired to tell me. After being with him a long time I bade him farewell, and turning my back upon him, made my way out of the building heedless of the calls of those by whom I passed. I never saw John Montieth again. Poor fellow, he died as became a soldier, and in him the country loses a noble man, a brave soldier, and a true patriot and defender.

On the 23rd, a committee of the Corn Exchange arrived in camp with hospital and other stores. This committee consisted of T. Horace Brown, A. McIlroy, Job Joins, P. B. Mingle, Lewis J. Baugh, & L. G. Graff. Professor Saunders, father of Capt. Saunders, the body of [whom], together with the bodies of the other officers obtained from the battlefield by Lt. Crocker was buried in the church yard adjoining the Episcopal Church at Sharpsburg, having disinterred his remains, left this morning (the 25th) with them for Philadelphia.[78] Mr. Ricketts and Norris Cummings are also here, making arrangements for the removal of the remains of Capt. Ricketts.

Thus after infinite labor which consumed every available leisure moment and many long hours of the night when all save myself were asleep, I have brought to an end this lengthy account of the "Antietam Campaign." I will add here, for fear the length of this letter causes you to forget it, that I still dislike letter writing and it is only the desire to gratify you and my friends that I force myself to write as I do. In conclusion I will further say that knowing you will expect a frank statement of my opinion as to the battle of Shepherdstown and where I honestly believe the blame for fighting it belongs, I will give it trusting that as in the past you will respect my confidence and not use me as authority should my criticism be adverse to my superiors.

However much I regret to say so, Col. Prevost, in my judgement, is entirely to blame for the disaster that overtook us at that place, and were it not that he is so seriously wounded I feel confident he would be court-martialed. Apart from his bravery, of which there is no possible question, he was not the man to command this regiment. It was too much for him. There appears to be a want of character so essential in a commander of troops. He is a theoretical soldier, good at arguing the results of this or that move, but never ready to make it himself. Now a thorough soldier, as all supposed Prevost to be because of his experience as an officer of Genl. Frank Patterson's staff during McClellan's campaign on Richmond, would never in the world have placed his regiment, as he did, on the summit of a precipitous bluff in the face of a numerous enemy, not withstanding the fact that he was ordered to do so. Some discretionary powers are left to commanding officers. A thorough, practical soldier, I say, taking in at a glance the situation and the utter impossibility of contending against such tremendous forces already plainly in view, would have instantly decided that it was no place to put a regiment, especially so knowing the movement to be one of reconnoisance only, and so have fallen back under cover of the brow of the hill, reported the fact, and withdrew his regiment. Col. Prevost, on the contrary, obeyed the order literally, using no judgment. Col. Barnes, commanding brigade, himself an old soldier who in obedience to orders made the crossing, as soon as he got a glimpse of the surroundings, ordered the whole command to fall back, which with exception of our regiment they did, recrossing the river without loss. The 118th being in the advance was actually forming on the summit of the heights when this order to retire was given, and although the firing had commenced, there was yet time to have withdrawn without serious loss had Col. Prevost accepted the order delivered to him. It appears that the officer charged with this duty, himself an old soldier, deemed it sufficient, owing to the confusion existing at the time he reached the regiment, to communicate the same to the first responsible officer he met with, to have the order obeyed. This officer happened to be Captain Bankson, who, near the right of the line, was superintending the loading of his men's muskets. He sent his Lieutenant, Kelly, to the Colonel with the order, but Col. Prevost haughtily declined to receive it other than from the staff officer himself. So the fight went on, and the slaughter took place. This is my individual view of the affair, but I am not an authority on such matters. I submit it, however, trusting the future will decide whether I am right or not.[79]

As I have said the colonel was not the man to have had command of this really fine regiment. Neither is Lt. Col. Gwyn fit for the position. He is very little better, to my mind, than Col. Prevost, although arrogance is his substitute for "force of character," which Col. Prevost is too much of a gentleman to have. This fellow, this Lt. Col., is indeed a low person, and feels his oats amazingly in his new position; the regiment, in my judgment, will never come to any good under him.

In my opinion, the soldier among the Field Officers is Major Herring, although he too has much to learn. He is, as far as I have been able to judge, impartial, just, dignified and compels respect, is strictly military, or wants to be, and will succeed. My idea is that he is the man to command us, and I feel confident that under him the regiment would achieve a record second to none. I do not think he would have fought at Shepherdstown. I think he would have sent back for instructions, reporting the situation. However, this is mere conjecture. He is always polite, kind, and sociable with me, apparently recognizing that I <u>know something</u> about tactics. I like him very much, but am careful not to let him see that I do. I rarely go to head quarters, and as a consequence am not in much feather with the Lieut. Col., who appears to want the officers to think him a <u>big thing</u>. "All of which is respectfully submitted"—I am dreadfully tired of this letter. . . .

>→●→O→●→<

Camp near Sharpsburg, Md.

September 23rd, 1862

Dear Jacob:

. . . We are all at 6's and 7's since the battle and are very uncomfortably located in camp owing to the non-arrival of baggage, tents, etc. My quarters are composed of boughs—good in the day time and clear weather, but somewhat cool at night, and should it rain, wouldn't amount to much as a place of shelter from the elements. My baggage I have not seen since leaving Fort Corcoran, and as a consequence, am pretty dirty and soiled. Indeed, I have worn the stockings completely off my feet, which are blistered and very sore. Of course, I will get my things as soon as the interminable tangle the wagons seem to be in can be unraveled, but my mess chest, of course, is abandoned, with all the good things it contains, including a pair of dress boots. My blankets also are with my valise, and these I miss really more than all else beside, excepting, now that I think of it, my man George, who has been lost to me for many days, and I fear harm has come to him. I make out but indifferently at cooking, but manage to get along some how or other.

But for all this I am ready again to try the issue with the rebels. Hang them! they are splendid fighting men. Genl. Lee is an able commander, and his retreat from Antietam most masterly. Indeed, he lost no material whatsoever, not even a baggage wagon, and but a few prisoners. Of some of these I learned the 22nd Virginia was at Antietam and lost heavily,[80] but I don't believe it, else we would know more about them. I have had but one letter from home, but presume there are many others awaiting distribution in the mail. By the way, from what I have written, I fear you will think me utterly destitute and may, perhaps, send some cloths. Do not do this, as I can replenish my underwear at the sutlers and get just what I need. You can, however, send my boot bill and Dr. Neill's bill also. I sincerely trust you will escape the draft, as this is no place for you. You are better at home "<u>as the only support of your mother, and she a widow</u>." . . .

Capt. Passmore's father is here, the captain being <u>SICK</u>. You better believe he is sick, and will be <u>worse</u> shortly, the coward. He ran away from his command in the face of the enemy, abandoning them on the eve of a battle while he made good his escape across the river. Will Conner[81] stood up to the work like a man and throughout the whole affair behaved well. Lt. West had a bullet to rip open his coat across his stomach and I had one through my coat tail; whether this mark of the enemy's esteem was received as I faced them, or whether, and most likely, when showing them a clean pair of heels, I will never know. . . .

>-+◆>-◦-<◆-+-<

Camp 118th Penna Vols.
Near Sharpsburg, Md.
October 5th, 1862

Dear Brother:

. . . All your favors recd. In reply to the inquiry contained in each as to how it is possible for me to keep up my courage and spirits, I will say that I am in better spirits than ever before and do not accept as final your deductions as to the impossibility of whipping the enemy. In regard to my courage, I believe I have never said much about that, thinking the proper thing in regard to it is to have others speak of it. I think, however, I feel pretty much as all others do when an action is about to be fought—a sense of duty and responsibility, a love of country, a desire to conquer and to show the enemy that we are made of one and the same stuff, as we certainly are, makes me toe the mark. I am not one of those who disparage the fighting qualities of the Confederates. They are a brave people, a very brave people, and splendid soldiers, to conquer whom many a bloody battle will have to be fought and many a life sacrificed. I am willing to take my chances and should I be spared to see the end, and there can be no possible doubt as to our final success, I will have a record to be proud of all my days, for it will, indeed, be a grand thing to conquer Lee's army.

My poor corporal John Montieth, or as I now know his name to have been, John Montieth Fullam, was buried in the church yard adjoining the Episcopal Church at Sharpsburg. If you remember, I stated in my letter descriptive of the Battle of Shepherdstown that in the interview I had with him, he tried so hard to make me hear and understand his last words, but that I was unable to do so, and his pitying look when I left him. Well I now feel certain his desire was to make me understand that his true name was Fullam, he having enlisted under his middle name so that his family could not find him. This is a great mistake for men to make, as it causes no end of trouble to their company officers, but to their own families also. I will write to his wife shortly and tell her the sad ending of as brave and good a soldier as ever grasped a musket. In his death he has shed lustre on his country and his flag, and glory and honor on the mother that bore him. So shall it be with all those who die in this cause. I presume his people have already learned of his death and that he was buried by my company with the honors due a soldier. . . .

>--+-+>--0--<+-+-<

Camp Near Sharpsburg, Md.
Co. H 118th P.V.
October 14th, 1862

Dear Bro:

I have just returned from a horseback ride of from 5 to 6 miles about the country adjacent to our camp, and among some of the regiments near us, and also to Sharpsburg, where I visited Lt. Purney Smith, who is rather comfortably located considering the crowded state of the town. His trouble is diarrhoea, which threatens to be chronic. The wound in the hand is healing nicely, but his general condition is bad, and I should think he ought to be sent home to his family and be made to stay there, but of course, it is next to an impossibility to have a man discharged just now, other than for wounds. . . .

On my return to camp found yours of the 9th inst. upon my table— i.e. folded green blanket—and will try and answer your questions. In regard to my commission, I authorized Capt. Passmore to get and deliver it to you, which he promised to do, although I do not think he will pay the least regard to my wishes. Before leaving camp he desired to know whether he could do anything for me in Philadelphia, and I spoke to him about my commission. Passmore is now at home or ought to be by this time, but I don't think he will trouble anyone, he wants to <u>remain quiet</u> for the present. He wants to be where wars and rumors of wars are not heard of. Rest and peace is his desire just now. Capt. Levis Passmore was discharged, honorably, I presume you may call it, because it was not by sentence of court-martial. It was thought best, for the <u>honor</u> of the regiment, to have him apply for his discharge after the following manner; that, having run away from his company while in the face of the enemy, he <u>finds him-self physically</u> unable in the future to attend to the duties incumbent upon a captain, or words to that effect, which was approved by the Lieut. Colonel commanding, who briefly stated by endorsement the reason why he was <u>requested</u> to resign, and the paper was again endorsed by the general "approved, this officer having deliberately left his company while in the face of the enemy, is no longer fit to associate with soldiers, his resignation is therefore accepted for the good of the service," or words to that effect, so he is <u>honorably</u> discharged and thus ends the career of as big a fraud and as great a coward as ever drew a scimitar. . . .

My associates, as you term them, are myself, principally, Commissary Sergeant John J. Thomas, when in camp, and Lieut. Wm. West, when I do any visiting, which is not often. I am to dine with him today, however. All other officers I know but am not intimate with. You say that I <u>appear</u> to be badly off for officers. Well! I not only <u>appear</u> to be, but am in an awful predicament as to help, and have been so since camp at Fort Corcoran, where Lieut. Batchelder left me, sick, since which I have not seen or heard of him, and have been deprived of his valuable services in which I stood so much in need, especially at Shepherdstown. Lieut. Smith was no help what ever, consequently all the labor and work has fallen upon me. Hence it is as I have before remarked, you should appreciate my letters and my friends should not complain if I neglect them. . . .

George is with me again, having been "lost, strayed or stolen" during the last campaign, and the world moves once more. During his absence I was like a fish out of water, a child without its mother. I was helpless to the last degree. But now that he is here, I am again all serene. George says that he has been offered much higher wages if he would leave me, but as the blind man said, he can't see it. . . .

. . . The regiment still carries the flag Aunt Sophia gave my company, and will continue to do so until the government gives us another. I have plenty of opportunities for regretting the good dinners so often had at her house, and feel sorry that I then made so little account of them as to leave the table while one morsel remained. Had I the chance now, I fear the government would lose the services of a captain at one sitting, as I would stuff to suffocation. Oh! for some blackberry pudding, my!!

To assist George I have a curious little nig called "Scipio Africanus," a most wonderful specimen of colored deformity I ever saw. He does the rough work about the house while George polishes it off, and occasionally "Scip" also. I always commend George in this, for Scip is disposed to be a "sassy" nigger. . . .

━┤━◆━○━◆━┤━

Camp 118th P.V.

October 20th, 1862

My dear Brother:

. . . What do you think of this idea of mine—that you address John Montieth's (Fullam's) widow a letter of condolence, stating that I desire you to write to her expressing my sympathy, etc.? Now do you know, I think this a good plan, as you can write so much better than I. I trust you will kindly take upon yourself to do the "condolence" business for me. Indeed I don't think I can do the occasion justice. If this strikes you favorably act at once. I am pleased to know that Auntie has attended to the sick of my company. They will appreciate any kindness from the captain's mother.

Confound the election! I don't want to hear anything about it. I presume the "nigger" worshippers have all been elected. I am a Democrat, first, last and all the time, but as long as the rebels are in arms I will sustain the government's efforts to put down rebellion—with my life if necessary. I think there should be but one party, one issue in the North as long as the war lasts. So hang the election, I say.[82] . . . Am not so well today. The soldiers enemy has taken me in reverse—the diarrhoea has captured me horse, fort and dragoon, and as there is no medicine handy, I have to obey literally the command "trot, march" a round dozen times daily. Will be all right again soon, as I am observing a rigid diet. John Thomas has been appointed 2nd Lt. Co. B, but assigned temporarily to my company. Of course I am perfectly delighted. Should the Corn Exchange send any of their members to visit us please send by them some brandy and tobacco. . . .

I desire to correct a statement made in a former letter as to the discharge of Capt. Passmore. I therein said he resigned—this is not so. At a meeting of the commanders of companies called by Lt. Col. Jas. Gwyn to take into consideration Passmore's case, it was the sense of the meeting that he should hand in his resignation in such form as stated to you, and until today I understood he had done so. He is discharged on Surgeons Certificate "for moral, mental and physical cowardice" with endorsements as stated to you. Dr. Joseph Thomas, our surgeon, himself told me this, and further added that Passmore willingly accepted this discharge. Pending approval by the War Department, he is at home. This is even worse than I had stated. For the good of our regiment I ask you to keep this to yourself.

>⊶⊙⊷<

Camp 118th Regt. P.V.
Near Sharpsburg, Md.
October 21st, 1862

Dear Brother:

. . . I have just received orders to prepare to pack up, three days cooked rations, officers baggage to be cut down etc. It can hardly be a reconnoisance, more likely a forward move across the Potomac. I somehow dread the passage of this river. It seems to bring disaster upon us every time we make it. Should I meet with misfortune in the ensuing campaign, I want you to attend to all business matters of mine, collecting my pay, settling all personal debts, and give the balance to Auntie. This I make [as] a general request, without again alluding to it in the future. As we are only to hold ourselves in readiness we may not leave here at all, or we may go into winter quarters, but this can hardly be, the weather so fine and the roads so good and hard. I will try and write again tomorrow if we do not move. However I really think I will be glad of a change, am tired of "observing" the enemy as we appear to be doing, would rather be on the move and letting them "observe" us for a little while.

I think from what you say that were I at home I could obtain a majority in some of the new regiments forming. I would gladly make the change if I could, as I am not at all at home here with these people. There appears to be so much jealousy and unkind feeling among the officers, and a good deal of favoritism, while there is so little of the true feeling of the comradeship that should actuate the true soldier. Good night—I am dreadfully tired.

>⊶⊙⊷<

Camp 118th Reg. P.V.
Near Sharpsburg, Md.
October 25th, 1862

Dear Jacob:

Marching orders [that I] recd. soon after I notified you of the order to pack up have been countermanded, although the order to be packed up still remains. We will be off shortly no doubt, as additional rounds of cartridges to the 60 each man already has have been issued, while we also keep the three days cooked rations on hand ready to issue at a moments notice. The inspection of corps, division and brigade, regiments, batteries, and trains has been regularly gone through with, and, in fact, everything put upon a war footing, ready to swing into motion at the command. Where our destination I cannot say, but of course Lee's army where ever it may be will be our objective point. The weather is all that could be wished for by our commanding general, so delightfully cool and bracing, making one feel equal to any undertaking. The roads are hard and in excellent condition for artillery and ammunition trains.

I will relieve your mind by stating that I have nearly recovered from the disorder of which I suffered, feeling none the worse for the severe wear and tear of my intestines and will be ready to face all fatigues of the coming campaign. . . .

I have for some days past been hard at work on my clothing return. It is almost an impossibility to account for every article drawn by me for the men since our organization, but this is what is expected of me, and I think beside the prisoners taken at Shepherdstown, the rebels will be accountable for an immense quantity of clothing also abandoned to them on that occasion. A battle helps along amazingly the quarter master and ordinance accounts, so that all the clothing I cannot account for will be charged up to Johnny Reb from whom the government can collect its little balance. John J. Thomas, Lieutenant of the 118th Penna. Foot is now on picket, hence this letter. Were he here, he would be proposing all sorts of outlandish excursions which would interfere with my clothing account, and you would get no letter. I must say, I enjoy being alone once in a while.

I have really nothing of interest to write about. Our life is very monotonous, the same thing over and over each day. . . .

I have lately made acquaintance of rather a pretty girl residing on the road to Sharpsburg, and as I stop daily to chat with her folks I have frequent opportunities to cultivate her. I find her to be a well disposed young damsel with large black eyes, large mouth, and large—no—small feet. She has a good voice and sings some. She tried "Oh, Forget Thee" on me the other day, and after recovering from the creeping sensation that pervaded my being during the operation, I informed her I thought a nightingale had warbled near me—she blushed and said shoo! Finding she did not have the correct words of the song I promised to have my folks at home get it for her. Please tell Auntie to do so and mail it to me. When it comes what a fine duet we will have. We are both good singers, at least you know that I am, and I can vouch for her voice sounding like a man filing a saw. . . .

>—+—‹›—O—‹›—+—‹

Camp 118th Regt. P.V.
Near Sharpsburg, Md.
Oct. 27th, 1862

Dear Jacob:

. . . We move from here today so the orders read, but until we actually make a start, I won't believe it. There is nothing so dilatory as marching orders, or should I say procrastinate instead of dilatory. I have not the faintest idea where we are to move to but of course it will be across the Potomac at some contiguous point. All along I have thought Harpers Ferry would be the place of crossing, it is fordable near there, I am told, and certain movements and activity in that direction makes me think so. Again the Loudoun Valley of Virginia has hardly been touched by our troops, and is an excellent country to march through, I understand; beside, a new route "on to Richmond" would be popular. However, take this for what it is worth, an individual opinion only, without rumor or any authority to back it up. I am no authority, you know. . . .

>—+—‹›—O—‹›—+—‹

Camp 118th Regt. P.V.
Near Sharpsburg, Md.
Oct. 28th, 1862

My dear Brother:

We are still here, or as has been facetiously remarked by the astute military critic—the private soldier, we are waiting until a rain storm again swells the Potomac, a piece of sarcasm indicating the temper of the men and their eagerness to be off. As this may be the last time I will have an opportunity of using pen and ink, at least for some time to come, I feel that I must, confidentially, put down in writing as a matter for future reference, should occasion require it, an incident that occurred recently in which I figured rather prominently, and the Lieut. Col., James Gwyn, appeared to [be] anything but an advantage before his officers and men. I have refrained mentioning this matter, preferring to let it drop, but the extreme kindness and consideration with which the Lieut. Col. treats me of late suspicions some underhand deviltry, some contemptible, unmanly and treacherous business to which he alone would stoop, and against which I must be guarded. He is capable of the most undignified and cowardly actions to gain his end, and that end, at this time, is to get rid of me, not by allowing me to resign, but to work me into some sort of trouble and thus get rid of me, so to speak.

It was on the night of Oct. 13th inst. when as "officer of the day" I was, as my duty required, visiting the sentinels around camp. Not the grand rounds, for it was too early for that ceremony, but merely a personal visit to ascertain from my own observation whether the men had received proper instruction, because they were comparatively green and not fully up in guard duties. I had been pretty well around camp and had just reached the sentinels on the right flank when I overheard a remark uttered by Lt. Col. Gwyn that caused me to stop and listen. It was about 10 o'clock and a bright light was in his tent which reflected against its canvas sides the forms of persons within. They were apparently officers from other regiments being entertained by Gwyn. From his remark I judged they had been heavily drinking and he had been talking of his previous service in the 23rd Penna. Regt., I believe it was, and finally ending by belittling his present command, saying there wasn't a <u>damn</u> officer in it who knew the slightest thing about tactics or any military matter, that they were all a pack of green horns, and that he alone was the only one at all up in camp and field duties, and as a consequence had the entire instruction of the regiment on his hands, why [it] nearly used him up. To illustrate how perfectly ignorant the officers and men were he would proceed with his friends to pass out at the nearest post by giving the wrong countersign, returning again in the same manner through some other post. A bet was made by one of the officers that he couldn't do it, whereupon the money, $10, was put up, and he then arose to put into execution his assertion, but before starting, another drink would be had all around.

My feelings can be imagined as I thus stood and heard this libel, this cowardly unjustified stigma by the commanding officer of our regiment. Especially was this galling to me, <u>as I held</u> the same opinion of himself as he did of the officers. I considered him an insufferable tyrant, a braggart, and anything but an officer and a gentleman. I at once hastened to the post nearest his quarters and after challenging the sentinel, instructed him in the proper manner of challenging more than one person approaching, stating he would be tested shortly, and to be on the alert. "Be particular," said I, "upon seeing several approaching who, when sufficiently near, challenge in a firm voice 'who goes there,' upon their reply, 'Friends with the countersign', reply, 'Halt friends,! Advance <u>one</u> with the countersign,' which being correctly given, say, 'Countersign is correct,' and allow them to pass. But should a wrong countersign be given, then keep the party and call loudly for the corporal of the guard, to whom when he comes, the party should be handed over, and your further responsibility ceases." "Be sure," continued I, "to challenge in a firm, quick and determined voice, as much depends upon the way you say it whether you are approached respectfully or not. Meanwhile I will take my place behind a tree to see that all goes on as it should." After a little delay, Lt. Col. Gwyn and his friends, mostly officers of the 1st Michigan Regt. of our brigade, came walking leisurely along, apparently engaged in an earnest conversation, and so approached the sentinel, who, in a voice loud, distinct, and determined, called out, "Who goes there!" Our <u>Friends</u> were rather startled by this unexpected and vigorous challenge and instantly slowed up in their gait and finally came to a sudden halt upon the command "Halt friends!" to reply of friends with the countersign. At the order to advance <u>one</u> with the countersign, Col. Gwyn himself advanced, and his towering form could be distinctly seen in the darkness, as with rapid stride he came up to the sentry with evident intention of passing him without giving the word, but was instantly checked by a bayonet thrust full up to his breast, and there was nothing else to do but give the countersign. My man had done so well, had challenged so grandly that I was in high glee and could scarcely retain myself but, gracious heavens! Gwyn, instead of giving the right password, said, "I am Col. Gwyn, you know me of course, put up your musket and allow me and my friends to pass," at the same time saying, "Come gentlemen, this way if you please." To my extreme mortification the sentry did as he was ordered, and bringing up his piece, deliberately marched off along his beat.

Gwyn's friends now approached, but at that moment I sprang from behind the tree, and with a voice made hoarse from suppressed rage called out, "Halt there, let no man stir. I will blow out the brains of any one that moves. Sentinel, call for the corporal of the guard." I then pulled out my Colt Navy revolver; the click of its trigger convinced these law breakers that I surely meant business. "Damn it!," I heard one of the friends say, "I knew we would get into trouble."

As we thus stood, an interesting picture was presented to the gaze of
Dr. Joseph Thomas, who in his shirt sleeves was in front of his tent, having
been disturbed by the sentinel's challenge and my angry tones, and the other
officers of the staff who also made their appearance, together with some of
the company officers not yet asleep, and a few men whose tents were near,
to all of whom the loud cry of the sentinel, "Corporal of the guard, post
10," made it apparent that something extraordinary had happened.

At this juncture Col. Gwyn, having regained somewhat his discomforture, said to me, "Well done captain, I commend you for your efficiency
and the excellence of your guard, whom I was testing as becomes my privilege, and I desire to say publicly to these friends of mine that no better
officer than yourself is in the service today. Come to my tent captain,
I have something further to say to you." "You will not stir," said I, "and I
will also show these friends of yours that notwithstanding your boast, there
is one officer at least in this command who understands perfectly his business and who while officer of the day and responsible for good order in the
camp knows how to enforce obedience to orders and military discipline
from all, be he colonel or private." "What do you propose doing?" said the
colonel in some alarm. "I propose putting you in the guard house for
drunken and disorderly conduct." "Captain, captain," said Dr. Thomas,
"you must not do this thing, permit the colonel to go to his quarters and
prefer charges against him, but you have no right to put your commanding
officer in the guard house." I said I knew my powers, and as this person
and his friends had so little respect for themselves, they should be treated
accordingly. Again the good doctor pleaded, as did also Lt. Crocker, who
came up on the scene at this moment. Finally thinking I had given them a
good fright just as the corporal came upon the ground, I yielded, and
allowed the colonel to go to his quarters, and after taking the names of his
friends, put them out of the camp. I ordered the corporal of the guard to
relieve post 10 and put the sentinel in the guard house until further orders,
after which I retired to my tent and at once commenced against Lt. Col.
Jas. Gwyn charges and specifications. Charge 1st—Conduct prejudicial to
good order and military discipline. Charge 2—Conduct unbecoming an
officer and a gentleman.

While hard at work I was interrupted by Lt. Crocker and Dr. Thomas
who commenced an earnest appeal for me to drop the matter, but I resisted
their importunities and after guard mount next day, went over to Col.
Barnes quarters and laid the case before him. His advice was to proceed

with the charges. On my return I was visited by Col. Gwyn, who ate such "humblepie" as never man did, saying among other things that I should consider his wife and children, that they would be disgraced, and finally, being joined by Dr. Thomas and Lt. Crocker who together made such entreaties, I withdrew the charges, and the moment I did so, I knew my own happiness was gone forever while I remained in the command. In Lt. Col. Gwyn I had an enemy for life who would use every opportunity to make life weary to me. I would be hateful to him but he would never show it on the surface—it would be only me who would understand his actions. I know my man, and my stay with the 118th Corn Exchange is not for long. Upon explaining how matters stood to Col. Barnes he remarked that I had made a great mistake and would regret it. No doubt, hereafter, Gwyn will avail himself of every opportunity to annoy me, but of course doing it in such a way that I alone will feel it. However, I may be wrong after all. This of course you must keep to yourself, but I feel better now that I have made you my confidant, as should I have further trouble with this blackguard Lt. Col. you will know the reason why.

Your letters of the 24th and 25th to hand. . . . I am somewhat surprised at your mention of McClellan's removal. Can it be possible there is such a rumor? You ask have I heard it; surely not, there must be some mistake. You allude, of course, to Rosecrans in the west, not our army.[83] A change of commanders with us would be most disastrous at this time. You will find you are certainly mistaken. Please don't allude to it again, it distresses me.

I have been very comfortable of late, indeed, ever since our tents came to hand. I have a nice little fire place built in rear part of my tent, and can keep as warm as you please both night and day. George and Scipio are constantly adding to my comfort, and, indeed I fear, spoiling me for rough work again.

CHAPTER 4

Fredericksburg
October 30–December 15, 1862

*M*cClellan had spent the six weeks following the Battle of Antietam resting his army and exchanging sometimes heated messages with an impatient administration in Washington. He complained of everything from his need for reinforcements (he outnumbered Lee by more than 30,000 men) to the overworked condition of his horses. Finally, on October 26, he began to cross his army over the Potomac near Harpers Ferry.

Lee's army was now encamped in the vicinity of Winchester, Virginia, farther away from Richmond than the Army of the Potomac, and acting on a suggestion from Lincoln, McClellan's plan was to march down the east side of the Blue Ridge Mountains and interpose himself between Lee and the Rebel capital, in the process disrupting Confederate supply and communication lines and forcing a battle. The key to the plan was to move quickly, however, and that element of urgency that characterized most of the successful commanders of the Civil War was simply not a part of McClellan's makeup. It took him nine days to complete his crossing of the Potomac, and when, after having marched his army just thirty-five miles in eleven days, he found Lee squarely across his path at Culpeper, his fate was sealed. On November 7 Lincoln relieved McClellan and replaced him with Maj. Gen. Ambrose Burnside, commander of the 9th Corps.

Donaldson's emotionally charged reaction to the change of commanders, the blame for which he places with Secretary of War Edwin Stanton, may seem extreme, but it probably reflects the general feeling of many of the Peninsula veterans who were still serving in the Army of the Potomac.

155

Camp 118th Regt. P.V.
at Snickersville, Va.
November 5th, 1862

Dear Jac:

We have been here two days after a hurried march from Sharpsburg, Md. I am in good health and just returned from a successful forage. I have been hard at work making out our pay rolls, an indication that the paymaster will be an incident before long. In future, direct all letters to Butterfield's Division,[1] Fitz John Porter's 5th Corps, Washington, D.C. The other day Lt. Col. Gwyn introduced me as the best captain in his command. Look out for squalls! Too much flattery is dangerous. Now for a short account of our movements.

Oct. 30th. Broke camp and moved at about 4 o'clock in afternoon, marching to within a few miles of Harpers Ferry, about 10 o'clock bivouacing on the property known as Bryant's Farm.

Oct. 31st. From this place, at sun rise, nature's grandest decorations in a thousand charms were spread out before our enchanted vision. No scenery in the world, I imagine, can surpass in loveliness that about Harpers Ferry. From our stand point, the eye first rested upon the now historic heights of Maryland and Loudoun, which from opposite sides of the Potomac rise up in bold array, covered with woods whose variegated verdure, at this late season, noted the lingering of summer amid a panorama of such magnificence that language fails to describe it. The lovely Blue Ridge Mountains extending away back into Virginia, and the Shenandoah River, which after forcing its way through them comes bounding along until it dashes into the Potomac, with Bolivar Heights beyond and the old town of Harpers Ferry at its base, with its old fashioned houses and long walls of the ruined arsenal, its tall chimneys still standing, while away beyond the Potomac River with its mountain ranges on either bank all make up a picture that must be seen and not described. It was a scene better calculated to impress one with the greatness of God, whose mercy permitted us to gaze upon his handy-work, rather than to realize that amid such scenes of loveliness his creatures were at this moment assembled to destroy each other. I have before attempted, in my poor way, a description of the scenery hereabouts, and yet were I now able to fully describe it, I could not possibly give you a single conception of its beauty.

We moved at 9 A.M. and crossed the Potomac at Harpers Ferry, but did not enter it. From the pontoon bridge we had a fine view of Maryland

Heights which towers 1000 feet above the river, but I much regretted our officers had not the opportunity of seeing Harpers Ferry and the old engine house of John Brown fame still standing. Upon arriving at the opposite side no time was lost in pushing on to the Shenandoah River over which we also crossed and at once found ourselves in the lovely Loudoun Valley. The Shenandoah is a beautiful stream and comes dashing and foaming along through innumerable rocks which everywhere fill its bed near where we crossed it. We took the road along the east base of the Blue Ridge, and after passing through the most fertile country yet experienced since our first <u>invasion</u> of the "Mother of Presidents," bivouaced near Hillsborough, a little bit of a town in Loudoun County chiefly noted for the innumerable number of roads that appear to centre there, one, the Leesburg Pike, recalled unpleasant memories of former experiences at a place of that name.

We found the country rich in everything, the soil being extremely fertile, vast quantities of turkeys, chickens, butter and eggs, horses, grain and everything a soldier could well wish for was crammed in every nook and corner of the county. As the inhabitants had never experienced the devastating march of large bodies of troops, they thought it only necessary to keep their poultry within enclosures and their barn doors shut to have their possessions undisturbed by the soldiers. Indeed so plentiful were the supplies that although Burnside's Corps had preceded us and had foraged liberally, when our turn came it really seemed as though no other troops had been before us, so vast was the accumulation.[2] The country is what would be termed rolling, I should say, and the grand old Blue Ridge, which by the way is called Allegheny north of the Potomac, with its heavy covering of timber, added wonderfully to the beauty of the country. Loudoun County appears to be interceded in every direction by a stream called Goose Creek, that is, if the inhabitants speak the truth, for on reaching a little stream, no matter where, and inquiring its name, "Goose Creek" is invariably given, until it becomes a by-word for the soldiers.

Nov. 1st. Remained in camp all day.

Nov. 2nd. Bright and early I received from Quarter Master Gardner[3] 6 pair shoes, 2 canteens and 2 haversacks being the best he could do in the way of filling my requisition for 20 pair shoes and many other needful articles! I allowed the men who stood in most need of them to draw lots for the shoes. We moved at 7 A.M. and passed through a country of the same lovely character as before. We halted and encamped at Snicker's Gap, with the little Snickersville village hard by. Again we had plenty of good things to eat, and as there appeared to be no restriction, we cleaned out the inhabitants of every thing in the way of edibles.

Nov. 4th. This day we remained in camp and commenced making out pay rolls. There was another occurrence which makes this day particularly noticeable. I loaned Private Ratzel[4] my last dollar! Poor fellow, he had an opportunity of purchasing from a member of a Massachusetts regiment of our brigade an article that he stood badly in need of, but had no money. I gave him the dollar, knowing I could get anything I wanted on credit. It is wonderful how these Yankees love to barter "and trade a spell."

George Slow, my good faithful colored servant, asked leave of absence to cross the mountains and visit his masters house once more; he would return before the army moved, or if not, would rejoin it. He was familiar with every inch of ground around where we then were, and had passed hundreds of times through Snicker's Gap, and he knew every by path for miles across the mountains. His family were still "at home," as he yet termed the residence of the Pendleton's near Winchester, where he was born and bred.[5] His old father, mother, and sister Frances were yet there, and he was so near to them that he would like to cross the mountains and see them. I told him it was a hazardous undertaking as the enemy were on the other side, and that the gap was full of them. Of course I knew better, as General Lee is too good a soldier to allow his army to be spread out along the mountains exposed to flank attacks, with exception of a few cavalry to watch the passes, his army must be in our front or else rapidly concentrating there. Our halt would seem to indicate such to be the case. However, I told him to go and get back as soon as he could. Now that there was a prospect of losing him I felt how necessary George was to my comfort, and I was extremely sorry that he cared to leave me. . . .

Nov. 5th. Still here, and have finished my pay rolls. I can say in conclusion that I never saw the army so full of enthusiasm as it now is, everyone anxious to meet the enemy and terminate the war by one grand battle. McClellan seems to have the final termination of the issue well in hand, and when we again meet Genl. Lee's army, they will suffer a defeat that will end their existence. We all feel confident of this, and should I be correct in this forecast of the future, McClellan will be, as he really is today, the greatest military chieftain of the age.

>──◆──O──◆──◀

Camp at Warrington,[6] Va.
November 10th, 1862

Dear Brother:

None of your favors to reply to—Genl. McClellan took leave of us today. The army is in tears—my heart is too full of bitterness to say more at present. Am still in good health, tho' much depressed—defeat is before us—how can I help feeling badly. . . .

>-·-◄►-·-O-·-◄►-·-◄

Camp 118th P.V.
Warrenton, Va.
Nov. 11th, 1862

Dear Jacob:

Feeling more composed today, I will take up the acct. of my doings since the 5th inst. If I remember rightly, I had parted with George Slow and finished my pay rolls when I last wrote.

Nov. 5th. Remained in camp as stated.

Nov. 6th. Broke camp at daylight and moved at the early hour of 6 A.M. Our march still continued through a lovely country, but provisions were not so plentiful as heretofore. A little after noon, George Slow put in an appearance, having marched all night to get up with the regiment, knowing we were about to move. How well posted the Rebs are, knowing more about our movements than ourselves. He came laden with spring chickens, home-made bread and the greatest treat of all—two pounds of print butter, sent to Capt. Donaldson with Mrs. Pendleton's compliments. This was truly receiving aid and comfort from an enemy. I was overjoyed to get this treat and forthwith spread some bread and reveled in the toothsome luxury. Why to speak truly I had actually forgotten that such a thing as butter existed. Besides all these things, George brought for himself a pigs-head to make "jowl" as he calls stewing it. He had had a grand time and his mistress was overjoyed to see him and to learn that he was kindly treated.

These people have an idea that we are brutes, and not susceptible to emotions of kindness. If they but knew the true feeling actuating the Union soldiers breast, they would find anything but the bitter hatred ascribed to us. It is all on one side—theirs. The intense hatred of the Southern people makes them do things unbecoming intelligent creatures, unworthy a race said to be fighting for their liberties, it does indeed, and I fear before the war is over they will have fallen very much in the estimation of the Yankee soldier. Indeed, it is tending that way now, for I occasionally hear the men liken mean and contemptible actions as worthy of "Johnny Reb." This is, of course, due to the leaders of the rebellion who inflame the people by every artifice of action and speech they can possibly do, but I can assure you who may think differently at home I have never heard during the whole time that I have been in the army a single expression of intense hatred expressed by our soldiers against the South, its people, or its soldiers.

We halted near Middleburg, another little town of Loudoun County. Our encampment was on the farm of a Mr. J. W. Patterson, which was well kept and in good condition.

Nov. 7th. Moved at 7 A.M. This day we acted as guard to the wagon train, a very laborious and fatiguing business, I can tell you. The trains have the exclusive right to the roads, while we on the "flanks" make one for ourselves through woods, underbrush and every conceivable obstacle. At first we moved slowly, owing no doubt to infantry and artillery ahead, but as these got away, the mules were whipped up and the poor dough boys, as the cavalry call infantry, had to trot along with them. No wonder the older regiments grumble and growl at such duty. . . . During our march it commenced snowing with such violence that we were compelled to camp in consequence at White Plains, by the way, a very appropriate name at this time. As this was early in the afternoon, we had ample time to prepare for the night, so Crocker, Thomas and I joined our pieces of shelter tent and made a most cozy sleeping place. George Slow built a huge log fire before the open door which added greatly to our comfort. During the afternoon Lt. Frank Gillingham,[7] 119th P.V., called to see me. I was sorry I could not entertain him with much beyond the regulation fare, hard tack, molasses and pork, as forage had been getting scarce for some days, and we were obliged to consume at one sitting George's contribution for want of transportation. So many troops had preceded us that the country was fairly eaten out. . . .

After Frank left, George informed me that there was nothing for tomorrow's breakfast but coffee. It is either a feast or famine with the soldier, but as far as I am personally concerned, it makes very little difference what I have to eat. In consequence, I suffer less than my brother officers. When nature informs me that my stomach is empty, I can make as enjoyable a

meal on crackers as others can on roast chicken and trimmings. The eating part
never bothers my army life. Short allowance prevailed throughout the brigade.
The men changed the words of a song which goes "Hard times! come again
no more," into the following, and sang it with much vigor and vim:

> "'Tis the voice of the hungry,
> Hard tack, hard tack,
> Come again once more!
> Many days I've wandered,
> from my little tent door
> Crying hard tack, hard tack
> Come again once more!"

This night's sleep was the most enjoyable I ever had, and as long as I
live I will never forget my refreshing and recuperating slumber at White
Plains, Va.

Nov. 8th. After waiting until the whole division had moved off, we
took up line of march at 7 A.M. acting as rear guard. This was somewhat
better than yesterday's duty, although it had its disagreeable side also, as we
were compelled to keep the stragglers up and look after things generally in
rear of the division. Towards afternoon the ammunition trains fell to us for
safe keeping, when our troubles began. We never reached bivouac near
New Baltimore until 10 P.M. and were fairly used up. I was too tired to
even ask the name of the place near where we halted, and after a cracker or
two and some coffee, turned into my overcoat and at once forgot my misery, the army, and all else beside.

Nov. 9th. We moved again at 7 A.M. As we were now with the brigade,
our march was a pleasant one. During the frequent halts I had leisure to
study yesterday's march from my Harper's Weekly map, which had already
stood me such good service, and found New Baltimore, our last nights
bivouac, to be a little place in Fauquier County. This map is wonderfully
correct, even the cross roads are correctly given and the little rivers and
streams are properly named. Although a small affair, I should think a map
of this kind would be invaluable and a handy thing for every general officer
to carry about him. We made a good march this day and halted at 7 P.M.
near Warrenton.

Nov. 10th. This day was the most emotional one yet experienced by
me during my army career. General McClellan, having been removed from

command, made a farewell review. How can I describe it, how can I tell the utter despondency of the soldiers, at the loss of their idolized commander? The news broke upon us like a thunder clap. Our general removed during an active campaign, taken from the head of the army when about to engage the enemy. Who ever heard of such a thing? Does history point to a like occurrence? The whole army was in tears, there were no exceptions. Even our field officers, who had served but a short time under him, and had not yet experienced the devoted attachment of the old Peninsular soldiers, were dismayed, discouraged and in tears.

I can better describe the true feelings of the army by giving my own at this most tragic period of its existence. When the news was first told me, I would not believe it, but when the order was promulgated and the final review ordered, I could not longer contain myself. I entirely lost my self control, lost my grip, so to speak, and gave way to tears of indignation and words of bitter reproach. Yes! I sat down and cried, and in my dire distress cared no longer to continue in the service. Could I have gotten home, I would have done so, as I no longer had heart to fight for such an ingrateful country. The army was losing the services of the most distinguished officer it had, the ablest soldier in the land. A man who had seen distinguished service in former wars, who had gained great knowledge of practical warfare during the Crimean War. The man whose single mind, as supreme commander, had set in the field and moved in unison the immense armies now under the government. A man who had <u>now</u>, under his immediate charge, an enthusiastic, well organized, invincible army, the very flower of the country ready, anxious, willing and confident. A man who had conducted a skillful campaign on the Peninsula, and who when about to realize the prize for which he had toiled and sacrificed so much, had been cruelly betrayed and deprived the support of an immense auxiliary force under Genl. McDowell, and was thus forced to retreat from before Richmond. All honor to him for his masterly retreat, all shame to the perfidious Stanton, Secretary of War, who defeated his plans and well nigh brought ruin on our country. Noble man, true soldier and patriot who, loving his country more clearly than his own honor, tamely submitted to that humiliation and now again this day to further outrage.

It must certainly have been with the advice and consent of Stanton, and after mature deliberation, repeated explanations and consultations the present campaign was entered into, with a full understanding of its hoped for results and probabilities. Instead of the support he fully counted on from the great Secretary of War, he was deprived of his command without notice or without cause. How can we expect to succeed? Whenever has success attended the movements of armies in the field when controlled by other than their commanding general? How can a civilian Secretary of War conduct a campaign from the seat of government? . . . I say that even to my uninstructed military mind, the idea of handling troops in the field by orders from the seat of government is simply ridiculous. Must our army be forever interposing between Washington and the enemy? Why not keep enough troops in the defenses of that city and let the commander of the Army of the Potomac pursue his own ideas as to how the campaign shall be carried out. I feel sure the result would be better for our cause, the army would then be at liberty to engage the enemy without regard to the Capital, and either defeat him or else tire him out. Such it seems to me is the true plan of our operations.

I have no confidence in Stanton. I think him a politician and an unscrupulous man who is all for self. He is jealous of McClellan and his popularity. He is afraid of him and the army who so loyally worship him. He fears ambition might make McClellan dictator, so he uses his authority while yet he has it, and crushes the only man who can lead this army to victory. I tell you frankly, had McClellan done this, had he placed himself at the head of the army and instead of marching on to Richmond turned against Washington, all would have followed, and instead of "hanging Jeff Davis to a sour apple tree," so much and so often advocated by word and song, it would be down with Stanton, down with the whole dishonorable crew who dare to dictate such humiliating orders to the most skillful soldier of modern times. In that crisis, I would have been there, I would have followed my beloved general and shouted myself hoarse at the discomfiture of "Stanton the Great," "Stanton the 1st," Stanton the unblushing humbug, low minded, unscrupulous fellow who thinks he knows more than anyone else in the whole country. Oh! how I hate and despise him! I care not whether you make public these sentiments. They are flagrant violations of the Articles of War, but they are held by the whole army, and the truth should be told, and the eyes of the long suffering people be opened to this man's crimes.[8]

And now to the man who will succeed Genl. McClellan, I will do him justice to say that we all think he had no hand in it. But we do not think he can command this army. Why the reputation he gained in his North Carolina campaign was not through any merit of his own. It was

Genl. Parke[9] and the late Genl. Reno, who lost his life at South Mountain, both young and skillful men who did all the work there and won for him the reputation of being a success. Time will show whether I am right in this, but of course you must understand I am not enough of a military man to discuss this point, and have only my feelings to guide me in my estimation of my generals, but I am learning soldiering fast. I find that I have again allowed my feelings to carry me away from what I intended to say. To sum up, the army is in a frightful state of disorganization, which probably is really a good thing just at this time for the officers, as it will require their whole time to get the men back again to proper discipline. I can say for myself that today I feel that I can do my duty if for no other reason than that by doing so it will please and gratify McClellan.

A sadder gathering of men could not well have been assembled than that of the army drawn up to bid farewell to its beloved commander. Our corps was reviewed in the morning, and as General McClellan passed along its front whole regiments broke and flocked around him, and with tears and entreaties besought him not to leave them, but to say the word and they would soon settle matters in Washington. Indeed it was thought at one time that there would be a mutiny, but by a word he calmed the tumult and ordered the men back to their colors and their duty. As he passed our regiment he was thronged by men of other commands, making a tumultuous scene beyond description. He was obliged to halt in front of us as Meagher's Irish Brigade were pressing on him to the extent that further progress was impossible. They cast their colors in the dust for him to ride over, but of course this he would not do, but made them take them up again. General Humphreys,[10] who was riding near McClellan, was forced by the crowd towards our line, and I heard him say to a mounted officer close by that he wished to God Genl. McClellan would put himself at the head of the army and throw the infernal scoundrels at Washington into the Potomac. This is history! and I give it here to show the wild excitement pervading all branches of the service, from the rank and file to the general officers—inclusive! Our regiment, except [for] vociferous cheering, made no demonstration.

At 12 M. Genl. McClellan met the officers of Fitz John Porter's Corps at the latter's head quarters and bade them good bye, and as he grasped each officer by the hand there was not a dry eye in the assemblage. Before parting he made a short address in which he said his removal was as much a surprise to him as it was to the army, but he supposed it was intended for the best, and as a soldier he had but to obey. He therefore urged upon us all to return to our respective commands and do our duty to our new commander as loyally and as faithfully as we had served him. By so doing we would pay him the greatest honor, and as he had only the welfare of his country at heart he would follow with his prayers and good wishes the future of the grandest army the continent ever saw. Jac, what do you think of this man? He had it in his power to be <u>dictator</u>, anything he chose to name, if he would but say the word, but he chose retirement rather than ambition—he was not a Caesar. General Porter remarked, as our brigade officers took leave of him, that it would be his turn next. I presume the <u>authorities</u>, i.e. <u>Stanton</u>, will kick him out because he is a friend of McClellan. I have no confidence in our future success. I believe the next battle will witness a terrible and bloody defeat for this army. I make up my judgment merely from my own feelings, and they are that in the next engagement I will want to know <u>all about a safe retreat</u>. My feelings are those pervading all ranks. How can Genl. Burnside remove this feeling before we meet the enemy? It is too short a time for him to gain the confidence of the men, and without that he had better fall back and get his army well in hand, rather than hazard a battle with unwilling troops. Please give me the cause that led to McClellan's removal, as we never see a newspaper. By the way, I have not had a letter from home, or anywhere else, since leaving Sharpsburg some two weeks ago. What the reason is I do not know, as our march would not prevent the mail from following. . . .

I do not know what the program is for our future, but hearsay has it that we advance tomorrow. This can hardly be so as it will take Genl. Burnside several days to take hold of things and to study the plan of the campaign. . . . I will feel obliged if you will mail a pair of buckskin gauntlets, open at the side. I will pay for them on payday. It is very cold weather to be out doors, day and nights together, and I suffer from my hands a good deal. . . . By the way, I forgot to mention that the snow has all disappeared, gone, the warm sun at midday dispersed it, cleaned it all away. An officer has just reported the enemy strongly entrenched at Gordonsville, where he awaits our coming; this through some of the communicative inhabitants of Warrenton. Have you seen Lt. Smith yet? Lt. Jno. Thomas desires to me to state, that in reply to a query in a former letter of yours, that upon close inspection, he is happy to report <u>no soldier bugs</u> present for duty, but that all are absent <u>with leave</u>.

I forgot to mention that Thomas, West, Binney and myself took dinner at the house of Ruddy White's parents in Warrenton. You remember he was killed at Shepherdstown. Warrenton is not much of a place, probably 4 or 5 hundred inhabitants, but is said to be the largest town in Fauquier County. It has quite a large frame hotel—Genl. Burnside's head quarters.

Upon taking command, Burnside organized his six army corps into three Grand Divisions. The 5th Corps, grouped together with the 3rd Corps, constituted the Center Grand Division, which was placed under the command of Maj. Gen. Joseph Hooker.

Donaldson immediately felt ill at ease with the new commanding general. "We do not think he can command this army," he had related to his brother upon Burnside's appointment, and later added prophetically, "We will be beaten, I feel sure."

Burnside abandoned McClellan's plan of advancing along the Orange & Alexandria Railroad through Culpeper east of the Blue Ridge, and instead headed southeast along the line of the Rappahannock River toward Fredericksburg. Once there, he intended to cross into the tidewater region of Virginia, with its shorter, water-based supply routes, and advance on Richmond from the east.[11]

When the lead elements of the Army of the Potomac reached the north bank of the Rappahannock opposite Fredericksburg on November 17, they found it lightly defended, but the pontoon bridges necessary to cross the river were held up by a nearly unbelievable set of blunders and red tape. By the time the bridges arrived on November 27, Lee had been able to get most of his force dug in on the heights behind the city. When Burnside was finally ready to cross, the Confederates were waiting.

Belle Plain, Va.
November 24th, 1862

Dear Brother:

. . . My last letter was from Warrenton, in which I gave account of the farewell of McClellan, and stated, I believe, that Genl. Fitz John Porter remarked to us his turn would come next. Well, it has! He has been relieved, as you doubtless know, and had <u>his</u> farewell review of the corps on Wednesday the 12th. A sad, sad review it was. Our people love Genl. Porter, and his departure from among us is the last straw to break the camel's back. We are a listless lot of soldiers I can tell you; whose turn comes next I would like to know. Saturday 15th inst. Genl. Hooker reviewed his Centre Grand Division, composed of the 3rd Corps, Genl. [Stoneman], 5th Corps, Genl. Daniel Butterfield.[12] Our Division is now commanded by Genl. Griffin[13] and brigade by Col. Barnes. Genl. Hooker remarked after this review, when meeting the officers of our brigade at his Head Quarters, that with his two splendid Army Corps he could go any where in the southern states and the whole rebel population couldn't stop him.

That we are not yet considered <u>veterans</u> by the older troops an incident which occurred at Sunday's inspection on the 16th will illustrate. We had just been formed on the color line, preparatory to wheeling into column for the ceremony of inspection, when the 13th N.Y. of our brigade passed by, with its "<u>gallant</u>" Col. Marshall at its head. They were marching in column of companies right in front, and were a little unsteady. Our regiment remained quietly watching them, Lt. Col. Gwyn evidently deferring our movement until they had passed. Col. Marshall, upon noticing their wavering line, called out in a loud, insulting voice heard by us all, "Steady there, steady, any one would suppose you were a parcel of Pennsylvania ragged a———— militia! Steady!" This from a regular officer, a graduate of West Point, it was unbecoming, uncalled for, and exceedingly ungentlemanly, and had I been in command of the 118th, he would have been called to an account for it, sure! But then Lt. Col. Jas. Gwyn is not on this sort of thing; rather fight, devil, and worry his subordinates. Since this time Col. Marshall has been known as the <u>Red Warrior</u> because of his fierce red whiskers.

<u>Nov. 17th</u>. We broke camp and amid a drizzling rain moved shortly after 6 A.M., and after marching through Warrenton, bivouaced at a little place called Elk Town situated on a little stream of dirty, muddy water. A few houses and barns constituted this <u>town</u>. Quite a number of roads cross one another at this place. I should judge we had marched in all about 12 miles this day. Here we stayed until about 11 A.M. the next day in order to allow the other divisions to get ahead, and then we pushed on, still amidst a drenching rain, and after floundering along for about 6 miles, reached "God knows what this place is called" about 6 P.M., encamping in the mud just where we halted. I never before saw such a place, and it being dark, there was no help out of our troubles, so [we] had to make the best arrangements we could for the night, and by putting down gum blankets had a soft bed of mud to sleep on, and a drenching rain to cool us off. "Mud camp" or "mud hollow" the boys call this place.

We stayed here until the next afternoon, Wednesday 19th, and then moved a few miles forward to a place called Hartwood Church. This is a lovely little backwoods one story brick church, with a little square belfry, capable of seating about one hundred people, and is planted right in the primitive forest. I don't know its denomination or where its congregation comes from, but presume from among the scattering farm houses around, of which it is in the centre. Strange scene this little house of God was witness-ing this day, artillery, cavalry, and immense bodies of hostile men making sacrilege its hallowed surroundings. Hartwood is in Stafford County (I am beginning to know a good deal of Virginia). We remained here until Sun-day 23rd, when shortly after 8 A.M. we moved, and after a 10 mile march encamped, as the heading of my letter shows, at Belle Plain. We are not at this place strictly speaking, but are nearer to Potomac Creek, but as our camp has not been named, I head my letter as near as I can to some desig-nated place. Belle Plain can be reached by boats and transports, which find good anchorage, via Potomac River and Aquia Creek. From the number of ammunition and supply trains here congregated, I take it this place will be the base of future operations.

You say you have met with Quartermaster Addicks, I wouldn't have much to say to him, as he is a great drunkard and decidedly on the borrow. Lt. Wm. West, I think, will be promoted shortly to Captain of his company. He deserves it, although being so extremely gentlemanly may militate against him with the Lt. Col. commanding. However, I will await the result with much interest, as I do not understand how he can be gotten rid of except for cause, and there is no cause other than I have stated. West is capable, efficient and a most excellent gentleman and soldier. . . .

My associates continue to be Jno. Thomas, Horace Binney III and Will West, rather an exclusive set, but I can not fraternize with the other officers. I am still of the same opinion, expressed some time since in a letter to you, as to the military abilities of our officers, both field and line. I feel very much alone in this regard, that I have no one whose opinion in tactical matters I can refer to, as superior to my own. This with all due humility. I will caution you, however, that this fact I want to be most sacredly kept, for I have no desire, not, indeed, any need to puff myself up. I merely state facts plainly and without reserve to you, my brother. Indeed Jacob, I do not like service in this regiment. Everything is so entirely different from the Cali-fornia Regiment that I fear I can not endure it. Lt. Col. Gwyn is so dicta-torial that it amounts to positive insult, and there are many other annoying things tending to make me very unhappy. I write with no desire to have you suppose I am dissatisfied with the service generally, or want to get home. It is not so. I feel that I would be unhappy in any volunteer branch of the army. I love the life of the soldier and would dearly like to be in the regular service. There, where discipline reigns, where every superior officer is an <u>authority</u> to appeal to, I could be what my dearest ambition longs to realize—an efficient, capable soldier, deserving recognition by these qualities.[14] Now in this command I feel have reached the top most round in ambition's ladder. Lt. Col. Gwyn does not like me, and I <u>despise</u> him, hence, although I obey literally his orders, I feel the time will come when I <u>won't</u>, thus, I say I am unhappy. However I will drop this subject, 'tis an unpleasant one, and will endeavor to discipline myself and endure to the end. . . .

. . . I am still in very robust health, and spirit, I was going to add, but I cannot in truth say this. I, like the balance of the army, am unsettled. . . . I regret very much that I did not get Mary Landell's cakes. I can assure her, even at this late time, they would be very acceptable. I would like to know, however, whether in making the "hasty cakes" time was wanting to wash her hands before mixing the dough. We are neat, particular people in the army, indeed very fastidious. Ask her whether she won't knit me a smoking cap, one of the pan-cake pattern, or, indeed, any pattern. If she has not this accomplishment, ask her to engage the services of some of her numerous female friends, and get me up something unique in red or other bright color. I am so very unfortunate in not having many female friends, not at least with whom I can take the liberty of asking such a kindness. . . .

From present indications, I think we will have a winter campaign. The enemy is in posession of Fredericksburg, while our army is opposite. I sincerely trust Genl. Burnside will not attempt taking the city at this time, as he will surely meet with defeat. He don't, he can't possibly know to what extent dissatisfaction exists in his army. How should he? There can be no possible doubt as to the result of an engagement at this time. We will be beaten, I feel sure. The men have lost that espirit de corps so essential to a fighting army, and until it is regained, Genl. Burnside had better sit right down and get his men in good humor again.

Our friend Jno. J. Thomas desires me to say that he cannot make so favorable a report as the last, in regard to the "soldiers companions." Upon close scrutiny of his mahogany colored underwear this A.M. he discovered a few hundred "soldier bugs," but as hundreds do not count for much, he soon removed them by a sharp application of hickory. He hopes to rest well tonight in consequence. You can direct as before—all letters will reach me with only the regiment as the address.

>─┤◆⟩─○─⟨◆┤─◄

Camp 118th Regt. P.V.
Near Falmouth, Va.
Dec. 8th, 1862

Dear Auntie:

Learning there would be a mail to start from here in a few moments, will take advantage of it and write you to know why it is I do not hear from Jac. I have written him repeatedly, but recd. no reply, wake him for me.

I think we will winter quarter here, at all events it looks very much like it. I can't see any strategy in squatting here in the cold. Do write me what on earth we are doing and when we will do it, as the folks at home know more about the movements than we who do the moving. It is hardly fair to say that we have "squatted" all the time, for since I last wrote you our brigade has been racing all over the country in our rear after Jeb Stewart's[15] cavalry, but as usual, like the city policemen, could not find any one of them about, altho' many traces of them were to be seen, especially at a place called Hartwood Church. It appears they gobbled a number of our cavalry who were loafing in the building instead of attending to duties outside. In this church, which, by the way, is without pulpit or seats, on the wall back of the channel is a half finished war like sketch in charcoal, done apparently by a master hand, and it is said our men were taken by Stuart as they stood around the officer who was making the sketch. That chap will have a chance now to draw upon his imagination in Libby as he speculates upon the "grub" he will receive there.[16] . . .

>—⊷—O—⊷—<

Camp 118th Regt. P.V.
Near Falmouth, Va.
Dec. 9th, 1862

Dear Jacob:

Owing to the absence of Capt. O'Neill, home on sick leave, I am acting as "Field Officer of the Day," and in consequence, am excused from all regimental duty. Thus having much leisure time on my hands I thought I could not better employ some of it than by writing to you. Being senior captain present for duty, I, together with ranking captains of other regiments, divide Field Officer duty with the various majors of the brigade, my tour of duty coming every 10 days or so, at which time I have entire charge of the sanitary, policing and guard duty of the whole brigade. I have just returned from visiting the different camps, giving to each regimental officer of the day instructions as to the proper policing of their quarters, and such other orders as Col. Barnes, the brigade commander desired me to communicate. It was with some misgivings that I summed up courage enough to get up on the quarter master's horse (a Field Officer of the Day upholds his dignity by being properly mounted) because I am not much of an equestrian, feel better on foot so to speak. But then it would be a big job to visit, on foot, all the different regimental guards, which, by the way, are turned out for the Field Officer by the call of the sentry, "Turn out the guard, officer of the day," when the regimental officer of the day approaches the guard house. . . .

Jno. Thomas and I took a ride over the surrounding country on Thanksgiving day, and got lost in the woods and did not get back to camp until nightfall. We were outside the pickets, altho' they did not alarm us, as we knew the enemy were across the river. Still for all that it was an unpleasant situation, and had it not been for the sagacity of our beasts, to whom we finally left the direction to be taken, we would have had to camp out all night. At several houses we passed we found the people very civil, especially the women, altho' to tell the truth, there were no others excepting an occasional old man. I attributed these civilities to the good looks of John Thomas, and to his insinuating manner.

You ask what are we doing? I refer you to the court-martial of Genl. Fitz John Porter[17] as to what our leaders are doing, and of course while they are lying and swearing away the life of this great man, this noble soldier, the army is wasting time in the face of a strongly entrenched foe, with an impassable river in his front. By our leaders I mean the fools at Washington, for of course I do not presume to say that the general who, in name, commands this army, has the remotest idea that he can order it to move. He, as well as every man and boy in the service, is aware that Stanton is the commander-de-facto. The patience of the soldiers may yet be tried too far—then look out for a second Cromwell and a dissolved rotten Congress. As I write these things, prudence tells me I do wrong, but I feel that I must speak my mind to you who appear to take so much pleasure in saying so many cruel things about the officers I think the most of. Now tell me why it is you think Genl. Pope such a good man? Surely we all know him to be an unmitigated liar, with his bombastic telegrams of imaginary victories. Explain to me how it is that you and the people in Philada. think him a great man? Or better still, do not answer the above, and do not again criticize our generals. No matter what their faults, I believe them all to be good patriotic men, striving in their best way to make war a success with us. I am no prophet, nor the son of a prophet, but I can predict certain defeat should Burnside attempt to attack Lee in his present entrenched position. I can't see, and here again comes in my want of military education, the necessity for an attack upon strong works. Why not move the army to one flank or the other of the Confederates, and make them let go of Fredericksburg and its entrenchments and come out and fight us? It seems to me that because the enemy builds large fortifications right in our path, that is no reason why we should attack them. If we get to their rear without fighting what good are the works?

It looks very much as though we would winter quarter here. I will be glad, as it will give my man George an opportunity to regain strength, for the weather is so very much against him that without shelter he cannot recover. We have been on a run after Stuart's cavalry since I wrote you, and after forced marches to Hartwood Church and vicinity, in which we saw no one, returned after an absence of two days.

Lt. Col. James Gwyn continues his persecutions. Today he sent an orderly to my quarters, and although I was standing just without my tent, the fellow entered without ceremony and proceeded to search it. Upon my ejecting him and demanding what he meant by such conduct, he said the colonel ordered him to search my quarters for a stolen stove. This was too much, so I proceeded to head quarters, and in a tone of voice anything but respectful, demanded to know the meaning of the insult put upon me. The Lt. Col., feeling perhaps he had gone too far, said no insult was intended, but that understanding a Sibley stove belonging to him had, by mistake, been delivered to my quarters, he had sent the orderly to see whether such was the case, and that the orderly had obeyed <u>literally</u> the instructions given him. Merely remarking that I regarded it an affront to have him believe I would keep the stove had it been so delivered, I without ceremony took my leave. Hatred was stamped upon every lineament of his countenance, but <u>Fear</u> kept him from resenting my unmistakable manner. I have this Gwyn in my grasp should I care to use what I consider a cowardly advantage. But I will wait and see. I have a grave charge of immorality against this fellow that would rid the service of him should I make the charge.[18] It may be necessary some day to do this, but I think should the occasion arise, I would rather retire from the service than do what I consider an unmanly thing. However, I feel that I will be obliged to open on him some day, and come home on charges for "disrespectful conduct towards a superior officer." . . .

Burnside's plan of attack against the well-fortified Confederate positions that lined the hills in back of Fredericksburg was not without merit. Had his orders been properly communicated and executed, his offensive might have succeeded. Maj. Gen. William B. Franklin's Left Grand Division, consisting of the 1st and 6th Corps, was to lead off the assault, crossing the Rappahannock below Fredericksburg. Once over the river, their goal was to break through the Rebel works that stretched southward along the line of the Richmond, Fredericksburg, & Potomac Railroad, and then wheel north, taking Lee's position in reverse.

Burnside hoped that Lee would be forced to send reinforcements to his right to parry the threat from Franklin, pulling troops from his lines near Marye's Heights directly behind the city in the process. Maj. Gen. Edwin Vose Sumner's Right Grand Division, composed of the 2nd and 9th Corps, would then attack Lee's weakened left and, as the plan went, force him to retreat. Hooker's Center Grand Division was to be held in reserve, ready to reinforce the attack from any point.

Things went wrong nearly from the start for the Federals. After some initial success below the city, Franklin failed to push his attack vigorously, and as a result, Sumner was faced with the well nigh impossible task of carrying the heavily defended positions on Marye's Heights. While wave upon successive wave of Yankees were mowed down in the face of overwhelming Confederate fire, the 1st Division of the 5th Corps was sent out from the city to reinforce Sumner. As the 118th Pennsylvania and their comrades in the 1st Brigade advanced up the sloping ground toward the Rebel lines, they passed their division commander, Brig. Gen. Charles Griffin, and heard him remark to no one in particular, "There goes one of my brigades to hell, and the other two will soon follow."[19]

Camp Near Falmouth, Va.
Dec. 16th, 1862

Dear Brother:

Once again we are at our old camp. The newspapers have given such accounts of our disaster at Fredericksburg that I need scarcely enter into details just now. However I have made some notes of our doings in this campaign and will make them the subject of a letter to Auntie, so will, therefore, merely outline experiences of the last few days. I have no comments to make—the army was glorious, nothing wrong with its material, but its strength and capabilities were misdirected, that is all. . . . Regimental loss 125 killed, wounded and missing. Maj. Herring shot thru' both arms—home.[20]

With this campaign I feel I have had enough soldiering in this regiment, unless a change of commanders can be had. Lt. Col. Jas. Gwyn is a drunken, dictatorial, worthless fellow, not fit to command gentlemen. I desire to know whether you can secure influence enough to have my resignation approved by the Sec. of War. I feel that I must leave this command upon the first opportunity. I forgot to state that I am entirely unhurt and in perfect health.

＞—＋◆＞—O—◇＋—＜

Camp Near Falmouth, Va.
Dec. 18th, 1862

Dear Brother:

Yours of the 9th and 13th to hand, and particular attention paid to contents of former. Note what you say relative to coming home. Of course you know I would be unwilling to do this other than in an honorable way. I will be glad if you can suggest any plan whereby I can be transferred or removed from this command. To be on the outs with the commanding officer forebodes a dark future. I feel sure of great unhappiness under Gwyn. I want to serve my country if I can, but am not willing to do so at the expense of my manhood. In other words, a check has been put to my enthusiasm, and I can gain no further promotion while Gwyn lords it here. I admit, frankly, that I am ambitious, and want to rise higher, feeling confident of my ability as an officer of higher grade than captain. I know too that the field officers of this command are cognizant of my fitness for command, but I feel that with the enmity of Lt. Col. Gwyn I am at a stand still. He knows my worth, and also, that by keeping me down, he can have no greater satisfaction. I wrote you hurriedly yesterday outlining the Fredericksburg fight. Am now preparing a full acct. of the battle which I will send to Auntie. I am so glad to know that you have heard from John. Poor dear boy, although he is a rebel, engaged in a wicked cause, he is a noble fellow—blood is thicker than water. . . .

＞—＋◆＞—O—◇＋—＜

Camp 118th Regt. P.V.
Near Potomac Creek Station, Va.
December 27th, 1862

Dear Auntie,

. . . Heretofore I have had but one uninterrupted career of success as a soldier since the time of my first enlistment, rising from the ranks to my present position by close attention to duty and by good conduct in times of trouble, and have been repeatedly complimented by my superior officers, upon many an occcasion, for gallantry both as an officer of the skirmish line and for the handling of my company under adverse circumstances in the face of the enemy. But I now come to a period in my military career that, for the first time, I gained anything but glory from my conduct in battle, and from the effect of the misfortune that befell me at Fredericksburg, I suffer a mental torture most distressing. I will try and state concisely the facts of the case and let you and my friends be the judges whether my conduct at that battle reflects upon me as a soldier. I feel much mortification at being compelled to explain my conduct in time of battle, but, as Major Herring remarked when talking over the affair with him, my previous record is so very brilliant that I should cease to worry, as all know me to be a good soldier and a brave man. I write plainly, and trust in speaking of myself as I do, I may be fully understood as not, in any way, trying to puff myself up or desiring to boast of myself. I believe, however, I have never been guilty of this, and the present occasion is the only one where in I have ever alluded to my personal qualities as a soldier. But, as I have said, I believe it necessary to be as concise as possible, and, therefore, state all the surroundings of the case in order to be fully understood, and mention these things by way of preliminary remarks. I believe I feel more keenly this trouble than any other that has ever befallen me, for the reason that having always held those around me to such a strict accountability for their conduct in battle, that I probably feel, in justice to them, that I am in duty bound to review my own conduct just as severely when called into question as upon this occasion, and to pass upon it just as severely as I would do upon the conduct of others who failed to do their whole duty. But to the story.

We remained in camp from the 2nd to the 11th inst. doing the usual camp duties, the only interruption to which was an order from Head-Quarters to prepare and have in readiness five days cooked rations, but as this order had been so often issued without any result following, we paid little attention to it, other than to have on hand the cooked rations required. But on this day (11th) at about 4 o'clock in the morning the sudden roar of cannon was heard, and the bugle sounding to "pack up" shortly after soon made things lively, and bustle and confusion reigned. We were ordered to leave everything standing and to march in light marching order, which portended, as we thought, a reconnoisance in force somewhere. Thinking it might be sometime before I would again see my quarters, I determined to put on a full change of clean undercloths, and as it was very dark I did not notice that I had placed my flannel shirt on wrong side out. When about to rectify the mistake, my man George stopped me, saying in his earnest way "Don't do that Captain, for it is bad luck to change a garment after having made a mistake in putting it on." To please him I did not take the shirt off, but the sequel proved George to be a bad Prophet. From the outset of this campaign things did not go right with me. I was exceedingly cross to the men for their tardiness in getting ready, and spoke to several of them sharply, a thing so unusual for me to do that there was much comment among them about it. I remember to have been particularly severe on Private Ayres[21] for his persistence in singing different religious tunes, which somehow irritated me a good deal. I did not like the man anyway, because he was so good at excuses, and then, too, he was such a remarkably good natured fellow with it all, always laughing whenever I spoke cross to him, which was pretty often, and I did not like him for that either. He was constantly endeavoring to be funny and to attract my attention, besides he was prominent among the Psalm Singers of the regiment, always singing in public like mad, a thing that gave him no standing among the duty loving men. Indeed, I did not consider him a manly soldier by any means. In fact, to sum up, although I had never been able to lay hands upon him for any willful neglect of duty, I was aware of his constantly shirking the same, and when called to account for dereliction he was sure to have some good excuse trumped up and I would be obliged to excuse him. I am very particular in stating all this about Ayres because I consider that by pure dumb luck the fellow got even with me afterwards, as I will show, and I tell it as rather a good point made on me.

I say the men generally annoyed me a good deal this morning and I went among them scolding right and left. Poor Lieut. Coane, too, came in for a share of this, and I made him look sharp, I tell you. We were not left long in doubt as to our destination, for as we moved out of camp at about 7 o'clock and fell into line with the other regiments of the brigade, instead of taking the old track towards Hartwood Church, which, somehow, we always thought was the true direction towards the enemy that is to have any success, we marched directly towards Falmouth and soon arrived on the heights overlooking Fredericksburg. All along the road as we passed there was every evidence of preparation, on a grand scale, for a great battle. Hospital tents were everywhere erected in favorable and convenient locations. Caravans of ambulances were parked in readiness for immediate service, whilst piles and piles of stretchers were being moved to the front for distribution among the troops, and last but not least, the accumulations of straw in bundles everywhere met with told us plainly as words could do that our leaders anticipated desperate and bloody work.

As was usual with him whenever we started on a march, and, indeed I may say, whenever a good excuse for doing so offered, our Lieut. Colonel, James Gwyn, who was in command, commenced filling up with rum, and by the time we got to Falmouth was pretty full of "Dutch Courage." This kept up all day, much to my wonder, as I did not understand how it was that his canteen held out so long, until I ascertained that it was by tippling with the Field Officers of other regiments that he managed to husband his own supply. This conduct on the part of Gwyn greatly disgusted us all, and went a great way towards increasing my annoyance. . . .

Our whole Centre Grand Division was massed here, and we could distinctly see the enemy's earthworks on the hills back of Fredericksburg. What under the sun could have induced Genl. Burnside to attempt storming them is beyond my comprehension. Why, even to one who knew scarcely nothing about the art of war the thing looked simply preposterous. The whole army could easily see the work laid out for them, and the men were anything but enthusiastic over it. They could tell at a glance how impossible it would be to take the works that had been quietly in progress of building for weeks, while their commander waited until their finish before attacking them. I learned this day that as early as the 21st of November Genl. Sumner had sent his Provost Marshal, General Patrick,[22] to summons Fredericksburg, and had been replied to by Genl. Lee declining to give the place up, and then the whole army settled down until Lee had covered the place with impregnable works before moving upon them. My God! what fearful blundering, what an infernal want of military skill the change of commander has brought us.

After waiting nearly all day and there appearing to be no prospect of our being moved away, I went up to the batteries to see what was going on. I found most of the guns of the 9th Corps, together with a number of heavy siege guns, in active operation shelling the city and fortifications opposite. The city of Fredericksburg lay stretched below my feet for at least a mile along the Rappahannock, whose banks were low on that side, and appeared to be quite a place of importance. Our batteries completely commanded it from the bluffs on our side [of] the river, which, by the way, seemed to be so very narrow, not as wide as our Schuylkill, I should say. The permanent bridges which lately spanned it were now utterly destroyed, nothing but the piers left standing. I saw the pontoon boats scattered along the shore where they had been left by the New York Engineer Corps, who were hugging shelter behind piles of lumber which, I think, formed the flooring of the bridges when laid. All their attempts to place the boats had resulted disasterously and [with] much loss of life, and the workers had abandoned the attempt as nothing could be done by reason of the terrific musketry fire which had driven them back so many times.[23] The enemy were in the houses and rifle pits along the river front. Whilst looking at these stirring scenes a large body of men rushed down the bluffs, and jumping into the boats, pushed them rapidly across under a galling fire, landed and drove the enemy from the river banks and houses, into, through and beyond the town. This most gallant deed was done by the 7th Michigan and 19th Massachusetts Regts., and was the most brilliant achievement of the campaign. . . .

The troops had remained at this place under arms all day, listening to the roar of the artillery, which up to this time never ceased for a moment, but as we could not yet distinguish any musketry firing, we presumed that our people had not, to any great extent, crossed the river, but judged they were doing so although it was nearly dark when the pontoons were laid. At about 5 P.M. we were called together and moved to the rear about a mile where we bivouaced in the woods for the night near a place called White House. I could never find out why this particular spot was so called, other than the fact of there being a solitary white washed shanty near where we rested. If there ever had been a settlement hereabouts, there certainly was none now; probably, and most likely, the soldiers had carried it away.

Dec. 12th. About 8 A.M. we moved again to the spot occupied by us the day before, stacked arms, and listened all day to the artillery duel. The troops under Sumner, in the meantime, were crossing into the city and taking position. During the day I went up again to the batteries and saw the troops passing over the pontoons amid the continual rain of shells from the enemy. The artillery of our whole army seemed to be concentrated along the bluffs, or Stafford Heights, as they are called, and belched forth great volumes of smoke as they threw their shells over the heads of the soldiers into the enemy's works, but as far as I was able to make out, without much damage to them. There was also a good deal of riding backwards and forwards of staff officers from the Phillips Mansion, Genl. Burnside's Head Quarters. As night approached we went into bivouac upon the spot we had been all day.

Saturday, Dec. 13th. Was ushered in with a heavy fog covering the face of the earth. I made an early start to Stafford Heights, and when between 9 and 10 o'clock the fog lifted a little, I looked upon a wonderful scene. I could see the enemy's batteries, extending along the heights in the rear of Fredericksburg, all ready to commence the work of death upon our army then crowding the city. The glitter of the arms of the soldiers flashed and blinded the eye, the city appearing to be literally packed with troops. At this moment the artillery on both sides commenced firing, which seemed to have the effect of again causing the fog to settle. I now went back to the command and as it was exceedingly monotonous doing nothing, I engaged in a game of cards with Capt. Crocker, Lt.'s Thomas and Kelly which soon became most absorbing, even to the exclusion of the stirring sights and scenes around us.

About one o'clock P.M. we were suddenly called to arms, when I again had occasion to speak to Private Ayres for his constant jabbering and singing, regardless of orders to keep quiet. I said I thought it more than likely within an hour or so, at least, we would be closely engaged with the enemy, and that I would then hear him sing another tune if his legs did not carry him in a contrary direction which, however, it was my purpose to prevent, as I was determined he should face the enemy for once in his life. For the first time the fellow looked "taken down," and remarked to the men near him, but just loud enough for me to hear, that "the Captain was down on him for some reason or other."

As we commenced moving off with the division I noticed that Lt. Col. Gwyn was again pretty full of liquor, which I was very sorry to see, because when under its influence he becomes very domineering, abusive, and even brutal. Moreover, I did not care to go into battle with a drunken commander.

We halted occasionally as the troops ahead became jammed in crossing the pontoon bridge, and upon one of these halts Crocker, Thomas, Kelly and I finished the game of cards that had been interrupted by the order to march. When just concluding the game, Maj. Herring chanced to pass along, and noticing us made some remarks about our indifference, saying that we had better be thinking of the approaching conflict and the part we would soon be called upon to take in it. As the game was ended we put up the cards, but not one of us could be induced to keep them. Capt. Crocker explained the situation exactly when he said he did not care to have the only thing found about his clothes, when dead, to be a Euchre deck. So, we threw them away and laughed at each other for being superstitious.

We soon commenced passing down from Stafford Heights on the way to the river bank, and the raging battle beyond Fredericksburg lay before us in all its grandeur and horror. We could see the blue lines of infantry moving quickly up the hill, and then as quickly melt away. I heard many comments from the soldiers as they gazed upon the battle and generally to the effect that they wished the troops then engaged would drive the enemy, a wish that was just a trifle selfish, it is true, but which expressed very generally the sentiments of the soldiers. They felt defeat before encountering it. As we moved over the pontoons, abt. 2 P.M., there were several attempts made by the drummers of the regiment to shirk, and among the number, young Booth of my company. I had to handle him pretty roughly to get him along, and then he succeeded in giving me the slip afterwards, just as we landed in the town, and I have never laid eyes upon him since. He is now marked <u>deserter</u> on my company rolls.[24]

The sight that now met our eye was a very remarkable one, indeed. The city had been thoroughly sacked. The household furniture of the whole place lay in the streets. In every direction could be seen men cooking coffee on a fire made from fragments of broken furniture and I actually saw horses feeding out of a piano, the instrument part of which had been broken out to make a feed box of the body. Books and battered pictures lined the streets, bureaus, lounges, feather beds, clocks and every conceivable thing in the way of furniture lay scattered on every side. The destruction was appalling and most wanton, even if justified by the usage of war.

We turned into a street that ran parallel with the river but very near the outskirts of the city, and were partially sheltered by the houses from the dreadful shells, although the bricks, window shutters and shingles were flying in every direction as they were knocked off by the enemy's shot. We halted in line and remained here some time. I entered a dwelling opposite to where my company stood and found everything in confusion there. Several cannon shots had passed thro' the upper rooms, and the floor of one of the back rooms where a shell had entered and burst was piled high with bricks, mortar and books. It was evidently the library of a person of culture, as I noticed upon the shelves still standing many well recognized works of the popular authors of the day. I took from the collection a nicely bound volume of Waverly (Ivanhoe) intending to retain it as a souvenir. Thus you see that even I, a commissioned officer, was guilty of vandalism, but I justified myself in this <u>theft</u> by believing the city would, certainly, be destroyed by

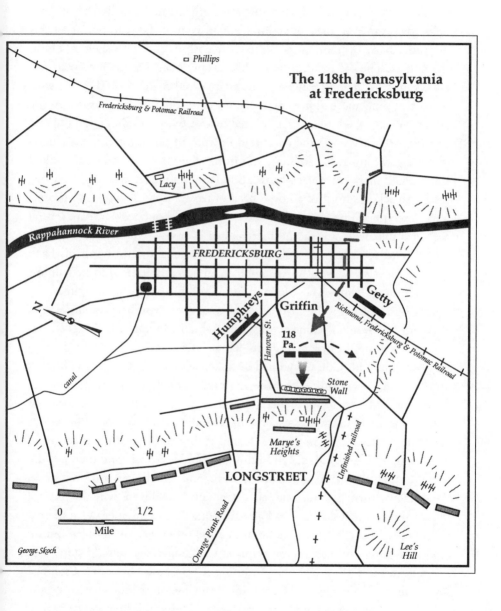

The 118th Pennsylvania at Fredericksburg

fire before we got through with it. However, I did not long enjoy the posession of the book as I lost it shortly after in the desperate charge we made up Marye's Heights.

A funny incident occurred just about this time. Usually the officer's colored servants, in time of action, remain well to the rear, but upon this occasion many of them crossed the river with us and took shelter behind the houses. The only exception to this was my man George Slow who was always up close during battle and never appeared to be afraid. He was with me at this time and had just taken my watch, money and papers, when my attention was called to another colored fellow, who, standing upon the end of a door that lay upon the pavement in front of the regiment, was laughing and grinning at the soldiers, and from where I stood, his teeth looked like a chalk mark on a black board. Suddenly a solid shot wizzed over our heads, struck the front of a house back of us, glanced, flew up into the air, and, descending upon the other end of the door, bounced Mr. dark several feet into the air. It was the funniest sight I ever saw. We just shouted with laughter to see the poor fellow fly through air and land upon his back about 10 feet away, with his woolly hair on end and himself turned almost white through fright. Maj. Herring added still further to the merriment by asking him, "What is the matter wid you honey, is you been foolin' with a torpedo?" The man hadn't words with which to express his disgust, but without waiting for orders to do so, left at once.

Meantime Lt. Col. Gwyn had been actively engaged in getting himself into proper condition to lead the regiment, and from the redness of his face, I judged he had succeeded. Whether it was the laugh that attracted him or his desire to impress us all with his indifference to danger, he, at this juncture, appeared upon the scene, and riding to the front and centre of the regiment commanded, "Attention!! Shoulder Arms!" and then put the men through the manual. When the command "Support Arms" was given he suddenly turned to me and said, "Captain Donaldson, why do you not repeat the command?" As I had already done so and my men were then at a "support," I replied that I had repeated the order. He again called out, in a loud tone, whilst his face was crimson with anger and rum, "I don't care sir, repeat it again." There being nothing for me to do but obey, I stepped out from the Company, and facing down the line, in as loud a voice as possible, gave the command to support arms. The whole occurence was so ridiculous that the men grinned audibly. Again addressing me, he said, "You will be careful, in future, to repeat the command," and then rode off, leaving the men still standing at support arms while he went away to get some more "<u>condition</u>."

Soon after we were ordered to load, and shortly afterwards our brigade moved off past Col. Barnes, our brigade commander, and staff, towards the main or principal street running through the city, out which we went to the front. The shot and shell flew over and amongst us, and it certainly did appear, as was afterwards said, that the Confederates had guns to cover each street leading out of the city. I noticed a number of men behind the houses at the corners of the streets, watching us as we passed by. They were stragglers, or men who had been "<u>in</u>" and were demoralized. Their silent, sullen aspect did not encourage us much. I also noticed two brass guns, well towards the end of the streets out which we were passing, firing at the enemy, but how in the world they were able to do so amid such a storm of shells was beyond my conjecture.

Some of the shells that struck near us performed many curious tricks. One, in particular, appeared to have come obliquely into the middle of the hard street, ricocheted, striking the front of a house up which it ran, tearing off a window shutter, then flew over to the other side of the way, striking the house opposite, and then down again into the street just missing my company, and then into the house it had first struck, coming to a stand still near the steps and not exploding, a fact I am happy to record of nearly all the shells thrown at us here. This tremendous fire had the effect of scattering my company somewhat and I was in momentary expectation that it, and indeed the whole command, would break to the rear. But beyond avoiding the centre and keeping to the pavements on either side [of] the streets, the men behaved splendidly.

As we debouched from the town we passed near a sign board, upon which was painted in big black letters Van Haugen's Variety Store. I had merely time to notice this as my company passed by, when a shell struck the sign, knocking it into fragments and hurling them over Co. K just in the rear of me, but hurt no one as far as I could ascertain. A moment after, a shell struck into the 1st Michigan Regt. of our brigade, which was immediately in the rear of us, killing and wounding 16 of its men, whose cries and shrieks could be heard above the roar of battle. Shortly we came to a swift running stream, which I afterwards found to be a canal, into which we plunged and crossed to the opposite side. As I splashed into the water I noticed Maj. Herring there, on horseback, urging the men forward and calling to them to close up. Col. Gwyn I did not see but presumed he was at our head. The tempest of shot was fearful at this point. Private John Mensing,[25] of my Co., met with a curious accident. As he ran forward with his musket aport, a shell struck and shivered it to pieces, but beyond a severe cut on the right hand, he was otherwise unhurt. Private John Fisher's[26] right arm was shot clean off below the elbow, and four of my sergeants were knocked down by the same shot and more or less bruised and hurt. My loss at this point was nine men.

We now came to a piece of level ground of about 400 yards in width, not so much as that probably, certainly not more, and just beyond was a rather abrupt rise in the ground which seemed to me as though the hill had been cut away. This was at the foot of Marye's Heights. The only chance we had to form line was on this little level piece of ground, exposed the whole time to the enemy's artillery. We succeeded in this after a fashion amid great confusion, and then hugged the foot of the hill—the abrupt cut alluded to when I had a chance to look beyond me. From this abrupt rise or cut Marye's Heights gradually rises. At the top and beyond is an elevated piece of ground which commands it. Nearly to the top is a stone fence behind which the Confederates lay, and from behind which they kept up a constant discharge of musketry. Before reaching this stone wall there was a board fence which greatly impeded the advance of the troops. Humphreys division, of our corps, had charged up the hill but a short time before us, and from the appearance of their men, who covered the slope, I judged that although they had not succeeded in carrying the heights, they were too proud to retreat and had thrown themselves down to avoid punishment, and there they were, hundreds, thousands of them, in plain view, flat on their faces. Will you believe it—they were dead, all dead men that I saw, but did not know it at the time.

Meanwhile, although our men hugged closely the foot of the hill, great confusion existed, until finally, without attempting to form them into anything like order, a charge was ordered, by whom I do not know, and, indeed, I did not hear the order at all, but took up the movement as I saw others doing. The regiment now became very much mixed, each man appearing to be on his own hook. By tremendous exertions I contrived to keep ahead of the company, and by doing so kept my men pretty well together. The fire of the enemy, at this time, was something appalling, and right into the teeth of the guns we moved up the slope. Soon we came to a brick yard with a brick kiln standing in it, from which the bricks were flying in all directions as the shot tore into it. Behind this kiln, the ground was literally packed with wounded who had crept there for shelter. Our line did not halt here but swept on past the place upward until we struck the board fence alluded to. In front of my company, the troops who had charged before us had stopped long enough to break it down, and the bottom board alone remained standing. The evidence of this delay was painfully evident, as the ground was thickly covered with dead as they lay heaped upon one another. Towards the left the fence was still standing, and the men instead of climbing laid hold of and broke it down. The whole line halted here not knowing what next to do, as no orders could be heard owing to the roar of battle.

At this moment, Sgt. Van Meter, of my company, who, along with the rest of the men near me, had thrown himself down behind the one board of the fence alluded to, was struck in the crown of the head, the ball passing directly through the brain. I had been sitting on a little knoll with Lieut. Wetherill and Lt. Binney looking at the enemy, and noticing the shot strike Van Meter, went to him to see the extent of his hurt. I found him still conscious altho' his brains were oozing from the wound.[27] Ascertaining it was impossible to extract the ball, I gave him some whiskey and went back to where I had left Wetherill & Binney, and was surprised to find that beyond this point, there was not a man of the regiment to be seen. A great number of the men from various companies, and many officers, still occupied the ground they had at first taken up, and of those who were more to my left and nearer to that portion of the regiment who had left us, I inquired what had become of the balance of the command. They all said they did not know. Finding myself alone, as it were, in a peculiar position, and in command of a large portion of the regiment, I gave the order to fall back to the brick kiln, which was done—precipitately.

Halting at this point for a moment until I determined what next to do, my peculiar position suddenly flashed upon me. It was a time requiring instantaneous action on my part, as the brick kiln could not possibly cover all those attempting its shelter. I again ordered the men and officers to the rear, but remained myself to see what was going on around me, and to think what was the next best thing for me to do. I had not a shadow of doubt but that the command had fallen back, and I considered my course, thus far, to have been the correct one. I now turned my attention to the wounded who lay in great numbers around me, and proceeded to make bandages from ribbons, quantities of which lay around still unwound from the blocks. How it ever got there I cannot imagine, unless it had been carried off by some thieving Confederate who finally hid it among the bricks until a

Sgt. John Van Meter, Company H, 118th Pennsylvania Volunteers. The carte-de-visite was taken in January 1863 while Van Meter was recuperating from his Fredericksburg wound. THE CIVIL WAR LIBRARY & MUSUEM.

better chance could be had for getting it away. At all events, I feel confident our men could not have brought it there. However, it was turned to a good purpose, and to its presence, seemingly Providential, many a poor fellow owes his life, as other material could not have been had at that time, and their life blood was fast ebbing away. This ribbon and my whiskey did faithful work behind the old brick pile.

While thus busily engaged, I noticed a new line of troops advancing up the hill, over the piles of dead, in pretty good order, their Colonel on horseback, a most fool hardy thing to do. Then a battery of 6 guns came dashing out into the clear space at the foot of the hill, just back of the brick yard. These guns were brass 12 lb. Napoleons and were wheeled into position in less time than I can write about it, and instantly, as it were, the horses were all killed, and the men took to their heels and ran away as fast as their legs could carry them, leaving their guns and their officers, who, by the way, stood their ground and cursed the men lustily, but to no purpose. The guns never fired a shot. It was no place for a battery, and the officer who ordered it there ought to have been shot. It was, without doubt, the grossest of all the gross mismanagement of this shocking battle, or slaughter, for at no time during the day did it rise to the dignity of a battle. The Confederates themselves actually stopped the fight because they were too tired to kill anymore. They were gourged with slaughter. The new line advanced to the brick yard when the officer on horseback was shot and fell headlong off his horse. This officer, I afterwards learned, was Col. Cross, 5th New Hampshire Regt., the same who was with me in the ambulance when I, with two other wounded officers, was being taken after the battle of Fair Oaks from Savage Station to White House on the Pamunkey River. If you remember, I told you of the kindness of this officer, who, although severely wounded himself, nevertheless helped to keep me from jolting over the corduroy roads, and was otherwise kind to me. It was remarkable that the next time I was destined to see him was to witness his death. Three of his men gathered up his remains and bore them to the rear.[28] His regiment now broke and scattered in all directions and the advance ended. I noticed a number of the 5th New Hampshire loitering behind and plundering the dead. Private John Smith[29] of Capt. Crocker's Co. K, who was with me, was so horrified at this that he rushed at them with his musket and drove them off.

After this, finding I could be of no further use to the wounded, I was about to retreat to the city, when I saw 1st Lt. Wilson of Co. A coming up the heights—alone. He appeared to be oblivious to the extreme danger he was in and would occasionally stop to look at some of the dead, apparently to ascertain their regiment. The enemy noticed him and commenced a rapid musketry fire, but he appeared to wear a charmed life. The dust flew up as the bullets struck around him and I stood transfixed, momentarily expecting to see him torn to pieces. At last he reached the brick kiln and appeared not to have known he had done an act of bravery that, I venture to say, not one single man of the thousands comprising both armies would have dared to have done. I asked him where he had been. He said the regiment had left the city before he was aware of it, and after a vain search, he was going to the front to see whether he could find it. I told him of my experience and stated that I believed the regiment had fallen back, certainly the greater part of it had. He replied he had met them, but as the Field officers were not with them, he concluded they must still be at the front, and he was going to satisfy himself on that point. I expressed my doubt of his ever reaching the front alive, and spoke of his rashness, as I firmly believed the regiment was in Fredericksburg. He replied he had no fear, and started off up Marye's Heights, alone, facing the whole rebel army, and no doubt drawing from them, as he did from me, admiration for the display of the greatest courage, the greatest bravery ever before shown, on either side. As a proof of this feeling, he lived to reach the regiment, and therefore, could not have been fired at deliberately by them after he left me, as he was in point blank range, and a child could have killed him with a musket. I frankly confess I could not have done this without a positive knowledge that my regiment was at the front. Had I known this to have been so, I would have reached it at all hazards, but not, I fear, as Lt. Wilson did.

I say he reached the regiment, which was so. It appears that when I went to Sgt. Van Meter, and whilst engaged with him, the regiment, or so much of [them] who saw the movement, as a command could not have been heard for any distance, moved off by the left flank for about 300 yds., along the site of the board fence, in order to seek cover by a slight elevation in the hillside, and when I looked I could not distinguish them from among the others, who, lying flat on their faces, covered the hillside, hence my belief that the command had fallen back. The length of time elapsing from that when the new position was taken up by the regt. had familiarized the officers somewhat with the danger, and upon looking abt. them afterwards, and seeing the solitary figure of Wilson wandering about, he was hailed, and thus is accounted for his ever finding the regiment. Poor Wilson, this was the first time during his connection with the 118th that he had ever done anything to distinguish or to bring himself into prominence, and he would undoubtedly have reaped the reward of such gallantry had it not been for his dissolute habits, which did not leave him, and his achievement lapsed into a nine days wonder and was soon forgotten, whilst his drunkenness continued, and, up to this time, as heretofore, he continued of no earthly use to the service.

After watching Wilson depart on his "fools errand," as I thought, I again took in the situation and concluded to go back to the city. Private John Smith, Co. K, who alone among the few of the regiment still remaining behind the brick kiln seemed to possess any degree of coolness, said he would remain and look after the men and assemble them, after dark, on the river bank by the pontoon bridge. Bidding them all to be of good heart as darkness would soon end the fight and their troubles, I gathered up my sword under my left arm and ran from behind the bricks. I presume I made some remarkable time in covering the ground intervening between the brick kiln and the foot of the hill, as it seemed to have taken me but a moment in getting over it. I made my way to the outskirts of town, and behind the shelter of the first houses I found assembled the officers of the regiment who had previously fallen back. We divided and proceeded to gather up the command, which we soon succeeded in doing, as a heavy guard was at the bridges preventing stragglers from crossing, and bivouaced them for the night on the bank near the bridge over which we had crossed. I afterwards found George and had a good square meal cooked. Little after dark I turned in, that is, wrapped myself up in my overcoat and slept soundly through the night.

December 14th. Bright and early Private Jno. Smith arrived with the balance of the stragglers. He reported that he had gone out during the night to find whether any of the regiment was still at the front, but could not find anything of them, and had slept out there. He further reported it certain death for anyone at the extreme front to move, so completely did the enemy command the ground. There was no communication whatever with the front.

After breakfasting I strolled thro' the town. It was Sunday. But what does a soldier care about the Lords day? The streets were lined with wounded and dying men. The ambulances and stretcher bearers were strained to their utmost capacity, and all that could be done was to gather the wounded under the shelter of the houses. The town was actually choked with wounded, every house, every room and every nook and corner being filled with the mangled fellows. Our loss was estimated at from 15,000 to 20,000 in killed and wounded. I passed through the town and gained a good position for seeing from a window of a house on the extreme outskirts. I could plainly see our men still lying flat on their faces, just where they had been the day before, and not one among them daring to lift up their heads for fear of the dreaded sharpshooters, the puff of whose rifle, seen at all points along the enemys lines, told, too well, that there was still uncovered portions of the person of many of our brave fellows. There was no artillery firing on either side.

An incident occurred whilst the men were at this point which I think will bear repeating. Towards noon the men appeared to suffer greatly from their constrained position, and Capt. Crocker, unable longer to remain so closely held to the ground, suddenly jumped up, and seizing the colors, jammed the staff into the ground a short distance in front of the line and then deliberately shook his fist at the enemy, calling them some very stirring names. As he came back to his place, a bullet struck and passed through his canteen, letting out the whiskey in a great stream. Lt. Kelly, who was quite near Crocker and who was equal to the emergency, rose up on his knees, seized and placed the canteen to his lips and finished it before Crocker knew what was the matter. Neither of these officers received the slightest injury altho' the firing was quite lively. Shortly after, Capt. Bankson, not to be outdone, jumped up, ran along the front of the regiment to the colors, seized and waved them backwards and forwards before the enemy, then stuck the staff in the ground and returned to his place without a scratch.

I forgot to mention that as I passed through the town to this point I learned that my friend Capt. Kennedy of the 1st Michigan had been mortally wounded and was lying in one of the houses in the centre of the city.[30] This was a great shock to me, as it was to all the officers of our regiment. Capt. Kennedy had made himself particularly agreeable to us ever since we joined the brigade, having been the first of the old soldiers to make our acquaintance, and was, in consequence, held in high regard by us all. He was a man of splendid presence, a jovial, kind hearted and brave gentleman, whose wise counsels will be greatly missed by those accustomed to consult him. I did not go to see him, fearing to intrude, as I was told he had made his peace with his Maker and was meeting death as a soldier should. His hurt was in the thigh, which a shell had dreadfully shattered, and his death, in consequence, would be lingering. Poor fellow! poor fellow! how well do I remember the last time I saw him, how vividly I can see him now, as standing in front of his company with drawn sword flashing in the sunlight, his cheerful face lit up with excitement, he unconsciously and calmly awaited his death wound at the foot of Marye's Heights.

I hung about the outskirts of the city all day, longing with my whole heart and soul to be with my comrades, and as darkness commenced to settle over the earth, I passed out over the battle field to find the regiment. It was a difficult task to do, and I wandered about not knowing where I was going. It seemed to me that I could find any other regiment of our division without much trouble, and it was not until near 10 o'clock that I met them on a road near Marye's Heights as they were returning from the front, having been withdrawn. I at once reported to Col. Gwyn, who greeted me by asking where I had been keeping myself, which so enraged me that I replied I had been keeping together the 225 men of his regiment that he had ran away from. Other words followed when I asked him whether he took exception to my conduct and if so my sword was at his disposal. He replied that he did not want it, and for me to go to my company, as he would see me again about the matter. I then went to the company and found several of my men who had succeeded in keeping with the regiment and who were delighted to see me, fearing that I had been killed. Among others who saluted me was Private Ayres, who bawled out at the top of his voice in unmistakeable sarcasm—"Capt., I have been at the front all the time." I had nothing to say. Ayres had the best of me.

I piloted the regiment to the bivouac on the river bank and was soon telling my friends of my experience. I found the loss of the regiment to be 125 killed and wounded. Among the very severely wounded of my company were Sgt.'s Crossley,[31] Joyce[32] and Van Meter, and Privates Robt. C. Bennett,[33] Jno. B. Fisher, Thos. Reynolds[34] and Timothy Tierney[35]. There are many others badly bruised and slightly wounded who will be ready for duty in a short while.

Monday Dec. 15th. The ambulances had been busy all night long removing the wounded to the other side of the river, and were still at it when we breakfasted. Our brigade was allowed to remain, resting, at this place all day. After thinking well over the conversation had with Gwyn the night before, I concluded to demand a Court of Inquiry, and about 10 A.M. went to where he was sitting and said that I considered his remarks had reflected on me and I desired to ask for a Court of Inquiry, which I believed was my privilege. He displayed a good deal of feeling, especially in manner, as he said he would rather let the whole matter drop, as he had not made any comment about my conduct, neither had he heard anyone else do so. I insisted, however, in my demand, when he said I should be accommodated. Meanwhile, I was to keep command of my company until after the campaign had ended, when I would be given a speedy hearing. I thanked him, and said if there was any blame to attach to the men and officers who had been with me, I desired to assume the whole of it. "Very well, sir," said he, "but remember you have brought this investigation upon yourself and you shall be 'put through'." I replied that that was what I most desired, and if there was to be any "putting through" done, that maybe I could do some of it myself, as I still retained the charges I had once before preferred against him, and, if he would remember, had withdrawn, <u>at his most humble request to consider his wife and children</u>. I then left him to think the matter over. It was my determination to have a fair hearing, and in order to do this, I had to use the weapons this drunken beast had put into my hands months ago, of which I wrote you a full account at the time.

Shortly after noon Genl. Burnside and staff passed down to the river and crossed over the bridge near us. The men stood and silently looked upon their commander—they had no bad words to offer him, nothing but pity. There was no soldier more respected in the whole army than Genl. Burnside, but he had now lost the confidence of the men and was of no further use to them. They felt, and by their silence, showed this. Burnside pulled his hat down over his face and looked neither to the right nor the left.

At dusk we were ordered to fall in and at once started again to the front, taking up a position in a street at the extreme rear of the city, as we afterwards learned, to cover the retreat of the army. We were ordered to lie down and keep extremely quiet. The tin cups of the men were taken off their belts so there could be no rattling, and every precaution was taken to maintain the greatest silence. It was a terrible night, the wind blowing a gale from the enemy to us, so that sounds at the front were quite distinctly heard by us. The window shutters banged and rattled, while occasionally a shot would be fired here and there on the picket line. We were without orders of any kind and did not know at what moment an attack would be made on us. Altogether it was a most horrifying night.

During the time we remained here I occupied the cellardom of a house in the centre of a row of nice brick dwellings, and directly opposite was a drug store. Notwithstanding the harrowing nature of our position, I could not but be amused at the sharp report, now and then, of bottles falling in the store, as some of the soldiers, groping their way along the shelves seeking something to steal, would knock them down. The Col. would command the officers nearest to the store to arrest these pilferers, and upon one occasion, I ran into the store, seized a fellow in the dark, who in violently shaking himself loose from me left in my grasp a bottle of Ayers Cherry Pectoral, which I quietly pocketed and afterwards mashed as I thoughtlessly threw myself down on the cellar door.[36]

About 4 A.M. we were suddenly called to arms and as suddenly moved off to the lower end of the town, where a pontoon bridge <u>had been</u>, but which was removed before we got there. We were then double quicked in another direction, and then back again, and finally we were just in time to reach the old bridge as the engineers were pulling up the planks. We lost no time in having them fix them again, and amid a drenching rain which had set in, we crossed to the other side. A happier set of men could not well be imagined, to have the river once more between us and the Confederates. It appears we were the last of the Grand Army to leave Fredericksburg, none remained but the poor pickets who were abandoned that the army might be saved, and of course were captured at early dawn. The officer who carried the order for us to retire had made a mistake as to the bridge for us to cross, naming the lower one when the centre bridge was intended, a mistake that came nigh being fatal for us, as the working parties on the different bridges went ahead thinking we were all right. We pushed right through to our old camp—near Stoneman's Switch. Just as we reached the other side of the river, Lt. Horace Binney, who had been sick all night, gave out, but as there were no ambulances at hand into which to put him, I relieved him of his accoutrements, and with his arm about my shoulders, struggled with him to camp, where I had George make him as comfortable as possible in my quarters.

I forgot to mention the return to duty of Lt. Batchelder, who joined the company at noon on this day (15th). For this I was truly thankful, for Batchelder was a skillful officer, well drilled, especially in skirmish work, was of fine personal appearance, and seconded me so ably, that I always felt sure of any work if he was with me. We had been old comrades and friends in the 71st and knew each other thoroughly. Batchelder has the clearest, most silvery toned and far reaching voice for command of any officer in the regiment. As I say, I felt rejoiced at his return from sick leave, and after seeing the company well fixed in camp, I turned it over to him and awaited the result of Court of Inquiry.

Nothing of moment occurred until the 20th inst., when at the order of the Colonel a meeting was held of the officers of the regiment who had been to the front at Fredericksburg to take into consideration my application for a hearing before them. The meeting was of short duration, when they unanimously declined to hear any statement from me, as there was no charge against me, neither did they consider that I had done anything at all that could call forth the slightest censure from the Colonel, as my reputation was established in the regiment. Adjutant Jas. Perot, in bringing this information from the officers meeting, said he desired to add his own personal regard and confidence in me and hoped that I would give the matter no further consideration. He also suggested the propriety of my addressing a letter to the Colonel expressive of my appreciation of the good opinion held of me by the officers, which I did, and in which I freely acknowledged that my lost opportunity at Fredericksburg was when Lt. Wilson left me at the Brick Kiln. . . .

A day or two after, we moved back to this place and regularly encamped for the winter in a lovely grove of Pine trees whose fragrance is something delicious. The men have built themselves substantial log houses, whose roofs, covered with shelter tents admitting both light and ventilation, present a scene of picturesqueness and comfort most enjoyable. Altogether our camp is beautifully situated and by reason of the sheltering pines is as warm as toast. The railroad, which supplies the army, is just a short distance in the rear of the camp, and greatly adds to the scene as the trains rush over the high trestle work crossing the Potomac Creek. By the way, this same trestle is a marvel of engineering skill, being at least 100 feet high, and built of pine trees placed on top of one another, and firmly braced. It was finished in one day by the builders, which to me is something stupendous in the way of rapid bridge building.

I believe I have stated fully all that has transpired on this wonderful campaign, and as I said in the commencement, I will leave it to you and to my friends to say whether I have acted badly and whether I am justified in thus distressing myself. However, I know one thing certain, and that is when next the opportunity presents itself, I will be found in the right place at the right time, or my life will answer for it. . . .

CHAPTER 5

The Mud March and Winter Quarters

December 26, 1862–April 23, 1863

*F*ollowing the defeat at Fredericksburg, the air that hung around the damp, smoky mists of the campfires of the Army of the Potomac was pierced with the clarity of hindsight.

Had Franklin thrown the bulk of his force into his attack below the city, Lee's flank might have been turned. Had Sumner attacked less determinedly on the right against the impregnable lines at Marye's Heights, many lost and crippled lives would have been saved. Or, as the historian Bruce Catton has suggested, had the assignments of the two Grand Division commanders been reversed, the cautious Franklin might have bumped up against Marye's Heights and pulled back, saving countless lives in the process, while the hard-charging Sumner could have brought the full force of four army corps against the Confederates' less easily defended lines on the left.[1] But these were the might-have-beens.

The reality was that by the time the Army of the Potomac pulled back across the Rappahannock on the night of December 15, almost 1,300 of its best officers and men had been killed outright, another 9,600 had been wounded, and nearly 1,800 were prisoners. Lee had lost less than half of what the Federals had, and although Burnside dutifully shouldered the blame for the defeat, it was little consolation to the soldiers in the ranks. Many, like Donaldson, longed for their recently deposed commander. "We must have McClellan back," implored a 5th Corps general. "His name is a tower of strength to everyone here."[2]

Camp 118th Regt. P.V.
Near Potomac Creek Station
December 26th, 1862

My dear Brother:

Yours of the 20th and 23rd inst. to hand and were gladly received. You may perceive by the heading that we have again changed camp, gone about a mile back, to obtain a better supply of wood and water. I have read carefully your remarks about my feelings for Lt. Col. Jas Gwyn, and answer all your questions by saying that there is an armed neutrality, so to speak, between us. Our ideas of military discipline are antagonistic and my subordinate position compels an obedience to <u>his</u> interpretation of a soldier's duty, consequently I am unhappy. Cringing, servile, slavish, humble, tale bearing and utter disregard for all that constitutes true manhood is not the idea I hold of discipline. The fact is our relations are somewhat strained, and although in a conversation lately had with him he assured me that he wanted to be a friend to me, but that I would not accept his advances, would lead others than the initiated to believe that I am forcing the quarrel. Gwyn and I can never agree, and as a consequence I must leave the service. I cannot do my whole duty under his command. But enough of this. . . .

In regard to your <u>favorable</u> comments on Genl. Burnside's letter, I can only add that I consider his "manly statements" as bosh, all bosh.[3] I presume you had a splendid Christmas. How you should rejoice in being at home, a free man, accountable to no one, with no brute of a soldier to tyrannize over you. The day passed as usual with us, with the exception of whiskey tippling indulged in by all, including myself. I thought a good deal of Auntie, and of how exceedingly low spirited she gets at this the happiest time of the whole year. Indeed I could for once truly sympathize with her, for it was anything but a happy time with me.

It is astonishing the extent to which drinking is carried on in camp, and were I so inclined there is no restriction or limit to the amount of whiskey I could drink. It appears to be a qualification in certain quarters to be able to carry an enormous amount of the beverage with the least possible exhibition of its side effects. It is a bad business I think. Sometimes I am so low spirited that I am sorely tempted to indulge largely in this favorite pastime, but I can scarcely think that to be the proper remedy for my <u>ailment</u>. The true course is for me to get out of this regiment, <u>honorably</u> if I can but somehow else if I can do no better. Time will give me the opportunity I sincerely trust. . . .

Our encampment is very beautifully located in a deep valley in the heart of a dense pine woods which are so sheltering and warm that at midday I run about in my shirt sleeves without discomfort. The rail road runs directly in rear of our camp. If you entertain an idea of visiting us, now is the time to do so. . . .

>–+‹›–O–‹›+‹

Camp 118th Regt. P.V.
Near Potomac Creek
Station, Va.
January 4, 1863

Dear Jacob:

Yours of the 29th was duly recd.—also package containing gloves—they came just in the nick of time, as the weather is getting very sharp. You did not state what was paid for them, please let me know and I will remit.

January 2nd. We had a <u>glorious</u> time—there being no less than <u>two tons</u> of boxes and bales received by the regiment from home. Every man and boy, it seemed to me, had a <u>roast turkey</u> and many other good things. Lt. Jno. Thomas' box was a marvel—there being no end to mince pies and segars it contained. We fairly gorged ourselves. . . .

Captain West is still very sick. I think his case serious and that he should be sent home. In the box received from his folks there was a smoking cap from his sister and a package of candy from Mrs. Flickever for me. I am very grateful for these kindnesses and can truly say that the candy has been enjoyed and the cap has been converted into a night cap by the "Little Captain" to whom it was addressed. Why in the name of peace I am called <u>little</u> passes me, as I stand 5 ft. 8½ in. in my government socks. It may be on account of my youthful appearance. Hang it! If I am a boy where did Genl. Jackson get all his men from?

I have just finished my <u>pay rolls</u> for November and December—nearly two days solid work, which although very tiresome is excellent practice for my handwriting, as this letter shows. You will not complain this time, I am sure. The regiment has never yet been paid off, which makes it rather "tight papers" with us. When the pay-master does put in an appearance he will settle up in short order having but one person to pay—Barney Hoops, Sutler. We are all mortgaged to him. . . .

There is much talk of our moving back to Alexandria for Winter Quarters. I give it no credence whatever, as it is not at all likely troops will be sent from here for garrison duty when the new regiments arriving at Washington could be utilized for that purpose, beside giving them every opportunity to learn the duties and the school of a soldier, so that in my judgment it is "Cook house" talk. . . .

>─┤◆>─O─<◆┤─<

Camp 118th Regt. P.V.
January 6th, 1863

My dear Brother:

Yours of the 3rd inst. just received. . . . I always write you freely as to my opinions, but of course, I am not the less a good soldier for having these feelings, as, save to yourself, I am careful to suppress them. I feel guilty, however, whenever I receive praise such as you send, as I am sure I do not deserve it.

Col. Gwyn appears to recognize my tactical ability and yesterday put the regiment under my command for battalion drill. I had Major Herring's horse, which, by the way, gave me more trouble to manage than did the regiment, but I succeeded in managing them both to my entire satisfaction. I will also add the officers gave me cordial and hearty support which made the afternoon drill a great success. After drill I held "Dress Parade," and at its close was warmly congratulated by Capt. Ned Landell[4] of Col. Ellmaker's 119th P.V., who came over to visit me. By the way, he looks in splendid health and I enjoyed his company for an hour or more. . . .

I have heard we will not be paid off until the 10th of March. If true this is indeed bad news. The Government must be hard up for money to keep us so long in arrears. I am entirely strapped. It is particularly hard on commissioned officers who are not rationed like the men, but have to provide for themselves. I am about out of credit, too, which makes it worse. Let me see! There is now 5 months pay due me. Well, it will come someday, and in the meantime I will trust Uncle Samuel and "shin around" for rations. . . .

This is written with watered ink, as are many of my letters, but I trust it will remain dark long enough for you to decipher what I say. After that it does not matter. We often run out of ink and have to divide it around, hence the watering. Good bye—I have run out of ideas.

>─┤◆>─O─<◆┤─<

Camp 118th Regt. P.V.
January 12th, 1863
Dear Jacob:

. . . Rumor has it that the Army of the Potomac is about to move, some say to again attempt the works at Fredericksburg, but this can hardly be so after its sad experience there. More likely a return to McClellan's plan of "on to Richmond" via Gordonsville, I think would be the proper and true road to that far off Capital of Rebeldom. I will however acquaint you of any preparations we make looking towards a winter campaign. . . .

It is extremely dull in camp, nothing at all transpiring to write about. I cannot do as you suggest; ask Col. Gwyn to approve my resignation. I would rather stay here to the end than be discharged through his instrumentality. I will not accept a favor from him. We will—you and I—abandon all further attempts at a discharge and await the turn of circumstances.

You ask whether the army is in better spirits. Well, I can hardly say. It certainly does not enthuse much when Genl. Burnside passes the camp. We see him often, but not the slightest notice is taken of him. How different it was when Genl. McClellan put in an appearance. Then the whole camp was alive, the men showing every evidence of pleasure at the merest sight of their beloved Commander. He is in our estimation the greatest General of modern times.

May I mildly suggest some other topic for your letters than your description of the battles of the west. We now have the papers and read all about them. I speak from purely a selfish motive, as I want to know all the news from home, and I never tire of reading that, no matter how many pages you fill. . . .

>-+-<>-+-O-+-<>-+-<

Head Quarters, Co. H 118th P.V.
Camp Near Potomac
Creek Station, Va.
January 13th, 1863
My dear Brother:

Not having had a letter from home for sometime, and learning the mail had arrived in camp, I proceeded to the Colonel's Head Quarters, and after ascertaining that during his absence the mail lay on his table undistributed, I entered, and a careful search found your welcome letter dated the 10th inst.

Hastening back to my quarters, I found the gentlemen I had left there still absorbed in "penny ante, subject to a raise." That is Captains Richard Donegan and Charles Fernald were hard at the little game of draw, while upon the lounge reclined Lieutenants Thomas and Hand, having been "cleaned out," to use the forcible language of the former. Even the sedate Lt. Batchelder was there also, and while never indulging in this soldiers pastime, yet countenanced it, this time, by his smile of approbation whenever the cautious Donegan occasionally went "one better" than the ambitious Fernald. Desiring to read your letter in peace and quietness, I asked the gentlemen [to leave], and after wishing me many good returns of my good fortune in getting a letter from home, left me alone to enjoy its contents.

I trust you will make a mental note of the foregoing "glimpse behind the scenes," and be convinced that to us every pleasure and amusement is as nothing when compared with the happiness of receiving a letter from home. Letters are the only source of actual enjoyment I have, and did you but know how disappointed I feel when I do not hear from you at least twice a week, I feel sure you would find time to indulge me that often. . . .

The camp of the 118th Pennsylvania near Falmouth, Virginia, during the winter of 1862–63. This previously unpublished sketch depicts the quarters of the field and staff officers of the regiment. The figure on horseback is believed to be Maj. Charles P. Herring, and the officer on the right is believed to be Lt. Col. James Gwyn.

Now I must insist upon the strict fulfillment of our compact—not to publish my letters without my full consent, and, therefore, you must withdraw your promise to Dr. R. Shelton McKenzie of the "Press."[5] For heaven sake, do not give him my letters; can't you see they are written in the fullest confidence? Were they published, people would think me the veriest egotist alive. There is nothing in them but self. While you and I know exactly the reason for this, others would say "this fellow carries on the whole campaign himself—alone." While my letters are merely descriptive of my personal experience, and are literally true, anyone reading them would feel that I said too much about myself. . . .

I don't think I told you of my man George's attempt at a surprise for me, in the matter of a stewed beef dinner. If I did, it will bear repeating. He succeeded admirably, so I am told, in preparing the savory dish, and in my absence set the table in a very elaborate way—table-cloth, plates, glasses, and a number of little side dishes or relishes of one kind and another. When everything was arranged to his entire satisfaction, he started off to hunt me up and the other members of my mess. I was detained at the Colonel's Tent, and George was away, in all, probably 10 minutes. During this time someone stepped into the tent and either devoured or else carried off everything to eat there was on the table. Poor George, when he discovered the sad havoc made with his good things, threw up his hands, lifting his hat the while, and exclaimed "Well! I never! I declare to gracious, der's been thieves around." I can not exactly tell upon who to fasten this mean trick, but I strongly suspicion the vainglorious Hand, and the consumate, consolidated old bummer Donegan to be the other. I have issued George the following order, borrowing the language of the illustrious father of his country— "Put none but Americans on guard tonight"—G. Washington. Hereafter George or his henchman Scipio Africanus will be about my Head Quarters all the time. Capt. West started for home today, poor fellow, he is very sick. Tell Auntie to go at once to see him, and report to me his condition. . . .

>-¡-◆>-◆-O-◆-¡-◄

Camp 118th Regt. P.V.
January 15th, 1863

Dear Brother:

. . . We are on the eve of a movement—all sick have been sent to the rear, and cooked rations on hand ready for immediate issue. A campaign is to be inaugurated—that is certain—but we have not much confidence in its successful termination. We don't believe in Genl. Burnside's ability to achieve anything very startling. Where we are to go I haven't the least idea, but so long as it is not against Fredericksburg I don't care. So do nothing until you again hear from me. I am writing this hastily for fear another opportunity will be wanting. . . .

You speak of Lieut. Davids being at home and of the kindly way he mentions my name. He is a man of few words, an earnest, honorable gentleman, and words of praise from him are golden. I believe it was through influence at Washington a leave of absence was granted him, as he never in the world would ask a favor of Col. Gwyn. I, having no such influence, cannot get home without the Colonel's consent. I will never get it, because I will never ask it, but would accept the leave were it tendered me.

What distressing news from the South and West, and how very difficult seems the task of subduing these energetic, brave, and I may say, wonderful Southern soldiers.[6] I continue in good health and do not, as one would suppose by my frequent and long letters, spend my whole time in writing. For instance, I gave a little set out last night to a few friends. It is true there was not much of a variety, but such as I had appeared to be enjoyed exceedingly, especially the butter punch. It was piping hot and made by George. I fear my friend Jno. Thomas was a little overcome by the insinuating beverage, as he has not reported for duty today.

The all absorbing question is where are we to move to! Is it forward or backward, advance or retreat? We are entirely at sea in regard to it. Do you hear any rumors at home? Surely some of the enterprising correspondents have been able to give their papers the cue? I am still on the "outs" with Col. Gwyn and rarely see him. I would not be surprised if we had it out some day, as he is too polite for anything with me. . . .

By the middle of January, Burnside had Lincoln's hesitant endorsement for a renewed offensive against the Army of Northern Virginia. Moving north and west along the Rappahannock, the Federals were to march around Lee's left and cross the river at Banks's Ford, flanking him out of his entrenchments and forcing him to either attack on the open ground west of the city or retreat southward.[7]

The movement, which commenced on January 20, began well, but on the first night out, a ferocious rainstorm set in, chilling the soldiers to the bone and turning the frozen roads on which the army was advancing into quagmires. "Misery loves company," wrote Donaldson, "and misery must have been satisfied that night." The

Army of the Potomac ground to a halt, and with the Rebels jeering at them from the south side of the river and plowing the earth around their intended crossing points into a bottomless swamp, the men were ordered back to their camps on January 22. Burnside resigned soon after, replaced by the ambitious Maj. Gen. Joe Hooker, commander of the Center Grand Division, and both armies settled into winter quarters.

From a military standpoint, the balance of the winter of 1862–63 was uneventful. The 118th Pennsylvania was posted along with the 5th Corps on a picket line stretching between Stafford Court House and Hartwood Church, breaking up the monotony with occasional reconnaissances into the surrounding countryside.

For Donaldson, the winter months were a time of soul searching. The tension between him and Col. Gwyn worsened daily, and though he did not wish to leave the service, he wanted desperately to leave the regiment, so much so that he tried, through unofficial channels, to resign his commission. "I am unhappy here," he wrote to Jacob, "and were I out of [the regiment], would at once apply for a position, no matter what the rank, in the California Regiment—my first, my only love." Donaldson's efforts were for naught, however, as Gwyn got wind of his unhappy subordinate's endeavors and made it clear to him that in no way would he endorse his resignation.

>-‹•›-•O-•‹•›-‹

Camp 118th Regt. P.V.
January 16th, 1863

Dear Brother:

Yours of the 13th inst. with Plitt Smith's[8] letter enclosed, to hand. I hasten at once to reply. I am sorry Smith says I must <u>at once</u> get leave of absence, and again, <u>that the delay of a day</u> may make a great difference with my chances. Now the "Fates" are against me, for how can I possibly do this? To ask for leave of absence on the eve of a movement would put a wrong construction on my motives. I can not do it, but will do the next best thing— enclose you my resignation addressed to the Sec. of War, trusting it will answer the purpose. You ask whether there is any <u>other</u> reason for my desiring to leave the service than my trouble with Col. Gwyn? I answer <u>No</u>! and will also add, I <u>do not</u> want to leave the service, but merely this regiment. I am unhappy here, and were I out of it, would at once apply for a position, no matter what the rank, in the dear old California Regiment—my first, my only love. Oh no, I do not want to leave the service. I love the life of a soldier and would like to make it my profession. With any other commander my ambition would be a transfer to the regular army, but with Col. Gwyn I am at a stand still. I feel there is treachery in all he says and does to me. He wants to lull my suspicions so that his revenge will be the greater when it comes. His manner just now is most gracious, his words most affable with me. But I know the rascal, the treacherous tyrant. Holding these feelings is it any wonder I want to get away?

Direct your letters as before, I will keep you posted as to our movements. We are all ready to leave, and could do so within an hour should the order come. What causes the delay I know not, but it is always so, we "dilly dally" until the enemy are apprised of our intentions, which makes the task so much harder to overcome. I am as usual in splendid health.

P.S. Orders have just been recd. to move at daylight tomorrow—good bye!

>—+—+>—+—O—+<—+—+—<

Camp 118th Regt. P.V.

January 19th, 1863

Dear Brother:

We are still here, in old camp, but under marching orders. I can give no explanation why we do not move. The weather is favorable and should be taken advantage of, because at this season of the year, it is hardly to be expected that good weather will long continue. Yours of the 16th inst. to hand with ten dollars enclosed, making in all twenty dollars I have received from you. Again I must thank you for your exceeding great kindness. Should this letter reach you in time please send balance in one dollar bills as it is difficult to get such large money broken without sacrificing a greater part of it in things really not needed.

This morning in passing near Col. Gwyn's quarters he called me and wanted to know whether he had been rightly informed that I was endeavoring to get my resignation through. Although taken by surprise, I did not for a moment hesitate, but met him squarely by saying that my brother was looking after the matter for me, that I was anxious to leave the service, and knowing how impossible it was to get a resignation through by the regular channels, was endeavoring to do so through influence at home. Without waiting his reply or seeking to notice that he would be angry at what I said, but rather that he would take it as a matter of course that an officer had the right to leave the service could he but get his resignation approved, I asked him whether it would be considered improper to apply for a leave of absence to visit Washington in order to see personally after my discharge. His face was a perfect study. It was very red, as from suppressed anger, yet it wore the appearance of doubt, seeming to say—can this man be deceiving me?, is he the innocent fellow he seems? Anyway, he said, with a little tremor of speech, always noticeable with him when excited, "You should have shown me your resignation, so that I could have endorsed it, but don't make application for leave, as I will certainly <u>not</u> approve it, at this time especially— for the reputation of the regiment, if for no other reason." Great Scott! didn't I read this fellow as I stood looking into his face? Let him endorse my resignation—forsooth! Well, I should rather think I wouldn't. And the "don't apply for leave, as I won't approve it"—speaks his true feelings— neither would he approve the resignation. No, it is not just yet that he wants me to quit the service, he must first get even—then I can go. Well, when he gets even with me, it will be because I let him, and it will be after his contemptible character has been shown up to the command. But how in the world did he know I had been trying to work my resignation through? A spy is somewhere near me, but who can it possibly be? I have so few friends, and have kept this matter so very close, that I am at a loss to quite understand it. Have you yet received my resignation? I do hope it will go through before Gwyn has time to stop it, as I know he will surely do if he can. All are well. Love to Auntie.

>─┼─◆>─○─<◆┼─<

Camp 118th Regt. P.V.
January 25, 1863

My dear Brother:

The newspapers, I presume, have been filled with the latest wonderful efforts of the <u>Great Successor</u> to Genl. McClellan, and glowing accounts given of how such and such a success would have occurred, had Burnside not been <u>stuck in the mud</u>. I can, however, confidentially assure you, had there been no storm to interfere with the late campaign, we would have been unsuccessful, because, like at Fredericksburg, Burnside delayed so long after giving notice of the intended movement that the enemy were fully aware of it and were prepared accordingly. Why! Oh! Why! don't they remove this comically incompetent general and if not McClellan, give us an officer we can have confidence in?

Well here we are back again at our old camp after the most wretchedly conducted campaign recorded in history. My mind is so shocked, my military pride so humbled that I care not to record the events of the past few days. I speak not only for myself but I voice the feeling of the whole army when I say, as I have before done, that Burnside is an utter failure. The men ridicule and laugh at and have no respect, at all, for him.

We struck tents about one P.M. Tuesday, January 20th and started off to the tune of the "The Girl I Left Behind Me." Every face was bright with the "devil [may] care" look of soldiers, perfectly indifferent to destination, nature of movement, or fate. No one cared, no one had confidence, and it made not the slightest difference whether they stayed in camp or inaugurated a campaign, it was all one and the same thing to them. The army had settled down into perfect indifference. We marched a distance of 5 miles and encamped in an extensive oak forest. It had been threatening rain all day, and towards dusk it came down, with high winds and torrents of rain as it can only rain in Virginia. It was impossible to sleep or even to keep dry, and the whole night long Thomas, Batchelder and myself marked time beside a fire that troubled George Slow to keep fit. Misery loves company and misery must have been satisfied that night. The men, being without shelter, stood up all night with muskets and cartridge boxes held close to their persons to keep dry, and just took the pelting, pouring rain as it came along.

The next morning, <u>Wednesday January 21st</u>, at daylight, everything was a sea of mud. A general order was read to the officers and as many of the men as could be gotten together setting forth the fact that the enemy were surprised and what Burnside intended doing when he crossed the Rappahannock and other chin music that set the men laughing.[9] "The old man is right," said one funny fellow, "the Johnny's will be surprised to find us stuck in the mud." Weary and wet we pulled out of bivouac an hour after daylight and commenced to wade in the mud. Heavens! what a scene. The mud was hub deep and wagons and artillery were stuck fast all around us. The guns had 12 horses to each but they could not get them along. In fact, the whole army that day was in a state of <u>heaving</u>, as it were, or to be more explicit, it reminded me of workmen lifting a heavy stone—for instance a "Now then, all together, heave!" and the army would advance a step. By the aid of well developed muscles and prodigious blasphemy three miles of Old Virginia's soil was covered that day. Could the southern press have seen us at this time, their appellation of "Mud Sill" as applied to the

Yankee soldier could very appropriately be changed to "puddle rangers." We bivouaced again in the woods and passed another night in marking time while it still poured and deluged beyond description. It was a kind of Noah's storm.

Thursday, January 22nd. We remained in bivouac, couldn't move, everything and every body stuck fast. The head of our army had reached the Rappahannock but were mired along its banks. The rebs, at Ellis Ford, where we were to cross, had a large board erected with "Burnside stuck in the mud" in large letters written on it. On another they had "Yanks, if you can't place your Pontoons over yourself we will send you a detail." They were seen busily plowing the ground over which we would have to pass had we forced the Rappahannock.

About noon of this day, an incident occurred which placed our brave!!! commander, Lt. Col. James Gwyn, in his proper light before the command. It appears that Gwyn and Col. Johnson of the 25th N.Y. having, as was their custom, been tippling quite freely, got into a discussion as to the relative merits of their respective pioneer Corps, and to settle the matter they selected two large trees of similar thickness and detailed a pioneer from each regiment to cut them down. They made a bet as to who could first cut down one of these trees, making it fall in a given direction. Fowler[10] was selected from our men and another Hercules from the New Yorkers, and at it they went. Fowler felled his tree in less than 10 minutes and made it fall as directed. The New Yorker was away behind and none of the conditions were complied with. As Fowler was wiping the perspiration from his face a New Yorker came up and laid claim to his axe, seizing it the while. A scuffle ensued which was speedily joined in by numbers of both regiments, and a fight took place involving the greater portion of both commands. I will add here that a full ration of whiskey had been served to the troops just before this incident occurred, which may account for the belligerent attitude of the two commands.

Into this fight, for some unaccountable reason, Capt. Crocker and Lt. Wetherill were drawn. Headed by these two officers the 25th was badly cleaned out and flew to arms. I shall never forget the appearance of Crocker, as after fighting his way through the Camp of the New Yorkers, he came back again driving all before him with his brawny fists and mighty strength. Not so Wetherill, who, by the way, had always a good deal to say about his prowess as a fighting man. The New Yorkers just swarmed upon and gave him a pretty thorough beating. He was handled pretty roughly and his return to our lines was more of a strategic retreat than the irresistible drive of Crocker. I took no part in this melee and as far as I know neither did my company, for I prevented them. I have since heard however, unofficially, that one or two of them had a crack at the "damn New Yorkers."

By the time the 25th went for their muskets the brigade was under arms and a battery near by was trained upon the Combatants. Two regiments were moved up and active preparations were made to quell the disturbance. When the officer commanding the battery gave the order to "load with canister," a stampede took place and the men separated to their own camps. Satisfactory explanation was made to the brigade commander, our regiment was moved away from the vicinity of the 25th, and the incident passed over.[11]

Now during this disturbance Gwyn and Johnson fell to abusing each other until Col. Johnson, a very great black guard, by the way, gave the lie direct to Gwyn, who stalked off in high dudgeon, breathing vengeance and calling out loudly, "I will call him out for this." A challenge was written and given to Maj. Herring to deliver. Word of this got abroad among the men and they crowded up around the Colonel's quarters, expressing in loud voice their appreciation of his conduct. Major Herring found Johnson and received his acceptance and at once reported to Lt. Col. James Gwyn, when that doughty individual immediately subsided, rum and all, and shortly after we had the unspeakable mortification of seeing him, with arms around Col. Johnson's neck, begging his pardon. So it all ended in a big drunk. Everybody got drunk, men and officers, ambulance and wagon drivers, black and white, all got gloriously drunk. How about myself? Well, you know I am a truthful James, and I will have to "fess up" and say I got pretty merry, but not being much of a drinking man, a little went a great way with me, and made me funny. We were all demoralized, no discipline, no confidence, no respect, no nothing. Let me pass by this disgraceful scene.

Friday, January 23rd. The whole army was ordered back and the campaign abandoned. The elements this time, and not the rebs, defeated the Army of the Potomac. It was soon learned that to order and to perform were two very different things. Although ordered back, the army couldn't go; it was stuck fast in the mud, and as our line of march was stretched out at least 12 miles, something would have to be done before the pontoon and artillery trains could be moved. Thereupon the whole army was set to building corduroy roads and before night completed from the front back to old camp a substantial log road over which the trains passed that night.

<u>Saturday, January 24th</u>. We marched back and as before stated are again occupying our old quarters. It has rained almost incessantly from the time we started up to the present time. This <u>Grand Movement</u> fully demonstrated that a winter campaign in Virginia is simply impossible. It is all very well to refer to other nations and to point to Napoleon's winter movements of large bodies of troops. Well, they had good <u>hard</u> roads to move on. . . . What a trump this campaign is for Genl. McClellan. Oh yes! he could move <u>last</u> winter, but wouldn't; Burnside, somehow, cannot this. . . .

I can answer <u>no</u> to the question whether our Corps has been ordered West. The 5th Corps, having the regulars attached to it, is the most important division of the Army of the Potomac. It cannot be detached.

I have received in all from you $20. You can forward the balance on receipt of this. Many, many thanks my good kind brother. No rumors of the pay master yet, he hasn't been seen outside of Washington for many a day, so I am informed. . . .

>─┤◆├─○─┤◆├─<

Camp 118th Regt. P.V.
January 27th, 1863

Dear Brother:

. . . You have for sometime in every letter alluded to current rumors of trouble in our regiment, of a Court-Martial of a Captain, and about other matters, [which], while not strictly facts, are so near them that without [entering] into an explanation I had to abstain from answering at all. Now, however, I feel at liberty to make known to you a little family history that passeth all understanding.

It appears that on the reconnoisance of Dec. 31st '62 of which I gave you an account,[12] Captain Fernald became so drunk as to be utterly incapacitated and was left asleep (drunk) on the banks of the Rappahannock when we forded it. He did not, of course, join in the expedition. On returning to camp, Gwyn, very properly, put him under arrest and preferred charges which would have cashiered him. But Fernald was not that kind of a man. He immediately brought counter charges against Gwyn,—For <u>drunkenness</u> in camp, in the field and before his regiment—For <u>immoral conduct</u> in having a woman in camp—in his tent—two nights at Sharpsburg, and for interfering with the guard while drunk at same camp—(my case), to all of which I was the principal witness, especially the charge of immoral conduct, being officer of the day at the time and instructed by Gwyn to remove the guard from before and rear of his quarters. These were fearful charges and caused Gwyn great annoyance.

After the interview with him in relation to my resignation, the day after, I think it was, <u>he sent</u> for me, and upon presenting myself at his quarters, said he desired to have a <u>private</u> conversation. I replied I could not possibly grant such a thing in view of the unfriendly feeling existing between us (I thought I had better come out with it). He said I was entirely mistaken as

Capt. Charles H. Fernald, Company D, 118th Pennsylvania Volunteers. THE CIVIL WAR LIBRARY & MUSUEM.

to him, that he had none but the most kindly feelings towards me and always intended to be my friend, but that I would not let him. However, he desired to hold an important talk with me, and wanted to know how it could be done. I declined further conversation except in presence of a witness. He said he was perfectly willing there should be a witness to all he had to say and proposed Lt. Wm. Gardner, Quarter Master, to which I assented. Now Gardner is about as two faced and unreliable a man as can well be found. He would lie out of a thing if it suited him, with unblushing face. He was a creature of Gwyn's, but a <u>professed</u> friend of mine. But he would let me drop if the Lt. Col. ordered him to do so. Oh! I know him well, as does also, Gwyn. Gardner was sent for and Gwyn explained why. Gwyn then opened the conversation with,

"Captain, do you know of charges preferred against me?"
"Yes," said I.
"By whom?"
"Yes," said I.
"Captain Fernald?" said he.
"Yes," I said.
"Do you know their nature?"
"Yes," I said.
"What do you know about them?" said he.
"I know," I said, "they will cashier you."
"That is not what I asked you," he said.
"Well then," said I, "read me the charges."

He then took them up and asked me what I know in relation to them <u>all</u>. I said I knew he was now the subject of an additional charge—that of <u>tampering with a witness</u>, that I wanted him to understand that I would not permit him to treat me in this way, that I was no boy, that he would find out what I knew of the charges when <u>the trial</u> comes off. It was a rich scene. He just laid back in his chair and glared at me. Then it was he unmasked himself and made no effort to suppress his hatred of me. I gave it back to him—<u>full</u>. I was boiling with rage and stood up before him with clenched hands ready to spring on him if he attempted any violence. Great Scott!! how fortunate I had a witness even though it was Gardner. He, poor fellow, was dumb founded, but got himself together enough to say, "Colonel, I don't think Captain Donaldson knows much about the matter." This proved to be the right thing, said at the right time. Gwyn immediately changed front and said, "Sit down Captain, I sent for you today more especially to say that I have noticed your soldierly qualities and can say, before our friend the Quarter Master, that you are without exception the best Captain in the line. Now I am disposed to award faithful services like yours. How would you like to be detached to Belle Plain on the Quarter Master General's staff?" "I should like it beyond anything," cried I, like a drowning man clutching at straws. I was too eager and showed my hand, or rather let him see how I longed to get away, and my sufferings under his command. He quickly said—"Or, how would you like a leave of absence for 10 days?" "I should like that too," said I. "Well make application," said he, "and I will approve it." He then arose and our interview ended.

Now the cunning rascal, he has learned that I know enough to throw him out of the regiment. He will have to withdraw the charges against Fernald in order to have Fernald do the same with him. Meanwhile, I am kept quiet—bribed, with a leave. I haven't got it yet, although I promptly sent it in. I did not ask it—he offered it. Did you ever know of such a rascal? Now Jac, how can I be a soldier under this tyrant? If he were a disciplinarian, a martinet, a soldier, I would be only too happy to put up with anything from him, but he is an arrant coward, drunkard and tyrant. I can't serve under him, and I don't see what I am to do. I can't bring charges against him—I have condoned them. I will go on to the end, until finally goaded on to the verge of despair. I will assail him before the regiment and be sent home, dismissed [from] the service. There is no other way open to me that I can see—except the one final muster out—that may come in battle.

I intend dropping the whole subject and will write no more about my resignation. I am in excellent health—low spirited though. Added to all this it is still raining hard.

>—+◆>—O—<◆+—<

Camp 118th Regt. P.V.
Feb. 3rd, 1863

Dear Brother:

. . . Sunday last, 1st inst., Captain Fernald withdrew his charges against Lt. Col. Jas. Gwyn, writing an apology for making them and giving a paper to Gwyn stating there was not a word of truth in any of the charges. Gwyn immediately withdrew the charges against Fernald, and gave him 10 days leave of absence. Fernald has lost character & honor here. Even Gwyn will despise him. Well, everything is now lovely—Gwyn, the tyrant, Fernald the cowardly, mean spirited apostate, Donaldson the contumacious witness— will all be found at home together, thus giving the lie to dame rumor that there is trouble in camp. Each of us will smilingly deny any trouble, for are we not fast friends and home together on leave? Surely it is so, for we have bought and sold each other. Think of it Jac, my being in such company. The thought is terrible . . . but I'll come home never the less should my leave be granted. . . .

>─┤─◆>─○─◆─┤─<

Camp 118th Regt. P.V.
Feb. 18th, 1863

Dear Brother:

Well, here I am again with the army after the happiest 10 days of my life spent with you all at home. It seems like a dream and yet I have substantial [proof] it is a fact that I have been at home—and didn't stay there. Well, I trust that you, Mr. Heaton & Mr. Sparks know what is best for me to do. My judgment was the other way, but why speak of it. I accept the present fact, that I am here, ready and willing, as in the past, to do my duty.

After leaving you on Monday . . . I arrived in Washington about 12 o'clock midnight, slept and took breakfast at the National and left at 8 A.M. for camp. Arrived about 1 P.M. at Aquia, remained there until 3 o'clock, without shelter, amidst a blinding snow storm, and then got upon the top of a car load of baled hay (no other accommodation) and after being snowed pretty well, and almost stiff with cold, finally arrived in camp. I had a grand reception. All seemed so glad to have me back again that it was at this time the homesickness began to leave me. There could be no mistaking the embrace of genuine affection by John Thomas. Poor old fellow, they tell me he has been like a calf without its mother. He would just drift around and didn't know what to do—or who to do it with. He hasn't left me since. He gets along side of me—close up, and makes me tell <u>all about it</u>, over and over again. He was here long before I was up this morning asking questions and listening to my story. Even Scipio was loud and boisterous with expressive exuberance. Lt. Batchelder has admired my hat so that he has had it on ever since. . . .

By the way, my bottle of brandy disappeared as suddenly after my arrival as though I had struck a temperance meeting. My!! it was just <u>spirited</u> away. The subject of bibibles naturally suggests edibles and I would like to ask how about those fried oysters you didn't eat Sunday night last. I wish to gracious I had them now. Love to Auntie, tell her I am <u>at home</u> again, and am well taken care of by my man Friday—George Slow.

►─┼─◄►─◄─O─◄►─┼─◄

Camp 118th Regt. P.V.
March 7th, 1863

Dear Brother:

All your letters to hand. In a letter written yesterday I gave Auntie an account of a spell of sickness I have been having, and although very much better I am still marked "quarters," but will take command of my company tomorrow. I don't like the idea of anyone commanding it, even for a day or two, but myself. I know just what to do with the men, and how to keep them sufficiently occupied all the time to prevent them from getting into mischief. Everyone has been most kind, and to Major Herring I am indebted for many little delicacies and a number of pleasurable moments spent in conversation with him. He has visited me twice each day. . . .

I am pleased to know you consider my picture good. I hesitated before sending it, but you now make me feel glad I had it taken. It represents me as I really appear when on the march, picket, or other active duty. Jno. Thomas' father has Scipio's picture, which as soon as he forwards copies I will send you one. It is very funny. I really think John Thomas will be off for home—<u>sure, this time</u>—either Monday or Tuesday. Be sure to see him and show him all the attention you can spare, as he is, without exception, the best fellow in the world. I am sincerely glad to know the slippers will arrive soon, I need them so much. . . .

I am writing hastily in order to reach <u>this</u>—<u>great important matter</u>— <u>Captain Crocker is at home</u>, and I particularly desire you to meet him. He is one of nature's noblemen and my dearest friend here—<u>a brave, honorable, noble gentleman</u>. <u>GWYN</u> is also in town, and leaves for Camp on Sunday. You know what I think of him. . . .

►─┼─◄►─◄─O─◄►─┼─◄

Camp 118th Regt. P.V.
March 9th, 1863

Dear Brother:

I write to say that I reported for duty this A.M. having entirely recovered from my sick spell, and am now in command of my company again. I am told by my friends that I have fallen away somewhat, but have no fear of a speedy restoration to my former "heft." . . .

><-+•>-•0-•<+•1-<

Camp 118th Regt. P.V.
March 16th, 1863

Dear Jac:

All your letters to hand. I have been unable to reply owing to the rebuilding of my quarters—the past week. I have now a substantial and well built house of logs, which is impervious to rain and wind, ventilation being secured by an open fire place and light from the canvas roof. I may add, confidently, that I am as comfortably housed as any officer in the corps. Lt. Batchelder was architect and Henry Q. Cobb[13] contractor and builder. I enclose you Batchelder's photograph. I consider it a good picture and a correct likeness.

Captains Wetherill & Fernald and Adjutant Charles Hand left for home yesterday—three jolly good fellows among themselves. The two captains may be set down about as follows—Wetherill—the most unmitigated growler and discontented man in the regiment, although claiming to be the best posted, the best drilled and the best boxer in the command. Confidentially, he amounts to nothing—is a great blower and is disliked by everyone. Capt. Fernald is a well posted tactician with commanding voice, but is utterly useless and unfit as an officer for two strong reasons. First—his inordinate love of rum which has caused the men to nick-name him Capt. Drinkall, and secondly, he is not a brave man, morally or physically. However it is best, all things considered, to be friendly with them should you chance to meet either. They both profess friendship for me and we get along very well together. . . .

I am once more in good health and appetite. Col. Gwyn's wife is here in camp. He has fixed up his quarters most elaborately—sumptuously I should say. I have not yet met the lady. . . .

As spring approached, the morale of the Army of the Potomac, which had been hovering dangerously low since Fredericksburg and the Mud March, began to rebound, and much of the improvement was directly attributable to the efforts of its new leader. Whatever shortcomings on the battlefield his tenure in command would eventually reveal, Joe Hooker proved himself to be an exceptionally able administrator. Deserters, who had been leaving the army at a rate of 200 per day in late January, soon found it impossible to get outside of army lines.[14] *A furlough system was inaugurated, allowing deserving men to visit home. Sanitary conditions were strengthened, resulting in shorter sick lists, and most important, the soldiers' diet improved, with fresh bread and vegetables being issued for the first time in months. Reviews were held when the weather turned milder, and a new sense of exhilaration crept back into the ranks. "Despondency and doubt," recalled a Maine officer, "had given way to pride and confidence."*[15]

> Camp 118th Regt. P.V.
> Near Falmouth, Va.
> March 17th, 1863

Dear Auntie:

. . . I feel first rate today and am fast regaining my lost weight and ruddy appearance. Am very sorry you continue to fret about me; it is a source of much anxiety knowing you to be so continually unhappy. You ought, on the contrary, to be brave for my sake, for surely my surroundings are sad enough at all times. . . .

As a proof of my improved bodily condition I have but to mention what I ate for breakfast this A.M. One pint of coffee, about thirty flannel cakes, one pound and a half of beef steak, half loaf of toasted bread, three sardines, some cheese, boiled tongue and dried sausage. I will have but a scant dinner today, owing to the absence of the entire force of niggers from the culinary department. Henry is washing, George is absent on furlough and Scipio Africanus is in the Guard House, so with borrowed help, will have to make out on stewed oysters, apple fritters, molasses and butter. The recipe for making apple fritters as prepared by George Slow for our mess, of three, is about as follows—Fourteen cups of flour, three pounds of dried apples—but then, you, an old housekeeper, must certainly know all about making these delicacies, although I do not remember ever seeing any. For supper I will have boiled Mackerel, buckwheat cakes, chocolate, toast and milk punch. Had the niggers been on hand would have had coffee, omelets, buckwheat cakes, egg nog and ash cake.

You will perceive I am in no danger of starving and will wager that as a Captain in the U.S.A. I live better than does the Commanding General of the C.S.A. By the way, a recipe for making Ash Cake might be useful to you—Take one half gallon of flour, three parts of milk, half pound of butter.

Mix well together with your hands, then make a large hole in the ashes, pour in your batter, cover up with ashes, let remain several hours and— there you are—something splendid, I can tell you. . . .

March 19th. We have been very busy lately, so much so as to interfere with the close of my letter. The Corps has been thoroughly inspected as to present condition for Field Service. Indeed, we were looked after most sharply, especially as to condition of ammunition in cartridge boxes, shelter tents and shoes. Most of my tents were condemned by Capt. Bankson, Inspector General, so that I will start on the Campaign with a full new set. Suppose we are preparing to move from here, although I only surmise it, not hearing anything to that effect—no orders etc. I have yet much to do and am only availing myself of a little leisure to close the letter before my books and papers are inspected. . . .

Now Auntie, I have written you a good long letter and once again tell you that I am all O.K. physically although tired of that everlasting drill, drill, drill all the time, drill, but presume it is for the best. Write soon to your affectionate son.

>-+-‹›-•-O-•-‹›-+-‹

Camp 118th Regt. P.V.
March 26th, 1863

Dear Jac:

. . . We have had a jolly time today. A grand review by Hooker after which Col. Gwyn gave an entertainment. I need not add when entertained by that officer there is no lack of ale & whiskey and as the officers were not at all abstemious there was much drunkenness in consequence. I was present. After our return from review the adjutant visited each officer in person, and presenting Lt. Col. Jas. Gwyn's compliments, desired his presence after 8 P.M. I had to go. To stay away would have been marked an affront. I therefore presented myself in full uniform, and wished the Lt. Col. many happy returns of the present occasion. He then extended the bottle and we all took a drink. I was also presented with a photograph of the gallant Lt. Colonel, which, by the way, is a most excellent likeness. I stayed about his quarters for some little time, in conversation with officers of other regiments, and after another drink all around, took my departure. . . .

>-+-‹›-•-O-•-‹›-+-‹

8

Camp 118th P.V.
April 4th, 1863

Dear Auntie:

. . . There is nothing new of much account, everything remains dull, stale and unprofitable, but anticipate and am ready for an advance movement which must come sooner or later. An important incident, by the way of change, would be a sight of the paymaster, still, notwithstanding the low ebb of our finances, we continue to live pretty well, as Planked shad for breakfast this A.M. will attest. In regard to my drummer boy Booth you so feelingly allude to, I have heard or seen nothing of him and have forwarded his descriptive list to the Provost Marshal so that he will be arrested as a deserter and sent to Fort Delaware. He is an infernal scoundrel and is marked "deserter" on my pay rolls, while his place has been filled by another so that, in fact, I do not want him back again.

What lovely weather we are having, the woods fairly teem with birds and the fields are beginning to put forth. Spring is upon us in all its glory. Ah, how many of us will live to see another. God grant that we all may. To see the soldiers now one would hardly think that ere many weeks thousands of them will be numbered among those who were. I never saw the army in such splendid condition and in such excellent fighting trim. I presume the Confederates are in just such good order. God! what a crush there will be when they come together. Have just learned that we are to be mustered on the 10th inst. which indicates a speedy movement. Where we are to move is what no fellow can find out, but I hardly think it will be Fredericksburg again. . . .

>-I-<>-O-<>-I-<

Camp 118th Regt. P.V.
April 5th, 1863

Dear Jacob:

. . . It has been snowing all night and there is now about a foot of slush on the ground. It only shows how very uncertain the elements are in Old Virginny. It is in the course of things for us to move shortly, but have no opinion as to where, but it must be a flank movement—we can't do Fredericksburg again. However, I don't know anything about it. Camp life is just now extremely dull—no news at all, and as the weather has put a stop to all out doors work, all manner of games are resorted to as a pastime. Of course there is a good deal of gambling going on, and nightly the "sweat cloth" is resorted to by the idle officers, while large sums of money change hands at Vantoon and other games of hazzard, Poker for instance. I do not wish to censure others and have it appear that I am the only saint in the regiment, so I "fess up" and candidly say I have tried all the different games of chance, but to a very limited extent, as I am but a poor card player. I made out but indifferently.

Tomorrow being Easter Monday there is to be two celebrations in our regiment by two different societies, "The Morning Glories" give an Egg Nog in the fore noon and the "4 o'clocks" a grand ovation in the evening. As I belong to neither of these organizations but am invited to both entertainments I think I will have to be on my guard lest I partake too freely of the tempting beverage. . . .

>-+◦>-O-<◦+-<

Camp 118th Regt. P.V.
April 12th, 1863

Dear Brother:

. . . We have been quite busy getting into shape for a new campaign. On the 7th President Lincoln reviewed our Corps and in splendid condition he found us. On the next day he reviewed the whole army. Poor man, how bored he must have been. Just to think how often he had to bow his head in acknowledgment of drooping colors and "Hail to the Chief" from every regiment. Well, it did us all good to see "Uncle Abe" taking the kindly interest he does in our welfare. It was a magnificent sight, however, the well drawn line of masses, doubled on the centre, while all was as quiet as death, as is usual on such occasions, every man looking straight to the front, no turning of heads as the President, Genl. Hooker & Head Quarter staff come sweeping along. There is no finer disciplined army on this or any other continent than the Army of the Potomac, and the 5th Corps, with its full division of Regular troops, is the peer of any similar body of armed men in existence today.[16] . . .

Enclosed find a photograph of Lt. Gardner—an excellent picture of an excellent Quarter Master. He was never good as a line officer. . . .

>-+◦>-O-<◦+-<

Camp 118th Regt. P.V.
April 21st, 1863

Dear Brother:

. . . There is nothing much to report since last I wrote. It is of course an open secret that we are ready for business, and, I take it, are only waiting dry weather to again measure our strength with the rebels. It is still raining, however, so that nothing can be done now. I will let you in to a State Secret, which you had better keep entirely to yourself, especially so far as Auntie is concerned—orders have been received to keep 5 days cooked rations constantly on hand. This you know means a move. I will try and give you timely warning.

Colonel Prevost, with his boy, Southy, arrived Sunday, 19th and took command. He looks badly and has his right arm in a sling, and uses his sword with his left. He really ought not to be here, but had to come for self preservation. On one of his many trips home, Lt. Col. James Gwyn, taking advantage of the War Department Order mustering out of the service all officers whose wounds prevent their return to duty after 60 days absence,[17] attempted to muster out Col. Prevost without communicating the fact to him. It was his intention to have had himself mustered Colonel at once, and so sure was he of the success of his unkind and ungentlemanly scheme that he had his mess chest painted with his name as Colonel on it. While he did not succeed in his own case, he did, however, have Captain O'Callaghan mustered out under the same law, and, as I have written you, Wetherill mustered in.[18] Some of Colonel Prevost's friends, Mr. Stephen Winslow[19] in particular, learning of this attempt to do a gallant officer so gross an injustice, had influence enough with Governor Curtin to put a stop to it and hasten Prevost back to his command. The few "Outcasts" (his friends, among the number, myself) are heartily rejoiced at this turn of affairs and we walk about once more erect feeling there is some balm still left in Gilead.

There is, however, some alloy with the perfect enjoyment. Col. Prevost does not in the least assert his authority. He has not yet rescinded the order for Major Herring to attend Reveille Roll Call.[20] He has not yet placed in his proper position our blackguard of a Lieut. Colonel who has wrought so much demoralization in this fine command. He has not changed a single thing, nor revoked a single obnoxious order issued by our former brutal commander. In all this Col. Prevost shows a lamentable weakness for which we in silence grieve, but with it all—he is Colonel commanding and the other fellow can do us no harm.

I forgot to mention that both Captains Sharwood and Crocker no longer affiliate with Gwyn. Nor do they even speak to him. I shall never forget the day of the arrival of <u>Gwyn's Mess Chest</u>. Up to that time he, Crocker, and Sharwood messed together & although there had been a growing dissatisfaction with these gentlemen at many acts of "His Grace Duke James," there had been no open rupture. These two Captains at once raised a row at the title of "<u>Colonel</u>" on the chest. Gwyn was yet away and I think it was Crocker who sent the news to Winslow which brought about the return of Col. Prevost. However, when Gwyn returned, an explanation was asked by Crocker & Sharwood as to the meaning of the large white painted letters of Colonel on the mess chest, a rupture took place between them which ended in their leaving his mess and coming over to <u>ME</u>. Think of it! Captain Sharwood said as he came to my tent with a large Pine Apple Cheese and many other good things—<u>late of their mess</u>— "Take me in Captain, take me in, our mess has broken up." He then told me of the quarrel had with Gwyn about the mustering out of Col. Prevost. So I now have that splendid gentleman for a mess mate and have gained two friends who are both willing and ready to oppose that <u>monster Lt. Colonel Gwyn</u>. Verily it is indeed an ill wind that blows nobody any good.

I have been on Picket towards Hartwood Church the past three days. Had command of the Division line of Pickets, covering a distance of at least two miles, through a wooded country with some clearings here & there, when advantage was taken of the fences in the vicinity to cover the men. I believe I have before described the spot. It is the only really pretty country around our army. We generally picket this flank of the army and locate hereabouts although at times we are more to the right of Hartwood, as for instance our late tour of duty. There are more houses to be seen hereabouts than nearer Hartwood, although there are not many in either direction. This has been an unpleasant experience for me, as I have been compelled to reprimand a number of officers for dereliction, and they [are] my friends too, but on a duty such as this, there cannot be allowed the slightest departure from strict discipline and the laws governing this the most important most vigilant of all duties a soldier is called upon to perform. . . .

I have just received an order to take charge of the late pickets and superintend the discharge of their pieces—or in other words—I have a firing party on hand, so will have to hurry and finish this long letter. The mail leave[s] before I would be back and I am anxious to get this to you. Enclosed find photograph of Lt. Coane of my company. I make no comment but merely say he is better adapted for a mercantile than a military life. I had nothing whatever to do with his appointment. He is Lt. Col. Jas. Gwyn's selection. . . .

>‑‑‑O‑‑‑<

Capt 118th Regt. P.V.

April 23rd, 1863

My dear Brother:

. . . I am very busy making out my Quarterly Returns of Clothing, which must be finished today. I therefore have time enough for just a short letter to you. We were all ready last night for a move, but a rain storm came up and put a stop to it. We have been and are now ready to move into active operations at a moments notice. You had better accept this letter as positive information as to our intentions and not expect another from me before hostilities open. We may leave at any moment, our wagons are packed, the sick have been sent to the rear, inspection after inspection of arms and clothing have been made, cooked rations on hand all the time, officers' baggage reduced, and, in fact, the weather alone keeps us back. I have no idea of our destination. It of course must be a flanking movement, or else an entire change of base somewhere. I am sorry I can't post you, but before you again hear from me we will in all probability be in the field.

Another infallible sign of the nearness of a new campaign is the presence among us of the Paymaster. I will send you <u>one hundred dollars</u>. I owe some $250 mess, servants, and regimental debts, and as I receive $504 in all I will be unable to do but little of my cherished plans for you all.

This is an extravagant regiment. The officers have assumed the debts of Addicks, our late Quarter Master, which will be pro-rated among us.[21] This I think is uncalled for. Why not let <u>his family</u> settle his thieving and scoundrilly and drunken contracts, or else let him suffer the penalty. However it was by a vote of the majority that this unbusinesslike transaction was perpetrated—or to repeat the argument of the "affirmative"—"to save the <u>HONOR</u> of the regiment."

I have under consideration an offer from Devitt & Co. to advance— monthly—my pay <u>to you</u>, one half to be given to Auntie, the other sent to me. They will charge 5 per cent for the advance. What do you think of it? Poor dear Auntie, I hope she is well again, but I can't help thinking of her condition when she learns that this vast army is again launched into the enemy's country. . . . Here with find photograph of Chaplain Wm.

O'Neill—a good man, I believe, but like his brother Captain Henry O'Neill don't know much about his tactics.[22] He considers loud, ranting, boisterous roaring and the frequent repetition of the name of the Lord goes a long way towards making up an interesting sermon. He don't amount to much as a preacher—is more on the "<u>blather</u>." Yet he is a good man, kind and willing. He is familiarly known among us as "<u>Holy Joe</u>." Still he is a good man—yes! a very good man. I have seen abler ones, however, but he will do. "Holy" looks after himself pretty closely. Well, that's nothing to his discredit—all preachers do that—they rather like to be comfortable. My health is splendid. . . .

CHAPTER 6

Chancellorsville
April 27–June 9, 1863

"*I* *never saw the army in such splendid condition and in such excellent fighting trim,*" *Donaldson had written early in April, and many of his fellow soldiers shared his sentiments. By the end of April, the rejuvenated 130,000-man-strong Army of the Potomac was again ready to cross swords with the Army of Northern Virginia. Lee's 60,000 men were entrenched in a twenty-five-mile line stretching south of Fredericksburg, and Hooker had settled on an intricate but well-thought-out strategy to force the Rebels out of their positions and into a fight on favorable ground.*

The main feature of Hooker's plan (which was vaguely reminiscent of what Burnside had attempted in his failed Mud March) called for three Union Army corps to march up the north bank of the Rappahannock well beyond Lee's left, cross the Rappahannock and Rapidan Rivers, and land squarely in rear of the Confederates. During this movement, which was to be conducted with the utmost secrecy, two other Union Army corps would cross the Rappahannock opposite Fredericksburg to keep Lee's attention away from the flanking column. The Confederates would soon find themselves trapped between the converging Federal wings, and with Yankee cavalry raids to the south cutting his supply and communication lines, Lee was to be left with the choice of either retreating or attacking the Army of the Potomac in defensive works on ground of Hooker's choosing.[1]

The initial phases of the campaign were carried out nearly flawlessly. By April 30 the 5th, 11th, and 12th Corps (the cumbersome Grand Divisions organized by Burnside had been done away with), some 40,000 men,[2] had advanced into the darkly forested Wilderness and reached the small clearing around Chancellorsville undetected. The men were in high spirits ("full of enthusiasm and anxious to get ahead into some open country," was how Donaldson described them), and none seemed more optimistic than Hooker. "The Rebel Army," he boasted on May 1, "is now the legitimate property of the Army of the Potomac."[3]

225

Reaching the cleared ground that lay between the eastern edge of the Wilderness and Fredericksburg would have been advantageous to Hooker, as it would have uncovered an additional crossing point for his reserves posted north of the Rappahannock and allowed him to bring the bulk of his troops into battle. But as the flanking force pushed east toward Fredericksburg on May 1, it met resistance from Confederate infantry who were finally alive to the threat behind them. This opposition, combined with an inaccurate report of heavy Rebel reinforcements moving against him, led Hooker to abandon the advance and take up a position in the Wilderness near the Chancellorsville clearing.[4] "Nobody but a crazy man would give such an order when we have victory in sight," exclaimed one incredulous corps commander when told of his superior's decision,[5] but Hooker had gained what he wanted—a defensive battle on ground he had chosen.[6]

Upon their arrival at Chancellorsville on April 30, Donaldson and the 1st Brigade were sent eastward along the Orange Turnpike toward Fredericksburg in support of a Federal cavalry probe. The following day, May 1, the brigade was sent along the River Road toward Banks's Ford but was pulled back when Confederate resistance grew stiff against Union columns advancing on parallel lines to the south.

Camp 118th Regt. P.V.,
1st Brigade, 1st Division, 5th Army Corps.
Near Potomac Creek Station, Va.
May 9th, 1863

Dear Auntie:

Again has another battle been fought, again have we been outrageously and disasterously defeated, and again have I been spared to tell you the mortifying tale. Indeed I fear my account of the Chancellorsville campaign will be a short one, for I can hardly bring myself to the task of narrating the events of this most inglorious defeat of as fine an army as ever trod God's green pastures. No, I will not call it defeat for the army, it was rather a defeat for our commanding general, more shame to him, the braggart. Our army was never at any time during the campaign repulsed, checked or defeated. One Corps (11th) it is true was dispersed, but its loss was of no moment, for another fresh Corps (Reynolds 1st) took its place immediately. No, we were commanded by a drunkard, and to rum alone the failure of this campaign must be placed.

When Genl. Hooker reached Chancellorsville with his army and witnessed the entire success of his well ordered plans, success overcame him and he, like many another successful man before him, made merry over the occasion, and commenced that infernal tippling which appears to be the orthodox thing among officers of high rank. They tipple because of success, they tipple because of unsuccess, they tipple because it is rainy, or because it is bright and clear. It is with them drink, drink, drink, always and all the time. From this cause alone Hooker lost his head, and the battle of Chancellorsville can be placed among the other thousands of disasters wrought by rum. I speak with a clear understanding of what I am saying, with a perfect knowledge of the penalty attached to the criticism of a superior, and I give you perfect liberty to repeat it upon all occasions and to use my name freely. I saw Genl. Hooker, during the heat of battle, guzzling (I can call it by no other name) wine instead of attending to his duties, and I saw him incapacitated for command by reason of strong drink—this I declair and affirm. I feel confident the historian will vindicate this army and lay the blame where it belongs, upon Genl. Hooker. Certainly the men blame him and as a commander he is of no further use to the cause and should be relieved before he can do any more mischief. He can never fight this army successfully. The men don't believe in him, they have lost faith, he had better go home.

But to my story. We were not at all surprised at the order to "pack up" which came sounding along on the morning of the 27th of April, as we had been keeping on hand for some time an eight days supply of cooked rations, keeping it always full and ready to issue. The men were in fine spirits, and the weather bright and clear. Indeed the whole army felt good. They had been well taken care of during the winter, had been fed upon full rations of everything a soldier could well desire. They had had a good jolly time and little work. The old despondency which had settled on the army after Fredericksburg had given place to a feeling of security and confidence. The army was well up in point of numbers; 120,000 infantry, 12,000 Cavalry and about 400 guns made up its strength, which compared to the Confederates in the late campaign was as 3 is to 1. We had seven splendid army Corps, 1st, Genl. Reynolds, 2nd Genl. Couch, 3rd Genl. Sickles, 5th Genl. Meade, 6th Genl. Sedgwick, 11th Genl. Howard, 12th Genl. Slocum.[7]

On this day's march the men suffered a good deal from heat, being pretty heavily ladened with ammunition and rations, and all along the ten miles of distance travelled, the roads were strewn with blankets, overcoats and every description of wearing apparel abandoned by the needless fellows who had preceeded us. The 5th, 11th, and 12th Corps appeared to be engaged in this movement and it was, indeed, a trial to the old soldier to

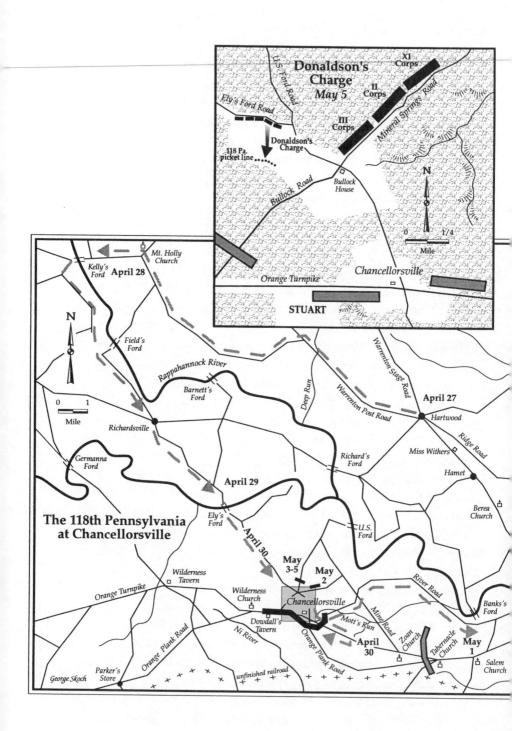

Donaldson's Charge
May 5

XI Corps
II Corps
III Corps

Ely's Ford Road
U.S. Ford Road
Mineral Springs Road

Donaldson's Charge

118 Pa. picket line

N

Bullock Road
Bullock House

0   1/4
Mile

Chancellorsville
Orange Turnpike

STUART

Mt. Holly Church

Kelly's Ford   April 28

N

Field's Ford

0   1
Mile

Rappahannock River

Barnett's Ford

Richardsville

Germanna Ford

April 29

Deep Run

Warrenton Post Road

Warrenton Stage Road

April 27

Hartwood

Richard's Ford

Miss Withers

Ridge Road

Hamet

The 118th Pennsylvania
at Chancellorsville

Ely's Ford

April 30

U.S. Ford

Berea Church

May 3-5

May 2

Wilderness Tavern

Orange Turnpike

Wilderness Church

Dowdall's Tavern

Ni River

Chancellorsville

Mott's Run

Orange Plank Road

April 30

Mine Road

Zoan Church

River Road

Banks's Ford

Tabernacle Church

May 1

Salem Church

George Skoch

Parker's Store

Orange Plank Road

unfinished railroad

be baffled in his conjecture as to our objective point, but of one thing this critic was well assured, and he gave it as a well digested fact, we were on the right path to have a successful bout with the rebels, because the old soldier knew that nothing could be done with them at Fredericksburg, so that the present movement looked like a "flank" one. Indeed it is very wonderful how accurately the old soldier will reason out a plan of a campaign without knowing anything at all about the movements going on around him. It is a great mistake to suppose the American soldier to be a mere machine only. They are excellent critics and their judgments sound. It has always been a source of surprise to me that our General Officers do not treat the men as Napoleon did. When on the eve of a campaign he would tell them just what he was about to do so that they went knowingly into it. However, war is a new business for our country to engage in and can only be mastered by experience.

We halted at Hartwood Church, having been leisurely marching since 10.30 A.M. At 7 P.M. we went into bivouac in the woods. We were very familiar with the spot having picketed here many times during the winter. You will remember I told you of the little brick church which gives the place its name, and of the capture of our cavalry picket here. It is one of old Virginia's beauty spots and is lovely even in winter. The surrounding forest trees are mostly of oak and at this time were beautiful in their fresh leafy abundance. Indeed all the earth seemed teaming with glorious virdure, while the delicious fragrance of wood-bine filled the air. The excitement of the march, the sights and scenes of lovely places passed and the romantic encampment amid my "old friends" the giant oaks, so stimulated my mind that, after seeing my men properly taken care of, I went away, apart from my comrades, and sat down alone with my thoughts, and noted the days experiences which I have just given you.

April 28. We did not move until 1.30 P.M., apparently to let the other divisions of our Corps get ahead, then, indeed, we did do some rapid marching. The men had, the day before, as stated, thrown away a great many articles that had encumbered them, but upon this day's march got themselves down to the lightest possible marching order, gum blanket, shelter tents and haversacks. Nothing of interest occurred, the men marched gaily along, there was some straggling but generally the whole division was in splendid spirits. We arrived and bivouaced near Kelly's Ford on the Rappahannock, at 9.30 P.M. making about 17 or 18 miles this day. This time, after a light supper, I made haste to get into my overcoat and was soon asleep.

<u>April 29</u>. We were up bright and early cooking coffee. I never saw the men in better humour and more anxious to move on. We formed line and started towards the Rappahannock at 7 A.M., but owing to the jam of troops ahead made but slow progress. When we arrived on the bluff overlooking the river the sight that met our view was indeed stirring. Stretched like a huge serpent far, far across the country, which was generally low, could be seen the troops which had preceded us, and it struck me as a very gratifying sign that they were well closed up and moving along with the swinging pace so noted in disciplined and confident troops. I felt a thrill of pride that I, too, belonged to this army and was almost willing to defy the whole world, for surely who could stand before such a magnificent array. Artillery, Cavalry and Infantry lay before my vision in the plain below. The men, as they arrived and caught a glimpse of the warlike panorama, were wild with enthusiasm and felt, as I did, that such a host could not be beaten, that victory must be ours.

At noon we passed over the canvas pontoon bridge at Kelly's Ford and hastened on after the other troops. . . .

It was nearly dark when we arrived at Ely's Ford on the Rapidan, which at 7.30 we forded. This stream is by no means a sluggish one, and is about as wide as our Schuylkill is at the Falls. It empties into the Rappahannock abt. two miles above U.S. Ford. The river appeared to be unusually high and came up to the men's waists, causing them to carry their cartridge boxes on their heads. I took off my pants and waded in my drawers, and had my dry pants to put on again when we landed on the other side. We bivouaced on the bluff above the river, and after dark kindled great fires by which the men were warmed and dried. During the fording of the river, and after, I did not hear a single grumble, the soldiers were as jolly as you please and full of fun and frolic. They went cheerfully into the river as men knowing that, thus far, they had outwitted and gained a substantial advantage over the enemy, for it was apparent to all now just what Genl. Hooker was driving at, to out flank Lee and crush him. Although tired I did not feel like sleeping, but while my linen was drying I sat by my log fire and thought over and noted the events of the past day.

By the passage of the Rapidan we were clearly in the enemy's country and the morrow would certainly develop him, and it was fair to presume, from the known character of our foe, that an engagement would take place. As I looked upon the sleeping forms of the men, I could not but realize how wonderfully indifferent to approaching danger soldiers become. They certainly knew that a battle could not be long delayed, and that many of them would never again see the setting sun. Yet here they were, peacefully slumbering as if no thought of the kind ever entered their minds. Soon I was joined in my lonely vigil by Capt. Crocker and together, smoking the calm meditative pipe, we sat up to a late hour over our camp fire which burned brightly, throwing weird shadows upon the surrounding trees, and in the genial warmth we recalled memories of mingled pleasure and pain, reviewing our past lives and forecasting the future.

April 30th. Everything was quiet, calm and beautiful as the sun arose and tinted the tree tops with its rich golden hues. I was already up, having been notified before retiring that our brigade would lead the van, and most likely our regiment do the skirmishing, and as I had already asked Col. Prevost, who I forgot to mention was in command, for the post of honor during this campaign, I took time by the forelock, packed up and gave my man George all unnecessary things that added to the weight I had to carry. Our Brigade swung into the road at 8 A.M. and with our regiment at its head moved briskly forward. It did not fall to our lot to act as skirmishers, but we were kept close to them as a support. It was with great difficulty in some places that rapid head way could be made owing to the dense thickets and underbrush which had to be penetrated by the skirmishers. Our brigade kept to the road, and it was with a sincere pride that, occasionally looking back, I noticed how well the men kept closed up ready for instant deployment into line of battle. Back of us again, at a distance of about half a mile, came the two other brigades of our division and two batteries of artillery. We were prepared to give a good account of ourselves should it become necessary before the corps could come up, and we felt satisfied when we caught a glimpse of the slender form of our division commander, Genl. Griffin, who was personally conducting this the advance of the whole army.

As we neared the Chancellorsville House, the skirmishers were momentarily brought to a halt by the sight of an earth work which had been hastily thrown up by the enemy. Genl. Barnes at once deployed the brigade at the double quick for action, and with muskets at the trail we moved forward after the skirmish line in a splendid line of battle. Seeing the movement going on ahead, Genl. Griffin ordered up the other two brigades at the double quick to support us. What a sight it was to behold as with glistening bayonets our line of battle burst from the woods into the clearing surrounding the Chancellor House, and saw that our skirmishers had cleared the earth work, and the rebels were in rapid retreat, while down the road amid clouds of dust thundered the 2nd and 3rd Brigades. Quite a number of the enemy's pickets had been taken in the morning and, indeed, for that matter we had been capturing prisoners ever since we commenced to move forward, and had at this time under guard several hundred of them. They were utterly surprised at our sudden advent and we judged, as a matter of course, it was a surprise to General Lee as well.

We reached the Chancellor House at 11 A.M. and halted in front of it for some little while, why I do not know, as the men were not tired, but full of enthusiasm and anxious to get ahead into some more open country. The Chancellor House was a large two story brick building with porches and wooden pillows [pillars], and was in the centre of a cleared space surrounded with dense woods and thickets. It struck me at the time as being a large summer boarding house, although I did not go to it to ascertain, because, I presume, I felt that I was too soiled and dirty, although we were directly in front and but a few feet from the house. Upon the upper porch were many ladies dressed in light summer cloths, who, with characteristic Southern female bravado, reviled us audibly, and wanted to know why we did not go on as General Lee was anxious to extend the hospitalities of the country. Our General Officers beginning to arrive and dismount, the porches soon presented a lively appearance, and I may add, a very pleasant one to the soldier who had not witnessed a scene so unusual and so domestic for many a long day. We were ordered forward, however, before our eyes were weary of the cheerful spectacle, and once more serious thoughts again engaged us.

At 2 P.M. we were brought to a halt by the sudden appearance of a piece of artillery rushing from the opposite side of the top of the high ground but a short distance from the foot of which we had but that moment arrived. Furiously lashing their horses the artillery drivers, amid clouds of dust, swiftly wheeled into battery, and as quickly our brigade, which in column had been marching along the road, deployed into line of battle in the woods on either side of the road, and before the gun could be fired, not a soul of them could be seen by the enemy. Our skirmishers had also slackened up and were but a short distance in advance, as they found the enemy to be waiting for them in a heavy skirmish line, evidently determined to contest our further advance. There being no firing going on, I went up to the skirmishers and found the opposing forces in close proximity, boldly facing each other, and standing bravely up, with muskets aport, as if they had been startled by each other's sudden appearance. The enemy was so close that a conversation could have been had without raising the voice above its ordinary tone. Neither side seemed capable of making the first move, they were, for the moment, paralyzed apparently. I was particularly struck with the attitude of the Confederate opposite to where I stood, as standing rigidly in the position he had assumed when our people came upon him, with right foot advanced, right hand against a tree as for support, his other hand grasping his musket at the middle, he presented the picture of utter surprise as though conscious of the awful predicament in which he found himself. What magic spell came upon these brave men and prevented an instant death grapple I can never know, but after a pause which seemed minutes to me, but which, in reality, was but a few moments, the enemy, still facing us, drew back and gradually disappeared into the depth of the thicket without a shot being fired on either side. This was the most remarkable incident thus far experienced in my military life.

Word was passed for the skirmishers to halt and General Barnes awaited the arrival of General Griffin, who soon made his appearance, and an earnest and hurried conversation was had which resulted in General Griffin sending back to General Meade for instructions. We rested here for a long time, time that could have been spent to better advantage in letting us get the high ground in front. Ah! how true it is that man proposes but God disposes. Here we were with the key to the whole field within our grasp, and [with] the elevated ground in our possession, the battle of Chancellorsville would never have been fought. Its vital importance was known to every man and boy in the brigade. We could have taken it beyond a doubt. We were crazy to get upon high ground out of this wilderness. But no! the battle is not always to the strong, and the Almighty took a hand here and discomforted our mighty host by making our great Captain [lose] his head and judgment just at the critical moment. At this very spot next day was fought one of the bloodiest fights which took place during this most bloody battle, and hundreds of precious lives were wantonly sacrificed for its possession.

While waiting patiently for something to turn up, we were greatly amused by the performance of our surgeon. Without appearing to notice the fact of the brigade taking to the woods, he came sauntering leisurely along on his horse, oblivious to sights and sounds, as meditating, in all probability, over the old problem of how to make pill opi answer as a remedy for all sorts and conditions of ailments, when he was rudely brought to his senses by the jumping of his horse, which had been shot by some bloody minded rebel who certainly must have recognized in the doctor a non-combatant, for no one could possibly mistake him for an Achilles, and just shot his horse out of pure mischief. At all events this is the interpretation we put upon it, and if it be the correct one, the reb must have been gratified at the celerity with which the good doctor dismounted and sought cover.

After waiting several hours the order came to fall back. I shall never forget the utter surprise with which the command was received by the men and officers. Indeed, the long halt had been a great mystery to us all, but to retire altogether after securing so much, to give up such commanding ground, was beyond the comprehension of even our diminutive military brains. Both Generals Griffin and Barnes appeared to be much chagrined, but General Meade's orders were, under no consideration, to bring on an engagement. No importance whatever was attached to the fact of the extreme silence of the enemy, thus denoting a want of strength and showing a desire to avoid a conflict if possible until reinforced. The one solitary piece of artillery that frowned down the road had done the business and held in check the advance of the Army of the Potomac already flushed with success and willing to move right up to the attack. No! I will not say the advance was checked, but rather the General-in-chief hesitated. It soon leaked out that General Griffin had urged the importance of this particular spot and in an agony of disappointment and mortification that his sound judgment should be set at naught, had staked his commission on the result of an attack by his division—but to no purpose. Genl. Meade's positive orders were not to engage the enemy, and thus was lost the golden opportunity at Chancellorsville, and thus commenced the series of gross blunders that cost the nation so much blood and treasure.

We fell back to the Chancellor House, the enemy not following or in any way attempting to molest us, and went into bivouac close to the rifle pits or small earth works near the house. The surrounding country now appeared to be filled with troops, showing a concentration of nearly the whole army at this point.

While busy with the company, attending to guard detail or other little matters that a captain has personally to see after, Col. Prevost came along and invited me to accompany him to General Hooker's Head Quarters. After hunting up Capt. Crocker and getting him to join us, we proceeded to find Head Quarters and were fortunate enough to find Col. Joseph Dickenson, General Hooker's Adjutant General,[8] and were informed that

General Hooker was too busy, just then, to be seen. The Colonel introduced us to General Sickles, who, without any of his staff and on foot, was leisurely sauntering to & fro on the road near where I understood Head Quarters were to be located. I found General Sickles to be an affable, pleasant man, not at all distant or hard to approach, as would have been supposed by reason of his rank. His salutation after shaking hands with us was, "I am sorry gentlemen that I have nothing with which to extend the hospitalities, have you Joe?," meaning Col. Dickinson. To which the latter replied by stating that the Head Quarter wagon had not yet come up, and with the exception of a bottle of Drake's Plantation Bitters, he too was without a suitable beverage. However, as it was the orthodox thing to do, we passed around the bottle which he took from his pocket, and each in turn strangled over the vile stuff, wiped our lips upon our cuffs, and pretended to look perfectly serene and happy.[9]

Shortly after our return to the regiment an order from General Hooker was read to the troops, in which he complimented them upon their brilliant achievements thus far, saying the Genl. Lee's army now belonged to the army of the Potomac; that Genl. Lee must come out and fight or else surrender; that he, Genl. Hooker, had done his part and he knew the men would now do theirs, and other like stuff which the soldiers call "chin music," meaning brag-a-docia.[10] When darkness came I again took up my usual position at the camp fire for a smoke and a review of the day's events, which I noted, and then turned in for a little sleep. It was long before slumber would come to my eyelids and I lay awake thinking of the order just read and wondering how General Lee would extricate himself from the toils he was then in.

Friday, May 1st. . . . Our Division remained quietly in its place until about 10 o'clock, when to the front heavy musketry firing was heard, and from its prolonged roar, we knew the battle was on. Soon word reached us that the regulars were attacking the high ground which, yesterday, we had failed to do, and a dreadful fight was in progress. We were moved out into the road near to where the regulars were then engaged, and halted for a time listening to the conflict. Nothing could be seen in the woods to the front where the battle was in progress, but owing to the clearness of the atmosphere the thin blue smoke could be seen rising above the thickets and hanging like a curtain over the contestants. The roar of musketry was appalling and the booming of canon deafening. No cheering was heard, nothing but the continuous roar of battle, as if 10,000 boxes of Fire Crackers were being set off at once about one's ears. This showed the stubbornness, closeness, and deadly nature of the struggle, neither side apparently making much impression on the other, but standing right up and taking punishment.

After momentarily expecting to be ordered in to take an active part in the fight, about 11 o'clock the order came to move and our whole division took up the march along the road leading towards Banks Ford. The route was indescribably lonely and desolate. The road for miles winds through a wilderness and is totally devoid of even a sign of human life. After a march of about 5 miles we came within sight of the Ford, and not finding the enemy, halted for a long time and amused ourselves with watching manoeuver of the balloon from which officers of our army on the other side of the Rappahannock were surveying the country, and, I should judge, finding very little to report about. Certainly they could see nothing of the movements going on because of the dense woods.

Finally, as there appeared to be nothing for us to do at this point, orders came to retrace our steps, which we did, arriving near the Chancellor House about 5 P.M., where we formed line of battle facing to the front as nearly as we could judge, for all points of the compass were lost in the interminable thickets. We moved forward for quite a distance, and at one place where it was more clear of brush and timber than usual, came upon a spot where a line of battle had halted some hours before. How plainly the half opened, rifled and abandoned line of knapsacks showed the preparation for the charge, and how dreadfully significant were the torn cartridge papers scattered just where the line had stood. Now, how changed, not a soul of all the hundreds of men who had stood here but a short time before were any where to be seen, no trace of them, no evidence of their advance or retreat was here, nothing but the abandoned knapsacks and torn cartridge papers to show that a line of battle had been here at all. I took from one [of] the knapsacks a small Bible and found it had once belonged to D.C. Thompson, Worth, Mercer Co. PA., Co. H, 134 Regt. Penna. Vols. I presume this man held on to his tobacco when he threw away his Bible, as there was none left behind, only evidences of there having been some in the knapsack. He also left several articles of underwear and from their cleanly and nicely made appearance, I judged he had some one at home to look after and keep him in repair.[11]

After going a short distance further we rested and threw out pickets. Of course we did not know whether we were up with and [had] joined the army or not. There appeared to be an anxious look on the countenances of the men as if they were becoming confused in the dense jungle. Soldiers like to know just where their enemy is and where their friends are also, but in this case they could not tell where either were, and were consequently nervous and restless. At dark General Barnes rode up to our regiment and said to Col. Prevost that we were far in advance of the army, that Sykes, after having secured the high ground, and when just about to sweep down and destroy the Confederates, preemptory orders came to retreat, which was obeyed against the protest of the General officers, the astonishment of the men, and wonder of the enemy, and that the orders for our advance to this position had not been countermanded and that we were entirely alone, outside of the army, and liable to be taken at any time. [Also,] that he would shortly send orders to withdraw which must be done directly to the rear, and work our way back silently and with great caution, and that the pickets must be abandoned without some self-sacrificing officer volunteered to notify and bring them in.

Now, as this conversation took place in my presence, I at once volunteered to notify the pickets of their danger, and as I was receiving instructions from the General how to proceed, a cannon shot was fired, followed by the most furious shelling I ever experienced. The red streaks of fire from the fuses could be seen coursing through the darkness, the vivid flash of the bursting shells and their horrifying shrieking shook the nerves of the stoutest and intensified the agony of suspense which nearly paralyzed us. This terrifying shelling was kept up for several hours,[12] during which time we were compelled to endure it as no orders came to fall back. Several men were killed and wounded in the brigade, but no one was hurt in our regiment. As soon as the firing commenced the men began felling the trees and slashing their branches, thus making an impenetrable abatis in front of the brigade.

This awful situation had, also, its ludicrous side, as is generally the case. Scipio Africanus, Lt. Thomas' colored boy, the most remarkable specimen or freak of nature to be called human I ever saw, of whom I believe I have already written you, became so demoralized by fear and clung so closely to me that, in order to secure a little comfort, I told him to go to the rear, at the same time pointing back of me. He started off with a furious rush and had not gone many feet when a shell came crashing along and burst directly in his path, its flash lightening up the trees and bushes and causing him to think it had been fired from a cannon to the rear of us. With his hair on end, dilated eyes and fallen jaw, he staggered back to me and shouted, so that the whole company could hear him, "Captain dare is no rear, dare is no rear."

About 10 P.M., the cannonade having gradually slackened, I started out towards the front to find the pickets and was soon utterly lost in the bush. However my true direction was soon ascertained by hearing the enemy singing and loudly talking. I could hear the creaking of gun carriages as they were moved off from the place they had just occupied. I could hear the driving of stakes, cutting of wood, and, as I have said, singing going on. I could plainly distinguish the words of the singer as he kept time on a banjo, and knew pretty well from this what troops were in our front. He sang to the tune of "Other Side of Jordan" with a chorus as follows:

> "The Louisiana boys air a coming,
> Never mind the Yanks, but get upon their flanks,
> Ho, ho, ho, ha, ha, ha,
> And you'll send them to the other side of Jor-dan."

During this time I had been making a slight descent and soon struck a bog, across which, I judged, another hill arose, on the crest of which, I presumed, our Confederate friends lay. It struck me at the moment that possibly it was for this very elevation the battle of the morning had taken place, although I could not be positive as we had approached the place from a different direction, and again, it being dark, I could not accurately judge. As I could go no further, and not knowing exactly what to do, but believing my chances good for a retreat in case I made a mistake, I called out, "Where is the picket line?," and instantly received a reply from a dear familiar voice which seemed close to me, "Which picket line?" I cautiously answered, "Is that you Crocker?" and received the welcome reply that it was, as he pushed through the jungle and joined me. I hastily informed him of the situation and although I tried to disguise it as much as possible, yet his generous, true and manly heart understood the motive which had led me to seek and acquaint him of his perilous position.

After he had quietly assembled the men, I guided them safely back and reached the regiment without accident at 3 A.M., just as they were moving off, and after a fatiguing march to the rear, reached and bivouaced on the road to Banks Ford. Not waiting or attempting to write this day's proceedings, I threw myself down upon the ground, just where we halted, and without protection of any kind at once fell into a deep sleep. I was very tired, mentally tired. My brain had been on the strain all day, trying to fathom our mysterious manoeuvers and to learn whether our army had been checked. I was otherwise greatly distressed and annoyed by our flounderings amidst the tangled thickets and woods, now forward, then back again, now here and now there, not knowing just where to locate the enemy or to expect his attack. If this was the case with me, a captain, what must have been the anxiety of our division General, for I do not think he knew any more than I did of what was expected of us.

On May 2 Lee seized the initiative "Fighting Joe" had handed him when he backed into the Wilderness and sent Stonewall Jackson's Corps on a flanking march around Hooker's unsuspecting right. At dusk Jackson attacked and crushed the Federal 11th Corps, in the process forcing Hooker to retreat into a U-shaped defensive position with his right resting on the Rapidan and his left on the Rappahannock. Despite the disaster to the 11th Corps, Hooker was still optimistic. Gen. John Sedgwick and the 6th Corps were due to come up behind Lee from Fredericksburg, and his cavalry were to have cut the Confederate supply line by this time. But Sedgwick was inexorably slow in attacking, and the Federal troopers had failed in their half-hearted attempts at disrupting the southern rail links.

On May 3 Hooker remained hopeful, with his army strongly entrenched and Sedgwick due at any moment. But Sedgwick was delayed, and without the relief the attack of the 6th Corps would bring, Hooker felt exposed. He ordered his lines to fall back yet again, this time into a more constricted defensive position, but in the course of the retreat, the Federals yielded the key artillery position at Hazel Grove.[13] The Confederates soon took possession of the ground, and at a crucial moment during this day's battle, an artillery round fired from Hazel Grove shattered a porch column against which Hooker was leaning, knocking him unconscious for a time and insensible for much of the day. No news was received from the cavalry, and by the late evening, Sedgwick's advance had been halted by Confederate resistance at Salem Church, well short of Chancellorsville. Hooker determined to occupy his defensive position for one more day in the hope that Lee would attack.[14]

Donaldson and the 5th Corps were held in reserve throughout May 2 and 3 and, as at Antietam, were merely spectators to the events that transpired around them.

May 2nd. At early dawn we were up and commenced entrenching our position, heavy logs being placed one upon the other until a breast work 3 feet high and at least a mile in length was completed. The men worked with the energy of despair to erect this covering, a pitiable change having come over their spirits from the day before. The backing and filling plan of action, substituted for the bold aggressive one, had made them timid and panicky, and I noticed with much chagrin that my own men were entirely changed in demeanor and in their tone of conversation. I overheard them calculating the chances for a successful retreat, I heard them repeatedly say to one another that Lee was too much for us, and we would all be slaughtered if we did not get out of this dreadful place, and a great deal more of like talk which gave me an insight into the demoralization that had taken place in the last 24 hours. I mention this with no desire to disparage my company, but because my men spoke the sentiment of the whole division. They knew something was the matter with the General in Chief, some bungle had taken place, and they were fast losing confidence.

After finishing the works, which took them nearly to the middle of the afternoon, the men rested behind them. During this time I made my notes of the preceeding day's events and studied our position as critically as possible. It did not take many minutes to decide that our position was untenable, as in front of some portions of the line the ground was much higher and our men could be picked off without much show for their lives. They saw this also, and were silent and sullen all day. However our breastworks were very substantially built, more so than upon any other portion of the line. This fact is accounted for by reason of it being the first attempt of the 118th to build entrenchments, hence more pains were taken, and more time spent on them than by the older troops.

Just before sunset I noticed there was considerable firing towards the right of the army which gradually grew louder and louder until towards dusk the roar of battle was something appalling, the loud piercing soul-harrowing cheers of the Confederates being heard above all other sounds. The absence of any like demonstration from our men told the story too plainly. We were being beaten. Just as darkness closed in we were hastily called into line and moved at the double-quick towards the Chancellor House, where in single line we occupied the breastworks just vacated by the troops who had that day built them.

Now commenced a series of tactics the like of which I never before saw and which so thoroughly demoralized the men that I doubt if they had been seriously attacked they would have made a respectable fight. First there was passed along the line from man to man an order to spread out and take more room; then, to turn the visor of their caps around so that the moon's rays would not be reflected; then again to keep perfectly still; then to lie down; then to stand up and come to a ready; then to sit down; then to man the breastworks again, and many other ridiculous orders which got the poor fellows worked up to such a state that it required the utmost exertion of the officers to keep them steady. I found by taking a musket myself and standing in the ranks with them, obeying literally all orders passed along, it had a good effect.

Meantime the roar of battle slackened somewhat and at about nine o'clock, I should judge, although I did not note the time, Genl. Howard, with a portion of the 11th Corps which had just been crumbled to pieces by the Confederates, passed through the line at a short distance to the right of our regiment, and they continued to pass for over an hour. They seemed to be in pretty good condition, although not in anything like regular order. They said nothing, but moved silently to the rear. After they had passed there suddenly came a lull in the storm of battle. There was not a sound to disturb the most sensitive ear. Indeed the silence was most oppressive, causing the men, without any instruction to do so, to speak together in whispers.

The night was a glorious one, the full moon shining brightly and making objects quite distinct in the surrounding woods. An occasional cloud would now and then obscure it, only to make its rays more brilliant as they again burst forth and illuminated the forest. About this time a slight noise was noticed in our front, and peering eagerly into the woods, we tried to make out what it was. Soon a voice called out for "the men not to fire," as it was General Griffin, who having been out a short distance to observe the character of the ground was now making his way back again, and as he passed along with but one of his staff with him, I could not but notice how very much better satisfied the men appeared at getting a glimpse of the man, of all men, they had the most confidence in. Indeed, I never before saw such devotion to any single individual as his division to Genl. Griffin, and it was deserved, too, because he is always the friend of the enlisted men and looks closely after their wants.

Again silence reigned, but at length there came borne upon the gentle breeze, that indescribable murmur as of the wind afar off sighing through the trees, but which experience taught me was but the hum of a large body of men in motion. Louder and louder the sound approached until it broke into a perfect roar made by the steady tramp of thousands of disciplined marching feet through dried leaves and twigs. We could distinctly hear the words of command given, and one loud voice in particular will ever, while memory lasts, ring in my ears the order, "Battalion, halt, front, on the centre dress." Then again after a little pause, "Battalion right shoulder shift arms," again a slight pause and, "Forward, guide centre march." This order was quickly followed by a tremendous musketry firing, followed by a crash of artillery that fairly shook the earth beneath us, then deafening cheers arose, this time from our men, and the battle was on again in all its wild fury, and raged in fierce tumult all night long. The attack was upon our immediate right and our regiment did not fire a shot.[15] Thus was passed the night of the 2nd of May.

May 3rd. The dawn of day found us still in line, although the battle had ended and all was hushed. The battle by moonlight had terminated favorably to our arms, the enemy being repulsed with great loss. We soon learned the full extent of the disaster which had befallen the 11th Corps and of the opportune arrival of the 1st Corps, and of the further contraction and concentration of the whole army. We had consumed our last ration during the night before and were now entirely without food. I speak more especially of the officers, although the men generally had a few crackers still in their haversacks. I personally had been without anything to eat since early last night, and noticing the comfort tobacco chewers derived from its use, I started in to try and see what effect the weed would have upon me. I am glad, or sorry, I don't know which, just yet, that I took to it so kindly and was able to stand right up with any old regular and "chaw" right along. It certainly was a great help to me and warded off hunger in a very marked manner. Strange to say I did not feel the slightest indication towards sickness, but on the contrary greatly relished my first chew of "flounder."

The first thing this morning Lieut. Batchelder confidentially informed me that he felt a presentiment he would be killed this day. Before we entered on the campaign he had been troubled with horrible dreams, representing himself as being shockingly wounded in the right leg, and has had a repetition of them several times since, and again early this morning when having fallen asleep he dreamed that the right leg of his pants was saturated with blood. He said the dreams had been so persistent that it annoyed him and thought he had better speak to me about it, and make arrangements in case his presentiment should be verified. He then told me of his private affairs, and what he wanted done in case the worst should happen. This statement, made by such a manly, dignified, able and brave a gentleman was not to be treated lightly. I listened attentively and did not attempt to make light of his statement, but merely remarking that dreams go by contraries, I suggested that he should cease to make a target of himself as he had been doing, and merely to attend to his legitimate business obeying orders only.

Lt. Batchelder was remarkable for his coolness in danger, his bravery and utter disregard for self in times of peril, yet, with all these most excellent traits he suffered from a weakness often noticed in men of his temperament & character. He has often told me that the first report of a gun, in battle, gave him a nervous pain in the stomach which required the exertion of his utmost will to prevent it from incapacitating him for duty. To this disorder I traced his troubled mind and his disturbed sleep, and I felt assured he was not the subject of any special forecast of fate. I remember to have read of this peculiarity among celebrated military men, and that even the great Napoleon was a martyr to this curious trouble.

At 5 A.M. we were ordered and moved towards the centre where the firing had already commenced. Here we waited a long time on the road leading to U.S. Ford, and listened to the awful roar of musketry firing. The occasional

Winfield Scott Batchelder, Donaldson's first lieutenant in Company H, 118th Pennsylvania Volunteers. He had served previously with Donaldson in the 71st Pennsylvania. Don Enders Collection, USAMHI.

whistling of bullets over our heads told of the closeness of the engagement in front, although the dense woods hid the battle from our sight, whilst the thin blue smoke above the combatants, which, gradually drifting towards and enveloping us, partly obscured the sunlit sky of as lovely a morning as ever dawned on these forests. The passing to and fro of mounted officers, the dashing by of aides and the rapid marching past of artillery and detachments of infantry indicated to our eager senses an impending climax.

At 8 A.M. we were placed in line with Sykes' regulars, and for two hours the men worked like beavers to cover their own and the regulars front with breastworks, whilst the regulars themselves remained at a rest. No want of energy from loss of sleep was apparent, but the men tugged and toiled eagerly, for they knew instinctively that the battle ahead was not a success. During this time troops were being constantly pushed out to the front and the battle each moment seemed to grow in intensity. There was no cheering on either side, as the fight seemed to hang in the balance. I noticed that as the other troops passed through, our men congratulated each other on the fact that this duty had not fallen to their lot, an evident lack of improved spirits most discouraging. After completing the breast-works the Regulars moved up to and occupied them, while we fell back again to the road and enjoyed a short interval of rest.

At noon we were called into line and moved by the flank towards the Chancellor House. As we approached this place the noise of the battle became most deafening, the air was filled with bursting shells and the cheering of the Confederates incessant. Just before arriving at our destination we saw approaching us thro' the timber, which at this point was rather free of underbrush than usual, four men bearing an officer on a stretcher. Captain Bankson called out and wanted to know whom they had. They replied, "Col. Collis of the 114 Penna." [16] "Is he shot?" said the Captain. "Shot in the neck," replied one of the men, whereupon they put down the stretcher and Col. Collis arose, and upon Col. Prevost asking where his regiment was, replied, "Just ahead, Sir, heavily engaged, but I being sick was obliged to turn over the command to Maj. Chandler and go to the rear." He exhibited his sword scabbard, much bent, as having been struck by a bullet. Without desiring to comment upon the conduct of this officer, I will say his whole appearance and manner at this time denoted fear of the most abject kind. The men smiled contemptuously as they passed him by, and I felt exceedingly sorry they had been a witness to the humiliating loss of honor and self-respect of a man so widely known as Col. Chas. H. T.

Collis.[17] I can add here that Maj. Joseph Chandler fought his regiment bravely after Collis left, and lost his life in so doing, his body being left upon the field in the hands of the enemy. A sad ending to the career of as fine a soldier and gentleman as ever entered the service. He was a man very well known to our officers, and, indeed, throughout the army. It had been the intention of the Corn Exchange to have given him the position of Lt. Colonel of the 118th, but which intention was frustrated by an influence which to-day must feel their mortifying mistake.[18]

We arrived at an open space in the vicinity of the Chancellor House, upon the margin of which Griffin's Battery was heavily engaged, and to the rear of which the great Field Hospital, with its crowds of wounded and its busy surgeons was located. Just as we reached this spot there took place a lively stampede among the doctors and attendants, who dropping their instruments rushed frantically to the rear. It appears that our line to the front had been beaten back far enough for the shells to reach and tear through the hospital, killing and wounding several of the surgeons, and as we passed through, I witnessed the unhappy sight of many of our wounded still further mangled and killed as they lay abandoned with their hurts but partially dressed.

We were ordered to lie flat upon the ground in rear of the guns which we were to support. The rain of shells at the time was something marvelous, indeed, so terrible and so accurate was the firing that our guns were speedily silenced. I looked along the line to see how the men were standing this ordeal, and was pleased to notice that very few were lying flat, but that most of them were crouching with muskets held upright in the attitude of soldiers alert for instant service. As I stood looking down the line I saw a shell strike an officer of the 1st Michigan as he lay upon his back reading a paper. It passed directly through his stomach, scattering his entrails on those around him.[19] Just then one of my men told me that Col. Prevost was calling me, and I went over to where the Field Officers were. They were behind a breastwork a little to the right and beyond our line where they had a commanding view of the whole situation. Col. Prevost called my attention to the conduct of Lieut. Batchelder and desired me to order him to his proper station. I then for the first time noticed this gallant officer who was then and had been for some time standing erect upon an artillery chest gazing through a pair of field glasses at the enemy and making himself a conspicuous object and drawing the fire of the enemy towards this particular spot. He was apparently oblivious to any personal danger, and upon my ordering him down said that I had no idea of the magnificient view he had obtained of the battle.

Meantime the artillery kept arriving and as battery after battery took position I could not but wonder at this massing of so many guns. The firing abating somewhat, I asked and obtained permission from Col. Prevost to advance towards the front and with Capt. Crocker proceeded towards a little white house, the property of a person by name of Burns, that occupied an angle of the breastworks which had lately been thrown up to and extended a little on the left of it.[20] Directly in the rear of this house a large tent was pitched which I soon saw was Head Quarters of the army. The flaps being up, we stopped to see what was the occasion of so many of the field and staff officers assembled both inside and around it. I saw General Hooker reclining, who, with a number of other officers, was busily engaged in drinking champagne, a basket of which liquor occupied the centre of the tent. Capt. Crocker was told by an officer present that General Hooker had just been stunned by a pillar of the Chancellor House striking him as he stood upon the porch of that building directing the fight. Upon Crocker remarking that he thought it more than likely the beverage the Genl. had taken was the cause of his prostration, the officer laughed and rode forward himself to get some [of] it.

This spectacle was in plain view of our regiment and could be seen by those who cared to look. Our Field Officers saw it, and I feel confident in asserting that they and all of those who witnessed this undignified sight felt how little the army could depend upon its leader for any future success.

The scene about this tent was altogether one of the most remarkable I ever saw. Officers were rushing to and fro in hot haste, artillery was dashing up and unlimbering, men by the hundreds, apparently without leaders, were passing rapidly to the rear, and riderless horses were wandering about, very many of them badly wounded. One horse in particular, with blood spouting from a wound in his chest came cantering up to an officer who was at the time sitting on his horse near me. I shall never forget the poor beast, he looked so intelligent and came so confidently towards us as if certain of help, and I am sure it made the same impression on this officer as it did on me, for suddenly pulling out his pistol he fired two shots into the poor animal's head and then rode away as if the sight was too much for him. Some time after I again noticed this horse as he would occasionally try to get upon his feet, only to fall struggling back again. Oh, would that my pen could but describe the scenes here enacted and others which shortly after followed. If I could only tell of every incident I witnessed in this dreadful panorama how many pages could I fill with the account of this disastrous day's work.

The battle was raging just ahead and the atmosphere was hazy from the smoke which enveloped us and which drifting aloft, hung above our heads like a canopy. Running forward to the front of Burns House, I gazed upon a battle scene the like of which I think has been given to very few to witness. The open ground of which I have spoken was about 150 yards in extent, and dipped somewhat towards the centre, then gradually rising terminated in a sparcely wooded elevation. The battle was plainly in view, and I could see our men with their lines nicely formed, who, with their backs towards us, were firing and loading as they slowly retired through the timber. Then came the waving battle flag, the gleaming muskets, and the butter nut and gray uniforms of the Confederates as their line of battle came in view in a fierce determined onset. On they swept, the men loading and firing as they came, the peculiar flash of their ram-rods being particularly noticed. Our line stood fast and their muskets spoke the notes of defiance, warning and death. There was a crash, a mingling of gray and blue and then cheers and cries, shouts, shrieks and shrill voices of command rent the air. My heart stood still, my blood fairly curdled, my breath came quick and fast, and the cold perspiration broke out all over me. God! did ever mortal see such a sight? I could see the bayonet freely used and I could note the ever advancing flag of the enemy as it pushed down the slope, now sprinkled with blood.

The piercing yells of the rebels now drown all other sounds as our brave fellows break and retreat towards us, closely followed by the victorious enemy who came on in a headlong, blazing charge. It was Tyler's brigade of the 3rd Division, 5th Corps that had made this fight, and now that all regular order was lost, they retreated precipitately towards and through the artillery which had been massed evidently in anticipation of this disaster. We had lost the Chancellor House and our army was being badly handled. So urgent was the necessity for an instant check to be given the enemy that many of our own men who had not yet reached the shelter of the guns were torn to pieces by the full charge of canister, which, at that moment, the artillery hurled into the advancing foe, and with that tremendous discharge the enemy's line was annihilated, but very few of them ever reaching their own people again. To add still further to the horror, the dried leaves in the woods took fire, and the wounded of both sides, friend and foe alike, were speedily burned to death.

So great had been my excitement that I had not noticed the extreme peril both Capt. Crocker and I had been in, and was only reminded of it just before our artillery opened by the death of a poor fellow who had almost reached the shelter of the house where we were standing. After the fight I made an examination of his body but could find nothing whereby to identify him, and he was buried just where he fell and not even a mound raised to mark his last resting place. Had his name been found I could have marked his grave and sent his people word of his death. But no, he now sleeps with the great army of unknown dead.

Shortly after, and while there was still great confusion, bustle and heavy firing going on on our left, I noticed a mob of cheering men moving along our front, from the left towards us. As they neared our regiment I saw they were dragging several pieces of cannon, which from the broken appearance of the muzzle of one of them, I judged they had seen some rough usage. I soon learned that these guns had been lately taken by a Captain of the 116 Penna. Regiment for which gallant exploit Genl. Hancock ordered them to drag them along the front of the army. We joined lustily in the cheering which marked the passage of these brave fellows.[21]

At 2 P.M. we were ordered a short distance to the rear and the men were allowed to make coffee. As I had no coffee nor anything else with which to make a meal, I wandered among the wounded in the Field Hospital where we bivouaced and did what I could to help the doctors, who had returned to their posts. . . .

Later in the afternoon we were informed that Genl. Sedgwick had crossed the river, taken Marye's Heights and Fredericksburg, capturing many prisoners and large quantities of artillery, and thus placing the Confederates between two fires.[22] I must confess we were greatly elated at this most unexpected success, and the news made us feel confident that the morrow would witness a new state of things and the final discomforture of the enemy. Just before dusk we were again moved up to the Burns House and put to work building breastworks. The men having now had considerable experience in this work soon constructed them by piling dead horses along the line and covering them with a foot or two of earth.

Thus closed this eventful day, and although very many of the officers, my friend Capt. Crocker among the rest, erected shelter tents, I was too tired to do so, but just rolled myself up in my overcoat and soon slept the sleep of the weary.

On May 4 Lee left a holding force to watch Hooker and his army around Chancellorsville and turned on Sedgwick, pushing him back to the Rappahannock under concentrated assaults. Faced with the now real prospect of heavy reinforcements

reaching Lee from the south and the 6th Corps isolated and hemmed in, Hooker
ordered his army to cross to the north side of the river on the night of May 5–6.[23]
"My God!," Lincoln anguished when informed that Hooker had been defeated.
"What will the country say?"[24]

Donaldson and a detachment from the 118th played a significant role in the
retreat, acting as rear guard for the army.

<u>May 4th</u>. This day, like its predecessors, was ushered in with a cloudless
sky. I soon noticed something was the matter with my friend Capt.
Crocker. He said he had spent a very uncomfortable night owing to the
uneven and yielding nature of the ground, and although he had several
times tried to remove the things which had annoyed him he was unable to
do so, and as soon as it was light enough, had made an examination of the
spot to see what in the world was the trouble. To his horror, he found he
had been sleeping upon the body of a dead man, who, having been hastily
buried, had but a thin layer of earth over him, and it was his nose and fingers that he had tried to pull away through the night, and his yielding
body that made his bed so spongy and springy. It was the first time I ever
saw the Captain disconcerted, but he certainly was this time. Who can
blame him and who would like such a mattress?

It soon became apparent that the enemy, far back in the woods—the
margin of which our pickets firmly held—had gotten our range exactly,
and from the tree tops at nearly a mile distant, their sharp shooters constantly picked off our men. Indeed the firing became so severe that we
were obliged to keep below the breastworks for safety, and yet we could
not see from whence the shots came.

About 11 A.M., whilst momentarily standing in an exposed place talking to Lieutenant Thomas, he was struck in the shoulder by a bullet,
which having traveled such a long distance was spent and did not penetrate
his clothing, but just gave him a severe blow and then fell at our feet.
Upon examining the missile we found it to be of the peculiar elongated
pattern used in the Berdan rifle and most likely was fired from one of those
terrible globe sighted weapons captured from our people.

About one P.M. General Whipple, General Hooker's Engineer officer,[25]
came out to where we were and leisurely walked his horse along our
breastworks. He was at once cautioned by the officers and advised at least to
dismount, but being so much under the influence of liquor as to be scarcely
able to sit on his horse, he did not heed nor reply but walked along to the

right of our regiment, where, halting his horse and facing the enemy, he swayed backwards and forwards in his saddle. Capt. Crocker had just remarked that the General was very drunk, when we saw the dust fly from his cloths and himself fall off his horse. Running to where he lay we found that he had been shot through the stomach and bowels, the bullet coming out at the small of the back.[26] Although he appeared to be perfectly conscious, he never spoke, never said one single word, or groaned, or betrayed the slightest concern at his condition. Soon, a stretcher having been sent for, he was carried back into the woods, and I witnessed the examination of his hurt by the surgeons, who, placing his face downwards on the stretcher made some little show of stopping the flow of blood, which however, was not much to speak of, as the wound bled internally. He died whilst they were working with him, not having displayed the slightest emotion of any kind.[27]

Again I returned to the breastworks and listened to the deep booming of the guns on our left, where Genl. Sedgwick and the enemy were struggling for the mastery. In our front with the exception of the sharpshooting there was nothing done until about 4 P.M. when the 2nd & 3rd Brigades of our Division commenced preparations for an advance. About 5 P.M. they moved out and our brigade at once spread and occupied their place and held ourselves in readiness to support the movement. It was [a] glorious sight to see these two heavy brigades in line of battle, their colors fluttering in the wind, and their muskets glistening in the bright sun light.

All things being in readiness the order to advance was given and I stood upon the breastworks with bated breath and watched the imposing spectacle. Nothing could exceed the steadiness of the troops and their correct alignments, no crowding, no pushing or elbowing, but just the slight touch of the elbow so noted in the well drilled, disciplined and self reliant soldier. There was no apparent hesitation, but with a ringing cheer they crossed the open ground and were soon lost to view in the woods. It was only a spurt.[28] Meantime the Confederate pickets and skirmishers kept up a lively fire until driven in, and then our ears were greeted by the awful roar of heavy musketry firing, as our people became engaged. We soon noticed the firing did not recede and indeed for that matter appeared to become more and more distinct, until our troops were seen slowly retiring from the timber and were soon again in their places behind the breastworks, having utterly failed to dislodge the enemy, who, by the way, did not follow them up very closely, thus showing a desire to avoid a general engagement. It seemed to me that the attack lacked spirit and energy, thus proving what I have before remarked, that our troops were not <u>now</u> in good fighting trim, they were dispirited and listless. The very men who had just obeyed the order to attack knew it would be a failure as they plainly saw that they were not supported and that even if they did meet with success they felt they would in all probability have to face back again in order to continue the inaugurated policy of the "defensive." So we again resumed our places, and crouching down behind the breastworks, listened to the distant battle on our left. So closed the day and the night passed uneventful with the exception of one or two alarms from the nervious pickets.

May 5th. Again the sun came to greet us, unclouded and gorgeously brilliant, gilding the tree tops, penetrating the vapors of the forest and glistening through the foliage. Shortly after dawn there took place a very heavy firing on the picket line, which lasted quite a little while, until finally the 1st Michigan pickets were driven in pell mell, and followed some distance over the open by the audacious enemy. After the Michiganders had gained the breastworks the artillery opened and for at least 15 minutes swept the margin of the woods causing the Confederates to hastily seek cover, but failed in driving them altogether from the edge of the woods, as the straggling but murderous fire of the sharpshooters constantly bore testimony among the artillerists.

Soon after the artillery ceased firing, Adjutant Chas. H. Hand came crawling along the breastworks to where I was sitting, and in his usual laughing but very annoying way said that a detail of 160 men and three officers had been ordered from the regiment to advance and wrest from the enemy the space just captured from the 1st Michigan, and that although it was not my tour of duty, I had been selected to command it, and that I might originate my own plans, and that he would do all in his power to further them. He concluded by adding, as was generally his custom when giving a disagreeable order, that he thanked God he was so situated as never to be called upon for a like duty. He meant to be funny, as he really was not cowardly, but bore the reputation of being an efficient officer. Being an adjutant, he was not liable for picket or skirmish work, excepting only when the whole command was on picket at one time, which was very seldom. I think he always tried to make a fellow feel as badly as possible without really meaning to be ugly. He certainly made it a point in saying disagreeable things to do so in such a manner that little chance for resentment was had. I told him to have the detail report to me, and in the meantime I would prepare my plans.

After he left I sat still for a little time and thought over the order just given me. True it was a splendid opportunity for distinction, as the advance would be made in the presence of the whole division, and in the presence of Genl. Griffin, from whom the order came, and who at this very time was waiting and watching among the cannon for us to go forward. Still I was not unmindful of the very great danger attached to the undertaking, nor at the still more dreadful and mortifying effect of a failure. The latter contingency, should it unfortunately happen, I calmly and deliberately determined not to survive.

In order to make success doubly sure, I went over to Col. Prevost and asked permission to select my own officers, which was granted, and I chose my Lieut., Batchelder, & Lt. John W. Thomas. Whilst receiving his instructions and arranging the necessary preliminaries, Capt. O'Neill, who, by the way, ranked me, volunteered to serve with the detachment provided I would permit him, or to use his language, he was "divilish tired of 'marking time' behind breastworks." I could not refuse, although to tell the truth, of all the officers of the regiment I would rather not have had him. Whilst he was bravery itself, that was all. He knew absolutely nothing about handling skirmishers, or, indeed for that matter, was the poorest tactician in the whole command. The men knew this and the soubriquet of "Owld Teddy" will illustrate in what estimation they held him. O'Neill was no soldier, but a good natured, well meaning, brave Irishman, who would rather fight than do anything else except tell about what they used to do in "Injee" when he served in Her Majesty's Foot. However I accepted his services and assigned him to the extreme right of the line, where I felt certain his fierce bravery would keep the men up from very pride, if for no other reason. Shortly after I saw him with his overcoat, haversack and shelter tent on, as though he were off for a day's march. When spoken to about his "get up" he replied "there is nothing like being in 'chewn' (tune)," meaning prepared for any emergency.

Maj. Herring, my mentor, my dear generous and devoted friend, took me aside and said that it was to him I owed this distinction and that he desired above all things that I should be successful, and that he felt that I would not disappoint the opinion he had formed of my ability for command, and that he held for me a high personal regard and esteem, and, he further added, confidentially, that to no other officer would he so confidently entrust the honor of the command about to be so desperately tested, as to myself. Need I say that whilst he spoke my blood tingled with pleasurable emotions entirely new to me, for I never before knew that I was held in such regard by this splendid man, this beau ideal of a manly soldier. I thanked him for his kindly words and assured him that my life would this day pay the forfeit should I prove unworthy the friendship he had just shown me. At parting he said he could do no more for me, that I was about to make for myself and for the regiment a name that all who knew me would feel proud of and that during the attack he would pray the Almighty to have me in His keeping.

I have before mentioned that the open ground dipped towards the centre. General Griffin's orders were that in case I met with a reverse to fall back and halt at this depression, when he would cover me with the artillery, and that the signal for the advance would be a red flag dropped by himself on the breastworks.

I now went back and found the men assembled in detatchments in rear of the regiment, and after ordering them to deploy as skirmishers, which had to be done on hands and knees, I passed along and spoke to nearly every one, explaining that at the signal, which would be my rising and giving the order to charge, they were expected to jump up and rush over the breastworks to the woods opposite, not stopping to fire, but merely to gain the edge of the woods where a better chance could be had with the enemy. I will add here that I was particularly struck with the behavior of the men, they appeared to have confidence in me and plainly showed it by their attention to what I said and by the business-like manner with which they grasped their muskets. I felt very proud, indeed, of my little command and was assured the honor of the 118th was in safe hands. You must bear in mind that my line extended about the distance of nearly three squares, the men being abt. five feet apart, and of course it took considerable time to get them into shape, but I was ably assisted by my officers and finally succeeded in having them all properly placed. Meantime we were constantly receiving the attention of the rebel sharpshooters, who appeared to find the weak spots in our defenses, much to our discomfort. Nothing, however, could be seen of the enemy, but the puffs of smoke from the bushes told too plainly they were in considerable force on the line we were expected to occupy.

Everything being in readiness I passed the word to General Griffin that I was ready, and shortly after saw a man rise up from the artillery and drop the red flag. Springing to my feet, in a moment I was on the breastworks, and turning called out, "Up men, forward, double quick, charge," the command being at once repeated in the clear ringing tones of Lt. Batchelder as he headed the terrible rush which was instantly made by the left of the line. Pausing long enough to take a hasty glance along the line, I found that whilst all were up and rapidly leaping the breastworks, the left was already in the advance, and I noticed the tall figure of Lt. Batchelder well ahead, swinging his sword about like a wind mill. Jumping to the ground I broke away and led the centre, which was something of a task to do, as the men literally rushed headlong after me. I never knew from whence came the impulse which drove them ahead but have since thought it was the appreciation of the importance of covering the open as quickly as possible that had something to do with it. Before we had gone half way I remember to have felt surprise that I had such difficulty in keeping ahead. I really did not give the men credit for the fiery vigor they now displayed, having so lately seen them stubbornly obedient to orders, only without enthusiasm.

The enemy's fire now became very severe and the whole edge of the woods seemed ablaze. I could hear the cheers and encouraging shouts of our brigade and I was terribly excited. I was keenly alive to everything that was happening, and I felt that I knew every man by name and had entire control of his actions. I called upon and urged the lagging ones, and noticed when anyone dropped out of the line. I knew just what every man was doing. As we proceeded I became aware that the men were bunching too much near me, and I tried to scatter them, but did not succeed very well. Soon the depression was reached and passed, the men showing no evidence of faltering, but pushed right on. As we neared the woods they redoubled their exertions and a number passed me, some of them firing their muskets, which was the only infringement of positive orders that occurred. A few more hurried stops and we were in the position lately occupied by the 1st Michigan, and the firing became most severe and destructive. My men were pretty well exhausted by the long run and many of them hugged the trees without doing anything but pant.

Just at the spot where I struck the woods was a large tree which was pretty well scored by shot, and behind its shelter four men struggled for place, the outer one, a very large man named George La Noir of Co. K[29] seemed determined to displace the others. Noticing this unseemly strife I laid hold of La Noir and dragged him into the line of fire, when he broke away and took to another tree in short order. I did a like service for two of the others, when the fourth, fearing perhaps that I wanted the tree for myself, ran off and took up a new position before I had time to stop him. However, I took the tree myself and established head quarters there, and then went along the line and found a number of instances where two or more had taken the same tree, thus losing the services of fully a dozen men who were unwilling to budge and afraid of being ousted by each other. I made short work of this and soon got the men down to good musketry firing.

I made no effort to force the woods, but soon heard Batchelder's voice far on the left as he directed the men to move forward. He was pushing on beyond where it was deemed the line should be, so I ran over to and withdrew him from the woods to its margin, ordering him to hold the same until I could get some entrenching tools. I then went along to where O'Neill was and found him hopping about like a mad man shouting, "Out Scout, bad luck to ye." It appears that a member of his Co., Tom Scout by name, was particularly disagreeable to him, and he was forever finding fault with him, and when angered or excited, called everyone by the name of

Capt. Henry O'Neill, Company A, 118th Pennsylvania Volunteers. Don Enders Collection, USAMHI.

Scout. Hence when the men refused to go beyond the edge of the woods he "Scouted" the whole of them and accused them of "marking time." I ordered him to hold on to the ground already gained and I would get him a few spades.

A little while after I noticed the enemy were falling back and that only an occasional slouched hat bobbing about among the bushes was all that could be seen of them. Taking advantage of the lull, I sent Lt. Thomas back to report that I had gained the woods and reestablished the line and wanted some picks and spades to make myself secure. These were at once sent me and after distributing them along the line I had the men dig themselves rifle pits. I had a pretty roomy one thrown up for myself and Lt. Thomas, who, by the way, although a most brave and fearless fellow, is also most exasperatingly fond of his comfort. After seeing a good wall of dirt thrown up against the tree, which by the way he did not seem in any haste to take advantage of, he went about gathering up a number of the Waverly Magazines which lay scattered among the dead that encumbered the ground. How they got there, whether by the Confederates or our own people, I cannot say, but there they were, all scattered about and Thomas appropriated all within reach. Along with the picks and spades came a line or two written by Maj. Herring congratulating me on the good record I had made for myself and the regiment.

During all this time I had never once been under shelter and, indeed, I was so very anxious about the success of my undertaking that I never once thought of personal danger, and it was only after having seen the men well covered and everything properly prepared to repel attack that the thought of self suddenly flashed upon me, and I sprang into my rifle pit as though I had been shot, and for a few minutes lay quite overcome with emotions at the contemplation of what I had accomplished and of my escape from any hurt.

As I lay here thinking of these things the men on my right called to pass the word not to fire, that O'Neill had agreed with the Confederate commanding the skirmish line in our front to discontinue firing, that they would not molest us provided we would do the same, and that in event of being relieved they would notify us in time and expect us to do likewise. I was glad of this arrangement, especially as it had been made by another than myself, as had I been approached with the proposition I would have had to decline holding any conversation with the enemy. The word was therefore passed and shortly after the men were sitting upon and around their rifle pits as unconcernedly as you please. The enemy did likewise and from where I sat I could plainly see one of them walking about quite near, without his musket, as though merely stretching his limbs a little. I forbid any conversation with them and ordered the men under no circumstances to leave their pits but merely to make themselves as comfortable as possible and be ready for instant action should it be necessary. O'Neill soon after reported to me that he had had a good talk with the Confederate officer who met him at a log midway between the lines; that he had explained just where his own line extended and O'Neill had done the same. The Confederate had added that he was opposed to picket firing except when absolutely necessary, and that he could see no necessity for it now, and also that his men were tired and he knew ours were also. O'Neill had acted very prudently, if it can be called prudence in holding conversation at all with an enemy with whom you are actually fighting, in declining to name his regiment, although, of course, the officer knew by his badge that he was in front of a portion of the 5th Corps.

For the rest of the day we had no firing on our line, but to the left the firing was very severe, and we also noticed that very many of the bullets exploded after passing beyond the line, thus showing the enemy to be using the English explosive ammunition that had run the blockade.

About 11 A.M. a mounted officer and two mounted men bearing a large white flag came slowly from our works, and crossing the open field, passed through the line on our left, after which the firing near us gradually slackened and finally ceased altogether. I learned the flag of truce was for the purpose of obtaining the body of Maj. Chandler, but I fear they did not succeed as they did not return, at least through our portion of the line.

I had now plenty of leisure to inspect this portion of the battle field, and I noticed that the fire which had burned so fiercely in the woods had not reached this particular locality. The vast number of dead that lay around showed how deadly had been the conflict. The Confederate dead greatly exceeded our own and presented a marked contrast, in their scanty cloths and equipment, to the well appointed Union dead. With my knees drawn up to my chin and my hands clasped around them, I sat for a long time leaning against the tree looking at the upturned faces of the dead. Great Heavens! how many they were and in what attitudes they lay. It was a dreadful sight to see them there, so quiet and to note the sprinkling of blue among the butternut and gray. I noticed one peculiarity with these dead men, and that was that our people invariably lay upon their sides, with knees drawn up, or else upon their faces, whilst the Confederates lay upon their backs with legs spread out and hands clenched, and some of them in their dying agony were clinching the branches of the bushes that drooped over time. As I had nothing else to do I tried to account for this peculiarity and finally concluded that the weight of cartridge box, canteen and haversack which our men carried and which invariably worked to the front when not otherwise controlled, as in time of battle, had something to do with it. The Confederates not encumbered by anything but a canteen and haversack, usually with nothing in it, and seldom by a cartridge box, having cartridges in their pockets, had fallen backward when shot. At least this is the way I interpreted the singular coincidence. . . .

Towards 2 P.M. it commenced clouding up rapidly, and from where I sat I watched the heavy dark gathering masses as they crowded and rolled over each other in one vast effort to overcome and obliterate "the luminary that made the day." The wind came with the gathering storm and the trees bent before its blast. Heavy, black, and lowering the storm burst upon us, and the rain fell in sweeping torrents as though the very windows of Heaven were opened. We were soon drenched to the skin and our rifle pits filled with water. This kept up for over an hour, when the storm settled into a continuously heavy pour.

Just before dark we were notified by the honorable fellows who had been confronting us that they were about to be relieved by the Mississippi troops and would advise us to seek cover and look sharp. As the enemy very soon again commenced firing we were obliged to bail out the pits and occupy them. I cannot describe the misery of the situation. The mud was appalling and as the temperature had greatly fallen, the men were soon stiff from the cold. To add still further to the discomfiture, the enemy discovered a new plan of harassing us. They would creep up quite close to our line, suddenly flash a lantern and fire a shot. In this way two of my men were hit, and by reason of the extreme watchfulness this procedure caused, the water gained in the pits and the poor fellows had to stand in it up to their waists.

O'Neill was the only one oblivious to the surrounding discomforts. Just before the storm burst, he had erected a shelter tent out in the open field to the rear of me, and upon the many blankets gathered he lay as dry as punk and as comfortable as could be. After dark he had the audacity to light a candle which he had with him and lay back reading his paper, unmindful of the shots fired at him. I can recall but one instance wherein he was at all disturbed, and that was when a few drops of rain fell upon him from a bullet hole just made in the canvas, and then his shadow pictured him as reaching up and stopping it with paper. To the repeated orders from me to put out his light he replied that he "didn't care a devil for the firing as he would much rather be shot than drowned entirely." I let him have his own way and he kept the light burning 'till it burned itself out.

Although it was very dark and the rain continued falling incessantly, the water, as it ran over the open field between us and our army, made a certain light upon the surface that reflected objects quite plainly.

About one o'clock A.M. I noticed an object moving cautiously toward us and I determined to learn what it was. Leaving Lt. Thomas in charge I walked back towards it, and as I approached I distinctly heard the click of a pistol trigger. Holding my own in readiness to fire I called, "Who goes there." "A friend," replied the deep toned voice of Maj. Herring, and my heart gave a leap of relief as I ran toward him. His greeting was most affectionate, as laying aside the stern soldier he met me as only a true friend could under such trying circumstances. He said the army had retreated and that we were abandoned on post that they might escape, but as he had urged my selection for this duty, he could not leave without first making me acquainted with the situation. Noticing that I shook and trembled a good deal, he asked whether I was hurt or sick. I replied, neither, but that I was very cold and hungry, and believed unnerved by the excitement under which I had been for so many hours, and by the great responsibility yet resting upon me; that I also believed the pleasure of seeing him and the appreciation of his kindly act of friendship had a good deal to do with it. Without replying he handed me his canteen and I soon felt very much invigorated by the long draft I took of its water and Jamaica Ginger contents, and from eating the two crackers he gave me of his scanty supply.

He then gave me a full account of what had happened, how that the rain had flooded the breastworks so that openings had to be cut to let the water out; how that the mud was knee deep everywhere, effectually preventing any movement of troops that might have been in contemplation; and how that the artillery and wagon trains had gone early in the afternoon and the troops after dark. He said that during the early part of the night, before our division had retreated and before it was known that the army was retiring, General Barnes had informed him of its withdrawal and desired him to take general command of the rear guard, using his judgment whether to abandon the pickets or try and bring them off. Being familiar with the exact location of my line he had posted himself on a few sacks of grain which lay in the open field about 50 yards in front of the breast-works, where with an officer whose name he could not now recall he had awaited the morning hours with the intention of informing me of the situation.

While listening attentively to the occasional shots on my line and gaz-ing anxiously over the field towards where I lay, he noticed a dark moving mass apparently coming from my direction, and thinking that perhaps the enemy had gotten through and was moving to the attack, he asked his companion to accompany him towards it for the purpose of finding out its true character. This the gallant gentleman declined doing, so he proceeded alone, and when near he commanded the object to halt, which being done, an officer advanced whom he found to be Col. Hayes of the 18th Massachusetts Regiment who had been detailed with his command to act as support to the skirmishers should they succeed in withdrawing. He had been floundering about for sometime trying to find the picket line and was utterly lost and bewildered. After explaining the position to the Colonel, he had suggested the placing of his regiment in line in front of the works to await the first movement I should make towards a retreat.

This being done he had sought me and now suggested keeping all this to myself and at day break do whatever I thought best about getting away. Although I felt very badly at thus being deserted, I told him I thought I could bring off my men safely. He further added that he would not inter-fere with me as I had already done so much and so well and that his only desire was to be near should I need help, and that the glory, reputation, and credit attending this final act in the great drama just enacted of a right belonged to me, and I should have it all. He then went back to the breast-works and I to my post where I sat through the two long dreary hours awaiting the time for action, and listening to the falling rain and the occa-sional picket shot. The one thought uppermost in my mind was that I was alone in the face of a victorious enemy, and that upon me rested the safety of the army and its trains & artillery. I was the Rear Guard.

It was near 3 A.M. when I awakened Lt. Thomas and told him just how things stood. I also acquainted Capt. O'Neill with the situation of affairs and ordered him to look after the withdrawal of the right of the line, but not to fall back until the word to do so was passed. I then saw Lt. Batchelder and together we laid the plans for retreat. I now passed along the line and acquainted the men with the state of affairs and ordered the removal of all tin cups and everything else likely to make the slightest noise. In a number of instances I found the men asleep, but it was always where two or more occupying the same pit had erected a slight protection against the rain while one of their number kept watch. At one of the pits near my own I had great difficulty in arousing the men, but finally succeeded in awakening Private Jno. Smith, Co. K, who with his usual activity assisted me in notifying the rest of the line. The man on post at Smith's pit was so benumbed with the cold and wet that he had to be abandoned when we finally retired.

At a little after 3 A.M. I silently withdrew from the rifle pits without the enemy's notice, and moved back over the muddy plain to the abandoned breastworks, where after placing my men to the best advantage, I awaited daybreak and the enemy. Meantime, as soon as they noticed me moving, the 18th Massachusetts fell back to the woods and took up a position in support.

Soon after it was light the Confederates discovered our absence and at once moved forward in pursuit. I soon saw that it would be impossible to stay where we were as the enemy's skirmish line covered nearly twice the distance that mine did and I would be flanked out of the woods in no time and perhaps taken, so I gave the order to fall back. After retreating about a half of a mile, I halted in a piece of thick woods through which our army wagon road passed, and facing about with my line across it, I awaited developments. I never in all my experience saw anything like the mud. It was something dreadful, it was knee deep and it is no exaggeration when I say that I saw a number of caissons and battery wagons abandoned because they were over axle in the mire. I never saw anything to equal this mud hole through which the army had retreated, and I very much doubt had it remained a day longer whether it could have withdrawn at all.

Shortly after, the enemy, in following the road as I anticipated they would do, came suddenly upon me and a fierce encounter ensued, resulting in their being estopped and brought to a stand still, when they in turn were attacked by Lt. Batchelder, who in a handsome manner pushed back for some distance a portion of their line. Maj. Herring now came up with a number of men with whom he desired me to relieve some of my exhausted ones. I sent the reinforcements to Batchelder with instructions to extend his line as much as possible with the extreme left well refused. Whether it was this movement that attracted the enemy's attention, certain it is that they precipitated a most furious attack upon me, causing some of Batchelder's men to give way and break in rather a panicky manner. The balance of the line with the assistance of Thomas and O'Neill I was able to hold well in hand.

At this juncture Colonel Hayes came upon the scene, riding forward pistol in hand, threatening and cursing the men for giving way and bidding both Maj. Herring and me to shoot down any who did not instantly halt and face about. I answered that my men would stick and that there was no need for violence, and indeed while I spoke the panic was stayed and the men were feeling up again towards the enemy. I will admit that just where Colonel Hayes came upon the ground, there was considerable confusion, noise and shouting, and things did look a little badly, but the men had rallied some-what, and were soon at it again, while a new turn to affairs was given. Shortly after Col. Hayes sent me a reinforcement from his regiment which I deployed along the whole line to strengthen it. I was now able to hold my own and did do so until ordered by Maj. Herring to fall back. . . .

I now commenced falling back fighting the whole way until I reached the edge of the woods near the river at United States Ford, where the army had crossed. From the woods to the pontoon bridge the ground descended gradu-ally and was utterly devoid of trees or other covering. I noticed that everything was perfectly clear on the bridge and that the artillery lined the hills on the opposite bank, and I rightly judged that it was placed there to protect me. The enemy again commencing to be active I gave the order to fall back which was quickly responded to, and I was soon out in the open ground with my line exposed to the enemy's musketry. I now gave the order to assemble, double quick on the centre, which was hardly accomplished when the artillery from over the river opened and swept the woods in my rear. Marching my men in quick time I without any further trouble reached the pontoons in safety and at once commenced tearing them up. It was now 9 o'clock A.M. & I shall never forget the scene as I stood on the bridge directing the work. The artillery roaring and the shells hissing overhead, the bustle and noise as the men pulled up the planks and lifted anchors of the boats, the swift flowing river, the heavily wooded hills and the dark lowering clouds and pelting rain, all made up a scene of dreadful grandeur. When my work was completed, I reported to Genl. Barnes and was at once the recipient of congratulations from him, Col. Prevost and Genl. Griffin. With the aid of detachments from different regiments of the brigade, I worked until near night in loading the pontoons, and then we started for our old Camp.

I was now pretty thoroughly exhausted, so after dragging along for a number of miles, I, together with Capt. Crocker, Lts. Thomas, Coane &

Batchelder, fell out of line and took shelter and rest at a little house in the neighborhood of Hartwood Church, where, after getting a pretty substantial meal of coffee and corn bread, we went to sleep in a wood shed attached to the house, and I declair that I never before enjoyed such a night of perfect rest like this.

In the morning we took up line of march for camp and had not proceeded many miles when we were overtaken by General Wadsworth[30] and staff, who inquired to what regiment we belonged. The ever ready Capt. Crocker said that we were officers of Col. Johnson's 25th N.Y. Regt. and had been compelled to straggle with a majority of the command, because the Col., thinking we could fly, had put spurs to his horse and ordered the regt. to keep well closed up and follow him. Genl. Wadsworth ordered one of his staff to take our names and make a note of the fact that the 25th N.Y. was very much demoralized, which fact he purposed bringing to the notice of Genl. Griffin. Of course we gave fictitious names and I presume Col. Johnson will get a severe overhauling, which, although he richly deserves it, is hardly a fair way to bring him into trouble. But then the honor of the 118th must be preserved at all hazards.

I forgot to mention that in the retreat from the breastworks I lost James McGinley of my company, but do not know whether killed or wounded. It has been reported to me that just after the enemy commenced firing he was seen upon his knees apparently binding up his foot. I trust he may have escaped death and is now a prisoner only.[31] You remember him, of course, he and I were clerks together in Alex. Heron Jr. & Co.'s office.

In the afternoon we reached camp where I found George prepared to receive me, and after partaking of a hearty meal, I turned in, and knew nothing more until 8 o'clock the next morning.

Following just four and a half months after the defeat at Fredericksburg, the reverse at Chancellorsville was singularly disheartening to the North. Lincoln had cautioned Hooker before the battle to put in all of his available men, yet the 1st, 5th, and a portion of the 2nd Corps, some 35,000 troops, either had been lightly engaged or saw no action at all. There were 17,000 Federals killed, wounded, or captured, and though Lee's casualties were less, just under 13,000, he suffered an egregious loss in the mortal wounding of his brilliant corps commander, Stonewall Jackson.

The Army of the Potomac, judging by the accounts it left behind, was certainly dispirited by the outcome of the battle, but this remarkably resilient group of soldiers had not lost hope. Just a week after returning to the camp of the 118th on the north side of the Rappahannock, Donaldson reported to his brother that "notwithstanding our discouragements we are fast recovering and could make a big fight today if we had someone to inspire us with confidence." A 6th Corps surgeon wrote at this time that "the health and spirits of the soldiers of the Corps had never been better, and in spite of the failure at Chancellorsville, they felt a great deal of confidence." [32]

The next month was a period of quiet recuperation for both the Yankee and Rebel infantries, but for Donaldson, a change took place that was to influence the remainder of his military career. On May 25 Colonel Prevost was forced by the wounds he had suffered at Shepherdstown to take permanent leave of the 118th, leaving Donaldson's nemesis, Lieutenant Colonel Gwyn, in command. "The regiment will become worthless," the dejected captain warned, "and will be torn to pieces by contentions and bitter feuds among the officers."

> Camp 118th Regt. P.V.
> Near Potomac Creek Station Va.
> May 14th, 1863

Dear Brother:

I presume you are quite uneasy by my silence, but I trust the volume! sent Auntie yesterday by Express will relieve you, and at the same time atone for my seeming neglect. I commenced that letter on Saturday the 9th and finished it Tuesday the 12th putting in many solid hours of writing. I had no intention of making it so lengthy when I commenced but I found I had so much to say that I really could have made it longer.

The army is in a very unsettled condition. The men are morose, sullen, dissatisfied, disappointed, and mortified. We are a good deal discouraged because we feel that we should not have lost the battle. I don't see how we can hope to succeed if we are not better handled. But at the same time it must be confessed we are a remarkable army. I doubt very much if any other could have sustained two such tremendous disasters as Fredericksburg and Chancellorsville and held together as we are doing. Why, do you know that not withstanding our discouragements we are now fast recovering and could make a big fight today if we had someone to inspire us with confidence? The enemy must have been badly crippled or else they would have followed up their success. But I presume Genl. Lee is soldier enough to know that an army able to withdraw from his front so successfully after sustaining so great a defeat must still be [in] condition to deliver another battle if pressed, with different results, possibly.

On the 8th an order came from brigade for the 118th to retrace their steps to United States Ford and bring in the Pontoon train we had neglected to guard, as it was reported it had been abandoned—stuck in the mud—near there, and was likely to fall into the enemy's hands. There was much grumbling in consequence. We could not but feel that all the rough work was heaped upon our regiment. We had no idea that it was expected of us to guard this train. Why was it Genl. Barnes did not look after this matter at the time instead of marching us to camp? And this recalls an incident that occurred after these same pontoon boats had been loaded by us after recrossing the Rappahannock on the 6th, which may account for the General's forgetfulness! and which I will relate just here.

After working and toiling like mules in loading the train our brigade was formed preparatory to its withdrawal to the old camp. There was a good deal of confusion in getting the regiments into proper alignment, especially with the 118th, and things became much jumbled. I had observed an officer on a white horse riding about ordering and blustering a good deal while we were loading the boats, and he was, at this time, dashing here and there scolding the men right and left. I didn't know who he was, but understood afterward he was a U.S. Engineer officer by name of Cogswell—a Lt. Colonel.[33] Well, anyway, in the midst of our backing and fumbling about, Genl. Barnes called out in a loud voice so that the whole brigade heard him. "Col. Prevost, why don't you get your regiment into line," and then followed it by calling to Col. Cogswell to take command of the 118th and get it into its proper line. Of course Col. Cogswell did no such thing because we succeeded in extricating ourselves. Now I mention this affair merely to show the "Forgetfulness" existing at this time with our brigade commander, for certainly the old gentleman was full of forgetfulness!! or something stronger, or else he would not have humiliated Col. Prevost as he certainly did.[34] I have never heard what came of this, but I feel assured Col. Prevost will or possibly has had the matter properly straightened out. Anyway it nettled me a good deal at the time and has been the subject of much comment among us since.

Well, to proceed, there was nothing else to do but to obey the order; so Major Herring, who was in command, asked for volunteers for this duty. I did so with several other officers and about half the regiment, and at 10 A.M. we moved out and leisurely trudged along to near U.S. Ford, and at 6 P.M., on the property of Miss Withers, at Bravere's Church,[35] we bivouaced for the night. I didn't see anything of the pontoons but learned in the morning they had gone ahead and were, in all probability, in camp. We were very comfortable that night, having shelter tents and blazing fires to keep us warm. Next day we returned to camp, arriving about 1:30 P.M.

We have also been engaged the last two days in a new line of duty—guarding the refractory 25th New York Regt. It appears this regiment's term of enlistment is out but the Government refuses to discharge them, claiming, I believe, a month's longer service. A revolt ensued, the men refusing duty, and the right wing of the 118th under Lt. Col. James Gwyn were ordered under arms to enforce discipline. Their camp was surrounded, the men compelled to leave their quarters, stack arms and moved into an open space and securely guarded by our regiment. The left wing under Maj. Herring relieved the right of this duty in the evening and were in turn relieved by the 1st Michigan under Lt. Col. Throup.[36] The next day Maj. Herring received an order from Col. Johnson, commanding the New Yorkers, to arrest 10 sergeants and a number of corporals and enlisted men named specially in an order from Genl. Meade, and to publicly pull their chevrons from off their uniforms and to closely confine them until further orders. This was a hard duty, as these men had been most excellent soldiers, having been in every engagement and skirmish with the Army of the Potomac to date, losing heavily, especially at 2nd Bull Run. They felt that the order to tear off their stripes was too severe when considering these facts, and petitioned Genl. Meade to permit them themselves to remove them. They drew up a petition to this effect enumerating their services and asked clemency in this matter alone. All other punishments they would submit to as they felt they were in the right. Major Herring took this petition himself to Genl. Meade's Head Quarters and after an interview succeeded in having the order modified as desired. The men themselves then took off their chevrons and they were then confined in the 118th Guard House. The different regiments of the brigade relieve each other in guarding this regiment. This is a sad affair. Candidly I feel that the New Yorkers are in the right and that justice should be done them. They are brave men who have served their country faithfully and well, and their case should be promptly looked into.[37] However much I or the members of our regiment sympathize with them, our duty is plain. We are ordered to suppress any disorderly demonstration and I fear should there be any attempt on the part of the 25th to openly resist their confinement they would be utterly destroyed. Such is military law. Our orders are plain and we will carry them out to the letter, right or wrong. . . .

I notice the newspapers give rumors of another movement by this army across the Rappahannock, or to quote them literally—"Hooker is again across." This is all bosh. Hooker has had enough of being across and so have we. I sincerely trust there will not again be any forward movement under Fighting Joe!!! No sir, we are safe and sound this side [of] the river. . . .

><+>+O+<>+<

Camp 118th Regt. P.V.
May 15th, 1863

My dear Jac:
    . . . In company with Capt. Crocker, this morning I went over to visit some of his and my own friends in Humphreys division. I was much surprised at the "lashions" of rum the famous 3rd Division had on hand. Either they are more abstemious than our own 1st division, or else, their opportunities for getting liquor surpasses ours, as the supply at each Head Quarters visited was simply marvelous. Had we partaken of the freely extended hospitalities I feel sure this letter would not have been written. As it was they deemed it advisable at Genl. Humphreys Head Quarters, where we made our last stop, to send us home in an ambulance. They are certainly lively and wide awake fellows in the 3rd Division, but once a year is about all the visiting I would care to make [to] these heroes of Fredericksburg. . . .

><+>+O+<>+<

Camp 118th Regt. P.V.
May 18th, 1863

Dear Jacob:
    . . . I have nothing—absolutely nothing new to communicate, but will fill the balance of this sheet with the latest rumors as to the 5th Corps, knowing you want to be posted all the time. The 5th Corps has been detatched, temporarily, from the Army, to guard the Rail Road from Aquia Creek to Falmouth, as well as to occupy the fortifications on the south side the Potomac Creek—all of which is deep strategy. Again, the Corn Exchange of Philadelphia has asked (and the request has been granted, only waiting certain little formalities of red tape for the order to issue) for a permanent detachment of the 118th from the Army of the Potomac in order to be brought into Pennsylvania to do guard duty in one of the Arsenals. This is a positive fact—I had the news from the Company Cook.

I still report present for duty each morning. I presume the city looks lovely just now. I would be pleased to know the styles for the present season both in men and womens wear. Fortunately we are not troubled much about the fashions here. We appear in the same "rig" both winter and summer, the old adage really applying in our case—What will keep out the cold will also keep out the heat. Give my love to Auntie. . . .

▸⊶⊷⊶O⊷⊶⊷◂

Camp 118th Regt. P.V.
May 23rd, 1863

My dear Brother:

Yours of the 19th inst. I found awaiting me on my return from the Potomac Creek where I had been indulging in a delightful bath, which by the way is an evening diversion after the duties of the day are over. This refreshes and invigorates me a good deal, and I always feel the better for it. I suffer a good deal from the heat during the day, which is intolerable, but the nights are cool and pleasant. I think the temperature of Virginia is pretty much that of Philadelphia—hot when it is hot, and cool and pleasant when such conditions govern the temperature—no middle course. . . .

I have nothing new to communicate, everything remains quiet along the lines. Thursday last we had a grand sword presentation to our General Barnes. It was a Grand affair. It seems to me that most all the officers of the army were present. In a previous letter I stated that the 3rd Division had monopolized the rum of the army—but I can now state that the old 1st Division has gloriously redeemed itself in that particular. Lt. Col. James Gwyn made the presentation, and did it handsomely too, I will say that for him. After a response by our brave old General, an entertainment was given which for lavish supply of edibles and bibables, beat anything ever undertaken in the army. In its preparation the conspicuous talent of the 118th was displayed.

Capt. Dendy Sharwood was Master of Ceremonies. He has had great experience as a provider and caterer, having been proprietor of Jones Hotel before the war, and a member of the Fish House Club. He is the most genial and uninsinuating host imaginable. There was no resisting his importunities to indulge in the good things provided, and he certainly did provide most royally. He evidently knew the capacity of his guests, and among many other beverages, had two barrels of Gin Cocktail, two barrels of Fish House punch, two of Claret punch and two casks of ale. Think of it! There was also enormous tubs of chicken salad, together with cold beef and boiled ham—ham sandwiches and everything solid to satisfy the cravings of the appetite Gin Cocktail was sure to produce. Heavens! what a drunken carouse ensued. Our brave Lt. Col. led off with a thorough and complete <u>inspection</u> of the gin cocktail barrels, followed by copious deluges of Fish House Punch, and as a consequence soon had a <u>lordly load on</u>. Other prominent officers of high rank soon joined him, and then the song and ribald jest made the air reverberate with shouts of hilarity. Earth! how the warriors did guzzle. The gin cocktail was first exhausted, then the other mixed beverages, and as night progressed the spacious tents of our brave commander were filled with a writhing mass of drunken men.

My friend Jno. Thomas was with "<u>the boys</u>," "close up," as he said, and before midnight was hail fellow with all the rank our corps could produce. He was a sight to behold as pushing and crowding hither and thither he would first seize a general officer, calling him familiarly by name, without title, and lead him to the Gin Cocktail barrel, across which the two would indulge in a social and friendly drink of its contents, and express mutual admiration for each other. This he would do with all colonels and generals he would find. All dignity was laid aside in one wild endeavor to make it a <u>pleasant occasion</u>. I finally saw him—arm in arm with Gwyn moving up to the ale cask, and—Great Scott!! calling him <u>Jim</u>—as true as I live, while Gwyn was trying to explain how it was he was so <u>fond</u> of Thomas. They quaffed two bumbers of ale in mutual pledges of eternal love and friendship, when Gwyn being called in another direction, I seized hold of Thomas and tried to get him to his quarters. The rum had done its work on the dear old fellow and he became violent at first, then merry—laughing and shouting. I could not manage him so I hunted up Captain Crocker, whom I found with a countenance like unto a light house, and got him to bear a hand in removing Thomas. There now ensued the funniest performance I ever witnessed. Thomas insisted upon climbing over the spruce hedge surrounding Genl. Barnes' Head Quarters, and of course we had to climb too; no sooner would he be over than he would clamber back again, and so kept it up for at least 8 or 10 times, ere he became so exhausted that with the aid of George Slow I got him to our quarters, and with his last remaining senses he declared as he shook his fist under my nose that "with these dirty pair of fives he had cleaned many a bar room in Philadelphia." I felt much relieved when I got him out of the way, for it was early yet, or, as Capt. Sharwood put it, it was "the shank of the evening," and I feared harm might come to him.

On my return to the Banquet Hall I found great numbers of the braves hors de combat among the horses of head Quarters. But the riot was still going on in the tents and it kept up till morning found fully near the whole congregation asleep on the floors, under the tables and on the ground surrounding. Need I add that I abstained from indulging in any of the beverage and as a consequence reported for duty the next morning. . . .

I enclose photographs of Capt. Fernald Co. D and Lt. White Co. G— both good pictures. I believe I have expressed myself in regard to Fernald,

One of Donaldson's closest friends in the 118th
Pennsylvania, Lt. John J. Thomas, Company B.
The Civil War Library & Musuem.

or old "Oscafoozel" as he is called. Lt. Jno. R. White is a most excellent fellow and a capable & intelligent officer. I wish there were more like him. I wish you would send me an album, say, like the one you have. Send it by Capt. Hunterson who is now in town. I have a great many pictures scattered about in my valise. Please give me a list of those sent you. . . .

If leaves of absence continue to be granted I think Thomas will be home before many days, now that he and Jim are so intimate. I will also see what I can do for myself in that line. . . .

⊱•⊷•⊙•⊶•⊰

Camp 118th Regt. P.V.
May 24th, 1863

King James now reigns!

"This man is now become a god; and Cassius is a wretched creature, and must bend his body."

Col. Prevost leaves us tomorrow in order to take command of the Invalid Corps at Harrisburg, PA.[38] The wheels of fortune have again put Gwyn in power, and for the little of heaven's peace and comfort we have recently enjoyed under Col. Prevost's dignified command, the vials of wrath will now be let loose and life itself will be burdensome to some of us, while all will be made miserable under this despot's reign. The regiment will become worthless, and will be torn to pieces by contentions and bitter feuds among the officers. The spy system will again be inaugurated and such men as Capt. Wetherill and other scum will boil to the top. The gentlemen and soldiers of the command, Maj. Herring, Doctor Thomas, Capts. Crocker, Sharwood, Davids, Lts. White, Thomas, Batchelder and others will be made to feel the iron heel of the tyrant. The drunken and worthless sycophants, fawners, and cringers will flock around head-quarters.

I have but one object now in life—to leave the command, honorably if I can, but leave it I will at whatever cost. My career as a soldier is at an end. Every indignity and insult imaginable will be speedily heaped upon me. There is no future for me, and rather than drag along as an hireling soldier, I will insult this brute before the whole command, and leave, by sentence of Court-Martial. These words will doubtless distress you, but you really cannot understand how very unhappy I am under the command of Gwyn. I have conscientiously endeavored to do my duty always and no one knows this better than Gwyn. He knows that I am capable of performing the duties pertaining to my rank, and that I am aware that he, himself, falls far short of the military knowledge requisite for a commander of troops to have. <u>Do not misunderstand me</u>—that I will <u>at once</u> inaugurate a system of defiant warfare against my commander. Not so, I will await the spring of the tiger—strike back—and retreat in as good order as possible. This may all take time, but the end will come—I feel it. My occupation is gone. My military ardor cooled. I would I were a civilian—a "counterpimper"— anything but a soldier just now. Thank goodness! I am not alone in my misery. Poor Crocker said when the news reached him—"God! but there will be heavy weather now!" It even seems as though the very elements were anticipating the cruel time before me, as the thermometer has steadily risen the last day or two, and we are literally scorched by the heat. It is something frightful. Please do not forget that I am waiting for a letter from home. I believe I do not receive a letter a week, on an average, the whole year round. This is a poor showing. You will have to do better than that, or else, I will retaliate.

Jas. McGinley—lost at Chancellorsville—has reported from Camp Parole. I feared the poor fellow had been killed. Love to Auntie.

>–·–◆–·–O–·–◆–·–◁

Camp 118th Regt. P.V.
May 25th, 1863

Dear Jac:

My letter of yesterday was written under pressure of excitement and agitation at the misfortune befallen our command in the retirement of Col. Prevost. Today, while in the main I feel uncomfortable and have lost heart in a measure, I desire to correct any impression I may have conveyed that I will abandon my line of conduct so far as acting the true soldier is concerned and antagonize the Lt. Colonel commanding. My heart is as cordially and firmly in the cause as ever, and I will do my duty always as heretofore, but I cannot but feel that Lt. Col. Gwyn and I are now face to face as bitter enemies, and in the struggle about to ensue one of us must give way. Were I to make the issue on charges I could bring against him the issue would not be doubtful, but as I do not care to do this, I will be the one to suffer and eventually to be overcome. All this would be avoided if the Lt. Colonel would accept my resignation, but it does not suit him to do so, knowing that my desire is to leave the command, and my anxious and most urgent wish is to go home, he takes delight in keeping me in the service under him. It is gall and wormwood to me, but nuts for him. . . .

Col. Prevost left us this A.M. and there was much sorrow at his departure, both among men and officers. Of course with a few of us the occasion was one of the deepest grief. We felt that we were now entirely in the hands of an unscrupulous, dastardly tyrant, and that henceforth, our lives would be made miserable. However there was one oasis in our desert of despair, and that was [that] Col. Prevost, at Harrisburg, could be of vast assistance to his friends. It was some consolation knowing this.

Well! I presume you are heartily tired and sick of all this—henceforth I will say as little as possible about my quarrel with Gwyn. Enclosed I hand you a photograph of Captain Richard W. Davids, Co. G. He is one of God's noblemen, a true soldier and a gentleman under all circumstances. He has little to say and but few associates. He is a reserved man. I enjoy his company greatly when I am favored with it, which is pretty often of late. Please place his picture conspicuously among my collection.

Today the weather is quite cool, and great coats are in demand. Wonderful climate this, from extreme heat to uncomfortable coolness in the space of a few hours. I understand that we change camp tomorrow—for sanitary reasons. Now this to my mind is simply absurd. If it be a fact, the change of camp will be the inauguration of a campaign. We are not supposed to be camped here for all time. The weather is favorable for the marching of troops, and that we will be off soon is reasonable to suppose. Where? is the problem. I have no idea of the next campaign. Indeed we are all at sea regarding it. It will largely depend on what Genl. Lee is doing, for certainly he does not intend to await behind the Rappahannock our movements. It seems to me he will more than likely force a passage of the river and engage us, as he did Pope, on the plains of Manassas. I do not think it is the intention of Genl. Hooker to again attempt the Chancellorsville or Fredericksburg Campaign. As I have said, I don't quite see what the next move will be, but think it probable Lee will demonstrate on our right flank and "spar for an opening" as the pugilists say. Well, I would much prefer him hunting us. We have tried the hunting business, and know all about it. It is his turn now. We will beat him, however, if he tries it on.

The near termination of "Camp near Falmouth" brings in review before me a period most eventful, and I may add—most enjoyable of my army experience. I look back to the time spent at this great camp with feelings of satisfaction. There has been social enjoyment here—unknown in previous Winter Quarters. With exception of two short campaigns, Fredericksburg and Chancellorsville, it has been one long series of pleasurable social enjoyment. . . .

>—+—+>—+O—<+—+—<

Head Quarters Co. 'H'
118th Regt. P.V. Flying Brigade
May 26th, 1863

Dear Brother:
        . . . The change of camp alluded to in my yesterday's letter turned out to be a heavy picket detail from this brigade. . . . You will observe from my daily correspondence that I suspicion a sudden move of the army. Candidly, I think there will be a change of base before long. We are doing no good here, with exception of covering Washington. . . .
        With exception of the movement on picket there is really nothing to write about. We are calmly, deliberately and with much resignation awaiting the pay master. In the event of his coming I will have paid me $250— or, more money than I ever before could call my own, but sad to relate, the major part of it is encumbered—mortgaged to the sutler—bad luck to him. . . .
        You ask what is the standard beverage of the army, what a question— Water—to be sure, but only because there is nothing stronger to be had without money. Whiskey appears to be the standard tipple with both officers and men. Restrictions and hindrance of one kind and another so hedge about the enlisted man that a full gratification of his natural appetite in this regard is hopelessly impossible. While with the officer, it is only a question of cash as to the quantity he can procure, and indeed not even that, for there appears to be no end of ways by which "shoulder straps" can obtain "commissary." Should the army remain in its present camp I feel assured I can obtain a leave of absence. In such case I will move rapidly in retreat towards the city of Brotherly Love and Sisterly affection. . . .

>—+—+>—+O—<+—+—<

Camp 118th Regt. P.V.
Near Morrisville, Va.
June 1st, 1863

Dear Brother:

You will perceive by the heading we are again on the move. We broke camp on the 29th ult. and after a march of 20 miles bivouaced near Grove Church, and moved again the next morning at 7 A.M. to and encamped at Morrisville at 10 A.M. We remained here until 4 P.M. yesterday, when after a march of some 4 miles we encamped at "Gold Farm" as our present camp is called, near Morrisville. Our location is about 6 miles from Bealton on the Orange and Alexandria R.R. and about 20 miles from Warrenton Junction. How long we will remain here is uncertain and what we are here for is quite unknown to us as yet. But the old soldier will soon get at the bottom facts—he is speculating on it now, and has conclusively summed up the evidence thus far adduced that our present movement has been caused by some activity of the enemy—possibly an extension of their forces towards our right flank, hence, a counter movement, in check. Subtle fellow is the old soldier. A knowing chap this very day said to me as I was watching the busy scene of erecting shelter tents—"I say Captain, General Lee is marching around our flank, see if he aint."

We have a lovely situation for our camp—so much so, indeed, as to make me wish to stay here the balance of the war, but, we are on no such picnic. . . .

>-I-<>-•-O-•<>-I-<

Camp 118th Regt. P.V.
June 2nd, 1863

Dear Brother:

We are all snugly settled, with camp laid out in the open field, and officers tents along the edge of an extensive wood. It is the most beautifully situated and best arranged encampment we have had since Camp Union, Philada. Major Herring, who has been in command since the 25th ult. when Lt. Col. Jas. Gwyn left for home on a short leave of absence, has taken special pride in making it as near regulation as a regimental camp can well be made, which means <u>perfection</u>. . . .

As is usual with me, I have visited a number of the farm houses near by and have talked to nearly all the F.F.V. female occupants willing to engage in conversation with the dreaded and despised Yanks, refusing as usual to enter their houses because I know that fear alone prevents them from forbidding me to do so, but at their doors have purchased milk and eggs whenever I could get them, calmly listening the while to their bitter reproaches, vouchsafing no reply and only occasionally asking a few questions about the enemy, which of course brings forth evasive answers or flat denials of all knowledge of them. The women of Virginia are a sour-visaged, caustic tongued, boldly insulting and defiant set, but nearly all are anxious to take our money whenever they have anything to sell. It strikes me as being rather remarkable that not withstanding all the newspaper abuse about the thieving, rascally, murdering Yankee violaters of female honor, the men invariably give the lie direct to these outrageous charges by deliberately running away on our approach and leaving their women and children to the <u>tender</u> mercies of the invader—knowing well—the infernal, lying, rascally scoundrels—that there has never yet been a case of abuse of defenseless females by our troops since the war began. Damn them—we are men, and brave ones too, and we always protect and treat with the greatest respect the families of these frauds who thus at a distance tell their people to <u>rise up</u> and defend their outraged hearth-stones. They must feel cheap, if there is any honor or feeling left among them, upon their return after we leave, to find their hearth-stones intact, their women and children in better circumstances than when they so cowardly left them. Bah! I am fast loosing all regard for this people. War is war, but we do not make it on defenseless women and children.

My feelings, I perceive, are getting the best of me, so I will "mark time" with a gentle admission that amid the excitement of a soldiers life, with its innumerable duties, ceaseless occupations and vicissitudes, I have leisure to envy you your good fortune in being at home, quietly enjoying the society of the prettiest girl in Pennsylvania. You can tell Annie Crossan that I will be a happy fellow if she will write to me now and then. I am in good health and ready for anything that may turn up.

>·|·◆◇·•O•·◇◆·|·◁

Camp 118th Regt. P.V.
"Gold Farm"
June 9th, 1863

Dear Brother:

We still remain in this lovely camp, doing nothing but taking all the enjoyment we can from our charming surroundings. How long it will last, or what we are here for is as yet the undeveloped object of our strategic inactivity. The weather is remarkably cool for the season, and we find large fires not uncomfortable. That there is something "stirring" going on the heavy and protracted cannonading seemingly 8 or 10 miles to the front surely indicates.[39] There has been a very mysterious movement of troops towards what I consider the front. Detatchments of Genl. Russell's brigade of the 6th Corps passed our camp yesterday, among them a portion of our old friends the 119th P.V. under command of Major Truefitt.[40] Our army appears to be divided. I don't know where the other corps are, they certainly are not here with us. It looks to me as though our commander is not yet fully assured as to the movements of the rebels. There is a good deal of uncertainty or rather mystery as to our future, but the tremendous artillery firing would indicate an endeavor to locate the enemy.

Lt. Col. Gwyn's return on the 3rd is about the only incident of note I have to mention. There has been very little camp work to perform and the usual picket duty has not been unpleasant, altho' being surrounded by guirrillas we are compelled to exercise vigilance. My health is perfect and my appetite keen, although with exception of strawberries I have now and then obtained from families my daily bill of fare has a good deal of sameness about it. If anybody is curious on the score of my housekeeping I will name the savory dishes which daily grace my table. Pork (salt), biscuit, fried—coffee—liberal supply, and will assure my friends at a distance who have never experienced a like repast that when I get home, and if I am blessed with a house of my own, I will be most happy to initiate them into the mysteries of Pork ala mode and other delicate miseries attending camp fare.

Your letter of the 2nd inst. to hand last night. I can answer most positively <u>NO</u>! to the query—"can't you get a leave of absence?" General Hooker has stopped giving any—on any pretense whatsoever. <u>We are</u> in "<u>observation</u>" and must be ready to move just as soon as he grasps the true situation of affairs. I have continued my visits to the families near by, purchasing strawberries or whatever else I can get with which to vary my diet—declining always invitation to go into the houses, which, by the way, is a concession extended, I am vain enough to believe, to myself alone, simply because I am polite, gentlemanly, and not obtrusive—but as before said, knowing how deadly they hate my uniform, I will accept no hospitality or kindness from them. I pay for everything I get. . . .

CHAPTER 7

Gettysburg
June 10–July 18, 1863

*F*illed with confidence by his Chancellorsville triumph, Lee boldly set his sights on
a second invasion of the North. In early June he began quietly pulling his divisions
from their positions near Fredericksburg and advancing them north via the Shenandoah
Valley.

Hooker, aware of activity in the enemy's camps but uncertain of Lee's intentions,
had sent his cavalry across the Rappahannock on June 9 to probe for information,
and he learned that the Rebels were again on the move. The Army of the Potomac
was soon in pursuit, as always staying east of the Blue Ridge Mountains and covering the capital as it slid northward. By a series of strenuous forced marches, which
Donaldson details, it was soon within striking distance of the Confederates.

During their advance, the 118th Pennsylvania and the rest of the 1st Division
were briefly detached from the 5th Corps to support Federal cavalry probes in the
direction of Ashby's Gap of the Blue Ridge Mountains, but by June 26 they had
crossed the Potomac and were on their way toward the Pennsylvania state line and
the crossroads market town of Gettysburg.

Once aware of their intentions, Hooker had conducted a skillful pursuit of the
Confederates, but in spite of this, both the administration and the soldiers in the
ranks lacked confidence in him. "We don't believe in him some how," Donaldson
wrote on June 25, later adding, "I doubt very much indeed whether a successful battle can be fought under him." The administration, namely Secretary of War Stanton
and General in Chief Halleck, were of a like mind. On June 27 an argument with
Washington over the disposition of the troops stationed at Harpers Ferry prompted
Hooker to tender his resignation, and it was quickly accepted. Pennsylvanian
George Gordon Meade, commander of the 5th Corps, was placed in command.

Camp Near Gum Springs, Va.
June 18th, 1863

Dear Auntie:

I have just time enough before the mail leaves to write you of our doings. I do not think letters are sent through to destinations but are detained at Washington for fear of giving information. The men write all the same and their people will get them later on. My last letter home was from Camp at Gold Farm near Grove Church in which I made mention of heavy firing heard in the distance. It turned out to be, as doubtless you know, a cavalry reconnoisance into the enemy's territory, resulting in the cavalry battle at Brandy Station. The enemy were roughly handled, Genl. Jeb Stuart's Head Quarter Wagon, with all its dispatches, was captured, from which it was learned the enemy were marching up the Shenandoah Valley.

June 10th. Our brigade was hurridly marched towards the front at Kelly's Ford to protect the recrossing of our cavalry. I, being Officer of the Day, was left in charge of the Camp with Lieut. Innman[1] as Officer of the Guard. Our troops returned again that evening at 8:30 without having been called upon to perform any special duty, as the rebs did not follow the cavalry. We remained in camp under marching orders until the Evening of the 13th when at 8 P.M. we broke camp and marched to the little village of Morrisville and bivouaced at 10 P.M. I am yet unable to see the utility of this short night march. It certainly made us very uncomfortable.

June 14th. We moved at 11 A.M. and poked along thro' Farquier Co., passing through Weavertown to Catlett Station, where we bivouaced at 7 P.M.

June 15th. Moved at 5 A.M. and bivouaced at Manassas Junction, Prince William Co. at 9 A.M. This place is close to Bull Run, the scene of the first great battle of the war, and later, on August 30th, 1862, it again witnessed the defeat of the Army under Genl. Pope. Strange as it may appear, the fence rails in the vicinity had not yet all gone, and as soon as the command broke ranks, the men made a rush for them. There was quite a nice house near our bivouac with the fences still intact, and as the men seized the rails a young darkey came out of the house saying—"Don't take de rails, my marster done and set me free and give me dis hyear house." One of the men said, "All right, snow ball, we only want a few to turn in half and we will give you back the ends, and if you are coming over to camp, just bring a few rails with you." "But I ain't coming dat way no how," said the dark, "no use talking to sodiers, dey march all day and den when night comes dey take all de fences away." At this bivouac water was so scarce that there was great suffering in consequence.

Our position lay along the margin of what appeared to be a dried up stream, and there being but a few stray stunted trees, very little shelter was had from the sun, which, fortunately however, was dimmed somewhat by haze. Toads in great numbers were seen hopping about in great numbers. To illustrate the extreme paucity of the water supply, I will illustrate that Capt. Donegan, having obtained enough barely sufficient to cook a cup of coffee, that gentleman was diligently engaged in cooling the beverage when I approached and engaged him in conversation regarding some matter of duty to be performed. As I seated myself beside him I noticed a toad hop into his coffee. Without interrupting the thread of his argument, he inserted two fingers into the tin and promptly threw out the scalded intruder, and then without the slightest compunction, drank off the beverage. Upon leaving I remarked that I sincerely trusted the good Captain would feel no inconvenience from the warts his person would soon be covered with.

June 17th. Broke camp at 6 A.M. and three hours later came upon and crossed Bull Run battle field near the Henry House. This frame 2 story building was just as it had been left after Pope's memorable battle of Aug. 30th. Torn and shattered by shot and shell, it yet appeared to be occupied, as a man in citizens dress stood in front of the doorway looking at us as we passed. It was at this spot that Buchanan's brigade of regulars stood fast amid the rout and disaster of Porter's Corps and the rest of the army and checked Longstreet in his headlong victorious charge thus saving the army and permitting its defeated battalions to escape across the fords and the stone bridge crossing the Bull Run Stream. The whole field was thickly strewn with leather accoutrements, shoes, canteens, rags of one kind & another and vast numbers of the dried skin covered remains of horses, the faded soil color of which, and the fact that the skin at all remained, a good deal surprised us.

We passed on through Centreville and bivouaced at this place at 6 P.M. There is heavy cannonading ahead as I write, the deep roar of the guns being distinctly heard. We are upon the direct road to Leesburg, so I am told, the famous little town where I was first incarcerated when a prisoner at Ball's Bluff, Oct. '61.

We suffered dreadfully on the march to this place for want of water and the intense heat. We have lost a dozen men or more in the brigade from sun stroke, and yesterday Lt. Col. Gleason of the 25th New York was overcome and died from the sun's effect, and as soon as we halted, was

Donaldson, taken in March 1863. THE CIVIL WAR LIBRARY & MUSUEM.

buried in a little church yard hard by.[2] The dust was most appalling and a fearful looking set we are anyway. By keeping wet leaves in my hat and boughs carried overhead I contrived to keep off the sun, and when I could do so I thoroughly wet my head and neck. It was a novel sight to see the mass of men carrying boughs and branches of trees. Truly we looked not unlike a walking forest. I cannot believe the rebs will be bold enough to invade Pennsylvania, as we are now up with them, but should they do so may they stay there until the last trump sounds.

There is a good deal of grumbling about Hooker and the men are about convinced he is not competent to handle them. McClellan would be the proper officer to command this army if there is any likelihood of a battle.

I do hope Jac has not gone to Harrisburg with the Gray Reserves. I will feel most anxious until I know positively he has not done so. He should remain home with you, two of a family are enough in this cause.[3] Do you think John can possibly be with Lee, because there will be a tight squeeze when these two armies come together and his luck would be to get hurt.

I have just learned that we will remain here today and leave tomorrow for Leesburg, from thence to Chambersburg will be the program. Where in the world is Lee heading to? I have only one set of cloths and <u>no</u> drawers and am therefore pretty well used up, awfully dirty, and run down at the heel, somewhat similar to my condition during the Peninsular Campaign. . . .

[P.S.] We were wagon guard from Manassas to this place.

>-+◆>-O-<◆+-<

Camp 118th Regt. P.V.
Thursday, June 25/63
Aldie, Va.

Dear Auntie:

My last was from Gum Springs, where we stayed until the afternoon of the 19th when at 2 o'clock, we started off, marched to this place and bivouaced at 5 P.M. Aldie, a little village of Loudoun Co., is picturesquely situated in a Gap of a range of hills, far beyond which looms up the Blue Ridge. It lies on the banks of a little stream which flows on through the Bull Run mountains and empties into Goose Creek, of which I believe it is a branch. I, however, did not ask the natives, as they would only say it was; every stream hereabouts bearing that name, I believe. The road, a good solid turnpike, divides into two just immediately outside of the town, one running to Ashby's Gap and the other towards Snickers Gap.

At this place we saw the band and remnant of Col. Duffy's 1st Rhode Island Cavalry.[4] The few survivors of this regiment were mostly wounded men, and one in particular, with no less than four distinct sabre cuts across the top of his head, gave me the following experience of his command. It appears this regiment had been posted in "observation" of the western approaches of Thoroughfare Gap in Bull Run Mountains on the 17th, with orders to join the cavalry column at Middleburg, a town some distance beyond Aldie. Meantime, Stuart's Cavalry had moved through Ashby's Gap of the Blue Ridge towards Middleburg on a reconnaisance to see what Hooker was about, and his advance had reached Aldie when suddenly Kilpatrick's troopers came upon it and drove them pell mell towards Middleburg. Near this place they however made a stand, and being reinforced, a terrific fight ensued, resulting in Stuart being driven into Middleburg. Meantime, Col. Duffié started to obey his orders, and the rebs, learning of the approach of a force to their rear [and] not knowing its strength, skedaddled from Middleburg, which Duffié at once took posession of. The rebs ascertaining the smallness of the force returned, and attacking them with their whole force, beat Duffié out of the town, compelling him to fall back the way he came. But upon this road the rebs had followed him from Thoroughfare Gap and he was caught between the two forces. It being at this time quite dark he halted and picketed for the night and early day found himself surrounded by the entire rebel cavalry. A bloody fight ensued in which the relator was sabred, as stated, and taken prisoner, and Col. Duffié's command destroyed.[5] Our wounded friend was then taken to Middleburg where he was recaptured by Pleasonton shortly after, who drove the rebs out of town and punished them severely. There was every evidence of hard fighting all around Aldie—great numbers of dead horses encumbered the ground, and quite a number of wounded men, upon litters of straw, lay along the roadside near the houses.[6]

We halted here all day of the 20th while the cavalry manoeuvered & reconnoitered, but at 2 A.M. of the 21st we were hurriedly assembled and at day break were well on towards Middleburg in support of Gregg's Brigade of Cavalry;[7] shortly after, we entered Middleburg. Beyond the town was an open country, then a woods and then quite a hill, up which the roadway ran. It was here the great struggle between Pleasonton & Stuart had taken place. The enemy's artillery upon the hill played upon the Union Squadrons in the open, and the fight was for the woods mentioned, which were finally taken and held by our cavalry. I never saw anything like the number of dead horses. The roads and fields were strewn with them. Just outside of Middleburg is a house, isolated and surrounded by a substantial fence. This was now torn down, excepting immediately in front of the house, and in the yard, grouped together, were no less than 18 dead horses of both forces, and in the roadway lay one horse in particular that had been struck by a 12 lb. round shot, full in the chest, which had torn completely through him, "from end to end," as the boy said, coming out below his tail, and lay upon the ground a foot or two beyond his body. What must have been the sensation of the trooper at that moment?

At about 8 o'clock our brigade pushed out from Middleburg and deployed, our regiment on the extreme right being carried well up and over the high ground overlooking the open country beyond and flanking Stuart's position. We were ordered to trail arms so that the enemy would not know the presence of infantry, but they saw us and commenced falling back. They were now attacked by the cavalry who, advancing at a trot with skirmishers in advance, rushed upon the retiring squadrons over the fields and up the ascending roadway, and I for the first time had a magnificent view of an Cavalry combat. I was surprised, although just why I cannot say, that mounted skirmishers preceded the advancing squadrons. It never occurred to me that cavalry required skirmishers at all. As I have said the sight was magnificent—the sabres flashed in the sun light as the men mingled together and fought in a writhing mass, cutting and slashing each other. Riderless horses ran to and fro over the fields, many of them covered with the blood of their late riders. Stuart's men were badly beaten, a part of their horse artillery being charged upon, the gunners sabred and two or three pieces taken, and the whole command beaten back some distance to a new position. We now took to the road and pushed on rapidly after the cavalry.

Soon we met Capt. Cadwalader of Pleasonton's Staff,[8] escorting through the fields along the roadway a batch of 50 prisoners—fine, sturdy fellows who, undismayed by their unfortunate condition, loudly praised the actions of our cavalry—the way they rode & fought. One fellow, as he passed, called out, "You'ns cavalry will soon be as good as we'uns." As soon as we came near the position of the enemy and began to deploy into the fields they left and retreated—it is true in good order, and without hurry, although hammered continually by our artillery, and did not again halt until Upperville was reached.

The country through which these movements had taken place was most beautiful and between Middleburg and Upperville is a succession of ridges and hollows and stone fences from behind which the dismounted enemy greatly annoyed our approaching cavalry. Our artillery was planted on one eminence after another and seemed to be admirably served the whole day long. The battle never tarried until Upperville was reached and then, the enemy making a stand, both bodies of cavalry entered the place at one and the same time. A terrific fight took place, sabre and pistol being freely used. The rebs dismounted and fought from behind stone fences while the roadway was jammed and choked by the contending combatants. Upon the approach of our brigade, or rather I may say, a little before we came near, the enemy broke and made a wild rush for the Gap, halting at the little hamlet of Paris, immediately in the defile, where their infantry came upon the scene, and the Cavalry battle ended. The developing of the infantry force was apparently the object of Pleasonton's movement. Of course, the valley on the other side [of] the Blue Ridge contained Lee's army.[9]

When we arrived at Upperville the fight was over and at 6 P.M. we bivouaced in the village. As we entered the place the first person I met was Maj. Ormsby Robinson[10] sitting on a fence, resting his great burly form. We had a little chat about the result of the fight and I learned the news from the folks at Pittsburg[h]. At parting we took a beverage or two to the health of the Crossan family.

This evening we made the acquaintance of Col. Taylor of the 1st Penna Cavalry,[11] who accepted our invitation to supper. He was very hungry, or to use his language, he hadn't eaten anything for Eleventeen years. Crocker prepared him a celebrated beverage which he had discovered and invented shortly after Chancellorsville, which he named "Hooker's Retreat." It consisted of whiskey, water and sugar, liberally coated with nutmeg. Crocker, Thomas and I, on the marches, always carry these "sundries," so that in case of separation we can still have a "Hooker's Retreat" at will. This beverage soon became famous in the command, but there is no one who can give it the exact manipulation that Crocker can. Well, Col. Taylor declaired it the finest beverage that he had ever "struck." Whether he intended to flatter or really meant what he said, it resulted all the same in Crocker being constantly engaged in shaking up a "Hooker's Retreat" for this fiery whiskered Colonel, who put it away and talked and talked until when he left us, you would have thought he was a sailor instead of a cavalryman, he pitched and tossed so. I believe, although he at first said he was so "confounded hungry," he got nothing but rum, which, however, apparently stayed his stomach.

Upperville is quite a smart little village in Fauquier Co. lying at the foot of the Blue Ridge and surrounded by highly cultivated farm lands in a country remarkable for its beauty and fertility. It has a population, I believe, between 2 and 3 hundred. Paris, the little village beyond, I did not get to, but am told its situation in the gap is most lovely. It is also in Fauquier.

June 22nd. We were aroused and moved off to the rear at 3 A.M. closely followed by the Cavalry, and that of the enemy too, the latter, however, keeping at a respectable distance until near Middleburg, when the rebs did likewise, our people suddenly broke to the right and left, unmasking a battery of artillery which let into the reb masses and put them to flight in short order. After this, beyond a little artillery practice at long range, the rebs generally behaved themselves.

At Middleburg we joined the two other brigades of our division and continued the backward march. Middleburg is a beautiful little borough in Loudoun Co. and one of its principal settlements. Like Upperville it is surrounded by tilled lands, stone fences and well kept farms. It has a few stores, a church or two, and a population of from 5 to 6 hundred. . . .

We reached Aldie at 5 P.M. and went into bivouac upon the right of the road, the regular division of Sykes being immediately across the road. The men at once began the erection of shelter tents, and I, after disposing of my sword and accoutrements, walked to the roadside to look at the regulars. I am always fond of watching these "silent machines"—there is never any bustle, noise, confusion or loud talking among them. Everything now was orderly and quiet, the guards amid their camps neat and clean, as though they had been in camp a long time. I say I always take pleasure in observing these men, and try to gather anything likely to aid me in disciplining my own men, but of course it can never be brought to the perfection of the regulars. There is such a marked difference between regulars and volunteers. They are hired soldiers, the volunteers are citizen soldiers only.

As I stood watching these people a cavalry company passed by, its captain in advance, as he should be, a tall fine looking fellow, with hand resting on right hip and sabre rattling and jingling. I recollect now that I noticed this man particularly for some reason, possibly because he turned his eyes upon me and appeared to note the troops forming their camp, at least I now think he did. He had a full round face, beard cropped close and a U.S. officers cavalry felt hat. . . . His men rode well together and there was an absence of noise and laughter usual with our cavalrymen. These men were quiet and appeared to notice nothing at all. I was so near the captain that I had a good square look at him. . . . I could have touched him with a sword had I one with me. Well, they rode by and disappeared to the rear out of sight. It wasn't long before there was a devil of noise to the rear, mingled with reports of fire arms, and then heavy explosions. It was Mosby and his men who had passed me, and who had attacked the 5th Corps trains, destroying some 40 wagons and doing very considerable damage generally, stampeding the teams and utterly confusing the teamsters.

Of course our cavalry were soon after him, but he got away in the direction of Snickers Gap, I believe. No matter how very much this man is hated by us, and called guerrilla, Mosby is certainly a remarkable man, indeed a wonderfully active and bold fellow.[12] His career is not unlike the Revolutionary partisan chieftain McLean, who gave the British then occupying Philadelphia so much trouble. Fortunately our wagons escaped destruction and the next day I had the satisfaction of a clean change of undercloths from my well stocked valise. The men are in a sad plight, however, and badly off for everything needful in a long campaign. My requisition made weeks and weeks ago was partially filled here. Some idea of the wants of the men can be had by what I recd. from the Quartermaster: 1 wool blanket, 13 Blouses, 8 pr. pants, 3 shirts, 17 drawers, 8 caps, 18 pr. shoes, 17 pr. socks, 2 Knapsacks, 7 Haversacks, 6 canteens and 4 shelter tents. These things were all that could be spared to my company.

I don't know how long we will remain in this camp, but not for very long, as I presume both Lee and Hooker are manoeuvering for position. For the first time in a long while, the army critic is "dead beat," nothing to say, no suggestions to make—bewildered. As for myself I can but say that I think that Pleasonton, having discovered the presence of the rebel army in the Shenandoah Valley, the main army will try and head him off at the Potomac, leaving either our Corps or the 6th, which, I am told, is yet far behind us, to cover the approaches to Washington. You can readily understand how completely at a loss we are to figure out the campaign and the object of our protracted stay at this point. I am in good health, and like all the rest of the brigade, in fine spirits, lacking only one thing to make us comfortable, and that is—faith in Hooker. We don't believe in him some how. Will continue to write at every opportunity.

Camp near Frederick, Md.
June 28th, 1863

Dear Auntie:

My last letter was from Aldie Va., which place we left two days ago, and after marching both day and night arrived here last P.M. We crossed the Potomac at Edwards Ferry, the ever to be remembered place whose proximity to Balls Bluff recalled so many harrowing reminiscences of that dreadful day in my early army life, when for the first time I realized what a fearful thing war was, where amid death and slaughter most appalling I won my officers commission, to receive it only after months of durance in Richmond, and hours and hours after we had left the Ferry behind, I was filled with the recollections of that time and [was] but dimly conscious of the ever advancing column [and] the rumbling of the guns and caissons. . . . I could see it all even in the hasty glance I gave the place as we hurried along and I then and there determined, come what may, never again to be taken prisoner.

Altogether, in some respects, this has been to me a most interesting march although it has been conducted upon the most economical plan imaginable as to the joys of the table, for I declair that but two meals have passed our lips in all this time. I forgot to mention we passed quite near to our old camp at Poolesville, Md., but it was too dark to see much of the spot. I would have liked, above all things, to have visited the grounds again, and to have stood once more upon the spot where trod our noble Baker, a chance missed, I fear, will never again be mine.

We forded the Monocacy River waist deep, there appearing to be no time for bridging the same, this extreme haste portending an anxiety to reach the "rebellious" most gratifying to the powers that be at Washington if they are aware of it, but extremely ruffling to the temper of us dough bellies as we poor infantrymen are called by those chicken thieves, the cavalry. . . .

We have not had any letters for a very long time and there appears to be no prospect of getting any until something is done to stop our onward rush and have the poor devil of a mail carrier catch up. "Old Four Eye," as General Meade is termed by the men, appears to be a man universally despised in the Corps. He certainly cares very little for the rank and file, and curses loud and deep are hurled at him, (for obeying instructions, as he must be doing), in marching us so tremendously. The men appear to lack confidence in their General Officers, and with the exception of Griffin and Sykes[13] are exceedingly dubious as to their capacity for command. Hooker has lost all command over the army and I doubt very much indeed whether a successful battle can be fought under him. On all sides is continually heard doubt as to Hooker knowing where he is and what he is about; all are convinced that he cannot locate the enemy. It certainly does appear as if the hand of Providence was directing the movements of the Confederates so as to give the lie to Hooker's slander of McClellan, for it is certain that Maryland and Penna. are invaded and "Old Hook" knows nothing about it. This is a fine condition of affairs truly, but give us back again Geo. B. McClellan and the Johnnies will soon show a clean pair of heels.

I am still in good health tho' worn quite thin by our tremendous marches, but am repaid for all by the happiness of getting out of Old Virginia. I sincerely trust I will never set foot upon her "sacred soil" again and hope that this war will now be terminated by a square stand up fight, give and take. I do not feel at all confident as to the result of an engagement just now, but if Lee is defeated he is so far from his base that his army will be taken or destroyed, and there is no other to supply its place. Lee must certainly have very many more men than we, as was made apparent by the vast clouds of dust over the tops of the Blue Ridge from his columns as they marched thro' Virginia parallel with our army on the other side of the mountains.

I do not know how long we will remain here but as our baggage train is ordered up, suppose it will be for some days, probably in order to concentrate and allow the enemy to develop his plan somewhat. As we are on the immediate outskirts of Frederick I will spruce up a little and take a run into town and look around upon civilization a while, and, it may be, get a substantial dinner somewhere. The army appears to be massing here as I have learned of the other Corps being encamped around and near us.

I have also learned just now that "Old Four Eye" did a pretty good thing with our Corps which accounts in a measure for our forced marches. It appears that Jeb Stuart with all the Reb cavalry forded the Potomac at Edwards Ferry just a short time ahead of us and that our Corps had been pushed between him and Lee, thus cutting off the latter from all means of discovering accurate knowledge of our whereabouts and throwing the former into an enemy's country from which it will be almost impossible to escape; at all events a wide detour must be made to avoid us and Lee will be compelled to fight or fall back for the want [of] this great auxiliary. I cannot see how so fine a cavalry officer could be trapped so nicely by the "doughbellies."

I presume the daily papers can inform you better than I what we really are doing, and I hope too they will give the public to understand that in the opinion of the army, Old Joe Hooker is a fearful fraud and by no means a match for the man he is climbing all over the face of the earth to find, and [who] when found, [is] just as likely as not to be scooped in by his honor the rebel chieftain. I will write at every opportunity, but before you hear from me again I hope a decisive battle will have been fought.

Because of the absence of most of his cavalry, Lee did not learn until the night of June 28–29 that the Yankees were north of the Potomac and close on his heels. As soon as he verified that the Federals were near, he ordered his widely scattered commands to concentrate at Cashtown, Pennsylvania, eight miles west of Gettysburg. Meanwhile, Meade, after a quick study of the separated positions of his seven army corps, decided to bring them within supporting distance of each other and advance toward Gettysburg. On the morning of July 1 Union cavalry scouting west of the town met Confederates advancing from Cashtown, and the three-day battle that would prove to be the bloodiest encounter of the war was under way.

The 118th Pennsylvania and the 5th Corps reached the outskirts of Gettysburg in the early morning hours of July 2, following an exhausting thirty-seven-mile march. After a few hours of sleep, the 5th Corps was advanced to a position supporting the Federal center.

As a result of the desperate fighting on the first day of the battle, Lee pushed the Army of the Potomac back into a defensive position that ran on the south from a small but commanding eminence known as Little Round Top north to Cemetery Hill. The line then U-turned to the south and east to cover Culp's Hill, which anchored the Federal right. Union major general Dan Sickles's 3rd Corps held the area around the Peach Orchard, located due west of Little Round Top, and his thinly manned line angled back to cover the Wheatfield–Devil's Den area.

On July 2 Lee ordered Lt. Gen. James Longstreet's 1st Corps to assail the Federal left, aiming his attack in the direction of Little Round Top and the ground north and west of it. At approximately 4 P.M., as the Confederate assault was gaining momentum, two brigades of Brig. Gen. James Barnes's 1st Division, 5th Corps, including the 1st Brigade with Donaldson and the 118th Pennsylvania, were ordered forward to plug a critical gap that had developed in the lines of the 3rd Corps in the woods to the west of the Wheatfield.

Donaldson's detailed letter of his experiences at Gettysburg was written two and a half weeks after the battle. Although the events were fresh in his mind, his account contains several errors, all of which are understandable given the rapidity with which the confusing events of July 2 transpired. Despite these occasional inaccuracies, his narrative is valuable nonetheless, as it sheds some needed light on the actions of his regiment, and of the 1st Brigade, in the landmark battle of the war.

On the field at Gettysburg
July 4th, 1863

Dear Jac—

Have been heavily engaged with enemy—Our Brigade is torn to pieces—
Our Regt lost three officers—and 35 men. Capt. Davids Co. G—killed,
Lt. Wilson Co. B wounded, Lt. Inman Co. F mortally—

Am unhurt—no one in the company hurt.

>—+—‹›—O—‹›—+—‹

On the field at Gettysburg
July 5th, 1863

Dear Jake—

Am well and unhurt—grounds encumbered with dead & wounded.
Enemy defeated. Greater battle than Waterloo.

There are two hundred dollars at Corn Exchange for you, get it.
Enclosed find Batchelder's picture.

>—+—‹›—O—‹›—+—‹

Camp 118th P.V.
Middletown, Md.
July 8th

Dear Jake:

Your favors June 26th, July 1st to hand this day, and as I have no paper
will have to use your letters—when you write send paper and envelop. It
has been raining now for 5 consecutive days and during that time I have
not been dry scarcely an hour, yet I still continue well.

To day we crossed the Blue Ridge amid a heavy rain storm. 'Tis now
clear and I trust will remain so. We have been marched night and day since
the battle but owing to the fearful condition of the roads could not make
much head way. Will write you a full acct. of the battle when we halt
somewhere. My boots have been worn out for some time and I am now
bare footed nearly. . . . Have received the cloths but have torn the drawers
climbing rocks etc. . . .

>—+—‹›—O—‹›—+—‹

July 11th, 1863
In line of battle at or near
Antietam Creek & 5 miles
from Williamsport

Dear Bro:

A most splendid sight—the whole army in line of battle offering to fight Lee who so far declines (3 P.M.). Troops in splendid spirits. Am well and nice and dirty & ragged. . . . Can't write much, expect battle every moment. Love to Aunty, tell her I am gay & happy. How are you?

>─◄►─0─◄►─◄

Camp 118th P.V.
Near Upperville, Va.
July 21st, 1863

Dear Auntie:

My last letter [to you] was from Frederick Md., since which it seems almost incredible that I have been amid such scenes of blood and carnage and yet escaped unhurt and am alive today and able to relate, as near as may be, what I actually witnessed in the late dreadful encounter. For a long time being without letter paper I have had to resort to whatever kind I could manage to obtain in order to pencil my daily experiences, and in consequence my haversack is quite full of scraps which I will copy now that we are to remain here for a day or two. I bought this paper and ink from a Yankee private of the 18th Mass. and it is wonderful to observe how ever ready the New England men are to make a trade, although most generally they contrive to get the best of the bargain, as in this case, I being compelled to come down handsomely for the luxury of ink and paper.

June 28th. This day General Meade was placed in command, an appointment most unlooked for by us all, and one not likely to inspire the greatest amount of confidence. It may be all for the best but certainly the appointment of McClellan would have filled the army with that "Esprit de Corps" so much to be desired just now. I asked leave of the Colonel to visit the city and learned that it was against positive orders for him to grant it, "but at the same time," said he, "if you particularly desire to visit town, you are old soldier enough to find a way to do so." Of course I found the way and went accordingly. I had a fine time with Capt. Crocker, Lieutenants Thomas and Gardner doing the town very thoroughly and winding up with a good meal at the house of an old gentleman, a friend of Crocker's, whose name just now escapes me.

June 29th. Commenced packing up at 8 A.M., moved thro' Frederick at 11 o'clock, the citizens lining the sidewalks and windows and very generally expressing wishes for our success. We reached Mount Pleasant at 2 P.M. and bivouaced beyond Liberty at 7 P.M. Our regiment lies upon the side of a little hill not far from the town but I am too tired to visit it and desire only rest.

This has been a hard march. It appears to be the endeavor of our new commander to test still further the marching capacity of this corps, and it is certainly very wonderful how the men keep up. I observe as the day advances that very many of them drop out along the roadside seemingly utterly exhausted, but after we have encamped for the day they come in before dark and roll call is sure to show all present in the morning. It is curious to observe the five minutes rest in each hour given to an army corps whilst on the march. The several divisions are stretched, one after another, along the road like a huge snake, and when the head of column halts, the balance keep closing in mass until there are thousands upon thousands of men jammed close together, stretched at full length upon the ground resting, according to instructions contained in a pamphlet written by Genl. Butterfield and issued to the officers to impart to the men, how to gain the greatest amount of rest in the shortest possible time.[14] As the different regiments close up and rest, the head of column moves off again, so that both ends of the snake are moving at the time the other part is resting, as it were. I say it presents quite a spectacle to sit and observe the vast concourse move away in front, whilst apparently no end of men are closing up in the rear, and all is bustle, noise and dust but just where you are while the space between you and the moving men in front is gradually diminishing.

The country thro' which we passed today is wonderfully abundant, the standing grain being in the finest condition and so dense and heavy. I noticed one peculiarity about straw that never struck me before, and that was its durability and toughness. It becoming necessary to make a short cut across the country, the head of column turned off the road at right angles thro' an immense wheat field, and altho' a whole division of troops had passed over it, making a lane thro' the grain of at least 40 feet, when our regiment arrived at the spot it presented a perfectly level appearance like unto a plank road, unbroken at any point and not all cut up as would have been supposed. It was very springy and delightful to march over. I could not but feel how urgent the necessity for destroying so many thousand bushels of wheat, the finest I ever saw.

June 30th. This day we were in the advance. Everything in the army is conducted in the fairest possible manner, each division of the corps having the advance every third day, and this rule is carried out with brigades and regiments. For instance, as I have said, we were in advance today, that is, our regiment of the brigade, our brigade of the division, our division of the corps. Tomorrow we will be in rear of the brigade, division, and corps. We were up at day break, hurriedly cooked coffee and moved at 4 A.M. By 8 o'clock we had reached Union Bridge, a distance of at least 12 miles. After a short rest we were off again and at 10 o'clock passed thro' Union-town without stopping, and with but few halts bivouaced at Union Mills at 6 P.M. Most of the regiment was detailed for picket duty but I remained in camp too much exhausted for any further action. Feeling alarmed at my utter prostration I had Dr. Thomas make an examination and he pronounced me perfectly sound but needing stimulants. After taking the usual "pill opei," I partook freely from a canteen of whiskey which I had carefully husbanded during the march, and arose the next morning feeling as "tight as a musket."

July 1st. I thought that in consideration of the tremendous marches we had been making lately, and of the great fatigue attending the same, the commanding general, in pity for our forlorn condition, had mercifully granted us a few extra hours rest. Subsequent events show the fallacy of my reasoning, and proved that that "thoughtful" officer was in truth preparing us for the champion march of the season.

We broke camp and moved at 10 A.M. previous to which orders were issued and read to the men that all officers were to march in rear of their companies and no one would be allowed to fall out under any pretence whatever, anyone disobeying this order to be shot on the spot. Straggling was to be put a stop to. I was detailed with the guard to bring up the rear of the brigade and was to enforce this order under penalty of arrest and court-martial. In no case was I to leave a live man behind, but was to press into the ranks anyone found skulking on the road, no matter to what command he might belong. Especially was I to seize all persons on detailed service, such as drivers of pack horses, cooks and other "noncombatants." My first capture was Private James Godfrey[15] of my company, for a long time detailed as driver of regimental head quarter pack horses. James was a poor, miserable, weak minded fellow, utterly unable to stand fire, and altho' stout in person was not so at heart. He cast a pitiful eye at me and in tones most distressed urged the necessity of protecting the property in his charge. Turning over the custody of the horses to a contraband happening near, I ordered the guard to push the poor fellow forward at the point of the bayonet. Shortly after a musket and accoutrements were procured for him, and he trudged along with us, a dejected, miserable fellow.

My next experience was with an Irishman belonging to a New York regiment, who despite all endeavors to urge him on, held back and detained me not a little. I was loath to use the pistol on him, for I was sure he was a good man, tho' somewhat demoralized by fatigue, who if left to himself would be up with his regiment at night, but my orders were so positive that as a last resort I placed two men behind him with leveled bayonets and ordered them to run him thro' if he did not move on. At this juncture General Sykes and his staff rode up and for quite a time witnessed my endeavors to get the stubborn fellow along, when suddenly speaking in a loud voice, the General said, "Go ahead captain and leave this man to me, I'll get him along." With that he struck the fellow several smart blows with a riding whip and ordered him to "double quick." Without stirring a foot faster and apparently not heeding the whip, the head strong good natured soldier, turning his head to one side and looking full in the face of the General, said, "I say Gineral, 'ave ye any tobacky about ye?" This speech, evidently uttered in all sincerity, was hailed by the General and us all with roars of laughter, whilst the general, putting spurs to his horse, said in passing me, "Captain, let the man go, I'll be responsible for him." I did as I was ordered, too glad to get rid of a disagreeable duty. I next captured the regimental barber, a fearful fraud of a fellow, and it did me good to lay violent hands on him and put him into the ranks.

As we crossed the line into Pennsylvania at 11, the colors were unfurled, drums beaten and the old Keystone State entered with great enthusiasm and loud cheering all along the line, the column pressing rapidly forward with ranks well closed up. Each one felt the new energy given by the settled purpose of our new commander and that it was evidently of great moment for the corps to make good time. Another feeling also appeared to animate the men, and that was the intuitive knowledge of the fact that the enemy had been positively located and we were being rushed forward by forced marches to strike them a deadly blow on old Pennsy's soil, so all felt that if a good fight could be made anywhere it would be here. Soldiers invariably constitute themselves critics of the objects and results to be derived from the various operations going on around them, and it is really wonder-ful the intelligence displayed, closeness of insight and accuracy of their pre-diction as shown by subsequent events. My detail was full of news all day, each one had to tell of a word dropped by passing aides as to our probable destination or what this or that officer said, and finally all agreeing that the rebs were being headed and brought to a stand.

As we neared Hanover Junction the first evidence of fighting could be seen, the fences in the vicinity being down on every side and dead horses scattered everywhere. The result of the encounter was easily ascertained by the C.S. branded on all the carcasses we passed near. It must have been a hot fight engaging most of the cavalry on either side, as the ground as far as we could see was much torn up, whilst the debris scattered about could only come from large bodies of men.[16]

We halted at Hanover at 4 P.M., our regiment being in an enclosed field on the outskirts of the town. Here we were surrounded by the eager wondering country people, who showed every degree of astonishment at the dusty travelled stained "walking arsenals," as one of them termed us. They closely examined the muskets, cartridges and bayonets, awhilst much amusement was afforded us by the deference, respect and awe evinced in the presence of an equiped soldier with "license to do murder," as one man facetiously remarked. They are a bright, quick people but are not at all interested in the war and its results. Among them were many ladies from the town who were much interested in our method of cooking, and asked a number of questions as to the food we had and how we prepared it. Capt Crocker, with his great, bright, bearded, jovial face as usual did the agree-able. He told them that our regiment was composed of the very best men from Philadelphia, gentlemen all, from the Colonel to the private in the ranks, but owing to our long march, the men did not present that natty appearance so looked for in the "best families," that fatigue and bad treat-ment had reduced their pride considerably, and as an illustration of how utterly lost to all feeling of self men become when upon so long and active a campaign, he turned to a wretched, miserable, ragged, dirty straggler who was stooping down near a little fire cooking a piece of meat upon a little stick, which continually fell into the fire, to be rescued again after some difficulty and well brushed with the sleeve of his dirty coat, and told them this man was the son of the Rev. Dr. Boardman of Philada. The ladies were much astonished to learn that this dreadful looking man was the son of so celebrated a divine.[17]

We rested until 9 P.M. when we again took up the line of march. It was a beautiful night and the scene so stirring. The moon mounted into the heavens and looked calmly down upon the moving mass of men. As we moved onward all was silence, nothing was heard save the steady monotonous tread of the moving troops or, perchance, the foot steps of the horse of some mounted officer. We halted at 3:30 A.M. in a piece of woods near the roadside, making a march this day of 37 miles. Just before halting it had been given out that McClellan had taken command, and an officer with a lantern read the order as we passed him. The men became perfectly wild with joy and the scene was very exciting where we halted. Here were divisions of infantry intermingled with artillery and cavalry cheering each other as they passed along, while the name of McClellan rang thro' the ranks. Every one seemed filled with enthusiasm, and each battalion as it moved past stepped to the encouraging shouts of thousands of voices in one grand chorus for "little Mac."[18] Most of the men went at once to making coffee, but I, wrapping my overcoat round me, coiled myself upon the ground and was soon asleep.

July 2nd. I slept about an hour then arose, brushed the dew from my hair and looked around me. The woods were a scene of busy stir, here and there the blue smoke was curling up in playful wreaths from our bivouac fires, while the men were cooking coffee or otherwise preparing to take the road again. About 5 A.M. our division moved out into the open ground beyond the woods and commenced to deploy for action, the regiments being formed at deploying distance in close column.[19] It was a beautiful sight to see, as far as the eye could reach, regiment after regiment in mass, with colors unfurled, upon a line as straight as a die, while the death like silence pervading all made the senses keen to note every trifling incident.

It took some time to satisfactorily arrange us, but finally the order came to move forward, and with a firm tread and muskets at the right shoulder, the movement commenced. Over fields and fences went the silent moving mass, while nothing was heard save an occasional caution from our Colonel as to the guide, and the singular noise made by the tramping of so many thousands of feet thro' the crushing leaves and grass, while the atmosphere was heavy with the pennyroyal smell so peculiar to all battlefields. As we gradually approached the rising ground in front, from beyond which musketry firing could be distinctly heard, a change of direction to the right was made, which after continuing for some time was changed again to the front.

We halted in a piece of woods to the front of which our army was then engaged, and from the length of time we remained here, I presume were upon the reserve. After listening for a long time to the intermittent firing, the battle suddenly became very animated, the deafening and unceasing roar of artillery making the earth fairly quake. By its long continuance and regularity, all felt that if not pushing the enemy they were certainly not getting the advantage of our people, and as we had received no orders to load, our help was evidently not needed. Drawing this inference I determined to avail myself of an opportunity to indulge in a bath, a pond of inviting water being but a short distance to the rear of our regiment. I stripped myself, rushed eagerly into the water and was soon splashing and dashing about like a dolphin, when noticing some very curious weeds sticking to my person, I hastened out to rid myself of them, when to my astonishment I found them to be leeches. I postponed further bathing. After this little episode nothing was to be done but to sit down and listen to the firing, which was now becoming terrible, the shells whistling above us and plunging away beyond our ammunition trains which were directly to the rear of us.

My feelings at this time can be readily described, as but one thought was paramount, a hope that the troops in front would be able to thrash the confederates without our aid, for with rest comes a dislike for bloody encounters. With this thought uppermost and while considering our probable chances for continuing this soft thing, even then, amid the thunder of the artillery bursting upon my ear, the missiles flying and the sound of musketry piercing the air, I, before I was aware of it, grew drowsy, my eyelids grew heavy and shut, thus closing out the warlike scene, and I was asleep. I know not how long I had been sleeping when suddenly I was awakened by the cry of "fall in," which was quickly responded to by all. As the men took their places in line, still laughing and jesting among themselves, the order to load was given, which at once put a stop to all trifling, and by its peculiar significance made the blood leap suddenly in the veins, and the choking sensation to rise in the throat, as each realized that we were about to take an active part in the battle going on in front. The enemy were shelling our lines furiously which seemed to indicate a general assault.

At 3:30 P.M. we moved by the left flank, and our regiment, being on the left of the brigade, of course now became the advance. Already the battle was raging fearfully ahead, and strings of ambulances with the wounded and mangled fellows were passing to the rear. As nearer and nearer we approached

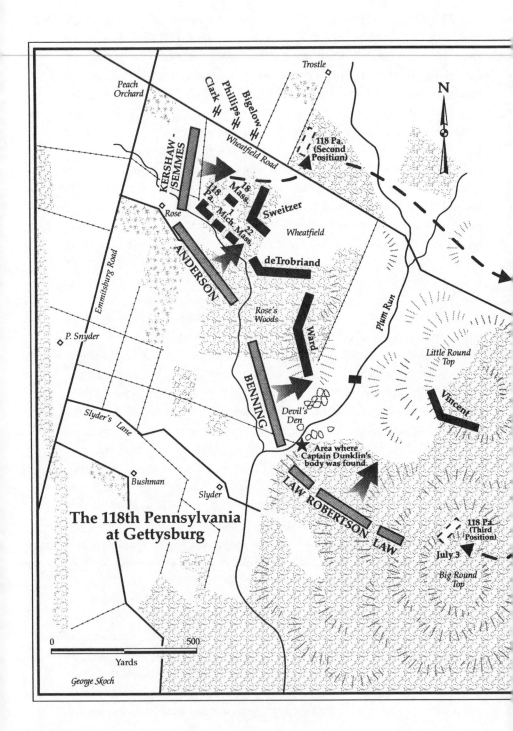

The 118th Pennsylvania
at Gettysburg

George Skoch

the field, shells could be seen bursting in vast quantities, while ammunition wagons and limber boxes were being hurried forward, and the usual confusion, noise and bustle of the rear of an immense army during a battle met our eye, and, I may add, left an unpleasant feeling upon us.

We now entered the woods which appeared to crown an eminence whose sides, full of rocks and boulders, sloped away towards the enemy, and were at once amid the dreadful bursting shells, which, however, flew past us and did no harm. At this point I saw an orderly leading a splendid black horse which was limping along on three legs, the other having been shot off at the hoof. Inquiring to whom it belonged, I learned that Capt. John Fassitte of General Birney's[20] staff, its owner, fearing harm would come to this fine animal, had mounted another and sent it to the rear for safety, but just as our column was reached, a shell had struck the poor beast and he would now have to be killed. At this moment Captain Crocker came to me and asked my opinion of the present movement. I replied that judging from the heavy musketry fire going on to the front, I had no doubt our movement was intended to support a threatened point, or to retrieve a disaster which had already happened; certainly the peculiar rebel cheer now heard above every other sound would indicate that they had been successful somewhere.

A few minutes after, we formed in line immediately to the rear of a very thin line of battle that looked to me like a skirmish line, which retired as soon as we were posted. Our brigade was now rapidly drawn up in the following order: 118th P.V. on the right, 22nd Massachusetts on the left, 1st Michigan in rear of the 22nd Mass., and the 18th Mass. in rear of the right of the 1st Michigan and left of our regiment. We had in our brigade all told but 425 men, the balance, having straggled during the night before, had been collected, formed into a stragglers brigade, and taken into a different part of the field. The reason the 1st Mich., and 18th Mass. were not in line was because the 2nd brigade crowded us to such an extent there was no room for them, and they therefore acted as supports. . . . Our position was in all respects a good one. We were on the edge of a heavy growth of timber, with rocks and huge boulders scattered about forming ample protection, and just beyond, the hill fell off to quite a slope, up which the enemy would have to reach us. Upon our immediate right a battery of brass guns was posted which was, even now, being served with wonderful rapidity.[21] Shortly before the engagement commenced on our part we were moved slightly to the rear, which allowed the 1st Mich. to get into line. . . . Nearly one half of our regiment [was] refused on the right in order to prevent flanking.

The skirmishers were but a short distance to the front, and I greatly feared many of them would be unable to get back, owing to the extreme eagerness of the men to open fire, and I particularly cautioned my company to be extremely careful and allow our people to get in before firing.

At this moment Private Jas. Godfrey, the man I had forced into the company the day before, came to me with his watch and pocket book, also a letter to his wife saying, "Here, Captain, take these things and if I get killed send them to my wife, I am going to show the boys how to fight today, I have been called coward long enough." I could not help smiling at what this action implied, altho' of course not so intended, as I was as likely to be killed as he, but taking him by the hand and giving it a good honest squeeze and a terrible shake, I said, "Well done Godfrey, I knew you were sound at heart and I will write to your wife of your conduct this day, here, take a pull at this," and stepping behind a tree I let him have my canteen. Well, I really thought the poor fellow would certainly choke in his eagerness to get the rum down him. When I thought he had enough I sent him back to the company, and shortly after saw him standing, in advance of all with sleeves rolled up, musket aport, and foot firmly planted awaiting the development of events. I now felt very badly for the skirmishers as I was sure Godfrey was certainly one of them.

During all this time the enemy were making their charge, and from the rapid firing of the battery on our right, I judged, were drawing closer and closer to our line, altho' as yet unseen by us. The roar of the artillery was deafening, and from the excited manner of the gunners all efforts had evidently failed to check the onset. The voice of the officer commanding the guns could be heard loudly calling for "canister," while the surrounding objects were becoming less and less distinct from the sulphurous smoke occasioned by such rapid firing. Soon was heard a startling volley of musketry towards the left of our brigade, another and another followed in a wild and continuous rattle as the enemy's column came within range. The scene now beggars description. The deafening shouts of the combatants, the crash of artillery, the trembling ground beneath us, the silent and stricken countenances of the men, the curtain of smoke over all and its peculiar smell, made up a picture never to be forgotten by any who witnessed it.

As the enemy's columns came nearer, the artillery was served with shell with short fuse, which burst at once upon leaving the gun, scattering destruction broadcast. Our skirmishers now came running rapidly towards us, and a moment after, the enemy's column was seen moving at a quick pace obliquely along our front, very many of them in their shirt sleeves, and all appearing to be loading and firing as they came steadily up the hillside in the face of the battery, which seemed to be their objective point.[22] Our regiment now opened and in a few minutes were at it pell mell loading and firing as rapidly as possible. So eager were the men to fight that I did not notice one of them taking advantage of the trees and rocks, but all standing bravely up to the work and doing good execution.

As I passed up and down in rear of the company speaking to the men and directing their firing, I noticed one of them like a blazing Vesuvius, standing a yard to two in front of all, begrimed with powder, hatless and shouting as he fired his piece, "Give them hell boys," and by his extraordinary behavior making himself the most conspicuous object in our whole line. It was Godfrey, who by his determined bravery had actually assumed a leadership among his hitherto jeering comrades, and now had several of them loading his and their own muskets for him to discharge. Passing thro' the line I took my place beside him to observe more closely the movements of the enemy, who were now so near that the countenances of many of them were quite distinct. I noticed one man in particular on the right of a division, as it seemed to me, with big broad brimmed hat on the back of his head, large black whiskers and eyes directed towards our regiment, as in evident fear of danger from that quarter, he looked the personification of physical daring as he rammed a cartridge into the musket he held at a trail. Altho' I know he was the object of several shots specially directed at him, yet I saw him gradually move away apparently unhurt, and finally with his comrades disappear altogether in the dense smoke of the guns.

Our line now became somewhat broken and open as the men, after firing, would step back to load, but this is generally the case in all stationary lines of battle. A cheer now broke forth, the smoke was rent, and the rebels dashed in upon the battery with a savage yell. The artillery men retreated somewhat to the rear dragging their guns with them by ropes, which in anticipation of a catastrophe had been fastened to them.

Running to the rear of my company to prevent any movement looking towards a retreat, for all saw that our position was now untenable as the cannon were virtually in the hands of the enemy, I was met by Capt. Richd. W. Davids, who was slowly walking towards me. Upon stopping to see what was wanted, he said, "Capt., I am hit." "Where?," said I. "Thro' the stomach and bowels," said he, at the same time placing his hand upon his waist belt. "You had better go to the rear," cried I, and he started to do so, but had not gone more than twenty steps before he fell, and I knew that death had come upon him. I was the last person he ever spoke to upon this earth, and mine the ears to hear the last utterance of as brave and noble a gentleman as ever trod God's green footstool.

Nothing could now stop the rebel onset, and the shouts of rage and defiance rose up amid the roar of musketry as they swarmed upon the cannon. In a moment our guns were lost and the enemy in fierce numbers were crowding upon our right and rear. Our line wavered, trembled and commenced to give ground, when Maj. Herring, in a clear and distinct

Capt. Richard W. Davids, Company G, 118th Pennsylvania Volunteers. He was killed at Gettysburg, July 2, 1863. THE CIVIL WAR LIBRARY & MUSUEM.

voice heard by the whole command above the din and roar of battle, cried, "Change front to rear on 10th company," and as upon parade the men performed the movement of swinging round to right angles with the line previously held, thus compelling the enemy to continue on a longer circle in order to outflank and get to our rear. This, however, they continued to do, and at last we were compelled reluctantly to fall back. Our retreat was as follows—1st Mich. and 118th P.V. immediately to the rear, the 18th and 22[d] Mass. by the left flank to the 3rd brigade. Our regiment was pushed back directly among the ammunition trains, but the men still kept up a straggling fire as they retreated.

Soon after we commenced to give way Maj. Biddle,[23] of Genl. Meade's staff, and I am not sure but the general himself, appeared and entreated, prayed and called upon the men for God sake to halt, not to give way, that this was the only portion of the line broken, to think of the safety of the ammunition train, that the whole army would have to retreat—but to no purpose, for with dogged silence the men retired slowly and without apparent panic or hurry, for they were perfectly well satisfied of the impossibility of longer holding their ground.

While this was happening, observing Capt. Crocker lingering behind, I allowed the men to pass me and went back to see what could possibly detain him amid such extreme danger. With a manner perfectly cool and collected he said it was too bad our boys had not stood their ground longer, and that he wanted to see how many the enemy numbered and what they would do next. It was a strange sight to look upon. The rebels were crowding up in great numbers but appeared unable to realize the extent of their success, and were standing cheering and yelling without attempting to pursue or even to fire upon our retreating line. Turning to me Crocker seized the pistol I held in my hand and discharged the two remaining barrels at the mass in front of us, then suddenly taking to his heels beat a rapid retreat quickly followed by me.

Our regiment continued to fall slowly back for a few minutes longer, when all at once it was brought to a stand still by a yell so fierce and terrible that the very blood seemed to curdle in our veins, while a sound as of a hurricane was swept towards us. It was the crushing of leaves and twigs made by the Pennsylvania Reserves coming up in mass, at the double quick, arms at the right shoulder, bayonets fixed and with Genl. Crawford on horseback at their head, hat in hand, waving it excitedly as he led the most terrific charge I ever witnessed. With diabolical screeches and shouts they pressed forward, struck the bewildered enemy and by very force of the onset sweeping every living thing before them, retaking the cannon, crushing under foot and bayonetting all who for a moment attempted a resistance and finally pushing back the whole rebel line up over and beyond a hill of considerable height upon our left which had evidently been occupied by them.[24] In the meantime the 2nd and 3rd brigade had been performing a movement rarely occuring in battle, resisting a bayonet charge; and it was give and take with them, no quarter being shown on either side. The 16th Mich. of the 2nd brigade was nearly annihilated, their colonel being bayonetted several times thro' the stomach and bowels as he sat on horseback, and died at his post, not having yielded an inch of ground.[25] This bloody work could not last long and the 2nd brigade gave ground slowly, and was about to retire altogether when a cheer arose, and a line of glistening steel was seen approaching. It was the 20th Maine, 83rd and 10th Penna. of the 3rd brigade, together with the Penna. Reserves, who, having just cleared our front, now did the same for the hard pressed 2nd.[26] I have been told that the 16th Mich. bayonetted every living rebel, wounded or unhurt, that fell into their hands, in retaliation for the loss of their Colonel. Such was the ending of this conflict from out of which our command so narrowly escaped annihilation or capture. We remained at the spot where we had halted and adjusted our line, while the 6th Corps, just arrived, formed line to our rear, and Penna. Reserves continuing to the front. After these dispositions we prepared for the night.

I must mention more prisoners had been taken than we had men in the brigade, these unfortunates being caught between us and the charging Reserves. I went among them eagerly questioning right and left for news of the 22nd Virginia Regt., and from what I could learn, that regiment is with Bradley Johnson and was not engaged today.[27] The prisoners, one and all, seemed rejoiced to have passed safely thro' such a "blazing Hell" as they termed the fire we poured upon them. They say we have no idea of the tremendous slaughter made among their people and are unable to explain how it was they escaped unhurt. One man told me they thought it was militia they were to encounter and rather took comfort from being beaten by old soldiers. About 8 o'clock P.M. the ammunition wagons unloaded at our regiment enough cartridges to have supplied a whole division. Surely this seemed to me a most uncalled for waste, as we really did not need more than an additional thirty rounds per man, and these boxes would therefore be abandoned when most probably some other portion of the field would need them.

At last the battle was hushed and all was still, night veiled the earth. Its gloomy shades were thickened by a sulphurous cloud that like a pall hung sadly over the field. The woods and fields were strewn with the wounded and dying, and with the ghastly forms of the dead. It is indeed remarkable that men can lie down and sleep so tranquilly when they know the danger that awaits them on the morrow, when they hear the cries of the already mangled, when they know that the dead lie strewn around and that with the early dawn of the coming day, the work of death will be resumed as all felt it would surely be, now that the whole army was up and the enemy had been repulsed.

July 3rd. At day break we were moved to the left and took position on the summit of quite a high hill[28] from which the Reserves had driven the enemy last evening, and we had now a commanding view of the whole field. The ground in front was heavily wooded and the enemy occupied the base of the hill, while our skirmishers were unable to push forward but a short distance from the line . . . [and] vast numbers of dead and wounded encumbered the ground, and to make the sight more horrifying, wild hogs were seen feeding on some of the badly torn bodies.[29] The troops who had occupied this place last night had erected a substantial stone breastwork from the loose boulders and broken fragments that covered the mountains.

Just after we had been established in our new position a rebel officer was seen leisurely walking towards our line, with his hands in pockets, segar in mouth and without sword or weapon of any kind, while his jacket was thrown open in careless abandon. The skirmishers allowed him to walk into their line, and he was greatly astonished and mortified to learn he was a prisoner. He said he was Genl. Heth's Adjutant General,[30] had left his command but a few minutes before and strolled along not supposing for a moment the "Yanks" were so near. He betrayed considerable feeling as he was led to the rear by two privates who were instructed to deliver him to Genl. Meade.

During the morning nothing of moment was done on either side and with the exception of a cannon shot now and then, everything remained perfectly quiet. Availing myself of the presence of the chaplain, who had come up in order to talk seriously to the men and distribute tracts among them, I wrote home that I had thus far escaped unhurt, the chaplain promising to forward any letters given him. Our men, wherever they could, gathered up the wounded enemy and carried them to the rear. I talked to one poor fellow who was shot thru' the breast, the lungs most probably, and who had been placed upon a stretcher and left to await the return of the ambulance men. He was suffering great anguish from thirst and was scarcely able to articulate his gratitude for the kindness shown by those from whom he had expected other treatment. The poor fellow was not as sanguine as he would liked to have been as to the final result of the battle, as our men looked to him so healthy, well fed and clothed, and yet capable of making a stout fight behind such splendid breastworks. He was an intelligent attractive man of about 45 years, and was exceedingly gentlemanly in his speech, always thanking us for any attention. I gave him some water and whiskey which appeared to help him considerably, and was sorry when compelled to leave him so helpless and alone.

About 1 o'clock, there suddenly burst forth the deafening crash of what appeared to me to be the whole of the enemy's artillery. I went to my post to see what was the occasion of this sudden concentration of the enemy fire that was making the ground rock as in the throes of an earthquake. The air was soon filled with a hissing, bursting torrent, while the men crouched low along the line. Standing on a rock I could see the smoke rising up along the whole of the enemy's position, and supposed they were about to try and beat us out by the weight of their artillery. The sun shone gloriously, making objects quite distinct in the distance, and I could see puffs of smoke from our own guns which were now replying. Retiring to the rear of our line, I sought shelter from the screaming and exploding shells, but could find none, so was compelled, along with many others, to sit still and endure this trial of the nerves for at least two hours. There was scarcely a second that we were free from shot or shell, and I never remembered to have seen so many solid shot thrown before. The missiles were sent one after the other so rapidly that a constant, prolonged and connected whizzing was maintained. Shells were exploded in front, now in the rear of us and frequently over our heads, solid shot came rushing madly, crashing and tearing among the trees, while the air was filled with fragments and the suspense was horrible to endure. During this time Capt. O'Neill and myself were sitting together on a piece of shelter tent which protected us from the damp ground. We had very little to say to one another and were very close together for protection, as it were. A shell bursting rather nearer than usual over our heads caused us to huddle still closer, while our very hearts ceased to beat as we listened to the singing of a fragment that seemed to be coming rapidly towards us. With one look we read in each others faces the alarm both felt, and saw the impossibility of avoiding the terrible death dealing missile. As we sat motionless—breathless,—it dashed furiously between my knees, and with a thud and splash of dirt, buried itself deep into the ground. I dug up the ragged piece of metal, felt its sharp edges, and put it into my haversack as a memento of the narrow escape I had made.

After enduring the fire of the rebels for at least two hours there was again a lull in the storm of battle, the artillery gradually slackened and finally ceased altogether. We could observe the field to be free from troops, the rebel infantry being within the woods. I now ran back to see after the poor wounded reb we had left on the stretcher, and found him torn to atoms and the stretcher to shreds. Poor fellow, he had been killed by his own friends, how terrible that must be, and what agony it must have been to him to have lain there fearful, not of his enemies, but lest he should be killed by his own people. Well, he was mortally wounded in the first place, and is now better off.

For a time everything continued to remain perfectly calm and quiet. Such quiet is always ominous; it betokens preparation for something of vital importance. Our own men we could not see owing to the woods, but the line could be easily traced as it stretched away to the right in the shape of an exceedingly shallow semicircle. We could clearly observe the movements of the enemy should they make any, and, I can add, all eyes were eagerly rivetted on their line to see what they would do next. About 4 P.M. they began to show themselves at the edge of the woods and to manifest signs of an intended attack. Our batteries again opened, but the rebs appeared firm and proceeded in two lines to advance in splendid order. There seemed to be a heavy body upon their rear and flank, apparently as supports, all forming a mass, I should say, of at least eight or ten thousand men, who were being pushed forward in the face of our whole army upon some point considerably to the right of our position. There was nothing to hinder anyone in our whole line from witnessing their advance, and the eagerness with which each man gazed upon this magnificent spectacle was evidence that all felt a terrible crisis was approaching. On every side could be heard men questioning the capability of our line resisting so tremendous an onset. After proceeding some distance to the front, the enemy appeared to move obliquely to the left, owing, no doubt, to the severe fire from the batteries near us. They again changed to the front, however, after proceeding a short distance, and came up in the face of all our artillery. They continued to move on unflinchingly, and it was a grand sight to see them, their splendid behavior calling forth bursts of admiration from us all. A piece of woods considerably to our right and beyond which the enemy's column soon passed shut out from our sight the finale of this desperate charge, but our ears were soon greeted by the tremendous roar of musketry, whilst a curtain of smoke ascended to the tops of the trees and remained there to tell us that a desperate fight was in progress. This state of things continued for some time and we were uncertain as to the result, when presently a few men were seen running from beyond the woods, followed by others, and at last whole clusters of the enemy were seen scampering to the rear as fast as possible, but it was also noticed that not one third of those who, but a few moments before had gone forward so bravely, returned; they had all been killed or wounded and the charge was unsuccessful. This latter fact we knew, as the enemy soon opened again their artillery fire to cover the retreat of their men, and we accepted the sign by giving a fearful shout for the victory gained.

July 4th. At 10 A.M. our brigade moved to the front in order to feel and develop the enemy. On reaching the slope and foot of the hill—what a sight presented itself. The ground was literally covered with shattered and shot torn limbs of trees, whilst there was scarcely room to move without treading upon the dead body of an enemy. As far as the eye could see the dead lay in all manner of shapes, some upon their faces, others upon their backs, and as incredible as it may seem, others still kneeling behind the rocks where they had taken shelter, some of them with their muskets still poised and supported by the rocks in readiness to fire, and who still kept their intent gaze along their pieces, but who had been stricken by death before they could discharge them, and who were so well balanced and looked so life like that the men instinctively avoided the leveled muskets as they came near them. Vast numbers of the enemy had hastily thrown up stone breastworks behind which to take shelter, but our marksmen had slain them, for there was no shelter from such a deluge of bullets, and again there were others who had clutched the leaves and grass in their death struggle, whilst their mouths were filled with the soil as they had literally bitten the dust, and all, nearly all of them, had tobacco between their teeth.

Just where we halted to allow the skirmishers to advance I noticed one spot in particular where apparently the enemy's line had halted momentarily in order to gather itself together for the desperate ascent of the hill. The ground was strewn with the bodies of men consisting, I could perceive, of a whole company which had been in the line of fire from our batteries and had received the content of a full charge of canister, killing every single one of them. I counted thirty seven bodies, all dressed alike, in a coarse dark material with black felt hats, seemingly new, and most probably taken from a store in Gettysburg or some other town. A little in front of these bodies, with his head resting on a stone, his body straightened out and hands folded across his breast, lay, as if asleep, one of the handsomest men I ever saw. Someone had arranged his body evidently with the intention of recovering it after the battle, but even this kind friend must surely have been killed, judging from the number of dead that marked the passage of this particular regiment. He appeared to be about 35 years of age, was dressed in gray cloth jacket and pants, neither showing much wear, and appeared to be at least 5 feet 10 inches in height, weighing, probably, about one hundred and seventy pounds. His face had been shaven upon the cheeks the day of his death, leaving a splendid luxuriantly flowing chestnut beard upon the chin. The ball that had slain him had pierced his heart, passing thro' a letter in his breast pocket from which I learned his name to be Wm. A. Duncan, Capt. 44th Alabama Regt.,[31] and dated from Selma. As usual with all dead soldiers his pockets were inside out, thus showing the plunderer had been around, tho' of course from among his own people, as our troops never occupied the ground. Sitting down I examined his body closely, and judging from the silken undercloths, he had evidently been a man of means and position in his community; in fact, a letter addressed to him was from some one in authority in his town, as it related to plans evidently suggested by the deceased for the capture of deserters who were occupying the hills around Selma. I cannot tell you how sad the fate of this fine looking soldier made me feel. Indeed I could picture to myself the anxiety of his family for intelligence from this terrible battle-field, and with no word received their confident belief in his capture, for surely some of his company would have escaped unhurt, and I could fancy the long lapse of years without one word, without one sign from their dear one, and their heart sickness from hope deferred. At parting I grasped his cold hand in mine and bid farewell to the noble form that lay stretched in death before me. . . .

I should mention that the apparent good condition of this particular body arose solely from the character of his wound. The ball, passing thro' his chest and heart, had caused internal hemorrhage, his veins therefore freed from blood, his body resisted longer the action of the weather than others shot elsewhere. One of my company asked my permission to take this dead officer's boots. I gave assent after observing the poor fellow had scarcely a piece of leather to his feet, and the last I saw of poor Dunklin was his fixed and glassy gaze towards heaven, and a pair of old worn out army shoes by his side. I trust his grave will be marked, as I left his name pinned to his coat so that at some future time his friends may be possessed of what remains of his handsome person, but I fear this cannot be done, as there are so many to bury that time will be wanting even to scatter a little earth over them all.[32]

We pushed on to the end of the woods without encountering the enemy, and found, just beyond, a field of grain in which lay the rebel sharp shooters. Our skirmishers, under command of Capt. Fernald and Lieut. Walters, advanced bravely into the field but were met by such a heavy fire they were compelled to take cover again. About this time large bodies of troops could be seen moving as if to flank us, while a line approached in front with evident intention to engage. Our orders being merely to develop the enemy and avoid an engagement, Col. Tilton, the brigade commander, gave the signal to retire, which we did, and went into bivouac in rear of the line of battle. Shortly after noon it commenced to storm, and the very flood gates of heaven seemed to open upon us. Each moment it increased in fury until every man was drenched by the cold rain. This continued the balance of the day and all night long, interrupting any further movement on our part and ending the greatest fight our army ever had since its organization.

Meade had handled the Army of the Potomac capably at Gettysburg, and after three horrific days of battle, the Confederates had lost more than 28,000 men, or one-third of their effective force, while the Federals had lost 23,000. After spending a day waiting for Meade to attack, Lee began his retreat to Virginia on the evening of July 4.

Meade's pursuit was cautious, and when he finally caught up with the Rebels on July 12 near the Potomac at Falling Waters, Maryland, he spent a day reconnoitering their formidable entrenchments fronting the river. By the time an advance was undertaken, on the morning of July 14, Lee had slipped back into Virginia, effectually ending the Gettysburg Campaign.

Up to this point in his correspondence, Donaldson had always recorded his experiences to his brother and Aunt through letters. His method, as he disclosed, was to jot his doings on scraps of paper and use these notes as the basis for his missives. Following Gettysburg, however, Donaldson began to keep a diary, and in the interest of time, he would occasionally tear the pages from the book and mail them home, in some instances accompanied by a letter.

July 5th. We remained all day of the 5th until 6 P.M. when having learned positively that Genl. Lee had retired, we moved back a short distance & took a path around the base of the mountain, crossing away to the left of the battlefield—2 Division leading. Reached the Emmitsburg Road and bivouaced at 11 P.M. on Marsh Creek, a little stream emptying into the Monocacy. This was a hard march. Genl. Griffin again took command. He had been on the field but declined to assume command until the battle was over. Quite a compliment to Genl. Barnes. This day was cloudy.

July 6th. Reville at 4 A.M. 10 A.M. changed bivouac about a mile in direction of Emmitsburg. Before dismissing battalion, Col. Gwyn had the Adjutant read congratulatory order of Genl. Meade to the troops upon their great victory. At its conclusion he rode to the front of regiment and taking his hat off called out, "Now men, three cheers for Genl. Meade; hip, hip"—but not a man moved in response, not a voice was heard, all stood still. "That," said he, "you won't cheer your commander, then I'll do it myself," and so he did, waving his hat and giving the regular orthodox cheers and tiger. No more cheering—there has been too many changes of commander, besides the army don't like Meade, they don't know much about him. Of all the General officers known to the army, with exception of the 5th Corps, he is least known of any of them.

July 7th. Raining. Reveille at 3 A.M. Moved at 4 A.M. and passed the line into Maryland at 6 A.M. There was a marked difference between the conduct of the troops at this time and that of July 1st on entering Penna. Now, no notice whatever was taken of the fact of leaving the State. After a forced march of 25 miles we halted and bivouaced within 5 miles of Frederick Md. at 7 P.M.—a hard march.

July 8th. Raining hard—dull, dreary day, but at 6 A.M. took up the march and at 10 o'clock crossed the Catoctin Mts. amid a violent thunder and lightning storm. Upon the summit we were amid the clouds and in the centre of the storm. The lightening tore and ripped through the clouds which were so dense as to resemble steam, and the rain in maddening torrents poured down the mountain pathways. As we descended the mountain side and reached halfway down, the clouds rolled back unfolding the glorious sun which spread its rays over the peaceful little village of Middletown, which looked just the same as it did in Sept. last, when on the march to Antietam we passed through it and brought out refreshed and invigorated the green things of the broad and beautiful valley below us. We passed through Middletown at 1.25 P.M. and bivouaced just outside the town.

July 9th. Clear and cloudy. Moved at 9.30 A.M., crossed the South Mountains and at 12.25 P.M. bivouaced to the west of Boonsboro. Detail of 125 from our regiment with others of the brigade on picket under command of Major, 1st Michigan. Genl. Barnes left for home on acct. of wounds recd. at Gettysburg.[33]

July 10th. Clear day. Reveille at 3 A.M. Moved at 7.15. Some conception as to the condition of the men's foot gear can be had from the fact that Maj. Herring told me he had made requisition for 154 pair of shoes. Crossed Antietam Creek, formed line of battle in two lines at 12 M., and rested & bivouaced about 5 miles from Williamsport. 3rd Brigade on picket.

July 11th. Near Williamsport. Moved at 6 A.M. and formed line of masses in double column in cornfield, and moved forward to support battery in orchard beyond. Remained until 5 P.M. then moved in line of double column across the country in N.W. direction for 2 miles and bivouaced on a high bluff near a little stream at 8 P.M. This day Senator Wilson, late Colonel, visited the 22 Mass. These troops in consequence were very happy, cheering continually and otherwise expressing joy. We all had a look at the Senator.[34]

July 12th. Sunday. Clear in the morning, rain in afternoon. 11 A.M. moved forward still in double column, halted and moved forward several times again until enemy's earth works were developed; halted and deployed for action. Occupied summit of quite an elevation down which and up to the enemy's works country was open & filled with stacks of wheat in which were reb skirmishers. 6th Corps join us on the right and 2nd Corps on the left. Genl. Meade and staff came upon the ground in front of brigade & watched the enemy thro' field glasses. He finally ordered 2 or 3 Co.'s to be detached from our regt. in support of skirmishers then in front. Right & left Co.'s E & B thrown forward, H in centre as support. Men moved into wheat field, some firing. At this time Q.M. Gardner came up & after little talk with friends, seeing engagement abt. to commence, said laughingly that his instructions were to keep out of _long_ cannon range, this was no place for him—so rode off—every one laughing. Meantime, had commenced clouding up. Chaplain O'Neill approached Genl. Meade, and with head uncovered asked the general whether a battle couldn't be fought as well the next day and not on God's Holy Sabbath. The Genl. good naturedly replied that he was like a man who had a contract to make a box—he had the four sides and bottom made & was abt. to put on the lid, hence the fight would take place. "Then," said the chaplain, "as God's agent I solemnly protest and will show you that the Almighty will not permit this to be done. Look at the heavens, see the threatening storm approaching," and sure enough in a few minutes it began raining with vivid lightning and pealing thunder. This was at 4.10 P.M. & it continued 'till night fall, of course, no movement could be made. The skirmishers, both sides, covered themselves with their blankets & stood looking at each other & trying to keep dry.

Regt. moved into woods on left & at 8 P.M. bivouaced. O'Neill & Crocker detached with 100 men for picket. Gwyn selected Crocker not withstanding he had just come off same duty. Maj. Herring explained situation to Gwyn, but he said he had selected Crocker especially, as an intrepid & skillful officer was wanted this night for that duty. This was a gross out rage & only done to make it unpleasant for Crocker who had this day refused to hold a conversation with Gwyn on some personal matter. Maj. Herring bid Crocker good bye, never expecting to see him again, as the firing was lively and Crocker always exposed himself so. He said he would pray the Almighty would keep him from harm. As he was unjustly dealt with I also was very indignant and kept awake all night listening to the picket firing from Crocker's direction. Gwyn finished up the shank of the evening as drunk as a lout. Don't know where in the world he manages to get his rum from.

July 13th. Rain. Commenced building breastworks of timber & earth— very solid & one of Capt. Martin's guns[35] was brought up & placed in interval reserved for it. Don't like the idea of breastworks. Looks like staying here. Certainly it cannot be possible that Lee will again assume the offensive. Besides, breastworks just now makes the men timid. We have been under the impression that Lee had been badly crippled and was anxious to get away. I don't know much about the science of the thing but it seems to me the proper plan would be to push ahead of him, cross the Potomac & attack his communications.—Pickets out all day.—At noon Genl. Meade passed along the line & examined our position. Chaplain O'Neill held a bray service— that is, he preached so loud that the whole brigade heard him. His text was "He that hath ears to hear, let him hear." None of us were deaf anyway. Afternoon, 3rd Brigade relieved our pickets. Still raining. Our Lieut. Binney of Genl. Neill's staff[36] visited us this P.M. Was awfully glad to see him. He was as jolly as ever.

July 14th. Still Raining. 6.20 ordered under arms in support of a reconnoisance by Genl. Crawford's 3 Division 5th Corps. Moved forward at 12 M., occupied enemy's breastworks, halted 2 P.M. at Williamsport. Picked up numbers of enemy's stragglers. Found that Lee had recrossed the Potomac during the night. Halted & issued rations. Capt. Sharwood rejoined the regt—had been left behind June 30th with attack of gout. He was at once made officer of the Day. Shortly after moved into wheatfield and bivouaced 7 P.M.

July 15th. Clear—Took up line of march at 4.10 A.M. Crossed & bivouaced at foot of South Mt. on the road to Burkittsville & Berlin at 5.30 P.M. Hard & trying march. Capt. Crocker, Lt. Walters, White, Thomas & myself only officers up. Rest straggled.[37]

July 16th. Clear. Few minutes before 5 P.M. took up line of march. Splendid road, 3rd Brigade in advance. Reached Burkhardtville[38] 6.30 A.M. Went into camp 9.15 A.M. near Petersville, Md. Wagons came up, no time for clean things. Lt. Batchelder quite sick, spitting blood, afraid he will have to be left behind. Will miss him dreadfully. During night rained very hard.

July 17th. Raining. Mustered by companies at Col. Gwyn's tent for May & June. Moved at 4 P.M., crossed the Potomac on Pontoons at Berlin at 5.25 P.M. Reached Virginia side at 5.30. Lovettsville at 6.45 P.M. An attempt was here made to destroy the village in retaliation for destruction of property in Penna. Genl. Griffin put an end to it—promptly. Lt. Batchelder very ill. Put him in the house of a lady who promised to take care of him.

July 18th. Clear—Moved at 5 A.M., bivouaced 9.30 A.M. 3 miles from Purcellville. Chaplain O'Neill, in view of the irregularity at Lovettsville, gave the boys a full half hours' of gospel truths from the text "For a man in authority saying to this one come & he cometh & to another go and he goeth"—special reference being had to the "going for the reb property." As I didn't go for anything I did not take his remarks as personal. He went for the boys, however.

CHAPTER 8

Boredom and Idleness
July 17–October 9, 1863

*F*ollowing *his crossing of the Potomac into Virginia after Gettysburg, Lee moved his army south to a position near Culpeper between the Rappahannock and Rapidan Rivers. Meade followed dutifully, and after a reconnaissance in force by the Federals on August 1, Lee decided that rather than face potential assaults with the Rapidan at his back, he would fall back to the more easily defensible terrain south of the river, in the process shortening and strengthening his lengthy supply line.*[1]

Faced with supply problems of his own and a loss of nearly one-third of his troops because of expiring terms of enlistment,[2] *Meade, on orders from the administration, settled in near Warrenton on August 9. With the exception of several minor actions, the ensuing two months were marked by almost complete idleness for both armies. As Donaldson describes, the sheer boredom of their situation led a number of officers of the 118th to seek excitement in other ways; in most instances, alcohol played a prominent part in their activities.*

The need to reinforce the army brought a new scourge with it—the substitute. The Union had passed a conscription act in March 1863, and if drafted, Northerners with the means to do so were allowed to hire replacements to serve their terms of enlistment. Additionally, sizable bounties, sometimes totaling over $1,000, were offered as incentives to new enlistees by local, state, and Federal governments. As a result of these practices, many of the new men who began to filter into the camps of the Army of the Potomac at this time were driven not by any desire to see the war through, but by purely monetary impulses. A small number of the recruits turned out to be good soldiers, but many of them were not ("a fearful lot of loafers, bummers, and substitutes" was how Donaldson described his new additions), and the net effect was a lowering of morale among the veterans. Sinking morale, as experience had proven in the winter of 1862–63, invariably led to increased desertions, something the already weakened Meade could ill afford, and he took forceful steps to quell the practice.

Deserters were caught, tried, and routinely executed during the months of August and September, and the ceremonies were usually held in the presence of large bodies of troops to set an example. In a very public display, which is fully described by Donaldson, five substitutes from the 118th Pennsylvania who had deserted were captured and put to death.

Colonel Gwyn left to recruit for the regiment in Philadelphia on July 22, and that duty, combined with several bouts of sickness, kept him away from the army until early December. Donaldson, needless to say, was not unhappy with the arrangement. Major Herring commanded the 118th while Gwyn was gone, and on several occasions when he was called away on picket or court-martial duty, he showed his high regard for Donaldson by placing him in command of the regiment, even though several captains outranked him.

> Camp 118th Regt. P.V.
> About 15 miles from the
> Potomac in old Virginia
> July 18th, 1863

Have just learned we are three miles from Perryville.

Dear Brother—

. . . We broke camp yesterday at Berlin about 3:30 P.M. and crossed the Potomac amid the curses and groans of the men who detest the soil of Virginia, and who declair that "Old Meade, the four eyed loafer" is again leading them to the graveyard of the Army of the Potomac (Fredericksburg). My own feelings at again entering the state can be imagined better than described. Even the name Virginia is hateful to me.

We encamped for the night at Lovettsville about five miles from the river, and this morning marched to this place. We are encamped on a hill covered with woods and have a beautiful view of Loudoun Valley—'tis a gorgeous picture, the lovely fields and noble mountains, the running stream and singing birds, contrast strangely with that portion of the old state we occupied last winter and spring. During our occupation of Lovettsville our men attempted to retaliate for the destruction of property in Pennsylvania, but happily for the credit of the 5th Corps our Generals were upon the scene of action in a thrice and put a stop to all such proceedings. I must confess I am opposed to all such actions and it distresses me not a little to see grain fields destroyed and houses burnt and pulled to pieces, but I presume such are the natural consequences of war, and those who are so unfortunate as to live upon the immediate route of the contending armies must suffer to a greater or less extent. We will remain here I think a day or two to enable the regiments to be mustered for pay and give the officers time to make out the necessary papers etc., etc. . . .

You are entirely mistaken in supposing we were not prominent in the late battle. The loss of 125 in the brigade is no indication that we were not in the heat of it. We were most fortunate in being protected by rocks and trees. We sustained a charge delivered by Anderson & McLaw's Divisions,[3] and at one time were nearly cut off by the enemy gaining possession of the guns on our right and front and pushing around our right flank. One thing I can add, that our brigade—with returned detachments and gathered stragglers since the battle—now numbers but barely 600 fighting men. The 1st Michigan came out of the fight with about a full company all told, officers and men.[4] I write in great haste, no time for corrections, and upon paper begged, borrowed or stolen, no matter how obtained so that I get it. I want to mention right here that shortly after we bivouaced, Crocker made a "Hooker's retreat" from the last drop of rum we have. We were a long time drinking it—merely sipped it, did Crocker, Thomas and [I].

[P.S.] Lt. Batchelder I had to leave in a private house at Lovettsville. He is dangerously ill. He will endeavor to make his way to Frederick, poor fellow. He is a splendid fellow and I think will not suffer long. Did you receive his photo, a good one, sent from Gettysburg?. . .

July 19th. Clear & very warm. Moved at 8.45 A.M. Rear Division & Rear Brigade passed through Purcellville 10.45 & bivouaced in woods beyond Perryville at 11.15 A.M. Orders recd. for a detail of 3 commissioned officers to bring conscripts to regt. Extraordinary conversation with Gwyn. Think I had better not enter it here, will think it over tonight.

July 20th. Clear & very warm. Reveille 2 A.M. Moved at 5 A.M., passed through Union, halted and bivouaced between Middleburg and Upperville at 12.30.

July 21st. Clear. In camp all day writing up Gettysburg letter—big job. Worked at [it] best part of the night.

July 22nd. Lt. Col. Gwyn, Adj't. Hand, Capt. O'Neill & 6 men including my Orderly Sgt. Crossley left for Philada 9 A.M. . . . Moved at 12 M., halted near Rectortown & bivouaced at 5 P.M. Our Chaplain again expounded the truth's.

July 23rd. Clear—Moved at 7 A.M. towards Manassas Gap. Went into line of battle in column by division at Wapping Heights in support of the 3rd

Corps, already engaged, 4.30 P.M. This was near Front Royal. Made frequent changes & advances. Had fine view of the battle—enemy posted on the side of hill. 3rd Corps line of battle plainly in view, with their skirmishers deployed & in action. Twas like a picture. The country very hilly & near the enemy much wooded, their artillery plainly in view. Could see them fire and observe effect of shot. As we moved to the front we passed through the Keystone Battery[5] standing ready for action. Up to date they had never fired a hostile shot; very anxious to engage. On the march to Gettysburg this & other battery's were at Centreville. They were ordered to join the 3rd Corps, but just as they were packing up Genl. Hays,[6] a brigade officer of 2nd Corps told them to wait as he had sent for a keg of rum for them to drink his health. This detained them, somewhat, and when they did get off they found that the 9th Mass. Artillery had been substituted in their place. They were then ordered to the defenses of Washington. The 9th Mass battery was badly crippled at Gettysburg, having quite a number of killed and wounded.[7] This Harry Carpenter[8] told me, and I saw many other friends as we passed through them. As we descended the hillside to the road below, we saw a dead reb lying full length in the road, and many wounded about in spots. We were not engaged.[9]

July 24th. Moved at 7 A.M. Immediately in our front was a heavily wooded mountain up which we were ordered to march. Formed Column by division and advance by the right of Column up & over the mountain

A heavily retouched carte-de-visite of Chaplain William O'Neill, 118th Pennsylvania Volunteers. THE CIVIL WAR LIBRARY & MUSUEM.

in support of the 2nd & 3rd Brigades. Genl. Ayres 2nd Division on our right. Fearful work forcing way through underbrush & timber. On arrival at top found enemy had retreated. Returned and moved back about a mile and bivouaced at 12.30.

July 25th. Clear. Reveille at 4 A.M. Moved at 7.30 A.M. Very warm day. 1st Brigade rear guard. 5.20 P.M. bivouaced at Orleans. Issued 2 days rations. Rained hard during night.

July 26th. Clear & hot. Moved at 5.30 A.M., 3rd Brigade leading. Bivouaced near Warrenton 11.30 A.M. Column by division. Occupied side of hill, no shade, fearful hot. This being Sunday our chaplain went for us, his text being last verse XXV Proverbs—"He that hath no rule over his own spirit is like a city that is broken down, and without walls." He attacked us in front, all along the line, worked around our flanks and got well into our rear, and as he let loose his reserves and routed us completely he hurled his Anathema Maranatha upon the evil doers until we couldn't rest. A man of powerful lungs is the Chaplain.

July 27th. Rations for one day issued. Moved at 5 A.M., halted & camped 3 miles below Warrenton at 9.15 A.M. Issued rations for 3 days. Rained heavy during night.

July 28th. Made ordnance returns & loafed generally.

>─┤◆>─O─<◆├─<

Camp 118th Regt. P.V.
Near Warrenton, Va.
July 28th, 1863

Dear Auntie:

I have just finished reading some of your letters kept with me and which I read over and over so often. I think of you constantly and wonder what you are doing, and long to be with you once more. I could now fully appreciate home and its comforts if it is ever my lot to get there again. How beautiful Philada. must look notwithstanding the intense heat, and how dearly I would love to see its dear acres of bricks and mortar, and how loath I would be ever again to leave it for this dreadful life. Indeed, Auntie, I do not think I am now as reconciled to Army life, after an experience of nearly three years, as I was at first. It is, of course, a free and easy way of living, but the surroundings tend only to develop all that is bad in human nature and the little good there is in man has a sorry chance among soldiers.

Do you recollect the laughs we used to have in days gone bye at 330 South 15th St. at my attitudenizing "Samson carrying of the gates of Gaza" and "Napoleon at Marengo" and other bloody fields, how I would feign indifference as he is supposed to have done, at the work of death going on around him, well, I little thought then that my attempts at being funny would ever be recalled to mind so vividly as they were at Gettysburg, where I lived to see Capt. Davids and Lieut. Wilson shot down on either side [of] me, the former killed outright, and to view with actual indifference an occurence that at any other time would have horrified me. . . .

Marching still marching appears to be the order of the day since we arrived again in Virginia, but I think we will now have to stop as our horses are giving out; they die by the hundreds daily. There is a wonderful unanimity abt. continuing the campaign further, or rather abt. marching anymore, and all are clamorous for rest, more rest, but of course we are not consulted as to our wishes in the matter, the same despotic military rule governing all things. Hence all are unhappy alike or rejoiced as the case may be. Taking it all together the past few weeks has been a fearful experience for the Army of the Potomac.

Has Crossley called upon you yet, he is charged with a few commissions from me, and also to deliver to you my account of the battle of Gettysburg which was entirely too bulky to send by mail. . . . I am at present really filthy dirty, not having changed my cloths for over two weeks, hence don't "essence of Jenny Lynd" much, you know. Capt. Sharwood beautifully expressed to his wife his and our own condition when he said, "I and all my comrades fairly stink, so foul are we all." Hot is no name for the weather we are having, it is roasting, the perspiration pours out of me by the quart and I am burnt to a lovely bronze color. We have feasted on black berries, there appearing to be no end of this delicious fruit, and no trouble to gather a plentiful supply. Orders have been received for a further movement into the enemy country, possibly the Rappahannock will be our objective point, at all events the "pursuit" will still be continued—at a safe distance.

If you have time I would like you to call at the Christian St. Hospital and see my Sergeant, Daniel B. Cobb, he is a good fellow and I want him looked after. Please send some postage stamps, want them worse than cloths, and am obliged to borrow so often that I feel ashamed. Send at least a dollars worth. Also have Jac send by mail a box of pistol caps. . . .

July 29th. Clear. Nothing to report. Storm coming up interfered with Dress Parade.

July 30th. Clear. General Griffin returned. Whiskey ration issued at "retreat."

July 31st. Cloudy. Whiskey ration issued this A.M.—good deal of rum abroad; officers somehow got badly loaded. Lt. Henry K. Kelly very full, Crocker straggling under a pressure of 60 lbs. to square inch. Thomas loaded to the point of explaining how he had cleaned various Bar rooms "with his dirty pair of fives." Fernald drunken as a boiled owl—Everybody full and all explaining it was to keep off Malaria. Dress parade a tremendous affair, officers unsteady as sailors. At command "present arms," Lt. Kelly knocked off his hat with his sword, and in attempting to regain it, first moved by the left flank, took wheeling distance, drew himself up in line of battle, and grounded arms. Riot act read him after parade; under arrest, awful time. Herring full of "war paint." How abt. myself? Well, I was always a George Washington. I had taken plugs from an old bottle half full of lemon peal to "take the rawness off the new commissary" as Thomas said, and whether it was the beverage or the lemon flavor I certainly felt duced unpleasant about the stomach, so much so that I had to refrain from "keeping my end up." Unlike Crocker, I hadn't a thirst on me that I wouldn't take a $1000 for. I passed the Major in review fairly well at "officers to front and centre." Capt. Sharwood detailed as acting brigade commissary. Orders recd. to move early tomorrow.

Aug. 1st. Clear—didn't move. Kelly awfully sorry—promised to be a good boy. Major H. let up on him. Celebrated his release from arrest by putting away half a canteen of rum—didn't affect him.

Sunday, Aug. 2nd. Company inspection by Maj. H. Good joke upon Sgt. Cassidy,[10] my company. His tin box removed from cartridge box & pack of cards put in its place. At the command "open boxes," Maj. H. & I passed to inspecting ammunition—should be 60 rounds in box. Noting the cards, Major asked, placing his hand on the sgt.'s box, "How many have you Sgt.?" "Sixty, sir," said he. "There should be 52," said the Major & passed on, much to the mystification of the Sgt. In the evening the Chaplain "sacrificed" the officers from a part of the 9th verse of XXIV Chap. Isaiah, "Strong drink shall be bitter to them that drink it." He spoke of the example set in high places by the constant indulgence in strong drink; appealed to the officers to set a good example in this particular to the men, and rated the Commissary for finding transportation for rum to the exclusion of bread. He made no head way with his hearers this time, as both men and officers would rather the rum than bread anytime.

Aug. 3rd. Broke Camp 6 P.M. by bugle from Division. The Division bugler is a bit of a humorist. He came out and planted himself conspicuously so that all could see him, then blew "Division Call." Of course everyone turned out and stood awaiting his next Call. This the fellow knew; was an anxious moment. There was a long pause; he wiped his bugle with his cuff, threw out his arms as if for a full breath, put the bugle to his mouth, then took it away again, looked around and laughed heartily, bending almost double in his mirth and clapping his hands in ecstasy as he noticed the faces of the whole division turned towards him. Then straightened himself and blew the "general"—"pack up, pack up." At its first note there was a derisive yell—"shoot him! stuff rags in that bugle! put him out," and the like. Took up line of March at 7 P.M. & bivouaced at 8.45 near Bealton Station.

Aug. 4th. Cloudy. Moved at 11 A.M. a short distance and established Camp by Column of Companies, officers on the flank. Artillery firing to the southward.

Aug. 5th. Clear. Nothing important. Major Herring Division officer of the Day.

Aug. 6th. Clear. Regt. paid off. Capt. O'Neill & Adj. Hand reported with 109 drafted men & substitutes, having lost 50 on the way by desertion. I recd. 12 out of the lot. Maj. H. called for commandants of Co.'s to assemble & choose their recruits. I didn't go; took those left. Every one of them informed me they had been officers in the 3 mo. service. One, Von Schlimbeck,[11] had been in command of a brigade in Blenker's Division, I believe. I noticed they styled each other as Col., Capt. and Lt. I had them brought to my tent, their descriptive lists filled up, and then informed them that there was but one Captain in this Co., and that—myself. I then turned them over to the Sergeant to find them quarters. They are a pretty stout lot of fellows, but appear to make light of their surroundings and act very impudently. I'll take that mob of them before 48 hours pass.[12] O'Neill and Hand returned again to Philada. I gave Charly Hand $200 for my mother.

Aug. 7th. Clear. Squad drills. I took the recruits and commenced the difficult task of setting them up as soldiers, a severe ordeal. At first there was some talking and laughing, but I speedily put a stop to it by calling the guard and landing two of them in the guard house, with orders to give them plenty of police duty. I noticed thereafter that they didn't appear to think it so funny. Afternoon heavy storm of rain & wind. Arbors all blown down. Recd. orders to move early next day.

    <u>Aug. 8th</u>. Reveille at 4 A.M. Moved at 6 A.M., halted at 9 A.M. in woods near Beverly Ford. We are abt. ½ mile from river—Rebs on other side. Cook House news—"will move to old Camp at Falmouth."

>-+-+>--O--<+-+-<

Camp Near Rappahannock
Station, Va.
August 8th, 1863

Dear Jac,

    . . . I congratulate you on escaping the draft. What a lucky fellow you are. The army is no place for you. . . .

    . . . It is very hot down here, or in the language of the Psalmist, "I seetheth like a steaming cauldron," and have to be led about lest I take cold. . . . You ask regarding Lukins. When I last saw him he was unconcious and the doctor told me he could not live, there was no hope, Typhoid fever.[13] How much better to die in battle; no camp sickness for me. I am well with exception of <u>Itch</u> which I have on my right hand, 4th finger, taken from one of the conscripts. This can readily be done in handling their muskets, which I have to do. The doctors laugh at me and say they can not prescribe a remedy, as they have nothing but "pill opei" in the hospital chest. A lively remedy that, for itch. Please see Dr. Gardner and get some of his powders. I am glad to know George Slow arrived safely. Poor fellow, he has been so faithful that I could not refuse him a furlough. He can come back when he tires of the city, which he will soon do.

    In my last I said I would acquaint you with an occurrence <u>that will</u> terminate my military career etc. etc. Briefly it is this—On the 19th July, an order was recd. to detail three commissioned officers and 6 enlisted men to Philada. to bring recruits to the regt. Col. Gwyn immediately detailed himself—<u>first</u>, then came over to my bivouac, and calling me aside, told me of the order and said he was so well pleased with my soldierly conduct that he had determined to make me one of the detail, and that there would be a vacancy in the majority of the regiment by reason of the advancement of himself and Major Herring, and he desired me to have the office. Of course he knew O'Neill outranked me but that would speedily be fixed by sending us both before an examining board, that O'Neill was totaly unfit for the position, and indeed for that matter, was worthless as a soldier anyway, he didn't know anything and would never learn. He added, "I will have the order made out at once detailing you." All the time he was talking I was looking him in the eye. I was so astounded that beyond thanking him I made no reply. I was astonished at two things—that he should think of me in connection with the detail, and that his upper front teeth were false. I had such a close look at him that I detected this fact. I believe no other man in the Command ever noticed it so very natural are they. Fortunately, most fortunately, on returning to Crocker and Thomas, who were dying to know what on earth Gwyn had to say to me so confidentially, I said that Gwyn was at some diabolical rascality regarding myself that would take our united talent to fathom. I then told them and was at once heartily congratulated. Crocker said Gwyn was trying to do the right thing; Thomas, that it was handsome of him, and much other encouraging talk did these two wise acres indulge in. Oh! how did they envy me, what a fine thing it was etc. etc.

Well, things went on as before, evenly and quiet along the line of the camp until the 22nd, when at 10 A.M. Major Herring sent for me and I then learned that Gwyn had at 9 A.M. gone to Philada. with O'Neill, Hand & Sgt. Crossley. This is such an indignity that it calls for prompt resentment, and I have mapped out a plan of revenge that I think will startle this drunken scoundrel and end my soldier life. On his return I will grossly insult him, on parade, before the regiment, tell him what I think of him, then retire under arrest, be Court-Martialed and quit his hated presence.

Please keep this to yourself and do not attempt to dissuade me. I will do it, so help me heaven. I will now dismiss the subject; don't allude to it, I will not reply. The end has come at last. I have told no one of my intentions. There has not been much of interest transpiring since my last letter.

Aug. 9th. Clear. Sunday—very critical Sunday morning inspection by Major Herring, 8 A.M. Arms, accoutrements in good condition, clothing well worn, Regt. in excellent physical health. A.M. Chaplain O'Neill preached from the XXXVI Chap. Ezekiel, 34 verse, "And the desolate land shall be tilled, whereas it lay desolate in the sight of all that passed by." These remarks were called forth by observing the barrenness of the Virginia lands in contradistinction to the fertile fields of Penna. and Maryland so lately passed through by the army. A moral was pointed to the barren and wasted hearts of his hearers which until the refreshing and invigorating dens of religion should come upon them would ever remain so and bear no fruit. As there was no place to go to, and no escape from his stentorian voice, the men and officers had to submit to having the Gospel pounded into them with the vigor of a man starting a bung from a cast. In the afternoon he again enfiladed us from the XXVII Proverbs, 3 verse. "A stone is heavy and the sand weighty, but a fool's wrath is heavier than them both." This time he tried to show the unwisdom of always complaining about that which is set for us to do, and illustrated his strong point by the parable of the wise and foolish men who built upon the rock and sand respectively, the strong point being his clever adaptation of the building materials of the text to the same materials in the parable. Crocker said this was Reciprocity, and immediately mixed a Hooker's Retreat all around, saying the Chaplain was trying to earn his pay anyway.

Aug. 10th. Clear. Squad drills in the morning; afternoon, Adjt. Walters read Articles of War to recruits. They are beginning to think things look a little serious.

>-+-+>-O-<+-+-<

Camp 118th Regt. P.V.
Near Rappahannock Sta., Va.
Aug. 10th, 1863

Dear Auntie:

. . . We left Warrenton on the 27th ult., passing thro' that place to about three miles beyond, encamped and was at once ordered on picket. Occupying a post on the main road about two miles from camp, I intercepted a fellow who was anxious to proceed beyond our lines, which of course I could not permit, and in fact put him thro' such a course of questioning as to whence he came and whither he was going that he became much alarmed at his position. Believing him to be as represented, a peddler of cutlery, I bought a six bladed knife for $1.50 and sent him back to town. You need therefore trouble yourself no further about getting me one. . . .

Aug. 6th, the regiment recd. a fearful lot of loafers, bummers and substitutes as recruits, 109 in all, and among them, falling to my share, were a Brigadier General, two Captains and several Lieut.'s. These chaps I have taken under my especial care and will continue so to do until I have fully impressed them with the knowledge that as former officers accustomed to power and consideration, they are now of no earthly account but to carry a musket in the ranks, obey orders literally, draw and eat the rations issued, growl to no purpose, and, when it becomes necessary, stand up and get

shot. Here is your fine chance for promotion, travel and study, as advertised
in the Ledger and other papers—such is life.

We are now encamped in the woods and have plenty of shade, but the
weather exceeds anything I ever experienced for heat, and in the mornings
there is a dense fog over the earth, making it very uncomfortable, if not
unhealthy. Indeed it must be so, as I learn there will be a ration of whiskey
issued to the men today, and we all know that is for the purpose of giving
them quinine, a goodly quantity of the latter being put into the barrel
before it is measured out. However if they put oil of vitroil in the rum the
men would drink it all the same. I will add that there are several members
of my company who invariably draw the ration and as invariably pour the
same upon the ground in full sight of the company. They are total absti-
nent fellows, Psalm singers generally and of not much account in time of
trouble. Not that I would have you to understand that a man, to be a good
soldier, must be a drinking man, but where a man is found brave, attentive
to his duties and a careful soldier, you will pretty nearly always find him to
be a modest man, saying little, taking his beverage in moderation when he
can get it, and, unlike the temperance men alluded to, does his devotions
in the privacy of his own tent, provided always he is a devout man. I do
not go much on the habitual Psalm Singer, he is generally a shirker, I am
sorry to say.

. . . I think it likely we will remain here sometime as the conscripts are
to be drilled and soldiers made of them, a task I fear which will bother us a
good deal. We have a matter of five quakers among the new batch, and
how to get them to take a musket is the mystery yet to be solved by our
commanding officer. They are willing to work, police the camp and go
into battle if necessary, but without arms, and they are apparently afraid of
no one or anything. They strike me as being brave men, refusing for con-
science sake to take into their hands the weapons of war their religion for-
bids them to do. In my opinion they should be sent home again, they are
Quakers, but not fighting ones. I am in splendid health. Write to me
often.

Aug. 11th. Clear. Very Warm. Dress parade without arms. Adjt. read
official hours for Camp duties. Capt. Crocker sent in his resignation. Maj.
Herring promised to approve and mail to Army Head Qur. Crocker feels
good. I wouldn't be surprised if it goes through, although Gwyn will stop
it if he hears of it.

Aug. 12th. Clear. Usual camp duties.

Aug. 13th. Clear. 5 Deserters returned to regiment by Provo' M. They were placed under heavy guard until further orders. I witness a revolting sight. Lt. Brown[14] has been drunk for weeks and for the last two days has not been out of his tent. I look in on him this morning and found him in a disgusting condition, maggots crawling all over him from accumulated filth.

Aug. 14th. Clear. Battalion Drill A.M. Recitations in Tactics & Army Regulations by company officers.

Aug. 15th. Clear. Orders recd. to move at moments notice. Lt. Thomas, Officer of the Day, had Lt. Brown stripped, thoroughly washed and cleaned. He was beastly drunk. Maj. H. visited him, destroyed his rum, ordered Brigade Com. not to sell him any more. Capt. Tucker,[15] Brigade Inspector, visited Regt., complimented Maj. H. on condition of men & camp.

>─┤◆>─O─<◆┤─<

> Camp 118th Regt. P.V.
> Beverly Ford, Va.
> Aug. 15th, 1863

My brave lad, [Jacob]

. . . The second Division (Syke's Regulars) of our Corps left yesterday for Washington D.C. and we have just received order to be ready to move at a moments notice.[16] I presume we will follow them, at all events I hope so—t'would be a large thing my boy. . . .

Am in excellent health and spirits, still have my hands full with the conscripts, five of whom are to be shot for desertion; t'will be an awful sight, but must be done. Love to Aunty and all my friends. Note—Have my sword fixed—get a scabbard steel bronzed—that is, a steel scabbard bronzed, with brass tips. Send it by some of the boys who are coming down. Horstman will fix it. I am now wearing Lt. McCutchen's[17] and have to give it to him in a day or so, and consequently will be without a sword. . . .

Sunday, Aug. 16th. Clear, rain at night. Dr. Kollock inspected recruits. Chaplain preached at Brigade Hd. Qurs. Although we could hear him roar, yet he was too far away to catch the words, for which we were all devoutly thankful. Poor man, he gives us no rest. The mosquitos are bad enough, but just to think of the way "his reverence" pesters us.

Aug. 17th. Clear. Maj. Herring Division Officer of the day. He made McCutchen tender his resignation and endorsed it "Respectfully forwarded

approved. This officer can be replaced by one better qualified for the position."
Arms issued to recruits.

Aug. 18th. Clear. In charge of the Regt. Maj. Herring at Court-Martial.
Witness against Lt. Brown of A, charged with <u>absence without leave</u>,
another way of getting rid of an officer without charging him with drunkenness. Also in the McCutchen case. This he had postponed pending his resignation. General Barnes returned. Great fuss made over him. 100 men detailed
on Picket, among them 50 recruits to learn the business. All under Capt.
Wetherill, Lts. Kelly & Young.[18]

Aug. 19th. Clear. Again in command of regiment. Maj. Herring at
Court-Martial—witness against substitutes.

>—I—<>—·—O—·—<>—I—<

Camp 118th Regt. P.V.
Beverly Ford, Va.
August 19th, 1863

Dear Brother:

Yours of the 18th inst. to hand—3.30 P.M.—Quick time isn't it? So
you are amused at the Diary and want it continued? It is from it I make up
my letters, or rather did, but have been unable to do much in the way of
letter writing lately, we move about so.

You think I have a grudge against the Chaplain. It is not so, I like him very
much, he is always polite and kind, and I treat him as becomes his cloth. But
I feel—indeed I know—he is about as competent a "Holy Joe" as his brother
is a Captain. His sermons do no good. He rants and fumes and there is nothing
in his argument. It is true he is not sent to the officers specially, but to the
masses. Your words make me confess to being somewhat insincere. I listen
to him preach and then ridicule him. I don't intend it, however, I merely
note my feelings regarding his teachings.[19] As to the other portions of my
diary, my strictures on my brother officers for their short comings, I explain
thus: My diary was not intended for your perusal, and I believe, also, that I do
not spare myself either, I am usually with the boys in all their frolics. I appreciate your comments and will send the pages occasionally, as written, provided
you allow no one to see them. As to orthography, I haven't time to be particular. As to the sword, please do as I request. It suits me better than the one given
me by Mr. Heaton and other kind friends. Beside, I have carried it thro' my
whole connection with this regiment. . . . There cannot possibly be much

trouble abt. attending to these simple requests. Much time has already been lost. I am wearing Lt. McCutchen's. He is in arrest for drunkenness. I shall never forget the ludicrous picture he presented when put under arrest on battalion drill. Major Herring rode up and said to him, "Mr. McCutchen, you are drunk sir"—but before he could proceed further, Mac, placing his hands to his mouth in imitation of a bugle, and working his fingers like the keys, played "sick call." It resulted in his arrest and <u>He will have</u> to go.[20] I carry his sword, it is a beauty, steel scabbard, brass bands and tip. I want mine made like it. . . .

I feel so rejoiced that you have heard of John. Did Mr. Goshorn give any particulars regarding his wounds? He must have been badly hurt to have been left with a family near Culpeper. Of course I am all impatience to know more. Don't you know what fight it was in which he received his hurt? Do you know his present rank? . . .[21]

Send Geo. Slow back to me. I cannot get along without him; besides, it is not unlikely we will move shortly, and I will need him then, of all other times. He can have another vacation when we get into Winter Quarters. Start him! to the front. We are having scorching weather. Oh! for a little sea air. . . .

<u>Aug. 20th</u>. Clear. Again in command. Major Herring at Court-Martial.

<u>Aug. 21st</u>. Clear. Lt. Wilson[22] returned from leave of absence. Picket returned at retreat.

Lt. Frank McCutchen, Company C, 118th Pennsylvania Volunteers. The Civil War Library & Museum.

Aug. 22nd. Clear. Squad drills in morning. Sgt. Stone[23] made Provo Sgt. to suppress gambling. Two men of G, one of K arrested. Maj. Herring made them hand over their winnings. Issued an order that all money used in that way would be confiscated to the Regimental Fund; he was determined to suppress gambling. Dress parade.

Sunday, Aug. 23rd. Clear, Very warm. Chaplain held service in 18th Mass. Seems to give us up as a bad lot. Clothing issued. Drew 2 Forage Caps, 11 Trousers, 17 Flannel Sack Coats, 9 Flannel Shirts, 20 Pr. Drawers, 3 pr. Shoes, 22 Gum blankets, 7 Knapsacks, 5 Haversacks, 12 Canteens, 3 Camp Kettles, 3 Mess Pans, 3 Camp Hatchets, 3 Hatchet Handles, 8 Shelter Tents, 1 Descriptive Book.

Aug. 24th. Clear. Rain at night. Squad Drills. Lt. Coane returned with detail. I am officially announced as Acting Major. Maj. Herring informed me that Genl. Barnes had sent for and notified him that the 5 deserters were to be shot. They were to be closely confined. He had also called upon Genl. Griffin who said the sentence was to [be] carried into effect on Wednesday between 12 and 4 o'clock, Capt. Crocker, Lts. Lewis, Bayne and Thomas and 24 men as guard—4 inside and 4 outer guards. Official order read on dress parade. Afterwards Major Herring read same to prisoners in presence of Chaplain O'Neill and German interpreter. Lt. Lewis searched prisoners and took everything away from them. One of the poor devils, a Jew, asked to have his pocket book returned. This Lt. Lewis was willing to grant, but Major Herring first looked carefully through it and found there in a lancet, which he removed, and then gave him his book. Poor fellow, after an examination he said it was of no use to him now. Q. M. Gardner sent to find a Catholic Priest—returned and reported couldn't find one.

Aug. 25th. Clear. Genl. Barnes visited prisoners. Maj. Herring sent Chap. O'Neill to Genl. Meade with application for respite to obtain Catholic priest and Jewish Rabbi. He returned with respite 'till Saturday.[24] Maj. Herring & Genl. Griffin selected site for execution and spot for graves. Orders recd. from Hd. Qurs. to make surroundings as imposingly stern and solemn as possible, no levity in camp, silence and close attention to duties, no leaving camp, no visitors allowed. Sent orders around at 10.30 P.M. for signature; Sgt. Major reported Capt. Fernald drunk and abusive, wouldn't sign. Maj. Herring took paper himself—Maj. had all his war paint on, will settle with Fernald in the morning.

>—⊷—O—⊷—◄

Camp 118th Regt. P.V.
Beverly Ford, Va.
August 25th, 1863

Dear Jacob

. . . A great tragedy will soon be enacted here. The deserting substitutes have been found guilty and are to be shot to death. Heretofore, although there have been many trials and convictions for such offenses there has been no execution of the sentence, as far as I can learn. The culprits have always been pardoned. But now the law is to take its course. These men have made "bounty jumping"[25] a business, and are to be punished. They are closely guarded, night and day. They are confined in a tent apart from the rest of the regiment, and an officer sits at the door all the time. Beside, there is a guard of 24 men surrounding their quarters, [and] they are also manacled. My God! what a wretched, horrible predicament they are in. Enough to move the heart of a stone. They have our most sincere sympathy, at the same time we approve the sentence. This has been a case of aggravated and systematic "bounty jumping," and they will be shot like dogs. Awful, most awful. I can write no more, the thought of this bloody execution sickens me.

Aug. 26th. Clear and cool. Regimental pioneers dig graves of the condemned. Major Herring telegraphed their friends and also sent a dispatch to the President asking clemency for the prisoners. Lt. Brown, who was under arrest, relieved from same by order of Genl. Griffin, but got drunk again and was immediately rearrested.[26]

Aug. 27th. Clear and Cool. Notwithstanding the awful tragedy so soon about to be enacted, there was a lively time at Division Head Quarters— a horse race between Genl. Griffin's mare and Capt. Bernard's[27] horse. Col. Hayes, Lt. Col. Throop, Col. Switzer[28] and Maj. Herring acting as judges. I did not see the race; was left in command of regiment, and strange to say—for an hour—in command of the Brigade, as I was the ranking officer in camp— so I was told by the Adjt. Genl. At 4 P.M. Father S. L. Egan arrived from Baltimore. He quartered with Major Herring.

Aug. 28th. Clear and Cool. Major Herring Division officer of the Day. Telegram received that Jewish Rabbi unable to reach camp as all passenger cars reserved for visitors to presentation to Genl. Meade.[29]

Saturday, Aug. 29th. Clear and Cool. From early morning busy with arrangements for the execution of prisoners. 20 men under Sgt. H. T. Peck[30] as bearers, 5 pioneers with spades, 5 with hatchets to close coffins, under Sgt. Moselander,[31] 30 men as escort under Capt. Crocker and Lt. Wilson. Rabbi Dr. Zould arrived and at 12:30 details with prisoners. Father Egan, Rabbi Zould and Chap. O'Neill sent to report to Capt. Orne, Division Provost Marshall, at house at 2nd Brigade Headquarters.[32] The 5th Corps paraded and formed—three sides of a square—in close column of divisions. Just before the prisoners were taken away, I noticed one of them without a neck tie, so pulling off my black silk handkerchief, I tied it neatly under the collar of his white flannel shirt. They were all in blue pants and white flannel shirts.

The place of execution was well adapted for such a scene. From the level plain where the graves were dug the ground rises slightly to Brigade Head Quarters, so that every man in the Corps had a clear and distinct view of all that took place. It took some time for the troops to assemble, and while they were still completing the formation, at 3 o'clock, the funeral procession appeared. Every detail had been arranged for the special object of making a solemn impression. There was an oppressive silence, not a sound was heard save the mournful notes of the Army Headquarters band playing the dead march from Saul, slow, measured, sorrowful. Deliberate and regular was the step of the band, which came first, sad and mournful was their music. Next came Capt. Orne, Division Provost Marshal, followed by the guard of 60 men. Then came two coffins borne by eight men, then two of the condemned with the rabbi. Major Herring had so arranged as to have the rabbi, representing the oldest faith, on the right. Then another coffin with 4 men and one prisoner, and then two more coffins borne by 8 men, two more prisoners, Priest and Chaplain. Each prisoner's hands were manacled behind him. Four of the condemned walked steadily and with apparent unconcern, one was weak and tottering and was with difficulty borne along, needing heavy support. Then came Capt. Crocker's escort of 30 men from the 118th. So the Column passed along the open front of the square and arrived at the graves in front of the Corps. The coffins were placed beside them, the prisoners seated on them. The firing party was halted about 30 paces in front, 12 men before each prisoner, and stood at "parade rest." At this juncture the 3rd Division arrived on the ground and hastily got into position. My God! think of the terrible thoughts of these helpless men as they marched to their graves, think of their awful condition as seated on their coffins they gazed at the twelve men standing before them sternly awaiting order to take their lives. Oh! it was a dreadful sight to see them there, swaying backwards and forwards so utterly helpless and forlorn.

This depiction of the execution, based on a sketch by Alfred R. Waud, appeared in the September 26, 1863, issue of Harper's Weekly.

Our regiment was posted close up to the graves, a little to the right of them, close enough to hear the earnest words and prayers of men of God who pleaded so fervently that God would have mercy on their souls. It was now drawing nigh to the limit of time set forth in the General Order of Execution—12 M. to 4 P.M. It was 3.45 o'clock and with but 15 minutes to finish Genl. Griffin's shrill and penetrating voice was heard breaking the awful silence—"Shoot these men, or after 10 minutes it will be murder, shoot them at once." The Sergeant of the guard hastened to bandage their faces with white cloths. Harper's and Frank Leslie's artists who, close up to the condemned with their easels had been busily sketching the scene, now rapidly packed up and withdrew. After a few parting words the ministers of the gospel stood aside and the poor fellows were left alone on the brink of Eternity. They hadn't long to wait. "Attention guard," in clear ringing tones called Capt. Orne, "shoulder arms." "Forward march," and the solid steady tramp of the detail sounded appalling on the ear. When within 6 paces, "Halt," ordered the Captain. "Ready." "Aim." "Fire," and sixty pieces flashed full in the breasts of the deserters, and military justice was satisfied. Four of the men fell back heavily on their coffins and rolled off to the ground, their heads striking the coffin lid making a dull sounding thud, while the bullets, passing through the bodies, were seen skipping and bounding over the open fields. One man, he upon the left, still remained in an upright position. "Inspection of arms," ordered Capt. Orne, and as the ramrods rang in the musket barrels, he, pistol in hand, with Surgeon Thomas, approached the upright figure. "Is this man dead?" he asked, for his orders were to shoot them to death, and had the musketry failed he would have had to use his pistol. "To all intents and purposes he is," said the surgeon, feeling the man's pulse and laying him gently back on the coffin. Of another who showed a movement of the limbs he said it was muscular movement only, the man was dead, and so on until all had been examined and pronounced dead. They were placed in their coffins and the names of each marked on them and buried. They were named Kuhn, Folaney, Walter, Rionese, and Lai.[33] The lines were now put into motion and the troops returned to their Camps to the tune of "The girl I left behind me." The poor Rabbi was sadly cut up. He had never before witnessed such a death scene. Hastening to the Major's tent, he gathered up his few traps and made for the train, anxious and eager to get away from such scenes of blood, as he expressed it. He was in such a hurry to depart that he left his pocket book behind.

Sunday, Aug. 30th. Clear and cool. Very quiet day in camp. I noticed in looking over towards the place of yesterday's execution that someone had placed two wooden crosses to mark the graves of the two Catholics. . . .

Aug. 31st. Clear and Cool. Regt. Inspected and mustered by Maj. Herring at 1 P.M. Today is the anniversary of the regiment leaving Camp Union.

>—•>•O•<•—<

Camp 118th Regt. P.V.
Beverly Ford, Va.
Sept. 5th, 1863

Dear Brother:

. . . Send at once my sword with steel scabbard, direct to Adams Express, Washington, to be called for, and send receipt. The sutler goes to that city on Monday and will get it for me. Do not disappoint as I am without a "Toad Sticker." Lt. McCutchen, whose sword I had whilst he was under arrest, has left the service and taken his sword with him. . . .

Sept. 1st. Clear and Cold. Genl. Griffin left for Washington, Genl. Barnes in command of Division and Col. Hayes, 18 Mass., in command of brigade.

Sept. 2nd. Clear. Usual camp duties.

Sept. 3rd. Clear and Cold. Camp duties. Rabbi telegraphed Major Herring for his pocket book, which was sent him. The Major also sent forward a document for the clothing packed at Camp near Falmouth.

Sept. 4th. Clear and Cold. Usual camp duties. Corporal Brooks, my company, applied for leave of absence for examination as an officer of Colored troops, under a recent order of the War Department.[34] He is an excellent man, well drilled, educated and a thorough soldier. I always used him as my "Fogleman." He will pass a successful examination, I am sure.

Sept. 5th. Clear and cold. 100 men under Capt. Donegan, Lt.'s Kelly and Brown out on picket.

>-+‹›-O-‹›+-‹

Camp 118th Regt. P.V.
Near Beverly Ford, Va.
Sept. 11th, 1863

Dear Brother:

. . . Last evening will ever be memorable in the history of the command as the "Dedication Night of the Haversack," as Crocker calls the new log house he has had constructed for himself. He gave a "free blow" to all his friends, getting out a substantial lunch and keg of beer, which he had ordered from Washington. I was a little late in getting to the entertainment, having been with Major Herring to call upon Col. Hayes, brigade commander, who, by the way, is a cultured gentleman of remarkably striking and soldierly appearance. He extended the hospitalities in a truly refined manner—beverage and segars—a cracker or two, served by a nigro servant gotten up most tastefully with clean white collar and gloves. The Colonel is a fluent conversationalist, engaging and winning. He acknowledged my introduction as the gentleman with whom he had a slight difference at Chancellorsville, and was pleased to remark that I had on that occasion, under his observation, handled my skirmish line in a soldierly manner. Jacob—I felt myself blushing at his words, and so long as he continued his praises, felt deuced uncomfortable. Major Herring was sensibly pleased that I should thus be complimented. The gallant Major rates me too highly, I must modestly confess.

The interview was terminated by the appearance of George Slow with a note from Crocker, asking my presence at his quarters. Excusing myself, I hastened back to camp, and as I neared it, I distinctly heard the uproar about the log house. The voice of dear old John Thomas was heard plainly above all, roaring to its full extent the only song he could sing:

In eighteen hundred and sixty-three
Hurrah! Hurrah!
In eighteen hundred and sixty three,
Hurrah! Hurrah!
In eighteen hundred and sixty three,
Abe Lincoln set the niggers free,
And we'll all drink stone blind,
Johnny fill up the bowl!

Upon entering I found the place filled with visitors, and Crocker, in red flannel shirt, "slinging beer" in tin cups, while the boys were loudly calling "Two beers here, Miller," and tapping on the logs and tables, making all the noise they could after the most approved manner of the Germans at Miller's Garden, 8th & Vine St. My appearance was the occasion of renewed "beer all around," and so the roar of song and jest continued until one after another of the invited, having drunk to sickness, retired, and relieving their overcharged stomachs around the "Haversack," staggered off to their quarters, leaving Crocker, Thomas and I pretty well tied up, too, although we didn't "spill" like the others. The immediate surroundings, next morning, reeked with the odors of beer, and presented a sorry sight. It looked, for all the world, as if a company of thieving cavalry had suddenly been stricken with an attack of Cholera Morbis around Crocker's quarters. It took the niggers an hour or more to clean up and bury the evidences of sea sickness thereabouts. So ended the "Dedication of the Haversack." Crocker was marked "quarters" and Thomas "light duty" the next day, whilst I, who can never do much in the intoxicating line, am fit for duty as usual. I stopped at "Millers" this morning for a beer as I passed by.

We have been living at the top of the market. Our larder has contained peaches by the basket, fresh tomatoes, chickens, eggs, fresh butter, and, by the way of side board, Drakes Plantation Bitters, Whiskey, Claret, Jamaica Rum, Brandy and Ice. That's so—we live, we do. Yesterday we gave the Purveyor an order for half dozen watermelons, basket of canteloupes, box of peaches, dozen chickens, 6 doz. eggs, and numerous other good things. Had for dinner yesterday Watermelon, lima beans and peas. This is the way to soldier. Talk about Washington at Valley Forge, why he couldn't cater around one side of us. Beside, all historical reports with the exception of Monmouth, he never did have any such weather as we are having, it was with him always raining, or freezing or snowing, with no chance to forage among the watermelon patches—besides, his men's feet were always bleeding. Well, we ought to whip the rebs on such rations, don't you think so? Enclosed I send you the countersign as it is given to each regiment in the field, also a photograph of my friend Capt. Tucker, Brigade Inspector, or, Military Paul Pry. Diary continued:

Sunday, Sept. 6th. Clear. Chaplain O'Neill preached in the morning to the Woolvareens [1st Michigan], afternoon at 2nd Brigade Head Quarters, evening to the heathen, i.e. 118th, XXVIII Ezekiel, part 26 verse. "And they shall dwell safely therein, and shall build houses and plant vineyards, they shall dwell with confidence." I don't know what it was all about as I didn't listen, but reference was had to "when this cruel war is over."

Sept. 7th. Clear and warm. Q.M. Gardner ordered to Washington, 3 days leave, to get regimental clothing stored there. Usual camp duties.

Sept. 8th. Clear and cool. Usual camp duties. Capt. Hunterson and Lt. Young returned from leave of absence.

Sept. 9th. Clear and Cool. 3 P.M. Brigade drill by Col. Hayes. Grand success, very interesting.

Sept. 10th. Clear and Cool. Usual camp duties. Q. M. Gardner returned, reported two carloads of storage.

Sept. 11th. Clear and Cool. Usual camp duties.

>─►─◦─◄►─┼─◄

Camp 118th Regt. P.V.
Beverly Ford, Va.
Sept. 14th, 1863

My Dear Jacob:

. . . This looks like business. We expect the arrival tomorrow of 200 Conscripts, and are making preparations for their reception. . . . Nothing new. My Diary says:

Sept. 12th. Clear in the morning, rain in the afternoon and during the night. Regt. partially inspected, rain interfered. Orders recd. to be in readiness to move in support of reconnoisance towards Culpeper C.H. Clothing from Washington inspected by myself, Lts. White and Wilson, found in excellent condition and so reported.

Sept. 13th. Clear, rain in afternoon. Chap. O'Neill preached in camp in morning—V Chap. St. Pauls Epistle to the Ephesians, 15th Verse. "See then that ye walk circumspectly, not as fools, but as wise." He very properly and wisely intimated that he could not possibly make plainer the words of the Great Apostle, but with great vehemence and much uproar tongue lashed the hardened wretches who had the temerity to withstand him for the half hour he tried to deafen them. In the afternoon he was at it again, somewhere in the Division, but couldn't tell exactly where, although we could hear him. In the evening, he "fibbled" away at us again, doing some very handsome "short arm practice and rapid countering," as Tom Hyer says.

Sept. 14th. Clear and Cool. Nothing new. Usual camp duties. Orders again recd. to be ready to move at moments notice. 22nd Mass. on picket, whole regt.

Sept. 15th. Clear and cool. 185 recruits recd. under charge of Capt. O'Neill. 97 drafted, balance substitutes. Mixed crowd, some bad fellows among them. They were distributed equally among the companies, arms and shelter tents issued them. Orders rec'd to be ready to move in morning. Off this time sure. This has been a busy camp. The regiment or details from it has been on picket 3 days and off six the whole time, then guard and police duty. Company, battalion and brigade drills filled in the spare time so that little time was left for frolic, but that little time was fully utilized. Situated close to the Rappahannock, not far from a piece of hard wood timber, we have been subjected to the dense, heavy fogs occurring in this region at this season of the year, hence a good deal of sickness has followed. Malaria, which caused an unusual issue of whiskey with its consequent—drunkenness. Our picket duty has been to the left of the line, on the river bank and sometimes branching off a mile or so across country, connecting with the other Corps pickets along the Orange and Alexandria R.R., the object being to guard the road and ford and prevent Mosby and other guirillas from raiding the supply trains.

Lt. Kelly gave me an amusing account of his experience on picket under Capt. Donegan Sept. 5th last. It appears that Donegan, after receiving instructions from the officer he relieved, by some mysterious and unaccountable misfortune, posted his men entirely wrong and upon a new line, inside the proper picket line, finally joining the pickets on the right near the Rail Road. The true line was supposed to be along the river and back through the country <u>near</u> the R.R. The balance of the division pickets, finding a gap existing, extended their intervals and covered it, thus leaving Donegan an interior line. Donegan, being in chief command, not comprehending the situation exactly, kept the matter to himself, and the men never knew the difference. The orders were to keep a sharp look out for guirillas. After locating the line, Donegan bothered no more about it, but selecting a cozy little grove well in rear of the center of the pickets, erected his shelter tent, built a fire, and made himself comfortable. He was not again seen during the 3 days they were out. Kelly, also ever anxious as to his own comfort, selected a vacant house hard by the right center of the line and established himself nicely in the parlor thereof, and made himself nicely at home. As there was no name on the front door he had his own tacked on it, with suitable "office hours" appended. There were a number of new men on duty, who, not being fully posted, required the constant attention of Kelly to protect them and prevent grouping too much. He finally succeeded in getting them instructed and alive to their responsibilities, and was just relaxing his vigilance somewhat, when Genl. Sykes appeared. It seems that this energetic chieftain, ever anxious as to the conduct of his Corps, had been visiting and inspecting the outposts, and with his staff was returning when he most unexpectedly met with another picket line. Astounded at this, he for a moment was under the impression that he had lost his way—got turned around, somehow. He was speedily undeceived, however, by the picket calling, "Who comes here?" The general then opened his overcoat, and putting it down from his shoulder, displayed his "passants," saying, "Now do you know me?" "No," said the man, "get down off that horse damn quick or else I send a ball through you." The General and staff dismounted. He was very wroth and said he had been in command of the Corps for several months and it was time that every man and boy in it should recognize him. One of the men on an adjoining post, in a clump of bush, hearing the altercation, called out, "Hallo, Billy, what kind of looking fellow is he, has he got big black whiskers?" "Yes," said Billy, "Then hold the son __ _ _____, you have got Mosby—call for the Corporal of the Guard." He did so lustily, and upon coming upon the ground the Corporal, recognizing the General, ordered the man to pass him. "Where is your officer?" said the General, and he was escorted to the <u>private</u> residence of Lt. Henry K. Kelly Esq.

who, notwithstanding it was not his office hours, made his appearance, hat in hand, on the front steps. The general asked, "Lieut, what in the name of God are you doing here?" meaning, of course, the picket line. Kelly, not rightly understanding the situation, thought he wanted his instructions, and innocently and school boy like rattled them off—"to arrest all persons outside the lines, look sharp after Mosby and other bushwhackers, all persons beyond lines to be treated as enemies. . . ." As he spoke the general looked at him with blank astonishment and contempt deeply stamped on every feature of his face, while the staff indulged in broad grins. The general remained for a moment speechless, too full of disgust to make any comment. "Great Heavens! what damn infernal stupidity," he said as he slowly rode off, leaving

Lt. Henry K. Kelly, Company G, 118th Pennsylvania Volunteers. THE CIVIL WAR LIBRARY & MUSUEM.

Kelly as proud as a pea-Cock in having answered the General so promptly, but somewhat confused as to his manner, and at a loss to understand why he was called stupid. He subsequently learned the above facts and laughs heartily at the disgust of the General at such a pack of fools.

Genl. Sykes is a martinet, a severe, unkindly man to all save the regulars. Himself a West Point graduate, a thorough soldier, brave and accomplished, in whom the men have the greatest confidence, fear, and respect, yet spoils it all by undisguised contempt and hatred of the volunteers. This the men know, so that there is no sympathy between him and them. He never speaks to an enlisted volunteer, and on the marches always halts amid the regular troops. Yet for all this we are proud of our commander, he looks well to the wants of us all, and handles us with skill and ability. We consider Genl. Sykes one of the great men of the army, but his manner being against him, he will never make a great name.

Longstreet's Corps was detached from the Army of Northern Virginia on September 8 and sent to support Braxton Bragg's movements against the army of Maj. Gen. William Rosecrans in North Georgia. Meade learned of the transfer several days later and shifted his army across the Rappahannock to face Lee from the north bank of the Rapidan.[35]

<u>Sept. 16th</u>. Clear and Cold—broke camp at 6.30, crossed the Rappahannock at 8.10 A.M. Col. Hayes in command of brigade. Bivouac near Culpeper Court House 12.30.

<u>Sept. 17th</u>. Cloudy. Moved at 7:15 A.M., passed through Culpeper and camped beyond the town. 1st Mich. and 18th Mass. on Provost duty there. Culpeper C.H. is not much of a place. 1000 inhabitants, I should say, living in rather neat Frame houses. I wouldn't call the place pretty, at least it does not strike me so. All the houses were closed as we passed through, and many of them deserted, I am told. I didn't see a citizen, male or female. I believe I am more disappointed in this place than any other Virginia town yet visited. The name is so high sounding, and it is such an old town; beside, it is a strategic point. "Oh, there's the rub," the weak joint in my military education. I strive so to understand the "science of warfare." Now what makes Culpeper a strategic point? My map is confusing. Other than as a centre from which many roads radiate, by which the various gaps in the Blue Ridge can be easily reached, I don't see but that we are in the position to be assailed in the rear, especially along our line of communication.

Sept. 18th. Heavy rain in the morning, clear in afternoon. Visited Culpeper to hunt up some old Richmond friends, found their houses abandoned. 3 P.M. division paraded to witness execution of a private of the 12th N.Y. shot for desertion.[36] We occupied a high ground overlooking a valley in which the execution took place. This was a sad affair. The prisoner was a brave man, a very brave man indeed to the last. He walked jauntingly along to the selected spot, refused to have his eyes bandaged, declined the services of a chaplain and <u>stood</u> looking at and facing the firing party. As the volley of musketry rang out in the stillness, a loud Oh! of mingled pity and horror involuntarily burst from the men. No matter what his crime, no matter how guilty, he was a bold, brave fellow, and we all felt sorry for him. . . . We returned to camp in silence, not a word was spoken, no sound save the dull heavy tramp of the battalions as they kept step to the shrill screech of the fife and drum of the Provost guard, who stepped off merrily to the tune of "Blow ye Windy Morning."

Sept. 19th. Clear. Whiskey ration served out. Haverstick[37] told me it had been heavily charged with quinine. There was a good deal of noise and rioting, but it calmed down as the effects of the rum passed off. Nothing of interest happened.

Sunday, Sept. 20th. Army regulations read to recruits by Sgt. Major. . . . Chaplain O'Neill preached in the morning. Beyond recording the fact I make no comment—his listeners had my most sincere and heartfelt sympathy. In the evening he expounded the truths to the 22 Mass.

Letter recd. from brother Jacob in which he, at some length, recounts the fact that I have degenerated as a soldier since my first enlistment giving as an illustration my frequent frolics, satirical mention of the Chaplain, and pointing to my entire avoidance of the war in <u>patriotically written letters</u>. Well, there is a good deal of truth in what he says. I believe I <u>have</u> changed; the poetry has been rudely taken out of me, all sentiment gone, and I see things differently. I believe the battle of Fredericksburg first gave me an insight into the manner with which the war was prosecuted. The Army of the Potomac is merely a political machine. We are moved forward and backward to suit the political situation. Earnest men like Genls. Meade, Hancock and Sedgwick, all true soldiers, are given to understand that the strategy will be supplied from Washington as the political necessities occasion it and they are to move in accordance therewith. If this were not so, why have we been loitering since Gettysburg, and what is the object of our present move? Surely there is nothing gained by sitting down here, only the political fact—that the army

<u>has advanced</u>. There is nothing in this fact. Let a Column of Cavalry raid our rear and we will come pelting back again. Again, if this were not so, Genl. Meade would be allowed to do what I am sure so upright and sincere an officer as he feels inclined to do. Move upon Lee's Army, fight it, fight it, no matter where, either destroy or so badly cripple it that upon the opening of the Spring Campaign, we will have a better chance of success. As it is, backing and filling, racing to the Rappahannock and back again to the Potomac will never end the war. I, an humble line officer with no military training, but as earnest in the cause as when I first entered the army, can see these things and I am discouraged, or as my dear brother says "luke warm." To my mind, with the enormous success at Vicksburg and Gettysburg, there remained but one thing to do—vigorously prosecute the War, recruit the armies, keep Lee employed, hunt him, not him us. As long as he is in the field there is a chance for the Confederacy—beat him badly to the entrenchments of Richmond and then destroy the country round about, everywhere, so that no crops can be raised, destroy, break down and burn everything likely to help the South. That is what I mean by vigor. Am I right in this? I think that I am, and I think, too, that our Generals would act something in this way were they left responsible for the movement of our armies. As it is now all that I have to think of is my own comfort. I <u>have</u> degenerated, and so has the army.

But what is the use of repining? I do what I am told to do, without ambition. I make no very great sacrifice of comfort, am sure of my rations and pay. What need a soldier care for more? As long as Uncle Sam's money bags hold out, this is well enough, but it can't last, there must be an end some day.

<u>Sept. 21st</u>. Clear and cool. Inspection of regt. by brigade inspector. Mr. Mitchener of the Corn Exchange arrived.

<u>Sept. 22nd</u>. Clear and Cool. Usual Camp duties. Orders recd. to issue 5 days rations for knapsacks and 3 days for haversacks.

<u>Sept. 23rd</u>. Clear and Cool. Lt. Binney visited camp. As usual he was heartily welcomed. Usual camp duties.

<u>Sept. 24th</u>. Clear. 400 men from the 118th and 200 men from 22 Mass. under Maj. Herring on picket. Returned 20th Maine and other detachments. Capt. Hunterson left in charge of camp. Our line extends well in direction S.W. of James City Court House, extending across country towards Raccoon Ford on Rapidan through a densely wooded and sparsely settled country. Maj. Herring's Hd. Qurs. at Mr. Chadwick's house, a fine

old Virginia mansion. The family have departed. I remained with him at Hd. Qur. 4½ P.M. with the Major visited the entire line. A number of nigros and stragglers picked up and sent in during the day.

Sept. 25th. Clear. On Picket. Made rounds with Major Herring— 10.30 A.M. and 11 o'clock at night. Found everything very, very satisfactory, men vigilant and well instructed. 4 men on each point.

Sept. 26th. Clear. On Picket. Rounds at 11.30 A.M. and 10.30 at night. Sent in colored men and stragglers.

Sunday, Sept. 27th. Clear. On Picket. Chap. O'Neill held service on part of the line, for once I did not hear him. Relieved by detachment under Lt. Col. Lombard[38] of the 4th Michigan. Returned to camp 3 P.M. Col. Hayes left for home on 15 days leave, Lt. Col. Sherwin,[39] 22 Mass., in command. After cleaning up and getting rested I was preparing to visit friends in another regt. I was informed that Alfred R. Tomlin[40] *[page obliterated],* a deserter from my company was *[page torn]* [present in the] Corps with an ambrotype outfit, & some of the men had had their picture taken by him. Reported fact to Major Herring & was ordered to arrest him. Waiting until it was dark, I, with a sgt. & 12 men, proceeded to the place, & after surrounding the tent, entered and arrested him. Everything was done quietly & expeditiously, no noise or commotion. Giving him time only to get his overcoat, I hurriedly returned & lodged him in the Guard House. He was very much surprised & is greatly frightened.

Sept. 28th. Clear. Grand review of Corps by Maj. Genl. Corterge of the Mexican Army.[41] On return regiment paid off by Maj. Holman,[42] with exception of Field and line officers, their pay being stopped by Genl. Ripley[43] owing to ordnance returns not being recd. Maj. H. telegraphed to Pay Master Genl. regarding it. Made out charges against Private A. R. Tomlinson. I fear if the matter is pressed, Tomlinson will be shot. I do not think he was aware of the gravity of his offense. I had a talk with the Major regarding him and will not press the case strongly. I have told him to make his defense ignorance of Army regulations, as evinced by his returning. He is very bitter against me although accepting my advice. I certainly have weakened very much regarding him and certainly do not want him shot. Will see that he is properly defended.

Sept. 29th. Clear. Dispatch recd. from Pay Master Genl. to pay officers.

Sept. 30th. Clear. Maj. Herring offers the Sgts. a gold medal for the best drilled Co. Officers paid by Maj. Holman on order from Ordnance Dept. that cause for stoppage has been removed.

Oct. 1st. Cloudy. Usual Camp duties.

>─┤◆├─O─┤◆├─◄

Camp 118th Regt. P.V.
Near Culpeper C.H., Va.
October 2nd, 1863

My dear Brother:

As it is raining hard and locomotion is anything but pleasant, I will devote a little of the enforced leisure to you. You have been a long time without a letter from me, although Auntie has heard regularly. My neglect no doubt caused you to write the "protest" to my present way of living and the "criticism" on my life as a soldier. What I think of that letter will be found in my journal. . . . You are right in some things and altogether wrong in others. Notwithstanding your deductions, I am still and will be while I remain in the service—a <u>soldier</u>. I couldn't be otherwise if I tried—it is my pride to be so considered, and until the return of Gwyn makes it incumbent upon me to altogether and at once <u>drop the military</u>, I will be attentive to duty, subordinate, and in every respect, a soldier. . . .

"How we live" would be an excellent title to a voluminous book on the subject that could be successfully written by any of our Mess. For example— a bird supper last night, and fried eels for breakfast. We breakfast at 10, dine at 5 and sup at 9 P.M. Supper is usually a cold set out, such as pickled salmon, cold chicken, sardines and chipped beef.

I am not, as you suppose, still acting as Field Officer, having been relieved of that duty since Sept. 5th. The appointment was only for the time Maj. Herring was on Court-Martial duty. We are—that is, the whole army— engaged in building substantial quarters. Our Mess is occupying temporary shelter during the construction of a commodious house, which we hope to have finished in a day or two. I really have nothing to add to my diary, it tells all about our doings since Beverly Ford Camp. Today Col. Tilton returned and again took command of the brigade. I am in excellent health. I enclose Sgt. Sylvester Crossley's photograph. Tis a good picture.

[P.S.] You say that the good living I enjoy should tell in my avoirdupois. Well, I weigh about 160 lbs., which speaks volumes. . . . I do indeed most cordially join in your wish that I could be at home during the coming election. I would dearly love to cast a vote for Andrew G. Curtin.[44]

The following undated passage was sent to Jacob Donaldson along with another of Donaldson's letters about this time.

I left this out in the last batch of notes sent you as being too <u>bad</u> to forward. You can see where I made the change. But after due consideration I think I had better let you have this account of the <u>battle of Fort Hunterson</u>. . . .

In view of the near probability of breaking up this camp, I will mention an incident that recently occurred which I had thought to suppress, but afterwards concluded to send as I have already mentioned a little of the inner life of a soldier of this command, wherein we are not depicted as forever on duty, strutting up and down on guard and otherwise behaving in a strictly military way, as our friends at home think we do.

A few days before Captain Hunterson left on leave for home, Capt. Crocker, Lieut.'s Worrell[45] and Walters and himself were indulging in a short "game of draw" in Hunterson's quarters, known as Fort Hunterson. I was present but not playing. Lt. Sam Lewis was reclining in his bunk lazily looking at the play and occasionally grumbling at the noise and racket made by the players. The canteen had been circulated pretty freely and the liquor was just making itself felt when a dispute arose between Hunterson and Walters, terminating in the latter saying that his uncle, Udmund Souder, had hired Hunterson to fill his (Walters) place during the formation of the regiment until he could join the command, being then an enlisted man in the 23rd P.V. ordered to the 118th as 1st Lt. This angered Hunterson and he grabbed Walters and put him out of the hut. Crocker interfered and insisted upon Hunterson keeping his hands off Walters. Worrell at this juncture mixed in, and being a very powerful man, altho' tall and spare, his gigantic strength also accentuated by nerve and rum, said he would knock Crocker down if he attempted to lay on Hunterson, and continuing, said Crocker had lorded it long enough anyway and it was time that someone should show him that he was not such a big thing anyway, that he proposed to take this task in hand and give him a damn good thrashing. Without further ceremony he made a dash at Crocker and caught him round the neck and by the side, intending to hurl him on his back. A mighty struggle ensued lasting but a few moments only, when Crocker, seizing him around the middle, raised him from the floor above his head and hurled him across the hut with such force as to break down all the bunks, including the one in which Lewis was. From among the debris Sam called out, "For heavens sake Crocker, don't break up everything." "Yes I will," he replied, "I'll smash everything in the damned old Fort."

A scene of indescribable confusion ensued, Crocker, following up his advantage, rushed upon Worrell, and gathering him up, proceeded to demolish the contents of the hut with him, finally ending by throwing him on the ground and sitting on his head. He then reached for Hunterson, and catching him by the legs, threw him violently and placed him beside Worrell. Then, wiping the perspiration from his head, called for a little beverage, as he felt tired. Lewis got out the best way he could, and I did the same, whilst Walters, standing amidst the ruins with his fists squared, called out to fetch the next champion. There had been no blows struck in all this disturbance, it was a trial of sheer strength, and the sequel proved there was no limit to Crocker's Herculean powers. The noise and confusion soon gathered about Fort Hunterson a number of the officers, among them Capt. Fernald, whose chief interest lay in rescuing the spilled rum. This he could not do, but espying a bottle of Jamaican Ginger upon the floor, half empty, he seized it and poured its fiery contents down his throat without halt, exclaiming, "Salvage—by Hookey." This was so supremely ridiculous, so worthy of Fernald, that we all burst into hearty laughter, and the bad blood between the combatants ended. Poor Sam Lewis declairs he would rather sleep in the weather than tent with Hunterson, who "never was and never could keep sober."

Oct. 2nd. Rained all day. Col. Tilton returned and took command of the brigade. Usual camp duties.

Oct. 3rd. Clear. Col. Tilton presented at Lt. Col. Sherwin's Headquarters with sword belt and spurs by the officers of the 22nd Mass. There was a "flowing bowl." I wasn't there, wasn't invited, none but Field Officers. 3 P.M.—250 men, 10 sgts., 17 corporals, 8 commissioned officers detailed from regt. on picket.

Sunday, Oct. 4th. Clear. Chaplain O'Neill undertook the difficult task of preaching to the specially sinful and stationed himself near the Guard House where those confined therein were at his mercy. He took his text—part of the 17th verse XIII Chap. St. Paul's Epistle to the Hebrews—"Obey them that have the rule over you and submit yourselves." After a boisterous harangue of half an hour it was suggested by one of those "who sit in the seat of the scornful" that had he said his words were taken from the Epistle to the Canadians, the prisoners would have been just as delighted, instructed and edified. In the afternoon he reached forth his hand to vex certain of the staff at Corps Headquarters, and in the evening he addressed the impious and atheists of the 22nd Mass.

Oct. 5th. Clear. Private Tomlinson tried before a Court-Martial sitting at 3rd Brigade Headquarters, Col. Chamberlain, 20th Maine, president,[46]

Capt. Sharwood, judge advocate. In my testimony I merely stated the facts as to his enlistment, desertion, and arrest, and in answer to a question stated he had been, whilst with me, obedient, attentive and evinced aptitude and the qualities to make a good soldier; that I knew of but one motive that could possibly have induced him to desert—homesickness, that I did not believe he was guided by a desire to secure a high bounty. In fact, I did all that lay in my power not to prejudice his case. However, he still holds bitter resentment towards me and in conversation with the men of my company blames me for putting his life in jeopardy.[47]

Oct. 6th. Clear. Pickets returned, quiet time. Regt. commenced building a spacious hall of logs for meetings and entertainments. Looks like permanent camp.

>-!-•>-•-O-•‹•-!-‹

Camp 118th Regt. P.V.
Near Culpeper C.H., Va.
October 6th, 1863

Dear Jac:

. . . I have been dilatory in writing of late, but pressure of business is my excuse. To the marching, picket and company duty there has been added the other and more and embarrassing one of a monthly settlement with the government for clothing, camp and garrison equipage recd., and, at the end of each quarter, with the Ordnance Department for muskets and accoutrements recd. and expended. It is now the end of the 3rd Quarter of 1863, and as a matter of course I alone have this added duty to perform, and it is by no means a light one. No one else can do it for me, and I may add it is a very difficult task to straighten the accounts and account for everything the soldier has belonging to the government. The marches, battles and receipt of new recruits in this quarter has complicated matters to such a degree that to use the expression of Capt. O'Neill, "me heart is nearly broke out of me body entirely."

Then too, I have been unsettled by the building of a new and commodious house. The materials for its construction have been almost entirely taken from the mansion of Col. Patton, the F.F.V. commander of the 22nd Va. Regt. (John's command).[48] This dwelling, a fine old Virginia structure, is just outside our lines, and as it has been abandoned by its people, it has fallen victim to the destroying soldiery. Had the family remained, no harm would have happened it. I am at a loss to understand why it is that in nearly every instance where isolated dwellings like this one are vacated by the families who should remain to protect [them] their properties are pretty thoroughly destroyed and those occupied untouched, that they still continue to leave their properties wholly abandoned. I have never yet learned of any vandalism perpetrated upon inhabited dwellings, but where the family has abandoned the property it is taken for granted they do so because of their intense hatred of the Yanks, hence a retaliatory measure in the destruction of the building.

The Patton house, when I first saw it, was certainly a lovely place, although the grounds were in a wild and unkept condition. The gate had been broken from the massive posts at the entrance of the grounds, and the house was open and somewhat disturbed, many of the windows out, but otherwise there was not much damage done. An old colored woman occupied a dilapidated shanty in rear of the house, and with her head wrapped around with a bandana handkerchief in true Virginny style, she sat rocking herself backwards and forwards lamenting the desolation and crying aloud that she "done and been born and raised here." I asked her about the Colonel and other members of the family and learned that as far as she knew "de Colonel was still in de army, but the family had done gone to Richmond." She, however, was so attached to the place that she wouldn't leave it. I asked her whether any of the officers of the 22nd had ever visited the mansion and learned that they had. She thought that she remembered that Capt. Donaldson was one of them. This of course is very uncertain, as the old woman didn't really remember much of the present but continued talking about the past, when "de lovely children were nussed and raised by her."

I have since visited the place again and found it a wreck, doors and window shutters all gone, floors ripped up, and nearly everything moveable taken away. Nearly all of the best furniture had been removed by the family. The front door lay broken on the porch, but the great old time brass knocker still clung to it. This I removed and had put on the door of my house, where the name of Patton showed to the unsympathetic soldiery how the mighty had fallen. I also secured two small bed steads, each post of which was surmounted by a quaint old brass ornament. . . . We also secured lambrequins for our sash windows, and brass andirons, fender and shovel tongues, and "spittoons," the latter interesting historical relics doubtless of the time when George Washington visited this dwelling and expectorated freely the juice of the weed into their broad open mouths. These things have made our house very comfortable. We have departed from the usual in our construction of the chimney. It is architectural at least. It is built inside and carried out through the rear wall towards the roof, thus saving heat and warmth and adding to our comfort. . . . This is the first chimney of the kind ever erected in the army as far as I know. Its design is entirely original reflecting much credit on the constructor, a fine fellow by the way, and no less a person than your brother. I am indebted to this happy inspiration by the thought of my uncomfortable experience with bad flues at Falmouth last winter.

Capt. Lemuel L. Crocker, Company K, another of Donaldson's close confidants in the 118th Pennsylvania.

I now come to a great scandal, and in the expectation of again offending, will relate what befell Crocker and myself last evening. Two days ago I recd. a written invitation from Clem. See of the 2nd Pa. Cavalry[49] to "visit the abode of opulence and refinement amid the fragrant atmosphere of the elevated and elegant aristocratic society of Culpeper's slate, on Monday evening the 5th inst." and, added he, "Full many a flower is born to blush unseen," that it was his intention to bring me forward and make me "shine in my proper sphere." In accepting his invitation I meekly suggested that I feared I was "like the Tulip, which when the sun shines upon it, it droops its lovely head and remains cast down." Well, I rather anticipated some deviltry and so took the precaution to invite Crocker, on my own account, to accompany me. No Tulip business about him, he promptly accepted without comment or question.

We quietly got ourselves up on the most "unanimous" manner, [and], saying "nothing to nobody"—ran the guard—fearing to ask permission to leave camp lest we should be refused, and arrived safely and unsoiled at a neat two story brick house, surrounded by porches, situated near the suburban end of the town. We made ourselves known, were admitted, and found a numerous assemblage of officers, mostly staff, and some remarkable females. I was presented to a Quaker like individual of some fifty summers, who was represented to be the "proprietor." I soon saw Clem See—this man of rum—and found him already full to begin with, which in the course of the evening made him a source of trouble an[d] annoyance, by reason of his excessive "chinning." Gracious Peace! how the rum did make him talk. It kept me busy dodging him. I didn't get along very well, at best. The staff officers, in boiled shirts and white collar, rather crowded me. Crocker, however, was not at all set back. He at once made himself at home and complimented each one of the ladies, and was received by smiles and bows. Finally pushing and shoving his way up to a female of whom I had strong suspicions that she was three parts nigro, he showered upon her a volley of compliments and audaciously took her hand to tell her fortune. Crocker is certainly a society man and no mistake—he just made the staff officers green with envy and livid with rage.

Things now commenced to look disagreeable—the staff were mad and no mistake—that the burley Crocker, a dirty, travel soiled, foot frogging infantryman should make such rapid time with the "pet of the ball," while their boiled shirts and white collars counted for nothing. Sherry wine was now introduced among the ladies and a good deal of whiskey got in among the officers—and some bad brandy. I as usual kept off this stuff, but Crocker took hold very lively every time the bottle came near him, excusing himself to the ladies saying he was not feeling well.

By and by one of the staff went up to the "landlord" and told him Crocker was insulting the lady he was talking to. I cannot say as to this, but the creature, having on an exceedingly low necked dress, no blame should possibly attach to the brave and gallant Captain if he did now and then take in the situation. I will incidently admit that Crocker, to use a homely expression, was certainly "very heavy" with the lovely, indolent, dark eyed mulatto—I mean octoroon— or, rather—native Virginia girl. He afterwards explained he was quoting, "Twer vain to tell thee all I feel or say for thee I sigh," etc. when the "old buffer" came up and said, "Friend, it is not for thine own health seeing thou hast drunk enough already, but rather for these my daughters with whom you parley," and with that he fetched Crocker a shot on the nose that unseated the doubty Captain. Recovering himself instantly he doubled the old fellow up and seated him on the coals in the fire place, where, becoming alarmed for the seat of his trousers, he was so diligent thereafter in his efforts to extinguish the fire in his clothes that he was out of the combat that ensued, a point in favor of Crocker, by the way, for he was a huge, broad shouldered fellow and would [have] aided materially in drumming him, had he been able to take a hand. Crocker then reached for the nearest staff officer and with him knocked over two or three others who made a rush at him.

The whole room now massed on Crocker. I of course took a hand and by way of diversion in Crocker's favor, rapped the officer nearest me two solid ones on the "nob." This turned about some of those assaulting Crocker, and a lively skirmish ensued in which I held my own pretty well until I was struck in my wounded arm a blow that entire[ly] disabled that member. I now made for the door but was headed [off] by a red whiskered Captain of Cavalry who wanged me pretty severely about the head until I fortunately got hold of a brandy bottle, when it became my turn for a while. Meanwhile there was a good deal of uproar, the women screaming and raising the devil general, while the whole batch of officers made at us two orphans as if we were wild beasts. However, Crocker fought his way to where I was, and kicking the door open, pushed me out, and then we both took to our heels, just as the Provost Guard came double quick upon the ground. The whole affair was disgraceful, and I am dreadfully mortified. I feel so badly about it that I tell it as a sort of confession. But Jac, my boy, amid all the humiliation there is one satisfactory thought constantly cropping out—the way Crocker "spoiled the

Egyptians"—the loafing staff officers. Why, when we arrived in camp, he had in one clutched hand the shirt front of one [of] the gentry and in the other a bottle of brandy his foresight led him to seize as he quitted the place. He was pounded a good deal about the body and head and is marked "quarters" today, whilest I, as usual, am marked "light duty" by the sympathizing and good Dr. Thomas.

The affair has gotten abroad and efforts are <u>being made</u> to bring to justice the two officers who so riotously broke up the "quiet little evening party." Of course the 18th Mass. and 1st Mich., on provost duty in the town, know who we are, but keep quiet about it and look elsewhere than the camp of the 118th for the offenders. The loafing staff officers put the whole blame on us. Clem See was too drunk to notice any unpleasantness, but when his attention was called to "his friends" and their names asked for, he was so ashamed of us that he said we were not there by his invitation—he didn't know us at all. Don't scold old man, I'll never do it again—neither will Crocker. He feebly remarked this morning that while there was very little fun without rum, it certainly did get a fellow into a deal of trouble. Cordially agreeing with him in this truism, I calmly put away the Hooker's Retreat he was mixing as he thus soliloquized. I presume you have heard enough from your repentant brother.

Oct. 7th. Cloudy. Orders recd. to haul no more logs or bricks. Mailed my ordnance returns. Mr. Tomlinson arrived in camp; avoids me, does not come near my quarters nor speak when I meet him in the Company street. I feel incensed at him and propose to let him understand that I am not to be treated in this way, but with respect. Later I concluded not to notice his disrespectful manner.

Oct. 8th. Snowing, didn't amount to much. Lt. Wm. F. Gardner mustered as Quarter Master. He has been acting as such for a long time. Battalion drill and usual camp duties.

Oct. 9th. Clear. Battalion drill in morning. Major Herring got Capt. Crocker to order Medals for Sergeants for best drilled company through Stephen N. Winslow of Philada. Commercial List. 10.15 P.M. Orders unexpectedly recd. to move at short notice. Much bustle and stir in camp. Such orders usually mean to move. During the day orders recd. that Private Sands, Co. F, a deserter, had been ordered to be shot on the 16th.[50]

CHAPTER 9

Bristoe Station
October 10–November 3, 1863

In response to the Union defeat at the Battle of Chickamauga on September 19–20, the Lincoln administration had determined to send reinforcements from the Army of the Potomac to help the besieged Army of the Cumberland at Chattanooga. On September 24 Meade reluctantly saw more than 16,000 of his veterans from the 11th and 12th Corps march away from the Rappahannock to the railcars that would take them west.[1]

Lee soon learned of the transfer and, sensing an opportunity to strike the Federals in their weakened state, ordered an advance around Meade's right on October 9 in hopes of getting into position behind him and offering battle on favorable ground. Meade was initially unsure of Lee's intentions, but by October 13 he was certain that the Rebels were beyond his flank and headed toward the capital. The Army of the Potomac was soon rapidly retreating, racing back along the general line of the Orange & Alexandria Railroad and angling to reach the heights of Centreville before the Confederates.[2]

The only serious engagement of the campaign occurred when Confederate corps commander A. P. Hill brashly struck what he believed was the Union rear guard at Bristoe Station on October 14, only to see two of his brigades nearly wiped out when the Federal 2nd Corps came up undetected on his flank. The retrograde movement to Centreville then resumed, and by the evening of October 15 the Army of the Potomac was firmly established behind Bull Run. Lee, seeing he could gain no advantage, soon fell back, destroying the Orange & Alexandria as far south as Rappahannock Station. By October 20 the Army of Northern Virginia was again behind the Rappahannock River.

Donaldson and the 5th Corps were not seriously engaged during the brief campaign, although the 118th Pennsylvania did suffer minor casualties when it was surprised by the advance of Hill's brigades at the Battle of Bristoe Station.

In the field near
Fairfax Station, Va.
October 16, 1863

Dear Brother—

Queer I haven't written you say? My dear brother, I have been on the
march, marching, night and day, getting only eight hours rest out of forty
eight. What think you of that? We have crossed the Rappahannock no less
than four times and was in action near Bristoe Station & no loss in our
regiment. We leave here today for I know not where—am almost dead
with fatigue. Will keep you posted as we move and send diary.

Oct. 10. Clear. Broke camp at 2 and moved at 3.45 A.M. Bid goodbye
to my comfortable quarters, "The Monitor," as it was named and started
on the march in direction of Raccoon Ford on the Rapidan. I was brigade
officer of the day. 8.30 A.M. arrived in vicinity of the Ford, a distance from
camp of from 4 to 5 miles, having passed thro' the picket line which apparently had been withdrawn inland somewhat. Here the brigade halted in
line until 2.30 P.M. I was ordered to take command of the skirmishers, and
with the division pioneers deployed along with them, to advance as near as
possible to the ford without attracting attention, and then to fall back gradually, felling the trees and blocking all the roads and by paths leading
through the woods. There was a good deal of mystery attending this movement. The fact that my skirmishers and pioneers were supported by the
brigade and I believe by the division made me suspicious that all was not as
it should be to our front, that the enemy were on the move or else we
were about to abandon this part of the country. After proceeding a good
long distance to the front, or as near to the ford as in my judgment I
ought to go, I set the men at work obstructing the roads and paths, and as
my task was accomplished fell gradually back and so on continuing the
work. The men worked with a will and I certainly had no apprehension of
cavalry or artillery following us very rapidly when my labors were through
with. It was a thorough job. I generally rode back and selected the new
places for the men to work.

On one of these trips to the rear I noticed that the road for quite a distance
lay through the open fields with nothing in the way of trees to obstruct it.
This could not of course be helped, but noticing a little further on a fine row
of maples, probably the finest trees of the kind I had ever seen, I rode up to
inspect them. They were quite large with heavy trunks and I would have

to put two men to each in order to expedite their felling. I was so enamoured of these fine trees that I looked about to see whether I could not in some way spare them, but there was nothing beyond for quite a smart distance and they would have to go. I declair I felt extremely sorry to cut them down, they were so grand, stately and shady.

Noticing a house at a little distance up the lane leading from them, I opened the gate and rode up to it, intending to say to the occupants, if they still remained, how truly sorry I was to destroy their property. Throwing the bridle over the post at the steps leading to the fine porch surrounding the house, I ascended and at first gently knocked on the door, but not receiving any response, I somewhat violently rattled the venetian blinds that closed the porch windows. Indeed for that matter all the windows in the house were tightly shut, inducing the belief that the place was vacant. As I was about departing the window was raised, the shutters unbolted, and a lady appeared who, with great dignity and in a calm but severe tone of voice said—"To what am I indebted for this intrusion?" I was rather startled at her sudden advent. She was decidedly the most refined and ladylike person I had yet met with in "my travels." Quickly removing my hat, and, by the way, I so remained uncovered during our brief conversation, I replied that I was then engaged, by orders from my superiors, in blocking the road and by paths by felling the timber to obstruct any possible advance of Lee's forces, and that, as she doubtless knew, for a long way there were no trees along the highway but those in front of her house. I was compelled to utilize them, but before doing so, being an ardent lover of trees, I came to say that I was actuated by no vandal desire to injure her property and that the stern requirements of duty alone compelled me to cut down her beautiful timber. That there was at least one tender heart among the legions of enemies surrounding her, and I sincerely trusted she would give me the credit of being loath to do her or indeed any lady an injury could I possibly avoid it. Having said all that I could possibly think of at the moment, I commenced backing away from her presence, bowing the while most graciously, when she said, "Stop, sir, I had been looking at you through the blinds before opening the window and fancied you were a gentleman, although disguised in the livery of Lincoln's spoilers. Your words have convinced me that my conjectures were correct." "Madam," said I, the hot blood rushing to my face, "the principles that actuate Mr. Lincoln in this cause and the uniform I have the honor to be clothed in do not require the slightest justification from me. Warfare on our part is honorable. I wish I could say as much for your president and the soldiers he arrays against us." I again assayed to withdraw when she added, "I have no intention of wounding your feelings, but it is so very uncommon to meet with a gentleman in your service." "Then Madam, you have never met with any of our soldiers. There is not one among them who would use such insulting language to one of your people trying to do what was honorable and right." She said, "From what state are you and kindly tell me your name so that when looking at my prostrate trees I can at least remember the officer who so politely and tenderly apologized for destroying them." "You mistake me Madam," said I, "I offer no apology for doing my duty, I am merely endeavoring to show you that I sympathize with you in the loss of these beautiful trees. My name is Donaldson, I am from Pennsylvania—Philadelphia. . . ."[3]

. . . [She said] that the trees I was about to cut down were dear, very dear to her and her sisters, that they had been raised under them and that she would do most anything to save them from destruction, that with the risk of being considered a traitor to the cause she could tell me something that would stay my destroying hand, that there was no force in front of me but some cavalry, that Lee's army was passing around us to the right, and that I need not cut down her trees as no troops would come this way. This was such startling information and told with such evident truthfulness that I did not for a moment doubt her, but forgetting my politeness in my eagerness to communicate what I had learned, I dashed down the steps, mounted my horse, and without saying goodbye or asking the name of the family rode rapidly to my line, ordered it to promptly assemble and return to the brigade, and then galloped back to the old mansion on the porch of which I had left Maj. Herring and hurriedly reported to him my interview with the ladies. Whether it was the information I had brought or whether Col. Tilton had recd. orders to do so the brigade certainly retreated at once. It was 2.30 P.M. when we started back and upon arriving at the old camp again recd. orders to move at a moments notice, while the teams were hitched up and at 9 P.M. moved hurriedly to the rear, taking with them the five prisoners under sentence of Court-Martial.[4] With much discomfiture we slept in the cold, cold "Monitor" with no covering but our overcoats and the heavens, our shelter tent roof having been removed.

Sunday, 11th. A most beautiful day. Moved at 6 A.M. As we left camp, one fellow, a stubborn dutchman, declined to leave—he was cooling coffee and would not until he had finished. To the repeated orders and urgent requests he replied—"Do you tink I am a plame fools to go away and leave my coffee?"

From the fact that he has not again been seen it is presumed he has been captured. All along the R.R. bags of grain abandoned by the teams were ripped open by the men and the empty sacks appropriated. We passed through Culpeper at 8 A.M., the 1st Michigan and 22nd Mass. joining us there. We never halted for a moment until Brandy Station was reached, a distance of nearly 10 miles in one single stretch. This I believe to be the longest consecutive marching without a halt we have yet made. I suffered a good deal from sore feet owing to delapidated boots—my first experience of a trouble of this kind. I however remedied it later on by fitting an insole of well soaped canvas which did very well.

At this place we took position in line of battle supporting the retiring cavalry and to protect the trains. There was considerable artillery practice at long range, mostly from the enemy who were pressing the cavalry closely. We fell back gradually and occupied rifle pits in front of the artillery. There was considerable cavalry fighting, charge and counter charge, and we stood watching the battle for a long time.[5] The enemy appeared in great force, their squadrons swarming to the front, and our horsemen were having a hard time of it, when Genl. Griffin, who had been standing near the guns

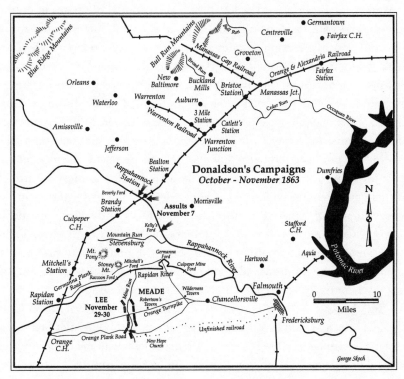

in rear of us, seeing an opportunity, ordered the battery to fire. The first shot was too high, merely taking off branches of the trees on the outskirts of which dense masses of the enemy's horse[s] were assembled. This practice didn't suit the general, and he called to lower the guns—"You are firing too high, just roll the shot along the ground like a ten pin ball and knock the trotters from under the 'sons of guns',," illustrating the order by stooping and trundling his hand as if in bowling, a favorite way he had of making his meaning plain. The next discharge was better, the shots went right into the masses, and the "sons of guns" broke from "four rounds into two ranks, right smart, git."

At 4 P.M. we retreated and crossed the Rappahannock at Rappahannock Station at 7.50 and at 9.30 occupied old camp at Beverly Ford. This was a tiresome and trying day and little rest was gained because of the cold and our uncertain and unsheltered condition. During the day Private Sands, under sentence of death, was placed in ambulance and kept with the regiment under heavy guard and ordered to be so confined until the 16th, the day of execution.

Monday, Oct. 12th. Clear. Left camp at 9 A.M. and recrossed the Rappahannock at Beverly Ford at 12.30 P.M. Formed line of masses in double column and with the 6th and 3rd Corps advanced in line of battle to the hill near Brandy Station occupied by us the day previous when we deployed for action. Our skirmishers were lightly engaged but further than that nothing occurred. Our march to this place was very laborious, being, the whole way to the open plain surrounding Brandy, through dense forests, which happily were pretty well cleared of underbrush. The advance of these immense Army Corps presented a gorgeous spectacle, and after the timber was cleared from the hill upon which we rested, the pageant was most imposing—the army offering battle with artillery at intervals through out its entire length, its lines beautifully dressed, colors fluttering in the breeze, made up a martial picture the mind loves to dwell upon, and in after years will recall as one of the remarkable displays of the war. There was no enemy in our front but cavalry. Here we remained until 1 A.M. at night, when we withdrew and again crossed the Rappahanannock at Beverly Ford, and at 6 A.M. rested and breakfasted at old camp.

Tuesday, Oct. 13th. Clear. Moved at 7.10 A.M., passed Warrenton Junction at 11.45 A.M. and bivouaced at Walnut Branch near Catlet Station[6] at 5.30 P.M. Fatiguing march—Rationed. On this march, with my compan[y] and other details, acted as Division flankers on the left flank of the marching column. Major Herring loaned me his horse Dendy, which being a spirited beast, strong and full of nerve, I had no difficulty in keeping both ends of my line in constant communication. I had the misfortune, however, to lose the Major's haversack attached to the saddle, for which I was extremely sorry and not a little mortified. Situated as we were, at a considerable distance from the column, I could see at a distance, away off, at intervals, what I took to be the enemy's trains. They may have been our own, however, although it was supposed the Confederates were marching parallel with us in their endeavor to gain our rear. At this time our lines must have been close together, as Genl. Griffin released Private Sands and ordered him to be equipped and put into action anticipated as we reached Catlett's.

<u>Wednesday, Oct. 14th</u>. Foggy and clear. Reveille at 4 A.M. Moved at 8.25 A.M. and halted at Broad Run near Bristoe Station. This could never have been much of a place in its best days, but it was now, as I believe I have before described it, in ruins. All the houses but one, and that some distance from the R.R., had been destroyed by fire, leaving nothing but chimneys to mark the site. It was 1 P.M., or near that hour I should judge, my watch having stopped, when we reached this place. We forded the stream and halted for dinner on the bluff beyond. The whole division was massed here and very soon innumerable little individual fires were kindled as they proceeded to cook coffee. We believed we were the rear of the army. As we passed down the road to the run, the trees along it had been nearly cut through, ready to block the road after we passed. Genl. Patrick, who on horseback was directing this measure, called to us to hurry up as he wanted to finish cutting down the trees. Hence we believed that we were the last of the retreating army.

Crocker, Thomas and I were sitting on the bluff overlooking the stream, road and country beyond, over which we had just passed. The country, unobstructed by timber, rose gradually from the stream to a piece of woods at considerable distance, through which the road led down which we had just passed. The intervening ground was rough and uneven, with every vestige of green grass and twig faded and blighted by the frost. As we chatted over our coffee, Crocker suddenly jumped to his feet calling out, "What's that coming across the field, look! It is a reb skirmish line." Sure enough we could see the line advancing, although not before noticed owing to their close resemblance to the color of the ground. As we looked a battery was seen to emerge from the timber and go into position, and a moment after a shot well directed ploughed into the crowded mass on the bluff. A stampede ensued the like I never before witnessed. So astounded were the men and so unprepared for such an attack that without waiting for orders they gathered up their traps, seized the boiling hot coffee pots, and grasping their muskets, made off at a mad pace. It was a spontaneous retreat, including all branches of the service—Artillery, without attempting to reply to the enemy's fire, Cavalry, General and Staff officers all took to their heels and beat a disgraceful retreat, crowding and pushing one another in painful disorder and eagerness to get beyond the range of the guns which plied them so unmercifully. Near where I also was running, a mounted officer, spurring and belaboring his horse to push its way through the frightened and crowded masses, had his arm torn off by a round shot and his bleeding and horrible appearance added to the panic. The retreat was not stayed until Manassas Junction was reached.

It appears that Hill's division of Ewell's Corps had pushed out from Warrenton to strike us in flank, and coming in our rear, attacked with the result related, not knowing the 2nd Corps was still behind. Neither did we know that Warren was yet in the rear, but I am told it was known to Genl. Sykes and he was waiting, in support, for the 2nd Corps to come up. It is a pretty muddle anyway. I don't understand how it is that if Sykes knew Warren was still behind why he retreated without first hearing from him.[7] However, I am away down in the ranks and how should I understand these things? No one questions Sykes—he is too good a soldier to take a panic. Where in the world did Warren come from and why did Genl. Patrick obstruct the road if he knew the 2nd Corps was to follow? As I think of it, I did no[t] see the trees actually felled, and it may be possible he only prepared them in readiness to throw down after Warren passed.

However, to continue, we reached Manassas Junction at 3.30 P.M. in pretty fair shape, formed line and stacked arms. There was tremendous artillery firing to the rear, the sounds indicating a general engagement which still more perplexed us. At 5 P.M. we were hurridly called to attention and the whole division, at "double quick," returned towards Bristoe Station, where upon arriving in sight of the battle, our artillery went into battery and became heavily engaged. We were not called upon to take an active part, but supported the 2nd and 3rd Brigades and had the disagreeable duty of sustaining an artillery fire for an hour or more. We were in a perfect hail of shells and round shot, but as far as I know no one was hurt in the regt., although the brigade lost 8 killed and 16 wounded, mostly the Massachusetts regts.[8] Warren defeated the enemy, capturing 5 guns, killing, wounding and capturing 1,500 men, including among the killed two or more general officers. Our loss was about 500.[9] As usual I went among the prisoners questioning and learning all that I could from them. Quite a number were North Carolina troops, the 6th being largely represented.[10] I have since been reminded that this was the command to which my friend Thomas Sugle[11] was attached as Major. I am sorry I did not think to ask about him. One of the captured cannon is a Wintworth gun,[12] the first I have seen of the kind.

We remained until 10 P.M. when we quietly withdrew and marched to and through Manassas Junction across Bull Run battlefield fording the Bull Run river waist deep and bivouaced near Centreville at 3 A.M. Of course in this long night's march all order was lost, the men making the best way they could to the rear. As we approached the bivouac near Centreville there was no way to distinguish the brigade and division's where abouts. To remedy this Genl. Griffin had the division bugler, at intervals, sound the Division Call, and brigades to do the same. By this forethought, being guided by the bugle calls, the men readily assembled in their proper commands. No time was lost in preparing food, but down upon the ground we fell, tired and weary.

Thursday, Oct. 15th. Cloudy. Moved at 9 A.M., passed through the 1st Corps entrenched at Centreville, also passed in position the 3rd, 2nd and 6th Corps. Saw the 71st P.V., Baker's California Regt., and had a warm reception from my many friends in this gallant command. It was evident I was not forgotten and was still appreciated there. My heart went out towards my old friends, my dear old regiment—would that I were with them now. Bivouaced in the woods at Fairfax C.H. at 1 P.M. It rained hard all night long.

Friday, Oct. 16th. Raining. Beef and whiskey rations issued. Busy all day in keeping dry under my shelter tent and in writing this journal. Amid a heavy downpour we moved at 6 P.M. back towards Centreville and bivouaced at 9 P.M. in column of divisions right to front. In this march, amid a pouring rain the whole time, we forded streams dreadfully swollen, were wet to the skin, miserable and dejected. To sleep was impossible so we huddled about the sickly bivouac fires all night long.

Saturday, Oct. 17th. Clear. Genl. Meade's Headquarters on our immediate left. Orders recd. for inspection. Had dress parade and inspection. About noon, as Crocker, Thomas and I were seated together drying our clothes and boots, Private Shields, a substitute of my company, asked permission to leave camp. This man, a big brawny fellow, so large and tall that he was on the right of the company, had given me a great deal of trouble by drunkenness. When sober he was quiet and inoffensive, and being a handsome soldierly fellow would have made a name for himself, but he was seldom so. In liquor he was a veritable devil incarnate. I told him I had no confidence in him and couldn't trust him for a moment out of my sight, that he could not leave the Camp. Muttering something about going anyhow, I called him back and told him if he left the Camp without my permission and got drunk again it would be his last offense, as I would kill him.

An hour or more afterwards it was reported to me that he was outside the camp limits, roaring drunk, and disgracing the regt. by unseemly language and conduct. I called the 1st sgt. and ordered him to take 12 men and bring him into camp and put him into the guard house. This they did using much force. After a time one of the men came running to me with the information that Shields had secured a musket and had intimidated the guard, captured the stacks of arms and [put] the whole force to flight. Not waiting to put on my boots, I ran in my stocking feet to the guard house and found Shields stalking about brandishing a musket and loudly calling to the men to come and fight him, that he could whip the whole of them and Capt. Donaldson to boot. Advancing rapidly I called [to] him to put down the musket. Declining to do this and actually turning upon me with the bayonet, I seized a musket from the stack, and avoiding his lunge, made at him with the piece clubbed. A struggle ensued between us. He was so very powerful that had he been sober he would have finished me in no time, but I had the advantage, altho he pressed me very closely. Finally, an opportunity offering, I brought my musket down upon his head and felled him to the ground. Shortening the piece I was about to run him through when Crocker seized me like a vice saying, "He is dead already." And so it seemed for the blood was pouring from the wound in his head and he was quite motionless. Summoning the doctor I had his hurt examined and learned that he thought his skull was fractured. I now reported to Maj. Herring who justified me in "quelling a disturbance and outbreak" and said he would await further reports from the doctor. I then returned to the man and urged upon the doctor to use his best endeavors to save his life, as I did not want his blood on my hands. He was taken away to the hospital at Centreville and I saw no more of him.[13]

This has aroused a good deal of feeling among other regiments camped near us, who not knowing the circumstances, brand me as the "man killer," and as I appear call out, there goes the "brave man killer," "down with the bloody Captain," "shoot him" and the like. I recd. a favorable report later on and feel relieved, although I certainly justify myself for this action. I have learned that Shields gets drunk on Jamaica Ginger, drinking a whole bottle at one time. This accounts for his violence. Pontoon trains just passed. After looking at them I inquired of the "prophets" what this might mean and learned from the company cook that he had heard it said—on good authority—we are destined for the Potomac by way of Gum Springs, Leesburg and Edwards Ferry.

Sunday, Oct. 18th. Clear. Reveille at 4 A.M., moved at 7 A.M. back to Fairfax C.H., arriving at 9 A.M. The "Strategists" of the regt. badly puzzled at this retrograde movement, but the wise old company cook let me into the secret (confidentially) that Lee was crossing into Maryland. Without orders to do so the men commenced preparing for a lengthened stay. I don't see why they thought so, but they certainly did. They commenced to align the tents, cut and haul cedar and spruce boughs for shelters, and generally stirred about, getting huge logs for camp fires and otherwise making themselves comfortable. I did nothing towards fitting up, neither did head quarters. I merely sat about the campfire, smoking pipe, and finally scribbled this journal. Later on—I visited Private Shields whom I found in an ambulance, not having been taken to the Centreville hospital as I supposed. He was perfectly sober and sane, and his head was tied up in bandages. I addressed him a few words regarding his habits of intemperance and my determination to quench his turbulent spirit of insubordination. He made but one reply and that to the point—in the next battle he would remember me, a threat that gave me a clear insight into his character. I said I would bear his threat in mind when he again reported to me for duty. The doctor said he would be fit for duty shortly. At all events, come what may, I am glad he is still alive. I am fully sustained by Major Herring and all the officers, but the men comment on my conduct as brutal—but I notice they move lively when I speak to them. Sent George Slow into Fairfax for supplies.

At 10 A.M. orders recd. to pack up. This was a disappointment to the men, they thought we would certainly stay at this place for a few days at least. About this time a rumour reached me that Genl. Lee had again invaded Maryland, and the cook said "we will be after him." I have about concluded that Genl. Meade, nor anybody else, knows nothing of what Lee is doing. At noon we moved to Fox's Mill and bivouaced at 3 P.M.[14] I don't know just where this place is or what is intended by the change. George Slow joined me here—he had secured 4 doz. eggs. Our bivouac is on an elevated piece of ground overlooking a wide expanse of beautiful country with lovely scenery. Heavy artillery firing is heard to our left. Presume we will remain here at least for the night. We are more of an outpost than a bivouac. Orders are to keep under arms. Recd. from the foragers fresh butter and milk & at 5 P.M. had supper of Pork & eggs, hard tack, butter and milk & coffee—not so bad. Have been informed that Mosby with about 400 men are hovering around us, and from where I am his horsemen can be plainly seen in the distance, at least those we saw are said to be Mosby's men. Shortly after, our cavalry passed and pushed out to the front, when the others disappeared, and if they were Mosby's gang they, as usual, escaped, for they are sound on the road system of Old Virginny. . . .

I forgot to note my horrible dream of last night. I was shot in the arm and had it amputated with all the attending terrors of the surgical table. I also came very near neglecting Chaplain O'Neill. He gave us a sermon without a text and for three quarters of an hour roared like the Bull of Bashan. Thomas suggested that hereafter at his services we wear little plugs of wood to fit the ears, with a string connecting them upon which should be suspended a printed card with this legend—"pull when you get through." What a spectacle we would present. I think it would discourage a less cheeky man than the good chaplain to have us thus stand until he finished his wrangle.

Monday, Oct. 19th. Clear. Had a grand sleep last night. Reveille at 4 A.M. Moved at 6 A.M. We are marching towards Centreville. Passed through Centreville 11:30 A.M. and at about a mile beyond the works took a road to the right, marched a mile, and are now at a halt for 5 minutes rest. Have just had a "Hooker's Retreat"—Crocker's mixing. Whole army appears to be concentrated here. 10 minutes later moved on in a course nearly due west, crossed Bull Run river twice and bivouaced on 2nd Bull Run field at 3 P.M., within a stones throw of the ruined house where I slept on my first march to this place as a Ball's Bluff prisoner, Oct. 1861. The ground is covered with bones of men and horses and vast quantities of debris. Visited the battlefield and located the spot where the brigade had fought in the 2nd Bull Run battle. The dead had been so carelessly buried that among the uncovered remains, that of an officer of the 1st Michigan who had been killed here was recognized by the formation of his teeth. Time was taken to more properly cover his bones and to mark his grave. At another place in one of [the] slopes or wash outs leading to the stream was found the remains of a cavalryman. The flesh had entirely disappeared from his bones but his uniform was still in fair condition and his sword was still belted around his waist. He had evidently been wounded and crawled to this spot in search of water. The bones of his legs protruded well beyond his pants, which were much shrunken, and his shoes were still on his fleshless feet. In attempting to lift his remains by the sword belt it all fell apart, so gathering them together as compactly as possible a little earth soon hid them from view.

Captain Bankson of the staff here met with an incident worthy of mention. When we crossed the Bull Run battlefield on our way to Gettysburg in June last, he dropped his pocket album containing the picture of his wife and children and did not miss it until after we had gone a days journey beyond. Today he rode over to the spot on the field where the brigade had rested and found the book. It of course was warped and twisted by the weather, but the pictures were recognizable. He was much rejoiced at finding it. Near our bivouac numbers of the unburied Confederate dead encumber the ground, representing, among others, the 11th North Carolina and 18th Georgia. I could spend a week going over the ground locating without trouble the different lines of battle as they stood on that fatal day. Fletcher Webster, son of Daniel Webster, is buried near our bivouac with his grave nearby and plainly marked. He was Colonel of a Massachusetts Regt.[15] Captain Crocker on picket.

Tuesday, Oct. 20th. Reveille at 1 A.M. Moved at 3 A.M. without breakfasting, 2nd Division leading our brigade, leading 1st Division. I was not at all disturbed by the sudden move as I had been on the move all night—with an irregularity of the bowels. Indeed I am quite under the weather, bad water, I presume, is the cause. 8 A.M. halted near a piece of woods close to the Alexandria and Warrenton Pike at a place called Groveton. Here we remained until 12 M. and then moved forward and at 3.30 halted on a spur of the Bull Run Mountains about 5 miles from Warrenton and but a very short distance from New Baltimore.

On our way we passed through Buckton,[16] a place of about 12 houses occupied by a few old men and women. I asked one of these "sharps"— "Where does this road go to?" He replied, "It stays where it is, don't go anywhere." "My friend, you had better restrain your tongue when those Massachusetts men come along, they will go for you," one of the men remarked to the old cock, [and also] that he was quite surprised at the growth of this place since he last visited it, and wanted to know whether there was not an old "widdy woman" in the place who wanted a stout active young husband, sound of wind and limb. To which the old fellow laughingly replied that he attended to the wants of all the "widdy women" hereabouts and up to date had heard of no complaints from them as to a want of consideration on his part. This sally produced a burst of laughter and the boys gave the good natured old fellow three cheers.

~~There has been some heavy cavalry fighting hereabouts and all through~~ the country passed the roads were strewn with dead horses. I played out entirely just as we bivouaced, the first time since I have been in the service. Don't feel at all like myself. We occupy a very commanding position and the scenery is lovely, made more beautiful by the setting sun. George Slow reports our larder in bad condition, 7 eggs and pint of whiskey constituting the store. Crocker has just given me a strong "Hookers Retreat" heavily coated with nutmeg and recommends sleep as a restorer. I have abandoned my boots, they could no longer be worn, and have on a pair of government shoes, which, although large (Hospital 10's) are splendid for marching. My pants however look as if they were cut in highwater.

Wednesday, Oct. 21st. Clear. Had a splendid nights rest. Slept sundown to sunrise and feel "cat bird." This camp is known as "Camp Near New Baltimore." Wagons arrived from Gainesville, rebs having torn up the Warrenton R.R. Rations issued and Dress parade and company inspection held. Ordnance returns for 3rd quarter '63 made out. New Baltimore, Fauquier Co. Va. but a short distance from us—is a small affair of abt. 15 houses and like all the towns in this state is deserted and looks worn out. No orders to move, indicating—nothing, as we may get out of this at any moment, can't tell. Have had a good days rest and feel well, but a good deal soiled and travel stained.

Following the Bristoe Station Campaign, Lee had retired the bulk of his force south of the Rappahannock River and in the process had destroyed a 20-mile section of the Army of the Potomac's main supply line, the Orange & Alexandria Railroad. Meade followed the retreating Confederates cautiously, rebuilding the railroad as he went, and by early November the Federals were in position near Warrenton, ready to assume the offensive.[17]

Colonel Gwyn remained absent from the regiment, and Donaldson, certain that sparks would fly upon his return, was discreetly attempting to arrange a transfer out of the 118th. His plans, however, were put on indefinite hold on October 29 when Lieutenant Colonel Herring was taken ill and placed Donaldson in command of the regiment. "How strangely command alters one," Donaldson wrote soon after. "I have to drop all levity and call to aid all the dignity I possess." His tenure in command was to be brief, though, as he was soon ordered away in charge of the division pickets, and Capt. Dendy Sharwood of Company C, who had been serving on the brigade staff, was recalled to lead the 118th.

Camp Near New Baltimore, Va.
October 22, 1863

Dear Brother:

. . . You <u>astound</u> me with the rumour that Genl. Meade is to be removed. Great Scott! what in the world do the authorities want? Of course, I ought not to be surprised at anything, but I am at this time sure. Candidly, we feel every confidence in Meade, and if anyone succeeds him but McClellan, the dissatisfaction will be intense. I notice by the papers that Genl. Rosecrans has been displaced and Grant put in his place.[18] Well, the Western field of action is too far away for me to rightly and clearly understand the situation. Of course the comments of newspapers cannot be relied upon. Rosecrans has always done so well, until very recently, that I considered him an able man. I don't want to criticize, but really the Government takes great chances in its numerous changes of commanders.

Anticipating the row that will surely ensue between Gwyn and myself upon his return, I have been quietly at work with my resignation, and if he will but stay away a little while longer, I feel assured of success. Of course you must keep this entirely to yourself. My grand scheme is to be transferred to another branch of the service, at a lower grade rather than not at all, to the Cavalry. I think I can make it. Candidly Jacob, I am very, very unhappy here. With exception of a very few officers I have no friends in this regiment. I do not and cannot mingle and associate with all the officers, and my inter-course with some of them is so very limited that it amounts to positive unfriendliness, so that I heartily desire to get away. I feel that I could do good service with some other command. Why just to think of the indignity of having O'Neill thrust upon me as Major. He don't know an earthly thing about manoeuvering and handling men, nothing about the tactics, and to think of him being in command with the lives of men in his charge. Great Scott! when will Gwyn cease to degrade his own regt. and belittle it among the other commands of the brigade! We will be the laughing stock of the whole brigade with this awkward, hulking Irishman in charge.[19] . . .

You say my letters, while accounting for my own doings and that of brigade, division, corps and army, rarely mention that of my own company. Well, frankly I am really more of a regimental than a company officer. I would do better in the field than in the Line. I am concerned more for the credit of the regiment and brigade then I am for my little company command. My desires are broader than this. I am naturally interested and concerned about the movements of the Corps as a whole. I feel that I would like to have com-mand of something larger than a company. Besides there is nothing to write about regarding my co. It is the same with them, one day with another. They are like all others, a shiftless set, so unthinkingly improvident. They would try the patience of Job himself, for they are a childish set of babies, so dependent. I presume I am in a measure to blame for this—I have spoiled them.

Oct. 22. Clear. Still in camp near New Baltimore—no orders to move. A detail of 200 men, including 60 from our regt. has been made from each brigade of the division to repair the Rail Road & build bridges. Have put up tent & am making myself comfortable. Made an entire change of under-cloths after a good wash all over and feel much better thereby. Recd. two letters from home with all the news—Brother Jacob still prods me about my irreverence and takes me to task for "unseemly and unsoldierly conduct" & again reminds me that I am "degenerating." He fails to see that I am older both in years and experience, that all sentiment has vanished, that I at last see the humbuggery of the "Grand Army's" manoeuvering to cover the Capital and the ridiculousness of the strategy as directed from Washington.

As an illustration—I as well as all the army know that had it been the desire to do so, no better chance to fight Lee could have been had than at Broad Run. This cannot be disguised or hidden from the men, they are an intelligent body. Our retreat from that place, to my mind, was simply disgraceful. Every-thing was in our favor. We were recovered from the Gettysburg fatigues, understood Lee's movement to be a "turning" one, were well posted in a posi-tion of great natural strength & advantage, had fought a successful fight at Bristoe, and above all, Lee [was] the assailant. Beside too, he has lost prestige, his name is no longer a terror, on the contrary, we know he has lost his grip by underrating us, even to calling us "these people"—contemptuous words unworthy the great man he is said to be. He deigns not even to call us soldiers & men. When a General does this, then is the time to meet him. Ours was at Broad Run. We could have beaten his army, we all feel confident of this, and the two Bull Run's could have been retrieved most signally.[20] I admit, of course, that the retreat as a whole was masterly, but we don't want to retreat. We lose heart & become demoralized. Thus it is—I have "degenerated." I am learning to become critical.

Have written Chief of Ordnance relative to arms & accoutrements belonging to my company, a discrepancy existing between previous & present statements. In order to harmonize things made affidavit before acting Adjt. Walters to effect that I abandoned two muskets on the march. Ordnance must be kept all right. Now feel a great quietude both in mind & body.

Poor old John Thomas, grumbling and grumbling, went along with the fatigue party, and his parting injunction was not to drink up all the rum in his absence. He will be gone two days, poor fellow. However I am told there are plenty of handsome females in the locality where he will be, and with his handsome youthful face and manly form a conquest will surely be made.

12 M. dined on hard tack, coffee & fresh beef, afterwards wrote Lt. Batchelder a short acc't. of our doings. This is a lovely day & strangely enough, I feel homesick. How beautiful Philadelphia must look. Visited Brigade and had a "Joe Hooker" with Sharwood. On returning looked over my album—they were all there—my girls.

2 P.M. Received a line from Thomas. He is about 6 miles from camp building corduroy roads. . . .

3 P.M. Shaved off my beard and now only have a mostache & Presbyterian whiskers. Paid ten cents for the job. Crocker says I look very youthful. Fussed about till 4 P.M. then fell to reading the "Christian Instructor," a paper sent Crocker each week by an admiring devine, Rev. McKnight of Philada. I must say while its purpose is certainly good it is not the kind of literature that finds ready circulation in camp. Passed it over to the Chaplain, it may be he can glean something new from it for his next encounter with the "toughs" of the 118th. Major Herring spent half hour with me and upon leaving took my corn cob pipe, a serious loss, for me and my pipe are two fearful old smokers. Usual company drill & dress parade. Retired at 7.30 P.M.

Friday, Oct. 23rd. Cloudy. Arose at 5 A.M. and washed my head with some of Thomas' whiskey. My hair has of late been falling out, rather a coincidence for so young a man. Brain worry, I presume, not piety the cause. After breakfast had mostache cut off lest it fall out also. After guard mount Major Herring ordered camp to be regularly laid out, officers tents on a line, company streets at proper distances & camp cleaned up generally. Herring recd. his commission as Lt. Colonel by mail from Gov. Curtin. Visited brigade, had a "Joe Hooker" with Sharwood, my own mixing. Learned we would probably move camp about a quarter of a mile beyond for better ground. There must be some mistake about this as we cannot be better located. To day it is cold and blustery, threatening rain. Proposed visiting Camp 155th P.V. but was refused permission to do so as <u>Lt. Col</u>. Herring is detailed on Court-Martial and wants me in camp. Fatigue party returned this P.M. with Thomas as mad as a hornet. He said he would rather fight than build roads. . . .

<u>Saturday, Oct. 24th</u>. Raining like Old Sam Hill. Compelled to so closely hug quarters and so cold that I remained in bed pretty much all the morning to keep warm. No rumors of moving, no camp gossip. Busily engaged writing up orders & fixing my papers generally. There is a good deal of this kind of work for a Captain. It is true I have a company clerk but I would just as soon do the work myself as to explain it to him. Col. Herring recd. notice of Col. Prevost's transfer to Invalid Corps, and of the discharge of Lt. DeBuck, for the good of the service, I presume, as he was utterly worthless and of no account or use as an officer.[21]

2 P.M. The "General" most unexpectedly sounded and at 5 P.M. we pulled out into the rain and mud. The roads in a frightful condition, knee deep with mud, so that slow progress was made, certainly not more than a mile an hour, not so much as that, I should say. I soon became drenched and as I had no boots my feet were soaking wet. 8.45 halted & bivouaced at Auburn.

<u>Sunday, Oct. 25th</u>. Clear. Last night was a dreadful experience—so wet & cold. Now, my dear brother, cannot you perceive why it is I "degenerate"? What earthly purpose was saved by this movement so late in the day—why not let the men have their shelter tents until morning & then move to this place? Certainly there was no emergency existing. One of my men, as he shivered over a sickly little fire, remarked in my hearing, "The Army of the Potomac is a damn humbug," to which another sang a reply in a voice tremulous with cold, "So say we all of us." It is clear and cold this morning. I took a Joe Hooker before breakfast to warm me up and then repasted on hard tack, pork & coffee, after which I took up my waist belt three holes, am getting so thin. We are in the mud ankle deep. Without adding it here the blueness of the atmosphere from curses loud & deep at our unhappy condition can be imagined.

12 M. General again sounded and for an hour and a half we floundered about in the "muck," as O'Neill says, 'til a contiguous wood was reached. It was all the while hard by, but we had to approach it in a soldierly manner. A great change for the better and a consequent revival of the men's spirits. Head Quarter tents not yet arrived, no shelter tents erected, men awaiting further instructions. Huge fires built & everybody steaming, like a laundry. I have an immense pile of oak blazing before my quarters. It feels so good. Auburn, "sweet village of the plain" I endeavored to find, but beyond an old delapidated machine shop could see nothing of it. We are delightfully situated in a dense woods, sheltered from the northern blasts. We are cozy

without our tents. I love a bivouac in the timber. Chaplain O'Neill preached a first class sermon in the evening, so stirring, so full of eloquence & pathos, abounding with rhetorical oratory. I never before appreciated his eloquence as on this occasion for I was asleep and didn't hear a word of it, neither did his uproar at all disturb my blissful slumber. Yet I am told he roared like the "Behemoth of Holy Writ." . . .

Monday, Oct. 26. Clear. . . . I slept well last night before the huge fire & was not at all inconvenienced by the cold.

12 M. With George Slow visited a large house a mile distant from camp. It was a lovely place, well shaded and beautifully situated, being off the road and removed from straggling soldiers. It was occupied by three females, one of whom was quite young, and upon my knocking at the door they all appeared. They were not particularly attractive, being dowdy and careless looking. I asked whether they would permit my man to grind an axe with the grindstone I saw in the yard, to which the young "beauty" with saffron hair and sore eyes replied "she didn't keep grindstones for Abe Lincoln." I for the first time lost temper with a woman and told her I regretted she was not a man that I could tweak her nose, that I was also sorry to find petticoats protecting so venemous a tongue, that she certainly represented the class nigroes term "poor white trash." She called me a "nasty Yankee cur" and I retorted by adding something about freckled faced, sorrel topped, sore eyed old quilt. I then directed George to use the grindstone and afterwards to break it. Goodness! but I was angry. I just stormed about the grounds "taking stock" & noted sheep, turkeys, ducks and chickens. I then went to the window and bawled in that I would send my men over and clean them out with orders to burn the house if they gave any impudence. The little sore eyed pullet wasn't afraid, she said, "Do it you dirty Yankee thief, do it."

At this juncture a wounded reb hobbled out on the porch and said although he was an inmate he was not related to the people of the house. He had been wounded in Kentucky and was stopping with this family for a time, that he certainly appreciated my feelings and offered an apology for the girls' rudeness, that I must attribute it to youth and bitterness caused by the war, that I had been respectful & should have been so treated and allowed to use the grindstone when I had clearly the right to do so unasked. He urged my doing so without further ceremony & that he was ashamed of these persons conduct and trusted I would not carry into effect my threat to burn the house. At these kindly words I surrendered and ascending the porch entered into conversation with him. I found him very civil and gentlemanly & frankly told him how uniformly insulting the females of the country were, how that I had invariably taken their abuse without retort, except in this instance, that I had been surprised into making a threat I had no intention of carrying out.

During this time George had finished his task and in skirmishing about picked up a dozen fresh eggs, after which I took leave of the civil fellow, wishing him a speedy recovery and shook off the dust of my feet on the message. It is surprising, the pluck of these women. I attribute it to the fact that they have learned we always respect females, and they take advantage of it.

Capt. Donegan held Dress Parade. It was bungled through some how. Donegan is not now nor ever will be a soldier of distinction. He don't look it either, the good old man. He is a close fisted old chap too. I once asked him some legal question, and would you believe it, he said as it was not a

Capt. Richard Donegan, Company B, 118th Pennsylvania Volunteers. Don Enders Collection, USAMHI.

military question but one of law, he would not answer it unless I gave him a fee of $5—Fact. Well, my opinion is if he is no better Lawyer than he is a soldier he wouldn't earn many fees of that amount.

<u>Thursday, Oct. 27th</u>. Didn't sleep much to speak of last night—it was so cold. Crocker had the best of it, he was in the middle, Thomas & I on the flanks. While it is true Crocker throws out a great deal of heat, it was neutralized by the keen wind which blew under the sides of the shelter tent, so that I was all but frozen. However it is my turn tonight for the middle place. Lt. or rather <u>Capt</u>. Kelly dropped in at our quarters & told us of his promotion and said in the envelop addressed to him was commissions for Lt. Bayne[22] as 1st Lt. of A and Sgt. Ashbrook[23] as 2nd Lt. of K, Crocker's Co., the latter a most excellent appointment. Ashbrook is a soldier and a gentleman, a very scholarly fellow and will make a most creditable officer. Gwyn ignored Herring entirely by sending to Kelly the commissions of these gentlemen. It is another evidence of his littleness. . . .

12 M. Wagons arrived with tents and baggage and if "Old Four Eyes" will permit and "Mr. Hawkins," as we call the cold, has no objection, a happy and comfortable night will be passed. . . . The best information I have as to [John's] whereabouts I gleaned from prisoners—Brockenridges brigade, Heth's Division, Ewell's Corps. If this be true then he was in the repulse sustained by that brigade in the 1st days fight at Gettysburg and was in the charge with Picket on the 3rd day.[24] Of course there is nothing authentic in this. I rarely see prisoners from Ewell's Corps. Hill's division of Longstreet's Corps is invariably in our front and appears to have been so always, so that we are actually on <u>intimate</u> terms.[25] The prisoners always appear to know us and say, "You'ns are 5th Corps, ain't you'ns? We'uns are always in front of you'ns," and appear to recognize in us friends. I have recd. blanks for pay rolls and will have a fearful job making them out. Clothing acct. with government to be settled this month also. See heavy work before me.

Well our friend Lee is again behind the Rappahannock, and as the weather is now settled, the wind having "hauled" not "backed" to Westward, a campaign can well be again inaugurated. We are prepared for it, well prepared for another <u>run</u> back to Washington just as soon as Lee's men are rested. All he has to do is to put the cavalry on our communication and, "presto," back we skedaddle. There don't appear to be any fight in the Army of the Potomac, or rather I shouldn't say that, for the men will fight, it is the leaders that are cautious. We will never do much until some determined man gets command & then catching us by the back of the neck, so to speak, holds us up and forces the fighting. However I have no right to comment. Genl. Meade is a good man and knows best. No orders, no news. Took a Joe Hooker at 6.30 & retired at 7 P.M. In the middle this time.

Wednesday, Oct. 28th. Clear. Didn't sleep well. Not withstanding was in the middle I was cold all night long. This too with two blankets over me. The wind blew the smoke from the camp fire directly into the tent which almost suffocated me. Crocker & Thomas slept like logs. . . .

Thursday, Oct. 29th. Clear. Had a refreshing nights sleep, arose at daylight and took a Joe Hooker in accordance with rules of the Mess. Lt. Col. Herring, who had been complaining for several days, was too unwell to leave bed this morning. He sent for me and put me in command.

12 M. I took full command of the Regiment in pursuance of orders issued by him. At 4.30 ordered and held Dress Parade which passed off creditably. At "officers to the front and centre" I explained the situation and asked for their support. Each and every one of them afterwards expressed their confidence in their young commander. How strangely command alters one. I have to drop all levity and call to aid all the dignity I possess. My heart is full of sympathy for Herring, he must be sick indeed to relinquish command during a campaign not yet ended. I am mindful too of my responsibility. Busy all day with Pay Rolls. As there is now nothing of interest to write about I propose hereafter to abandon this journal. Orders recd. to move at 7 A.M. Not withstanding my position as commander, I retired as usual with my friend Hooker.

Friday, Oct. 30th. Cloudy. The "general" sounded before daylight but we did not move before 10 A.M., and after a pleasant march of about four hours through a beautiful country, up hill and dale, we camped at 3 Mile Station on the Warrenton R.R. but a short distance from Warrenton Junction. It is a lovely situation and one in which I feel quite at home, we have been here so often. I was so busy with handling the Regt. that I neglected noting the exact time of our departure and arrival at this place. Col. Herring very sick and has asked for Surgeon's Certificate. Major Hooper, 1st Michigan,[26] assigned to muster the regiment. I procured some excellent butter from an old Irishman living at the switch. His habitation is a perfect picture of an Irishman's shanty with his pigs, dogs & pipe. Retired with faithful Joe after a days hard brain worry. I was so anxious to have the command behave well under me, and they did too.

Sunday, Oct. 31st. Rained like the devil all night, but broke away about 8 o'clock this A.M. Orders recd. for 4 pioneers with shovels to report to

Brigade Hd. Qrs. Lt. Col. Herring ordered me to fill the detail. Regt. mustered for pay by Maj. Hopper. Recd. orders to command Division Pickets. Had a serious talk with Col. Herring and suggested the recall of Capt. Sharwood to the regt.[27] I would be gone 3 days, probably, and as he is the ranking officer he ought to be placed in command. Herring thought so too. Sharwood has never been in command, was absent at Gettysburg, and now that he (Herring) is sick, it is an opportunity to establish the gallant Captain's reputation. He finally said he would see about it and I left feeling very anxious indeed abt. him. Should anything happen [to] my dear friend it would be a calamity beyond all others to me. He is very dear to me and I honor and respect him above all men.

It was with a heavy heart I led the 350 men to the picket line and relieved Capt. Allen, 44th N.Y.[28] He had placed his line with excellent judgment, skirting timber & covering the country from the high ground so judiciously selected. The line is nearly straight and was the most systematically and carefully arranged of any in my experience. . . . Visited pickets and outposts at 10 P.M. and slept part of the night. . . .

Sunday, Nov. 1st. Clear day. All quiet last night, nothing new today. Very lonely, not even the chaplain to devil us. Visited picket line twice and Grand Rounds at 10 P.M.

Monday, Nov. 2. Nothing of importance transpired. Splendid day and all quiet along the line. I did not sleep at all during the night. Visited outposts at 10 P.M. and fussed about afterwards among the Grand Reserve. I felt anxious somehow. In the morning word was received that Lt. Col. Herring had received leave of absence and would go home at once. Capt. Dendy Sharwood in command of the regiment and myself relieved. I am glad of this. Sharwood is an able man of middle age, scholarly attainments and manly presence. It is fitting he should have command.

Tuesday, Nov. 3rd. Splendid day. Word recd. that Herring would start for home this A.M. Expect to be relieved this morning. Recd. a funny letter from Batchelder.

10 A.M. Am relieved from picket and returned to camp. Found Herring had left for home in charge of Father Egan.[29] Washed, shaved and reported to Capt. Sharwood. Congratulated him and assured him of my support. He replied, "Poney, I will need your help." I took a Joe Hooker with him as the first evidence of the kind of support I would give him.

CHAPTER 10

Rappahannock Station and Mine Run

November 9–December 3, 1863

*T*he early November days were growing shorter and colder, and the soldiers in both armies surely would have been content to settle into camp for the winter. But Meade was under pressure to initiate an offensive against the Rebels ("The President desires that you will prepare to attack Lee's army," Halleck had telegraphed him in late October[1]), and by dawn on November 7 the Federals were poised for another strike.

The Confederates were strung out along the southern bank of the Rappahannock, but Lee had chosen to leave a bridgehead north of the river at Rappahannock Station, hoping that if Meade attempted a crossing he would be forced to divide his numerically superior force to deal with the stronghold.[2] Meade's plan was to divide his army into two wings (as Lee had wished), with one wing forcing a crossing of the river at Kelly's Ford, and the other attacking the fortified position at Rappahannock Station. Once both wings had effected a crossing, they were to link up and advance on Brandy Station.

Maj. Gen. John Sedgwick, commander of the 6th Corps, was given the responsibility of carrying the bridgehead at Rappahannock Station and was to use his own corps and the 5th Corps to carry out his objective. For Donaldson, the advance across the open fields north of the river was one of the more memorable experiences of his war service: "I gazed upon a pageant such as was never before seen by me, and a sight never to be forgotten by any one who beheld it."

Camp 3 miles from Rappahannock
Nov. 9th, 1863

Dear Brother:

In action at Rappahannock Station—am unhurt. Division on left 6th Corps. Charged over open fields exposed to fearful shelling. Lost only one man from my Company shot thro' the hand. Men struck on either side of me. It took good troops to face the shelling we recd. 6th Corps did the actual storming of the enemy's works, Got there first or was intended to do so. Will write full acct. as soon as I can. We are manoeuvering in the enemy's country, so look out for news. Sharwood commanded and did it bravely and well. Made a good name for himself. Regiment behaved admirably. Genl. Meade was cheered yesterday for first time, but not by us. We <u>stood fast</u>—no cheer from this Veteran brigade. Can't see it. If there is any good newspaper account of the fight send it to me. Want to see all about it. Love to Auntie. Have you seen Lt. Col. Herring & if so how is he?

⊱⊶⊷⊶○⊷⊶⊷⊰

Camp 118th P.V.
Kelly's Ford, Va.
November 11th, 1863

Dear Brother:

Your letter of the 7th inst. has just been handed me, and I am rejoiced at the blessed continuance in good health of the loved ones at home. In the newspapers I notice very little is said about our brigade in the late action at Rappahannock Station. That we participated prominently in that affair our loss shows plainly. While not nearly so large as the 119th P.V. or, indeed, as that of many other regiments in Elmaker's brigade, 6th Corps, still our loss is considerable considering that it was Elmaker's brigade that did the actual storming of the enemy's works.[3] Justice to our gallant regiment and to its gallant commander, Captain Dendy Sharwood ([Lt. Col.] Herring having left for home on the 3rd quite sick) compels me to give you a detailed account of the part taken by us in the battle, and the handsome manner with which the First Division, and indeed the whole 5th Corps, behaved on that occasion. I will endeavor to give you all the incidents which came under my observation in this action. It seems useless to write fully of our campaigns, movements and battles, because you at home generally know more of what we are doing at the front than we ourselves, and you will scarcely credit it when I tell you that after an engagement or movement of any kind, we always look eagerly for the [Philadelphia] "Inquirer" to find out what we have been doing and whether we have been successful or not, because many and many a time, when we were positive our movement had been <u>unsuccessful</u>, the newspapers tell us quite the contrary, and that we have <u>gained a great and substantial triumph</u>. Well, it is all right, I suppose, but I would like it better if all victories were as this one, a success that all know to be a real one, and no newspaper victory.

My last letter was from "Camp 3 Mile Station," Warrenton R.R., where we remained doing usual camp duties until the morning of the 7th. The weather had been generally quite pleasant and with exception of a remarkably fine brigade drill in the afternoon of the 6th, which did great credit to Captain Sharwood, we lazily passed the hours away.

The sun went down on the evening of the 6th in all its golden grandeur and "by the bright tracts of its fiery chariot, gave token of a goodly day the morrow"—(Shakespeare, Richard III eve before the battle of Bosworth field, I don't know if I have quoted it quite correctly, but look it up and let me know). There was not thought of hostilities or even a movement of any kind on our part, no one dreamed of the short, sharp and decisive campaign about to be inaugurated. On the contrary, we had retired to our beds speculating on the possibility of remaining here for the winter, and our minds were in composure, rest and ease, certainly far removed from battle, wounds and sudden death.

Thus it was that at 4.30 the ringing tones of the division bugle, on this cold Saturday morning of the 7th, sounding the division call, broke in upon our slumbers, rousing us from a deep sleep to eagerly inquire what it meant. Scrambling out in the dim light of the early morning, we were saluted again with reveille from the same bugle, followed at once by "pack up" or more properly "the General." The brigade and regimental buglers now took up the call and our camp was soon a scene of busy stir, men running about every where, and all anxiously inquiring what we were about to do or where going. Certainly it must be a forward movement, they said, as the enemy were known to be far away towards, if not actually beyond, the Rappahannock. Indeed the very fact of using the bugle to arouse the troops showed plainly the enemy was not within hearing. Soon word was received from Captain Sharwood that we were to move forward towards the Rappahannock in order, as he thought, to winter near that stream, an opinion seemingly born out by the fact that cooked rations had not been ordered. We were merely changing camping ground was the final conclusion arrived at by the officers grouped together in consultation.

At about 6 A.M. we were on the road and commenced marching over that same old hateful, well trodden, dusty track between Warrenton and the Rappahannock along the rail road so often described to you, every inch of which was unrelieved by anything pleasant for the eye to rest upon, with nothing but dust, dust the entire way, and not a drop of water to be had until the river was reached. Our regiment was on the advance and at a brisk pace we pushed along the Rail Road. The entire 5th Corps was in motion and we learned that the 6th Corps had preceded us an hour or more, but by a different road far to the right, and we saw nothing of them. For a mere change of camp, the early start and rapid marching of two immense army corps was rather a curious coincidence, thought I, "but did not the sounding bugle this morning portend peace and prove conclusively the enemy at least a days march away," still argued the officers. So on we trudged, all suspicions at rest, and had it been on any other than this road, it would have been a glorious tramp, the weather so cool and bracing, the men full of life and spirits as they moved along at a better pace that I had seen them do for many a long day. It seemed to be their desire to accomplish as much as possible of this miserable road before the sun was up to add its rays to the thick clouds of dust enveloping us. Soon Bealton Station was reached, or rather what was known to have been that place, for now everything was changed. I never saw such utter destruction as had been wrought here. Since I last saw it, whether by our troops or by the enemy I cannot say, but certain it is that the buildings were all burned, the rails torn up and carried off, ties burned, telegraph poles cut down, destruction and ruin everywhere.

Nothing of moment occurred until we halted a little before noon at the foot of a thickly wooded ridge, or hill, or hardly a hill either, but an unusual elevation of ground from among the miles of dead level surrounding it. As our division came up it took ground and stacked arms to the left of the line of battle of the 6th Corps, which was already on the ground and had leisurely awaited our arrival. The other divisions, also, as they arrived, moved off to the left and took position in line, so that as far as the eye could see to the left, the bright stacks of muskets extended, whilst the men lay down behind them. About this time some of my men, seeing there was not disposition to move forward, asked permission to cook coffee. Knowing they had had but a scant breakfast, I did not forbid them doing so, although I had received no orders as to how long we would be likely to halt here. Soon after, little individual fires were started here and there, the smoke of which no sooner commenced curling among the trees than a staff officer came dashing along, ordering the fires out and directing Captain Sharwood to report to brigade Head Quarters. The men threw themselves down upon the ground once more and contented themselves with munching hard tack. I sat down in front of the stacks and watched the scene around me. There was a good deal of moving backwards and forwards among the troops immediately to the right of us, a concentration, as it were, of a whole division, a heavy massing of men. But this soon subsided and we remained quietly watching and waiting for orders to go into camp, or else to move on again. This state of suspense lasted a good while, but finally we were ordered to "fall in" and officers to report to Captain Sharwood at the front and centre of the regiment. My surprise knew no bounds when informed that the enemy was just ahead, strongly entrenched, and that General Sedgwick, in command of both corps, intended storming their works. I do not think that we could have been more astonished had we learned that the war was over and we were to return home at once. The men, also, when informed of the work before them, were dumb founded. However, we did not have long to speculate upon the news, as we at once commenced forming line of battle, which when done, we again rested for a while in order, as we soon learned, to let the extreme left of our corps swing around in advance of the centre and right and envelop the enemy. I presume the same was done by the 6th Corps' right flank.

About 3 o'clock the order to load was given, and immediately after to move forward, which we did in good order. After going a short distance we commenced descending the other side of the elevation, and halted beyond the same in an open country, which as far as we could see in front of us, was dead level, perfectly barren and without shelter of any kind. The enemy's works were at least a full mile in front, quite extensive and formidable, occupying a ridge commanding every inch of ground over which we would have to pass to the attack. The rail road ran from us to them in nearly a straight line, and the right of our regiment, which was also the right of the Corps, rested upon but did not cross it. The ground was covered with a growth of long thick grass, from among which in the near distance could be seen the heads and pieces of our men forming the skirmish line. It struck me at the time that the line was exceptionally heavy, the men being so close together. Away beyond at the distance of a quarter mile or so, the enemy's skirmishers could be seen, who made no attempt to bring on a fight, but seemed merely to watch our movements. What a spectacle from the enemy's point of view was presented, even though it was of their foe preparing to assault them. Our line to the left extended in a beautiful and graceful curve, with left flank well advanced towards the enemy. The State and National Colors fluttering in the wind along the line, and the glistening pieces of the men as they stood with arms at the right shoulder ready for the word to move forward, was, indeed, a glorious and at the same time an awfully grand sight to gaze upon. The enemy still remained silent, apparently waiting until we came nearer before opening their guns.

At this juncture General Sykes rode up and inquired who commanded the regiment. Captain Sharwood, who remained mounted throughout the fight, and [was] the only regimental officer in our entire division who did so, rode up to him, and saluting, said that he did. General Sykes then told him that we would move at a quick pace, which his regiment must set, that the corps would guide on us; that the right of our regiment was under no circumstances to cross the Rail Road, but was to follow it as a guide only; that the 6th Corps left would rest upon the other side of it, and that the Captain must be exceedingly careful and not allow his men to incline to the right and interfere with the other corps, and that he would hold him personally responsible should they do so and jam the other troops; that it was important in the movement about to take place that the division on our right should be kept in good order and free from entanglement by the near approach of other commands. All this was said in my hearing, and is nearly verbatim. He then put spurs to his horse and with his staff rode out to a slight rise in the ground in front of the 6th Corps and nearly up to the enemy's skirmishers. This elevation slightly protected the 6th Corps from the ricocheting shots that were soon fired by the enemy. Captain Sharwood then gave the command to "guide centre" and cautioned the color sergeant to be careful and move directly to the front. I, being a senior captain and in command of the left centre Co., was now, at this command, obliged to take position in the front rank between Co.'s C and H, the two centre companies, and next [to] the colors, which were on the left of Co. C, color company. I was separated from them by one man only, Corporal Davis, color guard.[4] The Captain (who, by the way, always calls me "pony" because Lieutenant Thomas and I, both very young men, wear jackets alike, tight fitting and of the "nobby" staff pattern, as you know, very comfortable but in no sense regulation), taking position immediately in front about ten paces from the colors, turned on his horse and said, "Pony, I will rely upon you to see that the colors go forward in a straight line, and that they be kept well to the front." Assuring him I would do my best to keep them up, I turned and took a glance at the warlike scene.

It was an indescribable spectacle, grand, stirring, impressive, and from my position in the centre of two corps, I gazed upon a pageant such as was never before seen by me, and a sight never to be forgotten by any one who beheld it. Upon our right was Colonel Ellmaker's brigade, 6th Corps, in mass, and it appeared that the whole division was also heavily massed; certainly they were in several lines deep and close together. The burnished arms and every bit of metal on this splendid mass of men glistening in the nearly setting sunlight; the colors and lines so well dressed, and the faces of the men aglow with excitement, the ceaseless riding back and forth of mounted officers giving final orders made the blood tingle in my veins with a sensation of admiration at the picture. With our Corps the view was somewhat different; here the men were already formed in line, standing quietly gazing at the enemy's works, while the stillness of death reigned over all, yet the glow was on them also, its golden rays sparkling on the mica dust covering their uniforms made them appear as though they were profusely powdered with gold dust. In fact the whole landscape was covered with a golden glory. There was one sight that rather took the poetry out of my feelings when I recognized it, and that was the long line of stretcher bearers close up to the

Capt. Dendy Sharwood, Company C, commander of the 118th Pennsylvania at Rappahannock Station. He died November 21, 1863, as a result of exposure incurred in the field. THE CIVIL WAR LIBRARY & MUSUEM.

rear of the line of battle. The drummers and other non-combatants, much against their will, had been compelled to shoulder these implements and follow us as we advanced. Had they known when we halted that a fight was on the tapis, they would [have] made themselves scarce in no time.

If you remember, in one of my letters I mentioned the severe manner I had handled Private Shields, a substitute of my company, for drunkenness and mutiny. Well, afterwards, when I visited him in the hospital, he gave me warning in his brutal way that he would remember me in the next fight we would be in together. That, of course, meant he would kill me, a threat I at the time paid no attention to, as I did not think it likely we would be together again, because I felt sure he would die of his hurt. However, the man got well and was sent back to me, and at this very moment, being the tallest man in the company, was on the extreme right of it and next to me. Whatever made me think of his threat just then I cannot say, but I did, and I turned and looked at the fellow. He was as calm as a May morning, perfectly cool and rigid, in fact a splendid looking soldier. He appeared not to notice my scrutiny, so I said to him, "Shields, do you remember threatening me when I visited you in the hospital?" I had drawn my pistol at the thought of him, and was deliberating what to do. He said he did. "Well," said I, "I think you will have enough to do in a few minutes to protect your own life without attempting mine. I could shoot you down like a dog if I chose to, and be justified in the act, but you are not worth the exertion. Let the enemy waste their ammunition in killing you, for I won't!" I then dismissed him from my thoughts as the word came to move forward.

Our skirmishers arose from the grass and commenced firing, while the enemy lost no time in falling back. The whole line now stepped briskly forward, guiding splendidly on the colors and keeping well together. I never saw a handsomer sight, in fact, I never before saw the advance of so vast a line of battle. We had not gone very far when a puff of smoke was seen to arise from the rebel works, and a shot, well directed, struck the ground about 20 yards from our line, ricocheting over our heads and burst just beyond the stretcher bearers; another and another followed, all bursting close to the line. I was soon covered with the dusty soil dashed in our faces by the bounding shot, each of which seemed aimed at the colors. Unwavering, the line swept on, skirmishers well to the front, moving rapidly with arms aport. At every discharge we could see the flash from the cannon, they were now firing rapidly, and instantly the projectile burst near us. Ball after ball, shell after shell struck in quick succession, now whistling a few feet above or striking the ground and bounding over us, others tearing and shrieking along the ground, their bursting fragments singing in the air.[5] The first man struck in our regiment was Private McCandless of Captain Crocker's Co. K, his foot being taken off at the ankle by a shell.[6] He was rather an old and spare fellow who required a deal of urging to get along on the marches, and upon a former occasion he had abandoned his musket so often that at last Captain Crocker charged him with it. As he fell to the ground a rush was made for him by the frightened stretcher bearers, who were anxious to get away, and a fight ensued resulting in his being captured by several of them, and as he was borne away he yelled at the top of his voice for Captain Crocker to see that he still held on to his musket. This funny incident was told me by Crocker after the fight, I did not see it myself.

The firing now became very severe, and it was with the greatest difficulty the alignment could be preserved. The pressure also from the left was something fearful, as the men, for shelter, inclined towards the little hill in front, the same towards which General Sykes rode a short time before. Whilst I was shouting to the men to resist pressure from the left, and urging the color sergeant to keep steady to the front, Corporal Davis, who was shoulder to shoulder with me, was struck in the chest by a fragment of shell, and so tightly was he wedged between myself and the color sergeant that we carried him along for quite a distance before room could be had to let him drop. The colors were repeatedly struck and torn by fragments of shell, and the flying dirt dashed in our faces was like hail stones. The right of the regiment was now forced over the Rail Road despite all efforts of Captain Sharwood and the officers to prevent it, and at once commenced to jam the 6th Corps, which up to that time had been fired upon but little. Their alignment was soon broken and began to waver backwards and forwards as the men sought to rectify it. The enemy, perceiving this, opened upon them a tremendous shelling, which with wonderful accuracy burst in their midst. A great deal of disorder ensued but the men kept right on, striving to keep an unbroken front. Captain Sharwood was in a perfect frenzy and rushed his horse about, calling on the men to be calm, to be steady, and feel to the left. He also directed me to move ahead with the colors, which I did, and although the greater part of the regiment was forced across the rail road, the colors never were. It seemed to me that the enemy increased their firing and planted shells thickly among us.

About this time I noticed my friend Captain Crocker, and he was a grand sight to behold, as with overcoat closely buttoned around him, trousers stuffed in boots, swinging his sword about with his great muscular arm, he looked the very image of the daring soldier he was, as he stalked in front of his company cheering and directing the men to keep the alignment and not be forced across the rail road. A moment after we suddenly came upon a wide muddy ditch that traversed the country directly in our path. We were hastened into it without much time for thought by a sweeping discharge, and were at once floundering knee deep in slime. This fearful hole had not been noticed as it was hidden by the long grass through which we marched. Our whole line halted here and awaited further orders. Clambering to the opposite side of the ditch, I found Crocker standing and looking to the rear. So did I. I saw a section of brass guns coming obliquely across the field, from the right of our line, "hell to split," the horses lashed to madness, straining every nerve as they dashed along making the guns and caissons fairly jump from the ground. "Isn't that great?" said Crocker, and it was. Taking position on the left of our division, they went into battery and commenced firing with wonderful rapidity and accuracy, sweeping the enemy's parapets, making the dust leap up in great columns and driving the Rebs from their guns. The skirmishers who had passed the ditch and sharpshooters from our regiment soon made it impossible for the Rebs to use their guns.

After a little while, a column of troops from our right at the double quick moved up to the skirmish line, quickly followed by another column also at the double quick. The entire division on our right, it seemed to me, also moved forward at the double, and we then realized it was for them to storm the works, and right well they did it. A cheer and shout arose as the columns rushed forward, and the division following also taking up the cheer, sprang forward on the run. We were ordered to remain fast and were a witness of what followed. With cheers and yells the line moved rapidly forward amid a terrific crash of artillery and musketry. The enemy lined their works and poured a steady fire upon them. They worked like devils to overcome the onset, but with headlong fury the skirmishers rushed into and over the dry ditch surrounding the works, and clambering up the scoop, closed with the foe. We could see the hand to hand fight that ensued in the embrasures and on the parapet, the bayonet being freely used, until the supporting columns, like a great torrent, swarmed upon the works and rushed upon the cannon just as they were discharged, men being blown to atoms and death and carnage scattered broadcast. Yet the assault was not stayed, the gunners were slain and the cannon turned upon their late owners who were fighting fiercely to keep off the assailants.[7]

What followed was told me by an officer who participated in the final struggle. Up to the time of actual assault the Confederates had lost comparatively few men; there now ensued a bloody scene, one which generally follows successful storming of works. All orders were unheeded or at least not heard amidst the din and racket, and the resistance had so infuriated our men that they attacked the enemy with great fury. It seemed for a time that nothing could restrain them and they dashed upon the foe bayonetting and beating them down right and left, amidst the cries of officers to cease fighting and for the enemy to surrender. The curses and bitter oaths of the combatants, the dreadful noise and din was appalling. Then the left of our corps suddenly appeared and took the Rebs in rear, completely enveloping them, capturing the pontoons and cutting off all chance for retreat. They now broke and ran for the river, but were met by a solid wall of advancing troops steadily closing in on them. All resistance at once ceased and they threw down their arms and surrendered.

It was now nearly dark, the sun having gone down leaving a dull red light in the western sky suggestive of the bloody deed just enacted. The work of securing the prisoners and caring for the wounded at once commenced. Our loss had been severe and that of the enemy also. Indeed, the works seemed covered with bleeding and mangled forms alike of friend and foe. The prisoners were nearly 2,000 in numbers, belonging to Early's Division, Ewell's Corps, being the famous Louisiana Tigers, and Hoke's brigade of North Carolina Troops, all commanded by Colonel Godwin. They were loud in their praises of the handsome manner their works had been carried, and did not seem at all dismayed or cast down by their unfortunate condition. "Boys," shouted one, "we are all going to Washington to live on soft bread and fresh beef," and they all cheered.[8]

Shortly after the battle, General Sykes rode up, asked for Captain Sharwood, and said in language anything but that of an officer and gentleman, "Why in the hell did you allow your men to cross the Rail Road?" This so incensed the Captain that replying in his forceful way, he said, "General, if Jesus Christ himself had been in command of this regiment, he could not have prevented the men from seeking cover." "Well," replied the General, "if Jesus Christ could not have prevented [it], I am sure it was beyond your power to do so." Captain Sharwood was now the recipient of congratulations from the officers, this being his first fight, and shortly after from brigade and division commanders. He certainly displayed marked bravery and ability, leading the command close up to the enemy's works in a manner that inspired us all. To me the greatest wonder was that either he or his horse was not torn to pieces, the shells seemingly to burst beneath them. I shall never forget the hearty manner [in which] he took my hand after the fight, saying, "Pony, I am glad you are unhurt, from the way the shells burst around the colors at times, I was sure you were hit, and always felt so much relieved when I saw you step through the smoke again, for I depended on you to have the colors go straight up to the enemy. Thank you Pony, thank you for carrying out my orders." Think of the modesty of the man, giving me praise when it was he himself that had heroically managed with skill a trying situation, and won the confidence and respect of the men. This, too, was his first experience as a regimental commander. The good opinion of a man like Sharwood is worth a good deal to me. It makes a wonderful difference who commands in time of trouble.

The loss in our regiment was not so large as that of the 18th and 22nd Massachusetts, because the right of our line was protected after crossing the rail road.[9] It was quite plain to me now that the advance of the 5th Corps in the open field was intended to attract the enemy's attention, while the columns of assault were massing concealed by the hill side. After dark we retired to the woods again and bivouaced for the night. We slept supperless, our servants having remained well to the rear.

Following his reversal at Rappahannock Station, Lee fell back to the south side of the Rapidan River, while Meade, ever wary of his supply line, followed, continuing to rebuild the Orange & Alexandria Railroad as he advanced.

The Army of the Potomac went into camp in the vicinity of Brandy Station for several weeks, but by the end of November Meade was again ready to move. Beginning on November 26, the Federals were to cross the Rapidan well beyond Lee's right and concentrate swiftly via the Orange Turnpike and Orange Plank Road in rear of his position. Once there, Meade sought to use his numerical superiority to fall on Ewell's Corps before Lee's other corps, under A. P. Hill, could march to its support.

The success of the plan depended on speed and surprise, but by the evening of the first day of the movement, the Union advance had reached only several miles beyond the Rapidan crossings, and worse yet, Lee was fully aware of the danger to his flank. By the evening of November 27 the Confederate chieftain had pivoted his troops back into an exceedingly strong defensive line on the west bank of a small stream known as Mine Run and was confidently awaiting the Federal assault.

Capt. Dendy Sharwood, who had led the 118th Pennsylvania at Rappahannock Station, was fatally stricken by typhoid fever shortly after that battle, and both Colonel Gwyn and Lieutenant Colonel Herring remained sick in Philadelphia. Capt. Henry O'Neill, the senior officer present in the regiment, ascended to a short-lived and, as

Donaldson describes it, humorously inept stint as commander during the early stages of the Mine Run Campaign.

Sunday, Nov. 8th. Up bright and early this morning and had a good look at the captured entrenchments, and from them I could trace every foot of our charge across that dreadful field. What a fine chance the Rebs had at us, and I could, in my mind's eye, again see the advancing line. I failed to understand why the enemy did not abandon their works and fall back across the river, when they could plainly see they were about to be attacked by overwhelming forces, all seasoned troops. The works showed every sign of the battering they had received, especially about the embrasures, and the ground was strewn with all manner of articles in surprising number and variety which usually litter battlefields, such as canteens, haversacks, bits of leather, muskets, trinkets, diaries, lost by the wounded or abandoned in the hurry of a forced retreat, and it is equally surprising where it all comes from.

We started at 8 A.M. and marched to Kelly's Ford where we arrived at 11.30 A.M. I have so often described this place to you that of course its name is familiar to you. Before reaching here General Meade passed us, but the men took no notice of him, scarcely looking at "old four eyes," as he is called, because of the "specks" he wears, I presume. As he came up to the other troops their conduct was in contrast to ours, they closed around him and cheered lustily, throwing caps in the air and fairly mobbing him. It speaks well for the General, as the soldiers at first had very little confidence in him, there having been so many changes of commanders that the idea had taken firm hold of their convictions that a competent officer could not be found to lead them. General Meade, however, appears to be steadily winning his way into their confidence and many favorable comments are heard among the rank and file as to his ability to handle them. The old soldier, as I have often told you, is a sagacious fellow, and handles his superiors without gloves, so to speak. Of course this is to be expected in an army of as much intelligence as the Army of the Potomac, but he was clean beaten this campaign, the old soldier was, he didn't forecast worth a cent this time.

We crossed the Rappahannock at 12 M., and after marching about 5 miles bivouaced for the night. Crocker, Thomas and I made our three pieces of shelter into one tent, and were fortunate in getting a supply of good straw from a stack hard bye, which most unaccountably had not been destroyed, in great contrast to everything that could be destroyed. . . .

Monday, Nov. 9th. I arose bright and early after a refreshing sleep, had a good breakfast and then felt equal to any undertaking. I forgot to mention that our Division is now commanded by General Bartlett of New York.[10] I am not much given to hero worship; that was taken out of me when General McClellan was removed, and I have since been unable to bestow my affections on any one else, or as the old axiom has it, " first impressions are lasting." For some time we have been without our beloved General Griffin, whether sick or removed we do not know, but hardly removed I think, for he is too valuable and capable an officer to be dispensed with. Some say he has been detached on special duty at Washington, anyway, we all feel his absence, and if it is to be permanent, who ever succeeds him in command will [have to] be an able one to gain the affection of the men as General Griffin has done. However, General Bartlett made an impressive hit at the Battle of Rappahannock Station. It was the first time we had seen, and, indeed, ever heard of him, and just before the action commenced he rode out to the skirmish line with the old staff of General Griffin, and stood there for a little time looking through his field glasses at the enemy's works. It was just at the time the skirmishers commenced firing, and Captain Mervine, A. A. G.[11] said, "General Bartlett, you are on the skirmish line." "Gentlemen," said the general, turning to the staff, "I would advise you to seek cover and protect yourselves as much as possible. Come orderly, we will see what is going on." The effect can be imagined, each staff officer felt mortified and crest-fallen. This incident was soon noised about, much to the amusement of the men, upon whom it made a good impression.

Again, about 4 P.M. this day, he gave the division an insight into his character that has had a good effect. The men had been on short allowance for a day or two, and were grumbling because the commissary had not rationed them. It is said that General Bartlett had been much annoyed at this and used his best energies to get supplies. Be that as it may, upon passing through the brigade this afternoon he was assailed on all sides by the cry of "hard tack," which was at once taken up by the other brigades, and soon the whole division was yelling at him. It certainly was an amusing sight to see them swarm out of camp yelling and shrieking at the General. But he was equal to the occasion, for upon passing me he said in a very mild, polite tone, "Captain, can you direct me to your commanding officer's head quarters?" I informed him where they were, and he rode over and said to Captain Sharwood that he noticed the men needed discipline and more work, and ordered him to drill the regiment for an hour. Riding off he did a like service for the rest of the division, which was soon hard at work with battalion movements. The men took it in good part and jestingly said they were not drilling "Hardee" but "Hard Tack."[12] I do not think there will ever again be a desire to jeer "the old man" on the question of rations or on any other subject.

In the midst of the drill the bugle sounded the general or "pack up," when a scamper took place for camp, and in less than an hour we were rapidly marching again to Kelly's Ford, where we recrossed the river in the dark, and after a march of about two miles inland, bivouaced at 9 P.M. for the night near the wagon train, which, by the way, delighted us to see. It snowed quite freely during the afternoon and evening, or as the southerners say, "evening and night," being the first we have had this season. As I sat smoking my pipe beside the glowing campfire, the mysterious movements of the past two days quite took possession of me. I was soon joined by Captain Crocker and Lieut. Thomas and together we attempted the solution of the late strategy. After a few pipes and a thorough warming we arrived at the Bunsbyran decision "that if so be the commanding general knew what he was about, why so, if not so, why so also," and then turned in, boots and all, leaving my man George Slow and one or two of his colored friends to keep up the campfire.

Tuesday, Nov. 10th. We passed a wretched night, it was so bitter cold that everything was frozen hard. We were without blankets and although we slept close together, and it being my turn to sleep in the middle, I arose chilled to the bone and so stiff I could hardly walk. A rousing fire was made and in about an hours time we thawed out. . . .

What General Meade's intentions are regarding our future I have no means of knowing, but presume we are to guard the ford. When speculating upon our position and surroundings I feel mystified. We are certainly far away from any base of supplies, the nearest is Warrenton, and that, you know, is a long way off. The rail road, too, I am sure cannot be repaired short of two weeks, pending which we will have been out of food. I cannot understand what it all means. Again, I can fancy Mr. Sparks saying a soldier should not speculate on the causes and reasons for the movements ordered by his commanding officer. To this I plead that just now having nothing else to do, I naturally feel interested in my surroundings and cannot refrain from reasoning out the situation.

We are but a short distance from our old camp at Gold Farm, an account of which I gave you on our march to Gettysburg. Rumor has it that it is quite possible we will move to Fredericksburg. I would regret this as I have no desire to ever again visit this "grave yard of the Army of the Potomac." Captain

Fernald met with an accident which I think will unfit him from further duty in the command. Like myself, he arose this morning well chilled by the frost, and as he is a very intemperate man, his physical condition [is] not first class, so that slipping on the ice the bones in his left leg were fractured and he will have to be sent home.

Wednesday, Nov. 11th. I arose this A.M. at daylight, called the regimental barber and had my head shampooed, then took a ramble over the hills, and upon returning sat down to a substantial meal of hard-tack and coffee, since which I have devoted myself to you, and presume ere this that you are as heartily tired of reading as I am of writing this letter. I don't improve any in my love of letter writing, and only continue them, as I do not construe this as in any sense a desire to put an end to all correspondence, for I know how anxious you all are to hear from me, and as a dutiful son and brother I will continue to write regularly. My desire is to convey the idea that it is not an easy task for me to write. I go to a great deal of trouble and spend a great deal of time in having [to] correct the matter of which I write and describe. This letter, for instance, was written on pieces of paper at the close of each day, and is now copied and elaborated, although in great haste. You will please make allowance for any mistakes, and attribute them to my uncomfortable surroundings, or more properly, I should do as you do when making up an account, mark it E.O.E. I suppose Auntie will desire most of all to know about my health, and I can assure her that I continue in the enjoyment of this blessed boon, and can add that I have nothing in the world to worry me or to complain of. . . .

>―◆―O―◆―<

> Camp 118th P.V.
> Kelly's Ford, Va.
> Nov. 18th, 1863

My dear Brother:

No letters for a week. Is anything wrong? Have been dreaming lately of John, have you had any bad news from him?[13] What is the matter anyway? Anything wrong at home, anything the matter with Auntie? Surely you are not so busy that a few minutes could be spared to let me know that you are all well, or otherwise. Truly someone has "degenerated" besides your brother.

>―◆―O―◆―<

Camp 118th Regt. P.V.

3 miles South of Kelly's Ford, Va.

November 20th, 1863

My dear Brother:

Yours of the 17th to hand last night, and was much relieved in consequence, it being the first letter I have had from home for a long time, and since the recent news from Western Virginia, I had feared the worst. Do you know I fancied the reason I did not get letters was because you had received news of John's death, and that it had killed Auntie, and you hesitated writing me. Think of it—what forebodings. I was very much distressed and contemplated something desperate, such as an underground plan for reaching home. My mind has been in a wretched state anyway lately. I had a terrible dream of John. He appeared to me with a man under sentence of death in our regiment. John looked so natural, but I could not speak to him and in my agony to do so awoke. From this dream I reasoned he had been wounded, probably, in the late battle. I trust that he is safe, for, indeed Jacob, I dearly love my rebel brother. Poor Captain Rufner—he was such a staunch friend whilst I was in Richmond. So he is dead. Well, such is the fate of war.[14] How well I remember at the American House, Richmond, getting into Major Barley's[15] new cloths. John had remarked when they arrived "here is a suit of cloths that no Yankee will ever get into." I had the laugh on him that time. I made him put them on, just to see how he would look in Confederate Gray. You know, his own regiment was uniformed in "Lincoln Green."[16] We went out into the streets together. How handsome he looked, he had such a fine figure. I thought at the time how noble he would appear in Uncle Sam's livery. Tell me all Mr. Goshorn writes about, or better, send his letter. I wish John were a prisoner.

We are again across the Rappahannock River, and are making preparations for a move <u>forward</u>. That suits me, forward is the word. I believe in continuous fighting until one side or the other is destroyed. The pontoons have been taken up, and it looks as if we were come to reside for some days at least. I do hope we will keep the Rappahannock permanently. . . .

. . . Old Teddy O'Neill, or Philem, as we call him, is a regular old farce at commanding. We are all bunched up in a heap, no order or alignment like the other regiments of the brigade. Old Teddy says he "don't care a divil.". . .

Camp 118th Regt. P.V.
Near Paoli Mills, Va.
on the banks of Mountain Run
Nov. 25th, 1863

Dear Brother:

My two previous letters were from "the devil knew where," but today I am able to locate the camp as above. We broke Camp at Kelly's Ford at 7 A.M. on the 19th and moved to this place, occupying the rebel Winter Quarters which, by the way, are substantially constructed—all of wood. No canvas; shingle roof, doors & sash. I had no idea they could make so good a job as they have done. They just got them completed in time for our occupancy. Why they did not destroy them is the mystery that confuses us.

I told you of "owld Teddy's" arrival, or old "Philem" as Crocker calls him. Well, "the likes of it you never see." He beats the deck for style. I shall never forget his advent in camp. We scarcely knew the old Paddy. He was decked out in tinsel and gold from head to foot. Cap with gold braid on top & sides—"rigulation" he calls it. Double breasted "Stern Cooler" as he calls this jacket, with sleeves heavily gold braided to the elbows, and sky blue pants with gold stripe down the sides and such damnable top boots, the "likes" you again would never see. Why, hang me if they don't come up to his "cooler" entirely. As we turned him around about and took in his gorgeousness, he said, as he planted his seven league boots into the soil, "It is all rigulation, every mothers son of it." He looked for all the world like a Punch and Judy soldier. "This is the way we used to dress in Injee," said he, "and it was a beautiful sight entirely to see the 'callants,' as he termed the officers, "paraded on occasions of state. I disremember now just when it was, but it was when the Governor General made a Mason of the Rajee. The Lift Tenant General in command was kivered with his medals and his medallions and his sash and his plumes, and the Foot and the Horse and the Artillery were out in full rigiments. The Rajee came down with his camels and his aliphants and his whole ratinew, and there was bowing and scraping and damn humbuging over the owld divil until our regiment was reached and then at command they let out of them such a screech that it made the aliphants cock up their trunks and trumpet like the divil, and the camels and the ratinew fooster and fumble about and tremble at Her Majistic Foot. Och! there was a divil of a time." Well I can add there is a "divil" of a time with us, "the likes of which you never see." Mounted on his horse you see nothing but his gold laced "Cooler," top boots and sword, carried at right shoulder shift. He has no particular word of command. It is just as it happens.

In an attempt at batallion drill the other day, he closed the exercise by a review—"the likes you nivir see." We were in line, and he gave all the commands himself to move us off, then rode ahead Don Quixobly to have us pass him in review. He commanded, "break into open column of companies, right in front, the kivering sergeants will be responsible for the distance, march," all in one breath. After we had passed in review he commands, "halt, disperse and be damned to you." . . . After passing in review the command is always marched to their quarters and there properly dismissed. Not so with Teddy—he didn't think of that, he just "dispersed" the command then and there, and the men went to their quarters helter skelter, every man laughing and shouting "bully for old Teddy." Nice state of affairs, and such is discipline under "old Philem." How degraded and humiliated we all feel. But enough of him. I am so full of shame and mortification that I can scarcely write about it.

Sharwood is dead! Sharwood is dead! is the lamentable news we have. . . . On his return from Brigade to command he tented with me. I shall never forget his last day with me. In the afternoon he came into my tent, and gathering together all the blankets carefully wrapped himself in them, laughing and talking the while. His last words were, "Poney, I'm sick, got a cold and want to sweat it out. Mix me a double distilled Joe Hooker. Make it stiff, make it stiff, Poney, make me a bowl full." I did so, and he drank it all. Then covering up his head, fell asleep and never again woke to consciousness. The next day I had him taken to brigade Headquarters, and he was subsequently, as you know, sent home to die, I am told as he reached the house. Blinding tears fill my eyes as I now write. I haven't words, Jacob to tell you of my grief. I have lost a friend, and a friend such as he cannot be spared or replaced. He is gone forever, and I grieve "in sack cloth and ashes." Noble, generous, gallant, kind and faithful friend, how sadly missed, how deeply regretted by all, not myself alone. He died at one P.M. Saturday, November 21st, 1863 of Typhoid Fever.

<u>Nov. 26th, 1863</u>. I start this diary with the hope that I may be able to keep it up during the campaign just inaugurated. I will not promise to note each days events as they occur, at their close, but will do the best I can towards that desirable end. As we are rationed for 10 days and have no supply trains other than ammunition, I take it this movement is to be a hurried one. The old soldiers have not yet fairly grasped the situation and so I cannot

give the object of the present operation, but will use the overheard expression of an old campaigner—"it is to be a turning one, most likely on the approved Confederate plan." Broke camp at Paoli Mills at 7 A.M., marched to and crossed the Rapidan at Culpeper Mine Ford—some call it "Gold Mine Ford"—but I think Culpeper is right. However, I will correct it as soon as I learn the name for a fact. We pushed through forests so dense that for a space of a few feet only on either side [of] the road the underbrush could [only] be penetrated by vision. The road was good, the pace fairly well maintained, although numerous little halts occurred as the troops became jammed. We finally struck the Stevensburg Plank Road and after a lengthy march along it, halted at 10 P.M. near Chancellorsville.[17]

Nov. 27th. I was very tired last night and slept but poorly until towards morning when George Slow threw his blanket over me while he cooked coffee and prepared breakfast, then did I sleep good. At 7 A.M. the regiment was detached as flankers. Old Philem, in making the necessary preparations, assigned me to the centre, Donegan the left, and himself on the right. This, he said, was to be an important "juty," requiring us to "look sharp and not be marking time," "and Kelly," continued he to that unhappy Captain who had come under his displeasure somehow, "you'll just be after keeping on the line and not be prancing about picking out dry places, but mind and look sharp Kelly." He don't like Kelly for some reason, possibly because he "sasses" back. Well, we had a "divil of a time" in deploying but finally "dispersed and spread out" to his satisfaction on the left flank of the marching column. The march commenced and was necessarily slow because the flankers had to push their way through timber and underbrush which made most uncomfortable marching, besides, the trains were with the column, which retarded the column.

After marching along the Germanna Plank Road until the intersection of the Orange Plank Road was reached, we made an abrupt turn to the right into it, the flankers following the general direction of the column. I had passed the junction and had gotten well on in the new direction when I suddenly became aware that all was not as it should be. There was much noise and confusion in the direction of the marching column, although we could not see them. Loud tones of command, such as "halt," "front," "steady there," "close up," "load at will," "load," and finally away off towards the head of column a single cannon shot boomed sullenly. The flankers halted, then towards the Germanna Plank Road, but beyond towards the enemy, quick and rapid firing, lasting a few seconds only, was heard. I knew that something had happened. I couldn't tell what so I pushed on to find O'Neill but he was so far away that I abandoned the attempt and struck out for the column, which I found—in line of battle—a short distance from us. I then learned that our wagon train had been attacked. Running back to the flankers I gave the order to "left wheel," "double quick," and faced them in the direction from which we had come, or rather, as many of them as heard me. As we proceeded I made my way to the left to find Donegan, but didn't find him. I was in a perfect stew of excitement. As I approached the Germanna Plank Road I met a staff officer making his way towards me with orders to retire the skirmish line to its place on the flank. I forgot to mention that just as we began the left wheel, one of the men called out, "There goes a reb," and sure enough I saw a man and woman hurrying rapidly through the woods. They disappeared instantly.

After the flankers had returned to their places, I went back to the junction and learned the cause of the trouble. It appears that as the leading wagon reached the Orange Plank Road, instead of turning to the right as the troops had done, two men suddenly jumped from the bushes, and springing into the wagon beside the driver with leveled pistols, compelled him to drive straight ahead. This he did, and the succeeding wagons of course followed on after him. No one knew there was anything wrong in this until Capt. Bankson, Inspector General, came along, and inquiring why they did not follow the column, the ruse was discovered. Then the rebs, lining the road ahead, opened fire and shot the mules, which was the musketry I heard. I am told that at this juncture Lt. Col. Sherwin came up, and noticing a cavalryman seated on his horse at the junction, drew his pistol and demanded him to open his Union overcoat. This not being instantly complied with he seized him by the collar, and tearing open the coat, discovered the Confederate uniform beneath. Promptly shooting the fellow through the head, he hauled his body to the ground where it lay when I visited the spot, and where we left it.[18] Not being able to withdraw the wagons, Capt. Bankson had large fires built under them, their canvas covers fired, and exploded them all. I have heard the number lost variously stated, but I think there must have been at least 25 wagons destroyed. I will be unable to tell possibly until I see Bankson. This was a bold move of the rebs, and if by Mosby it only proves how very fearless he is and with what contempt he holds us. I cannot help admiring that fellow, he is certainly a wonderfully energetic soldier.[19]

The column kept to the Plank Road whilst the flankers struck a Rail Road Grade or unfinished R.R. embankment running parallel with the road, of

course unencumbered by woods. The bold Teddy occupied it. This roadway ran for a long distance below the surface, but Teddy kept right along it
and of course, as a matter of protection, we were simply of no earthly
account, as we could see nothing. Becoming uneasy, I worked my way to
O'Neill and asked why he did not put the men on the surface and not
march them in the Rail Road cut. He replied, "To the divil with them, if
there are an enemy about they will find us just as readily in the cut as if we
were out of it," that they were a bold set of divils anyway and we were just
getting even with them because they couldn't see us at all and didn't know
a divil about us. "Why Major," said I, "it is not for them to see us so much
as it is for us to see them, and how in the name of God are we to do it if
you keep us below ground?" "Well," said he, giving his immense nose a
knowing tap with his finger while his eyes guided right and left—he is
goggle eyed you know—"I was afraid the spalpeens would see the enemy,
and if they did do so, every mothers son of them would skeedaddle like the
divil, they ain't worth a divil anyway, only fit to draw and eat rations, bad
luck to them, so if they do not see the enemy they will stay where they
are, bad [luck] to them for a set of lame ducks." Then he added, "Where's
that old woman Donegan and what in the divil did he let the wagon train
get captured for, the old pirate? I told him it rather reflected on him as he
was in command. "On me, is it? To hell with them, do they think I was
bothering about a lot of bushwhackers, and when did you see Kelly larst?
Oh! that Kelly is an owld divil, tell him I want him, I want to keep my
eyes upon him." As I could make nothing out of our commanding officer,
I "marked time" til the centre reached me & then told Kelly that Old
Philem wanted him, to which he characteristically replied, "Does he? Well
then, let him halt the line 'til I reach him." Kelly was about as disgusted a
man as I ever saw.

Towards dark we reached a place called Hope Church[20]—this I learned
since but didn't know it at the time. I only knew that after sending
Thomas back to communicate with the column, and he reporting he had
gone a mile or more and couldn't see anything of it, Teddy then suddenly
freed the skirmishers to the front, and moving out of the cut proceeded
across country in skirmish array towards a little house seen in the distance
occupying the summit of an extensive knoll. He halted on a line with the
house and Kelly, Walters & I then examined it. The doors & windows
were closed. One of the men with his musket pried open a window shutter which was pretty high from the ground, and giving Walters a boost,

that energetic officer jumped inside. A "divil" of noise ensued as Walters in the darkness fell over and smashed an old fashioned spinning wheel. We could hear him muttering something about the damned old plunder barking his shins. He opened the door and we found the house had just been deserted in evident fear at our sudden appearance. Upon a refrigerator in one corner of the kitchen lay a chicken, just cleaned & ready for cooking, which Walters instantly seized and shoved into his haversack before the watchful eye of Old Teddy discovered it. The table was set with bread ready cut and coffee, or what appeared like it, in the cups. We didn't stop to examine its quality, but downed it off hand. Someone said the chicken & coffee might be poisoned, to which a reply was made that it made no difference, we could look into the matter when more leisure was had. The ceiling was hung with strings of dried fruit, and in the loft was walnuts, shell barks and chestnuts. In another room was a double bed, neat and clean, with a blue and white cotton counterpane over it. O'Neill said he would make this house his head quarters, and feeling tired, would turn in, if anything happened during the night to let him know, and to "look sharp." Then eating a scanty supper, he turned in, boots and all, and pulling the covers over him, was soon asleep.

I busied myself along the line, giving instructions and cautioning the men to be watchful. After seeing everything snug, even to visiting Donegan who still remained on the left, I went back to the house and with Kelly and Walters spent the night cracking nuts upon flat irons and talking over the events of the day. The chicken was cooked & eaten and all the bread too. There was one conclusion privately arrived at, which was that O'Neill was unfit for command, that we were unsafe under him, and were in a "divil of a fix generally," that we would wait until we rejoined the brigade when action would be taken at once. Our position was certainly alarming. Here we were in the enemy's country, away, God knows how far, from the army, and were free from attack only because we were a line of infantry skirmishers supposed to be the advance of a large body of troops. So we reasoned. The enemy had seen us, that we knew, so we grumbled and grumbled the night through.

Nov. 28. Broke cloudy, threatening rain. Away off on the edge of a piece of timber along the ridge of high ground in our front was plainly seen the enemy's cavalry in skirmish line, extending along our entire front. There they sat and watched us, and here we stood, not knowing what the devil to do. They were wondering, no doubt, at the infantry so unexpectedly confronting them. "I'll be damned if Owld Teddy hasn't been connecting his line with the enemy's," said one of the men. It did look like it certainly. "Well," said I to Philem, "what are we to do now?" "Observe the divils till further orders," said he, and so we did—and closely too, lest we should be gobbled.

Towards noon Old Teddy concluded we were doing no good here, so after going to the rear of the house and shaking his fist at the "dirty black-guards," gave the order to retreat, still keeping up our skirmish formation. Just as the line started it commenced raining, and the men covered themselves with gum blankets. We had not fairly started when Old Teddy came dashing out of the house and ordered the line to halt. He said somebody had stolen the coverlet from off the bed and he wanted it returned. "Bring it back Kelly," said he, "and put it where you got it. Do you want them to think us a set of thieves and divils? Put it back at once." How in the world he knew Kelly had the coverlet I cannot tell, but think he merely surmised it. He blames everything on Kelly. Sure enough Kelly had it snugly rolled in his gum blanket. He replied, "Why damn it Major, it is not wantonness, I need the thing." "Put it back Kelly, do you mind?" And as Kelly left to do so, he turned to me and said, "That Kelly is a divil, and I wouldn't be surprised if he had a flat-iron in each pocket, the thief of the world." This was dangerous talk, as I had purloined an awl-pien of bees wax and some needles & thread for a work basket. I kept quiet and was not suspected.

We did not rejoin the brigade until 3 P.M. when Robinson's Tavern[21] was reached. Here we bivouaced. As soon as possible the officers congregated and after a short discussion sent word to Col. Tilton, commanding brigade, that there was serious trouble in the command, and if he could possibly do so, would he kindly visit us. He responded at once, and finding all the officers together in earnest consultation, rode up, saying kindly, "Why, what is the matter gentlemen, what is the trouble?" Crocker, as spokesman, then explained the situation: that we had no confidence in Major O'Neill, and desired him to give us a commander under whom we could do our duty intelligently. O'Neill was present and said not a word. Neither did Tilton appear to consider him. "Well gentlemen," said he, "this is most extraordinary conduct on the eve of an engagement, and were it not that all the officers are concerned in it, [it] might lead to serious consequences. I, however, appreciate your feelings and do not care to jeopardize the efficiency of so excellent a regiment as the 118th, so we'll do as you say. Whom do you want?" "Lt. Col. Throop of the 1st Michigan," said we. He then went away and shortly after returned with Col. Throop, and made known to us he had persuaded that gentleman to command us. Throop then said that of course he preferred to remain with his own command, but at the urgent solicitation of Col. Tilton had consented to take command of us upon one condition only—that it should be by the unanimous desire of the officers, including Major O'Neill. "Certainly," said that Christian Knight, "certainly. . . . I don't care a divil under whom I serve [just] so that he gives us a chance to fight. Certainly I will serve under you, with pleasure too," whereupon following the lead of Crocker we all shook hands cordially with the gallant Colonel and pledged him our hearty obedience and cooperation. Great Heavens! how relieved we felt, and so happy too. Why it was such a signal success that Crocker proposed, then and there, to shake up a Joe Hooker all around, including our new commander Lt. Col. Throop. To the credit of the officers be it said they did not take up Crocker's very generous offer, so that Thomas, Kelly, Crocker & myself withdrew to a sheltered spot, [and] indulged copiously with blissful Joe for at least half an hour, during which time that old Drunkard got on most familiar terms with us, did good old Joe Hooker.

Nov. 29. Moved at 7 A.M. about 2 miles in direction of Orange Court House and came upon the enemy strongly posted on the opposite side of Mine Run. They occupied a series of ridges just back from the stream. The country beyond and on our side too was densely wooded. Between the enemy's position and the Run the ground appeared marshy up to the base of the ridges. Indeed, from the very first we were appalled at the apparent impregnable position Lee had selected. The spot where we halted and went into line of battle was called Chestnut Hill; whether the name [was] given by the men or really its true name I don't know. It was also a high ridge, but commanded by the enemy. They were seen busily felling trees, throwing up entrenchments and tearing down the few houses obstructing the range of their guns. Here we "marked time" the balance of the day and all night, much to the disgust of the old gossips who began to get the hang of the operation. It was evident to all that whatever our purpose it had miscarried, as Lee was not surprised, if it was the intention to do so. There he was confronting us, ready & willing, and we at a stand still. Great Scott! how we do blunder. Somebody had made a mistake sure. If it was thought to catch Lee napping we didn't do it. We will have to move quicker if we want to get the better of that old fox.

Nov. 30. Exceedingly Cold. About 2 A.M. we were ordered into line, knapsacks and everything unnecessary to carry piled and the march taken up towards our right. We came upon the ground already occupied by the 6th Corps, massed, and stripped for action. We formed upon their left in masses of battalion doubled on the centre, and moved to the edge of [the] timber, a thick pine growth, to await daylight and the signal to charge. I, being in command of the 1st Division [of the regiment], took some of the men and removed the fence rails in our front, also cutting down a good deal of underbrush. I had provided myself with a camp hatchet in lieu of a sword, which by the way [came in] very handy, although it certainly was not rigulation. The weather was extremely cold, so much so that the men were in danger of freezing.

At early dawn the enemy's position could be seen. During the night they had greatly strengthened it by formidable earth works and by damming the Run so that it had filled & spread into quite a river. Col. Throop called the officers to the front, and in a manly, soldierly way said, "Gentlemen, the orders are that at the sound of two guns from Warren's position we are to move forward and charge the enemy there," pointing to the entrenchments. "Do you see those works? We either sleep to night on the other side of them— or else on the slopes leading to them." My God! what a dreadful task laid out for us. Immediately to our front, across the Run, the ground ascended to nearly an angle of 30 degrees—base, rough & barren without shelter or protection of any kind. I can truly say there was not an officer or man in the division but that felt it now simply impossible to carry such entrench- ments. It could not be done, it were madness to attempt it, worse than at Fredericksburg to allow it. The men at once fell to labeling themselves, writing name & address on paper which they pinned inside their coats. Crocker took a fools cap sheet and in bold characters gave his name & address, ending with "was this day mustered out [of] the service, Nov. 30th, 1863." He placed this length wise over his breast, pinning it fast and buttoning his coat over it. I wrote a few lines to the effect that I was killed in this impending assault and asked the finder of my body to kindly send this paper to my friends. Every man in the command felt that death would surely be met with on these terrible slopes. But I did not hear any one decline to go forward. No one thought of backing out.

The hours wore on apace, but no signal gun was fired. We waited in silence and fear until it gradually dawned upon us that the contemplated charge had been abandoned. Soon the artillery opened on the enemy, but by battery, not the signal guns, alone. This firing was replied to very lively by the rebs, and then got serious. As we lay crouching to avoid the shells,

Private Hyatt[22] of my company, who had carried his knapsack, was kneeling upon it tightening the blanket roll strap when a solid shot dashed into the ground beneath him, coming out again beyond him and taking the heel of one of his shoes. The concussion lifted him up at least a foot, but he was not hurt apparently, only paralyzed both in body & speech. Hyatt was a great blower and a great coward, and at the time of the mishap—the dangerous charge being abandoned—was loudly telling what he would do should the order be renewed. His speech was interrupted so suddenly that it caused a laugh, the cannon ball seeming to say as it tore the ground— Liar. I had him taken to the rear on a stretcher, he was unable to walk. One of the regiment went into the battery on our left to watch their firing. He had not been there long before both legs were carried away by a round shot. The cold became more intense and the suffering greater, no fires being permitted. I gathered a pile of rails with which I made a pretty snug shelter and busied myself with this journal. It was soon learned that Genl. Warren, upon whom rested the responsibility of the assault, decided it as improachible and failed to order it.[23]

The 119th is on our right and we have had a chance to see & meet with old friends. . . . I have just returned from a reconnoisance conducted by Walters & myself. Walters asked me to stroll out with him and have a look at the enemy. He was mounted on Charley Hand's spirited little horse, while I, on foot, kept close to his side. We passed beyond the timber and descending the slope leading to the Run took up a position well down its sides. Here Walters took out a pair of field glasses and surveyed the enemy. They were plainly to be seen sitting in their works watching us. It was soon evident we had attracted their notice as the bullets began to strike uncomfortably near. Still Walters did not move. I remained at the horse's head, facing the enemy. Again and again did the bullets strike, now under and now alongside the horse, while many went singing by in close proximity. Still he looked steadily through the glasses, and the suspense became somewhat annoying. A voice was heard calling, "Come in here, don't you know you are making a target of yourselves." At this we turned and walked slowly back again to our lines in safety, receiving a cheer and a wave of hats from the rebs. It is true they were a good way off, which accounts for our not being hit. When we were fairly under cover I asked Walters why he continued so reckless after recognizing the fact that we were objects of special attention from the rebs. He replied, "You are the ranking officer and I was waiting for you to suggest retiring." "Had I known you were waiting for me," said I, "we would have dusted long before." At dark, or say 5 P.M., we drew back and marched again to our old position at Chestnut Hill where knapsacks and blankets were resumed, and a little rest and comfort secured.

Dec. 1st. We remained here all day. In the afternoon fires were allowed and at dusk the artillery, after being masked, was withdrawn. The cannon was masked by inclining logs together with a third behind, so that at a distance it would resemble guns & trail. Large fires were made and at 6 P.M. we withdrew. The whole army was retiring, and being crowded together slow progress was made, there being so many intervals of halting and marching that the whole night was consumed in reaching the Rapidan. At one point along the route we came to a burning tavern, whether Robinson's or not I cannot say as it was pretty well consumed when we got to it. The weather was biting cold. . . . *[next line illegible]* . . . so that we enjoyed a warmth so greatly needed, but rather an expensive treat for somebody.

Dec. 2nd. Crossed the Rapidan at Germanna Ford at 4 A.M. and at 5 o'clock bivouaced near there at a place called Coney Mountain.[24] 8 A.M. moved to near Stevensburg and bivouaced at noon.

Dec. 3rd. Moved at 8 A.M. Crossed the Rappahannock at Rappahannock Station at 2 P.M. Bivouaced at 4 P.M., camped at Beverly Ford.

CHAPTER 11

Confrontation, Dismissal, and Exoneration
December 4, 1863–March 3, 1864

*T*he Army of the Potomac had crossed to the north side of the Rapidan following the Mine Run Campaign, and the soldiers were soon peacefully reposed in the vicinity of Brandy Station, Virginia, where they would remain, for the most part undisturbed, for the next five months. In the camp of the 118th Pennsylvania near Beverly Ford, however, the solitude was only temporary.

As early as December 1862 Donaldson had predicted to his brother that the animosity that existed between him and Colonel Gwyn would eventually force him into a confrontation with his superior that would lead to his dismissal from the service.

After a four-and-a-half-month absence because of recruiting duty and illness, Gwyn returned to the camp of the 118th on December 4. Following a brief but contentious meeting with the colonel that day, Donaldson decided that as long as the regiment remained under Gwyn's control, he would never be able to serve peaceably in it. Accordingly, as he recounts below, he set into motion a premeditated chain of events that would permanently remove him from what he felt were the petty tyrannies and harassments of his adversary and ultimately spell the end of his Civil War service.

Camp 118th P.V.
near Beverly Ford, Va.
December 6th, 1863

Dear Brother:

Finis—to my military career. The end forshadowed for a year past and certainly predicted for months as drawing nearer to hand, has come, and, with but a very short interval to arrange the preliminaries, I will be out of the service. I will briefly narrate how it all came about, and how I fully, suscinctly, clearly, distinctly and with deliberation carried out the program so solemnly prearranged.

Our drunken autocrat Gwyn arrived in camp on the 4th inst. With the exception of myself the officers turned out to greet him. I remained steadfastly in my quarters. However after pondering well my future course regarding him, I finally concluded that, in view of our peculiar and remarkable condition, being commanded by an officer from another regiment, I was after all glad to have one of the Field Officers to again command us and therefore towards evening proceeded—alone—to the Colonel's tent to tell him so. He was alone and merely looked up at my entrance. I said, "Colonel, you doubtless remarked my absence from among the officers who greeted your return to camp." He said he had noticed it. I continued that in view of all that had transpired between us and the bitterness of my feeling towards him I could not consistently welcome him back again, but that after hours of reflection and deliberation I deemed it best to appear and say what I truly felt to be the case, that I was glad to be again commanded by our rightful and proper officer, and would take occasion if not too late to do so to add my congratulations upon his promotion. Had a bombshell struck him it could not have produced greater effect than this pretty little speech did. "Damn you, sir, I want nothing from you, it was no promotion—it was my right to be Colonel. I have been kept out of it long enough and I will not receive congratulations from a man who writes cowardly articles about me to the newspapers." "Colonel," said I, "You know that it is not I who writes these articles. I have given every evidence that I am not afraid to openly disagree with you. You know that Stephen Winslow of the Philada. Commercial List is the author of them, and I solemnly declair that I never in my life addressed a single line to any newspaper on any subject, much less to criticize you."[1] "I don't believe you," said he, "it is you who have done this, and I want you to leave my quarters at once else I will call the guard and have you thrust out." "All right," said I, "I will take occasion to let you hear from me but not in the newspapers, and if you will but waive rank will settle our quarrel speedily—" "Leave me, leave me," said he, "I will no longer have anything to say to you"— and I left—in a frame of mind anything but angelic.

I kept my quarters pretty closely until today—Sunday. An inspection had been ordered to include also all recruits—they previously to be examined physically and passed upon by Dr. Thomas. These new men were therefore assembled at the Surgeon's headquarters and my Sergeant—Crossley—who by the way is a most exasperatingly slow man—thick headed and although apparently working like the very devil is always behind in everything—had been the very last to get his men to the doctor and as a consequence they were being examined when the call sounded for parade—I was in my quarters awaiting the time to appear and take command of the company when "to the colors" sounded and I went out to see what delayed the company's formation. I found the men scattered about the company street and not yet in line. Hurriedly asking where Sgt. Crossley was I learned he had not yet returned from the Surgeon. I called the company together and without waiting for the recruits proceeded out the company street toward the parade ground. At this juncture Crossley joined and took his position at the head of the company. I now noticed the regiment formed, a space left open for my company—and Col. Gwyn at his post. As I came forward he turned and noticing my approach hastily called out for the regiment to close up and fill my interval. When I had nearly reached him he said, "You being late Capt. Donaldson will take your company to the parade ground and drill it for two hours." I replied, "Colonel, why not punish me, it was no fault of the men that we are late. Beside it is Sunday and contrary to regulation to do any work on this day." "Do you refuse to obey me, sir," said he. "Yes," said I, striding rapidly toward him. "I do, and I propose to tell the command what I think of this drunken Irish loafer, and I tell you I will not be insulted by a Major General much less by this incompetent, drunken, immoral, damned infernal scoundrel, this Jim Gwyn, this coward and tyrant." With that he made at me, laying his hand upon his sword as if to draw it. Whereupon I drew my pistol and continued, "Damn you you infernal drunken blackguard, if you draw your sword on me, I will shoot you down like a dog." Then turning to Lieut. Coane I told him to take the company to the parade ground and stack arms there, but not to drill it as it was against army regulations. Meanwhile Gwyn called lustily for the Corporal of the guard, and ordered the Adjutant to assemble the whole guard and arrest me. I said, "Now then you Irish scoundrel, I will retire to my quarters, where I will await your blackguard pleasure," and I did so.

As soon as I reached my tent it was surrounded by the guard and the Adjutant, trembling like the hound he really is, stood outside and asked me for Heaven's sake to give him my sword, and not to get him into any trouble. I passed it out to him, but declined to give up my pistol saying I deemed it best to keep it, as I might want to use it on the carcass of our Irish Colonel, and that if he or any of the guard attempted to take it from me I would shoot the first that entered the tent. The pistol, at this writing, remains in my possession. A guard is upon me, but most singular, and I may add, most mortifying too, they display sympathy for me, which is anything but that intended by my actions—they have in subdued tones told me that under no circumstances would they fire on me, should anything occur whereby they were ordered to do so. I replied that they were soldiers, sentinels, and guards, and must obey all orders, that I was not for a moment to be considered by them, and finally, that I forbade them speaking to me, as it was improper and uncalled for, that I was a prisoner, their prisoner, and they must treat me as such, that my quarrel was with the Colonel and they would do me a favor not to express sympathy for me or in any way show that they were other than true soldiers. They were placed as guards over me and should conduct themselves as such regardless of any other feeling than that of duty, and especially were they not to attempt to talk to me. "Be soldiers, men," said I, "under all circumstances."

Now that the affair is over I feel a joyful sense of relief from a most depressing weight of pent up emotions, and were it not unseemly would sing and dance for very joy—I tell you Jac I am happy that my release from this cursed regiment is so nigh at hand. I will be arraigned, Court-Martialed and dismissed [from] the service. My conduct today, in a strictly military sense, deserves greater punishment. I really ought to be shot to death by musketry, but a court cannot be assembled in this division that would do that. I am too well and favorably known, and my simple statement of long continued oppression, insults, and ill treatment by this fellow who seldom, if ever, draws a sober breath would carry any court. Therefore a dismissal—alone—will be the verdict.

Should I choose to do so, I could make a stout defense, even the threat to shoot my superior officer would & could be treated lightly. I can beat him at the trial—But I will not defend myself. I will gladly welcome any punishment that will rid me the presence of this hated Irishman. Indeed, for that matter, I could bring countercharges of gross immorality—occupying his tent with a lewd woman at camp near Sharpsburg—and ordering me as officer of the day to remove the guard from his quarters so that he would not be disturbed in his lustful amours, getting Maj. Herring to sleep elsewhere that same night than in his tent adjoining the Lt. Colonel's. I could charge him with repeated drunkenness, both on and off duty, especially upon an occasion of battalion drill at Camp near Falmouth when he fell from his horse. I could charge him with tampering with the guard, as you know, and of grossly immoral conduct in camp near Falmouth with a wife of an orderly Sergeant, who was then in camp, and with many other charges enough to kick him out of the service—but I have in a manner condoned these faults, by not bringing charges long since, especially when Capt. Bankson urged me to do so. But I have no disposition to fight this rascal. I want to get away, I am unhappy here. It is without exception the most dreadfully demoralized command in the service. Bickerings and quarrelings, hatred, jealously and malice are abroad among us everywhere. All the officers are at loggerheads. The intense hatred felt towards each other can never be subdued but by the grave—it will last for ever—there can be no union of officers after the war, they cordially hate and despise one another, and this feeling will be carried into their homes and survive all other recollections of the <u>Noble 118th</u>. I doubt whether throughout the Army of the Potomac, or indeed of the whole army of the United States, there exists today a regiment so torn to pieces by internal dissensions as this famous Corn Exchange regiment—and all brought about by its disreputable commanding officer JIM GWYN—the Irish blackguard Colonel. This letter I mail with an impression that its contents will be scanned by Gwyn, and if you do not receive it I will know he has taken it from the mail. . . .

Now as to your conduct—merely lay the facts before Mr. Sparks and my friends and take no other action. After all is over, I will appeal to President Lincoln, and I feel assured that notwithstanding his manifest duties and trials—he will accord me a hearing, and will relieve me from any orders attending a dismissal from the service. I have a strong case and can present it faithfully to this truly good man. I will write you continually, as to my condition, and will post you as to the time of trial. Finally let me assure you that I am satisfied with myself, although fully alive to the grave offense committed. It was premeditated and determined upon long, long before as you know and I only awaited the opportunity.

>-+-+>-O-<+-+-<

Camp 118th Regt. P.V.
Beverly Ford, Va.
December 9th, 1863

Dear Jacob:

Capt. Henry K. Kelly, Co. G left this day for home on leave of absence for 10 days. He will <u>probably</u> see and tell you of my glorious assault upon our <u>Irish Beast</u>. . . .

The first evidence of the "Beast's" line of action towards me happened today. Crocker & Thomas left this A.M. for picket duty after making everything snug in the new loghouse we have been building. After they had gone I moved in and proceeded to make myself comfortable. The Adjutant and Officer of the Day appeared and informed me that by the "Beast's" orders I was to return to my old quarters. I did so. This, an old shelter tent, is only serviceable to me as a cover from the impertinent gaze of the curious both of our own and other regiments. The latter are not at all restricted in their desire to view the quarters of the "Lion" of the brigade. Yes, it has come to this, that I am lionized. My tent has no fireplace and is kept warm by basins of hot coals which the indefatigable George supplies both day & night unceasingly. Should a heavy and prolonged rain storm set in I will be in a sorry plight as the canvas is too old and worn to shed the rain. However, I complain not. I am in no sense a martyr. I had foreseen the likelihood of harsh treatment and am not disappointed. I welcome it too, as my release will bring with it comforts so long denied me. I am as happy as a lark. I still see no good reason for making a defense.

Shortly after returning to my old quarters I was the recipient of an unasked indulgence that contrasts strangely with the "Beast's" severity of an hour ago. A deputation from my company was allowed an interview with me. They came to express the sympathy of the company in my troubles and their urgent desire to aid and assist me in any way that lay in their power, adding they felt that in defending them I had brought this serious trouble upon myself. I thanked them for their kindly words and added that they could greatly assist me by being true, conscientious soldiers, obedient and willing, showing no disrespect or displaying any feeling towards the commanding officer, but to accord him on all occasions respectful behavior. I feel greatly gratified at this evidence of good will from my men.

Should you see Col. Herring please make known to him my present condition. I have nothing else to communicate. I still sleep soundly and eat appetizingly.

>-+-+>-O-<+-+-<

Camp 118th Regt. P.V.
Beverly Ford, Va.
December 10th, 1863

Dear Brother:

. . . I do now, and have since, and at the time of my assault upon the "Beast," confessed my very unsoldierly conduct. I am fully aware that I was wrong in thus attacking him, but knowing, I still did it deliberately, knowingly, willfully, and I still see no reason to repent my course. Had I to do it again I would certainly act as I then did—assail him publicly. I have abandoned the profession of a soldier, did so when I attacked him. My only fear is that he may desire to compromise, but should this happen, I say now— No Sir, I am for Court-Martial. I want to get away. I wouldn't be in the least surprised if his cowardly heart urges him to make settlement with me. He knows the damage I can do him. . . .

I have not yet been served with a copy of charges, and from their delay presume they are being carefully <u>compiled</u>, and <u>competent</u> witnesses (Sergeants anxious for promotion) schooled and instructed. I am extremely anxious for a speedy trial and want the "Beast" to "come to time." . . .

>-·-◦-·-<

Camp 118th Regt. P.V.
Beverly Ford, Va.
December 14th, 1863

My dear Brother:

. . . I need no money as I will employ no counsel and make no defense. You must just let things take their course. <u>I want it so</u>. I could make a hot fight were I disposed to do so, but I want to go home. It is charity to let me do so, so give up your cherished plan of aiding me.

I had a little fun all to myself yesterday. Fearing the "Beast" might still be disposed to let up on me, I played a little game to see what I could do towards further irritating him. I sent up a paper asking the Beast to remove the guard from my quarters. He sent it back endorsed

Respectfully returned—the guard will not be removed, any officer threatening to shoot his commanding officer should be kept under guard to prevent his escape from justice.

This is what I supposed he would do, so I then carried out my further plan. After dark, to show him how inadequate his guard was to keep me confined should I care to leave, I boldly walked out of my tent and paid Capt. Crocker a visit of an hour. I did this also to have him add an additional charge of "breach of arrest." However, I am now mindful of the fact that it was not a breach of arrest as I was under guard, and not on my honor. While at Crocker's the Adjutant happened in there and saw me. Had the devil himself been there he could not have been more surprised. He shortly took himself off to tell the "Beast" the story of my "escape from justice." However, I left too, not caring to involve my friend in any difficulty. The effect of this little escapade has been to strengthen the guard, 4 now being over me, with the additional duty of opening my tent door each morning and loading their muskets in my presence, while the officer of the guard loudly instructs them to fire upon me should I attempt to leave my quarters. However this will not deter me whenever I want to go out.

Crocker told me that the "Beast" says firmly he is determined to have me shot, that a dismissal will be no punishment, but that a public example shall be made of such gross insubordination and <u>mutiny</u>. Well I will welcome even that rather than stay longer [under] this adulterous viper. But have no fear, it is rather amusing than otherwise to know that I still have the power to annoy him. . . .

>-+>-O-<+-+-<

Camp 118th Regt. P.V.
Near Beverly Ford, Va.
December 15th, 1863

Dear Brother:

I have been furnished with "Charges and Specifications." It is a formidable document covering several pages of foolscap, and contains enough counts to shoot me. I cannot, however, help being amused at the termination of each specification—"damn you, I will shoot you, I wouldn't be insulted by a Major General," or words to that effect, seemingly to apply to the exalted <u>future</u> rank of the adulterous plaintiff, whereas I intended to show how very little he really was. My criticism is the charges and specifications are too finely drawn, showing malice and extreme personal hatred which will of themselves go far toward mitigating extreme punishment. Now see if I am not correct.

That I will be dismissed [from] the service is apparent, and in anticipation, Crocker has given instruction to Stephen N. Winslow to see to it that the Philadelphia Press and Washington Chronicle will withhold mention of the fact. I will hasten to the President and make my defense before him. I am now engaged in collecting testimony of my previous good character as a soldier from those under whom I have served and will greatly rely upon a letter to be sent Genl. Isaac J. Wistar.[2] I will arrange with you as soon as practicable from whom to get other testimony, and will reverse the court's findings. I can't help but do this as I have been too good a soldier. My record must count for something. I cannot hope to do much here—I don't want to. . . .

For the first time I begin to chafe and feel a little anxious at the delay. I want the thing over. I am exceedingly desirous to get away from scenes of turmoil and daily petty quarrels, bickerings and fighting, envy, jealousy, hatred and ambitions, [and the] designs of unprincipled men such as the officers of this regiment. This, Jac, is the true inwardness of the finest regiment from Pennsylvania. Its usefulness and efficiency is impaired by the constant quarrels of its officers. I am now and have long been heart sick with such scenes. No wonder poor Sharwood died—he was the subject of abuse from the Beast's gang of drunkards. Promotions are now made from among those who toady to him and who show capacity for rum drinking—real merit counts for nothing. Take the case of Jno. R. White. He is not a rum drinker—this is a mortal offense with the "Beast"—and to refuse to drink with him—a sufficient reason for dislike. Crocker, as you know, has made many and various attempts to resign. Capt. Bankson worked himself out of the regiment <u>avowedly</u> because he could not live at peace with the Beast. These things have been suppressed, and I should probably not now mention them, but I trust you will not make use of it as I do [not] care to injure the regiment. It is only its commanding officer I wish to reach.

There has been a slight change made in my treatment due I am told to the persistent exertions in my behalf by my good friend Dr. Thomas. I now have but one guard over me and am priviliged to sniff the pure air outside my tent door. . . .

I still remain well. Lt. Col. Herring is expected tomorrow. I am sure he will visit me, although I shall not ask him to do so.

>─◆>─○─<◆─<

Camp 118th Regt. P.V.

December 19th, 1863

Dear Jac:

. . . There is nothing new to communicate. I live fairly well and spend the day generally in walking up and down before my tent, say a distance of ten feet, more or less, at a trip, and occupy my sleeve cuffs alternately in wiping my nose. . . . It has become an absolute necessity to pace up and down, for I really do think I would freeze if I didn't. What think you of this shelter for zero weather? An open work out shelter tent, two blankets and an overcoat, and yet strange to say, I could do with less and not really suffer. . . .

My "little difficulty" remains as before. Crocker, as Judge Advocate, has not recd. instructions as to my case. The Court has adjourned until Monday. I don't exactly favor this, it is too quiet to suit my idea of business. . . . I feel in first class spirits, indeed I have done so all along, and especially so now that I am likely to be at home <u>soon</u>. . . .

This is written with my gloves on. I wish you could send me a pair of woolen ones, say of some dark color, as unlike military ones as possible. No more soldier business for me, not here anyway.

What follows is Donaldson's retelling of his court-martial proceedings. Some of what he relates differs materially from the official court transcription made at the time of his trial. Though Donaldson was almost wholly certain that his actions on December 6 would result in his dismissal from the service, he seems to have found it necessary to color his account of the trial, possibly to impress Jacob, by stretching the truth in several instances, as indicated in the end notes.

Camp 118th Regt. P.V.

December 21st, 1863

Dear Jac:

. . . My trial came off today, not, however, before Crocker's Court, as had been anticipated, but at 3rd Brigade Hd. Quarters, and before a Court composed of entire strangers to me. So far as I know, with exception of Col. A. E. Welch,[3] its president, I never before saw any of its members, certainly was unknown to each and every one of them. This was a great move for the "beast," a great triumph, so to speak, as he knew I could not be convicted before a jury composed of officers selected from my own brigade where I am so well and favorably known. However, it was, also, agreeable to me as it insures my speedy return home.

I should judge Hd. Quarters 3rd Brigade to be all of two and a half miles from here, and I was compelled to walk that distance surrounded by a heavily armed guard under command of the officer of the guard. As a consequence I was stared at like a common felon. There was none to do me the smallest service had I required it. To one less self reliant this apparent utter abandonment by my friends would have been very depressing. Even Lt. Col. Herring, who I am told is in camp, was not seen by me. This I attribute to a desire on his part not to be called as a witness in my behalf, for should I have called him, he would have testified most favorably and flatteringly in my interest, but, in doing this, he would have exposed himself still further to the abuse of the cowardly rascal who has us all in his power. So also my friends, my intimates, they one and all stood aloof, none volunteered to assist me, I was utterly alone. But as for that I have never asked them to help me, so fearfully cowed are they all by this imperious monster. I merely mention these facts because I could not help but notice their absence and because you will naturally ask where were your friends, where Col. Herring. Jac, they one and all acted wisely. There was nothing to be gained by bringing them into court, but much misery and sorrow and trouble would have been their lot had they testified in my behalf. And again, this is entirely my own private matter, and I have no desire to bring into it any of those I so dearly love, honor and esteem.

Upon arrival at 3rd Brigade Hd. Quarters I found the Court adjourned for a few minutes having just disposed of a case, and I stood at a fire near by awaiting my turn. . . .

A little incident occurred when the Court convened that I think most unwittingly placed me rather favorably before it. I was notified the Court had resumed its sitting and was ready to proceed with my case. Not being posted how to act or to whom to report, I went into the tent, saluting the assembled officers, and taking the only vacant seat beside the president, awaited the "first move" in my trial. It appears that judging from the gravity of the charges, a burly, rough and ready prisoner was expected, and when I entered and took my seat, I was presumed to be a new member of the Court, or a witness in the impending trial, certainly not the prisoner. At all events, for a moment or two quiet prevailed, when the judge advocate remarked that he hoped the pending case would not detain them very long, as they had been so eminently successful in disposing of the others so speedily that he trusted short work would be made of this one, to which another replied that they couldn't be very long in convicting this officer, which when done would make a clean record of convictions in every case brought before them. I was rather disconcerted upon hearing this avowal, and hastily getting to my feet, said, "Pardon me gentlemen, I am a prisoner here, but I do not for a moment suppose you intend insulting me or even to pre-judge my case." You should have seen the confusion that ensued. Col. Welch, speedily regaining his composure, said he begged my pardon and was not aware I was the officer about to be tried, that notwithstanding the remarks just made I could rest assured of a fair and impartial trial. I remarked I was not familiar with trials by Court-Martial, and being sent for was under the impression my standing was known to the Court. I would therefore with his permission retire until they were ready to proceed. "No, no," said the Colonel, "we will proceed at once, call Col. Gwyn who brings the charges against this gentleman." This was done, and the tent door being thrown open, his "beastliness" entered.

Jac, he is a magnificient specimen of physical manhood. He has a decided "presence" which was never more clearly shown than at this time. All eyes were turned upon him—he cowed the Court. His presence simply crushed them to such an extent that I called out, "Don't be alarmed gentlemen, he is harmless," which was another surprise. Gwyn fairly glared with rage. His face became scarlet and he said, "I trust, sir, I will have the protection of the Court." I answered quickly before Col. Welch could reply, "He needs it, as his guard of six men are not with him now and I might hurt him." Col. Welch then cautioned me that my conduct was unbecoming, and I replied that I knew "this person" much better than he or the Court did. Gwyn said if I was allowed to proceed in this manner he would have to ask that I be sent to my quarters and the trial go on without my being present. I answered back that I would be a "good boy." But I had already done the mischief, I had belittled my adversary, the great and mighty autocrat, before the Court. Its effects were marvelous, and had I forseen this auspicious beginning, I verily believe, I would have retained able counsel and utterly demolished this "big nothing."[4] However, I had won the sympathy of the President, that I saw at once. He afterwards, as the trial progressed, showed it more than once.

In order to recover somewhat from the effects of this first encounter, Gwyn put his hand into his coat pocket and produced a bunch of segars which he handed the judge advocate and each member of the Court, and then putting several in to the hand of Col. Welch, asked that gentleman to "ask the Captain to smoke." This he did, to which I replied I scarcely supposed this great warrior would care to have me smoke his "sixers." This last shot seemed rather to squelch the "beast" as he sat down, and picking up the Army regulations from off the table, shook and trembled with suppressed rage as he nervously turned its pages.[5]

The charges and specifications were then read, to which I firmly and most decidedly [replied] "not guilty." Gwyn was then called. His testimony was short but full of venom and lies. He commenced by first stating that he sincerely trusted I would not question him as he had no enmity towards me and did not desire to answer questions that would injure me in the sight of the Court. I interrupted, "You are impertinent sir, and I will do as I please with you on the witness stand as I deem best for my case." The judge advocate said if I continued my line of conduct he would be compelled to have me put in writing questions I desired to ask the witness, upon which he first would pass. I pleaded ignorance of the rules, and being without advisers was doing the best I could in my own defense by showing my supreme contempt for this person and his glaring presumptions. After a further caution by the President, Gwyn proceeded.[6]

He told of the Sunday inspection scene, how that I had cursed him in the hearing of the whole command and had threatened to shoot him then and there and afterwards, that I always neglected my duties & that he had to reprove me upon many occasions for such neglect. My face, I presume, showed my utter astonishment at this statement and I asked him whether he knew he was under oath. He said he knew it. "Then," said I, "you don't know its meaning. Will you state what duties I ever neglected and name the occasion when you had to reprove me for any unsoldierly conduct?" He was a long time in answering and then said, "I trust the Captain will not press this question, I trust he will withdraw it." "No sir," said I, "I demand an answer, and remember if you do not speak the truth I will see that charges be preferred against you for perjury." The judge advocate ruled this question in its present shape as improper. I then asked the question without the threat. Said he, "You always send your Company out to drill under Lieutenants while you remain in your quarters." "Is that all?," said I. "Well, seeing that during most of the time I have been with this regiment I have been without Lieutenants, you must mean that I let the sergeants drill the Company." "I mean," said he, "you do not yourself drill the Company." "I would like to ask another question," said I. "As you have been but little with the command during the time it has been in [the] field, being home so very often, how do you know that I remained in my quarters?" "I am kept well informed of all that transpires during my absence." "Oh?"

said the judge advocate. I replied as I didn't care to have it appear that Gwyn was on trial instead of myself I would ask no more questions. The judge advocate then said sternly, "Hereafter you will submit to me in writing the questions you desire to ask the witnesses."[7] Gwyn's testimony was a failure. Apart from the fact that I had been insubordinate at Inspection he made but a sorry figure with his other statements. I believe he got the worst of the encounter.

That cowardly sneak, Adjutant Hand was next called. He related arresting me, and although not hearing the words attributed to me by the Colonel, swore that I afterwards threatened to take the life of Gwyn. He felt assured I meant to do so and was only prevented by the guard. When asked whether I wished to cross examine, I wrote on a piece of paper, "No, I don't care to make a greater liar of this drunken idiot." The judge advocate returned the paper to me saying it was contemptuous and improper, and another such action would lead him to remove me from the Court.[8]

At this juncture Dr. Joseph Thomas was called, and although he was Gwyn's witness, never did man do more to injure a case than the good doctor. He gave a lucid and absolutely true account of that Sunday morning trouble, [and] gave also a description of my character and standing in the regiment and brigade, told what he thought of my angered expression at the time, and gave a history of what led up to my quarrel with Gwyn. He spoke of my youth, my previous service, my unwillingness to defend myself and of his request not to be called by the prosecution. As he spoke, Jacob, I was completely unmanned—tears I could not suppress welled up and ran down my face. Against all propriety I rose up and exclaimed, "Thank you, my friend, thank God there is one friend honest and true enough to speak a word in my behalf." There was a scene in the Court. The Judge Advocate called for my guard to remove me; he got right up and stormed saying that I had gone far enough. The Court was cleared and whatever took place afterward I do not know. When it resumed its sitting I was allowed to stay. Great Heavens, if I had a lawyer then to take up my case how I could have beaten this loafer. How Gwyn scowled at the Doctor, and under what lasting obligations I will ever be to this good man's friendly help just in the pinch of time. There was very little direct questioning of Thomas. He took his departure and I felt that I did not now care what else was said. My case had been explained to the Court.[9]

Sgt. Major Seesholtz[10] called, sworn. He gave an acct. of the formation of the regiment for inspection and added that "as soon as the Captain was ordered to drill his company, in passing me he said I will be damned if I do, I'll be damned if I give a command, that it was damned foolishness, or damned foolish, I cannot tell which. He was from 4 to 5 paces from company and from 15 to 20 paces from me and other enlisted men of the regiment." I really did not care to bother much with this fellow, so just to make him nervous I asked him whether he had notified me that recruits would be excused. He replied, "I think I did, I don't know." I asked where was I at the time he alleged I used profane language in the hearing of the men. "In front of the Color line," said he, "and it was said loud enough for me to hear." "What distance is there," I asked, "between the officer's tents and the Color line?" The judge advocate asked the object of this question. I said I wanted to show that the man really did not know the meaning of a pace, a rod, or a distance of any kind. "25 to 40 paces," said Seesholtz. "You are sure of this distance?" said I. He replied, "It might have been more or less than 19 or 20 rods, I am not a good judge of distance." "Are you sure you notified company commanders that recruits would not come out on inspection?" He replied, "I think I had such instructions and delivered them." "You're a bully Sergeant Major," said I aloud.

Sergeant Crossley (of my Co.) called and testified word for word as follows—"Capt. Donaldson, on being told to drill his company, at first said, 'Yes sir,' then changing the direction of the Company he declaired he would not, and then speaking to me said, 'I might drill it.' He then fell to the rear and walked off some paces and followed the Company at some distance. The Company, on coming near Head Quarters, the 2nd Lieut. came up and the Captain ordered him to drill the Company. At this juncture the Colonel again ordered him to take command and drill it. Capt. Donaldson then stepped to the front of the Company, when the Colonel said, 'Do you intend obeying my orders?' I did not hear the conversation, but the Capt. said it was unjust to punish the Co. for his faults. I did not hear the Captain say you, meaning the Colonel, are a damn fool, or it is damn foolishness. He was about to give a command to the Company when the Colonel again ordered him to drill it."

Sgt. Leo, Orderly Sgt. Co. B,[11] called. "On Dec. 6th, on coming into line the Colonel ordered him to drill the Co. for two hours, then he would inspect it. Capt. Donaldson ordered his Orderly Sgt. to take and drill it, and said he would be damned if he would, or 'I will be damned if I will.' He said it was a damn foolish order, or that the Col. was a damn fool, or words to that effect. This was in hearing of the enlisted men. I heard it while he was passing our company. He said it was an improper order and <u>looked</u> dis-respectful towards his commanding officer." I asked him, "How does a man look when he is disrespectful?" He replied, "Men have different styles of looking disrespectful."

Chaplain Wm. O'Neill called. "I don't remember the date. It was Sab-bath morning. I heard Col. Gwyn ask the Captain why he was not drilling his company. 'Didn't I order you to drill your company?' said he. Capt. Donaldson said, 'Yes, you did, but I do not want my men to suffer for my offenses,' or something to that effect. Capt. Donaldson said you have insulted me and that I will not permit a Major General to do [this], much less you. I have no recollection of hearing him use profane language."

So closed the prosecution. The judge advocate then said, "We will now call the witnesses for the defense." I asked whether I could make a statement. He said, "No!" I said inasmuch as I was defending my own case I was under a great disadvantage. I merely desired to state why I will not call any witnesses for defense. The Court was cleared and after a very short time resumed again its sitting. When the President said, "What is it you wish to say about your witnesses?" I said I have no witnesses to produce, nor any defense to make, and that I sincerely trusted the Court could see its way clearly to dismiss me from the service, or in any other way to get me out of the house of bondage. Col. Welch said it would never do for me not to defend myself, that if I was not prepared he would adjourn the Court until Wednesday so that I might procure my witnesses; that I was in duty bound, having pleaded "Not Guilty," to protect myself. I urged that I was very unhappy and desired to go home—or to be shot—anything to rid me of the service. I could no longer remain in the regiment. It would be charity as well as justice to dismiss me. During the conversation Gwyn had left that tent. "Well," said Col. Welch, "the Court will adjourn 'till Wednesday next in order to allow the Captain time to make his defense." The judge advocate said, "If you do not intend calling witnesses, make a statement of your defense in writing, as you will not be allowed to speak. I tell you this because you seem to be unacquainted with the rules governing Courts-Martial."

Of course Jac, there is no help for me now. A dismissal is sure to follow this trial. It has been shown that I was disrespectful to my commanding officer, and as I declined to make a defense, there is nothing else for the Court to do but find me guilty. I have, however, saved myself from being "Cashiered," and will go at once to the President and make my defense before him, and reverse the findings of the Court. As soon as I learn the result I will telegraph you from Washington where I will hurry at once. . . .

I think I have written about all I know of the trial, and [am] very tired. It is a long distance to and from 3rd Brigade Hd. Quarters. As I left there on my return the members of the Court noticed me marched off under the guard of four men and one officer. I paid no attention to anyone, but buttoning my greatcoat closely around me, retired in silence, speaking not a word till I reached my quarters.

>—↔—O—↔—<

Camp 118th Regt. P.V.
December 23rd, 1863

. . . I made my statement this morning before the re-assembled Court. I don't know whether it went for much, as all could see I did it only in deference to the wishes of Col. Welch. This worthy man is evidently interested in my welfare, and I do not believe the Court is badly disposed towards me. But in the absence of any endeavor on my part at a defense, there remains nothing for them to do but to find me guilty according to the evidence. So be it. I am at this moment either a soldier or else a civilian— the latter I hope. . . .

Statement of the accused, F. A. Donaldson, Capt. Co. H, 118th Regt. P.V.

The accused desires to avail himself of the courtesy always extended in like circumstances to make a statement of the facts connected with the charges which have been preferred, to review the testimony adduced at the trial, and thus furnish a plea in mitigation, in extenuation, or entirely to overthrow the allegations against him. In doing this he regrets that he is obliged, in order to furnish a clear understanding of the case, to allude to his superior officer in a manner which would otherwise or at other times be altogether unwarranted and improper.

The charges and specifications are of a very grave and serious character, and very voluminous, embracing five charges and fourteen specifications, although the transactions of that sabbath morning as shown by the witnesses called by the Government were brief and simple, entirely out of proportion to the magnitude of the charges. The facts as elicited by the witnesses were these: On the morning of the 6th of December there was the usual Sunday morning inspection. The Orderly Sergeant of Co. H, which the accused then commanded, being at the surgeons quarters attending to the examination of the recruits, was a little late in getting the company out, having just started from the Co. Street as the others were forming in line. The Colonel, on learning that it was Co. H, immediately ordered the line to close up, and as they were closing up in obedience to his order, the accused appeared on the ground with his company and was reprimanded in the presence of the entire regiment, and ordered as a punishment to drill the company two hours, and it is respectfully submitted whether the punishment ordered was not too severe for the offense committed, and as the fact of the Company not being promptly on the Color line is the base of the charge of neglect of duty, it is contended that the 1st Charge is not sustained.

The evidence goes on to show that the Company was then turned over to the 1st Sergt. who proceeded to drill it as directed. The Adjutant was then sent to the accused with an order from the Colonel to drill the Company, which he was proceeding to do when called to the Colonel and the conversation about a previous insult occurred, and the accused was then placed in arrest so that he could not obey the order to drill his company. The Second charge of disobedience of orders is thus disposed of.

The accused, upon being deprived of his sword and ordered into arrest, went to his quarters, where he endeavored to calm his agitation produced by the indignities he had received by walking in front of his tent, as he supposed he had a perfect right to do. When he was told by the Adjutant that a guard was to be placed over him, when this additional insult was put upon him, he is alleged to have threatened to shoot the guard, placing his hand upon his holsters as if to put his threat in execution, although the guard was not yet posted. There is not the slightest evidence that the accused made the least resistance or exhibited any mutinous conduct to justify the placing of guard over him. The especial attention of the Court is called to the testimony of Surgeon Thomas, an officer above suspicion who gave in his account of the affair with no fear or favor, and who explained why the Company was late and expressed his belief from a knowledge of Capt. Donaldson and his manner at the time that he had no idea of shooting the Colonel, "Although," he said, "the Colonel is pursuing me and must let me alone." The specifications of the remaining charges being a mere repetition of the former are not alluded to further than to call attention to this fact.

In the list of witnesses placed upon the charges and specifications were included quite a number of line officers, and as the language alleged to have been used was in the presence of the whole regiment, it gave to the charges an amount of respectability of which they are deprived when it is remembered that the witnesses called were mostly Sergeants—the Sgt. Major and two Orderly Sgts.—whos[e] commissions are trembling in the balance, and the question to be or not to be is an absorbing one with them, and depending perhaps upon the acuteness of their hearing, or ability to decide by the countenance as to respect or disrespect. Why were the line officers who were there and saw it all not called? Dr. Thomas was called because he was the only witness who heard a word about shooting Colonel Gwyn, and he looked upon it as something of no importance whatever, that the accused did not intend to put into execution. The whole feeling of the accused was that he had been wronged, that he was required to punish his company for something for which they were not to blame. No witnesses have been called by the defense except the Chaplain, who heard the conversation but did not hear the profane expressions attributed to the accused. It was supposed that all the witnesses on the original paper would be present, but as they were not, it was not deemed advisable to delay the Court by sending for them.

The reason that no testimony was offered as to the unusual character of the punishment ordered by Col. Gwyn [was] because every member of the Court is perfectly competent to decide on that point. Every officer knows whether it is proper for a commanding officer to reprimand his officers for slight offenses in the presence of the command and can judge what must have been the feelings of an officer who had always endeavored to do his duty to be thus summarily dealt with. The accused must have been a poor scholar not to have learned during the years he has been serving his country in the field that the first and last duty of a soldier, be he officer or private, is obedience to the commands of the superior, but he has yet to learn that subordinates have no rights which their superiors are not bound to respect.

Gentlemen of the Court, there is a solution to this whole transaction which you will allow to be briefly and respectfully recapitulated. Colonel Gwyn, returning from a long absence in Philadelphia where he had been eminently successful in recruiting, [arrived] to find his regiment in [the] command of an officer detailed for the purpose from another regiment; it was evidently his duty to do something to impress the command with the idea that their Colonel was among them, and that he would command them and do it well. He knew and felt that he was the Colonel of the regiment, that he could and ought to have the entire command, and he had a laudable ambition to be respected, and felt that something must be done to secure it. Some example must be made, and in his zeal to reestablish himself as a disciplinarian the reins of government were seized too roughly, and an example to be held up was sought too eagerly. Like Napoleon when he defended the assembly from the populace by firing solid shot into the masses, he desired to place his signet upon the regiment and let them know that in him they had a commander indeed. Unfortunately, thus far for the accused, circumstances gave him the opportunity for reprimand, for a signal display of his authority, and it is submitted whether if Col. Gwyn had been cool and dispassionate he could not have afforded to wait until the morrow before giving the Company a punishment by drilling. Why did he thus order the Company for punishment when the Captain was alleged to be the party to blame?

No one will be deceived by the verbiage of the Charges and Specifications, they are drawn out and extended to cover as much space as possible to serve to make the offence appear equally extensive. This is a true solution of the difficulties of the case; the whole thing has been overdrawn, too highly colored, magnified beyond its real importance. The placing of a single sentry before the tent of the accused ostensibly to prevent his escape, but really to prejudice the case in the eyes of others to give the impression that a very heinous crime had been committed, and the fact that in a written appeal to have the sentry removed the accused incidentally stated that if a sentry walking in front of his tent was intended to prevent his escape that all must see it to be wholly inadequate to such a task, the incongruity was immediately rectified and an additional sentinel placed in the rear, both of them being required to load in the presence of the accused. This item is a key which unlocks the <u>animus</u> of the Charges and Specifications.

In making up the findings of the Court, if it has been proved by the evidence that either of the Charges or any of the specifications are true, the accused begs to have the Court remember the provocations that were offered, and to take into consideration his services in the past. In conclusion the accused returns his thanks for the courtesies which have been extended to him, and desires to express his regrets that he has felt obliged to occupy so much of the attention of the Court, and so much of the time of the reviewing officers in making the statement, but he has felt impelled to say this much, trusting it will have just and due influence in the decision of the case.

➤─┤◆├─O─┤◆├─◄

Camp 118th Regt. P.V.
December 27th, 1863

Dear Jacob:

. . . Christmas passed as do all <u>legal</u> holidays with us—quietly. I was, however, not neglected. I had a partridge for breakfast, a glass of superior old brandy, and a heavy cut of cake—pound cake. Crocker did the partridge, Dr. Thomas the rum, and my company the cake. These good things were received in boxes, per express from home.

You ask the meaning of "oskerfoodle." Well, it is a term used by the soldiers to denote drunkenness, or rum, according as it is applied. Thus, Adjt. Hand was "oskerfoodled," meaning that he was drunk, a condition that he is in pretty much all his time just now. . . .

>-+◆>-○-<◆+-<

Camp 118th Regt. P.V.
December 28th, 1863

Dear Jac:

. . . I have been pondering the question of leave taking with my company, and think it not unlikely I will write them a letter to be read after my departure, something like this—In bidding them farewell I will make no mention of my troubles, will speak only of my sorrow at parting from them, speak of them as good disciplined soldiers of whom I always was, and still am, so proud, that for the old soldiers of the company a bond of true friendship and brotherly affection will always hold [a] place in my heart, that I will always be glad to take them by the hand and welcome them as dear friends who have shared with me so many perils and hardships. Of the new men, that their conduct has always been such that gives them an equal share with their older comrades of my lasting regard. I will then lecture them upon the <u>first</u> duty of a soldier—<u>obedience</u>, and urge upon all to do as well in the future as they have with me, that in me they will always have a friend upon whom they can confidently rely should they need my aid or assistance or desire anything to be done for them at home, and now conclude by adding the eagerness with which I will scan the daily paper for news of my dear old comrades in the coming campaign. What think you of all this? Or do you suggest a more formal leave taking, a word to each with a manly grasp of the hand? Tell me, what do you counsel, and what is the proper thing to do?

Seven men of Donaldson's Company H, in the winter of 1863–64. None of the individuals are positively identified, but the soldier seated at left is likely Sgt. Owen D. Roberts, and the figure seated at center is probably Lt. (formerly Sgt.) Sylvester Crossley. Don Enders Collection, USAMHI.

You will scarcely credit it, I dread the time to approach that causes me to leave these brave fellows. They are my creation, they are soldiers of my own making, and it is with no little pride that I say it—a braver, better, or more honorable set of men no captain ever commanded. I have great respect for my company—in other words, <u>they are soldiers</u>. . . .

Camp 118th Regt. P.V.
January 5th, 1864

Dear Jac:

. . . Gwyn has obtained 10 days leave of absence, poor fellow; he has been in camp nearly one month—needs rest—must go home. . . . Last night a few of his <u>personal and intimate friends</u> presented him with a gold watch and chain. The presentation was made by Capt. Hunterson. It must have been of <u>choice language</u> considering the orator's abilities. The result was a glorious drunk. The <u>friends</u> were carried home and put to bed. I am told the rum ran full and free as water. The watch cost $175.00—I did not subscribe (loud laughter), neither did the Lt. Col. or the rest of us. . . .

Lt. Brown, the consolidated, unanimous drunkard, has recd. an honorable discharge. He is one of the "friends." Think of it! To my certain knowledge he never did a full days duty during the whole time, as an officer, he was with us. I have seen him so drunk that a detail had to be made [to] clean him. Think of this fellow getting an honorable discharge from the service he has so signally disgraced. But he was one of the Friends of the commandant. . . .

Donaldson was found guilty on December 23 of all of the charges brought against him by Colonel Gwyn, and was sentenced to be dismissed from the service. In accordance with military custom, the sentence was approved by President Lincoln. Donaldson did not learn of the verdict until sometime after January 9, the date of his final (unincluded) letter from the Army of the Potomac.

In early February, following what was surely a joyful reunion with Eliza and Jacob in Philadelphia, Donaldson hastened to Washington, D.C., to attempt, with the assistance of influential family friends, to secure a meeting with the president and have his dismissal reversed.

Metropolitan Hotel, Washington D.C.
February 4th, 1864

My dear Brother:

I arrived here about seven o'clock this morning. I slept well during the ride from Philadelphia, and felt as fresh as a daisy all the morning. I took breakfast at the hotel and certainly developed an appetite for the good things set before me. . . .

After breakfast I called upon Mr. Thomas Webster[12] but he was "non est come at a bus" and had been for a good while. This was unfortunate. Next I made an effort to see the Hon. Chas. O'Neill, M.C.,[13] from Philadelphia, and succeeded, after a little diplomacy, in securing a short interview with that genial gentleman. He was at breakfast, so I waited until he was through and then introduced myself. He received me most affably, but at the same time I thought he seemed bored, certainly what he said was of the wet blanket order. He could give me no assurance of a successful endeavor on my part to appeal to the President. Among other things, he said I might just as well go home as to wait about the Capital for an audience with Mr. Lincoln, that I could not aid my own cause one particle, that it would take time and I must have patience, that he had many similar cases that must first be attended to before he could possibly interest himself in my affairs, and that in any event it was highly problimetical whether I succeeded in my desire should I be fortunate enough to see the President. However he took all my papers, including my letter to the Hon. John W. Forney,[14] which letter I was loath to part with.

I listened respectfully to what he said, and then, in reply, told him I was not to be judged by my looks, that I was a person of some energy and would have an audience with the President whether he contributed to that end or not, that once in the presence of this good man and allowed to briefly plead my own case I was not without heart of enlisting his sympathies in my behalf, and that I would not go home until the object of my visit was attained, that I had powerful friends yet to see, but considered it my duty first to call upon him, the representative of my congressional district, that I had no intention of inconveniencing him with my troubles, but would at once seek elsewhere for help. Mr. O'Neill showed surprise at my vehemence, and added in conclusion he would give my affairs his earliest attention. Now just think of it—he had but a moment before he told me it would take time, and that I had better go home—and then, after I pitched into him, said he would give my affairs his earliest attention. . . .

>—1—4>—0—<4—1—<

Metropolitan Hotel,
Washington D.C.
February 5th, 1864

My Dear Brother:

My letter of yesterday doubtless caused you some uneasiness, and I fancy you will be impatient for news of today's experiences. Well then, not to keep you in suspense, I have been imminently successful. . . .

Mr. O'Neill was profuse in his greeting and gave me a segar, which I took and lit from his. He said all the cases ahead of mine had been disposed of and he was at leisure to give his immediate personal attention to my affairs. He would arrange with Mr. Webster, Mr. Forney, and Sec. Montgomery Blair[15] for an interview with the President the first of the week, and would notify me when to be on hand. Think of it! Did you ever hear of such a worker as the Honorable Charles O'Neill? All cases ahead of mine, which only yesterday he said would take time to dispose of, had been adjusted by this lightning worker, in the wee hours of last night, apparently. . . .

>—+—◆>—O—◆+—+—◄

Metropolitan Hotel,
March 3, 1864
Washington D.C.

My dear Jacob:

At last I have won!! I am too excited, or rather too exultant to calmly and deliberately write how it all came about, but I will not keep you another day in suspense. I will not return home until tomorrow probably.

As per appointment I met Mr. O'Neill, Mr. Webster, Mr. Forney at "Willards" this morning at 10 o'clock and proceeded to the White House, where we were joined by Sec. Montgomery Blair. There were a goodly number awaiting an audience with the President, but we had precedence and were ushered into Mr. Lincoln's private office, where we took seats and awaited the approach of this great man. I had not been coached, nor were any suggestions offered as to the line of procedure in presenting my case. In fact I did not know what was to be done or what was expected of me. Mr. Webster has since told me it was purposely done, that it was thought best for me to make my appeal perfectly free and without preparation, because no one was more susceptible to downright honest unstudied, innocent candor than the President, and none more ready to detect dissimulation than he.

After a little time Mr. Lincoln came into the room when we all arose. The size of the President nearly overcame me. He was, apparently, the tallest man I ever saw, and so thin too and so ugly. He had a long black double breasted frock coat which hung like a wrapper on his lean frame, and it was positively the dirtiest coat I ever beheld for a man having any pretentions to gentility, much less the President of the United States of America. Before he came into the room I was rather impressed by the occasion and honor of meeting the President. But when this homely, dirty, shabby, lean, lanky man appeared I lost all sense of the dignity of the surroundings and found myself filled with amazement that this was indeed Abraham Lincoln, President of the United States. Gracious! Jacob, with all due respect to Mr. Lincoln, how can foreign nations, or indeed our own people, have respect for institutions when such a slovenly careless man is the first gentleman of the land. Although I have frequently seen Mr. Lincoln, it has always been at a distance, but I never for a moment conceived him to be the uncouth, the common man I found him to be when face to face with him. I was the worst disappointed man conceivable. Indeed, although I have gained my object, it has been at the expense of my loyalty to a Republican Form of Government. I will tell you my reason for this when I get home. Now all this is about the personal appearance of Mr. Lincoln. Now for the other side.

He shook hands with the gentlemen present, and when I was presented, as I did not do so, merely out of respect—he approached and gave me one single up and down pump handle style of shake hands, and laying the other hand on my shoulder, still retaining hold of the hand he had shaken, led me to a seat immediately in front of his own, where the light could shine right on my face. I felt the warm blood coursing through my veins, but it was not from bashfulness or modesty, but from a recognition of his kindly act of encouragement. But I did not need to be assured, I was perfectly under self control.

Mr. Forney at once proceeded with the object of our visit. He said—about as follows—"Mr. President, the young gentleman we have just presented to you is here for the simple purpose of appealing to you for justice in a matter that is as life and death to him. I will let him tell his own story, but will say that I have known him ever since he wore slips, and up to the present time have known nothing of him but what is honorable, manly and to his credit. Mr. President, look at him, his face bespeaks [what is] honest, upright, pure and manly. I will let you into a secret, but it is to be held sacred for a time at least, and that is he is engaged to be married to a lovely, beautiful young lady, a personal friend of my family. She too I have known from infancy. The match is in every way most proper, suitable, and to be desired by both families, but the Captain most positively refuses to wed unless the stain upon his honor first be removed, and I cannot blame him."

Mr. Blair then said his attention had been called to my case by persons who usually refrain from interfering in military matters, but this being a case that in their judgment should be referred to you for consideration, and I strongly urge your Excellency to do all that lay in your power to right a gross wrong done to this young man.

Mr. O'Neill said he thought there never had been a case of the kind that had called forth so largely the sympathies of the citizens of Philadelphia, and especially those of his district, where Captain Donaldson resided. He had petitions from clergymen, doctors and merchants asking [his] interest in behalf of <u>my friend Frank</u>.

Mr. Webster said I was a kinsman of his and the family were greatly distressed in consequence of this trouble. He then made, at considerable length, the record of my family, spoke of Harry Donaldson's death at Savage Station, and heaven only knows how many more of the family he had killed off before he was through.

By this time I was nearly <u>done</u> for with astonishment at the bald face lying of these men. I had never before seen Forney in my life, am not engaged to be married to anyone, much less a relative of his.

Mr. Lincoln said, "Now Captain just tell me as briefly as possible your trouble—from the very beginning." I then stood up, assuming the position of a soldier, and told my story. Mr. Lincoln listened without comment to the end. He rested his chin on his hand and looked right at me. Whether his thoughts were following my words or were far away I cannot say. He was apparently giving close attention to my speech. I said I had been tenderly reared by a fond mother, and was the Benjamin of her flock. That I had enlisted—among the very first—spoke of Colonel Baker, my capture at Ball's Bluff, imprisonment at Richmond, my exchange and promotion by Colonel Isaac J. Wistar, wounding at Fair Oaks, again promotion, but this time by an order of the War Department to another command, the 118th Penna. Vols., a new organization then forming, my many altercations with Col. Gwyn, the character of that person, my appreciation of the responsibilities of rank, and consequently my contempt for this man whose principal claim to command was capacity for absorbing liquor. That I had made no defense at my trial because it was before strangers and not the officers of the brigade entitled to try me, and that I determined to cast myself upon the generosity of himself and ask for a review of my case with this statement of facts. This is about the substance of what I said, but I think the way I said it had an effect, because I was lost to all save the one pervading thought of making my case as strong as I could.

When I was through, Mr. Lincoln sat for a moment or two and then said, "Let me have your papers." I gave them to him, and taking a lead pencil from his pocket, wrote upon the front of the package "Judge Advocate General Holt will favorably consider this petition, A. Lincoln," and handed me the package again saying, "I think you have made out a case for clemency, take these papers to Holt, who will notify you of the result. Now young man, inasmuch as I have done you a service, I want you to promise me one thing. Mr. Forney says you are engaged to be married. Now I want you to go right home, marry the young lady, and have lots of children, all of them boys, because the war bids fair to be prolonged indefinitely and we will need all the men we can get."

Mr. O'Neill said, "By the way Captain, you have in your pocket the resignation of Captain Wetherill of the 118th. Please give it to the President for acceptance." I did so, and without a moment's hesitancy he approved it, and Wetherill was out of the service.

Jacob, I have learned one thing most positively—there is nothing like looking after your own affairs. Had I long ago gotten leave of absence and forced my way into the presence of the President, or had had Mr. O'Neill to take my resignation to him, I would have been spared all this trouble. I came away disappointed at the appearance of the President but nevertheless entertaining kindly feelings towards him. I think he belongs to the common people, has a sympathetic heart and is probably not bull dog enough to master the knobby problems thrust upon him. I may not get home tomorrow, but when I do will give you fuller details of my long battle to reach an audience with the President.

EPILOGUE

*D*onaldson's efforts in reaching the President were rewarded, and though he was not successful in gaining an outright honorable discharge, he was informed, in armyspeak, "that the disability resulting from his dismissal was removed," by order of the War Department, effective March 28, 1864. "The effect of a removal of disability," explained the War Department, "was to remove the stain of the sentence" and to declare the volunteer officer "qualified to re-enter the service, if desired. It is a measure of reparation, equivalent, practically, to an honorable discharge." It is not known whether Donaldson made any attempt to reenter the service; in the unlikely event that he did, he left no record of it.

As with many veterans of the Civil War, the details of the captain's postwar life grow more obscure with the passage of years. Some particulars, however, are known.

Immediately after the war, Donaldson entered into the insurance business with two of his superiors from the 118th Pennsylvania, Col. Charles Prevost and Lt. Col. Charles P. Herring. Prevost had ended the war commanding the 16th Regiment Veteran Reserve Corps at Springfield, Illinois, and was brevetted to the rank of brigadier general. Herring, who was also brevetted to brigadier general, had lost a leg at Dabney's Mill, Virginia, during the fighting there on February 6, 1865. After a year in partnership, Donaldson struck out on his own (he left Prevost and Herring on good terms, remaining fast friends with both men until their death) and in 1866 founded Francis A. Donaldson & Company Insurance, which he successfully headed for the next fifty-one years.

Donaldson became active in the Pennsylvania National Guard, serving variously as lieutenant, adjutant, and captain in the 1st Regiment from 1868 to 1872. He was also involved in veterans organizations as a member of Philadelphia Post No. 2 of the Grand Army of the Republic, and he held several offices within the Pennsylvania Commandery of the Military Order of the Loyal Legion of the United States. He *also worked with several veterans of the 118th Pennsylvania in writing their Regimental History, albeit as an unmentioned contributor, and corresponded with soldiers from both sides to flesh out details mentioned in his letters. Throughout his life, Donaldson visited several of the battlefields he had fought on as a young man and was present for the dedication of the 118th Pennsylvania's monument at Gettysburg in 1884, as well as for the fiftieth anniversary commemoration of the battle in 1913.*

In 1872 Donaldson married Mary Heyburger Landell, and the union produced two sons, Francis Adams, Jr., born in 1875, and Wharton Landell, born in 1880, and a daughter, Kate Beresford, born in 1876. Donaldson applied for a pension in 1878 because of his war wound, claiming "severe weather neuralgia" in his limb and that he was "compelled to support the arm when walking or when long on his feet." The pension was granted at half disability in 1879 at the rate of $7.50 per month, with the rate increasing over time to $50 per month in the 1920s. A physician who examined him in 1888 noted that he was "a healthy looking, robust man."[1]

Donaldson's Confederate brother, John, served as captain of Company H of the 22nd Virginia until he was captured at Cold Harbor, Virginia, on June 3, 1864. Initially imprisoned at Point Lookout, Maryland, John was soon transferred to Fort Delaware, thirty-five miles south of Philadelphia.[2] Strenuous efforts apparently were made to secure his release, as John, writing to Jacob in 1897, recalled that "Auntie, on her knees to Mr. Lincoln, could not have me paroled." The Donaldson family surely visited him as often as possible during his captivity, and he took the oath of allegiance and was released on June 10, 1865. John entered into business in Cincinnati in the years after the war, later relocated to Philadelphia, and died in Atlantic City in 1901.

Little is known postwar of Donaldson's eldest brother and chief correspondent, Jacob, or Aunt and stepmother, Eliza Ann Nice. Jacob wed later in life and passed away in 1915; Eliza died in 1907.

Donaldson and his nemesis, Colonel Gwyn, appear to have crossed paths twice during the remainder of their lives. Gwyn had gone on to compile an admirable service record throughout the balance of the war, was wounded in the Wilderness, and had led two separate 5th Corps brigades into battle. For gallant and distinguished services at Peebles' Farm, Virginia, on September 30, 1864, he was brevetted brigadier general, and he was brevetted major general at the Battle of Five Forks, Virginia, on April 1, 1865, for the same reason. The first encounter between the two men took place soon after the war and resulted in Donaldson being physically restrained from confronting his former commander. The second incident, which was distinctly less acrimonious, occurred six years before Gwyn's death.

Philadelphia, Pa.
February 18, 1907

Whilst on an open Chestnut Street car, July 2, 1901, at 9th Street, General Gwyn got on, and without noting me, apparently, took a seat next to me. Always a large man during the war, he at this time was particularly so, having gained in weight as his years advanced. We were crowded somewhat, and naturally both turned to look at each other. I said, "General, do you recall me?" "Perfectly, Captain, perfectly," he replied. "It has been many years, General, since we met, and I feel grateful that time has wrought so little change with me that you so readily recognize me. I may add that with exception of additional weight, you too are not much changed." He replied that appearances were deceptive, that he was far from well, was suffering from diabetes and could not expect many years of prolonged life, that he had been recently living with his daughter at Collingswood, I think he had said, but was now living at the Red Lion Hotel, this city.

I remarked that I was glad of this opportunity for talking with him, that I had long since removed from my mind all bitterness of feeling engendered by my military life in the 118th Penna. Regt. and could now look back with regret at my hasty temper and consequent insubordination that led to so much trouble—but that I was not wholly to blame, that he, himself, so much older that I, should have used different methods to bring me under discipline. "Well," said he, "I am an old man now, 73 years (12 years older than me) and I find that I have not changed much since war times. You know Captain, I was a pretty free drinker whilst in the service, and I kept it up until about a year ago, when I had to refrain because of my health, but I propose to celebrate the coming 4th of July by getting 'pretty full' and having a royal good time." "I wouldn't do that general, it is undignified, unnecessary, and besides, you have just stated that a year has elapsed since you took a drink of liquor. Rum was the cause of much trouble to us all during our army life, and it should have been dispensed with when the war was over." He made no reply to this. "By the way Captain, I am told that you are married." "Yes," said I, "and have three children, two sons and a daughter. My eldest son is in business with me, as a partner, at 216 South 3rd Street." He said he would call at my office during the forenoon and be presented to my son. "Not so," said I, much to his astonishment, "on the contrary, if you should honor me by a visit, I will be pleased to present my son to you." This seemed to mollify his rising ire, and he replied that he had heard of my goodness and charities to the soldiers of the regiment, noticeably to

Private Henry Steiner,[3] and as the late commanding officer he thanked me for my kindness to the poor old fellows.

He did call at the office and I duly presented my son Francis. He remained about an hour and we parted in the friendliest manner imaginable. To Francis' inquiry as to how it was possible for me to meet and receive General Gwyn with such apparent cordiality, I replied that whilst it was true that for years I held malice, bitter hatred and all uncharitableness towards this man for the many wrongs done me whilst under his command, resulting in a personal encounter shortly after the war necessitating my being placed under heavy bonds to keep the peace against him, with a final "treaty of peace," as it were, between our mutual friends, that should we chance to meet upon the public highways we were to pass each other without noticing—yet—I had long since forgiven him and blamed myself a great deal for hasty temper and too high a standard placed upon my superior officers—that I wanted to be at peace with all men.

Donaldson passed away on May 3, 1928, at the age of eighty-seven, survived by his wife, three children, six grandchildren, and one great-grandchild. He was laid to rest beside Jacob, John, and Eliza in Philadelphia's West Laurel Hill Cemetery. In his obituary it was stated that he had been "a man of great force and determination of character, [and] of great energy of action—one of those who achieve success by indomitable force of character and concentration of purpose."[4] The soldiers he had served with, whether or not they had liked and respected him, probably would have agreed.

NOTES

INTRODUCTION

1. Francis Adams Donaldson Papers, The Civil War Library and Museum, Philadelphia (cited hereafter as FAD Papers, CWLM). Except where noted, all of the material used in the preparation of this introduction is taken from the Donaldson Papers.
2. Terry D. Lowry, *22nd Virginia Infantry* (cited hereafter as Lowry, *22nd Virginia*) (Lynchburg, VA: H. E. Howard, 1988), 2.
3. Noyes Rand to FAD, January 1904, FAD Papers, CWLM.
4. Lowry, 22nd Virginia, 145.
5. Survivors' Association, *History of the 118th Pennsylvania Volunteers Corn Exchange Regiment, from their First Engagement at Antietam to Appomattox. . . .* (cited hereafter as Survivors' Association, *118th Pennsylvania*) (Philadelphia: J. L. Smith, 1905), 145–46.
6. Harold Adams Small, ed., *The Road to Richmond* (cited hereafter as Small, *Road to Richmond*) (Berkeley, CA: University of California Press, 1939), vii.

CHAPTER ONE: BALL'S BLUFF, CAPTIVITY, AND RETURN

1. Harry C. Blair and Rebecca Tarshis, *Lincoln's Constant Ally: The Life of Colonel Edward D. Baker* (Portland: Oregon Historical Society, 1960), 124–25.
2. Isaac Jones Wistar, *Autobiography of Isaac Jones Wistar: 1827–1905; Half a Century in War and Peace* (cited hereafter as Wistar, *Autobiography*) (Philadelphia: Wistar Institute, 1937), 13–14.
3. Frank H. Taylor, *Philadelphia in the Civil War, 1861–1865* (cited hereafter as Taylor, *Philadelphia in the War*) (Philadelphia, 1913), 86.
4. Munson's Hill, Virginia, was located approximately seven miles northwest of Alexandria on the Leesburg and Alexandria Turnpike. George B. Davis et al., eds., *Atlas to Accompany the Official Records of the Union and Confederate Armies* (1891–95; reprint, *The Official Military Atlas of the Civil War,* New York: Fairfax Press, 1983) (cited hereafter as *O.R. Atlas*), plate VII, map 1.
5. William P. Tomlinson, thirty-two, of Philadelphia, served as captain of Company I until his discharge on November 20, 1862, due to "partial loss of sight and total night blindness" suffered soon after the Peninsula Campaign. Compiled Service Record, Record Group 94, National Archives (cited hereafter as CSR, RG94, NA); Samuel P. Bates, *History of Pennsylvania Volunteers, 1861–1865* (cited hereafter as Bates, *Penna. Vols.*) (Harrisburg, PA: State Printer, 1869–71), vol. II, 823.
6. Lewinsville, Virginia, was located midway between the Georgetown and Leesburg and Alexandria Turnpikes, approximately ten miles west of Washington. Ibid.
7. Brig. Gen. William Farrar Smith of Vermont commanded a division of the Army of the Potomac at this time. U.S. War Department, *The War of the Rebellion: A Compilation of the*

Official Records of the Union and Confederate Armies (Washington, D.C.: Government Printing Office, 1880–1901) (cited hereafter as *O.R.*; all references are to ser. I), ser. I, vol. V, 17.

8. Joseph Pascoe was a nineteen-year-old Philadelphia native. CSR, RG94, NA.

9. Garick Mallery, twenty-nine, of Philadelphia, was seriously wounded in the wrist and thigh at White Oak Swamp on June 30, 1862. His leg wound precluded further infantry service, and he mustered out of the 71st in February 1863 to accept a promotion to the lieutenant colonelcy of the 13th Pennsylvania Cavalry. CSR, RG94, NA; Bates, *Penna. Vols.*, vol. II, 820, vol. III, 1272; *Annual Report of the Adjutant General of Pennsylvania . . . for the Year 1866* (cited hereafter as *Adj. Gen. of PA, 1866*) (Harrisburg, PA: Singerly & Myers, 1867), 371.

10. Sgt. William Sloanaker, twenty-three, of Philadelphia had been promoted to orderly sergeant of Company H in August 1861. He was captured at Ball's Bluff later in the year and was discharged from the 71st in June 1863. CSR, RG94, NA.

11. Edmond Ford, twenty, of Philadelphia, would later be captured at Ball's Bluff. He became a clerk in the Medical Directors Office in Philadelphia upon his exchange in February 1862 and was discharged in July 1863 to enable him to reenlist as a hospital steward. CSR, RG94, NA.

12. The "House of Lords" was the nickname Donaldson and his comrades had conferred upon their mess.

13. Pvt. Joseph Payran, nineteen, of Philadelphia. CSR, RG94, NA.

14. Pvt. Joseph White, forty-two, of Philadelphia. CSR, RG94, NA.

15. Lt. William C. Harris of Company H, a native of Philadelphia, was captured two weeks later at Ball's Bluff. Upon his parole in January 1862, he was assiged to a skeleton regiment of returned prisoners that was being organized but that never completed its formation. He was discharged upon his resignation due to disability in February 1863. Harris was a close friend of Donaldson's, and he published an account of his experiences as a prisoner of war, titled *Prison Life in the Tobacco Warehouse at Richmond* (Philadelphia: G. W. Childs, 1862). CSR, RG94, NA; Bates, *Penna. Vols.,* vol. II, 820.

16. Berdan's Sharpshooters were an elite regiment of marksmen formed with companies from various Northern states at the outbreak of the war. Named for their flamboyant, self-promoting colonel, Hiram Berdan, they participated in all of the major battles of the Army of the Potomac. They were noted as much for their distinctive green uniforms as for their combat abilities. For a well-written history of their service, see Charles A. Stevens, *Berdan's United States Sharpshooters in the Army of the Potomac, 1861–1865* (cited hereafter as Stevens, *Berdan's Sharpshooters*) (St. Paul, MN: Price-McGill, 1892).

17. Robert A. Parrish, thirty-nine, had served as captain of Company B until his election as major in June 1861. He tendered his resignation on July 15, 1862, because of his desire to raise a new regiment and "because of the strong prejudice against me by Col. Wistar and [brigade commander] General Burns (which has barred all hope of promotion for me in this Regiment)." CSR, RG94, NA.

18. Adj. Charles S. Newlin, a twenty-one-year-old Philadelphian, was promoted to the captaincy of Company C on February 15, 1862. He was later captured during the Peninsula Campaign on June 30, 1862, and following his parole in July was mustered out of the 71st as a supernumerary. CSR, RG94, NA.; *Adj. Gen. of PA, 1866*, 368–69.

19. The Cameron Dragoons, named after then Secretary of War Simon Cameron, were recruited predominantly in Philadelphia in the summer of 1861 and were later officially designated as the 5th Pennsylvania Cavalry. Bates, *Penna. Vols.*, vol II, 569.

20. William E. A. Bird, at this time sergeant major of the Cameron Dragoons, eventually rose to the captaincy of Company B. He was discharged on January 8, 1865. Ibid., 578–84.

21. This mishap occurred essentially as Donaldson describes it; however, Federal losses totaled five killed and seventeen wounded. For reports on this action, see O.R., vol. V, 217–20; Stevens, *Berdan's Sharpshooters*, 8; Charles H. Banes, *History of the Philadelphia Brigade* (cited hereafter as Banes, *Philadelphia Brigade*) (Philadelphia: J. B. Lippincott & Co., 1876), 20–22.

22. *O.R.,* vol. V, 290.

23. Poolesville, Maryland, located twenty-five miles northwest of Washington, D.C.

24. Francis J. Keffer, thirty-six, was the captain of Company N. He was captured at Ball's Bluff in October 1861. Upon his exchange, he served as provost marshal of the Department of Annapolis until his muster out in July 1864. CSR, RG94, NA.

25. Twenty-three-year-old Charles W. Smith of Philadelphia was originally commissioned as captain of Company C and served as such until his promotion to junior major of the 71st in July 1861. He was honorably discharged in October 1862 due to ill health. CSR, RG94, NA; Bates, *Penna. Vols.*, vol. II, 801.

26. Augustus Stiles, a twenty-three-year-old carpenter from Massachusetts, had been promoted to 4th sergeant of Company H in August 1861. He deserted from the 71st near Falmouth, Virginia, on January 7, 1862. CSR, RG94, NA.

27. Pvt. James M. Chapman, twenty-six, was captured at Ball's Bluff and was later wounded in the ankle at White Oak Swamp on June 30, 1862. The Chicopee, Massachusetts, native deserted from the regiment on January 7, 1863, but returned and was discharged on a Surgeon's Certificate of Disability in July 1863. CSR, RG94, NA.

28. Frank S. Urie of Chester County, Pennsylvanias, had originally enlisted as 4th sergeant of Company H and was promoted to the second lieutenancy of the company in August 1861. He was slightly wounded at the Battle of Ball's Bluff. Later, as captain, he commanded Companies R and A. Urie resigned on account of ill health and was honorably discharged on July 27, 1862. CSR, RG94, NA.

29. Charles P. Stone, thirty-seven, was a Massachusetts native and an 1845 graduate of West Point. At this time he commanded a division in what would eventually become the 2nd Corps of the Army of the Potomac, to which Baker's Brigade had been attached. Following the ill-fated action at Ball's Bluff, Stone was made a scapegoat for Baker's mistakes and was incarcerated for more than six months, although no charges were ever brought against him. Stewart Sifakis, *Who Was Who in the Civil War* (cited hereafter as Sifakis, *Who Was Who*) (New York: Facts on File, 1988), 626.

30. Charles H. T. Collis, twenty-three, an Irish-born Philadelphian, was at this time in command of an independent company of Zouaves d'Afrique that had been recruited to serve as a bodyguard for Gen. Nathaniel Banks. In the summer of 1862 Collis was authorized to recruit his command into a full regiment, which became the 114th Pennsylvania Volunteers. Taylor, Philadelphia in the War, 124; Roger D. Hunt and Jack R. Brown, *Brevet Brigadier Generals in Blue* (cited hereafter as Hunt and Brown, *Brevet Brigadier Generals*) (Gaithersburg, MD: Olde Soldier Books, 1990), 123.

31. Donaldson's first cousin, Henry Clay Donaldson, was a twenty-two-year-old Philadelphia native. He had enlisted as a private in Company R of the 3rd California Regiment, which was later officially designated as the 72nd Pennsylvania Volunteers, on September 27. Promoted to 3rd sergeant of his company of April 1, 1862, he was shot in the stomach at Savage's Station on June 29, 1862, and "died in an ambulance and was buried on the roadside during the retreat wrapped in his overcoat and blanket." His family was unable to locate his remains. CSR, RG94, NA; Jacob Donaldson to John P. Donaldson, July 25, 1862, and January 14, 1863, FAD Papers, CWLM.

32. Morris Stradling, nineteen, of Philadelphia. CSR, RG94, NA.

33. James Marsden, a twenty-one-year-old prewar engraver, survived this wound and was discharged on August 11, 1862. CSR, RG94, NA.

34. No compiled service records have been found for Pvt. John R. Harvey or Pvt. John B. Survey, but both men were listed on the state rolls as having been killed at Ball's Bluff. Pvt. John Johnson was mortally wounded in the action and died the following day. Bates, *Penna. Vols.*, Vol. II, 802; CSR, RG94, NA.

35. Charles Jaggard, forty-two, of Philadelphia. CSR, RG94, NA.

36. Capt. Louis Bieral, a thirty-four-year-old New Yorker, was wounded at Ball's Bluff when he was knocked down by an artillery horse. He resigned his commission on April 12, 1862, due to ill health. CSR, RG94, NA.

37. Milton Cogswell, thirty-six, an 1849 graduate of West Point and native of Indiana, was captured later in the action. He returned to the army following his exchange in September 1862, serving in a variety of assignments in both the volunteer and regular services. In 1869 he was awarded the brevet of brigadier general of volunteers for his services at Ball's Bluff. Hunt and Brown, *Brevet Brigadier Generals*, 120.

38. Thomas H. Whitehouse, a twenty-seven-year-old private of Company H, was eventually exchanged and returned to the 71st, only to be wounded and captured at Antietam. He again was exchanged and returned to the 71st but deserted at an unspecified date. CSR, RG94, NA.

39. Col. Winfield Scott Featherston, a forty-one-year-old Mississippian and prewar congressman, commanded both the 13th and 17th Mississippi at Ball's Bluff. John L. Wakelyn, *Biographical Dictionary of the Confederacy* (Westport, CT: Greenwood Press, 1977), 184.

40. Col. Erasmus R. Burt, a former state auditor of Mississippi, was mortally wounded while commanding the 18th Mississippi. He died on October 26. Robert K. Krick, *Lee's Colonels: A Biographical Register of the Field Officers of the Army of Northern Virginia*, 4th ed. (cited hereafter as Krick, *Lee's Colonels*) (Dayton, OH: Press of Morningside House, 1992), 77.

41. Brig. Gen. Nathan G. Evans, thirty-seven, of South Carolina, was an 1848 graduate of West Point and was in overall command of the Confederate forces at Ball's Bluff, Sifakis, *Who Was Who*, 208.

42. Otho R. Singleton, forty-seven, a former congressman from Mississippi, commanded Company C of the 18th Mississippi. He was elected to the Confederate States Congress shortly after Ball's Bluff and served in it throughout the remainder of the war. Dunbar S. Rowland to F.A.D., October 19, 1917. FAD Papers, CWLM.

43. Capt. Wiley A. P. Jones of Company B of the 17th Mississippi resigned his commission sometime before the end of 1861. Dunbar Rowland, *Military History of Mississippi, 1803–1898* (reprint, Spartanburg, SC: Reprint Company, 1978), 82.

44. Pvt. Solomon McDonald, twenty, was one of Donaldson's mess mates. Following his exchange in February 1862, he was posted to guard duty at the U.S. Army Laboratory in Philadelphia. CSR, RG94, NA.

45. Twenty-six-year-old Thomas Coke Johnson of Georgia was later killed in action at Mechanicsville, Virginia, on June 26, 1862. Krick, *Lee's Colonels*, 210.

46. John B. Andrews, twenty-four, of Iredell County, North Carolina, commanded Company C of the 4th North Carolina until his death in July 1862 as a result of wounds received at Gaines' Mill, Virginia, on June 27. Weymouth T. Jordan and Louis H. Manarin, *North Carolina Troops, 1861–1865: A Roster* (Raleigh, NC: State Department of Archives and History, 1973), vol. IV, 35

47. Donaldson was mistaken about being initially held captive in Castle Thunder, which, although located on Cary Street in Richmond, did not open until August 1862. In all probability, he was first imprisoned in Mayo's Navy Tobacco Factory on Cary Street and then transferred, as he relates, to Ligon's Warehouse and Tobacco Factory at 25th and Main Streets. Sandra V. Parker, *Richmond's Civil War Prisons* (cited hereafter as Parker, *Richmond Prisons*) (Lynchburg, VA: H. E. Howard, 1990), 3, 6, 12.

48. Christopher Quarles Tompkins, forty-seven, of Matthews County, Virginia, was an 1836 graduate of West Point and had recently resigned his commission as colonel of John Donaldson's regiment, the 22nd Virginia, purportedly as a result of repeated disputes

with his brigade commander, former Virginia governor and U.S. secretary of war John
B. Floyd. Lowry, *22nd Virginia*, 6, 21, 202.

49. The 22nd Virginia had been detached from Floyd's Brigade on December 16 and sent
to Lewisburg, in southwest Virginia, to defend Greenbrier and Monroe Counties. Ibid., 23.

50. The narrator, Noyes Rand, has confused Ligon & Co.'s Tobacco Warehouse, where
Donaldson was confined, with Libby Prison, an infamous Federal officers' prison that
was not opened until March 1862. Parker, *Richmond Prisons*, 9.

51. In a postwar letter written to Jacob Donaldson, John Donaldson recalled securing
Frank's parole: "I shall never forget how he looked as he was brought in to me between
two Confederate soldiers in . . . prison. I saw him pass the window outside, a Reb with
a gun on each side of him. How I shook with emotion as he came towards me and as I
folded him to my heart the tears streamed down my face. He did not know I had his
parole in my pocket. Do you know Jack he was the only Yank that was ever paroled in
the City of Richmond during the war? How I don't [know]. General Lee's letter and
my interview with the secretay of war, Judah P. Benjamin, opened the prison door. I
remember so well when I entered the Secretary's room—he was alone sitting at a table.
The first thing he said was, 'Take a seat, sir.' I expected to stand in his presence, but this
remark made me feel at my ease at once. He had my papers open on the table before
him. He spoke to me in such a fatherly way. Asked how it was I was in the Confederate
service, he then said, 'If I release your brother on parole will you be responsible for
him?' A smile was on his face as he said this. . . . Poor dear old fellow. I loved my
brother and the regret of my life will always be our estrangement for so many years. . . ."
John P. Donaldson to Jacob Donaldson, March 1, 1897, FAD Papers, CWLM.

52. Levi Welch had served as 3rd Sergeant of Company H of the 22nd Virginia until his
discharge due to disability in November 1861. Appointed to the Virginia Military Institute,
he participated with the cadets in their distinguished action at New Market, Virginia,
on May 15, 1864. His brother, Lt. James C. Welch, had been killed in action while
serving with the 22nd Virginia at Scary Creek, West Virginia, on July 17, 1861. Lowry,
22nd Virginia, 206.

53. Donaldson is referring to Charlestown, located in present-day West Virginia.

54. 1st Lt. Marine C. Moore of Philadelphia was killed on picket duty on June 8, 1862.
Adj. Gen. of PA, 1866, 371; *Adj. Gen. of PA, 1863*, 296.

55. Israel B. Richardson, a forty-six-year-old Vermonter, commanded the 1st Division of
the 2nd Corps; Connecticut native John Sedgwick, forty-eight, commanded the 2nd
Division. German exile Louis Blenker's 10,000-man division was soon detached from
the 2nd Corps to reinforce Maj. Gen. John C. Fremont's unsuccessful operations in
West Virginia. William W. Burns, thirty-six, of Ohio had assumed command of the
Philadelphia Brigade upon Baker's death at Ball's Bluff. Edwin Vose Sumner of Massachusetts, commander of the 2nd Corps, was, at age sixty-five, the oldest active Federal
corps commander. Richardson, Sedgwick, and Burns were all graduates of West Point.
Sifakis, *Who Was Who*, 92, 543–44, 578–79, 634–35; O.R., vol. XI, pt. 1, 10; pt. 3, 52–53.

56. George Slow had been born in 1830 on H. N. Pendleton's Westwood Farm in Jefferson
County, Virginia. Captain Urie left the service in May due to illness, and George became
the paid servant of Donaldson throughout the balance of his army career. Donaldson
grew quite attached to George and, at the end of the war, secured employment for him
as a coachman with a wealthy Philadelphia family. Upon Slow's death in 1900, Donaldson
wrote that he was "irreproachable in character, kindly, manly, brave, faithful, true, always
to be depended upon, [and] was endeared to me not only for these sterling qualities but for
the tenderness with which he watched over me, a young soldier, and for his unassailable
honesty, unhesitating willingness in the performance of his duties, and furtherance of
my comfort." FAD Papers, CWLM.

57. Capt. Alfred C. Hills, thirty, was originally first lieutenant of Company H. Promoted to
captain of Company M in July 1861, he was transferred to the captaincy of Company

C in July 1862. He resigned one month later to accept a position as aide-de-camp on the staff of Maj. Gen. Nathaniel Banks. CSR, RG94,NA.

CHAPTER TWO: YORKTOWN AND FAIR OAKS

1. Stephen W. Sears, *George B. McClellan: The Young Napoleon* (New York: Ticknor and Fields, 1988), 180.
2. Col. Turner G. Morehead, a forty-eight-year-old native of Maryland, commanded the 106th Pennsylvania; Col. Joshua T. Owen, forty-one, originally from Wales, led the 69th Pennsylvania; and Massachusetts-born Col. DeWitt C. Baxter, thirty-three, commanded the 72nd Pennsylvania. Hunt and Brown, *Brevet Brigadier Generals,* 41, 429; Sifakis, *Who Was Who,* 39, 482.
3. Donaldson erred here. Brig. Gen. Samuel P. Heintzelman at this time commanded the 3rd Corps of the Army of the Potomac, not a division of Sumner's 2nd Corps.
4. In the fall of 1861 rumors had reached Confederate major general John Magruder that the Federals planned to use the historic city of Hampton as a settlement for runaway slaves. Rather than see what he considered to be an indignity put upon the town, the native Virginian ordered it burned. Stephen W. Sears, *To the Gates of Richmond: The Peninsula Campaign* (New York: Ticknor and Fields, 1992), 28.
5. John T. Greble, a native of Philadelphia and an 1854 graduate of West Point, was killed at the Battle of Big Bethel on June 10, 1861—the first regular army officer to die in the war. He immediately became a martyr to the Union cause. Benson J. Lossing, *Memoir of Lieutenant Colonel John T. Greble of the United States Army* (Philadelphia: Privately printed, 1870).
6. Winfield Scott Batchelder, a twenty-three-year-old Philadelphia bookkeeper, remained with the 71st as sergeant major until August 20, 1862, when he resigned to accept the first lieutenancy of Donaldson's Company H of the 118th Pennsylvania. Donaldson valued him highly, noting while they served together in their second regiment that he considered Batchelder "the superior of any company officer" in that command. CSR, RG94, NA; Office of the Adjutant General, Muster Rolls, 118th Pennsylvania Infantry, Pennsylvania State Archives, Record Group 19, Harrisburg, Pennsylvania (cited hereafter as MR Harrisburg; references are to specific companies).
7. Donaldson is utilizing a shortened version of the word "spondulix", which was a slang term for money.
8. Brig. Gen. Francis E. Patterson, a forty-one-year-old Philadelphian and son of Maj. Gen. Robert Patterson, was unassigned at this time but would soon assume command of a brigade in the 3rd Corps. Sifakis, *Who Was Who,* 491.
9. 2nd Lt. George W. Kenney, a nineteen-year-old prewar student from Philadelphia, was soon promoted to the first lieutenancy of Company N. He was killed in action at the Battle of White Oak Swamp on June 30, 1862. *Adj. Gen. of PA, 1866,* 373; *Philadelphia Evening Bulletin,* July 10, 1862.
10. Kentucky native Willis A. Gorman, forty-five, who had raised and led the 1st Minnesota Infantry at the beginning of the war, commanded the 1st Brigade of the 2nd Division of the 2nd Corps. Sifakis, *Who Was Who,* 256–57.
11. Brig. Gen. Napoleon Jackson Tecumseh Dana of Maine was an 1842 graduate of West Point. He at this time commanded the 3rd Brigade of the 2nd Division of the 2nd Corps.
12. The 5th Wisconsin was the only regiment from that state attached to the Army of the Potomac at this time, and it was assigned to Brig. Gen. Winfield Scott Hancock's division of the 4th Corps. I have been unable to locate any references to Indians serving in the regiment.
13. Though Donandson was not at this time actively courting her, nor was he at any time throughout his war service, this is one of the few references he makes to his future wife, Mary Landell, whom he wed in 1872.
14. Both the Union and Confederate armies in the East had been experimenting with balloons as a means of reconnaissance since the early stages of the war. What Donaldson witnessed

was one of three ascensions made from the Rebel lines at this time by Confederate balloonist John Randolph Bryan. For more on Bryan's activities in the Peninsula Campaign, see J. Randolph Bryan, "Balloon Used for Scout Duty," *Confederate Veteran* 22, no. 4 (April 1914): 161–65.

15. "The towers were built in the timber, and one of them was a hundred and fifteen feet in height. From their top one could look down into the enemy's works and observe their movements. When they appeared above the tree tops, the enemy shelled them, but it did not interfere with their completion. . . ." W. W. H. Davis, *History of the 104th Pennsylvania Regiment* (Philadelphia: J. B. Rogers, 1866), 53–54.

16. Union naval forces under the command of Flag Officer David G. Farragut had run the defenses of New Orleans and seized the key Southern port city on April 25.

17. Confederate brigadier general Gabriel Rains had mined the approaches to Yorktown with unexploded artillery shells, commonly called "land torpedoes," which proved deadly to more than a few Yankees. Their use was soon discontinued, as officers of both sides considered their employment as unethical. Robert U. Johnson and Clarence C. Buel, eds., *Battles and Leaders of the Civil War* (cited hereafter as Johnson and Buel, Battles and Leaders) (New York: Century Co., 1887), vol. II, 201; Warren H. Cudworth, *History of the First Regiment (Massachusetts Infantry).* . . . (Boston: Walker, Fuller & Co., 1866), 159–60.

18. This individual, by virtue of his skill as a marksman and the fact that he was black, had attracted much attention among the Berdan Sharpshooters in the previous several weeks, although he was firing at the Union pickets from such a long distance that the Berdan men thought it a waste of ammunition to reply to his shots. Eventually, however, the man became emboldened by his success and began to fire from closer range, and as recorded by Donaldson and described by the regimental historian of the Berdan Sharpshooters, "his fate was sealed. The result was finally announced . . . one morning in camp that 'a scouting party having cornered the nigger in a chimney top a quarter of a mile distant, where he had been concealed, finally brought him down,' and thus ended his sport with his life. . . . Sergt. Andrews of Company E discovered the fellow in the second story of the old chimney . . . and with the aid of his fine telescope, found him firing through a hole in the back of the fireplace." No mention is made of the subsequent death of the Berdan Sharpshooter in the regimental history, however. Sgt. William G. Andrews, the man credited with killing the black Confederate, went on to serve until his discharge as captain in 1864. Stevens, *Berdan's Sharpshooters,* 55–56, 514.

19. Brig. Gen. William B. Franklin of Pennsylvania commanded what at this time was known as the 1st Division of the 1st Corps although it was soon to be combined with Brig. Gen. William F. Smith's division of the 4th Corps to form the 6th Corps.

20. On May 6 Franklin's Division, which was to be supported by the 2nd Corps divisions of Sedgwick and Richardson as well as Fitz John Porter's 3rd Corps division, was sent up the York River to Eltham's Landing in an attempt to intercept the Confederate retreat from Williamsburg. Franklin's reinforcements failed to materialize, however, and under the cover of Union gunboats, he entrenched and was attacked on May 7 by Maj. Gen. William H. C. Whiting's division. Federal casualties in the brief action amounted to 186; the Confederates lost 48 and their line of retreat was not disturbed. The rumors of atrocities mentioned by Donaldson were unfounded. *O.R.,* vol. XI, pt. 1, 613–33.

For more on this action, see Newton M. Curtis, *From Bull Run to Chancellorsville: The Story of the Sixteenth New York Infantry* (New York: G. P. Putnam's Sons, 1906), 96–103; James I. Robertson, Jr., ed., *The Civil War Letters of General Robert McAllister* (cited hereafter as Robertson, McAllister Letters) (New Brunswick, NJ: Rutgers University Press, 1965), 151–54.

21. White House belonged not to Gen. Robert E. Lee, but to his eldest son, William Henry Fitzhugh "Rooney" Lee, who was at this time serving as colonel of the 9th Virginia Cavalry.

22. Pvt. John Greene of Company D of the 69th Pennsylvania. Joseph R. C. Ward, *History of the One Hundred and Sixth Pennsylvania Volunteers* (Philadelphia: F. McManus, Jr. & Co., 1906), 43.

23. Lieutenant Greenhill is unidentified.

24. Robert E. Lee was at this time serving as military advisor to Confederate president Jefferson Davis and was not present at the engagement at West Point. Interestingly, however, at least two other Federal officers, including Army of the Potomac commander George B. McClellan, were under the impression that Lee was in command of the Confederate Army at this time, a position he would not assume until June 1. See Stephen W. Sears, ed., *The Civil War Papers of George B. McClellan: Selected Correspondence 1860–1865* (New York: Ticknor and Fields, 1989), 244–45, 248; Robertson, *McAllister Letters*, 151.

25. On May 15 the Philadelphia Brigade had moved from its camp at Eltham on the Pamunkey River eight miles west to the vicinity of New Kent Court House. Banes, *Philadelphia Brigade*, 62.

26. Confederate forces under Gen. P. G. T. Beauregard had concentrated at Corinth, Mississippi, following their narrow defeat at the Battle of Shiloh, Tennessee, on April 6–7. After a long siege by Union troops under Maj. Gen. Henry Wager Halleck, Beauregard slipped away undetected on the night of May 29–30. Shelby Foote, *The Civil War, a Narrative: Fort Sumter to Perryville* (New York: Random House, 1958), 381–86.

27. Sedgwick's Division had moved from its camp near White House southwestward to Bottom's Bridge on the Chickahominy River on May 21. Banes, *Philadelphia Brigade*, 62.

28. Donaldson is likely referring to a brief artillery duel near New Bridge on the Chickahominy between U.S. Regulars under Brig. Gen. George Stoneman and Confederate cavalry under Col. Beverly H. Robertson. No casualties were reported. *O.R.*, vol. XI, pt. 1, 655–57, 663.

29. Col. Isaac Wistar of the 71st had been prostrated by typhoid fever on May 3 and was unable to return to the regiment until mid-July. Wistar, *Autobiography*, 43–44.

30. Albert P. Schurtz, a twenty-three-year-old prewar teacher, had mustered in as first sergeant of Company I and is listed on the regimental rolls at this time as first sergeant of Company D. Schurtz had been captured at Ball's Bluff and was in all likelihood acting as lieutenant of his company pending a commission. He was discharged on March 12, 1863, but reenlisted the same day as a sergeant in the Regular Army. In 1864 he was serving as a clerk in the adjutant general's office in Washington, D.C. CSR, RG94, NA.

31. Prior to the 1860 presidential election, elements of the former Whig and American parties formed the Constitutional Union party and nominated Tennessee slaveholder John Bell for president and Massachusetts native and former Secretary of State Edward Everett for vice president. Their intent was to draw support away from Lincoln's power base in the North and elect a compromise candidate, but they failed, garnering less than 3 percent of the popular vote. James M. McPherson, *Battle Cry of Freedom* (New York: Oxford University Press, 1988), 221–22.

32. Maj. James Madison DeWitt was honorably discharged on July 19, 1862. Bates, *Penna. Vols.*, vol. II, 834; Adj. Gen. of PA, 1866, 374.

33. The Trent House was located approximately one-half mile south of Grapevine Bridge. *O.R. Atlas*, plate XIX, map 1.

34. Col. John Cochrane commanded the 1st U.S. Chasseurs, which were later officially designated the 65th New York Infantry. Both they and the 23rd Pennsylvania were part of Brig. Gen. Erasmus Keyes's 4th Corps.

35. Pvt. George W. Jones, a twenty-one-year-old Philadelphia bartender, deserted from the 71st in late July 1862. He returned in April 1863, was transferred to the 69th Pennsylvania in June 1864, and mustered out in July 1865. CSR RG94, NA.

36. Donaldson is in error here, as the line of advance of Sedgwick's division did not take them past Allen's Farm, which was located approximately one mile south of where the battle was taking place. The Adams House was the structure nearest to where the 71st

went into action, and it is to this that Donaldson is likely referring. *O.R. Atlas*, plate XIX, map 1; Francis A. Walker, *History of the Second Army Corps in the Army of the Potomac* (New York: Charles Scribner's Sons, 1886), 36.

37. Donaldson is referring to a subdivision of his regiment, not to a division of the corps.

38. Capt. John Markoe, twenty-two, a Philadelphia native and prewar student, commanded Company A of the 71st. He was wounded later in the battle but recovered and was promoted to lieutenant colonel. Discharged by special order in February 1863, he was brevetted brigadier general at war's end for his services at the Battle of Fredericksburg. Hunt and Brown, *Brevet Brigadier Generals*, 379.

39. Thomas Ashton of Philadelphia had been appointed first lieutenant of Company A by Pennsylvania governor Andrew G. Curtin on January 1, 1862. He resigned his commission immediately after the Peninsula Campaign due to ill health, "which," he wrote, "has utterly unfitted me for duty." CSR, RG94, NA.

40. This is the same individual identified in note 29.

41. Dr. Martin Reizer was at this time serving as assistant surgeon of the 72nd Pennsylvania. He was promoted to surgeon on August 4, 1862, and mustered out with his regiment in August 1864. *Adj. Gen., of PA, 1866*, 374.

42. Donaldson's reference is to the opium pill, which was a commonly prescribed remedy for a variety of ailments in the Civil War era. He also later refers to it as "pill opi." George Worthington Adams, *Doctors in Blue: The Medical History of the Union Army in the Civil War* (New York: Henry Schuman, 1952), 51, 116, 119, 228.

43. Clement Biddle Barclay was a prominent citizen of Philadelphia who counted among his friends Maj. Gen. George McClellan and Pennsylvania governor Andrew Curtin. He devoted much of his time and considerable fortune to the Northern war effort both privately and through public charitable organizations such as the United States Sanitary and Christian Commissions. William Brooke Rawle, *A Refutation by William Brooke Rawle of Certain False Statements Made by Corporal Andrew Jackson Speese Regarding the History of the Third Pennsylvania Volunteer Cavalry Regiment* (Philadelphia: n.p., 1907), 41.

44. The United States Christian Commission was founded in New York City shortly after the war broke out, with the goal of providing spiritual and material assistance to needy soldiers. Members of the organization performed a variety of services, from feeding and caring for wounded and sick soldiers to distributing religious tracts and writing letters home for them.

45. Edward E. Cross, thirty, of Lancaster, New Hampshire, is one of the more colorful figures to emerge from the lore of the Army of the Potomac. A prewar adventurer, writer, and Indian fighter, he raised and molded the 5th New Hampshire Regiment into one of the finest infantry units in the Federal service. Recovering from his leg wound received at Fair Oaks, he returned to fight at Antietam, where he was again wounded, and at Fredericksburg, where he was wounded for the third time. After again recovering, Cross fought at Chancellorsville and led a 2nd Corps brigade through the maelstrom of the Wheatfield at Gettysburg, where he was fatally wounded only a short distance from where Donaldson was then fighting. William Child, *A History of the Fifth Regiment New Hampshire Volunteers in the American Civil War, 1861–1865* (cited hereafter as Child, *Fifth New Hampshire*) (Bristol, NH: R. W. Musgrove, 1893), 211–25, 311–15.

46. William Glenny, thirty, a prewar clerk and farmer, had been wounded at Fair Oaks on June 1. He returned to the 64th New York following his recovery and eventually rose to the colonelcy of the regiment. He was brevetted brigadier general at the close of the war for gallant and meritorious service. Hunt and Brown, *Brevet Brigadier Generals*, 234. For several interesting photographs of Captain Glenny displaying his Fair Oaks wound, see Michael Winey, "Empire State Soldiers: Images from New York's Bureau of Military Statistics," *Military Images*, 11, no. 4 (January–February 1990), 22.

47. Dr. John Neill of Pennsylvania, who had charge of the Cherry Street branch of the Broad Street Hospital, was later brevetted lieutenant colonel for faithful and meritorious

service. He was mustered out in August 1865. Taylor, *Philadelphia in the War*, 228; Francis B. Heitman, *Historical Register and Dictionary of the United States Army* (Washington, DC: Government Printing Office, 1903), 742.

CHAPTER THREE: ANTIETAM AND SHEPHERDSTOWN

1. FAD Papers, CWLM.
2. Survivors' Association, *118th Pennsylvania*, 632.
3. Lt. Col. Charles F. Ruff of the 3rd U.S. Cavalry mustered in many of the officers of the 118th. He superintended the volunteer recruiting service in Philadelphia until early 1864. Taylor, *Philadelphia in the War*, 268; Hunt and Brown, *Brevet Brigadier Generals*, 523.
4. Fort Albany was located just south of the Columbia Turnpike approximately two miles west of the Potomac River. *O.R. Atlas*, plate VI, map 1.
5. Donaldson's aunt, Sophia Donaldson, had presented this standard to him while he recruited his company in August. It was carried by the regimental color guard through all of the engagements of the 118th until just before the Battle of Chancellorsville in May 1863, when new national colors were received. Donaldson then entrusted the flag to Sgt. Henry Q. Cobb of Company H, who carried it in his knapsack until his discharge in October 1863. The remnants of this flag, which Donaldson had preserved and framed, are on display at The Civil War Library and Museum. FAD Papers, CWLM; Richard A. Sauers, *Advance the Colors: Pennsylvania Civil War Battle Flags* (Harrisburg, PA: Capitol Preservation Committee, 1991), vol. II, 386–89.
6. Upon assuming command of the Army of Virginia in July 1862, Maj. Gen. John Pope issued an order that, in addition to indirectly criticizing McClellan, essentially unfavorably compared the Union's eastern armies to their western counterparts. Newspapers North and South widely reprinted the order, reporting incorrectly that Pope had issued it from his "Headquarters in the Saddle," which led to the oft-repeated comment that he "had his headquarters where his hindquarters out to be." Bruce Catton, *This Hallowed Ground: The Story of the Union Side of the Civil War* (New York: Doubleday & Company, 1956) 154.
7. This was Fort Corcoran, located approximately one mile north of Arlington, Virginia. *O.R. Atlas*, plate VI, map 1.
8. A Massachusetts officer from the brigade the Pennsylvanians were to be assigned to later recalled that though he felt the rank and file of the 118th were brave and patriotic, the officers were "unfortunately not as a class experienced or practical," and he found them "unequal to their responsibilities." Edwin C. Bennett, *Musket and Sword* (cited hereafter as Bennett, *Musket and Sword*) (Boston: Coburn Publishing Co., 1900), 87.
9. John Montieth Fullam, a twenty-two-year-old bartender from Philadelphia, was mortally wounded less than two weeks later at Shepherdstown, Virginia. MR Co. H, Harrisburg.
10. James S. Wheeler, twenty-seven, of Philadelphia, was eventually demoted to private and discharged for disability in January 1863. MR Co. H, Harrisburg.
11. 2nd Lt. Purnell W. Smith, a thirty-year-old Philadelphian and prewar clerk, was slightly wounded at Shepherdstown, Virginia, and resigned on December 1, 1862. MR Co. H, Harrisburg; Survivors' Association, *118th Pennsylvania*, 723.
12. Sgt. John H. Keener, a thirty-two-year-old salesman from Baltimore, was promoted to quartermaster sergeant in October 1862 but was reduced to the ranks in early February 1863. He transferred to the Veteran Reserve Corps in October 1864, where he served out his term of enlistment. MR Co. H, Harrisburg.
13. Levis Passmore, a twenty-four-year-old self-described "gentleman" from Philadelphia, commanded Company E of the 118th. For reasons that Donaldson explains more fully in subsequent letters, he was discharged on October 11, 1862. MR Co. H, Harrisburg.
14. John V. Hunterson of Philadelphia, a thirty-two-year-old prewar bricklayer, assumed command of Company E upon Capt. Levis Passmore's resignation and led it until his discharge

for disability in February 1865. Hunterson had served previously as first lieutenant of Company F of the 23rd Pennsylvania, which was then commanded by the 118th's liuetenant colonel, James Gwyn. MR Co. H., Harrisburg; Survivors' Association, *118th Pennsylvania*, 705.

15. Samuel N. Lewis, eighteen, of Philadelphia, was seriously wounded at Shepherdstown, Virginia, but returned and was promoted to the first lieutenancy of Company E in March 1863. He was later transferred to the 1st Brigade staff of Brig. Gen. Joseph Hayes in the fall of 1863 but resigned due to wounds and sickness and was honorably discharged in November 1863. MR Co. E, Harrisburg; Survivors' Association, *118th Pennsylvania*, 641, 681.

16. Henry O'Neill, thirty-eight, was a native of Londonderry, Ireland, and had served in the British Army for twelve years before his immigration to America in 1860. Eventually rising to become senior captain of the 118th, he commanded Company A until his promotion to major on November 1, 1863. Brevetted to lieutenant colonel to date from December 2, 1864, he mustered out with the regiment in June 1865. MR Co. A, Harrisburg; Survivors' Association, *118th Pennsylvania*, 641, 681.

17. Thomas Scout, a twenty-eight-year-old engineer from Philadelphia, remained a private in Company A until May 20, 1865, when he was finally promoted to corporal. MR Co. A, Harrisburg; Survivors' Association, *118th Pennsylvania*, 683.

18. 1st Lt. Alexander Wilson, forty, of Franklin County, Pennsylvania, worked as an attorney until his commissioning in Company A. He resigned from the 118th and was honorably discharged on June 23, 1863. MR Co. A, Harrisburg.

19. 2nd Lt. George Alfred Schaffer, a nineteen-year-old native of Philadelphia, resigned his commission in January 1863. MR Co. A, Harrisburg.

20. Dendy Sharwood, a native of England and prewar hotelier and engineer, led Company C until his death in November 1863, which resulted from exposure incurred during the actions near the Rappahannock River in the late fall of that year. MR Co. C, Harrisburg; Survivors' Association, *118th Pennsylvania*, 653.

21. Fifty-one-year-old Richard Donegan commanded Company B of the 118th until his discharge due to disability on March 31, 1864. He had been an attorney before the war. MR Co. B, Harrisburg; Survivors' Association, *118th Pennsylvania*, 688.

22. Richard W. Davids, thirty-seven, a native of New York who resided in Philadelphia at the outbreak of the war, remained first lieutenant of Company B until January 12, 1863, when he was promoted to the captaincy of Company G. He was killed at the Battle of Gettysburg on July 2, 1863. Survivors' Association, 118th Pennsylvania, 646–47.

23. Horace Binney, twenty-two, another "gentleman" of Philadelphia, was promoted from second lieutenant of Company B to first lieutenant of Company C following the Battle of Shepherdstown on September 20, 1862. In August 1864 he was promoted to the captaincy of Company D. He mustered out with the regiment in June 1865 and was brevetted major to date from March 15, 1865. MR Co. B, Harrisburg; Survivors' Association, *118th Pennsylvania*, 694.

24. 1st Lt. Lemuel L. Crocker, thirty-two, a prewar merchant, had moved to Philadelphia from his birthplace in Albany, New York, ten years before the war. He served in Company C until just after the Battle of Shepherdstown, when he was promoted to captain of Company K. He served as such until his resignation in February 1864. Crocker was to become one of Donaldson's closest friends throughout his service in the 118th. Survivors' Association, *118th Pennsylvania*, 640.

25. 2nd Lt. Frank McCutchen, a nineteen-year-old clerk from Philadelphia, resigned his commission in Company C in September 1863. He had, as Donaldson notes, served in Capt. Joseph Knap's Battery E of the Pennsylvania Light Artillery. MR Co. C, Harrisburg.

26. Twenty-one-year-old Courtland Saunders, scion of a wealthy Philadelphia family, was a prewar teacher and had authored a Latin text. He now commanded Company G and would be killed in the action at Shepherdstown. MR Co. G, Harrisburg.

27. Capt. Joseph W. Ricketts, twenty-six, of Baltimore, commanded Company K of the 118th until his death at Shepherdstown. Survivors' Association, *118th Pennsylvania*, 644.

28. William M. McKean, a twenty-eight-year-old agent from Philadelphia, was the first lieutenant of Company K. Severely disabled as a result of wounds received at Shepherdstown, he resigned his commission and was honorably discharged on March 25, 1863. MR Co. K, Harrisburg; Survivors' Association, *118th Pennsylvania*, 735.

29. 2nd Lt. Joseph Mora Moss, Jr., nineteen, of Bradford County, Pennsylvania, was a prewar clerk and student. He was mortally wounded at Shepherdstown. MR Co. K, Harrisburg; Survivors' Association, 118th Pennsylvania, 653.

30. William West, a twenty-two-year-old Philadelphian, served as first lieutenant of Company G until his promotion to captain on November 1, 1862. He resigned his commission due to disability and was discharged on January 12, 1863. MR Co. G, Harrisburg; Survivors' Association, *118th Pennsylvania*, 717.

31. J. Rudhall White, twenty, a native of Warrenton, Virginia, had served briefly in the Confederate cavalry prior to his commissioning as second lieutenant of Company G. He was killed at Shepherdstown. Survivors' Association, *118th Pennsylvania*, 653–54.

32. Courtney M. O'Callaghan, a twenty-three-year-old merchant from Philadelphia, was the captain of Company I of the 118th. He was so severely wounded at Shepherdstown that he was unable to return to duty and tendered his resignation effective February 14, 1863. MR Co. I, Harrisburg; Survivors' Association, *118th Pennsylvania*, 729.

33. 1st Lt. Alfred N. Wetherill, twenty-three, a prewar druggist and Philadelphia native, assumed command of Company I upon Captain O'Callaghan's resignation. He served as captain until his honorable discharge in February 1864. MR Co. I, Harrisburg; Survivors' Association, *118th Pennsylvania*, 729.

34. Charles H. Fernald, a thirty-six-year-old Philadelphia bookseller, commanded Company D of the 118th until his honorable discharge in February 1864. MR Co. D, Harrisburg; Survivors' Association, *118th Pennsylvania*, 699.

35. Albert H. Walters, a twenty-year-old Philadelphia clerk, had served as a private in the 23rd Pennsylvania prior to his commission in Company D of the 118th. Promoted to the captaincy of Company A on February 10, 1864, he was brevetted major to date from July 6, 1864, for "gallant and distinguished services" during Grant's Overland Campaign. He resigned and was honorably discharged in February 1865. MR Cos. D & A, Harrisburg; Survivors' Association, *118th Pennsylvania*, 643.

36. Seventeen-year-old Samuel M. McIntire of Philadelphia, yet another of the 118th's "gentlemen," served as second lieutenant of Company D until his discharge on April 13, 1863. MR Co. D, Harrisburg; Survivors' Association, *118th Pennsylvania*, 699.

37. John Bankson was a twenty-seven-year-old prewar Philadelphia merchant. He commanded Company F of the 118th until March 1863, when he accepted a staff assignment with the 1st Brigade, 1st Division, 5th Corps because of his unwillingness to further serve under Lieutenant Colonel Gwyn. In July 1863 he was appointed acting inspector general of the 1st Division, 5th Corps. He resigned and was honorably discharged in March 1864. MR Co. F, Harrisburg; Survivors' Association, *118th Pennsylvania*, 710.

38. 1st Lt. Henry K. Kelly, twenty-seven, of Philadelphia, was promoted to the captaincy of Company G in October 1863 and led it until his capture at Cold Harbor, Virginia, in June 1864. Sent to a succession of prison camps, he was exchanged in December 1864 and honorably discharged the following month. Survivors' Association, *118th Pennsylvania*, 642.

39. Charles H. Hand, a twenty-seven-year-old clerk from Philadelphia, had served previously with the 75th Pennsylvania until he was commissioned second lieutenant of Company F of the 118th. Captured at Shepherdstown, he was soon paroled, and in January 1863 he was promoted to adjutant. He was eventually awarded the brevet ranks of captain and major and was mustered out with the regiment in June 1865. MR Co. F, Harrisburg; Survivors' Association, *118th Pennsylvania*, 681, 711.

40. Charles F. Dare, a twenty-year-old druggist from Bridgeton, New Jersey, was later promoted to hospital steward, 1st Brigade, 1st Division, 5th Corps. In April 1864 he was made executive steward of the 1st Division, 5th Corps hospital. He mustered out of the service in June 1865. MR Co. H, Harrisburg; Survivors' Association, *118th Pennsylvania*, 645.

41. Probably 1st Lt. Frederick K. Mears of the 9th U.S. Infantry. Francis B. Heitman, *Historical Register and Dictionary of the United States Army. . . .* (Washington DC: Government Printing Office, 1903), 700.

42. The numerous hose companies that populated the city of Philadelphia in the mid-nineteenth century were an outgrowth of the early citizen-led bucket brigades and fire companies formed in the 1700s. The Phoenix Hose Comapny, to which Major Herring belonged, was located on the north side of Filbert Street above 7th Street. Thomas Scharf and Thompson Westcott, *History of Philadelphia, 1609–1884* (Philadelphia: L. H. Everts & Co., 1884), vol. III, 1884–1902.

43. Dr. Joseph Thomas, a thirty-two-year-old native of Doylestown, Pennsylvania, had been wounded in the Seven Days' Battles while commanding Co. H of the 3rd Pennsylvania Reserves. He was promoted to surgeon of the 1st Brigade, 1st Division, 5th Corps, and in the spring of 1863 he advanced again to surgeon in charge of the 1st Division, 5th Corps hospital, in which capacity he served until his muster out in June 1865. "No officer of the regiment," recorded the historians of the 118th, "commanded a larger measure of respect and confidence." Survivors' Association, *118th Pennsylvania*, 641.

44. John M. Kollock, twenty-six, a native of Delaware, was promoted from assistant surgeon of the 118th to surgeon of the 50th Pennsylvania in September 1864. After an acquaintance of several months, Donaldson wrote (in an unincluded portion of a letter) that Kollock was "an excellent physician and surgeon . . . a rattling good fellow, full of fun, and [he] sings a good song." MR Field & Staff, Harrisburg; Survivors' Association, *118th Pennsylvania*, 681.

45. Assistant Surgeon Nelson L. Rowland, twenty-four, was discharged for disability in December 1863. MR Co. K, Harrisburg; Survivors' Association, *118th Pennsylvania*, 681.

46. Adj. James P. Perot, thirty-seven, was a prewar Philadelphia businessman and one of the founders of the Philadelphia Corn Exchange, which raised the 118th. He was severely wounded and captured at Shepherdstown, and his injuries precluded a return to active service. He resigned in January 1863. Survivors' Association, *118th Pennsylvania*, 652.

47. Thomas H. Addicks, twenty-six, of Philadelphia, tendered his resignation less than one month later, on October 4, 1862, MR Field & Staff, Harrisburg.

48. Donaldson began writing his account of the Antietam Campaign on September 23 and completed it on October 5. The narrative takes up nearly fifty pages of writing paper.

49. John J. Thomas, a nineteen-year-old Philadelphian, was promoted from regimental quartermaster sergeant to second lieutenant of Company B on October 22, 1862. Wounded in the Wilderness in May 1864, he was discharged three months later. Thomas was to become one of Donaldson's closest friends in the regiment. MR Co. B, Harrisburg; Survivors' Association, *118th Pennsylvania*, 689.

50. George W. Agnew of Philadelphia was a private in Company G of the 2nd Pennsylvania Cavalry. Bates, *Penna. Vols.,* vol. II, 343.

51. Brig. Gen. John H. Martindale of New York, an 1835 West Point graduate, was absent from the brigade at this time. He was trying to clear his name of charges against him by 5th Corps commander Fitz John Porter that stemmed from an incident in the Seven Days' Battles. Col. James Barnes of the 18th Massachusetts led the brigade in his stead. Maj. Gen. George W. Morrell, forty-seven, of New York, was an 1835 graduate of West Point who had assumed command of the 1st Division, 5th Corps in May 1862. McClellan had no stronger supporter among his corps commanders than forty-year-old New Hampshire native Fitz John Porter, an 1845 graduate of West Point who had led the 5th Corps since its formation in May 1862. Sifakis, *Who Was Who,* 455, 436, 515–16.

52. Lt. Col. William S. Tilton, a thirty-four-year-old Boston merchant, had been wounded and captured earlier in the war at Gaines Mill during the Seven Days' Battles. He was promoted to the colonelcy of the 22nd Massachusetts on October 17, 1862, and later commanded the 1st Brigade at Gettysburg. Sen. Henry Wilson of Massachusetts was originally commissioned as colonel of the 22nd Massachusetts, but the appointment was merely symbolic. He retained his senate seat and resigned his commission in October 1861. James S. Barnes, a fifty-five-year-old native of Springfield, Massachusetts, was an 1829 West Point graduate who had been appointed colonel of the 18th Massachusetts at the outbreak of the war. He was elevated to command of the 1st Brigade, 1st Division, 5th Corps soon after the Peninsula Campaign and led it at Antietam, Fredericksburg, and Chancellorsville. Wounded at Gettysburg while commanding the 1st Division, 5th Corps, he did not return to active service. Thirty-three-year-old Elisha G. Marshall of New York, an 1850 graduate of West Point, led the 13th New York. Charles A. Johnson, thirty-six, of Utica, New York, was a great-grandson of President John Adams. Johnson was wounded while commanding the 25th New York at the Battle of Hanover Court House on May 27, 1862. The 1st Michigan had lost its colonel at the Second Battle of Bull Run two weeks earlier, and in the absence of other field officers, Capt. Emory W. Belton, twenty-three, of Chelsea, Michigan, led the regiment. Lt. Col. George A. Varney, a twenty-eight-year-old prewar grocer, commanded the 2nd Maine. Hunt and Brown, *Brevet Brigadier Generals,* 315, 380, 619, 633; Sifakais, *Who Was Who,* 33; Adjutant General of Michigan, *Record First Michigan Infantry Civil War, 1861–1865* (cited hereafter as Adjutant General, *First Michigan*) (reprint, Detroit: Detroit Book Press, n.d.), 13.

53. Donaldson does not exaggerate the effect of this march upon the regiment, as the following incident recorded in the regimental history illustrates: "One weary, dusty private, trudging solemnly and slowly along the road, near nightfall, struggling against the heat and his own demoralized condition, met General Morrell, and, touching his hat, said: 'General, can you tell me where the 118th Pennsylvania is?' 'Certainly, my man' replied the general, seriously, 'everywhere between here and Washington.' The saddest thing about the matter is that the general told the truth. Reclining against fences or meditating under apple trees, the 118th averaged about one hundred to the mile." Survivors' Association, *118th Pennsylvania,* 30–31.

54. In an effort to permanently separate and defeat in detail the scattered commands of Lee's army, McClellan, with full knowledge of his opponent's dispositions, attacked the gaps of South Mountain on September 14, resulting in the Battle of South Mountain. He was ultimately successful in forcing three of the key passages, but skillful resistance by the outnumbered Confederates provided Lee with time to concentrate his forces and move to Sharpsburg. The Federals lost a total of 1,813 men in the action; the Southerners lost 2,685. Thomas L. Livermore, *Numbers and Losses in the Civil War in America, 1861–65* (reprint, Dayton, OH: Press of Morningside House, 1986), 90–91.

55. Virginia-born Jesse L. Reno, thirty-nine, an 1846 graduate of West Point, was mortally wounded in the fighting at Fox's Gap on South Mountain while commanding the Federal 9th Corps. Sifakis, *Who Was Who,* 537.

56. Boonsboro Gap was more familiarly known as Turner's Gap. The National Road crossed South Mountain at this point.

57. Maj. Gen. Joseph Hooker's 1st Corps had crossed Antietam Creek on the afternoon of September 16 and skirmished sharply with the Confederate left flank.

58. "Cook house," meaning a rumor started by the camp cooks.

59. Rush's Lancers, a Philadelphia-raised regiment, was officially known as the 6th Pennsyvlania Cavalry.

60. Maj. Albert Arndt of New York City commanded the 1st Battalion of New York Light Artillery and was mortally wounded on September 17, dying on September 18. *O.R.,* vol. XIX, pt. 1, 342; Frederick Phisterer, *New York in the War of the Rebellion 1861–1865* (cited hereafter as Phisterer, *New York in the Rebellion*), 3rd ed., 5 vols., (Albany: J.B. Lyon Company, 1912), vol. II, 1550.

61. Maj. Gen. Ambrose Burnside of Indiana, an 1847 graduate of West Point, commanded the 1st and 9th Corps at Antietam. The 9th Corps had carried the bridge over Antietam Creek that ever after bore Burnside's name. *O.R.*, vol. XIX, pt. 1, 93.

62. This was likely the John Otto farmhouse, as its position was closer to the 118th's position at this time than any other structure on the battlefield. See *O.R. Atlas*, plate xxviii, map 6.

63. Richard L. Sanford, a thirty-year-old barber from Philadelphia, is listed on the rolls as a corporal of Company E at this time. He was discharged as a result of his wound on March 16, 1863. MR Co. E, Harrisburg; Survivors' Association, *118th Pennsylvania*, 705.

64. Lee's proclamation, though not stated as Donaldson describes it here, can be found in *O.R.*, vol. XIX, pt. 2, 601–2.

65. Notwithstanding this episode, eighteen-year-old Sgt. Thomas M. Coane, a prewar Philadelphia clerk, was promoted to second lieutenant of Company H to date from December 8, 1862. Wounded at Spotsylvania on May 10, 1864, he recovered and on June 19, 1864, was promoted to first lieutenant. He was honorably discharged in October of the same year. MR Co. H, Harrisburg; Survivors' Association, *118th Pennsylvania*, 723.

66. Capt. Horatio Gates Gibson commanded Batteries C and G of the 3rd U.S. Horse Artillery. *O.R.*, vol. XIX, pt. 1, 180.

67. Cpl. Daniel B. Cobb was promoted to first sergeant of Company H in January 1863 and served with the regiment until a wound received at Peebles Farm, Virginia, in September 1864, which necessitated his transfer to the Veteran Reserve Corps. The twenty-year-old clerk was a native of Philadelphia. His brother, Henry, was a sergeant of Company H. MR Co. H, Harrisburg; Survivors' Association, 118th Pennsylvania, 723.

68. Lt. Louis R. Fortescue, a signal officer attached to McClellan's headquarters, and his superior, Capt. Benjamin Franklin Fisher, were on the Maryland side of the Potomac River observing the errant fire of the Federal gunners. In a postwar letter, Fortescue recalled that he and Captain Fisher, "by aid of their long range telescopes, saw that the shells from one of our batteries of 20 pdr. Parrotts were dropping short of the enemy and were apparently doing much execution among the men of the 118th. Capt. Fisher at once reported the fact to the Captain of the Battery, who directed a higher elevation of the pieces, but it was too late to prevent the fearful slaughter that followed from the musketry fire of the enemy." Louis R. Fortescue to John L. Smith, June 30, 1886, FAD Papers, CWLM.

69. John B. Fisher, a twenty-four-year-old prewar clerk, served in Company H until his arm was shot off at Fredericksburg on December 13, 1862. The Philadelphia native survived the wound and was discharged in January 1863. MR Co. H, Harrisburg; Survivors' Association, *118th Pennsylvania*, 725.

70. Relations between the 118th and the veterans of the brigade had not improved in the two weeks that had followed the rookies' less-than-friendly introduction in Washington, D.C., and the reception that awaited some of the demoralized Pennsylvanians as they reached the Maryland side of the Potomac did little to help the situation. A member of the 22nd Massachusetts recalled that "as the remnants of the various commands were being collected after crossing, a little short major of the One Hundred Eighteenth, dripping with water from head to foot and followed closely by a few of our gallant Corn Exchange comrades, turned, and waving his drawn sword in their direction, shouted in a high, squeaky voice,—'Fo-o-o-l-low me, a-l-l that are left of the gallant C-o-orn Excha-a-ange!' It was much too much for our boys, and the Sharpshooters in the canal, and they burst out laughing. Perhaps this served to open wide the wound. Suffice it to say, whenever on picket, scrambling for water at a small spring, gathering rails, or 'reaching' for straw, there were numerous collisions, although no bloodshed, between the two commands." John L. Parker and Robert G. Carter, *Henry Wilson's Regiment: History of the Twenty Second Massachusetts Infantry, the Second Company Sharpshooters, and the Third Light Battery in the War of the Rebellion* (cited hereafter as Parker and Carter, *22nd Massachusetts*) (Boston: Regimental Association, 1887), 201.

71. Donaldson significantly overstated the loss in his company. Actual casualties were one killed, eight wounded, and three missing, for a total of twelve—the fewest number of casualties of any company in the regiment. Fighting from the kneeling position does indeed appear to have paid off for the members of Company H. Brevet Brigadier General Charles P. Herring Papers, Civil War Library and Museum (cited hereafter as Herring Papers, CWLM).

72. William Pheeney, a twenty-three-year-old shipwright from Philadelphia, was discharged as a result of this wound on February 28, 1863. MR Co. H, Harrsiburg; Survivors' Association, *118th Pennsylvania, 723*.

73. James McLenaghan, thirty-five, of Philadelphia, was discharged for disability on February 7, 1863. MR Co. H, Harrisburg; Survivors' Association, *118th Pennsylvania, 727*.

74. Pvt. James Nelson, a twenty-six-year-old weaver from Philadelphia, transferred to the Veteran Reserve Corps in March 1864. MR Co. H, Harrisburg; Survivors' Association, *118th Pennsylvania, 727*.

75. Pvt. Charles O'Neill recovered from his wound and was promoted to corporal upon his return to the company. The nineteen-year-old jeweler served throughout the remainder of the war and mustered out with the regiment in June 1865. MR Co. H, Harrisburg; Survivors' Association, *118th Pennsylvania, 723*.

76. Pvt. George Steinmayer, a forty-four-year-old bricklayer and Philadelphia native, was discharged for disability on March 4, 1864. MR Co. H, Harrisburg; Survivors'Association, *118th Pennsylvania, 728*.

77. Pvt. Henry T. Gale, thirty-one, a machinist from Philadelphia, had been reduced to the ranks from his original rank of sergeant on September 1, 1862. While recovering from this wound, he deserted from a Philadelphia hospital and joined another regiment but was captured in May 1864. MR Co. B, Harrisburg; Survivors' Association, *118th Pennsylvania, 725*.

78. Capt. Courtland Saunder's father, Ephraim Dod Saunders, was a prominent Philadelphia clergyman and philanthropist. As a memorial to his fallen son, he donated land and buildings valued at over $100,000 to found Presbyterian Hospital in Philadelphia, which continues in operation today. For details of an encounter the distinguished Boston man of letters Oliver Wendell Holmes, Sr., had with the elder Saunders as he bore his son's body home, see "My Hunt after the 'Captain,'" *Atlantic Monthly* 10 (December 1862): 760.

79. In a letter to Donaldson detailing his role in the battle, Capt. Walter S. Davis, a staff officer attached to the 1st Brigade, 1st Division, 5th Corps, recalled: "I was the officer who notified Genl. Barnes of the approach of the enemy, and I also sent word to Genl. Porter that with the force we had it would be impossible for us to hold our position. When the order came to Genl. Barnes to retire in good order across the river, . . . he gave me orders to go to the 25th and 13th N.Y. Regt.'s saying . . . that he had sent orders to all the other regt's. In passing your regiment I saw that they were not retiring . . . and gave the order to the first officer I saw, directing him to communicate it to the Colonel, and then hurried on to the 2 regt's on the extreme right. On returning with those regt's I saw what I supposed to be the skirmishers of the 118th coming down over the bluff. Many of the men of the 118th were then crossing over on the dam. The two N.Y. regt's went lower down the river, thereby escaping the fire of the enemy. I have always had the impression that Col. Prevost did not receive a proper order to retire. . . . That whole movement was a mistake and I shall never forget how anxious I felt when I saw the enemy forming in the cornfield and how hard it was to convince Genl. Barnes that there was a larger force in our front. I knew that the Cavalry had informed Genl. Porter that there were not troops anywhere near, and that was why Barnes did not have any fear of being molested. . . . I was in 32 battles and Shepherdstown was the biggest blunder of the lot." W. S. Davis to FAD, May 26, 1883, FAD Papers, CWLM.

80. The 22nd Virginia Battalion was present at Antietam, not the 22nd Virginia Regiment, to which John P. Donaldson belonged. The fact that the two units bore the same number proved confusing to Donaldson in subsequent battles as well.
81. Pvt. William D. Connor, an eighteen-year-old farmer of Company H, served in the 118th until his transfer to Company I of the 2nd Regiment, Veteran Reserve Corps in February 1864. MR Co. H, Harrsiburg; Survivors' Association, *118th Pennsylvania,* 725.
82. Contrary to Donaldson's predictions on the outcome of the fall 1862 elections, many of the Northern states that had helped to elect Lincoln, including Pennsylvania, reversed their stance, and the Democrats made substantial gains in the House of Representatives. The inability of Union armies to achieve a complete victory in either theater, combined with the human toll of the war, was the underlying cause behind the electorate's rejection of the Republicans. James Ford Rhodes, *History of the United States from the Compromise of 1850 to the Final Restoration of Home Rule at the South in 1877* (Boston: Macmillan Company, 1910), vol. IV, 163–70.
83. Union major general Don Carlos Buell's failure to vigorously pursue and defeat retreating Confederates under Braxton Bragg after the Battle of Perryville, Kentucky, on October 8, 1862, led to his replacement by Maj. Gen. William Starke Rosecrans on October 24.

CHAPTER FOUR: FREDERICKSBURG
1. Brig. Gen. Daniel Butterfield, a thirty-two-year-old politically well-connected New Yorker, had succeeded Maj. Gen. George Morell in command of the 1st Division on November 1 and led it for but a short time until his promotion to command of the 5th Corps on November 16, replacing Fitz John Porter. Sifakis, *Who Was Who,* 97.
2. The man charged with the unenviable task of trying to discipline the foragers of the army, Provost Marshal General Marsena Patrick, wrote in his diary at this time that he was "distressed to death with the plundering and marauding of the army—I am sending out detachments in all directions and hope to capture some of the villains engaged in these operations." David S. Sparks, ed., *Inside Lincoln's Army: The Diary of General Marsena Rudolph Patrick, Provost Marshal General, Army of the Potomac* (New York: Thomas Yoseloff, 1964), 171. For more comments on the abundance the soldiers encountered on this march, see Frederick L. Hitchcock, *War from the Inside: The Story of the 132nd Regiment Pennsylvania Volunteer Infantry. . . .* (cited hereafter as Hitchcock, *132nd Pennsylvania*) (Philadelphia: J. B. Lippincott, 1904), 96–100; Child, *Fifth New Hampshire,* 145–47; Regimental Association, *Under the Maltese Cross . . . Campaigns 155th Pennsylvania Regiment* (cited hereafter as Regimental Association, 155th Pennsylvania) (Pittsburgh: 155th Regimental Association, 1910), 87–88.
3. William W. Gardner, a twenty-two-year-old Philadelphian, was originally the second lieutenant of Company I. He had been promoted to first lieutenant of Company G on November 1 and was at this time acting as quartermaster, a position he would be confirmed in on January 8, 1863. He served in that capacity throughout the remainder of the war, mustering out with the regiment on June 1, 1865. CS, RG94, NA.
4. Alfred Ratzell, a thirty-three-year-old prewar plasterer, was wounded at the Wilderness in May 1864. Recovering, he was captured at Cold Harbor on June 2 but subsequently returned to the 118th and was transferred to the 91st Pennsylvania in June 1865. MR Co. H, Harrisburg; Survivors' Association, *118th Pennsylvania,* 727.
5. The Pendleton Farm lay approximately seven miles east of Winchester on the road connecting Berryville and Charlestown. *O.R. Atlas,* plate LXIX, map 1.
6. Donaldson is referring to Warrenton, Virginia.
7. Frank C. Gillingham of Philadelphia served as first lieutenant of Company K of the 119th Pennsylvania until his discharge for disability in June 1863. There were numerous mutual

acquaintances among the officers of the 118th and 119th Pennsylvania, as many had served together in the Philadelphia-based Gray Reserves militia before the war, and each regiment considered the other its sister unit, even though the 119th was attached to the 6th Corps. Bates, *Penna. Vols.* vol. IV, 27; Survivors' Association, *118th Pennsylvania,* 104–5.

8. Many of the veterans of the Army of the Potomac, and especially those who had served in it since its inception, shared Donaldson's feelings of disgust at McClellan's removal, although with the value of hindsight, their recollections are markedly more tempered than Donaldson's. See James I. Bowen, *History of the Thirty-Seventh Regiment Massachusetts Volunteers in the Civil War of 1861–1865. . . .* (Holyoke, MA: Clark W. Bryan & Co., 1884), 94–95; J. Harrison Mills, *Chronicles of the Twenty First Regiment New York State Volunteers. . . .* (Buffalo: Gies & Co., 1887), 316–17; Richard Moe, *The Last Full Measure: The Life and Death of the First Minnesota Volunteers* (New York: Henry Holt and Company, 1993), 204–5.

9. John Grubb Parke, thirty-five, a Pennsylvania native and 1849 graduate of West Point, had commanded a brigade under Burnside during his successful operations along the North Carolina coast earlier in the war. He was at this time serving as Burnside's chief of staff. Sifakis, *Who Was Who,* 487–88.

10. Pennsylvanian Andrew Atkinson Humphreys, fifty-two, an 1831 West Point graduate, at this time commanded the 3rd Division, 5th Corps. Ibid., 325.

11. William Marvel, *Burnside* (cited hereafter as Marvel, *Burnside*) (Chapel Hill, NC: University of North Carolina Press, 1991), 163–64.

12. Massachusetts-born Joseph Hooker, forty-eight, an 1837 graduate of West Point, had recently ascended from command of the 5th Corps to command the Center Grand Division, which, as Donaldson notes, consisted of the 3rd and 5th Corps. George Stoneman, forty, a New Yorker and 1846 West Point graduate, had assumed command of the 3rd Corps on October 30. Sifakis, *Who Was Who,* 317–18, 627.

13. Thirty-six-year-old Charles Griffin of Ohio, an 1847 graduate of West Point, would lead the 1st Division of the 5th Army Corps throughout most of the remainder of the war. He had served in the prewar army and early in the conflict as an artillery officer and was tremendously popular with the soldiers who served under him. Ibid., 268–69.

14. The tendency of the Federal officers who shared Donaldson's political proclivities (Democrat, pro-McClellan, and anti-abolition) to gravitate toward the notion of serving in the Regular Army was not uncommon. The Regulars, unlike the more patriotically driven volunteers, served not to further a cause or advance a political objective, but because their chosen occupation was that of a professional soldier. This single-minded devotion to duty, one author has noted, provided a fixed point of reference that did not change with the political climate or the whims of successive commanding generals, and was therefore admired by soldiers who less than wholeheartedly supported Republican war aims. See Mark DeWolfe Howe, *Justice Oliver Wendell Holmes: The Shaping Years, 1841–1870* (Cambridge, MA: The Belknap Press of Harvard University Press, 1957), 82–85.

15. Donaldson is referring to the distinguished cavalry leader of the Army of Northern Virginia, Maj. Gen. J. E. B. Stuart.

16. The artist referred to by Donaldson was Capt. George Johnson of Company F of the 3rd Pennsylvania Cavalry. He, along with four of his brother officers and seventy-seven enlisted men of the regiment, was surprised and captured as described on November 28 at Hartwood Church by Confederate cavalry under Brig. Gen. Wade Hampton. For a full explanation of the event, see O.R., vol. XXI, 13–16; Regimental History Committee, *History of the Third Pennsylvania Cavalry Sixtieth Regiment Pennsylvania Volunteers in the American Civil War, 1861–1865* (cited hereafter as Regimental Committee, *3rd Penna. Cav.*) (Philadelphia: Franklin Printing Co., 1905), 172–77.

17. Fitz John Porter, the former commander of the 5th Corps, had been charged with misconduct and disobedience of orders at Second Bull Run by Gen. John Pope. A court

composed of officers hand picked by the anti-McClellan secretary of war, Edwin Stanton, immediately dispelled any hope Porter had of exoneration, and he was cashiered on January 21, 1863. After a long struggle, Porter succeeded in having the case reopened, and in 1878 he was cleared of all charges and recommissioned in the Regular Army. For a full treatment of this affair, see Otto Eisenschiml, *The Celebrated Case of Fitz John Porter: An American Dreyfus Affair* (Indianapolis: Bobbs-Merrill, 1950).

18. Donaldson does not elaborate here on the charges of immorality he could bring to bear against Col. Gwyn, but in later letters he relates that they include "having a woman in camp—in his tent—two nights at Sharpsburg" and "interfering with the guard while drunk at same camp."

19. Robert Goldthwaite Carter, *Four Brothers in Blue, or Sunshine and Shadows of the War of the Rebellion: A Story of the Great Civil War from Bull Run to Appomattox* (cited hereafter as Carter, *Four Brothers in Blue*) (reprint, Austin, TX: University of Texas Press, 1979), 213.

20. Actual losses for the 118th Pennsylvania at Fredericksburg were five killed, fifty-six wounded, and thirty-seven missing or captured, for a total of ninety-eight. Major Herring was astride his horse when he was shot in the right arm. "This is awful," said a soldier as the major was hit. "This is what we came here for," said Herring who, soon after dismounting, was shot again, this time in the left arm. Herring recovered from his wounds, however, and was back with the regiment by mid-January. O.R. vol. XXI, 135; Survivors' Association, *118th Pennsylvania*, 129.

21. Lorenzo W. Ayers, a twenty-year-old gardener from Philadelphia, served uninterruptedly in Company H until his muster out with the regiment in June 1865. MR Co. H, Harrisburg; Survivors' Association, *118th Pennsylvania*, 724.

22. Brig. Gen. Marsena Patrick of New York, a fifty-two-year-old graduate of the class of 1835 at West Point, had been serving as the provost marshal general of the Army of the Potomac since October 1862. He continued to serve as such throughout the remainder of the war. Sifakis, *Who Was Who*, 490.

23. The 15th and 50th New York Engineers suffered combined casualties of eight killed and forty-eight wounded in their attempts to lay pontoon bridges for the crossing into Fredericksburg. O.R., vol. XXI, 129.

24. Joseph E. Booth, a sixteen-year-old Philadelphia butcher, was, as Donaldson mentions, the drummer from Company H. He had been captured at Shepherdstown, and although Donaldson was under the impression that he deserted, he eventually did return to the regiment, as he is mentioned in a later letter. Booth was discharged due to disability in June 1863. MR Co. H, Harrisburg; Survivors' Association, *118th Pennsylvania*, 724.

25. Eighteen-year-old John F. Mensing, a prewar shoemaker from Philadelphia, was more seriously wounded in action at Spotsylvania Court House in May 1864 while serving with the 5th Massachusetts Battery. His father and older brother, both named Thomas, also served under Donaldson in Company H. MR Co. H, Harrisburg; Survivors' Association, *118th Pennsylvania*, 724, 726; [Regimental Committee], *History of the Fifth Massachusetts Battery . . .* (Boston: Luther E. Cowles, 1902), 818.

26. John B. Fisher, a twenty-four-year-old Philadelphia clerk, was discharged as a result of this wound on January 9, 1863. MR Co. H, Survivors' Association, *118th Pennsylvania*, 725.

27. Sgt. John Van Meter, a twenty-three-year-old sailmaker from Philadelphia, survived this fearful wound and was discharged in March 1863. MR Co. H, Harrisburg; Survivors' Association, *118th Pennsylvania*, 723.

28. Donaldson was in error. Col. Edward Cross of the 5th New Hampshire was indeed severely (though not mortally) wounded at Fredericksburg, but it was impossible for Donaldson to have witnessed it. The 5th New Hampshire formed a part of the 1st Brigade, 1st Division, 2nd Corps, which assaulted Marye's Heights at approximately 12:45 P.M. The 118th Pennsylvania was not sent into action until 3:30 P.M., long after the attack of the 2nd Corps. Additionally, Cross led his regiment into battle on foot and was not mounted. Several separate Federal assaults were attempted after Donaldson had

reached the area where the 118th halted, but it is difficult to ascertain the identity of the officer he saw wounded. Vorin E. Whan, Jr., *Fiasco at Fredericksburg* (State College, PA: Pennsylvania State University Press, 1961), 83–88, 96–99; Child, *5th New Hampshire,* 153.

29. John L. Smith of Company K was a plucky sixteen-year-old Philadelphian who had been employed as a huckster before his enlistment in December 1862. He would be promoted to corporal in March 1865 and mustered out of the service four months later. Smith published the three editions of the Regimental History of the 118th Pennsylvania and was also a contributor to the work, though he is often erroneously credited as the author. MR Co. H, Harrisburg; Survivors' Association, *118th Pennsylvania,* 736.

30. Capt. J. Benton Kennedy, twenty-three, of Jackson, Michigan, had mustered in as second lieutenant of Company D of the 1st Michigan in September 1861 and was promoted to first lieutenant in January 1862 and to captain in July. He died as a result of his wound on December 16, 1862. Adjutant General, *First Michigan,* 72.

31. Sylvester Crossley, a twenty-two-year-old whitesmith from Philadelphia, recovered from his wounds and in January 1864 was promoted to second lieutenant of Company H. He was captured at Bethesda Church, Virginia, in June 1864 and was held in a series of prison camps until February 1865, when he escaped from the Federal officer's prison at Columbia, South Carolina, reaching safety with Sherman's army soon after. He resigned and was honorably discharged in April 1865. MR Co. H, Harrisburg; Survivors' Association, *118th Pennsylvania,* 723; Noble D. Preston, *History of the Tenth Regiment of Cavalry, New York State Volunteers . . .* (New York: D. Appleton and Company, 1902), 568–71.

32. Sgt. Hazleton Joyce, a twenty-one-year-old Philadelphia carpenter, deserted from the military hospital at Point Lookout, Maryland, on March 1, 1863, while recovering from his wounds. MR Co. H, Harrisburg.

33. Pvt. Robert C. Bennett, thirty-one, a carpenter and Philadelphia native, recovered from his wounds and in January 1864 was promoted to first sergeant of Company H, a position he held until his muster out in June 1865. MR Co. H, Harrisburg; Survivors' Association, *118th Pennsylvania,* 723.

34. Pvt. Thomas J. Reynolds, an eighteen-year-old packer from Philadelphia, returned to the company and served with it until his discharge in June 1865. MR Co. H, Harrisburg; Survivors' Association, *118th Pennsylvania,* 727.

35. Pvt. Timothy Tierney, forty-three, a native of Ireland, had been employed as a harness-maker before the war. He was discharged for disability on February 27, 1863, most likely as a result of his Fredericksburg wounds. MR Co. H, Harrisburg; Survivors' Association, *118th Pennsylvania,* 728.

36. More than a few of the soldiers of the 118th, and indeed, many of the Army of the Potomac, were foraging through the abandoned shops and homes of Fredericksburg. Driven by hunger earlier in the day, Pvt. John Smith of Company K set out to find something to eat. "I went into a number of houses," he wrote, "but I could find nothing that I wanted. Everything was confusion and everything of use had been taken or thrown into the street. I got into a flour store and took a quart cup full of flour and went quickly to my company and . . . mixed the same up to make some slapjacks, made from flour and water. They apparently baked all right, but as they became dry, they cracked, and to my utter disgust I found that it was plaster [of] paris. Had I found that fellow who was selling plaster [of] paris for flour that morning, it would have gone hard with him. . . ." John L. Smith to Hannah Smith, December 26, 1862, John L. Smith Papers, Historical Society of Pennsylvania, Philadelphia (cited hereafter as Smith Papers, HSP).

CHAPTER FIVE: THE MUD MARCH AND WINTER QUARTERS

1. Bruce Catton, *Never Call Retreat* (New York: Doubleday & Company, 1965), 22–23.
2. Emerson Gifford Taylor, *Gouverneur Kemble Warren: The Life and Letters of an American Solider, 1830–1882* (Boston: Houghton Mifflin, 1932), 97.
3. Bothered by newspaper reports critical of the administration's role in prodding the Army of the Potomac to its defeat at Fredericksburg, General Burnside wrote a public letter

to General in Chief Halleck on December 17, in which he assumed sole responsibility for the reverse. The letter was published widely in northern newspapers, and many, like Jacob Donaldson, reacted favorably toward it. Captain Donaldson obviously felt otherwise. The letter is reprinted in O.R., vol. XXI, 66–67.

4. Edward A. Landell of Philadelphia was a boyhood friend of Donaldson's and had recently been promoted to the captaincy of Company I of the 119th Pennsylvania. He later served in brigade-level staff assignments in the 6th Corps, attaining the rank of major, and was brevetted lieutenant colonel and colonel at the close of the war. Mary Landell, whom Donaldson would wed in 1872, was Edward's sister. Edward A. Landell Military Escutcheon, CWLM; Bates, *Penna. Vols.,* vol. IV, 25.

5. R. Shelton McKenzie, a British-born journalist and author, was literary editor of the *Philadelphia Press.* Thomas William Herringshaw, *Herringshaw's Encyclopedia of American Biography of the Nineteenth Century* . . . (cited hereafter as Herringshaw, *Encyclopedia of American Biography*) (Chicago: American Publishers Association, 1907), 608.

6. Donaldson is likely referring to reports that had followed the Battle of Stone's River, or Murfreesboro, Tennessee, which had been fought from December 31, 1862, to January 2, 1863. Confederate general Braxton Bragg had prematurely notified Richmond that he was victorious over Union forces under Maj. Gen. William S. Rosecrans, but the bloody battle was essentially a draw. Almost 30 percent of the forces engaged became casualties in the three-day battle.

7. Marvel, *Burnside,* 197.

8. Plitt Smith, ostensibly an influential friend of the Donaldson family, is otherwise unidentified.

9. Burnside's General Orders No. 7, dated January 20, 1863, although not written as Donaldson here describes them, are in O.R., vol. XXI, 127.

10. Pvt. William Fowler, a thirty-one-year-old laborer from Baltimore, was a member of Company F. The regimental history of the 118th contradicts Donaldson and records that the man chosen to fell the tree was Pvt. Daniel Oakley of Company B, but this may result from the fact that Private Fowler deserted from the regiment on July 1, 1863, during the march to Gettysburg and was not heard from again. Survivors' Association, *118th Pennsylvania,* 162.

11. Sgt. Major Walter Carter of the 22nd Massachusetts wrote that this fight involved not only the Pennsylvanians and New Yorkers, but the entire 1st Brigade, and that at the height of the altercation, Captain O'Neill of the 118th pulled his pistols and threatened to shoot the belligerents of the 22nd if they did not desist. "This," Carter went on, "was too great a temptation for some of our whiskey-laden pugilists, one of whom stole up behind him, and sent him sprawling in the mud by a dexterous blow behind the ear. The only wonder is that the pistols did not go off and kill somebody." Carter, *Four Brothers in Blue,* 226. For more on this affair, see Survivors' Association, *118th Pennsylvania,* 162–64; Parker and Carter, *22nd Massachusetts,* 244–45.

12. On December 30 the 1st Division had been ordered to Richard's Ford on the Rappahannock to support a cavalry probe toward Warrenton. Most of Donaldson's lengthy letter detailing this uneventful move has been omitted.

13. Twenty-one-year-old Henry Q. Cobb, a plumber and native of Philadelphia, was a sergeant of Company H. He was discharged for disability in late October 1863. His brother, Daniel, was also a sergeant of Company H. MR Co. H, Harrisburg; Survivors' Association, *118th Pennsylvania,* 723.

14. Stephen W. Sears, *Chancellorsville* (cited hereafter as Sears, *Chancellorsville*) (Boston: Houghton Mifflin Co., 1996), 18, 70.

15. Small, *The Road to Richmond,* 81.

16. The sheer size and grandeur of this two-day review of the Army of the Potomac by President Lincoln left a lasting impression on even the most hardened veterans. For soldiers' comments on the event, see Hitchcock, *132nd Pennsylvania,* 191–99; George F. Sprenger, *Concise History of the Camp and Field Life of the 122d Regiment, Penn'a Volunteers.* . . .

(Lancaster, PA: New Era Steam Book Print, 1885), 254–56; Allan Nevins, ed., *A Diary of Battle: The Personal Journals of Colonel Charles S. Wainwright, 1861–1865* (cited hereafter as Nevins, *Diary of Battle*) (New York: Harcourt, Brace & World, 1962), 177–78.

17. General Orders No. 100 from the War Department, dated August 11, 1862, stipulated that officers who had been absent for more than sixty days due to wounds or disease contracted in the service were to be discharged so that their positions could be filled by more able-bodied men.

18. Capt. Courtney O'Callaghan of Company I had been severely injured as a result of having been driven over the bluffs at Shepherdstown. Alfred N. Wetherill, his first lieutenant, was mustered in as captain of the company to date from February 15.

19. Vermont-born Stephen Noyes Winslow, thirty-seven, was a journalist with the *Philadelphia Commercial List*. Herringshaw, *Encyclopedia of American Biography*, 1025.

20. Following a verbal disagreement with Gwyn in mid-January (Herring had refused to take a drink with him to celebrate the promotion of a lieutenant), Maj. Herring had been ordered by the lieutenant colonel to personally superintend all company roll calls, and was told that if he failed to do so, he would be reported by the orderly sergeant of the company from which he was absent. Gwyn's order created quite a stir in the camp of the 118th, especially among the officers. "Do you see the refinement of cruelty and indignity put upon the major?" Donaldson wrote in an excised portion of a letter to Jacob soon after. *"To be reported by an enlisted man.* To be present, no matter what the weather, at early morning roll call."

21. Thomas H. Addicks, who Donaldson previously described as a "drunken loafer," had resigned his commission as quartermaster on October 4, 1862.

22. William O'Neill, thirty-one, was a native of Ireland and the brother of Capt. Henry O'Neill of Company A. A Methodist, he had joined the regiment on January 29 and served with it throughout the balance of the war. Donaldson has much to say in future letters about the chaplain. Survivors' Association, *118th Pennsylvania,* 652.

CHAPTER SIX: CHANCELLORSVILLE

1. Sears, *Chancellorsville,* 131–32, 181.
2. Ibid., 143.
3. Ernest B. Furgurson, *Chancellorsville, 1863: The Souls of the Brave* (cited hereafter as Furgurson. *Chancellorsville*) (New York: Alfred A. Knopf, 1992), 111.
4. Sears, *Chancellorsville,* 210–11.
5. Furgurson, *Chancellorsville,* 129.
6. Sears, *Chancellorsville,* 169.
7. John Fulton Reynolds, a forty-two-year-old Pennsylvanian and 1841 West Point graduate, had commanded the 1st Corps since just after the Battle of Antietam. Probably no other corps commander then serving in the Army of the Potomac was more highly regarded. Darius N. Couch, forty-one, of New York, commanded the 2nd Corps. The 1846 West Point graduate later became so disgusted with Hooker's leadership at Chancellorsville that he transferred out of the Army of the Potomac. Daniel E. Sickles, forty-three, one of the North's so-called "political generals," was a prewar New York congressman and one of Hooker's intimates. He had led the 3rd Corps since early February. Pennsylvanian George Gordon Meade, forty-seven, an 1835 West Point graduate, had assumed command of the 5th Corps several weeks after the Battle of Fredericksburg and would, about seven weeks after Chancellorsville, replace Hooker in command of the army. Oliver Otis Howard of Maine had been posted to command of the 11th Corps on April 12. Howard, thirty-two, was an 1854 graduate of West Point, and his performances while leading his corps both at Chancellorsville and Gettysburg were suspect. Henry Warner Slocum, thirty-five, a New York native and 1852 graduate of West Point, had been promoted to command of the 12th Corps in October 1862. Like his 2nd Corps counterpart, Darius Couch, Slocum was so disillusioned by his experiences under Hooker at Chancellorsville

that he sat out the early stages of the 1864 Atlanta Campaign rather than serve again under "Fighting Joe." Sifakis, *Who Was Who,* 146, 321, 440–41, 539–40, 594, 598–99.

8. Lt. Col. Joseph Dickinson, thirty-two, was a Philadelphia native who had begun his war service as a lieutenant in the 26th Pennsylvania, and he was now serving as assistant adjutant general, not chief of staff, to Major General Hooker. Dickinson would be brevetted to the rank of brigadier general at the end of the war and was awarded the Medal of Honor for his services at Gettysburg. Hunt and Brown, *Brevet Brigadier Generals,* 162.

9. I have been unable to reconcile Donaldson's account of this encounter involving Sickles with any of the written records describing the battle. In his official report, General Sickles states that he reported to Hooker at Chancellorsville at 9 A.M. on May 1, the day after Donaldson places him at Hooker's headquarters. I can offer two explanations. Sickles, well known for his close relationship with his mentor, Hooker, could have ridden in advance of his corps, which had been ordered to U.S. Ford on April 30, for a direct consultation with the commanding general. Or, more likely, Donaldson simply confused the date on which this episode actually occurred. In either event, there is little doubt that what Donaldson describes actually did take place, as nearly every other detail of his experiences at Chancellorsville agrees with those in numerous other written accounts. *O.R.,* vol. XXV, pt. 1, 384.

10. Hooker's General Orders No. 47, dated April 30, stated that as a result of the previous three days' movements, the enemy "must either ingloriously fly, or come out from behind his defenses and give us battle on our own ground where certain destruction awaits him." Ibid., 171.

11. Pvt. David C. Thompson of Company H, 134th Pennsylvania Volunteers, survived his regiment's nine-month term of enlistment and mustered out of the service three weeks after Chancellorsville on May 26, 1863. Donaldson restored the Bible to Thompson's family in 1902, unfortunately several years after Thompson's death. FAD Papers, CWLM; Bates, *Penna. Vols.,* vol. IV, 298.

12. Donaldson modified this sentence in later years, changing "was kept up for several hours" to "continued for at least an hour."

13. Sears, *Chancellorsville,* 312.

14. Ibid., 388.

15. The action that Donaldson heard in the late evening of May 2 was an attempt by Dan Sickles's 3rd Corps to link up with the main army. Sickles was nervous about being cut off as a result of the rout of the 11th Corps, but his night attack was poorly managed and unsuccessful. Ibid., 300–2.

16. Col. Charles H. T. Collis of Philadelphia had originally led an independent company of Zouaves d'Afrique, which in September 1862 was expanded into the 114th Pennsylvania Volunteers. Donaldson previously mentioned seeing then Captain Collis outside of Washington, D.C., in October 1861. Taylor, *Philadelphia in the War,* 124.

17. The charge that Donaldson levies here against Collis, namely that he was drunk during the Battle of Chancellorsville, is one that would randomly plague the young colonel throughout the rest of his life. Collis was, in fact, placed under arrest following the battle and charged with "misbehavior before the enemy." Collis states in his official report (which his brigade commander, upon receiving it, characterized as "a complete romance from beginning to end") that he "was carried off the field insensible, suffering from exhaustion." When brought to trial, Collis successfully defended himself against the charge, sometimes from a stretcher in the courtroom, as he was then suffering from a full-blown case of typhoid fever, the early stages of which had apparently prostrated him during the battle. Dr. Ed Hagerty, who has closely studied the Collis court-martial and supplied me with the details of the case, concludes from all of the existing evidence that Donaldson's judgment of Collis's condition was misinformed.

In the mid-1880s, when he applied for membership in the Military Order of the Loyal Legion of the United States, a Union officers' veterans group, Collis was initially rejected, the reason being given that his conduct at Chancellorsville was the subject of a court-martial. Collis then assembled and privately published a detailed defense of his conduct at the battle, accompanied by numerous endorsements, and was eventually admitted to membership in the Loyal Legion. *O.R.*, vol. XXV, pt. 1, 422–25; Dr. Ed Hagerty to editor, May 9, 1993; Charles H. T. Collis, *Letters and Testimony Presented by Charles H. T. Collis Defending Himself against Accusations Made to the Military Order of the Loyal Legion as to His Military Record* (New York: n. p., 1891).

18. Joseph S. Chandler of Philadelphia had served as a captain in the 75th Pennsylvania until his promotion to major of the 114th in September 1862. He had been wounded previously in the war at Fredericksburg.

19. What Donaldson may have seen was the death of Capt. William G. Hewins of the 18th Massachusetts. His was the only fatality recorded among the officers of the 1st Brigade, 1st Division, 5th Corps, and the date of his death, May 3, coincides with Donaldson's account. *O.R.* vol. XXV, pt. 1, 186.

20. This structure was also identified in various Union and Confederate reports of the battle as the Bullock House, Chandler House, and White House. The two-and-a-half-story whitewashed wood building was the property of Oscar Bullock, a Confederate soldier, and stood in the southern angle of the intersection of the Bullock and Ely's Ford Roads, approximately three-quarters of a mile northwest of Chancellorsville. Noel G. Harrison, *Chancellorsville Battlefield Sites* (Lynchburg, VA: H. E. Howard, 1990), 11–15.

21. Donaldson is slightly confused about what he witnessed. The 5th Maine Battery of the 1st Corps, posted near the Chancellor House, had all of its officers shot down and its enlisted men either wounded or driven off under concentrated Confederate artillery fire. Details from the 53rd, 116th, and 140th Pennsylvania regiments, along with a portion of the 63rd New York, were ordered in by General Hancock and saved the guns from imminent capture, physically dragging them back to the Federal lines. "Passing out of the woods and into the open space near the Bullock House," recalled one of the rescuing party, "the regiment was met by General Sickles, who, rising in his stirrups, called for three cheers 'for the regiment that saved the guns.'. . ." *O.R.*, vol. XXV, pt. 1, 327–29; St. Clair A. Mulholland, *The Story of the 116th Regiment Pennsylvania Volunteers in the War of the Rebellion* (Philadelphia: F. McManus, Jr. & Co.) 100–101.

22. Sedgwick and the 6th Corps had overrun Confederate positions on Marye's Heights on the afternoon of May 3 and advanced as far as Salem Church. Lee, confident that he had Hooker on the defensive, left a holding force to watch the entrenched Federals in the Wilderness and by the evening of May 4 had pushed Sedgwick back across the Rappahannock, punishing him severely in the process.

23. Sears, *Chancellorsville*, 422, 427.

24. Lincoln quoted in John Bigelow, Jr., *The Campaign of Chancellorsville: A Strategic and Tactical Study* (cited hereafter as Bigelow, *Chancellorsville*) (New Haven, CT: Yale University Press, 1910), 434.

25. Brig. Gen. Amiel W. Whipple was not, as Donaldson believed, attached to Hooker's staff but commanded the 3rd Division of the 3rd Corps. The forty-seven-year-old Massachusetts native was an 1841 graduate of West Point. Sifakis, *Who Was Who*, 708.

26. A Maine private serving with Whipple in the 3rd Corps expressed seemingly callous amazement at his wounding: "How any bullet ever pierced General Whipple's armor of dirt is a mystery of mysteries. I considered him perfectly safe from any missile weighing less than a ton, having a casing of dirt of unknown thickness supposed to be invulnerable." Ruth L. Silliker, ed., *The Rebel Yell & the Yankee Hurrah: The Civil War Journal of a Maine Volunteer* (Camden, ME: Down East Books, 1985), 83.

27. In late May 1885 Donaldson revisited the Chancellorsville battlefield in company with other veterans of the fight and was given information that led him to modify his statements on the circumstances surrounding the death of General Whipple. "During the ride to Fredericksburg," he wrote, "I gave my letter descriptive of the battle to Judge

Fell to read. He had been a captain in the [122nd] Penna. Vols., Whipple's Division, 3rd Corps.

"In my letter I state that General Whipple . . . was drunk when killed near the Burns House. Judge Fell, who was also present when the General was shot, said I was certainly in error regarding the incident, that General Whipple . . . was not in liquor as stated by me, although he could readily understand why one not familiar with the General might be led to suppose that he was. He was a man of slow habit and unsteady seat on horseback, and was not intoxicated at the time alluded to. He did not die upon the battlefield as was stated by me, but lived for three days and died in Washington, D.C.

"I cheerfully make this correction and am only too glad to know I was in error as to General Whipple being in liquor. I would not intentionally cast an unjust reflection upon anyone, least of all a General Officer who lost his life in his country's cause. I was but twenty-two years of age when the battle of Chancellorsville was fought and was deeply impressed by the sights and scenes surrounding me. I had a most exalted appreciation of a General Officer's grade, and when noticing anything that at all lessened the standard I set upon his rank, I was greatly shocked. Hence it was that I mentioned so critically the supposed intoxicated condition of General Whipple. As to his dying on the field, the surgeon told me and others standing near the General would die in a few minutes." Memoranda dated June 1, 1885, FAD Papers, CWLM.

28. Only Col. James M. McQuade's 2nd Brigade of the 1st Division was engaged in this charge. *O.R.,* vol. XXV, pt. 1, 518.

29. Pvt. George W. LeNoir, an eighteen-year-old wheelwright from Philadelphia, was wounded later in the war, at Spotsylvania Court House on May 18, 1864. He recovered, returned to the regiment, and mustered out in June 1865. MR Co. H, Harrisburg; Survivors' Association, *118th Pennsylvania,* 739.

30. Brig. Gen. James S. Wadsworth of New York commanded the 1st Division of the 1st Army Corps. O.R., vol. XXV, pt. 1, 174.

31. As Donaldson has surmised, twenty-year-old Cpl. James McGinley of Philadelphia was captured during the battle, but he was exchanged and returned to the regiment in late May. He served out the balance of his enlistment and mustered out in June 1865. MR Co. H, Harrisburg; Survivors' Association, 118th Pennsylvania, 724.

32. George T. Stevens, *Three Years in the Sixth Corps* (cited hereafter as Stevens, *Three Years in the Sixth Corps*) (Albany: S. R. Gray, 1866), 216.

33. I have been unable to identify any engineer officer, volunteer or regular, with the surname of Cogswell.

34. The scene at U.S. Ford on May 6 apparently was far from inspiring. A sergeant major attached to one of the Massachusetts regiments of the brigade wrote that while at the Ford, "the officers behaved shamefully; got drunk and used the men like brutes. . . . I saw a lieutenant colonel of the One Hundred and Eighteenth Pennsylvania whip our Major's servant into some work, and I was disgusted with the drunken brute. . . . The brother of the young man, Lieutenant R. of our regiment, resented the insult, when General B. [Barnes] rode up, reeling in his saddle, and informed him (R.), with a swing of his stick, that if he didn't go to work too, he would put it over him also. . . . I saw Colonel J. [Johnson] of the Twenty-fifth New York ride up to a group of officers and soldiers . . . and rising in his stirrups he said: 'Hic! you are a disgrace to your country, go to work! Hic!!' And straight-way rolled off his saddle, a beastly sot." Carter, *Four Brothers,* 261.

35. The home of Miss Withers was located on the Warrenton Road, midway between Hartwood Church and Berea, not Bravere's Church, approximately five miles northeast of U.S. Ford. *O.R. Atlas,* plate XXXIX, map 3.

36. William A. Throop of Detroit, a twenty-four-year-old prewar merchant, had originally served as captain of Company F of the 1st Michigan. Wounded at Gaines' Mill in June 1862, he was promoted to major in August of that year and to lieutenant colonel in

March 1863. He was wounded again at Gettysburg, Cold Harbor, and Petersburg before his promotion to colonel in December 1864, and he was brevetted to the rank of brigadier general in March 1865. Hunt and Brown, *Brevet Brigadier Generals,* 616; Adjutant General, *1st Michigan,* 133.

37. The refusal of some of the two-year and nine-month troops then attached to the Army of the Potomac to continue to serve after they felt their term of enlistment was up was a somewhat common occurrence in May and June 1863. Hooker had been concerned enough before Chancellorsville about some 2nd Corps regiments to recommend that they be relegated to support roles, and one 5th Corps regiment, the 5th New York, actually marched off the battlefield on May 4. In a letter home at this time, a member of the 118th mentions guarding not only the mutineers of the 25th New York, but also portions of the 12th, 13th, and 17th New York, all of which were two-year regiments. A similar incident was also taking place elsewhere within the brigade at this time, wherein 120 men of the 2nd Maine who thought they had signed on for a two-year term of service, but who in actuality had enlisted for three years, were put under guard by the 118th until they were forcibly transferred for the balance of their term to the 20th Maine. *O.R.,* vol. XXV, pt. 2, 267; Bigelow, *Chancellorsville,* 417; J. L. Smith to Mother, May 17, 1863, Smith Papers, HSP; John J. Pullen, *The Twentieth Maine: A Volunteer Regiment in the Civil War* (cited hereafter as Pullen, *Twentieth Maine*) (Philadelphia: J. B. Lippincott Company, 1957), 77–81.

38. Donaldson has previously alluded to Prevost's weakened condition. The colonel had returned to the regiment prior to Chancellorsville without giving his Shepherdstown wounds sufficient time to heal, for fear of being mustered out of the service. The rigors of the campaign proved to be too much for him, however, and he returned to Philadelphia to recuperate more fully.

    Although Prevost departed on May 25, his resignation did not take effect until September 30. He was subsequently commissioned colonel of the 16th Regiment, Veteran Reserve Corps, and for a time commanded the Confederate prison camp at Elmira, New York. Upon his honorable discharge in June 1865, he was promoted to brevet brigadier general. His war wounds continued to afflict him throughout the rest of his life, and he died from their effects in 1887, partially paralyzed and blind. Survivors' Association, *118th Pennsylvania,* 637–38, 681.

39. Donaldson was hearing the reverberations from the largest cavalry battle of the Civil War, the Battle of Brandy Station. The newly organized Cavalry Corps of the Army of the Potomac, under Brig. Gen. Alfred Pleasonton, had forded the Rappahannock early on the morning of June 9 and surprised Confederate troopers under Gen. J. E. B. Stuart, resulting in a daylong series of attacks and counterattacks. Although the Southerners were ultimately victorious, pushing the Federals back across the river, it was only by the slimmest of margins, and though the Union cavalrymen were narrowly defeated, their morale was bolstered tremendously. For the first time in the war in the East, they had met their adversaries on open terrain, in nearly equal numbers, and came within a hairbreadth of beating them.

40. Henry P. Truefitt of Philadelphia had captained Company G of the 119th Pennsylvania until his promotion to major in April 1863. He was killed in action while commanding the regiment at Spotsylvania Court House on May 12, 1864. *Adj. Gen. of PA, 1866,* 665.

CHAPTER SEVEN: GETTYSBURG

1. 2nd Lt. Barzilia J. Inman of Company F had been promoted from sergeant in January 1863. The thirty-nine-year-old tailor had resided in Philadelphia before the war but was a native of North Carolina. He was honorably discharged in March 1864 due to wounds received at Gettysburg. MR Co. F, Harrisburg; Survivors' Association, *118th Pennsylvania,* 711.

2. Shepard Gleason, twenty-five, of Rochester, New York, had served as first lieutenant and captain in the 25th New York before his promotion to major in September 1862. He was

likely acting as colonel or lieutenant colonel at the time of his death. Phisterer, *New York in the Rebellion,* vol. III, 2020.

3. The Gray Reserves were a well-known Philadelphia militia unit that at this time was en route to Harrisburg, Pennsylvania, to be mustered in as the 32nd Regiment, Ninety Day Militia, United States Service. Officered and manned by the upper echelons of Philadelphia society, the Reserves served in the defenses of Harrisburg and on minor reconnaissances until their muster out on August 1. Although Jacob Donaldson had served in the Gray Reserves in a similar role during the Antietam Campaign, he was not with them at this time. Taylor, *Philadelphia in the War,* 249–250.

4. This was twenty-eight-year-old Col. Alfred N. Duffié, a French-born cavalryman who in the past two weeks had been demoted from command of the 2nd Division of the Cavalry Corps to command of the 2nd Brigade of that division and finally down to command of his old regiment, the 1st Rhode Island Cavalry. Edward G. Longacre, *The Cavalry at Gettysburg. . . .* (cited hereafter as Longacre, *Cavalry at Gettysburg*) (Lincoln, NE: University of Nebraska Press, 1993), 50, 91, 104.

5. The 1st Rhode Island Cavalry, trapped as it was between two converging forces at Middleburg on June 17, suffered casualties of 6 killed, 20 wounded, and 210 captured out of 275 engaged. Ibid., 109–13; Frederic Denison, *Sabres and Spurs: The First Regiment Rhode Island Cavalry in the Civil War. . . .* (Central Falls, RI: First Rhode Island Cavalry Veteran Association, 1876), 239.

6. What Donaldson witnessed around Aldie was the aftermath of a duel on July 19 between Union cavalrymen under Brig. Gen. David McMurtrie Gregg and Confederate troopers under Gen. Jeb Stuart. Each side suffered roughly 100 casualties in the action. Longacre, *Cavalry at Gettysburg,* 121–24.

7. Col. John Irvin Gregg of the 16th Pennsylvania Cavalry commanded the 3rd Brigade of the 2nd Division of the Cavalry Corps, which, in addition to his regiment, consisted of the 1st Maine, 10th New York, and 4th Pennsylvania regiments. *O.R.,* vol, XXVII, pt. 1, 186.

8. This was likely Capt. Charles E. Cadwalader, of the Philadelphia-raised 6th Pennsylvania Cavalry. He was at this time serving as an aide-de-camp to Hooker, not to Maj. Gen. Alfred Pleasonton, who headed the Cavalry Corps.

9. Supported by the infantry of the 1st Division, 5th Corps, cavalry leader Pleasonton had pushed Rebel horsemen under Jeb Stuart back through Middleburg and Upperville in a daylong series of hard-fought skirmishes on June 21, in hopes of probing the gaps of the Blue Ridge Mountains, which shielded Lee's advancing infantry in the Shenandoah Valley. Casualties for the Federal forces totaled 157; Stuart reported 250 captured. Longacre, *Cavalry at Gettysburg,* 126–29.

10. Ormsby Robinson of Allegheny County, Pennsylvania, had been promoted from captain of Company G of the 3rd Pennsylvania Cavalry to major on December 11, 1862. He mustered out of the service in August 1864. Regimental Committee, *3rd Penna. Cav.,* 566–67.

11. John P. Taylor, thirty-six, of Mifflin County, Pennsylvania, was at this time in temporary command of the 1st Brigade, 2nd Division of the Cavalry Corps. Longacre, *Cavalry at Gettysburg,* 119.

12. Col. John Singleton Mosby and elements of his 43rd Virginia Cavalry Battalion were active along the Little River Turnpike, on which the 5th Corps was moving on June 22. Following a botched ambush set for them by Federal cavalry that morning, Mosby and a group of approximately twenty men raided east along the turnpike, capturing a number of supply wagons and mules. See John S. Mosby, *Stuart's Cavalry in the Gettysburg Campaign* (New York: Moffat, Yard & Company, 1908), 72–76; Hugh C. Keen and Horace Mewborn, *43rd Battalion Virginia Cavalry Mosby's Command* (Lynchburg, VA: H. E. Howard 1993), 70–71; Virgil Carrington Jones, *Ranger Mosby*) (Chapel Hill, NC: University of North Carolina Press, 1944), 141–44.

13. Delaware native George Sykes, forty-two, an 1842 West Point graduate, would on this day, June 28, be promoted away from command of his beloved Regular Division and

given command of the 5th Corps in place of General Meade, who replaced Hooker in command of the Army of the Potomac.

14. Maj. Gen. Dan Butterfield, who had served as Hooker's chief of staff and was now acting in the same capacity to Meade, had published a widely circulated infantry manual earlier in the war. In it, he advised the commanding officer of the regiment leading a march to "sound the halt half an hour after the column has fully started, and once an hour afterward, giving a halt of five minutes each time." Daniel Butterfield, *Camp and Outpost Duty for Infantry* (New York: Harper & Brothers, 1862), 35.

15. James Godfrey, a thirty-six-year-old New Jersey native and prewar cordwainer, died on November 13, 1863, in a Philadelphia hospital. MR Co. H, Harrisburg; Survivors' Association, *118th Pennsylvania*, 725.

16. Union brigadier general Judson Kilpatrick's 3rd Division of the Cavalry Corps had been scouting northern Maryland and southern Pennsylvania in search of the advance elements of Lee's infantry and on June 30 had encountered Jeb Stuart's cavalry at Hanover, Pennsylvania. After a daylong fight in which the Northerners lost approximately 200 troopers and the Southerners 150, Stuart broke off the engagement and moved north toward York in a futile attempt to link up with infantry under Maj. Gen. Jubal Early. Longacre, *Cavalry at Gettysburg*, 172–79.

17. Henry Augustus Boardman was a noted Philadelphia Presbyterian cleric and author, but Captain Crocker was evidently having some fun with the women of Hanover, as Dr. Boardman's son, if he indeed had one, was not serving in the 118th. Herringshaw, *Encyclopedia of American Biography*, 1025.

18. The false report that McClellan had been reappointed to lead the Army of the Potomac was repeated to many units on their march to Gettysburg and appears to have been spread predominantly among regiments of the 5th and 6th Corps. One member of the brigade recalled its effect on the men differently, however: "[McClellan's] name had lost its magical impact, for beyond a few feeble cheers from some of the commands, the column stalked on in moody silence." Parker and Carter, *22nd Massachusetts*, 244–45. For more on soldiers' reactions to the announcement, see Theodore Gerrish, *Army Life: A Private's Reminiscences of the Civil War* (Portland, ME: Hoyt, Fogg & Dunham, 1882), 101; Survivors' Association, *History of the Twenty Third Pennsylvania Volunteer Infantry, Birney's Zouaves* (cited hereafter as Survivors' Association, *Twenty-third Pennsylvania*) (Philadelphia: n. p., 1903), 93; Regimental Association, *155th Pennsylvania*, 154; Johnson and Buel, *Battles and Leaders*, 301.

19. In a postwar alteration to his letter, Donaldson added the words "in line of masses" after "in close column."

20. John B. Fasset of Philadelphia had served as a lieutenant and captain in the 23rd Pennsylvania before accepting a position as aide-de-camp on 3rd Corps Maj. Gen. David B. Birney's staff. Discharged in 1864, he would receive the Medal of Honor thirty years later for his actions at Gettysburg. Survivors' Association, *Twenty-Third Pennsylvania*, 220; Harry W. Pfanz, *Gettysburg: The Second Day* (cited hereafter as Pfanz, *Gettysburg*) (Chapel Hill, NC: University of North Carolina Press, 1987), 407–8.

21. This was Capt. John Bigelow's 9th Massachusetts Battery, which had recently been posted to the Army of the Potomac as part of the Artillery Reserve.

22. One week after the battle, Pvt. John Smith of Company K recorded that the 118th "advanced out and were formed in line of battle in the shape of a bent pin and finally the rebs came down the hill in front of us in droves and we opened fire on them very lively. I loaded and fired fifteen times. They were so thick that you could shut your eyes and fire and could hit them, and they jumped behind every tree and stump for cover and halted at the edge of the woods. . . ." John L. Smith to Hannah Smith, July 9, 1863, Smith Papers, HSP.

23. Maj. James Cornell Biddle, aide-de-camp on Meade's staff.

24. At dusk, Brig. Gen. Samuel Wylie Crawford of Pennsylvania led elements of his 3rd Division (commonly known as the Pennsylvania Reserves) of the 5th Corps on the charge that Donaldson witnessed, pushing Confederate troops from the valley fronting Little Round Top back through the Wheatfield, effectively ending Southern resistance on that portion of the field on July 2. See Pfanz, *Gettysburg,* 391–402.

25. Donaldson's recounting of the complex events that occurred on other portions of the battlefield on July 2 is hindered by the fact that he, like almost every other foot soldier, had a firsthand knowledge of only what took place directly in his front. Although his version of the actions on that day is confused, it is interesting in that he was almost surely repeating information that was believed to be true at the time he wrote his letter. To clarify, portions of Col. Strong Vincent's 3rd Brigade, 1st Division, 5th Corps, actually undertook and were not resisting a bayonet attack on Little Round Top. Col. Jacob B. Sweitzer's 2nd Brigade of the 1st Division had been sent into the Wheatfield to support several 2nd Corps regiments that were under pressure, but the brigade was soon isolated and forced to fall back. Some vicious hand-to-hand fighting ensued, and Col. Harrison Jeffords of the 4th, not the 16th, Michigan was bayonetted and mortally wounded while on foot trying to retrieve his regiment's fallen colors. Ibid. 290–94.

26. Once again, the confused events of July 2 are largely to blame for Donaldson's misstatements. The 20th Maine (which had conducted the aforementioned bayonet charge) and the 83rd Pennsylvania were firmly ensconced behind their breastworks on Little Round Top at this time and did not participate in this charge. Nor did the 10th Pennsylvania Reserves of the 3rd Division, which at this time was being sent to the support of the troops occupying Little Round Top. In all probability, Donaldson was referring to an extension of the charge of Crawford's Pennsylvania Reserves, supported by 6th Corps troops, which cleared the ground to the front and left of Little Round Top of Confederate resistance. Ibid., 393–404.

27. The 22nd Virginia was at this time posted near New River in Greenbrier County, West Virginia. Lowry, *22nd Virginia,* 42.

28. Big Round Top.

29. Lt. Barzilia Inman of Company F had been wounded and left between the opposing lines, where he lay throughout the evening of July 2. "That night," he later wrote, "a number of stray hogs came to where I lay and commenced rooting and tearing at the dead men around me. Finally one fellow that in the darkness looked of enormous size approached and attempted to poke me—grunting loudly the while. Several others also came up, when, waiting my chance, I jammed my sword into his belly, which made him set up a prolonged, sharp cry. By constant vigilance and keeping from sleeping I contrived to fight the monsters off till daylight." Survivors' Association, *118th Pennsylvania,* 249.

30. Maj. R. H. Finney is listed as Heth's adjutant general at this time, and no mention of his capture was made in Heth's after-action report. O.R., vol. XXVII, pt. 2, 639.

31. William A. Dunklin of Selma, Alabama, had entered the Confederate service as second lieutenant of Company G of the 44th Alabama on April 18, 1862. He was promoted to first lieutenant of the company on August 30, 1862, and less than one month later, on September 23, was advanced to captain. The 44th Alabama suffered heavily at Gettysburg, losing 24 killed, 66 wounded, and 4 missing or captured, for a total loss of 99 men out of 363 engaged. A blood-soaked letter Donaldson took from Captain Dunklin's pocket is affixed to one of the pages of his second bound volume of letters opposite his Gettysburg letter. CSR, RG94, NA; John W. Busey and David G. Martin, *Regimental Strengths and Losses at Gettysburg* (cited hereafter as Busey and Martin, *Regimental Losses Gettysburg*) Hightstown, NJ: Longstreet House, 1986), 247; FAD Papers, CWLM.

32. In 1882 Donaldson began corresponding with state authorities in Alabama to try to locate the family of Captain Dunklin. He eventually was put into contact with John Haralson,

a self-described "kinsman" of William Dunklin and the executor of the deceased officer's estate, and via an edited copy of his Gettysburg letter, Donaldson was able to provide the family with the details of the captain's death and burial, which up to that time had been unknown by them. Captain Dunklin had left a wife and three daughters, and the family was so grateful for the information Donaldson had provided that he was invited to the wedding of one of the girls in 1883. FAD Papers, CWLM.

33. Brigadier General Barnes, although but slightly wounded in the leg, returned only briefly to the Army of the Potomac upon his recovery. He was thereafter assigned to administrative duty in Washington, where he served for the remainder of the war. Pfanz, *Gettysburg,* 261–62.

34. The regimental history of the 22nd Massachusetts records that Senator Wilson visited the regiment on July 12. Parker and Carter, *22nd Massachusetts,* 352.

35. Capt. Augustus P. Martin of Massachusetts commanded the artillery brigade of the 5th Corps, which at this time consisted of five batteries. Pfanz, *Gettysburg,* 233, 239, 450.

36. 1st Lt. Horace Binney of Company C was at this time temporarily attached to the staff of Brig. Gen. Thomas H. Neill, who commanded the 3rd Brigade, 2nd Division, 6th Corps.

37. Donaldson does not exaggerate the effect of this trek on the regiment, seasoned though they were by the hard marches of the Gettysburg Campaign. A sergeant of the 118th wrote that "four Fifths of our men . . . could not stand the march and fell out of the ranks. . . . I am the only sergeant in [my] company at this moment (the others are somewhere back on the road—used up)." Sgt. Henry Peck to Mother, July 16, 1863, Lieutenant Henry T. Peck Letters, 1st Regt. NGP Library, Philadelphia (cited hereafter as Peck Letters, NGP Library).

38. Donaldson is referring to Burkittsville, Maryland, approximately ten miles west of Frederick.

CHAPTER EIGHT: BOREDOM AND IDLENESS

1. William D. Henderson, *The Road to Bristoe Station.* . . . (cited hereafter as Henderson, *Bristoe Station*) (Lynchburg, VA: H. E. Howard, 1987), 25–26.

2. Freeman Cleaves, *Meade of Gettysburg* (cited hereafter as Cleaves, *Meade of Gettysburg*) (Norman, OK: University of Oklahoma Press, 1960), 191.

3. The assault that the Pennsylvanians defended against on July 2 was conducted by Brig. Gen. Joseph B. Kershaw's brigade of South Carolinians, who were a part of the division of Maj. Gen. Lafayette McLaws. Maj. Gen. Richard H. Anderson's division was not engaged in the Wheatfield area; however, Brig. Gen. George T. Anderson's brigade did attack the 2nd Brigade, 1st Division, 5th Corps, which was posted in the Wheatfield on the immediate left of the 1st Brigade. Pfanz, *Gettysburg,* 314, 385, 459.

4. Donaldson was correct in stating that the 1st Brigade had lost 125 men at Gettysburg. The 118th Pennsylvania had lost 3 killed, 19 wounded, and 3 captured, while the 1st Michigan, which went into the battle with 145 men, lost 42. Busey and Martin, *Regimental Losses at Gettysburg,* 247.

5. Capt. Matthew Hastings's Keystone Battery Independent Artillery had been organized for a one-year term of service in Philadelphia in August 1862. The battery had served in the defenses of Washington, D.C., until it was posted to the Artillery Reserve of the Army of the Potomac during the Gettysburg Campaign. Taylor, *Philadelphia in the War,* 275.

6. Brig. Gen. Alexander Hays of Pennsylvania commanded the 3rd Division of the 2nd Corps at Gettysburg. *O.R.,* vol. XXVII, pt. 1, 176.

7. The 9th Massachusetts Battery had lost eight men killed, eighteen wounded, and two missing during its obstinate stand around the Trostle Farm at Gettysburg. Donaldson was apparently unaware that this was the battery he had mentioned in his Gettysburg letter as having supported the 118th during its fight in front of the Wheatfield. Busey and Martin, *Regimental Losses at Gettysburg.* 260.

8. Harry Carpenter, a twenty-one-year-old Philadelphian, served with the Keystone Battery throughout its one-year term of service. MR, Keystone Battery, Harrisburg.

9. As the Army of Northern Virginia retreated southward, Lee used the natural protection afforded by the Blue Ridge Mountains to shield his army from the Federals, who were following on a parallel line, staying between the Confederates and Washington, D.C. Meade sensed an opportunity on July 22 to cut off a portion of Lee's army by thrusting west through Manassas Gap, and what Donaldson witnessed was the attempt by the 3rd Corps under Maj. Gen. William French to carry out Meade's orders. French, however, bungled the movement badly, and the Confederates continued their retreat undisturbed.

10. Andrew Cassidy, a thirty-six-year-old weaver and native of Scotland, was one of the original sergeants of Company H. He had been captured at Shepherdstown and was later wounded in the Wilderness in 1864. He mustered out with the regiment in June 1865. MR Co. H, Harrisburg; Survivors' Association, *118th Pennsylvania,* 723.

11. Frederick Von Schleumbick was a twenty-one-year-old native of Germany who listed his occupation as a soldier. He served with the 118th through the end of the war, mustering out in May 1865. MR Co. H, Harrisburg; Survivors' Association, 118th Pennsylvania, 728.

12. The levies of drafted men who arrived in the Army of the Potomac at this time were received with circumspection by the veteran troops, and usually with good reason. A member of the regiment wrote that the substitutes sent to the 118th were "as villainous a looking set as I ever saw. They came into the service for the money they got and are about to get, and that is all they care for it. Forty out of 160 for our rgt. deserted on the way here, one was fired on and killed at Vine Street wharf for attempting to desert. We have our camp guard quadrupled, and have loaded muskets on post. None of the substitutes are allowed to pass the guard line upon any account. They are nearly all Dutch and Irishmen. It is almost an insult to the men of our regiment to put such characters beside them. . . ." A soldier in Company E also noted that one of the substitutes sent to the 118th was a member of the 13th North Carolina who had been captured at Chancellorsville. Sgt. Henry Peck to Mother, August 6, 1863, Peck Letters, NGP Library; Francis H. Lincoln to Isaac, August 23, 1863. Lewis Leigh Collection, United States Army Military History Institute, Carlisle Barracks, PA. For additional comments on the reactions of the veterans to the substitutes and draftees, see A. M. Judson, *History of the Eighty-Third Regiment Pennsylvania Volunteers* (Erie, PA: B. F. H. Lynn, 1865), 76–77; Andrew E. Ford, *The Story of the Fifteenth Regiment Massachusetts Volunteer Infantry in the Civil War, 1861–1864* (Clinton, MA: W. J. Coulter, 1898), 290–91; Martin A. Haynes, *A History of the Second Regiment New Hampshire Volunteer Infantry in the War of the Rebellion,* 2nd ed. (Lakeport, NY: n. p., 1896), 206–7.

13. Pvt. Alfred N. Lukens, a twenty-two-year-old Philadelphia clerk, had died at Washington, D.C., on July 31. MR Co. H, Harrisburg.

14. 2nd Lt. James Brown of Company A, originally a corporal of Company D, had been promoted to his present rank in March 1863. This was not the last time the intemperate habits of the twenty-seven-year-old prewar grocer would get him into trouble. MR Cos. D & A, Harrisburg.

15. This was Capt. Louis N. Tucker of the 18th Massachusetts. The thirty-year-old prewar clerk from Milton, Massachusetts, had been wounded at Fredericksburg and was later wounded again in the Wilderness. He mustered out of the service with the rank of brevet major in September 1864. *Massachusetts Soldiers, Sailors and Marines in the Civil War* (cited hereafter as *Mass. in the War*) (Norwood, MA: Norwood Press, 1931), vol. II, 357.

16. In response to the Conscription Act, draft riots had broken out in New York City in mid-July 1863. The Regular Division of the 5th Corps was detached from the army at this time and sent to the city to help civil and state authorities prevent further outbreaks of violence. Timothy J. Reese, *Sykes' Regular Infantry Division, 1861–1864.* . . . (Jefferson, NC: McFarland and Company, 1990), 266–68.

17. Lt. Frank McCutchen of Company C was another officer of the 118th who was under arrest for drunkenness at this time; Donaldson was borrowing his sword until he returned to duty.

18. 1st Lt. Charles M. Young of Philadelphia, thirty, had served as a sergeant in the 23rd Pennsylvania before his commissioning in Company K of the 118th in January 1863. Promoted to the captaincy of the company in February 1864, he was mortally wounded at Peebles Farm, Virginia, on September 30, 1864. Survivors' Association, *118th Pennsylvania*, 735; CSR, RG94, NA.

19. Donaldson was not alone in his opinion of Reverend O'Neill. Sgt. Henry Peck wrote in early September: "I do not go much to hear our Chaplain. His manners are too unpleasant for me. He is no doubt sincere and earnest, but I think he has mistaken his profession. His style of teaching is a sort of forcing one. He seems to want to drive his arguments into his hearers' minds by means of physical strength, as one would drive a wedge into a log, for the greatest virtue of his preaching is his extremely loud utterance. . . . His strong Irish accent together with his ungraceful manners have the effect of making much dislike for him." Henry T. Peck to Mother, September 7, 1863, Peck Letters, NGP Library. For differing opinions on O'Neill's abilities, see Parker and Carter, *22nd Massachusetts*, 357; Bennett, *Musket and Sword*, 181–82.

20. Lieutenant McCutchen was allowed to resign from the service as a result of his "having been declared by his Regimental Commander to be wholly incompetent." Special Orders #194, 5th Army Corps, September 4, 1863, in Regimental Letter Book, 118th PA, Record Group 94, National Archives (cited hereafter as 118 PA Letter Book, NA).

21. No record exists of John Donaldson's having been disabled in any way at this time, and his 22nd Virginia was far from Culpeper, campaigning in western Virginia in late August 1863. Lowry, *22nd Virginia*, 43–44.

22. 1st Lt. James B. Wilson of Philadelphia, thirty-eight, a prewar carpenter and Mexican War veteran, was originally first sergeant of Company A. He was promoted to second lieutenant of Company K in October 1862 and to first lieutenant of Company B in January 1863. He was returning to the regiment after recovering from wounds received at Gettysburg. Promoted to the captaincy of Company C in January 1864, he was brevetted major later that year and mustered out with the regiment in June 1865. MR Co. A, Harrisburg; Survivors' Association, *118th Pennsylvania*, 649–50.

23. Charles F. Stone was a forty-two-year-old prewar salesman from Philadelphia. He had been promoted to a sergeancy in Company B on May 1, 1863, and he served in that rank until his muster out in June 1865. MR Co. B, Harrisburg; Survivors' Association, *118th Pennsylvania*, 689.

24. The appeal of the condemned deserters was sent to General Meade on August 25: "General—We, the prisoners, implore your mercy in our behalf for the extension of our sentence, so that we may have time to make preparations to meet our God; for we, at the present time, are unprepared to die. Our time is very short. Two of us are Roman Catholics; we have no priest, and two are Protestants, and one is a Jew and has no rabbi to assist us in preparing to meet our God. And we ask mercy in behalf of our wives and children, and we also desire you to change our sentence to hard labor instead of death, as we think we have been wrongfully sentenced; as we, being foreigners, were led astray by other soldiers, who promised us there would be no harm done." Survivors' Association, *118th Pennsylvania*, 296–97.

25. As the amount of money offered as an inducement to enlist increased, bounty jumping became a widespread problem. Men would enlist in a regiment, collect the proffered bounty, and desert at the first opportunity, oftentimes repeating the process until they were caught.

26. On the same day Lt. James Brown was rearrested for drunkenness, he addressed an apologetic letter to Major Herring:

> Feeling deeply mortified and humiliated by the course of conduct pursued by me after my return to the Regiment, I sincerely wish permission to offer an apology to you, and request forgiveness from you, for the

same, pledging myself that as long as I am in the Regiment, I will not only never allow myself to be in the same condition, but that Liquor shall never enter my lips. I trust that God will give me strength to keep my resolutions, and promises to you, and that from henceforth I may be a reformed man. I would most respectfully ask to be released from arrest, and have an opportunity by my future conduct to regain your confidence and the reputation I have lost. . . .

Herring was apparently unswayed by Brown's contrition, and the lieutenant was soon tried, found guilty, and sentenced to be dismissed. Before the sentence could be carried out, however, the court findings were disapproved by General Griffin, and Brown was again returned to duty. His dissolute habits continued, though, and on January 4, 1864, over General Sykes's signature, the following order was issued from 5th Corps Headquarters: "James Brown, having tendered his resignation and being declared by his regimental commander to be a habitual drunkard, he is discharged [from] the military service of the United States." Herring Papers, CWLM; 118PA Letter Book, NA.

27. Boston native Capt. George M. Barnard, Jr., twenty-four, of the 18th Massachusetts, had been wounded earlier in the war at Second Bull Run. He was promoted to captain from first lieutenant in November 1862, mustered out of the service in September 1864, and was brevetted to the rank of colonel. *Mass. in the War,* vol. II, 364.

28. Col. Jacob B. Sweitzer of the 62nd Pennsylvania was the commander of the 2nd Brigade, 1st Division, 5th Corps. Sifakis, *Who Was Who,* 637.

29. General Meade had commanded the Pennsylvania Reserves earlier in the war, and on August 29 they presented him with a sword, sash, belt, and spurs valued at over $1,000. Cleaves, *Meade of Gettysburg,* 192–93; Nevins, *Diary of Battle,* 277–78.

30. Twenty-two-year-old Henry T. Peck, a prewar Philadelphia druggist, was at this time serving as sergeant major of the 118th. Originally a sergeant in Company K, Peck was captured at Shepherdstown and would later, in August 1864, be promoted to first lieutenant of Company C. He acted both in that capacity and as regimental adjutant until his muster out in June 1865. MR Co. K, Harrisburg; Survivors' Association, *118th Pennsylvania,* 645–46.

31. Sgt. David Y. Moselander of Company B, a thirty-two-year-old customs house employee and Philadelphia native, was promoted to his current rank on May 10, 1863. He mustered out with the regiment in June 1865. MR Co. B, Harrisburg; Survivors' Association, *118th Pennsylvania,* 689.

32. The clergymen assigned to serve the spiritual needs of the prisoners were the Reverend Constantine L. Egan, a Catholic priest from St. Dominic's Church in Washington, D.C., and Rabbi Benjamin S. Szold of Baltimore. Chaplain O'Neill of the 118th counseled the condemned Protestants. Capt. James D. Orne, twenty-five, of Springfield, Massachusetts, had served as second and first lieutenant of Company A of the 18th Massachusetts before his promotion to staff duty with the rank of captain in March 1863. He mustered out as captain of Company F of the 18th in September 1864. George Levy, "President Lincoln Rejects an Appeal for Mercy" (cited hereafter as Levy, "Lincoln Rejects an Appeal") *The Lincoln Newsletter* 8, no. 3 (Fall 1994): 1, 4–7; *Mass. in the War,* vol. II, 356.

33. The men who were executed were Charles Walter (also known as C. Zene), a twenty-nine-year-old German bookkeeper; Emil Lae (also known as E. Duffie or Duffe), a thirty-year-old German clerk; George Kuhn (also known as G. Week), a twenty-two year-old Prussian barber; John Rainese (also known as Gion or George Rionese), a twenty-three-year-old Italian; and John Folaney (also known as Faline or Geacinto Lerchize), a twenty-four-year-old Italian. Walter and Lae were Protestants, Kuhn was Jewish, and Rainese and Folaney were Roman Catholics. Incredibly, the brother-in-law of one of the men (which one is unknown) was taken from his sickbed and forced to witness the execution, then returned to the hospital, where he later died.

The manner in which the trial of these unfortunates was conducted is suspect. None except Folaney spoke or understood English, yet no interpreter was provided during the proceedings. None of the five were represented by an attorney during their trial, nor were they ever advised of their right to a lawyer. The men were tried separately, and at least two of the trials lasted no longer than twenty minutes. Additionally, the Articles of War, which stipulate that death is the penalty for desertion, were never read to the convicts between the time they arrived in camp and their desertion. A simple under-standing of the consequences of desertion might have served as a deterrent to the men, provided regulations had been followed and the Articles read and interpreted to them.

In a letter to Donaldson in 1886, Chaplain O'Neill wrote that the execution of the five men "ought <u>not</u> to have taken place. You as an officer of the 118th are in no wise involved in the condemnation or execution of those men . . . but few of the officers of the 118th knew anything of the dark features connected with the execution as I did." Levy, "Lincoln Rejects an Appeal," 4–6; Robert I. Alotta, *Civil War Justice: Union Army Execu-tions under Lincoln* (cited hereafter as Alotta, *Civil War Justice*) (Shippensburg, PA: White Mane, 1989), 77–80; Herring Papers, CWLM; FAD Papers, CWLM.

34. William H. Brooks, a nineteen-year-old scroll sawyer from Philadelphia, was discharged from the 118th on November 10, 1863, to accept a captaincy in the 32nd United States Colored Troops. MR Co. H. Harrisburg; Survivors' Association, *118th Pennsylvania,* 723.

35. Andrew A. Humphreys, *From Gettysburg to the Rapidan: The Army of the Potomac, July, 1863 to April, 1864* (cited hereafter as Humphreys, *Gettysburg to the Rapidan*) (New York: Charles Scribner's Sons, 1883), 11.

36. Pvt. George Van, a twenty-two-year-old farmer from Company D of the 12th New York, had been tried and convicted of desertion on August 13, 1863. General Orders, Army of the Potomac, January to December 1863; Alotta, *Civil War Justice,* 82–83.

37. Pvt. Albert Haverstick, a twenty-year-old prewar Philadelphia clerk, was a member of Donaldson's Company H. He had been on detached service in charge of the adjutant general's office of the 1st Brigade, 1st Division, 5th Corps since January 1863. Haverstick would later be posted to the Headquarters of the Army of the Potomac and was eventu-ally made chief clerk of the Adjutant General's office there. He mustered out with the regiment in June 1865. Survivors' Association, *118th Pennsylvania,* 643–44.

38. Lt. Col. George W. Lombard of Hillsdale, Michigan, was originally the captain of Company E of the 4th Michigan. He had commanded the regiment since July 2, 1863, and was killed in the Wilderness on May 5, 1864. Jno. Robertson, *Michigan in the War* (cited hereafter as Robertson, *Michigan in the War*) (Lansing, MI: W. S. George & Co., 1880), part II, 65–72.

39. Lt. Col. Thomas W. Sherwin, twenty-two, of Dedham, Massachusetts, was a prewar teacher who had worked his way up from adjutant of the 22nd Massachusetts to his current rank. He had been wounded and taken prisoner during the Peninsula Campaign and mustered out with his regiment in October 1864. *Mass. in the War,* vol. II, 651.

40. Alfred R. Tomlinson was a twenty-one-year-old clerk from Philadelphia who had originally enlisted in Company H on August 12, 1862. He had been listed on the company rolls as a deserter since September 9, 1862. MR Co. H, Harrisburg.

41. "El General José Cortez," wrote an aide attached to Meade's Headquarters, "chevalier of some sort of red ribbon and possessor of a bad hat," reviewed part of the 5th Corps on September 28. George R. Aggasiz, ed. *Meade's Headquarters, 1863–1865: Letters of Colonel Theodore Lyman from the Wilderness to Appomattox* (Boston: Atlantic Monthly Press, 1922), 23–24.

42. Maj. Oliver Holman of Massachusetts served throughout the war as an additional paymaster of volunteers. *Mass. in the War,* vol. VI, 765.

43. James Wolfe Ripley, a sixty-eight-year-old Connecticut native, had been serving in the army continuously since his graduation from West Point in 1814. He had been relieved

as chief of the Ordnance Department two weeks earlier on September 15. Sifakis, *Who Was Who,* 545.

44. Pennsylvania governor Andrew G. Curtin, a staunch Republican, was a favorite among soldiers from his state, and Donaldson, despite his self-professed Democrat leanings, admired him greatly. Curtin won reelection by a 15,000-vote majority in November. William B. Hesseltine, *Lincoln and the War Governors* (New York: Alfred A Knopf, 1948), 326–29, 336, 344.

45. 2nd Lt. William W. Worrell of Company E had originally served as first sergeant of Company I; he had been promoted to his current rank in October 1862. The twenty-five-year-old Philadelphian was forced to resign on April 1, 1864, to support his family due to his father's loss of sight. CSR, RG94, NA.

46. Col. Joshua L. Chamberlain, thirty-five, of Brewer, Maine, was to become one of the most celebrated volunteer officers of the Civil War. At this time he commanded the 20th Maine; he would later lead the 1st and 3rd Brigades of the 1st Division, 5th Corps. He ended the war as a brevet major general and was selected by Grant to oversee the Confederate surrender proceeding at Appomattox. Sifakis, *Who Was Who,* 113.

47. Donaldson makes no other mention of the trial of Private Tomlinson in subsequent letters; however, the *History of the 22nd Massachusetts* provides a good overview of the case and its outcome:

When the One Hundred and Eighteenth Pennsylvania or "Corn Exchange" Regiment was formed there were more men to offer as recruits than could be taken, and though all signed the enlistment rolls, when the regiment was mustered into service the supernumeraries were rejected. One boy was extremely anxious to go, and followed the regiment to camp and to Washington. The muster-in took place at Washington, and he, finding himself among the rejected ones, followed the regiment to the cars on its way to the front, bade them good-by, and then returned to Philadelphia. He was a photographer, and in the fall of 1863, one year after his rejection, he obtained permission to visit the army professionally, and while we were near Culpeper set up his camera and commenced to take portraits. He paid an early visit to his old friends, and was warmly welcomed. One of the One Hundred Eighteenth, however, remembering that a reward of thirty dollars was paid for information that would lead to the detection of a deserter, reported the photographer as a deserter. His captain objected to preferring charges, but the informer persisted, and the artist was arrested. He was the most surprised man in the camp. He had tried to join the regiment, but was not permitted, and now to be arrested as a 'deserter' was terrible. Had he been a deserter he would not have come back in citizens' dress to his own regiment. His father came on to help him, but there is very little a citizen can do in a court-martial. The facts were presented as strongly as possible, but that was a hard court. While the army was moving about from Culpeper to Fairfax Court-house and back to Three Mile Station, he was not even under guard, but allowed to go on parole of honor, and there were hundreds of opportunities to escape, and he was even advised to do so by well meaning friends. But no; he said he was innocent, and he should face the court, whatever they might do to him. The result was announced at Three Mile Station; he was found guilty, and sentenced to serve out the term of his regiment without pay. The poor fellow was nearly beside himself with grief and shame, and if his cries on that night (for he could not control his feelings) affected the members of the court as it did his comrades, they must have repented of what they had done.

The historians also noted that Col. Joshua Chamberlain of the 20th Maine was president of the court and Capt. Dendy Sharwood of the 118th was judge advocate, and that though "this court may have been distinguished for justice, [it was] not for mercy. . . . But few of the Twenty-second came before this tribunal, for which we were grateful." Parker and Carter, *22nd Massachusetts*, 378–79.

48. This structure was in all likelihood the property of Col. George Patton's father, P. F. Patton, as Colonel Patton had relocated to present-day West Virginia in 1856. Spring Farm, as it was called, employed twenty-one slaves and covered 700 acres. Lowry, *22nd Virginia*, 2; Krick, *Lee's Colonels*, 299–300; Daniel E. Sutherland, *Seasons of War: The Ordeal of a Confederate Community, 1861–1865* (New York: Free Press, 1995), 30.

49. Clement R. See of Philadelphia was at this time first lieutenant of Company F of the 2nd Pennsylvania Cavalry. Promoted to captain in April 1864, he was wounded at Saint Mary's Church on June 24, 1864, and discharged the following September. Bates, Penna. Vols., vol. II, 340.

50. English born Pvt. Thomas Sands of Company F, a twenty-seven-year-old sawmaker, was released from arrest by General Griffin on the eve of the upcoming action at Bristoe Station to fight in the ranks. He seems to have acquitted himself well, as his sentence was overturned and he returned to serve with the regiment until he was wounded at Dabney's Mills, Virginia, on February 6, 1865. He was discharged due to disability on August 25, 1865. MR Co. H, Harrisburg; Survivors' Association, *118th Pennsylvania*, 715.

CHAPTER NINE: BRISTOE STATION

1. Cleaves, *Meade of Gettysburg*, 195.
2. Henderson, *Bristoe Station*, 140.
3. The next seventeen and a half lines of this letter, which was written in pencil, have been erased. The 1892 edition of the Regimental History of the 118th, however, gives at least a partial glimpse of what Captain Donaldson deleted:

> "From Philadelphia!" she exclaimed. "And have you relatives in our service?" "Yes," said he [Donaldson]. "I have a brother." "And to what regiment does he belong?" "The 22nd Virginia." "Is his name John? and do you remember his watch and anything about it that could specially identify it?" "Yes," he responded. "He carried an open-faced, old-fashioned gold watch, which, when I last saw it, bore the name of his father, John P. Donaldson, engraved on the inside." With this she hurriedly left, and, entering the house, called to another lady, whom she afterwards presented as her sister, to come down-stairs at once; that there was a Federal Officer upon the porch whom she was satisfied was the brother of Captain Donaldson, whom they knew. The captain wanted to know more of his brother, who, a resident of Charleston, Kanawha county, west Virginia, when the war began, had drifted into the enemy's service and of whom he had since heard but little. The lady told him his brother had been severely wounded in one of the recent engagements, and, fortunately, had fallen into their hands. He had been an inmate of their home for many weeks, and but for their care might have died.

Donaldson's brother, Jacob, had notified him in mid-August that John had been wounded and left with a family near Culpeper (see Donaldson's August 19, 1863, letter to Jacob). Jacob was mistaken, though, about John's having been wounded, and my guess is that Donaldson did not discover that Jacob was in error until sometime after the 1892 edition of the history was published, upon which he altered his original letter. As to the details of the interview between Donaldson and this woman, I would add that either Donaldson highly embellished his account of the conversation or the woman possessed both a vivid imagination and a poor memory. Survivors' Association, *Antietam to Appomattox with 118th Penna. Vols., Corn Exchange Regiment. . . .* (Philadelphia: J. L. Smith, 1892), 314–315.

4. Donaldson's reference to the five prisoners under sentence of court-martial is unclear. The only individual I have been able to identify is the aforementioned Pvt. Thomas Sands of Company F.
5. Elements of the 1st Cavalry Division of the Army of the Potomac under Brig. Gen. John Buford fought a series of delaying actions against Confederate cavalry under Gen. Jeb Stuart in the vicinity of Brandy Station on October 11. Buford's report is in *O.R.*, vol. XXIX, pt. 1, 347–51; Stuart's is on 439–53.
6. Catlett's Station lay along the line of the Orange & Alexandria Railroad, approximately thirteen miles northeast of the Rappahannock River. O.R. Atlas, plate VIII, map 1.
7. Donaldson is correct in his assessment of Sykes's actions on October 14; however, he is slightly confused about the forces that attacked the Federals. As the Army of the Potomac retreated northward along the Orange & Alexandria Railroad, the Confederates were moving in a parallel line of march to the west. Sykes's 5th Corps had been ordered to keep within supporting distance of Warren's 2nd Corps, which, as it followed Sykes, was acting as rear guard for the army. As reports, which turned out to be misleading, reached Sykes that the head of Warren's column was in sight, Sykes prematurely resumed his march toward Manassas, distancing himself from Warren and creating a gap between the two corps. Meantime, Confederates of Henry Heth's division of A. P. Hill's Corps spied the rear of the 5th Corps moving off, and, thinking it the rear of the Federal Army, attacked. In their haste to take advantage of the confusion their advance had created, the Rebels failed to notice Warren's men concealed behind the embankment of the O&A and suffered severe losses in consequence. Humphreys, *Gettysburg to the Rapidan,* 22–30; *O.R.,* vol. XXI, pt. 1, 240–43, 277.
8. The history of the 22nd Massachusetts notes that there were no casualties in the 1st Brigade and "several men killed and wounded in the second and third brigades." Sykes made no report of the action. Parker and Carter, *22nd Massachusetts,* 375.
9. Federal losses at Bristoe Station were 50 killed, 335 wounded, and 161 missing and captured, for a total of 546. The Confederates lost 136 killed, 797 wounded, and 445 missing and captured, for a total of 1,378. Included among the Southern wounded were Brig. Gens. Carnot Posey, William W. Kirkland, and John R. Cooke. Posey later died from his injuries. *O.R.,* vol. XXIX, pt. 1, 250, 427, 429–30, 432–33.
10. Donaldson was mistaken. The 6th North Carolina was serving in Richard S. Ewell's 2nd Corps and was not engaged at Bristoe Station; however, nearly all of the captives taken by the Federals were North Carolinians. Ibid., 400–401, 433.
11. Thomas Sugle is unidentified.
12. Donaldson's reference is to the English-made Whitworth rifled cannon, a distinctive-looking field piece noted for its range and accuracy. The Confederates employed two Whitworths at Bristoe Station, but their commander states in his after-action report that they "fired 8 shots at the enemy, without loss." The Federals reported the capture of five artillery pieces at Bristoe but did not detail the type of guns taken, although it seems likely that if they had captured a gun as unique as the Whitworth, it would have been cause for notice. On the other hand, and in support of Donaldson's observation, a correspondent writing on the battle from the Army of the Potomac on October 15 recorded the capture of "one large Whitworth gun, two fine Rodman's, and three brass field pieces . . . one of [which] was so badly broken up as to be worthless, and was left

upon the field." Ibid., 278, 290, 436–38; Frank Moore, ed., *The Rebellion Record: A Diary of American Events.* . . . (New York: D. Van Nostrand, 1864), vol. VII, 545.

13. Pvt. James Shields, a twenty-five-year-old Irish-born sailor from Philadelphia, had joined the regiment on July 15, 1863, and apparently was a chronic troublemaker. He recovered from his run-in with Donaldson and transferred to the 5th Massachusetts Battery in December 1863, but the change in organizations failed to change his habits. The next time the men of the 118th saw Shields after his transfer was while on the march, as they passed his battery in park. Shields was lashed, spread-eagle, to the spare wheel of one of the guns, which, when turned a quarter sideways, was a punishment that grew excruciatingly painful and was designed, as the regimental historians noted, to "have broken the rebellious spirits of the most hardened offenders." Shields deserted from his battery in late January 1864 but was recaptured in Philadelphia in July of that year, tried for desertion, and dishonorably discharged. The wonder is that he wasn't shot. MR, Co. H, Harrisburg' Survivors' Association, *118th Pennsylvania,* 331, 727.

14. Fox's Mill was located at the intersection of Ox Road and Difficult Run, about two miles northwest of the Little River Turnpike near Germantown, Virginia. *O.R. Atlas,* map VII, plate 1.

15. Col. Fletcher Webster was mortally wounded in the fighting at Second Bull Run on August 30, 1862, while commanding the 12th Massachusetts Infantry, but his body was disinterred soon after its burial on the battlefield and conveyed to Massachusetts. See Wiley Sword, "Col. Fletcher Webster's Last Letter," *Blue & Gray Magazine* 8, no. 1 (Fall 1995), 20–27.

16. Probably Buckland or Buckland Mills, located on the Warrenton Pike midway between New Baltimore and the Manassas Gap Railroad. *O.R. Atlas,* map XLV, plate 6.

17. Martin F. Graham and George F. Skoch, *Mine Run: A Campaign of Lost Opportunities, October 21, 1863–May 1, 1864* (cited hereafter as Graham and Skoch, *Mine Run*) (Lynchburg, VA: H. E. Howard, 1987), 8–9.

18. Following his defeat at Chickamauga in late September, Maj. Gen. William Starke Rosecrans concentrated the remnants of his Army of the Cumberland at Chattanooga but failed to properly defend the heights surrounding the city, allowing Confederates under Gen. Braxton Bragg to lay siege. Rosecrans was replaced by Grant on October 19.

19. Although Colonel Prevost had not served with the 118th since the close of the Chancellorsville Campaign in May, his resignation from the regiment did not take effect until September 30. The promotions of Lieutenant Colonel Gwyn to colonel, Major Herring to lieutenant colonel, and Capt. Henry O'Neill of Company A, the senior captain of the regiment, to major were effective to date from November 1, 1863. As future events proved, Donaldson was correct with regard to his misgivings about O'Neill's fitness to command.

20. Donaldson's analysis of the opportunity that Meade missed in giving battle at Broad Run is remarkable astute. No less a soldier than Maj. Gen. Andrew A. Humphreys, Meade's chief of staff and a highly respected military engineer, wrote twenty years after the fact that it would have been fortunate for Meade if he had halted at Broad Run and ascertained Lee's whereabouts instead of continuing the retreat toward Centreville. Humphreys, *Gettysburg to the Rapidan,* 20–21.

21. Thirty-seven-year-old Edmund DeBuck of Philadelphia had been promoted from sergeant major to second lieutenant of Company I in November 1862 and was advanced to first lieutenant in February 1863. During a reconnaissance in late 1862, Donaldson noted, in an unincluded letter, that then Sergeant Major DeBuck had tried to ford an icy stream by floating himself over on a log, but when about midway across, "he lost his balance and fell, head over heels, into the water amid the derisive shouts of the men. DeBuck is no favorite and I verily believe everyone rejoiced at his discomfiture." Survivors' Association, *118th Pennsylvania,* 682 and 729; FAD Papers, CWLM.

22. Nathaniel Bayne, a twenty-two-year-old prewar tailor from Delaware, was originally a sergeant in Company C. He was promoted to second lieutenant of Company I in

March 1863, to first lieutenant of Company A in October 1863, and to the captaincy of Company I in August 1864. Bayne was wounded at Dabney's Mills, Virginia, on February 6, 1865, and mustered out with his company on June 1, 1865. MR Co. C, Harrisburg; Survivors' Association, *118th Pennsylvania,* 645, 682, 729.

23. Twenty-two-year-old Joseph Ashbrook had been promoted from sergeant of Company C to second lieutenant of Company K to date from December 6. The prewar clerk was a native of Philadelphia and had been wounded at Shepherdstown. He would succeed Donaldson as the captain of Company H in November 1864. MR Co. C, Harrisburg.

24. Donaldson has once again mistaken the 22nd Virginia Battalion, which at Gettysburg served in John M. Brokenbrough's brigade of Henry Heth's division of A. P. Hill's Corps, for the 22nd Virginia Regiment, to which John belonged.

25. Neither D. H. Hill nor A. P. Hill ever served under Longstreet once he became a corps commander, and Longstreet's Corps was not attached to the Army of Northern Virginia at this time. Gen. A. P. Hill commanded the army's 3rd Corps, and most of the prisoners taken at Bristoe Station were of Heth's division of Hill's 3rd Corps.

26. Thirty-year-old Maj. George C. Hopper of the 1st Michigan had begun the war as a first lieutenant, and before his promotion to major in March 1863, he had been wounded at Gaines' Mill and wounded and captured at Second Bull Run. He mustered out of the service in September 1864. Adjutant General, *1st Mich.,* 66.

27. Capt. Dendy Sharwood of Company C had been acting as commissary for the 1st Brigade, 1st Division, 5th Corps until his recall to the regiment.

28. Capt. Campbell Allen, a thirty-one-year-old native of Albany, New York, commanded Company F of the 44th New York. Phisterer, *New York in the Rebellion,* vol. III, 2294.

29. This is the same individual Donaldson had identified in the previous chapter as having attended to the two condemned Catholic deserters before their court-martial sentence was carried out. Following the execution, Father Egan was invited by the colonel of the 9th Massachusetts Infantry (a predominantly Irish regiment) to become chaplain of their unit. He served in that capacity until the 9th's term of service expired in June 1864, whereupon he was commissioned field chaplain by the War Department and served on the staff of Maj. Gen. Charles Griffin until the end of the war. In the relatively short time he spent with the army, Egan made a good impression upon the soldiers he served, according to Sgt. Henry Peck of the 118th. "The preachers have deserted us entirely," he wrote in early 1864. "The few that we do have, the boys say, are marked inspected and condemned, and that is why they are here, for they will not be tolerated at home. . . . They are not only poor preachers, but are the most careless looking men in the army. Some are even ragged. . . . I believe they are here only for the money they get. They ought to be our finest gentlemen, fit to be respected and associated with. There is one exception in the case of a Catholic Chaplain in our division, Father Egan, and he is greatly liked, notwithstanding the usual prejudices. How very strange it is that no Protestant clergymen of ability will come here where they are so much needed." Daniel George MacNamara, *The History of the Ninth Regiment Massachusetts Volunteer Infantry . . . June 1861–June 1864* (Boston: E. B. Stillings & Co., 1899), 343, 429; Sgt. Henry Peck to Mother, February 21, 1864, Peck Letters, NGP Library.

CHAPTER TEN: RAPPAHANNOCK STATION AND MINE RUN

1. Graham and Skoch, *Mine Run,* 5.

2. Ibid., 6.

3. Col. Peter C. Ellmaker led the 3rd Brigade of the 6th Corps, which was made up of the 6th Maine, 49th Pennsylvania, 5th Wisconsin, and his own 119th Pennsylvania. The brigade lost 264 men in the action, with the 119th Pennsylvania, the 118th's "sister" regiment, losing 7 killed, 37 wounded, and 1 captured. O.R., vol. XXIX, pt. 1, 559.

4. John C. Davis, a twenty-five-year-old locksmith from Philadelphia, was wounded later in the battle. He returned to Company C in February 1864 and mustered out with the regiment in June 1865. MR Co. C, Harrisburg.

5. One of the substitutes who had recently joined Company K of the 118th was a young Irishman who had served previously on a monitor in Charleston Harbor, South Carolina. During his tenure in the navy, he was subjected to bombardments by the large-caliber Confederate coastal batteries, so when the Pennsylvanians began to dodge the fire of the Rebel fieldpieces, it was too much for him. "What the divil are ye dodging for," he chided his comrades, "they're nothing but pays [peas] sure they're shootin at us." Sgt. Henry Peck to Mother, March 16, 1864, Peck Letters, NGP Library.

6. George McCandless of Philadelphia, a forty-two-year-old Irish-born farmer, had been wounded and captured earlier in the war at Shepherdstown. After his return, he deserted from the regiment during the march to Chancellorsville. He survived this wound and was mustered out due to disability on May 3, 1864. MR Co. K, Harrisburg; Survivors' Association, *118th Pennsylvania,* 740.

7. A common misconception about Civil War combat is that hand-to-hand fighting was routinely engaged in, while in fact it occurred only rarely. The battle at Rappahannock Station, however, *was* one of those infrequent instances, and Donaldson does not overstate the ferocity of the assault. For descriptions of the fighting, see William E. S. Whitman and Charles True, *Maine in the War of the Union.* . . . (Lewiston, ME: Nelson Dingley, Jr. & Co., 1865), 158–60; George W. Bicknell, *History of the Fifth Regiment Maine Volunteers.* . . . (Portland, ME: H. L. Davis, 1871), 262–77; Stevens, *Three Years in the Sixth Corps,* 283–88.

8. The attack at Rappahannock Station was very ably carried out, as Donaldson relates, by Peter C. Ellmaker's and Emory Upton's brigades of the 6th Corps, supported by elements of the 5th Corps. Union losses were 37 killed, 376 wounded, and 6 missing, total 419; Confederate losses, which occurred in the brigades of Harry T. Hays and Robert F. Hoke, were 6 killed, 39 wounded, and 1,629 missing, total 1,674. O.R., vol. XXIX, pt. 1, 558–60, 616.

9. The 118th lost but two men wounded in the battle, the 22nd Massachusetts lost eight wounded, and the 18th Massachusetts lost two killed and fourteen wounded. Ibid., 558.

10. Joseph J. Bartlett, a twenty-eight-year-old prewar attorney from New York, had risen from a captaincy in the 27th New York to his present rank of brigadier general. He would go on to hold important brigade and divisional commands within the 5th Corps throughout the balance of the war and was one of a handful of officers chosen by Grant to oversee the surrender proceedings at Appomattox. Sifakis, *Who Was Who,* 36.

11. Twenty-six-year-old Catharinus B. Mervine of Utica, New York, had served as sergeant major, first lieutenant, and adjutant of the 14th New York before his promotion to captain and assistant adjutant general in July 1862. He died of disease on August 17, 1864. Phisterer, *New York in the Rebellion,* vol. 1, 510; vol. III, 1909; vol. V, 4295.

12. Confederate general William J. Hardee had authored *Hardee's Rifle and Light Infantry Tactics* while serving as a major in the U.S. Army in 1855. *Hardee's Tactics,* as it came to be known, was the most widely used infantry manual on both sides during the war, and Donaldson's reference is to this volume. Patricia L. Faust, ed., *Historical Times Illustrated Encyclopedia of the Civil War* (New York: Harper & Row, 1986), 338–39.

13. Donaldson's uneasiness about his Confederate brother was not unfounded. John had been wounded in the side and shoulder while in action at Droop Mountain, West Virginia, on November 6. Lowry, *22nd Virginia,* 145.

14. Seven individuals by the name of Ruffner served with the 22nd Virginia, but only one, David Ruffner, attained the rank of captain. He survived the war and lived until 1897. Ibid., 190.

15. Major Barley is unidentified.

16. John Donaldson's Company H of the 22nd Virginia was originally uniformed in "dark [olive] green broadcloth," with matching green overcoats. Ibid., 3.

17. Donaldson was mistaken. The road that the 118th had struck after crossing the Rapidan River was the Germanna Plank Road, and they followed it until they reached Wilderness Tavern, about six miles west of Chancellorsville, on the evening of November 26. *O.R. Atlas,* plate XXXIX, map 3; Survivors' Association, *118th Pennsylvania,* 355.

18. The regimental history of the 22nd Massachusetts records that Lieutenant Colonel Sherwin, who commanded that regiment, borrowed a gun from a nearby sharpshooter during the skirmish with the Confederates and killed one of the raiders. Parker and Carter, *22nd Massachusetts,* 383. For a description of a similar incident on this march by a 1st Corps soldier, see Rufus R. Dawes, *Service with the Sixth Wisconsin Volunteers,* 2nd ed. (Marietta, OH: E. R. Alderman & Sons, 1936), 227.

19. It was not Mosby but the cavalry brigade of Brig. Gen. Thomas L. Rosser that attacked the 5th Corps trains. Rosser reported that he destroyed thirty-five to forty wagons and captured eight wagons filled with ordnance, seven ambulances, 230 mules and horses, and ninety-five Federals, all at a cost of two killed and three wounded. *O.R.,* vol, XXIX, pt. 1, 904.

20. This was New Hope Church, which was twelve miles west of Chancellorsville on the Orange Plank Road. *O.R. Atlas,* plate XLIV, map 3.

21. Robinson's Tavern, also known as Robertson's Tavern, lay three miles due north of New Hope Church on the Orange Turnpike. Ibid.; Graham and Skoch, *Mine Run,* 41.

22. James W. Hyatt, a thirty-six-year-old clerk originally from Jefferson County, Virginia, recovered from the effects of this shell but was captured later in the war in the Wilderness. He died in prison at Andersonville, Georgia, on December 3, 1864. MR Co. H, Harrisburg; Survivors' Association, *118th Pennsylvania,* 372.

23. While Meade was highly displeased with Warren's decision to call off the attack at Mine Run, the soldiers in the ranks were greatly relieved. "What glorious news it was to us all," remembered a New Jersey infantryman, "the countermanding of the order to charge! Our noble country would have known of a greater slaughter than at Fredericksburg, and men and officers felt thankful that we resumed our position behind the breastworks." William P Haines, *History of the men of Co. F . . . 12th New Jersey Volunteers* (Mickleton, NJ: C. S. Magrath, 1897), 53. For more soldiers' comments on the improbability of Federal success at Mine Run, see A. M. Stewart, *Camp, March, and Battlefield; or Three Years and a Half with the Army of the Potomac* (Philadelphia: J. B. Rodgers, 1865), 366; Gilbert Adams Hays, *Under the Red Patch: Story of the Sixty Third Regiment Pennsylvania Volunteers, 1861–1864* (Pittsburgh: Sixty Third Pennsylvania Volunteers Regimental Association, 1908), 217–18; James M. Greiner, Janet L. Coryell, and James R. Smither, eds, *A Surgeon's Civil War: The Letters and Diaries of Daniel M. Holt, M. D.* (Kent, OH: Kent State University Press, 1994), 161–62; Carter, *Four Brothers in Blue,* 374.

24. Probably Stoney Mountain, located several miles due south of Stevensburg. O.R. Atlas, plate LXXXVII, map 2.

CHAPTER ELEVEN: CONFRONTATION, DISMISSAL, AND EXONERATION

1. An anonymous letter from "an officer of a Pennsylvania regiment in the Army of the Potomac" was published in the *Philadelphia Evening Bulletin* on September 16, 1863, and in it was contained the following veiled reference to Colonel Gwyn:

> I tell you that the soldiers from our state know Andrew G. Curtin. He
> has been with them, visited them to know and find out their wants, and
> on the battlefield, in the hospitals, we are watched and cared for. I speak
> the sentiment of the soldiers of Pennsylvania, when I ask the people of
> the state to re-elect him. I can except one who was the commanding
> officer of one of our regiments, who after the battle of Gettysburg
> 'thanked God he was not a Pennsylvanian.' He has now an important

command. I think he is an isolated case, and as he has his commission from Governor Curtin, he thinks that the Governor is of no further use to him, and probably might not advocate his re-election. . . .

At the time the letter was published, it was clear that Colonel Prevost would never return to the 118th, and the article was seized upon by several influential Philadelphians and forwarded to Governor Curtin in hopes of dissuading him from promoting Lieutenant Colonel Gwyn to the vacant colonelcy. Despite Donaldson's claim that Stephen Winslow authored the letter, it was signed by "L.," who in all likelihood was Capt. Lemuel Crocker of Company K, a close friend of Winslow's and no favorite of Gwyn's. Pennsylvania State Archives, Governor's Correspondence Files, 118th Regiment, Record Group 19, Harrisburg, PA.

2. Copies of any correspondence Isaac Wistar, Donaldson's former colonel in the 71st Pennsylvania, may have sent have not been found; however, a number of prominent citizens of Philadelphia signed a letter that was sent to President Lincoln in late January attesting to Donaldson's "character, temperance, and true loyalty." FAD Papers, CWLM.

3. Lt. Col. Norval E. Welch, twenty-six, of Ann Arbor, Michigan, commanded the 16th Michigan. The prewar attorney was killed at Peebles Farm, Virginia, on September 30, 1864. Robertson, *Michigan in the War,* part II, 187–94.

4. Donaldson was nominally represented at his trial by Surgeon Isaac Stearns of the 22nd Massachusetts. Dr. Stearns offered no recorded counsel or advice, however, so Donaldson is technically correct in relating to his brother that he had no lawyer.

5. None of the dialogue Donaldson recounts between him, Colonel Gwyn, and Colonel Welch is part of the official court-martial transcript. Court-Martial Proceeding of FAD (cited hereafter as FAD Court-Martial). Record Group 153, National Archives, Washington, D.C.

6. Neither Donaldson's interruption nor the advisement by the judge advocate, Capt. Amos M. Judson of the 83rd Pennsylvania Volunteers, is part of the trial transcript. FAD Court-Martial.

7. Donaldson's statement of the judge advocate's instructions notwithstanding, he was allowed to continue to verbally cross-examine the prosecution's witnesses. FAD Court-Martial.

8. No record exists of Donaldson's submitting this written statement. FAD Court-Martial.

9. Neither Donaldson's outburst nor the clearing of the court was recorded in the trial transcript. FAD Court-Martial.

10. Isaac Seesholtz of Catawissa, Pennsylvania, a twenty-five-year-old prewar student, had enlisted originally as a corporal of Company C. By the end of the war, he had worked his way up to the captaincy of Company K. He was wounded at Shepherdstown in 1862 and at Hatcher's Run in 1865. MR Co. C, Harrisburg; Survivors' Association, *118th Pennsylvania,* 650, 695.

11. Henry F. Leo, twenty-seven, was a prewar stonecutter and native of Philadelphia. As Donaldson has earlier predicted, Leo was promoted to the first lieutenancy of Company B in March 1864 and to captaincy of the company in November. He mustered out in June 1865. Interestingly, one month earlier Leo had been dropped from his company rolls as a deserter after having failed to report back to the regiment from an eight-day furlough granted in early August 1863. No charges were preferred, however, and a notation on his service record states that he was dropped by mistake. CSR, RG94, NA.

12. Thomas Webster is unidentified.

13. Charles O'Neill, forty-two, represented the 2nd Congressional District of Pennsylvania in the House of Representatives. The Republican served fifteen terms in the House beginning in 1862. Herringshaw, *Encyclopedia of American Biography,* 705.

14. In addition to his position as secretary of the U.S. Senate, Lancaster, Pennsylvania, native John Weiss Forney, forty-six, was the publisher of the *Philadelphia Press* and the *Washington Chronicle*. Ibid., 373.
15. Montgomery Blair of Kentucky was serving as postmaster general in the Lincoln administration at this time.

EPILOGUE
1. Pension Record of FAD. Record Group 15, National Archives, Washington, D.C.
2. Lowry, *22nd Virginia,* 145.
3. Twenty-one-year-old Henry Steiner of Company C, a prewar cordwainer, had been shot in the right breast at the Battle of Fredericksburg on December 13, 1862. As a result of the wound, his right arm was rendered useless, and he was discharged on February 26, 1863. A surgeon who examined him one month later noted that, in addition to lung damage, several ribs were fractured and, worst of all, the wound was still open. In a pension affidavit filed in 1889, Steiner complained of severe pains in his breast, weakness of lungs, and heart trouble. He died in March 1900. Pension Record of Henry Steiner. Record Group 15, National Archives, Washington, D.C.
4. *Journal of Commerce* (Philadelphia). May 12, 1928.

BIBLIOGRAPHY

MANUSCRIPT COLLECTIONS

Francis Adams Donaldson Papers. The Civil War Library and Museum, Philadelphia.

Brevet Brigadier General Charles P. Herring Papers. The Civil War Library and Museum, Philadelphia.

Capt. Alfred C. Hills Manuscript. Army of the Potomac Collection, Chicago Historical Society, Chicago.

Francis H. Lincoln Papers. Lewis Leigh Collection, U.S. Army Military History Institute, Carlisle Barracks, PA.

Sgt. Wilfred McDonald Diary. Center for American History, University of Texas at Austin.

Lieutenant Henry T. Peck Letters. 1st Regt. Infantry NGP Library, Philadelphia.

John L. Smith Papers. Historical Society of Pennsylvania, Philadelphia.

UNPUBLISHED PRIMARY SOURCES

General Orders. Army of the Potomac, January to December, 1863.

Pennsylvania State Archives. Governor's Correspondence Files, 118th Regiment. Record Group 19, Pennsylvania Historical & Museum Commission, Harrisburg, PA.

Pennsylvania State Archives. Muster Rolls, 118th Pennsylvania Infantry. Record Group 19, Pennsylvania Historical & Museum Commission, Harrisburg, PA.

Pennsylvania State Archives. Regimental File Box, 71st Pennsylvania Infantry. Record Group 19, Pennsylvania Historical & Museum Commission, Harrisburg, PA.

United States. Department of the Interior. Pension Records (Record Group 15), Military Service Records (Record Group 94), Court-Martial Records (Record Group 153). National Archives, Washington, DC.

United States. Department of the Interior. Regimental Letter and Indorsement Book, 118th Pennsylvania Infantry. National Archives, Washington, DC.

NEWSPAPERS AND PERIODICALS

Harper's Weekly
Journal of Commerce (Philadelphia)
Philadelphia Daily Evening Bulletin

BOOKS AND ARTICLES

Adams, George Worthington. *Doctors in Blue: The Medical History of the Union Army in the Civil War*. New York: Henry Schuman, 1952.

Adjutant General of Michigan, *Record First Michigan Infantry Civil War, 1861–1864*. Reprint. Detroit: Detroit Book Press, n.d.

Aggasiz, George R., ed. *Meade's Headquarters, 1863-1865: Letters of Colonel Theodore Lyman from the Wilderness to Appomattox*. Boston: Atlantic Monthly Press, 1922.

Alotta, Robert I. *Civil War Justice: Union Army Executions Under Lincoln*. Shippensburg, PA: White Mane, 1989.

Annual Report of the Adjutant General of Pennsylvania . . . for the Year 1863. Harrisburg, PA: Singerly & Myers, 1864.

Annual Report of the Adjutant General of Pennsylvania . . . for the Year 1866. Harrisburg, PA: Singerly & Myers, 1867.

Banes, Charles H. *History of the Philadelphia Brigade*. Philadelphia: J. B. Lippincott & Co., 1876.

Bates, Samuel P. *History of Pennsylvania Volunteers, 1861–1865*. 5 vols. Harrisburg, PA: State Printer, 1869–71.

Bennett, Edwin C. *Musket and Sword*. Boston: Coburn Publishing Co., 1900.

Bicknell, George W. *History of the Fifth Regiment Maine Volunteers. . . .* Portland, ME: H. L. Davis, 1871.

Bigelow, John, Jr. *The Campaign of Chancellorsville: A Strategic and Tactical Study*. New Haven, CT: Yale University Press, 1910.

Blair, Harry C., and Rebecca Tarshis. *Lincoln's Constant Ally: The Life of Colonel Edward D. Baker*. Portland: Oregon Historical Society, 1960.

Bowen, James I. *History of the Thirty-Seventh Regiment Massachusetts Volunteers in the Civil War of 1861–1865. . . .* Holyoke, MA: Clark W. Bryan & Co., 1884.

Bryan, J. Randolph. "Balloon Used for Scout Duty," *Confederate Veteran* 22, no. 4 (April 1914): 161–65.

Busey, John W., and David G. Martin. *Regimental Strengths and Losses at Gettysburg*. Hightstown, NJ: Longstreet House, 1986.

Butterfield, Daniel. *Camp and Outpost Duty for Infantry*. New York: Harper and Brothers, 1862.

Carter, Robert Goldthwaite. *Four Brothers in Blue, or Sunshine and Shadows of the War of the Rebellion: A Story of the Great Civil War from Bull Run to Appomattox*. Reprint. Austin, TX: University of Texas Press, 1979.

Cattell, Alexander Gilmore. *An Address at the Unveiling of the Monument . . . to Commemorate the Heroic Services of the Corn Exchange Regiment, Delivered at "Round Top" on the Gettysburg Battlefield*. Philadelphia: Commerical List Printing House, 1884.

Catton, Bruce. *Mr. Lincoln's Army*. Garden City, NY: Doubleday, 1951.

———. *Glory Road*. Garden City, New York: Doubleday, 1952.

———. *This Hallowed Ground: The Story of the Union Side of the Civil War*. New York: Doubleday & Company, 1956.

———. *Never Call Retreat*. New York: Doubleday & Company, 1965.

Child, William. *A History of the Fifth Regiment New Hampshire Volunteers in the American Civil War, 1861–1865*. Bristol, NH: R. W. Musgrove, 1893.

Cleaves, Freeman. *Meade of Gettysburg*. Norman, OK: University of Oklahoma Press, 1960.

Collis, Charles H. T. *Letters and Testimony Presented by Charles H. T. Collis Defending Himself against Accusations Made to the Military Order of the Loyal Legion as to His Military Record*. New York: n.p., 1891.

Cudworth, Warren H. *History of the First Regiment (Massachusetts Infantry).* . . . Boston: Walker, Fuller & Co., 1866.

Curtis, Newton M. *From Bull Run to Chancellorsville: The Story of the Sixteenth New York Infantry.* New York: G. P. Putnam's Sons, 1906.

Davis, George B., Leslie J. Perry, Joseph W. Kirkley, and Calvin D. Cowles, eds. *Atlas to Accompany the Official Records of the Union and Confederate Armies.* Washington, DC: Government Printing Office, 1891–95. Reprint. *The Official Military Atlas of the Civil War.* New York: Fairfax Press, 1983.

Davis, W. W. H. *History of the 104th Pennsylvania Regiment.* Philadelphia: J. B. Rogers, 1866.

Dawes, Rufus R. *Service with the Sixth Wisconsin Volunteers.* 2nd ed. Marietta, OH: E. R. Alderman & Sons, 1936.

Denison, Frederic. *Sabres and Spurs: The First Regiment Rhode Island Cavalry in the Civil War.* . . . Central Falls, RI: First Rhode Island Cavalry Veteran Association, 1876.

Eisenberg, Al, ed. "Finis—to My Military Career: Captain Donaldson's Feud," *North South Trader* IX, no. 2 (Jan.–Feb.1982): 8–11.

Eisenschiml, Otto. *The Celebrated Case of Fitz John Porter: An American Dreyfus Affair.* Indianapolis: Bobbs-Merrill, 1950.

Faust, Patricia L., ed. *Historical Times Illustrated Encyclopedia of the Civil War.* New York: Harper & Row, 1986.

Foote, Shelby. *The Civil War, a Narrative: Fort Sumter to Perryville.* New York: Random House, 1958.

Ford, Andrew E. *The Story of the Fifteenth Regiment Massachusetts Volunteer Infantry in the Civil War, 1861–1864.* Clinton, MA: W. J. Coulter, 1898.

Furgurson, Ernest B. *Chancellorsville, 1863: The Souls of the Brave.* New York: Alfred A. Knopf, 1992.

Gerrish, Theodore. *Army Life: A Private's Reminiscences of the Civil War.* Portland, ME: Hoyt, Fogg & Donham, 1882.

Graham, Martin F., and George F. Skoch. *Mine Run: A Campaign of Lost Opportunities, October 21, 1863–May 1, 1864.* Lynchburg, VA: H. E. Howard, 1987.

Greiner, James M., Janet L. Coryell, and James R. Smither, eds. *A Surgeon's Civil War: The Letters and Diaries of Daniel M. Holt, M.D.* Kent, OH: Kent State University Press, 1994.

Haines, William P. *History of the Men of Co. F . . . 12th New Jersey Volunteers.* Mickleton, NJ: C. S. Magrath, 1897.

Harris, William C. *Prison Life in the Tobacco Warehouse at Richmond.* Philadelphia: G. W. Childs, 1862.

Harrison, Noel G. *Chancellorsville Battlefield Sites.* Lynchburg, VA: H. E. Howard, 1990.

Haynes, Martin A. *A History of the Second Regiment New Hampshire Volunteer Infantry in the War of the Rebellion.* 2nd ed. Lakeport, NH: n.p., 1896.

Hays, Gilbert Adams. *Under the Red Patch: Story of the Sixty Third Regiment Pennsylvania Volunteers, 1861–1864.* Pittsburgh: Sixty Third Pennsylvania Volunteers Regimental Association, 1908.

Heitman, Francis B. *Historical Register and Dictionary of the United States Army.* Washington, DC: Government Printing Office, 1903.

Henderson, William D. *The Road to Bristoe Station.* . . . Lynchburg, VA: H. E. Howard, 1987.

Herringshaw, Thomas William. *Herringshaw's Encyclopedia of American Biography of the Nineteenth Century.* . . . Chicago: American Publishers Association, 1907.

Hesseltine, William B. *Lincoln and the War Governors.* New York: Alfred A. Knopf, 1948.

Hitchcock, Frederick L. *War from the Inside: The Story of the 132nd Regiment Pennsylvania Volunteer Infantry.* . . . Philadelphia: J. B. Lippincott, 1904.

Holmes, Oliver Wendell, Sr. "My Hunt after 'The Captain.'" *Atlantic Monthly,* 10 (December 1862): 738–46.

Howe, Mark DeWolfe. *Justice Oliver Wendell Holmes: The Shaping Years.* Cambridge, MA: The Belknap Press of Harvard University Press, 1957.

Humphreys, Andrew A. *From Gettysburg to the Rapidan: The Army of the Potomac, July, 1863 to April, 1864.* New York: Charles Scribner's Sons, 1883.

Hunt, Roger D., and Jack R. Brown, *Brevet Brigadier Generals in Blue.* Gaithersburg, MD: Olde Soldier Books, 1990.

Johnson, Robert Underwood, and Clarence Clough Buel, eds. *Battles and Leaders of the Civil War.* 4 vols. New York: Century Co., 1887.

Jones, Virgil Carrington. *Ranger Mosby.* Chapel Hill, NC: The University of North Carolina Press, 1944.

Jordon, Weymouth T., and Louis H. Manarin. *North Carolina Troops, 1861– 1865: A Roster.* 11 vols., Raleigh, NC: State Department of Archives and History, 1961–87.

Judson, A. M. *History of the Eighty-Third Regiment Pennsylvania Volunteers.* Erie, PA: B. F. H. Lynn, 1865.

Keen, Hugh C., and Horace Mewborn. *43rd Battalion Virginia Cavalry Mosby's Command.* Lynchburg, VA: H. E. Howard, 1993.

Krick, Robert K. *Lee's Colonels: A Biographical Register of the Field Officers of the Army of Northern Virginia.* 4th ed. Dayton, OH: Press of Morningside House, 1992.

Levy, George. "President Lincoln Rejects an Appeal for Mercy." *The Lincoln Newsletter* 8 no. 3 (Fall 1994): 1, 4–7.

Livermore, Thomas L. *Numbers and Losses in the Civil War in America, 1861– 1865.* Reprint. Dayton, OH: Press of Morningside House, 1986.

Longacre, Edward G. *The Cavalry at Gettysburg.* . . . Reprint. Lincoln, NE: University of Nebraska Press, 1993.

Lossing, Benson J. *Memoir of Lieutenant Colonel John T. Greble of the United States Army.* Philadelphia: Privately printed, 1870.

Lowry, Terry D. *22nd Virginia Infantry.* Lynchburg, VA: H. E. Howard, 1988.

MacNamara, Daniel George. *The History of the Ninth Regiment Massachusetts Volunteer Infantry . . . June 1861–June 1864.* Boston: E. B. Stillings & Co. 1899.

Marvel, William. *Burnside.* Chapel Hill, NC: University of North Carolina Press, 1991.

Massachusetts Soldiers, Sailors and Marines in the Civil War. 8 vols. Norwood, MA: Norwood Press, 1931.

McPherson, James M. *Battle Cry of Freedom.* New York: Oxford University Press, 1988.

Mills, J. Harrison. *Chronicles of the Twenty First Regiment New York State Volunteers.* . . . Buffalo: Gies & Co., 1887.

Moe, Richard. *The Last Full Measure: The Life and Death of the First Minnesota Volunteers.* New York: Henry Holt and Company, 1993.

Moore, Frank, ed. *The Rebellion Record: A Diary of American Events.* . . . 11 vols. New York: G. P. Putnam, 1861–63; D. Van Nostrand, 1864–68.

Mosby, John S. *Stuart's Cavalry in the Gettysburg Campaign.* New York: Moffat, Yard & Company, 1908.

Mulholland, St. Clair A. *The Story of the 116th Regiment Pennsylvania Volunteers in the War of the Rebellion.* Philadelphia: F. McManus, Jr. & Co., 1903.

Nevins, Allan, ed. *A Diary of Battle: The Personal Journals of Colonel Charles S. Wainwright, 1861–1865.* New York: Harcourt, Brace & World, 1962.

Parker, John L., and Robert G. Carter. *Henry Wilson's Regiment: History of the Twenty Second Massachusetts Infantry, the Second Company Sharpshooters, and the Third Light Battery in the War of the Rebellion.* Boston: Regimental Association, 1887.

Parker, Sandra V. *Richmond's Civil War Prisons.* Lynchburg, VA: H. E. Howard, 1990.

Peck, Henry T. *Historical Sketch of the 118th Regiment Pennsylvania Volunteers.* n.p., 1884.

Pfanz, Harry W. *Gettysburg: The Second Day.* Chapel Hill, NC: University of North Carolina Press, 1987.

Phisterer, Frederick. *New York in the War of the Rebellion, 1861–1865.* 3rd ed., 5 vols. Albany, NY: J. B. Lyon Company, 1912.

Powell, William Henry. *The Fifth Army Corps (Army of the Potomac).* . . . London: G. P. Putnam & Sons, 1896.

Preston, Noble D. *History of the Tenth Regiment of Cavalry, New York State Volunteers.* . . . New York: D. Appleton and Company, 1892.

Pullen, John J. *The Twentieth Maine: A Volunteer Regiment in the Civil War.* Philadelphia: J. B. Lippincott Company, 1957.

Rawle, William Brooke. *A Refutation by William Brooke Rawle of Certain False Statements Made by Corporal Andrew Jackson Speese Regarding the History of the Third Pennsylvania Volunteer Cavalry Regiment.* Philadelphia: n.p., 1907.

Reese, Timothy J. *Sykes' Regular Infantry Division 1861–1865.* Jefferson, NC: McFarland and Company, 1990.

Regimental Association. *Under the Maltese Cross . . . Campaigns 155th Pennsylvania Regiment.* Pittsburgh: 155th Regimental Association, 1910.

Regimental Committee, *History of the Fifth Massachusetts Battery.* Boston: Luther E. Cowles, 1902.

Regimental History Committee. *History of the Third Pennsylvania Cavalry, Sixtieth Regiment Pennsylvania Volunteers in the American Civil War, 1861– 1865.* Philadelphia: Franklin Printing Co., 1905.

Rhodes, James Ford. *History of the United States from the Compromise of 1850 to the Final Restoration of Home Rule at the South in 1877.* 7 vols. Boston: Macmillan Company, 1910.

Robertson, James I., Jr. ed. *The Civil War Letters of General Robert McAllister.* New Brunswick, NJ: Rutgers University Press, 1965.

Robertson, Jno. *Michigan in the War.* Lansing, MI: W. S. George & Co., 1880.

Rowland, Dunbar. *Military History of Mississippi, 1803–1898.* Reprint. Spartanburg, SC: Reprint Company, 1978.

Sauers, Richard A. *Advance the Colors: Pennsylvania Civil War Battle Flags.* 2 vols. Harrisburg, PA: Capitol Preservation Committee, 1987, 1991.

Scharf, Thomas, and Thompson Westcott. *History of Philadelphia: 1609–1884.* 3 vols. Philadelphia: L. H. Everts Co., 1884.

Sears, Stephen W. *George B. McClellan: The Young Napoleon.* New York: Ticknor and Fields, 1988.

———, ed. *The Civil War Papers of George B. McClellan: Selected Correspondence, 1860–1865.* New York: Ticknor and Fields, 1989.

———. *To the Gates of Richmond: The Peninsula Campaign.* New York: Ticknor and Fields, 1992.

———. *Chancellorsville.* Boston: Houghton Mifflin Company, 1996.

Sifakis, Stewart. *Who Was Who in the Civil War.* New York: Facts on File, 1988.

Silliker, Ruth L., ed. *The Rebel Yell & the Yankee Hurrah: The Civil War Journal of a Maine Volunteer.* Camden, ME: Down East Books, 1985.

Small, Harold Adams, ed. *The Road to Richmond: The Civil War Memoirs of Major Abner R. Small of the Sixteenth Maine Volunteers. . . .* Berkeley, CA: University of California Press, 1939.

Sparks, David S., ed. *Inside Lincoln's Army: The Diary of General Marsena Rudolph Patrick, Provost Marshal General, Army of the Potomac.* New York: Thomas Yoseloff, 1964.

Sprenger, George F. *Concise History of the Camp and Field Life of the 122d Regiment, Penn'a Volunteers. . . .* Lancaster, PA: New Era Steam Book Print, 1885.

Stevens, Charles A. *Berdan's United States Sharpshooters in the Army of the Potomac, 1861–1865.* St. Paul, MN: Price-McGill Company, 1892.

Stevens, George T. *Three Years in the Sixth Corps.* Albany: S. R. Gray, 1866.

Stewart, A. M. *Camp, March, and Battlefield; or Three Years and a Half with the Army of the Potomac.* Philadelphia: J. B. Rodgers, 1865.

Survivors' Association. *Antietam to Appomattox with 118th Penna. Vols., Corn Exchange Regiment.* Philadelphia: J. L. Smith, 1892.

Survivors' Association. *History of the 118th Pennsylvania Volunteers, Corn Exchange Regiment. . . .* Philadelphia: J. L. Smith, 1905.

Survivors' Association. *History of the Twenty Third Pennsylvania Volunteer Infantry,* Birney's Zouaves. Philadelphia: n. p., 1903.

Sutherland, Daniel E. *Seasons of War: The Ordeal of a Confederate Community, 1861–1865.* New York: Free Press, 1995.

Sword, Wiley. "Colonel Fletcher Webster's Last Letter." *Blue & Gray Magazine* 8, no. 1 (Fall 1995): 20–27.

Taylor, Emerson Gifford. *Gouverneur Kemble Warren: The Life and Letters of an American Soldier, 1830–1882.* Boston: Houghton Mifflin, 1932.

Taylor, Frank H. *Philadelphia in the Civil War, 1861–1865.* Philadelphia: Published by the City, 1913.

U.S. War Department. *The War of the Rebellion: A Compilation of the Official Records of the Union and Confederate Armies.* 128 vols. Washington, DC: Government Printing Office, 1880–1901.

Wakelyn John L. *Biographical Dictionary of the Confederacy.* Westport, CT: Greenwood Press, 1977.

Walker, Francis A. *History of the Second Army Corps in the Army of the Potomac.* New York: Charles Scribner's Sons, 1886.

Ward, Joseph R. C. *History of the One Hundred and Sixth Pennsylvania Volunteers.* Philadelphia: F. McManus, Jr. & Co., 1906.

Whan, Vorin E., Jr. *Fiasco at Fredericksburg.* State College, PA: Pennsylvania State University Press, 1961.

Whitman, William E. S., and Charles True. *Maine in the War of the Union. . . .* Lewiston, ME: Nelson Dingley, Jr. & Co., 1865.

Winey, Michael. "Empire State Soldiers: Images from New York's Bureau of Military Statistics." *Military Images* 11, no.4 (January–February 1990): 22.

Wistar, Isaac Jones. *Autobiography of Isaac Jones Wistar, 1827–1905: Half a Century in War and Peace.* Philadelphia: Wistar Institute, 1937.

INDEX

Numerals in bold typeface indicate a depiction or illustration of the corresponding individual. FAD is Francis Adams Donaldson.